ROUTLEDGE HANDBOOK OF SPORTS PERFORMANCE ANALYSIS

Edited by
Tim McGarry, Peter O'Donoghue
and Jaime Sampaio

Routledge
Taylor & Francis Group

LONDON AND NEW YORK

First published 2013
by Routledge
2 Park Square, Milton Park, Abingdon, Oxfordshire OX14 4RN

Simultaneously published in the USA and Canada
by Routledge
711 Third Avenue, New York, NY 10017

First issued in paperback 2014

Routledge is an imprint of the Taylor and Francis Group, an informa business

© 2013 Tim McGarry, Peter O'Donoghue and Jaime Sampaio

The right of the editor to be identified as the author of the editorial material,
and of the authors for their individual chapters, has been asserted in accordance
with sections 77 and 78 of the Copyright, Designs and Patents Act 1988.

British Library Cataloguing in Publication Data
A catalogue record for this book is available from the British Library

Library of Congress Cataloging in Publication Data
Routledge handbook of sports performance analysis /
edited by Tim McGarry, Peter O'Donoghue and António Jaime de Eira Sampaio.
p. cm.
1. Sports—Psychological aspects. 2. Sports—Physiological aspects.
3. Achievement motiviation. 4. Coaching (Athletics)
I. McGarry, Tim. II. O'Donoghue, Peter. III. Sampaio, António Jaime de Eira.
GV706.4.R69 2013
796.01—dc23
2012030823

ISBN 978–0–415–67361–7 (hbk)
ISBN 978–1–138–90820–8 (pbk)
ISBN 978–0–203–80691–3 (ebk)

Typeset in Bembo
by Swales & Willis Ltd, Exeter, Devon
Printed and bound by CPI Group (UK) Ltd, Croydon, CR0 4YY

CONTENTS

Contents

Contents

FIGURES

TABLES

ACKNOWLEDGEMENTS

The editors would like to express their sincere thanks to all of the people who helped during the writing and production of this handbook. In particular, we would like to thank those authors from around the world who have contributed chapters to the handbook. It has been a privilege to work with such a talented and knowledgeable team. We also wish to thank Josh Wells, Simon Whitmore and their colleagues from Routledge for their assistance during the planning and developing of this handbook.

FOREWORD

Ian M. Franks

In 1979 I was in a rather unique and some would say enviable position at the beginning of my academic career: a coach of international athletes and a researcher of skill acquisition and motor learning at a major university. This would seem to be the perfect symbiotic relationship. I could apply my research in a sport specific context and ask what I believed to be relevant research questions in the laboratory. Moreover, the Coaching Association of Canada, Sport Canada and several sports governing bodies were willing to fund sport research. This was therefore an ideal time to develop a Centre for Sports Analysis (University of British Columbia) with the goal of improving performance in a variety of national sports. These were lofty goals, especially as the research was to be driven by questions from the sport and not from the sport scientists. Development of these research questions into operational experiments and solutions proved to be a major challenge which involved many hours of discussions with coaches of national teams. It became clear, however, that the main obstacle for coaches was the accurate, objective and reliable analysis of game or match performance, be it to provide feedback for players and coaches after performance or to develop a model of criterion performance with data gained from major international competitions.

Following the lead of such people as Rudolf Laban and Charles Reep, I set about using a pencil and paper checklist to record significant events that occurred during sports as diverse as fencing, field hockey, water polo, wrestling and soccer. During the event I would ask my research assistants to record all the significant events (along with time of event) that occurred in a specific sport. While after the event I would rely heavily on videotape slow motion manual playback to confirm the accuracy of the recordings and to select outtakes for use as feedback for athletes and coaches. This process was extremely time-consuming. The problem was that there were too many events and not enough research assistants. Given the preponderance of computers that had been established in Kinesiology laboratories for several years, especially in the areas of biomechanics and human motor control, the solution to this problem was not difficult to find.

In 1980 Dave Goodman from Simon Fraser University and a system analyst Paul Nagelkerke joined the Centre to help me develop an interactive computer-video capture program using an Apple II micro-computer. This system would allow one analyst to record multiple time-event pairs and then summarize these events after competition. More relevant was the system's ability to automatically find instances of performance that required review on the video tape.

A paper ("Computer assisted sport evaluation") that outlined this system and its use in collecting game related data from all of the games in the 1982 FIFA World Cup was presented at the "Micro-computers in Sport" conference organized by Liverpool University in 1983. Although there was a dearth of papers at this conference that actually had used computers to record game related data, it was clear that several research laboratories in the UK, Europe and North America were about to embrace this technology and make it a critical component of sport performance analysis. Notably Mike Hughes was leading the way in the UK in his laboratory at what was then known as Liverpool Polytechnic (later Liverpool John Moores University). Mike went on to organize the First World Congress of Notational Analysis of Sport at Burton Manor in 1991 and in the same year he formed the International Society of Notation Analysis of Sport (later to become the International Society of Performance Analysis of Sport).

What followed was an explosion of sport related data collected by many and varied methods from different laboratories all over the world, most of them computer based. It is no surprise therefore that the technology for collecting this data has become extremely sophisticated and researchers involved in information technology and engineering have solved the majority of the problems related to reliability and accuracy as well as those of context variability. Systems can now seemingly collect *all* game related information. For example, in a soccer game all player's, referee's and the ball positions can be obtained in real time allowing time-motion, as well as technical and tactical information to be extracted automatically from the game and be available at any time during or after competition. Issues related to system expense, portability and usability will be solved in short order and perhaps we are now close to realizing what Tim McGarry and I forecast in a paper we wrote for Science and Soccer (Second Edition) in 2003. In this chapter we advocated a true interdisciplinary approach to performance analysis of sport.

"The behaviour of an athlete in sport competition is the product of many complex processes. The aim of various disciplines within the sports sciences is to understand these processes at a fundamental level. Match [performance] analysis might help to integrate the separate contributions from various disciplines" (page 274).

We illustrated this by describing a futuristic scenario whereby sport analysts, physiologists, biomechanists, mathematicians, physiotherapists and coaches would come together to break-down game performance from the observed behavioural data in order to uncover the processes that were responsible for either good or bad performance. This is now possible and in certain sports has already been used to good effect. In fact the following pages of this text are an excellent example of the progress that has been made by researchers in this field over the past 30 or more years.

Technological advances have now allowed scientists to answer most of the questions that have been generated by the coaches and players of these various sports. These types of questions while of immense value to sport may not be of critical importance to the scientist. Questions that speak to understanding human behavior in the specific contexts of sport are much more challenging to the researcher, although they may not be seen as being relevant to the people directly involved with athletes in sport. However, this type of discovery research has far reaching consequences for future application to solving practical questions in all types of situations, sport being just one. It is clear that discovery enquiry into more global issues surrounding active human involvement in sporting pursuits has begun and is seen in the following pages of this text albeit to a lesser extent than may be warranted given the preponderance of sport data now available.

While this text makes a valiant attempt at addressing these more general (and some may say esoteric) questions the work still appears to be in its infancy. This is somewhat surprising given the much earlier work of researchers such as Reep, Pollard and Benjamin (*Journal of the Royal*

Statistical Society, 1971, 623–629) and Gould and Greenawalt (*Journal of Sport Psychology*, 1981, 283–304) who used game related information to model team and individual performance. Let us hope that this text paves the way for a more concerted effort by sports scientists to engage in an examination of the underlying mechanisms responsible for sport performance. However, the large inductive leap to the generalized applied setting should be accompanied with caution. It becomes easy to speculate that models of behavior that can account for task specific findings, can also apply to most sport situations. This type of speculation is too readily taken as fact by coaches and players and therefore it is incumbent upon the sport science community to engage in task specific applied research to test these assumptions made from discovery research. To this end the following pages offer much in applied research and some tentative theoretical modeling of sport performance. It is a laudable attempt to cover all aspects of Sport Performance Analysis and the editors should be commended for bringing together the work of some excellent sports science researchers.

INTRODUCTION

Jaime Sampaio, Tim McGarry and Peter O'Donoghue

Sports performance analysis is interdisciplinary in nature and defies accurate (or unambiguous) definition. This said, the research presented in this handbook stems largely from previous empirical investigations of sports performance with a view on providing objective description of sports behaviour action variables in practice and/or competition. The aim of performance analysis is two-fold: to advance scientific understanding and to assist sports practice by providing the coaching process with augmented information. The process of labelling and recording the identified action variables was commonly referred to as 'notation', influenced by earlier developments in dance notation by Rudolf Laban, resulting then in *sports notation analysis* in reference to this method. In short, sports notation analysis is the predecessor of sports performance analysis.

Research in sports performance analysis developed a foothold in the 1980s, in large part because of work by Mike Hughes and others. The start of the next decade witnessed the First World Congress of Notational Analysis of Sport in 1991, organized by Mike Hughes on behalf of Liverpool John Moores University (formerly Liverpool Polytechnic) at the Burton Manor Conference Centre in the Wirral (UK). These Congresses have since continued on a bi-annual basis (or thereabouts) and serve as key markers in promoting and developing international research interest on this topic, culminating in its formal introduction into the research and/or teaching programs at various European academic institutions. During this period, common interests between sports notation analysts and sports biomechanists resulted in a shift from sports notation analysis to sports performance analysis. Thus, performance analysis may draw upon several scientific disciplines as various aspects of sports performance are investigated in practice and/or competition for knowledge advancement. Effective bi-directional dialogue among sport scientists, coaching staff and athletes allows for the fomenting of ideas and the bridging of scientific knowledge in sports practice for the benefit of all parties.

Summaries of sports performance analysis research are provided in three textbook references: *Notational Analysis of Sport* (First Edition – Hughes and Franks, 1997; Second Edition – Hughes and Franks, 2004), *The Essentials of Performance Analysis: An Introduction* (Hughes and Franks, 2008) and *Research Methods for Sport Performance Analysis* (O'Donoghue, 2010). Also, academic journals such as the *Journal of Sports Sciences*, the *European Journal of Sport Science*, the *International Journal of Performance Analysis in Sport* and the *Journal of Quantitative Analysis in Sports* offer outlets for the publication of new research in sports performance analysis. In fact, the latter two journals serve this specific purpose, as their titles indicate.

Research in sports performance has increased at accelerating pace, in part due to new technologies opening access to new data, more accurate data and greater volumes of data, as well as new data analysis. Examples include video analysis systems and global positioning devices, among other techniques, that enable accurate movement description in automated (or semi-automated) fashion, and computer software advances that allow for user-friendly, advanced data processing and statistical analysis. These advances in hardware and software alike have facilitated research advances by offering new opportunities. This continuing development of accurate descriptions for sports behaviours facilitates sports-specific theoretical approaches for the ultimate benefit of sports practice. The aim of this handbook is to present some of the knowledge gleaned from these research advances by gathering varied contributions from international multi-disciplinary teams that report state-of-the-art developments within their domain expertise as it pertains to various aspects of sports performance.

There are five different sections in the organization of this handbook. The first section addresses some theoretical aspects that underpin sports behaviours such as decision making, skill acquisition and coordination within and between persons from various perspectives using complex system approaches. The second section addresses measurement and evaluation of sports performance, including considerations of performance indicators, performance 'profiling' techniques and other collective variables for describing and understanding sports behaviours. The third section presents an update on how sports performance analysis research can be used in sports practice, by considering various professional contexts, including coaching, media and high-performance management. The fourth section reports various contributions of sports performance analysis, including 'situational' variables (i.e. context – e.g. home/away, score line, time line, etc.), technical effectiveness, game tactics and strategy, creativity, expertise and attention. The fifth section is dedicated to applied sports performance analysis and reports on recent developments in several sports. The handbook concludes with brief, high-level commentary from the editors on various aspects of sports performance analysis.

SECTION I

Theoretical aspects of sports performance analysis

1

GETTING ON THE RIGHT TRACK

Athlete-centred practice for expert performance in sport

David T. Hendry and Nicola J. Hodges

UNIVERSITY OF BRITISH COLUMBIA, CANADA

Summary

In this chapter, we offer guidelines for optimizing practice based on empirical studies of motor learning and a review of various practice methods. In so doing, we tie motor learning literature to developmental models of expertise in sport based on early specialized practice. We attempt to show how increased knowledge of skill acquisition and athlete-centred practice principles can enhance the quality of information provided to athletes for learning. Athlete-centred practice structuring can facilitate learning through the development of technical and tactical competencies, and increase robustness in the face of competition pressures, as well as encourage short- and long-term engagement and motivation. This is broadly achieved through a focus on the development of the athlete as a cognitively engaged problem solver. Knowledge of long-term practice pathways is necessary for practitioners as they work on developing athletes from an early age and as they make decisions concerning how much to practice and when. With respect to skill development, skill transfer and long-term engagement in sport, we argue that early specialized practice designed to promote activities which encourage cognitive effort, problem-solving behaviours and engagement on behalf of the athlete should be seen as the goal of the development of sporting excellence.

Introduction

For a long time, the general perception of the best athletes in the world was one fuelled by language of inbuilt talents and predispositions that were necessary possessions for attainment of success. In the past few decades, in no small part due to the research of Ericsson and colleagues, this view on expert performance has been somewhat de-cloaked. What have almost come to be universally recognized as the most important components to success are the amount and type of practice. This has led to a surge of interest in the discovery of best methods for practice, as well as the optimal practice pathway for attaining elite levels of performance in sports. In the first part of this chapter, we review various practice methods and their implications for skill development and optimization of athlete performance. In the second part, we tie these methods to models of long-term athlete development and make recommendations for performance analysts based on principles of athlete-centred practice.

Practice methods

Demonstrations

Demonstrations are perceived as fundamental to skill learning and, in many sport situations, they are considered the most appropriate way of instructing. Essentially, a demonstration provides the learner with a visual template for a desired movement, helps to emphasize key movement features and/or conveys a strategy for goal attainment (Hodges and Franks, 2002). Visual demonstrations are thought to reduce cognitive processing demands when compared to other types of instructions (Newell, 1985). There have been a significant number of reviews showing the potential benefits of observational practice for motor learning (e.g. Ashford *et al.*, 2006; Hodges *et al.*, 2005; Maslovat *et al.*, 2010; McCullagh *et al.*, in press). Although this technique has met with considerable success, below we outline methods which appear to best engage the learner with solving the motor task and avoiding learner dependencies on the coach.

Providing demonstrations *after* a practice attempt, rather than *before* an attempt, encourages the athlete to think and engage in the learning process. 'Retroactive' demonstrations provided after, rather than 'proactive' demonstrations provided before, function more like feedback and are assumed to aid retention through enhanced cognitive effort and what is termed 'retrieval practice' (Richardson and Lee, 1999; Patterson and Lee, 2005). There is some debate as to whether demonstrations in general should be provided early or late in practice. It appears that they are most beneficial when given early in practice then faded out, especially for acquiring new skills. Interspersing demonstrations with physical practice attempts early and during practice also seems to be the best method for promoting motor skill learning (e.g. Carroll and Bandura, 1990; Weeks and Anderson, 2000; see also Ong and Hodges, 2012, for a review).

When performers are given control over when to receive demonstrations, not only do they show better retention and transfer to similar variations of the skill, they also tend to ask for this information on a relatively small amount of trials (about 10 per cent: Wrisberg and Pein, 2002; Wulf *et al.*, 2005). Although there is some evidence that more skilled individuals request this type of information more frequently for practice of new skills (about 20 per cent of trials: Hodges *et al.*, 2011), inhibiting the tendency to show and tell frequently during practice and giving the learner control over when demonstrations in practice are given appears to positively impact learning.

Showing someone what to do might incidentally convey what they should avoid doing. Although this could speed acquisition, in motor learning research there is considerable evidence to show that techniques which might prove best for rate of acquisition and short-term performance gains are not typically the best for long-term retention (see Schmidt and Lee, 2011). Errors in performance are not considered detrimental if the learner is aware of the error and has the tools to correct it. In coordination research, the avoidance of certain types of errors has been shown to negatively impact on acquisition rate and the dispensing of ineffective movement techniques (Hodges and Franks, 2000, 2002).

People also learn from watching incorrect or suboptimal performance, such as watching peer models (e.g. Shea *et al.*, 1999; Shebilske *et al.*, 1992). Seeing a combination of correct and incorrect learning models allows the goals of the action to be accurately conveyed and also encourages the observer to be an active observer, engaging in the problem-solving process needed for the detection and correction of errors (e.g. McCullagh and Caird, 1990; Rohbanfard and Pro-teau, 2011). Variability in the types of demonstrations provided also alerts the athlete to other potential solutions for achieving a goal which may be suited to the athlete's current capabilities, body constraints or practice conditions (such as a muddy field). By directing attention towards a particular model or one 'correct' technique, the individual is inhibited creatively and has less chance to vary their practice. With access to video editing technologies, another technique which engages the learner and aids creativity in attaining success is to provide demonstrations that only show the desired outcome effects (e.g. the flight of the ball or the kicking foot in a soccer kicking task requiring the ball to go in the air, e.g. Hodges *et al.*, 2005, 2006).

In summary, demonstrations can promote skill development and engage the athlete if they are provided sparingly, are based on the learner's perceived needs and engage problem-solving activities through techniques such as learning models or outcome models. In Table 1.1, we have summarized various practice methods and techniques associated with their delivery. These have been subdivided into those we consider to be more athlete- versus coach-centred in terms of the involvement of the athlete in how the practice is structured (i.e. low or high). When the coach directly determines how, what and when activities are practised, showing what to do and continually correcting or preventing errors, then this is considered to be a highly structured coaching environment. In comparison, a more athlete-centred learning environment is one where the learner is actively involved in how to practice and learning what to do, fostering long-term learning, transfer and engagement.

Table 1.1 Summary of various practice variables and associated methods which could be considered to be more athlete-centred (low structure), whereby the learner is actively engaged in the learning process, in comparison to techniques that would be considered more coach-centred (high structure), where the learner is less involved and engaged in practice

Athlete-centred (low structured)	*Coach-centred* (high structured)
Demonstrations	
Retroactive	Proactive
Athlete-directed scheduling	Coach-directed scheduling
Learning models/variable demonstrations	Expert/correct models
Instructions	
Low explicit rules	High explicit rules
Externally focused	Internally focused
Use of physical/task-constraints	Low use of constraints
Feedback	
Faded feedback	Feedback on every trial
Descriptive feedback	Prescriptive feedback
Athlete-chosen amount/when/type	Coach-chosen amount/when/type
Practice organization	
Random practice of different skills	Blocked practice of different skills
Variations in practice of one skill	Constant practice of one skill
Error enhancement	Error restriction
Athlete-chosen organization	Coach-chosen organization

Instructions

Much of what we have said about demonstrations holds for instruction. However, there are a couple of important research findings with respect to instruction. The first is the repeated finding that a learner's focus of attention has a significant impact on performance and learning. Small changes in the focus of instructions from the body (internal) onto the effects of the action (external) can change how well a skill is acquired and retained (for a review, see Wulf, 2007). In throwing tasks, such as the forehand Frisbee disc throw, internally focused instructions might be 'accelerate first your elbow and then your wrist' or 'lead into the action with your elbow', whereas an external focus directs the performer's attention towards the intended effects, such as 'step into the throw and release the disc as though you are snapping a wet towel' (see Ong *et al.*, 2010). Directing attention externally can be beneficial for skilled and less skilled athletes, in comparison to internally focused or no-attentional focus instructions, although it appears that instructions which direct attention internally, onto the movement (e.g. the hand in batting or the foot in soccer dribbling), are more harmful for skilled than novice performers, in comparison to other attentional focus manipulations (Beilock *et al.*, 2002; Ford *et al.*, 2005; Gray, 2004). One reason why externally focused instructions work is that they encourage an appropriate level of movement control, one that is directed at attaining the task goal, but not at movement prescriptions and body-related techniques.

Instructions have also been shown to affect performance under pressure. In their work on implicit learning, Masters and colleagues have shown that during stressful conditions performers re-invest attention towards previously learned explicit rules about the technical aspects of an action (for a recent review, see Masters and Poolton, 2012). This re-investment of knowledge can cause disruption in what are regularly 'automatic' processes. Under stress or pressure, performance is thought to regress to an earlier performance level (e.g. Baumeister, 1984), which might be more akin to irregular movements characterized during early learning (e.g. Fuchs, 1962; Deschamp *et al.*, 2004). Individuals that exhibit high levels of re-investment have been shown to rely on more explicit information to control action than low re-investors during stressful situations (Masters, 2000; Masters and Maxwell, 2004). Liao and Masters (2002) showed that the greater the number of rules acquired during learning, the poorer was performance under pressure. These pressure costs were most apparent when instructions were internally focused and provided early in practice (Ong *et al.*, 2010). Consequently, learners and practitioners should be mindful of the amount of explicit rules or instructions given during practice. Although a number of methods have been proposed that lead to a reduction in explicit knowledge accrual and disruptions under pressure (e.g. dual-task learning, errorless learning and analogy learning; see Lam *et al.*, 2010, Liao and Masters, 2001, and Poolton *et al.*, 2006), such methods can be hard on the learner, making acquisition extremely effortful and not always as productive as non-instructed or instructional methods, at least for regular tests of retention. However, resistance to psychological pressure (Hardy *et al.*, 1996; Liao and Masters, 2001; Masters, 1992; Mullen *et al.*, 2007) and even physiological fatigue (Masters *et al.*, 2008; Poolton *et al.*, 2007) might be worth the associated slower learning costs, so long as the athletes can remain motivated and engaged.

A theoretical approach which has the potential for decreasing prescriptive instruction and keeping the performer's attention directed to external features is the constraints-led approach, initially developed by Newell (1985) and adapted to sport by Davids *et al.* (2008). In the constraints-led approach, a change in movement can be brought about by careful manipulation of three interacting factors: *environment*, *task/goal* and *person*. In addition to the altering of sensory information, such as vision, environmental constraints include field dimensions, playing surface and weather conditions. Person constraints refer to the characteristics of the learner, such as stature and psychology. Task constraints are often manipulated by the coach through the adaptation of rules or equipment. Through the interaction of these constraints, learners are directed towards strategies for bringing about movement solutions and/or effective decisions. For example, placing a barrier between a target and a ball conveys to the kicker that the ball has to go up to a particular height. The distance of the target to the ball will also constrain how the ball is or can be lifted (such as a scoop, chip or follow-through kick; see Hodges *et al.*, 2006). In this way, the athlete is guided to a task solution but they are actively involved in deriving the solution. The interactive nature of constraints means that constraining one factor is likely to influence the other. Reducing the dimension of the field of play (environmental) in a soccer possession exercise (task) will likely reduce opportunities in identifying passing alternatives, reduce decision-making time and increase the relative timing of the passing movement (person). In this scenario, players will have to actively seek solutions to deal with the increased temporal demands, such as limiting their touches or repositioning.

One of the key aspects of a constraints-led approach is to set up parameters that are appropriate to the learners' needs. A greater number of options should be included for advanced learners, while options should be limited for beginners (Schöllhorn *et al.*, 2009). These ideas of matching challenges to participant's needs, such as the need to acquire a skill and hence have reduced demands, or the need to learn and refine a skill and hence be challenged, are also at the core of the Challenge Point Framework (Guadagnoli and Lee, 2004). In this framework, information is considered a constraint on learning (see also Hodges and Franks, 2004). Careful consideration of constraints should place the learner at the forefront of the learning experience.

In summary, instructions should be provided to engage the learner in the processes needed to learn and retain skills and, importantly, transfer skills to new learning situations (see Table 1.1). Instructions should not be considered the default way of changing a skill and consideration should be given to altering constraints to bring about a movement solution. Given the requirements of athletes to perform under competitive pressures, techniques which reduce the emphasis on explicit, rule-based knowledge will be most beneficial for training.

Feedback

Feedback is information relating to how a skill was performed and its effectiveness. The way feedback is presented and its content can also have significant implications for learning, the engagement of the learner and the skills developed. Some of this information is a naturally available consequence of performing (termed 'intrinsic feedback') but often the coach augments this feedback in terms of the success of the action or outcome (termed 'augmented feedback'). Feedback can promote efficient learning, ensure correct development of the skill and influence motivation to persist with practice (for recent reviews, see Magill and Anderson, 2012; Williams and Hodges, 2005). The most critical finding to underline with respect to feedback provision is the need for it to be provided sparingly. Providing augmented feedback after every trial can accelerate performance. However, feedback itself serves to guide the learner to the correct solution, such that the learner has not learned to perform the action when feedback is no longer available. This developed dependency on augmented feedback is known as the guidance effect (e.g. Salmoni *et al.*, 1984; for recent reviews, see Magill and Anderson, 2012; Wulf and Shea, 2004). Continued and significant provision of augmented feedback reduces the capacity of learners to actively engage in the problem-solving process. Problem solving through error detection (e.g. was there something wrong with my action and its outcome?) and correction (e.g. what do I need to change?) is vital to skill learning as constant augmented feedback is not possible in competition situations. Individuals should be actively encouraged to develop these problem-solving skills through prediction of what their actions will feel and look like when success is achieved.

Skill level and the complexity of the motor skill affect how feedback should be provided. Early in learning, feedback may be required more frequently (Wulf *et al.*, 1998) and 'faded out' over time in order that learners become self-equipped to detect and correct errors. Adopting this technique of giving and then reducing feedback will help provide learners with a basic grounding of the fundamental elements of the skill, arguably developing motivation to continue to practise through competency attainment (Deci and Ryan, 2008). The skill of the coach is to determine the correct amount and schedule of feedback as a means of facilitating learning without negatively compromising the development of the athlete and their ability to correctly interpret intrinsic feedback.

The precision and nature of feedback can also affect learning. Providing individuals with prescriptive feedback about what to do can further reduce the problem-solving activities of learners to a greater extent than descriptive feedback, which refers to what went wrong with the skill (Wulf and Shea, 2004). During tasks that are difficult or during the early stages of learning, participants may require more prescriptive feedback to improve performance and maintain motivation, whereas later in learning the feedback should be more descriptive (Wulf *et al.*, 1998). As tasks become more advanced, or as performance improves, the feedback may need to become more precise in order to match the goals of performance. If performance plateaus, then this is a potential sign that alternative sources of feedback are required to move to a new level. As a general rule, feedback should decrease in its frequency and increase in its precision as skill develops. There should be a progressive shift from prescriptive (i.e. this is what you should do) towards descriptive feedback (i.e. this is what you did do) as a means of developing skills, retention and effective problem solvers.

Providing learners with the choice of when to receive augmented feedback underlines the athlete-centred principle of effective practice. In self-regulated practice, the athlete determines when to receive feedback or the type of feedback. This method has shown to be effective for promoting learning and transfer to new performance contexts (Chiviacowsky and Wulf, 2002, 2005). In a novel throwing task, Janelle *et al.* (1997) showed that participants who were able to choose when they received feedback about success improved more during performance and retention than a 'yoked' group who followed the same feedback schedule as the choice group. Research on self-regulated feedback provides some interesting insights into the preferred mode and frequency of feedback. Self-regulated participants prefer to receive feedback after perceived successful (or low error) trials (Chiviacowsky and Wulf, 2002, 2005). This tendency appears to show a learning strategy that could be thought of as counterintuitive to traditional coaching techniques, whereby feedback is typically provided immediately after unsuccessful or erroneous attempts (i.e. Adams, 1971). Preference to receive feedback after successful trials may facilitate motivation through developing a sense of competence. Therefore, in addition to the information-giving role of feedback, the reinforcing and motivational role of feedback should be highlighted. There is some evidence that more skilled performers seek information rather than necessarily reinforcement (Hodges *et al.*, 2011) but careful study of domain experts with respect to feedback has not been undertaken. This motivational role of feedback for aiding motor skill acquisition has received renewed attention. In one study, it was found that providing participants with 'positive' feedback about performance (i.e., informing learners that they were more accurate than their peers irrespective of whether this was true), rather than the reverse or even withholding this information, resulted in improved learning (Wulf *et al.*, 2010). Because the 'positive' group outperformed the 'negative' group, this is more than just a competition effect, but rather appears to be related to positive affect associated with affirmation of competency (Lewthwaite and Wulf, 2012).

In summary, augmented feedback is a powerful learning tool if administered in a way that promotes cognitive effort on the part of the learner and if it is delivered positively or provided based on the directions of the athlete. The techniques that best promote this type of learning, which we have defined as low structured, are summarized in Table 1.1.

Practice organization

An understanding of the organization of practice conditions is another critical variable in optimizing athlete learning and development. A well-studied practice variable that has shown to be relatively robust among sports and across individuals relates to the variability in the scheduling of practice conditions, referred to as the 'contextual interference' (CI) effect. When multiple skills are presented in a variable or random order (high CI), although the rate of acquisition may be slower in comparison to a low variable or blocked order (low CI), in retention tests the reverse pattern is seen. More random practice schedules result in better retention of the skills than more blocked schedules (for reviews, see Lee and Simon, 2004; Lee, 2012). Consequently, coaches and athletes should aim to avoid repetitious blocked practice and instead include a variety of skills within the same session. One exception to this may occur in the early stages of learning when reducing the amount of variability in practice appears to be beneficial to help individuals stabilize a skill (see Guadagnoli and Lee, 2004; Shea *et al.*, 1990). Indeed, this strategy of adopting a more blocked practice in early learning before progressing to a more randomized schedule was spontaneously adopted successfully by expert musicians when learning an unrelated throwing skill (Hodges *et al.*, 2011).

One of the proposed mechanisms underlying the beneficial effects of variations in practice of different skills is related to the idea that is it beneficial to 'forget' and 'recall' skills from trial to trial so that retrieval processes are strengthened, again promoting strong problem-solving abilities in the athlete. When one skill is continually practised, there is not the same effort in retrieving and remembering what to do. Although practice is easier, retention and transfer are poorer (Lee and Magill, 1985). In addition to practising different skills in a more variable/random order, there are also advantages with practising the same skill under different variations. This might involve shooting skills from different distances or to different targets. Introducing variability into practice trials forces performers into making slight adjustments to their movements and their motor commands, resulting in more adaptable movement patterns particularly suited to dynamic conditions of competition. There has been considerable empirical support for learning advantages associated with variable rather than constant practice conditions (i.e. performing a singular skill with no variations in conditions), particularly for transfer of skills within the range of variations practised (Lee *et al.*, 1985). Variability of practice is based on the idea that experience adapting to different sensorimotor conditions strengthens the representation of movements for the parameters practised (Salmoni *et al.* 1984).

Somewhat more recently there has been evidence that variability not ostensibly related to the task goal can also facilitate skill learning and retention across different skill levels. The augmenting of error and the encouragement to practice in a manner that leads to variation in the movement technique have shown some promise for aiding acquisition and improvements among new learners and more skilled performers. Error augmentation techniques are based on principles of aiding processes related to the detection and subsequent correction of errors. By making errors larger early in practice (or later), then the learner is forced into determining how to adapt and correct, potentially making them more able to apply these methods when the errors are reduced (e.g. Huang *et al.*, 2007; Patton and Mussa-Ivaldi, 2004). An additional method which has garnered some empirical support is termed 'differential learning' (Schöllhorn *et al.*, 2006). Here, random variability is introduced into training through encouragement to perform variations of a movement from trial to trial, so avoiding repeated attempts to produce a 'correct' or desired movement. In comparison to more traditional types of practice, repetition and corrective feedback are avoided. The principles behind this technique are based on concepts of constraints (Davids *et al.*, 2008). Because of the variability inherent in performance contexts, performers need to be able to quickly adapt their actions to fit the current environmental and task demands unique to competitive sport. It is important to find the optimal levels of variability that challenge the learner, but do not overly challenge the learner. However, too much augmented variability can be as bad, or potentially worse, than too little (Edwards and Hodges, 2012), such that the coach and/or athlete needs to be prepared to adapt their training methods to accommodate for differences between individuals and within individuals across training sessions.

As discussed earlier, the athlete might also be one of the best judges as to when they should vary their training. Allowing the learner control over when to switch between practice of different skills has been shown to benefit learning. Keetch and Lee (2007) showed that, irrespective of the overall amount of variability in the practice of three different skills, learners who were allowed to choose the order with which to practise showed better retention than individuals not given this choice. Giving the performer autonomy over the learning environment appears to carry certain advantages over and above those gained from merely varying the amount of feedback, demonstrations or variability. Based on Deci and Ryan's (2000, 2008) framework on fundamental psychological needs, Lewthwaite and Wulf (2012) argue that this autonomy benefits motivation to learn and improve, leading to intrinsically motivated individuals who participate for the inherent value of the sport and not for external rewards. Again, in Table 1.1, we have summarized these practice organization techniques which best encourage skill development and athlete engagement under the heading 'athlete-centred'.

Practice pathways

As the quality of youth development programmes improve, performance analysis techniques are increasingly employed with younger athletes and teams. Consequently, analysts are required to have a greater understanding of the long-term athlete development process. In the following section, we briefly detail how practice, and the structure of practice, fits into current conceptualizations of sports development and the attainment of high levels of skill. We evaluate research that has implications for the amount and types of practice which are considered important for athlete development across a longer time span.

Practice amount is important

There is considerable evidence showing that the greater the amount of time spent in 'deliberate practice' activities (i.e. highly relevant structured practice engaged in by performers for the primary purpose of improving performance), the greater the chance of success and achievement of expertise (Ericsson *et al.*, 1993). By way of illustration, in Figure 1.1, we have presented accumulated practice hours from three different levels of competitive swimmers in Canada (International level, Junior National level or University-Varsity/Club level, adapted from data published in Hodges *et al.*, 2004). Although all athletes had accumulated a significant amount of time practising swimming (over 5,000 hours), there were two notable findings. International

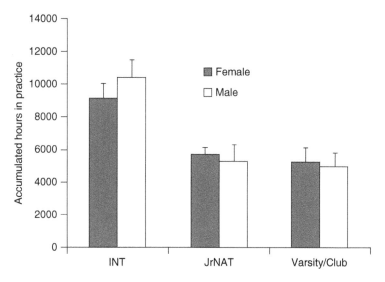

Figure 1.1 Average accumulated hours in practice (and SE bars) for three skill/age groups of swimmers. INT = International senior competitors. JrNAT = National and International competitors at the junior level – U16 yr. Varsity/Club = University 'senior' swimmers

athletes had accumulated almost twice the amount of practice as their less elite peers (University), despite being approximately the same age. These amounts were close to 10,000 hours of practice, an amount suggested as a rough estimate of the number of hours of specialized, highly relevant practice necessary to achieve expertise (Ericsson *et al.*, 1993; see also Simon and Chase, 1973). Second, although the Junior National swimmers were on average 4–5 years younger than the other athletes, they had already accumulated the same amount of practice as the University swimmers. These data and data from many other sports support this relationship between the need for high amounts of practice within a sport and success (for reviews, see Hodges and Baker, 2010; Ward *et al.*, 2004). Consistently, successful athletes can be differentiated from their less successful peers, at relatively young ages, in terms of the accumulated practice in their chosen sport. Therefore, there appears a need to engage in significant amounts of practice early to accrue the requisite practice needed for success. This has been termed the early specialization pathway, typified by early involvement in a single sport (~5 or 6 years), coupled with high amounts of focused, high-intensity practice (Baker *et al.*, 2009).

Athlete-centred practice is important

There has been recent debate about the type of practice activities that aspiring athletes should partake of early in their careers. Rather than encouraging the acquisition of high amounts of structured, or coach-led practice, researchers have proposed that there are benefits to be gained by high amounts of 'deliberate play' (unstructured) activities, early exposure to a large variety of sports and low amounts of coach-led practice. In Table 1.2, we have provided a schematic of these different types of practice with play and highly structured coach-led activities as opposite anchors of a continuum of such activities. The purpose of this table is to highlight the fact that athlete-centred, coach-directed practice is a middle-ground approach to structuring practice.

Table 1.2 Continuum of practice activities ranging from unstructured (i.e. deliberate play) to highly structured (i.e. coach-led practice with low variability and high instruction content)

Unstructured	Low structured	Structured	Highly structured
Deliberate play	**Self-led practice**	**Coach-led practice** *Athelete centered* (High variability, Low instruction/feedback)	**Coach-led practice** *Non-athelete centered* (Low variability, High instruction/feedback)

Deliberate play and unstructured practice

The term 'deliberate play' (Côté, 1999) is used to distinguish it from childhood play. It involves early developmental activities that are highly enjoyable versions of unstructured games, such as street soccer (Côté *et al.*, 2007). According to Côté *et al.* (2007: 186), deliberate play affords participants '. . . freedom to experiment with different movements and tactics and the opportunity to innovate, improvise and respond strategically. It also allows children to perfect skills that would not be practiced in organized situations.' This statement is often contextualized as opposite to what happens during deliberate practice. However, we argue that deliberate practice is not the antithesis of deliberate play, but rather the best type of practice is that which is athlete-centred, allows freedom in selection and promotes thought, active involvement and variability in how practice is structured. Neither play nor practice necessarily promotes these activities.

There is some evidence that deliberate play-type practice activities (i.e. low-structured game playing in basketball) resulted in better tactical game intelligence in comparison to more traditional structured practice (Greco *et al.*, 2010). However, significant issues with the design and terminology in this study make generalizations difficult. Evidence also exists suggesting that play-type activities (i.e. unstructured, non-coach-led activities) within the primary sport are important for later success. For example, Ford *et al.* (2009) showed that early experiences in unstructured types of practice (before 13 years) were predictive of later success in soccer (i.e. being offered a professional contract). One argument for the encouragement of early play/ unstructured types of practice is that it promotes intrinsic motivation, by virtue of the fact that play is engaged for fun and for its own intrinsic value (Côté *et al.*, 2012; Soberlak and Côté, 2003). However, there is little to no evidence to support this suggestion. This issue of motivation and engagement is obviously a critical variable to consider if one wishes to recommend a particular practice pathway and promote commitment to practice.

Early sampling and diversified sports experience

Based on analysis of practice profiles of elite performers, there is some evidence that early diversification in many sports can positively impact later success in sport (Abernethy *et al.*, 2005; Baker *et al.*, 2003; Soberlak and Côté, 2003). However, the evidence is far from clear and a diverse sports background does not appear to describe practice profiles of elite soccer players or gymnasts (Ford *et al.*, 2007, 2009; Law *et al.*, 2007).

Benefits of early sampling of different sports have been proposed to result in positive transfer of tactical and physical skills, development of creative-type skills and enhancement of long-term motivation. In a review of cross-training effects, Loy *et al.* (1995) concluded that transfer occurs primarily during the early stages of development, due to improvements in physical skill. With respect to transfer in technical skills, the motoric transfer between two tasks is thought to be small, unless the tasks share almost identical features (Schmidt and Young, 1987). Cross-training and early diversity could have potential benefits for injury prevention. There is evidence that repetitive-use injuries in children in the United States of America are increasing, especially in sports such as swimming, baseball and gymnastics (Brenner, 2007; Dalton, 1992; Law *et al.*, 2007). The assumption is that a wide, diverse participation will offset some of these potential injuries, but that only holds if the athlete actually does less specialized training.

In a study of world-class Australian national team athletes, Baker *et al.* (2003) reported a negative correlation between early breadth of exposure to other related sports (i.e. team ball sports) and the amount of sport-specific training required to obtain expert-level proficiency. This finding suggests that specialized practice could be offset by early (tactically related) sport diversity. The authors speculated that the transfer was cognitive (i.e. better decision skills) and physical (i.e. fitness related). There is some evidence supporting the transfer of tactical knowledge across sports (e.g. Abernethy *et al.*, 2005; Berry *et al.*, 2008; Smeeton *et al.*, 2004), although a specialist advantage is still noted. Similarly, in studies of 'creativity', described as varying, rare and flexible decision making in complex game situations (Memmert and Roth, 2007), transfer of tactical creativity between handball, soccer and field hockey was noted. However, the largest improvement in tactical creativity was generally in the primary sport that had been physically practised. Consequently, while transfer from other domains could potentially play a role in skill development, there is neither strong nor sufficient evidence supporting diversity at the expense of specific practice for sport-specific improvements.

In summary, there are two proposed practice pathways to the development of expert performance in sport. These pathways are primarily differentiated in terms of their early emphasis (or not) on structured (coach-led/adult-organized) deliberate practice type activities in one sport, so termed 'specialization'. In our view, the important distinction to be made with respect to practice and models of athlete development is not whether practice is coach-led or not, or specialized versus diversified, but whether the practice is structured to promote athlete-centred learning. This is likely to involve a mixture of play-type activities, self-directed practice and coach-led practice that is based on motor learning principles discussed in the first part of this chapter (i.e. variability, choice and cognitive effort; see also Tables 1.1 and 1.2).

Concluding remarks

We have reviewed two lines of research which suggest guiding principles for practice and motor skill development and the delivery of information by practitioners and analysts. This research was discussed with respect to short- and long-term engagement and the development of skills that aid technical and tactical proficiencies. As originally suggested by Ericsson *et al.* (1993), the best type of practice is 'deliberate' practice that is effortful and designed to improve performance. There is overwhelming evidence that practice which puts the learner at the forefront of the learning process and which is designed to foster effort, particularly cognitive effort, leads to better learning outcomes. As a means of engaging athletes in the error detection and correction process, the coach and/or performance analyst must be aware of this evidence and consider how information is presented. We have integrated and summarized these practice methods and pathways with respect to a continuum of structured-type practice activities (see Table 1.2). Unstructured or low-structured activities include activities such as deliberate play and self-determined practice. Even though coach-led formal practice might be considered 'structured', it is possible for the coach to primarily play a guiding role in setting up effective practice that allows and encourages an athlete to learn and improve through self- and coach-guided methods of problem solving, thus being relatively low in structure. Only participation in highly structured practice (as shown on the right of Table 1.2), at least early in development, would be expected to have negative consequences for long-term retention and engagement in sport.

According to the Developmental Model of Sports Participation (DMSP) for elite performance proposed by Côté et al. (Côté, 1999; Côté et al., 2007, 2012), there are two distinct pathways towards reaching an eventual expert level of performance. These pathways emerge through early and continued specialization or early sampling/diversification of different sports and high amounts of play followed by late specialization. The major difference between the two pathways is the time (age) when specialization in one sport should begin, associated expectations for engagement in 'deliberate practice' and predicted outcomes with respect to long-term participation and motivation. We argue that early specialized practice that is athlete-centred will promote long-term engagement and, arguably, better foster the acquisition and mastery of technical skills necessary to succeed in sport. Advantages of early specialization seem to show up in the data repeatedly, in as much as many hours of 'good' practice are necessary to compete at the highest levels, especially in sports where there is a large participation base. However, more rigorous research is required to test ideas about the relationships between early specialization and technical and tactical skills development and, perhaps more importantly, the development of intrinsic motivation.

In conclusion, as player development programmes begin to focus on increasingly younger athletes, performance analysts and coaches should be aware of the evidence showing that an early start age, coupled with high amounts of deliberate practice, most often describe people who have reached success in sport (e.g. Bloom, 1985; Starkes and Ericsson, 2003; Ward et al., 2004). Early specialization seems to be the norm rather than the exception in the attainment of elite levels of performance skill. Côté et al., however, advocated a skill pathway that de-emphasizes early specialization in a single sport with coach-led structured practice; the rationale for this approach based on concern for potential negative effects of early specialized practice, such as decreased motivation and burnout. We argue that the critical issue is not so much whether an athlete specializes early, or whether the practice is coach-led, but rather what the practice activities entail and whether they promote cognitive effort, engagement and athlete-centred learning. As a key part of the athlete-centred learning process, performance analysts should be acutely aware of the benefits of early specialization and endeavour to focus efforts towards promoting practice methods that show positive effects with respect to motor skill learning, transfer and engagement.

References

Abernethy, B., Baker, J. and Côté, J. (2005) 'Transfer of pattern recall skills as a contributor to the development of sport expertise', *Applied Cognitive Psychology*, 19: 705–18.

Adams, J.A. (1971) 'A closed-loop theory of motor learning', *Journal of Motor Behavior*, 3: 111–50.

Ashford, D., Bennett, S.J. and Davids, K.W. (2006) 'Observational modeling effects for movement dynamics and movement outcome measures across differing task constraints: A meta-analysis', *Journal of Motor Behavior*, 38: 185–205.

Baker, J., Côté, J. and Abernethy, B. (2003) 'Learning from the experts: Practice activities of expert decision makers in sport', *Research Quarterly for Exercise and Sport*, 74: 342–7.

Baker, J., Cobley, S. and Fraser-Thomas, J. (2009) 'What do we know about early sport specialization? Not much!', *High Ability Studies*, 20: 77–89.

Baumeister, R.F. (1984) 'Choking under pressure: Self-consciousness and paradoxical effects on incentives on skillful performance', *Journal of Personality and Social Psychology*, 46: 610–20.

Beilock, S.L., Carr, T.H., MacMahon, C. and Starkes, J.L. (2002) 'When paying attention becomes counterproductive: Impact of divided versus skill-focused attention on novice and experienced performance of sensorimotor skills', *Journal of Experimental Psychology: Applied*, 8: 6–16.

Berry, J., Abernethy, B. and Côté, J. (2008) 'The contribution of structured activity and deliberate play to the development of expert perceptual and decision-making skill', *Journal of Sport and Exercise Psychology*, 30: 685–708.

Bloom, B. (1985) *Developing Talent in Young People*, New York: Balantine.

Brenner, J. (2007) 'Overuse injuries, overtraining, and burnout in child and adolescent athletes', *Pediatrics*, 119: 1242–6.

Carroll, W.R. and Bandura, A. (1990) 'Representational guidance of action production in Observational Learning: A causal analysis', *Journal of Motor Behavior*, 22: 85–97.

Chiviacowsky, S. and Wulf, G. (2002) 'Self-controlled feedback: Does it enhance learning because performers get feedback when they need it?', *Research Quarterly for Exercise and Sport*, 73: 408–15.

Chiviacowsky, S. and Wulf, G. (2005) 'Self-controlled feedback is effective if it is based on the learner's performance', *Research Quarterly for Exercise and Sport*, 76: 42–8.

Côté, J. (1999) 'The influence of the family in the development of talent in sport', *Sport Psychologist*, 13: 395–417.

Côté, J., Baker, J. and Abernethy, B. (2007) 'Play and practice in the development of sport expertise', in G. Tenenbaum and R.C. Eklund (eds), *Handbook of Sport Psychology* (3rd ed.), (pp. 184–202). New York: Wiley.

Côté, J., Murphy-Mills, J. and Abernethy, B. (2012). 'The development of skill in sport', in A.M. Williams and N.J. Hodges (eds), *Skill Acquisition in Sport: Research, Theory and Practice* (2nd ed.), (pp. 269–86). London: Routledge.

Dalton, S.E. (1992) 'Overuse injuries in adolescent athletes', *Sports Medicine*, 13: 58–70.

Davids, K., Button, C. and Bennett, S. (2008) *Dynamics of Skill Acquisition. A Constraints-Led Approach*, Champaign, IL: Human Kinetics.

Deci, E.L. and Ryan, R.M. (2000) 'The "what" and "why" of goal pursuits: Human needs and the self-determination of behavior', *Psychological Inquiry*, 11: 227–68.

Deci, E.L. and Ryan, R.M. (2008) 'Self-Determination Theory: A macrotheory of human motivation, development, and health', *Canadian Psychology*, 49: 182–5.

Deschamps, T., Nouritt, D., Caillou, N. and Delignières, D. (2004) 'Influence of a stressing constraint on stiffness and damping function of a ski simulator's platform motion', *Journal of Sports Sciences*, 22: 867–74.

Edwards, C.L. and Hodges, N.J. (2012) 'Acquiring a novel coordination movement with non-task goal related variability', *Open Sports Science Journal*, 5: 59–67.

Ericsson, K.A., Krampe, R.T. and Tesch-Römer, C. (1993) 'The role of deliberate practice in the acquisition of expert performance', *Psychological Review*, 100: 363–406.

Ford, P.R., Hodges, N.J. and Williams, A.M. (2005) 'Online attentional-focus manipulations in a soccer-dribbling task: Implications for the proceduralization of motor skills', *Journal of Motor Behavior*, 37: 386–94.

Ford, P.R., Le Gall, F., Carling, C. and Williams, A.M. (2007) 'A cross-cultural comparison of the participation histories of English and French elite youth soccer players', in T. Reilly, F. Korksusz and E. Ergen (eds), *Science and Football VI* (pp. 109–12). London: Taylor & Francis.

Ford, P.R., Ward, P., Hodges, N.J. and Williams, A.M. (2009) 'The role of deliberate practice and play in career progression in sport: The early engagement hypothesis', *High Ability Studies*, 20: 65–75.

Fuchs, A.H. (1962) 'The progression-regression hypotheses in perceptual-motor skill learning', *Journal of Experimental Psychology*, 63: 177–82.

Gray, R. (2004) 'Attending to the execution of a complex sensorimotor skill: Expertise differences, choking, and slumps', *Journal of Experimental Psychology: Applied*, 10: 42–54.

Greco, P., Memmert, D. and Morales, J.C.P. (2010) 'The effect of deliberate play on tactical performance in basketball', *Perceptual & Motor Skills*, 110: 849–56.

Guadagnoli, M.A. and Lee, T.D. (2004) 'Challenge point: A framework for conceptualizing the effects of various practice methods in motor learning', *Journal of Motor Behavior*, 36: 212–24.

Hardy, L., Mullen, R. and Jones, G. (1996) 'Knowledge and conscious control of motor actions under stress', *British Journal of Psychology*, 87: 621–36.

Hodges, N.J. and Franks, I.M. (2000) 'Focus of attention and coordination and bias: Implications for learning a novel bimanual task', *Human Movement Science*, 21: 231–58.

Hodges, N.J. and Franks, I.M. (2002) 'Modeling coaching practice: The role of instruction and demonstration', *Journal of Sports Sciences*, 20: 1–19.

Hodges, N.J. and Franks, I.M. (2004) 'Instructions, demonstrations and the learning process: Creating and constraining movement options', in A.M. Williams and N.J. Hodges (eds), *Skill Acquisition in Sport: Research, Theory and Practice* (pp. 145–74). London: Routledge.

Hodges, N.J. and Baker, J. (2010) 'Expertise: The goal of performance development', in D. Collins, A. Abbott and H. Richards (eds), *Performance Psychology: A Practitioner's Guide* (pp. 31–46). Edinburgh: Elsevier Publishers.

Hodges, N.J., Kerr, T., Starkes, J.L., Weir, P. and Nanandiou (2004) 'Predicting performance from deliberate practice hours for triathletes and swimmers: What, when and where is practice important?', *Journal of Experimental Psychology: Applied*, 10: 219–37.

Hodges, N.J., Hayes, S.J., Breslin, G. and Williams, A.M. (2005) 'An evaluation of the minimal constraining information during movement observation and reproduction', *Acta Psychologica*, 119: 264–82.

Hodges, N.J., Hayes, S.J., Eaves, D., Horn, R. and Williams, A.M. (2006) 'End-point trajectory matching as a method for teaching kicking skills', *International Journal of Sport Psychology*, 37: 230–47.

Hodges, N.J., Edwards, C., Luttin, S. and Bowcock (2011) 'Learning from the experts: Gaining insights into best practice during the acquisition of three novel motor skills', *Research Quarterly for Exercise and Sport*, 82: 178–87.

Huang, F., Patton, J.L. and Mussa-Ivaldi, F. (2007) 'Interactive priming enhanced by negative damping aids learning of an object manipulation task', *Conference Proceedings IEEE Engineering Medical Biological Society*, 1: 4011–4.

Janelle, C.M., Barba, D.A., Frehlich, S.G., Tennant, L.K. and Cauraugh, J.H. (1997) 'Maximizing performance effectiveness through videotape replay and a self-controlled learning environment', *Research Quarterly for Exercise and Sport*, 68: 269–79.

Keetch, K. and Lee, T.D. (2007) 'The effect of self-regulated and experimenter-imposed practice schedules on motor learning for tasks of varying difficulty', *Research Quarterly for Exercise and Sport*, 78: 476–86.

Lam W.K., Maxwell, J.P. and Masters, R.S.W. (2010) 'Probing the allocation of attention in implicit (motor) learning', *Journal of Sports Sciences*, 28: 1543–54.

Law, M.P., Côté, J. and Ericsson, K.A. (2007) 'Characteristics of expert development in rhythmic gymnastics: A retrospective study', *International Journal of Sport & Exercise Psychology*, 5: 82–103.

Lee, T.D. (2012) 'Contextual interference: Generalizability and limitations', in A.M. Williams and N.J. Hodges (eds), *Skill Acquisition in Sport: Research, Theory and Practice* (2nd ed.), (pp. 79–93). London: Routledge.

Lee, T.D. and Magill, R.A. (1985) 'Can forgetting facilitate skill acquisition?', in D. Goodman, R.B. Wilberg and I.M. Franks (eds), *Differing Perspectives in Motor Learning, Memory and Control* (pp. 3–22). Amsterdam: North-Holland.

Lee, T.D. and Simon, D.A. (2004) 'Contextual interference', in A.M. Williams and N.J. Hodges (eds), *Skill Acquisition in Sport: Research, Theory and Practice* (pp. 29–44). London: Routledge.

Lee, T.D., Magill, R.A. and Weeks, D.J. (1985) 'Influence of practice schedule on testing schema theory predictions in adults', *Journal of Motor Behavior*, 17: 283–99.

Lewthwaite, R. and Wulf, G. (2012) 'Motor learning through a motivational lens', in A.M. Williams and N.J. Hodges (eds), *Skill Acquisition in Sport: Research, Theory and Practice* (2nd ed.), (pp. 173–91). London: Routledge.

Liao, C.M. and Masters, R.S.W. (2001) 'Analogy learning: A means to implicit motor learning', *Journal of Sports Sciences*, 19: 307–19.

Liao, C. and Masters, R.S.W. (2002) 'Self-focused attention and performance failure under psychological stress', *Journal of Sport & Exercise Psychology*, 24: 289–305.

Loy, S.F., Hoffman, J.J. and Holland, G.J. (1995) 'Benefits and practical use of cross-training in sports', *Sports Medicine*, 19: 1–8.

Magill, R.A. and Anderson, D.I. (2012) 'The roles and uses of augmented feedback in motor skill acquisition', in A.M. Williams and N.J. Hodges (eds), *Skill Acquisition in Sport: Research, Theory and Practice* (2nd ed.), (pp. 3–21). London: Routledge.

Maslovat, D., Hayes, S.J., Horn, R. and Hodges, N.J. (2010) 'Motor learning through observation', in D. Elliott and M.A. Khan (eds), *Vision and Goal-Directed Movement: Neurobehavioral Perspectives* (pp. 315–40). Champaign, IL: Human Kinetics.

Masters, R.S.W. (1992) 'Knowledge, (k)nerves and know-how: The role of explicit versus implicit knowledge in the breakdown of a complex motor skill under pressure', *British Journal of Psychology*, 83: 343–58.

Masters, R.S.W. (2000) 'Theoretical aspects of implicit learning in sport', *International Journal of Sport Psychology*, 31: 530–41.

Masters, R.S.W. and Maxwell, J.P. (2004) 'Implicit motor learning, reinvestment and movement disruption: What you don't know won't hurt you?', in A.M. Williams and N.J. Hodges (eds), *Skill Acquisition in Sport: Research, Theory and Practice* (pp. 207–28). London: Routledge.

Masters, R.S.W. and Poolton, J.M. (2012) 'Advances in implicit motor learning', in A.M. Williams and N.J. Hodges (eds), *Skill Acquisition in Sport: Research, Theory and Practice* (2nd ed.), (pp. 59–75). London: Routledge.

Masters, R.S.W., Poolton, J.M. and Maxwell, J.P. (2008) 'Stable implicit motor processes despite aerobic locomotor fatigue', *Consciousness & Cognition*, 17: 335–8.

McCullagh, P. and Caird, J.K. (1990) 'Correct learning models and use of knowledge of results in the acquisition and retention of a motor skill', *Journal of Human Movement Studies*, 18: 107–16.

McCullagh, P., Law, B. and Ste-Marie, D. (in press) 'Modeling: Is what you see, what you get?', in J.L. Van Raalte and B.W. Brewer (eds), *Exploring Sport & Exercise Psychology* (3rd ed.). Washington, DC: APA.

Memmert, D. and Roth, K. (2007) 'The effects of non-specific and specific concepts on tactical creativity in team ball sports', *Journal of Sports Sciences*, 25: 1423–32.

Mullen, R., Hardy, L. and Oldham, T. (2007) 'Implicit and explicit control of motor actions: Revisiting some early evidence', *The British Journal of Psychology*, 98: 141–56.

Newell, K. (1985) 'Coordination, control and skill', in D. Goodman, R. Wilberg and I. Franks (eds), *Differing Perspectives in Motor Learning, Memory and Control* (pp. 295–317). Amsterdam: North-Holland.

Ong, N.T. and Hodges, N.J. (2012) 'Mixing it up a little: How to schedule observational practice', in A.M. Williams and N.J. Hodges (eds), *Skill Acquisition in Sport: Research, Theory and Practice* (2nd ed.), (pp. 22–39). London: Routledge.

Ong, N.T., Bowcock, A. and Hodges, N.J. (2010) 'Manipulations to the timing and type of instructions to examine motor skill performance under pressure', *Frontiers in Movement Science and Sport Psychology*, 1: 1–13.

Patterson, J.T. and Lee, T.D. (2005) 'Learning a new human–computer alphabet: The role of similarity and practice', *Acta Psychologica*, 120: 267–87.

Patton, J.L. and Mussa-Ivaldi, F.A. (2004) 'Robot-assisted adaptive training: Custom force fields for teaching movement patterns', *IEEE Transactions on Biomedical Engineering*, 51: 636–46.

Poolton, J.M., Masters, R.S.W. and Maxwell, J.P. (2006) 'The influence of analogy learning on decision making in table tennis: Evidence from behavioural data', *Psychology of Sport & Exercise*, 7: 677–88.

Poolton, J.M., Masters, R.S.W. and Maxwell, J.P. (2007) 'Passing thoughts on the evolutionary stability of implicit motor behavior: Performance retention under physiological fatigue', *Consciousness & Cognition*, 16: 456–68.

Richardson, J.R. and Lee, T.D. (1999) 'The effects of proactive and retroactive demonstrations on learning signed letters', *Acta Psychologica*, 101: 79–90.

Rohbanfard, H. and Proteau, L. (2011) 'Learning through observation: A combination of expert and novice models favors learning', *Experimental Brain Research*, 215: 183–97.

Salmoni, A.W., Schmidt, R.A. and Walter, C.B. (1984) 'Knowledge of results and motor learning: A review and critical reappraisal', *Psychological Bulletin*, 95: 355–86.

Schmidt, R.A. and Young, D.E. (1987) 'Transfer of movement control in motor learning', in S.M. Cormier and J.D. Hagman (eds), *Transfer of Learning* (pp. 47–79). Orlando, FL: Academic Press.

Schmidt, R.A. and Lee, T. D. (2011) *Motor Learning and Control* (5th ed.), Champaign, IL: Human Kinetics Publishers.

Schöllhorn, W.I., Beckmann, H., Michelbrink, M., Sechelmann, M., Trockel, M. and Davids, K. (2006) 'Does noise provide a basis for the unification of motor learning theories?', *International Journal of Sport Psychology*, 37: 1–21.

Schöllhorn, W.I., Mayer-Kress, G., Newell, K.M. and Michelbrink, M. (2009) 'Time scales of adaptive behavior and motor learning in the presence of stochastic perturbations', *Human Movement Science*, 28: 319–33.

Shea, C.H., Kohl, R. and Indermill, C. (1990) 'Contextual interference: Contributions of practice', *Acta Psychologica*, 73: 145–57.

Shea, C.H., Wulf, G. and Whitacre, C. (1999) 'Enhancing training efficiency and effectiveness through the use of dyad training', *Journal of Motor Behavior*, 31: 119–25.

Shebilske, W.L., Regian, J.W., Arthur, W. and Jordan, J.A. (1992) 'A dyadic protocol for training complex skills', *Human Factors*, 34: 369–74.

Simon H.A. and Chase, W.G. (1973) 'Skill in chess', *American Scientist*, 61: 394–40.

Smeeton, N.J., Ward, P. and Williams, M. (2004) 'Do pattern recognition skills transfer across sports? A preliminary analysis', *Journal of Sports Sciences*, 22: 205–13.

Soberlak, P. and Côté, J. (2003) 'The developmental activities of professional ice hockey players', *Journal of Applied Sport Psychology*, 15: 41–9.

Starkes, J.L. and Ericsson, K.A. (2003) *Expert Performance in Sports: Advances in Research on Sport Expertise*, Champaign, IL: Human Kinetics.

Ward, P., Hodges, N.J., Williams, A.M. and Starkes J.L. (2004) 'Deliberate practice and expert performance: Defining the path to excellence', in A.M. Williams and N.J. Hodges (eds), *Skill Acquisition in Sport: Research, Theory and Practice* (pp. 231–58). London: Routledge.

Weeks, D.L. and Anderson, L.P. (2000) 'The interaction of observational learning with overt practice: Effects on motor skill learning', *Acta Psychologica*, 104: 259–71.

Williams, A.M. and Hodges, N.J. (2005) 'Practice, instruction and skill acquisition in soccer: Challenging tradition', *Journal of Sports Sciences*, 23: 637–50.

Wrisberg, C.A. and Pein, R.L. (2002) 'Note on learners' control of the frequency of model presentation during skill acquisition', *Perceptual & Motor Skills*, 94: 792–94.

Wulf, G. (2007) *Attention and Motor Skill Learning*, Champaign, IL: Human Kinetics.

Wulf, G. and Shea, C.H. (2004) 'Understanding the role of augmented feedback: The good, the bad, and the ugly', in A.M. Williams and N.J. Hodges (eds), *Skill Acquisition in Sport: Research, Theory and Practice* (pp. 121–44). London: Routledge.

Wulf, G., Shea, C.H. and Matschiner, S. (1998) 'Frequent feedback enhances complex motor skill learning', *Journal of Motor Behavior*, 30: 180–92.

Wulf, G., Raupach, M. and Pfeiffer, F. (2005) 'Self-controlled observational practice enhances learning', *Research Quarterly for Exercise and Sport*, 76: 107–11.

Wulf, G., Chiviacowsky, S. and Lewthwaite, R. (2010) 'Normative feedback effects on learning a timing task', *Research Quarterly for Exercise and Sport*, 81: 425–31.

2

IMPROVING ANTICIPATION AND DECISION MAKING IN SPORT

Joe Causer[1] and A. Mark Williams[2]

[1]LIVERPOOL JOHN MOORES UNIVERSITY, UK

[2]BRUNEL UNIVERSITY, UK

Summary

Traditionally, athletes and others involved with sporting organizations have tended to overlook psychological aspects of performance such as anticipation and decision making in favour of improving physical attributes and/or technical ability. However, as individuals proceed to the upper echelons of sport, differences in physical and physiological characteristics appear less likely to discriminate, while the importance of other components, such as the ability to anticipate and make decisions, is magnified. The nature of sport means high levels of uncertainty, requiring athletes to anticipate action requirements before selecting the most appropriate response from a range of possibilities. In this chapter, we outline key perceptual-cognitive skills involved in sport. We highlight how these perceptual-cognitive skills may be measured and enhanced through specific training interventions.

Introduction

In sport, athletes confronted with complex and rapidly changing environments are often required to make critical decisions in high-pressure, temporally constrained scenarios (Williams, 2000). Inherent limitations in reaction time and movement time necessitates that successful athletes must anticipate or predict future events based on limited preparatory information (Hagemann *et al.*, 2006). In order to deal effectively with such constraints, athletes rely on a range of perceptual-cognitive skills. These skills include the ability to recognize advance (i.e. early arising) visual information cues, identify patterns/structure in play and an awareness of likely event probabilities (Causer *et al.*, 2012).

Expert athletes can reduce the amount of information processed to create a coherent perceptual representation by selectively attending to more pertinent cues (Williams *et al.*, 2009). Furthermore, task-specific knowledge built up through experience is thought to help expert players attend to these more pertinent areas of the display, making it easier to surmise situational probabilities from events previously experienced, allowing for more effective processing of contextual information (Williams, 2009). This ability, which in lay terms is often referred to as 'game intelligence', is thought to develop through experience from the accumulation of hours spent in deliberate practice (Ericsson *et al.*, 1993). However, researchers have also highlighted the potential effectiveness of systematic training programmes in facilitating the more rapid acquisition of these skills (Causer *et al.*, 2011; Smeeton *et al.*, 2005).

In this chapter, we outline key perceptual-cognitive skills that underpin superior anticipation and decision making in sport. We provide an overview of the equipment and methods used to capture and analyse performance in both laboratory and field settings. Practical implications for performance analysts and sports performance are discussed. In finishing, we outline how data captured using these methods may be used to design training interventions that can improve performance in various sporting contexts.

Anticipation and decision making in sport

In many domains, researchers have argued that the ability to make decisions and anticipate future demands are the most important factors underlying expertise, particularly in situations with limited time to respond and/or when life is at threat (Causer and Williams, 2012). In diverse fields such as military combat (Ward *et al.*, 2008), law enforcement (Vickers and Lewinski, 2011), medicine (Joseph and Patel, 1990) and sport (Williams and Abernethy, 2012), scientists have attempted to identify how these skills differentiate experts from their less-expert counterparts. Several distinct differences in perceptual-cognitive expertise are evident across skill levels (Williams, 2009).

Ericsson and Kintsch (1995) suggested that experts acquire sophisticated complex skills for storing information in long-term memory in accessible form that enable the processing limits on working memory to be either bypassed or changed (increased). These skills promote rapid long-term memory encoding and enable selective access to this information when required, hence expanding the available capacity of short-term memory for information processing (Ericsson and Lehmann, 1996). With extensive practice, experts index information in such a way that they can successfully anticipate future retrieval demands. It is furthermore suggested that retrieval cues in short-term working memory facilitate immediate and efficient access to information stored in long-term memory (Ericsson and Kintsch, 1995). This expansion of working memory provides the expert performer with greater capacity to engage in planning, reasoning, evaluation and other key activities needed for elite performance (Ericsson and Delaney, 1999). A brief overview of the key perceptual-cognitive skills that underpin superior anticipation and decision making is provided below.

Identifying familiarity in sporting action

It appears that experts are better than novices at recognizing and recalling structure in evolving sequences of sports action. Methods borrowed from cognitive psychology, such as recognition and recall paradigms, have been used to illustrate that experts exhibit superior domain-specific memory compared to non-experts (de Groot, 1964; Simon and Chase, 1973). In sport, North *et al.* (2011) recruited expert and less-expert soccer players to view dynamic film stimuli and anticipate event outcomes. Previously viewed and novel sequences were presented in film or point-light display format with players represented as points on a background display. Participants were required to indicate if they recognized the film clip (i.e. shown previously). Experts demonstrated superior anticipation accuracy and better discrimination between previously seen and novel stimuli. These findings suggest that experts developed more complex memory structures, which enabled them to predict event outcomes more effectively than their less-expert counterparts. The authors argued that experts pick up relational information between players in order to make effective recognition judgments, whereas less-expert players rely on structural or superficial information. Preliminary findings suggest that the ability to recall and recognize patterns of play transfer across similar sports (e.g. netball to basketball) (Abernethy *et al.*, 2005; Smeeton *et al.*, 2005).

Knowledge of situational probabilities

It has been reported that expert performers are able to make use of expectations or situational probabilities to facilitate anticipation in sport. The experienced performer can use his/her superior knowledge base to dismiss highly improbable events and allocate attention to more likely occurring events (Gottsdanker and Kent, 1978). Alain and colleagues (Alain and Proteau, 1980; Alain and Sarrazin, 1990; Alain *et al.*, 1986) showed that expert racket players could accurately predict the outcome of rallies before they ended. Players evaluated the probability of each possible event that could occur in any given context and then used this information to maximize the prediction of subsequent behaviours and outcomes. Similarly, Ward and Williams (2003) reported that elite soccer players were superior to novice counterparts at identifying players who were in a better position to receive the ball and applied a more refined probability hierarchy to decrease the decision threshold necessary to predict successfully. Expert players were better at determining the importance of each option presented, effectively priming the search for new information and ensuring that the most pertinent contextual information was extracted.

The effect of contextual information has been investigated in other sports, such as cricket (McRobert *et al.*, 2011) and tennis (Crognier and Féry, 2005). Crognier and Féry (2005) employed three different subjective context-related manipulations to examine effects of visual information on anticipating outcomes when playing tennis against an opponent. They reported more accurate final ball location predictions during the high-initiative (high-context) condition in which a participant viewed the preceding shots by the opponent, as compared against the moderate-initiative and weak-initiative conditions. The high-initiative condition allowed the participant to control the rallies so that their opponent was on the defensive prior to the end of the rally. This condition also contained subjective context information on the strengths and weaknesses of the opponent and their relative position on court in relation to the participant. In comparison, the moderate-initiative and low-initiative conditions required either the participant or the opponent to set the ball; therefore, it contained no rallies and thus no subjective context information before vision was occluded and the participant was asked to anticipate the location of the opponent's final shot.

McRobert *et al.* (2011) reported similar findings in cricket, with expert batters showing greater prediction accuracy, more effective search behaviours and enhanced verbal reports on thinking. Moreover, when the opponent was viewed multiple times (high context), mean fixation time was reduced. Also, all batters demonstrated improved performance and different thought processes in the high-context condition compared to low context when they responded to the opponent without having seen them bowl previously. The above studies demonstrate how context-specific information influences performance in dynamic sporting tasks.

Picking up advance information (advance cue utilization)

Advance cue utilization refers to picking up information early in an action sequence (Abernethy, 1987). Jones and Miles (1978) examined whether tennis players could anticipate successfully the direction of serves based on advance information. Film clips were occluded 42 ms before and 126 ms and 336 ms after ball–racket contact. Expert players were better than novices at predicting direction of serve in the −42 ms and 126 ms occlusion conditions, whereas no differences in scores were evident in the 336 ms condition. These results suggest that expert tennis players were superior to less skill players in the use of advance information to predict serve direction. Similar work has been conducted in other sports using both temporal (e.g. selectively editing a film into time phases where progressively more of a movement is presented) (Abernethy, 1990; Abernethy and Russell, 1987; Farrow *et al.*, 2005; Salmela and Fiorito, 1979; Williams and Burwitz, 1993) and spatial (e.g. masking/occluding important areas/cues in the visual field) (Abernethy and Russell, 1987; Causer and Williams, under review; Williams and Davids, 1998) occlusion paradigms.

The visual system

Scientists have recorded eye movements to investigate the gaze characteristics used in sport (Janelle *et al.*, 2000). (See Figure 2.1 for example of an eye-movement recording.) A particular focus has been on identifying how visual search characteristics differentiate expert and novice performers. Mann *et al.* (2007) conducted a meta-analysis of nearly three decades of empirical work in this area. Although the strategies employed are task-specific, experts often exhibit fewer fixations of longer duration than non-expert comparison groups. While not a direct measure of attention *per se*, the longer the eye remains fixated on a given target the more information is thought to be extracted from fixated cues in the display. Fixation location is assumed to reflect the important cues used in decision making, whereas fixation duration (search rate) is thought to reflect the information-processing demands placed on the performer. Experts have been reported to use 'visual pivots' or 'anchor points' (Ripoll *et al.*, 1995; Williams and Davids, 1998; Williams and Elliott, 1999) to reduce the amount of eye movements required, thus reducing the demands on information processing and improving processing efficiency.

Figure 2.1 An illustration of eye movement data being gathered in the sport of curling. The image in the top left-hand corner presents the curler at the moment of releasing the stone, whereas the image underneath presents the performer's pupil and corneal reflection. The image on the right is picked up by the head-mounted scene camera, with the cross-hairs representing the curler's point-of-gaze

In summary, thus far we have identified some of the key perceptual-cognitive skills that underpin superior anticipation and decision making in various sporting environments. Specifically, we have identified how experts can have a significant advantage over less-experts in many situations by picking up advance visual information cues, using knowledge of likely event tendencies, and identifying familiarity with evolving action sequences. In the next section, we identify key skills and attributes that can be used to develop systematic training programmes to enhance anticipation and decision making in athletes.

Identifying information using advanced statistical techniques

Principle component analysis (PCA) is a common statistical technique used in biomechanics analyses for finding patterns in data. In brief, PCA is used to reduce large numbers of variables to smaller numbers of components that account for the majority of variance (for a review, see Daffertshofer *et al.*, 2004). Performance analysts too may have access to large databases involving, for example, kinematic joint data of individual players for movement technique analysis (e.g. from motion-capture systems, such as Vicon or Qualisys systems). The same holds for movement analysis of single and/or multiple players (e.g. from motion-tracking systems, such as Prozone or Amisco). As noted, PCA may be used to identify key components that account for the majority of variance in data. Ultimately, this approach could highlight key areas for attention during training, for instance, as well as in scouting future opponents.

Cross correlations can also be used to identify patterns, consistencies and relationships between variables. Cross-correlations are based on the assumption that linear relationships exist between two sets of kinematic time series data (e.g. joint pairs), but do not assume that these variables change in synchrony during the movement (Mullineaux *et al.*, 2001). By introducing time lags between data sets and calculating the corresponding correlation coefficients, researchers can obtain an indication of the type of relationship between body segments, the degree of linkage between body segments and the stability of coordination patterns when applied to repeated trials (Temprado *et al.*, 1997). For example, cross-correlations could be used to determine the consistency of a tennis player's serve or a cricket bowler's release action. Using high-speed video cameras and cross-correlation techniques, small temporal and spatial inconsistencies can be highlighted. Comparison between successful and unsuccessful trials, or training and competition scenarios, can determine the most efficient and/or effective technique for an individual. Coaches can then use this information to ensure this technique is reproduced consistently.

Protocols to measure advance cue utilization

Established video-based protocols can be used to assess anticipation and decision making in sport. These methods would require video footage of a certain skill or series of actions – for example, a series of soccer penalty kicks. Video information could then be edited temporally and/or spatially in order to assess anticipation and decision making – of the soccer goalkeeper given the above example. Information access (visual cues) and time available will influence perceptual strategies and so occlusion techniques can be used to manipulate these constraints (for a review of available procedures, see Carling *et al.*, 2009; Williams and Abernethy, 2012). Temporal occlusion (see Figure 2.2) is used to manipulate the time course of access to cues and has been used frequently to distinguish between skill levels (Jackson *et al.*, 2006). The temporal occlusion paradigm can also be used *in situ* using liquid crystal goggles that are capable of transitions between transparency and opacity within 5 ms (Milgram, 1987). Liquid crystal goggles provide an important advance in efforts to replicate the natural environment. The spatial or event occlusion (see Figure 2.2) technique is used to mask certain information in the visual field. A decrease in performance relative to a non-occluded control condition suggests that the occluded area contains key information concerning that particular movement.

Using these techniques, performance analysts can identify critical visual cues, as well as what time in the action sequence this information becomes important. Information derived can subsequently be used to create training programmes to improve attention on specific information in order to enhance anticipation and decision making. Soccer goalkeepers may fixate on a certain part of a penalty taker's posture that enables good anticipation of direction and flight characteristics of the ball. This technique can also be used to demonstrate how deceptive movements in sport can be anticipated. For example, a player executing a dummy pass in rugby may exhibit certain postural cues that are inconsistent with a 'normal' pass. The process involved in identifying these differences may then allow players to practice avoiding negative effects of deceptive movements by opponents.

Situational probabilities

The actions of opponents can be coded and a database established to identify trends or preferences for individuals and/or teams. In so doing, both general tactics as well as specific tactics based on, say, the score and/or time in a given game might be developed. By identifying patterns in advance, players and coaches are able to prepare for the most likely events. In cricket, knowledge of previous batting behaviours of opponents in terms of shot selection, target areas, ball end point and so on, for example, may provide the captain of the bowling team an advantage when setting field positions and instructing bowlers. Similarly, tennis

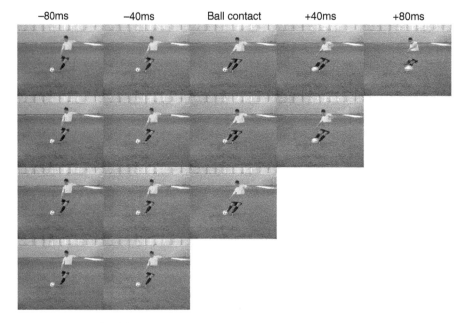

Figure 2.2 An example of the temporal and spatial occlusion paradigms with images occluded at various time points relative to ball–foot contact and spatial occlusion of the hip region

serves from an upcoming opponent may be coded to identify if a particular type of serve is preferred at critical game points, so offering the player a possible advantage in anticipating various aspects of the serve (e.g. direction, speed and/or spin). Thus, recording of performance data over time may allow for patterns of play, or tactical idiosyncrasies, to be identified. By comparing successful and unsuccessful events, critical behaviours and other variables prevalent in effective performances might be established. With this knowledge, alterations to key performance variables can be targeted in future events to increase the probability of successful performance.

The results or outcomes of games may be predicted or forecasted using techniques such as time series analysis, regression analysis and artificial neural networks, among others. These techniques have previously been used to predict scores in soccer games (Stefani, 2003) and attendance in baseball games (Siegfried and Eisenberg, 1980), and to investigate the effects of feedback in motor skill acquisition (Blackwell *et al.*, 1991).

In summary, skill acquisition specialists are concerned with understanding how information from the environment might best be used by athletes. The techniques identified in previous sections illustrate what information is available and how athletes might be guided towards attending to and exploiting this information. Performance analysts have the important task of identifying structure in seemingly otherwise random complex environments. Using data from training and games, models of behaviours can be created and performance outcomes forecasted, thus providing coaches with information regarding possible tactics derived from trends in opponent behaviours. Gathering data and modelling performances allows for effective tactics, behaviours and structures to be identified that can assist in developing technique and tactical awareness in players. In collaboration with coaches and skill acquisition specialists, performance analysts can be involved in developing and implementing training programmes that facilitate more rapid acquisition of perceptual-cognitive skills in athletes.

Training anticipation and decision making

Several researchers have examined the potential of training perceptual-cognitive skills in sport (Causer *et al.*, 2012). Williams *et al.* (1999) suggested that perceptual training programmes should use expert search patterns as models of perceptual performance, and so include tasks that contribute to developing a comparable knowledge base upon which these search strategies are based. Perceptual-cognitive interventions that help develop the knowledge base underlying expert perception have more practical utility in aiding acquisition of expert performance than clinically based visual skills training programmes that focus on improving visual function (Williams and Grant, 1999).

The majority of training studies in sport have utilized video-based simulations including instruction and varying amounts of feedback. These training programmes attempt to highlight links between important display cues and outcome (Ward and Williams, 2003). Williams and Burwitz (1993) applied the temporal occlusion paradigm to a penalty kick in soccer. Novice goalkeepers showed significant improvements in anticipatory performance when the relationship between important postural cues and penalty kick outcome were highlighted. More recently, Savelsbergh *et al.* (2010) attempted to modify visual search behaviours of inexperienced soccer goalkeepers in order to improve performance. The goalkeepers were required to anticipate penalty kick direction from video clips projected onto a screen and respond by moving a joystick. The perceptual learning group viewed clips that highlighted key information from the run-up sequence, the training group viewed the unedited videos and a control group performed the pre- and post-tests only. The results showed that visual search behaviours of the perceptual training group changed significantly and improved initiation of the joystick movement. This initiation coincided with the timing of the most important visual information and led to significantly better performance than the training and control groups.

Raab *et al.* (2005) compared the effectiveness of decision training and/or behavioural practice in elite table tennis players. Twenty table tennis players were assigned to either a behavioural or a decision training group. The behavioural group received technical training at regular intervals emphasizing targeting accuracy in the forehand and backhand strokes. The decision group received the same training as the behavioural group for the first four weeks and in the remaining five weeks were provided with video feedback and modelling orientated towards improving transitions between backhand and forehand. The two groups were assessed on how well they performed strokes technically and on their ability to make the best tactical decisions in competitive game situations. The behavioural group ranked last in tactical decision making and second in technique, while the decision-trained group ranked first in tactical decision making and third in technique. These results show that the combination of technical training and tactical decision making was more successful than technical training alone.

Williams and Grant (1999) provided a detailed review on research in perceptual training. The authors noted the potential of perceptual training programmes but also identified certain shortcomings, not least omission of control and/or placebo groups in several studies. Furthermore, transfer and/or retention tests had not been used adequately in previous research examining whether training facilitated improvements in real-world contexts as well as whether these improvements manifested themselves long term. Williams *et al.* (2003) addressed these limitations while using a training programme for the penalty flick in field hockey. Laboratory and field-based measures of anticipatory performance were recorded in a training group, a placebo group and a control group. The training group was exposed to video simulation training with key information cues underlying anticipation identified; the placebo group viewed an instructional video focusing on the technical skills involved in hockey goaltending; and the control group completed the anticipation tests only. Participants who underwent the training programme significantly improved performance beyond that of the placebo and control groups in both laboratory and field-based tests. These findings provide strong evidence that cognitive interventions highlighting the most informative cues and corresponding action requirements, whether by video simulation or by instruction *in situ*, have practical utility in facilitating perceptual skill in sport (Scott *et al.*, 1998; Tayler *et al.*, 1994).

Concluding remarks

In this chapter, we have outlined some of the key perceptual-cognitive skills underpinning anticipation and decision-making in sport. The role of these different perceptual-cognitive skills in performance is well documented in the research literature, but application of this knowledge to develop training programs is not well-established. Although we have reported a number of attempts to develop training simulations under controlled conditions, there remains a paucity of documented case studies involving the use of these training interventions with high-performance athletes. Performance analysts, supported by skill acquisition specialists, have a pivotal role to play in help to bridge the gap between ongoing research work and the translation of new knowledge into applied interventions that may be used at the 'coal-face' in high-performance sport.

References

Abernethy, B. (1987) 'Anticipation in sport: A review', *Physical Education Review*, 10: 5–16.

Abernethy, B. (1990) 'Expertise, visual search and information pick-up in squash', *Perception*, 19: 63–77.

Abernethy, B. and Russell, D.G. (1987) 'The relationship between expertise and visual search strategy in a racquet sport', *Human Movement Science*, 6: 283–319.

Abernethy, B., Baker, J. and Côté, J. (2005) 'Transfer of pattern recall skills may contribute to the development of sport expertise', *Applied Cognitive Psychology*, 19: 705–18.

Alain, C. and Proteau, L. (1980) 'Decision-making in sport', in C.H. Nadeau, W.R. Halliwell, K.M. Newell and G.C. Roberts (eds), *Psychology of Motor Behavior and Sport* (pp. 465–77). Champaign, IL: Human Kinetics.

Alain, C. and Sarrazin, C. (1990) 'Study of decision-making in squash competition: A computer simulation approach', *Canadian Journal of Applied Sport Science*, 15(3): 193–200.

Alain, C., Sarrazin, C. and Lacombe, D. (1986) 'The use of subjective expected values in decision making in sport', in D.M. Landers (ed.), *Sport and Elite Performers* (pp. 1–6). Champaign, IL: Human Kinetics.

Blackwell, J., Simmons, R. and Spray, J. (1991) 'Time series analysis of knowledge of results effects during motor skill acquisition', *Research Quarterly for Exercise and Sport*, 62: 10–17.

Carling, C., Reilly, T. and Williams, A.M. (2009) *Performance Assessment for Field Sports*, London, UK: Routledge.

Causer, J. and Williams, A.M. (2012) 'Professional expertise', in P. Lanzer (ed.), *Catheter-based Cardiovascular Interventions – Knowledge-based Approach* (pp. 97–112). New York: Springer.

Causer, J. and Williams, A.M. (under review) 'Sports clothing and disguise: playing tricks on the eyes', *British Journal of Psychology*.

Causer, J., Holmes, P.S. and Williams, A.M. (2011) 'Quiet eye training in a visuomotor control task', *Medicine & Science in Sports and Exercise*, 43(6): 1042–9.

Causer, J., Janelle, C.M., Vickers, J.N. and Williams, A.M. (2012) 'Perceptual training: What can be trained?', in A.M. Williams and N.J. Hodges (eds), *Skill Acquisition in Sport: Research, Theory and Practice* (pp. 306–24). London: Routledge.

Crognier, L. and Féry, Y. (2005) 'Effect of tactical initiative on predicting passing shots in tennis', *Applied Cognitive Psychology*, 19: 637–49.

Daffertshofer, A., Lamoth, C.J.C., Meijer, O.G. and Beek, P.J. (2004) 'PCA in studying coordination and variability: A tutorial', *Clinical Biomechanics*, 19(4): 415–28.

de Groot, A.D. (1964) *Thought and Choice in Chess*, The Hague: Mouton.

Ericsson, K.A. and Kintsch, W. (1995) 'Long-term working memory', *Psychological Review*, 102(2): 211–45.

Ericsson, K.A. and Lehmann, A.C. (1996) 'Expert and exceptional performance: Evidence of maximal adaptation to task constraints', *Annual Review of Psychology*, 47: 273–305.

Ericsson, K.A. and Delaney, P.F. (1999) 'Long-term working memory as an alternative to capacity models of working memory in everyday skilled performance', in A. Miyake and P. Shah (eds), *Models of Working Memory: Mechanics of Active Maintenance and Executive Control* (pp. 257–97). New York: Cambridge University Press.

Ericsson, K.A., Krampe, R.T. and Tesch-Römer, C. (1993) 'The role of deliberate practice in the acquisition of expert performance', *Psychological Review*, 100(3): 363–406.

Farrow, D., Abernethy, B. and Jackson, R.C. (2005) 'Probing expert anticipation with the temporal occlusion paradigm: Experimental investigations of some methodological issues', *Motor Control*, 9: 332–51.

Gottsdanker, R.M. and Kent, K. (1978) 'Reaction time and probability on isolated trials', *Journal of Motor Behavior*, 10: 233–8.

Hagemann, N., Strauss, B. and Cañal-Bruland, R. (2006) 'Training perceptual skill by orienting visual attention', *Journal of Sport and Exercise Psychology*, 28: 143–58.

Jackson, R.C., Warren, S. and Abernethy, B. (2006) 'Anticipation skill and susceptibility to deceptive movement', *Acta Psychologica*, 123: 355–71.

Janelle, C.M., Hillman, C.H., Apparies, R.J., Murray, N.P., Meili, L., Fallon, E.A. and Hatfield, B.D. (2000) 'Expertise differences in cortical activation and gaze behavior during rifle shooting', *Journal of Sport and Exercise Psychology*, 22: 167–82.

Jones, C.M. and Miles, T.R. (1978) 'Use of advance cues in predicting the flight of a lawn tennis ball', *Journal of Human Movement Studies*, 4: 231–5.

29

Joseph, G.M. and Patel, V.L. (1990) 'Domain knowledge and hypothesis generation in diagnostic reasoning', *Medical Decision Making*, 10: 31–46.

Mann, D.T.Y., Williams, A.M., Ward, P. and Janelle, C.M. (2007) 'Perceptual-cognitive expertise in sport: A meta-analysis', *Journal of Sport and Exercise Psychology*, 29: 457–78.

McRobert, A.P., Ward, P., Eccles, D.W. and Williams, A.M. (2011) 'The effect of manipulating context-specific information on perceptual-cognitive processes during a simulated anticipation task', *British Journal of Psychology*, 102(3): 519–34.

Milgram, P. (1987) 'A spectacle-mounted liquid-crystal tachistoscope', *Behavior Research Methods, Instruments and Computers*, 19: 449–56.

Mullineaux, D.R., Bartlett, R.M. and Bennett, S.J. (2001) 'Research design and statistics in biomechanics and motor control', *Journal of Sports Sciences*, 19: 739–60.

North, J.S., Ward, P., Ericsson, K.A. and Williams, A.M. (2011) 'Mechanisms underlying skilled anticipation and recognition in a dynamic and temporally constrained domain', *Memory*, 19(2): 155–68.

Raab, M., Masters, R.S.W. and Maxwell, J.P. (2005) 'Improving the "how" and "what" decisions of elite table tennis players', *Human Movement Science*, 24: 326–44.

Ripoll, H., Kerlirzin, Y., Stein, J. and Reine, B. (1995) 'Analysis of information processing, decision making, and visual strategies in complex problem solving sport situations', *Human Movement Science*, 14(3): 325–49.

Salmela, J.H. and Fiorito, P. (1979) 'Visual cues in ice hockey goaltending', *Canadian Journal of Sport Sciences*, 4: 56–9.

Savelsbergh, G.J.P., van Gastel, P.J. and van Kampen, P.M. (2010) 'Anticipation of penalty kicking direction can be improved by directing attention through perceptual learning', *International Journal of Sport Psychology*, 41(4): 24–41.

Scott, D., Scott, L.M. and Howe, B.L. (1998) 'Training anticipation for intermediate tennis player', *Behavior Modification*, 22(3): 243–61.

Siegfried, J. and Eisenberg, J. (1980) 'Measuring and forecasting demand: a case study of baseball attendance', *Business*, 30: 34–41.

Simon, H.A. and Chase, W.G. (1973) 'Skill in chess', *American Scientist*, 61: 394–403.

Smeeton, N.J., Williams, A.M., Hodges, N.J. and Ward, P. (2005) 'The relative effectiveness of various instructional approaches in developing anticipation skill', *Journal of Experimental Psychology: Applied*, 11(2): 98–110.

Stefani, R.T. (2003) 'Estimating the probability of a home win, draw and away win in soccer', Paper presented at the International Statistical Institute, Berlin, Germany, August.

Tayler, M.A., Burwitz, L. and Davids, K. (1994) 'Coaching perceptual strategy in badminton', *Journal of Sports Sciences*, 12: 213.

Temprado, J.J., Della-Grast, M., Farrell, M. and Laurent, M. (1997) 'A novice-expert comparison of (intra-limb) coordination subserving the volleyball serve', *Human Movement Science*, 16: 653–76.

Vickers, J.N. and Lewinski, W. (2011) 'Performing under pressure: Gaze control, decision making and shooting performance of elite and rookie police officers', *Human Movement Science*, 31(1): 101–17.

Ward, P. and Williams, A.M. (2003) 'Perceptual and cognitive skill development in soccer: The multidimensional nature of expert performance', *Journal of Sport & Exercise Psychology*, 25(1): 93–111.

Ward, P., Farrow, D., Harris, K.R., Williams, A.M., Eccles, D.W. and Ericsson, K.A. (2008) 'Training perceptual-cognitive skills: Can sport psychology research inform military decision training?', *Military Psychology*, 20: S71–S102.

Williams, A.M. (2000) 'Perceptual skill in soccer: Implications for talent identification and development', *Journal of Sports Sciences*, 18: 737–50.

Williams, A.M. (2009) 'Perceiving the intentions of others: How do skilled performers make anticipation judgments?', *Progress in Brain Research*, 174: 73–83.

Williams, A.M. and Burwitz, L. (1993) 'Advance cue utilization in soccer', in T. Reilly, J. Clarys and A. Stibbe (eds), *Science and Football II* (pp. 239–43). London: E & FN Spon.

Williams, A.M. and Davids, K. (1998) 'Visual search strategy, selective attention and expertise in soccer', *Research Quarterly for Exercise and Sport*, 69: 111–28.

Williams, A.M. and Elliott, D. (1999) 'Anxiety, expertise and visual search strategy in karate', *Journal of Sport & Exercise Psychology*, 21: 362–75.

Williams, A.M. and Grant, A. (1999) 'Training perceptual skill in sport', *International Journal of Sport Psychology*, 30: 194–220.

Williams, A.M. and Abernethy, B. (2012) 'Anticipation and decision-making: Skills, methods, and measures', in G. Tenenbaum and R. Ecklund (eds), *Handbook of Measurement in Sport and Exercise Psychology* (pp. 191–202). Champaign, IL: Human Kinetics.

Williams, A.M., Davids, K. and Williams, J.G. (1999) *Visual Perception and Action in Sport*, London: E & FN Spon.

Williams, A.M., Ward, P. and Chapman, C. (2003) 'Training perceptual skill in field hockey: Is there transfer from the laboratory to the field?', *Research Quarterly for Exercise and Sport*, 74(1): 98–103.

Williams, A.M., Huys, R., Cañal-Bruland, R. and Hagemann, N. (2009) 'The dynamical information underpinning anticipation skill', *Human Movement Science*, 28: 362–70.

3

THE INTENDING–PERCEIVING–ACTING CYCLE IN SPORTS PERFORMANCE

Duarte Araújo[1], Keith Davids[2] and Pedro Passos[1]

[1]TECHNICAL UNIVERSITY OF LISBON, PORTUGAL
[2]QUEENSLAND UNIVERSITY OF TECHNOLOGY, AUSTRALIA

Summary

Whereas behavioural scientists have tended to emphasize the personal constraints of performers in attempting to understand perception and action in sport, from an ecological dynamics perspective, skilled behaviour consists of intentional adaptation to the constraints imposed by the environment during task performance. Ecological dynamics integrates an information-based approach to perception with a dynamical systems orientation to action. For a given task, a performer and the performance environment are treated as a pair of dynamical sub-systems that are coupled and interact mechanically and informationally. Their continuous interactions give rise to behavioural dynamics, a vector field with stable, avoided and changing system states. Sudden transitions in behaviours indicate that decisions emerge in the 'intending–perceiving–acting cycle'. These ideas imply that there should be a strong emphasis on the specificity of the relations between the individual and the environment in designing representative settings both for experiments and for practice in sport.

Introduction

The ability of humans to select behavioural patterns that are tightly coordinated with the environment, when trying to achieve specific performance goals, has long been a concern for behavioural scientists. The production of stable yet adaptive behaviours raises two constituent issues. First, it implies the coordination of action, exemplified when the neuromusculoskeletal components of the body become temporarily organized into coordinated movement, or by the coordination patterns that emerge from the interpersonal interactions between players in sports teams. Second, it implies perception, such that information about the world and the body enables actions to be selected and adapted to environmental conditions. The problem of intentionality and decision making is thus grounded on the problem of the coupling between sub-systems involved in perception and action (Warren, 2006).

From an ecological dynamics perspective, skilled behaviour consists of intentional adaptation to the constraints imposed by the environment during task performance (e.g. Araújo and Davids, 2009). The influential work of Kugler and Turvey (1987) drew attention to the role of information in guiding action, originally argued by Gibson (1979), but went further in modelling how human action is constrained by laws of non-linear dynamics. Gibson's (1979) suggestion was that, rather than being localized in an internal structure, control is distributed over the performer–environment system. For Warren (2006), the structure and physics of the environment, the biomechanics of the body, perceptual information about the state of the agent–environment system and the demands of the task all serve to constrain behavioural outcomes. Adaptive behaviour, rather than being imposed by a pre-existing structure, emerges from this confluence of constraints under the boundary condition of a particular task or goal.

The link between information and action during sport performance

In ecological dynamics, perception refers to how animals, including humans, can be aware of their surroundings. For example, during locomotion, a performer can visually regulate their actions by detecting information from the optic flow. Optic flow is created by patterns of light available at a point of observation, structured by particular performer–environment interactions. In optic flow, particular reliable patterns of optical structure, called *invariants*, are relevant to guiding activity. Outflow and inflow are distinct forms of optic flow that inform the performer whether he/she is moving forwards or backwards. Flow is structured by the texture and objects that we encounter as we move around a performance environment (e.g. gaps, people, terrain) and allows us to discover invariants to regulate activity (Carello and Turvey, 2002). In order to effectively guide their activities, performers need to know more than just *what* they are approaching (i.e. perception for object identification). They also need to know *how* they are approaching (i.e. the spatio-temporal characteristics of how they are addressing a feature of the performance environment). Are they moving too fast? Do they need to adjust that approach? Should they slow down or speed up? Turn? Stop? For example, as a skilled rugby union player runs with the ball towards a group of defenders, he/she makes subtle adjustments to behaviour in order to control the impending collision. The player needs to maintain enough speed to engage them, but not so much that physical contact occurs. Effective performance requires that he/she knows when to adjust running-line trajectories in order to avoid being tackled.

Optical structure relevant to negotiating the environment has been identified and provides examples of quantitative invariants. The optical quantity called τ is specific to when a point of observation will contact an upcoming surface. As the performer approaches the defenders, their optical projection on the retina magnifies. The speed of approach affects this rate of retinal image expansion, regulating the change in optical area per unit of time. The quantity τ is given by the inverse of the relative rate of the retinal expansion – how long it will take until there are no units of time left (Lee, 1998). As our rugby player slows down (or speeds up), the rate at which τ approaches zero changes. The rate of this change (that is, the derivative of τ) is specific to when to pass the ball to a support player or when to change running-line trajectory to avoid collision. It quantifies whether the observer's kinetic energy is being dissipated (e.g. by braking) at a rate sufficient to stop movement before contact occurs. These descriptions of global optical structure capture situations when an observer is approaching a surface. But they are also relevant to a surface or object, such as a ball, approaching the point of observation. Local disturbances of optical structure are relevant to the guidance of interceptive behaviours and can be described in terms of τ and its derivative, providing specific information to the performer on when and how the interception of an object, individual or surface will occur.

These theoretical ideas have been exemplified in research by Correia *et al.* (2011), who analysed time series positional data of rugby union players from video footage of competitive performance. The τ value of the distance–motion gap between an attacker (first receiver) and his closest defender was calculated, along with the duration of the next pass made by that attacker to a teammate (second receiver). Results revealed that the initial τ value predicted 64 per cent of the variance observed in pass duration. A qualitative distinction of τ dynamics between two periods of the approach between the attacker and the defender was also observed (Figure 3.1). The degree of variability or dispersion in the entire time series of τ data (inter-trial variability) was compared between the period up until the first receiver got the ball (i.e. approach 'Without ball' – left-hand side of Figure 3.1) and after receiving the ball from the onset of the second phase of play (i.e. approach 'With ball' – right-hand side of Figure 3.1). To clarify, time zero refers to the time when an attacker who will perform a pass received the ball. The phase before time zero is termed 'Without ball', since the attacker whose pass is under analysis is without the ball during this initial period. Before the attacker receives the ball at time zero, both players are approaching each other. Then, during the phase 'With ball' (when the attacker has received the ball), the players continue approaching until the attacker releases the ball (i.e. makes the pass). Results showed that the point-by-point mean τ values computed were greater for the first period of approach than for the second phase. These data suggested that the time-to-contact values between the attacker and the defender may provide information about future pass possibilities. Moreover, these periods displayed dissimilarities in the point-by-point mean and standard deviation bands. The higher inter-trial variability during the approach 'Without ball', compared to a low variability in the approach 'With ball' indicates that these τ data points tend to be much closer to the mean τ in the approach 'With ball'. Correia *et al.* (2011) argued that the informational fields constraining attacker–defender interaction may be viewed as a convergent channelling of possibilities towards a single pass solution (Figure 3.1).

While all performers need to perceive information on openings and obstacles to locomotion, what counts as an 'opening' on field necessarily differs between individual performers. How perception is 'individualized' is addressed next, together with the concept of affordance.

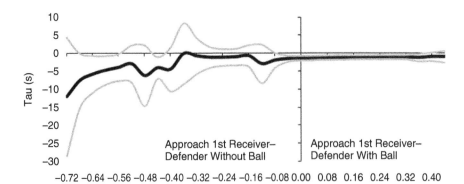

Figure 3.1 Point-by-point τ average band (M±SD) of the distance–motion gap between the 1st receiver and the defender. The mean is the black line, and the standard deviations are the grey lines. X = 0 marks the instance the 1st receiver receives the ball from the onset of the second phase of play, i.e. beginning the part of the approach 'With ball'. (From Correia *et al.*, 2011.) See text for further details.

Affordances

Affordances are possibilities for action in a particular performer–environment setting (Gibson, 1979); they are what an arrangement of surfaces/textures/objects offers to a performer. Whether a hurdle, for example, is a 'running over' place or a 'jumping off' place is not determined by its absolute size or shape but how it relates to a particular performer, including that individual's size and agility and style of locomotion. The assumptions central to Gibson's (1979) theory of affordances are that: (a) actor-scaled properties of the environment afford a given behaviour to a performer; (b) informational invariants in energy arrays specify an individual-specific action; and (c) provided observers have perceptual machinery sensitive to this information, they are able to perceive an affordance (Gibson, 1979; Withagen and Michaels, 2005). The theory of affordances is based on the dual interdependence of perception and action, where affordances are the primary objects of perception, and action is the realization of affordances.

These ideas were exemplified by Esteves *et al.* (2011), who studied 1 vs 1 basketball sub-phases and showed that decisions made by an attacker to drive to the left or right of a defender were affordance-based. These investigators showed that the specific posture adopted by a defender guided the decisional behaviour of the attacker. Both novice and intermediate attackers made the same affordance-based decisions by driving to the side of the defender's most advanced foot, but only at small values of interpersonal distances. Leftward drives emerged at smaller angles, which corresponded to the defender having his right foot advanced. Rightward drives occurred at larger angles, which corresponded to the defender having his left foot advanced. The use of this posture information by attackers trying to dribble towards the basket was not specific to expertise levels. This observation indicates how contextual information (e.g. posture of defender) directly helped to guide decisional behaviours – a finding in line with data from other studies (e.g. Cordovil *et al.*, 2009). Decisions on drive direction when dribbling, in both skill groups, was based on transient postures emerging from immediate defenders. By acting on an affordance related to the information available in a performance context, performers can rely on information about a future state of the player–environment system, a functional way to control ongoing actions and achieve task goals. The perception of affordances depends on the level of attunement of an individual to relevant properties of the environment, acquired through experience and learning (Fajen *et al.*, 2009). The fact that both groups acted on the posture information in a similar way indicates that novices may have been attuned to the relevant information sources even before the coupling of their perceptions and actions was fine-tuned.

Affordances exist on a continuum of action. For example, Pepping and Li (2005) showed that, for a performer, the distinction between two affordances for a standing reach and reach-and-jump action is not obvious: in the case of overhead reaching, as the required reach height approaches the maximum standing reach height, performers begin to exploit additional degrees of freedom until finally a critical boundary value is met at which an alternative reach-and-jump action emerges. As van der Kamp *et al.* (1998: 352) argued, action-scaled or 'body-scaled ratios can be used as a critical determinant of action choice – a change beyond the critical ratio value demands a new class of action'. Van der Kamp *et al.* (1998) highlighted that this process of switching between movement patterns emerges from changes in the constraints imposed upon action for each individual. This explanation clarifies that individuals do not engage in conscious and rational mental calculations, comparing the current body 'object-to-reach' ratios with an internal representation of a critical ratio, and deciding on the basis of this comparison which action to execute. Rather, action may be considered an emergent process, under constraints, which harnesses intrinsic self-organization processes.

Action self-organization

Inspired by Gibson's (1979) ecological psychology and the work of Bernstein (Bernstein, 1967), Reed (1996) argued that skilled behaviour requires subtle resource usage, asserting that behaviour is not intrinsically mechanical, but functional. He argued that, in the course of evolution, selection pressures gave rise to different action systems, enabling performers to establish new functional relationships with their performance environments. Whereas Gibson's theorizing on affordances was primarily concerned with how they are perceived, Reed addressed how affordances are utilized. During performance in sport, resources can emerge from the performer (e.g. height, velocity) or from the environment (e.g. adherent floor, jumpable obstacle). Thus an action should not be considered as a simple displacement of anatomical parts of the body because complex biological systems exhibit the capacity for stable and unstable patterned relationships to emerge between system parts through self-organization (Davids *et al.*, 2001). In the example of reaching and jumping, at the point of bifurcation (i.e. the critical ratio), the probability of using overhead reach and reach-and-jump actions is the same. An accidental fluctuation or perturbation to the system constrains the decision to use one or other action mode. Bifurcations show how open systems (e.g. biological systems which are sensitive to energy exchanges with the surrounding environment) often have several options in particular environmental conditions (Araújo *et al.*, 2006). For example, when an athlete is running to gain possession of a ball in soccer, and suddenly slips, self-organized inter-limb coordination can occur, to compensate for the effects of gravity and to re-equilibrate the performer vertically.

In nonlinear dynamical movement systems, this type of re-organization process can occur in several functionally appropriate ways. Non-linear dynamics is a branch of physics that provides a formal treatment of any system which is continually evolving over time, and which can be formally modelled as a numerical system with its own equations of motion (Araújo *et al.*, 2006). Within this framework, the behaviour of any living system can be plotted as a trajectory in a state space: the set of all states attainable by the system, together with the paths to them. Resting states of the system are attractors. A physical system can have one or more attractors. The number and layout of these attractors influence the overall functioning and behaviour of the system (Kugler *et al.*, 1990). In human movement systems, attractors are roughly equivalent to functional states of coordination of system degrees of freedom (Kelso, 1995). For example, when dribbling in ball sports, this idea can be captured by the relative positioning of an attacker with the ball faced by a defender. When the defender matches an opponent's movements and remains in position between an attacker and the goal, the form of this dyadic system remains stable (despite changes in specific variables describing its organization).

Self-organization processes emerge from the dynamics of open systems that intrinsically and autonomously create and destroy such stable system states. Transitions between states of organization (order–order transitions) occur at the timescale of perception and action, exemplifying interactions between athletes and the environment. These interactions initiate system trajectories from one marginally stable dynamic mode to another, providing the basis for athletes to select functional coordination modes. Structurally stable states of ordered behaviour are created or destroyed with reference to changes in the perceptual field (e.g. optic flow), allowing a performer to switch between different stable modes of behaviour. For example, a player who dribbles past an opponent near a goal area in hockey creates a transition region. In order to facilitate a transition, the attacker has to de-stabilize a stable state of system organization such as not approaching the goal until he/she can dribble past the defender, changing the dyadic system to a new state where he/she is approaching the goal.

The constant (re)structuring of system organization and behaviour emerges under the influence of constraints, which can simultaneously limit and enlarge the system's range of behavioural possibilities. Bottom-up constraints are responsible for the initial formation of macroscopic order among system microcomponents (e.g. physiological processes of the athlete). While this is occurring, top-down constraints can 'enslave' the microcomponents into the macroscopic whole (e.g. competing at altitude). In this way, human behaviour can be constrained by the specific performance context in such a way that states that emerge are those that contribute to the performer–environment system's desired behavioural goal. When microcomponents interact and bottom-up constraints produce macroscopic wholes, these large-scale patterned entities use top-down constraints (e.g. intentions) to regulate the organization of system microcomponents (e.g. motor system degrees-of-freedom) (Kelso and Engstrøm, 2006).

Intentionality and sport behaviour

The perceptual control of action and the enhancement of the quality of perception by exploratory activity are specified by initial conditions and constraints that are bounded by the goals aimed by the performer. Intentional constraints may be seen as goal-state attractors arising through the dynamic interplay of constant energy exchanges between a performer and the environment (Kugler *et al.*, 1990). According to Kugler and Turvey (1987), internally stored energy flows provide a source of force that can be controlled by the performer in sport and which can actively utilize or compete against external forces (e.g. a runner using or braking against gravitational forces when running downhill). With the capacity to delay the use of energy flows, a movement system becomes less reactive in a mechanical sense, but more active in biological purpose. Thus, internal forces can be directed to compete actively with external forces in achieving specific goals. The intentional dynamics that emerge during performance are the consequence of a movement system's ability to use energy tactically, to anticipate outcomes, and to choose among options. Some aspects of intentional behaviour refer to an interior frame of reference (e.g. the biological systems of the attacker), and others refer to an exterior frame (e.g. the situation confronting an attacker, which includes the position of the net/goal and defender). To intend a performance goal, a performer needs to select an initial condition that permits attainment of a specified final condition under the laws of physics. With each step closer to the goal, the information must become ever more specific, narrowing the range of possible action paths, until ultimately, at the final moments of goal accomplishment, an emergent performance path becomes uniquely defined.

The individual can use his or her internal potential only at choice points (Kugler *et al.*, 1990). Decisions arise at those points along a trajectory at which the system must expend internal energy to keep moving in the same mode towards the same target, or where it can counter the work done on it by an exterior gradient. Structurally, these choice points in the field are bifurcation points that act as attractors. They imply choices because there is insufficient information in the field to define uniquely a future path. In a one-on-one dribbling situation in sport, the defender seeks to maintain system symmetry, but the attacker is looking for a way to achieve his or her goal (of scoring), thus needing to choose a different path than desired by the defender. Due to the existing symmetry of a dyadic system in which a defender confronts an attacker, there is not enough information to select a path in advance. Consequently, the selection of a goal path for the attacker is an emergent process.

In order to achieve a final goal, nonlinear behaviours will result if there is a competition between attractors (i.e. if there are multiple sub-goals to be satisfied). The player–environment system that is established during dribbling in ball sports can facilitate our understanding of how the selected actions that emerge from player–environment interactions can contribute to achievement of an intended goal. With this approach, predicting a given behaviour requires precise and complete specification of a performer's initial conditions (including historical context), current (and largely private) mental states and the environmental context. Because these factors interact nonlinearly to constrain behaviour, incomplete knowledge of even a small detail may be enough to impair the ability to precisely predict emergent behaviour. However, it is clearly important to consider the dynamics of athlete–environment interactions in order to understand decision-making processes in sport (Araújo *et al.*, 2006).

For example, Cordovil *et al.* (2009) studied effects of task and individual constraints on decision-making processes in basketball. When specific instructions were manipulated, they observed effects on emergent behaviour of the dyadic system. Moreover, when body-scaling of participants was manipulated by creating dyads with different height and arm span relations, results indicated that height had a greater effect on emergent dynamics of decision making in dyads. When attackers were considerably taller than defenders, there were fewer symmetry-breaking opportunities than in other combinations (see Figure 3.2).

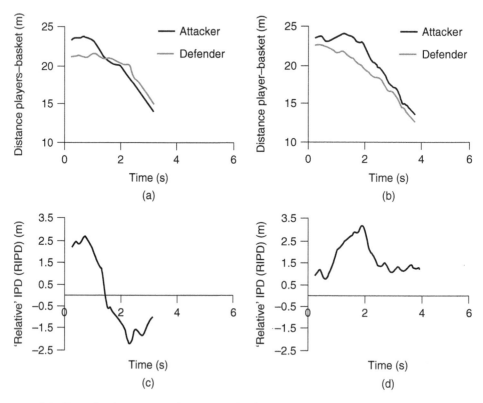

Figure 3.2 Example of situations with symmetry-breaking (graphs on the left) and without symmetry-breaking (graphs on the right). Graphs A and B show the players' distance to the basket over time, and graphs C and D show variations in the 'relative' interpersonal distance (RIPD) values in the same situations. To identify symmetry-breaking, one should look for a crossing of the lines that represent the trajectories of an attacker and defender on the graph of the players' distance to the basket, or for a negative value for 'relative' interpersonal distance. (From Cordovil *et al.*, 2009.)

The ecological dynamics of behaviour in sport

The key to studying a performer–environment system in sport then is to make the dynamics underlying the system's behaviour observable. Araújo, Davids and colleagues, in conjunction with others, have used this approach to study performance in sport (e.g. Araújo *et al.*, 2006; Davids *et al.*, 1994, 2001; Handford *et al.*, 1997; McGarry *et al.*, 2002; Palut and Zanone, 2005; Passos *et al.*, 2006; Schmidt *et al.*, 1999). An attraction of dynamic models is that they can explain different decisions by means of the same underlying process of emerging and decaying attractors. The behaviour of an identified system collective variable over time can often be described by a gradient equation. More precisely, if the system variable of interest (i.e. a collective or coordination variable or order parameter) is denoted by 'x' and the potential function is denoted by 'V', then the evolution of 'x' over time can be expressed by the differential equation (3.1).

$$dx/dt = - dV/dx \qquad (3.1)$$

A value of 'x' for which the derivative 'dx/dt' is equal to zero is an equilibrium point and corresponds to a steady state of the system. If that value is a minimum of 'V', then it is a stable region (i.e. an attractor); if the value is a maximum of 'V', then it is an unstable region (i.e. a repellor). A simple interpretation of equation (3.1) consists of identifying 'x' with the coordinate of a small ball which moves in the potential landscape. In line with this principle, a model proposed by Tuller *et al.* (1994) was established to study speech perception, namely the discrimination between the words 'say' and 'stay', when an acoustic parameter was varied. Listeners perceive the word 'say' at short silent gaps after the 's' noise and they perceive the word 'stay' at long silent gaps, implying the presence of two attractors (say and stay). If 'x' is a variable characterizing the perceptual form, then the potential function 'V' can be written as equation (3.2).

$$V(x) = k \, x - (x^2)/2 + (x^4)/4 \qquad (3.2)$$

where 'k' is a control parameter (gap duration). Equation (3.3) follows from equations (3.1) and (3.2).

$$dx/dt = - k + x - (x^3) \qquad (3.3)$$

This model has since been used in studying transition behaviours in other movement tasks, such as shifting between walking and running (Diedrich and Warren, 1995), selecting to start on the right or left in a sailing regatta (Araújo *et al.*, 2003, 2006) and in action selection in rugby union (Araújo *et al.*, 2009). The characteristic nature of the attractor states for V(x) is such that for all states within an attractor well, the system will tend to be pulled towards the minimum of the well. Once the system is caught in an attractor well, it will tend to drift towards the minimum (where V(x) = 0), and then meander (stochastically) around this minimum. The system is considered to have settled when this situation occurs (i.e. when the system is caught in an attractor well). It is assumed that a decision has been made (i.e. a new behavioural pattern initiated) as soon as the system has settled. The system is assumed to start in some initial state, x_0, and stochastically change over time until it settles and a new pattern is initiated.

Building on the notion of a potential landscape, Schöner *et al.* (1992) modelled the acquisition of an intrinsically unstable coordination mode by introducing the complementary concept of intrinsic dynamics. Intrinsic dynamics reflect the learner's inherent coordination tendencies (resulting from a mix of innate biological constraints, development and previous learning) as he/she starts out to learn a new coordination pattern.

The conceptualization of learning as a modification of an individual's intrinsic dynamics implies that learning a new coordination pattern not only leads to improved performance of the learned pattern, but may affect the performance of other patterns as well. In other words, learning a particular coordination pattern may have both positive and negative transfer effects. Although more needs to be understood about such transfer processes in the context of learning sport skills, coaches should be aware that such effects may occur, especially when athletes engage in skills or activities involving topologically similar coordination patterns (e.g. badminton and tennis; rugby union and Australian Rules Football). Moreover, all learning processes emanate from existing intrinsic coordination tendencies, never from a 'blank slate'. Although one can measure those coordination tendencies only under special circumstances, they always affect the dynamics of learning. As a consequence, some coordination patterns are easy to acquire by some individuals, but hard for others.

Concluding remarks

The production of stable yet adaptive behaviours implies the coordination of action, where the individual selects action modes, and it implies perception, where information is selected (picked up) from the environment in order to guide action. The problem of intentionality and decision making is, thus, grounded on perception and action cycles (Araújo *et al.*, 2006). From an ecological dynamics perspective, skilled behaviour consists of continuous intentional adaptations to the constraints imposed by the environment during task performance (e.g. Araújo and Davids, 2009). The implication is that the structure of the environment, the biomechanics of the body, perceptual information about the state of the performer–environment system and the demands of the task all serve to continuously constrain behaviours. Adaptive behaviours, rather than being imposed by a pre-existing structure (e.g. memory), emerge from this confluence of constraints under the boundary condition of a particular task.

References

Araújo, D. and Davids, K. (2009) 'Ecological approaches to cognition and action in sport and exercise: Ask not only what you do, but where you do it', *International Journal of Sport Psychology*, 40: 5–37.

Araújo, D., Davids, K., Rocha, L., Serpa, S. and Fernandes, O. (2003) 'Decision making in sport as phase transitions', *International Journal of Computer Science in Sport*, 2(2): 87–8.

Araújo, D., Davids, K. and Hristovski, R. (2006) 'The ecological dynamics of decision making in sport', *Psychology of Sport and Exercise*, 7: 653–76.

Araújo, D., Diniz, A., Passos, P., Davids, K. and Fonseca, S. (2009) 'Decision-making as transitions in a course of interaction in sport', presentation at the Joint Annual convention of the Society for Mathematical Psychology and the European Mathematical Psychology Group, Amsterdam, Netherlands, August.

Bernstein, N. (1967) *The Co-ordination and Regulation of Movements*, Oxford: Pergamon Press.

Carello, C. and Turvey, M.T. (2002) 'The ecological approach to perception', in L. Nadel (ed.), *Encyclopedia of Cognitive Science*. London: Nature Publishing Group.

Cordovil, R., Araujo, D., Davids, K., Gouveia, L., Barreiros, J., Fernandes, O. and Serpa, S. (2009) 'The influence of instructions and body-scaling as constraints on decision-making processes in team sports', *European Journal of Sport Science*, 9(3): 169–79.

Correia, V., Araújo, D., Craig, C. and Passos, P. (2011) 'Prospective information for pass decisional behaviour in rugby union', *Human Movement Science*, 30: 984–97.

Davids, K., Handford, C. and Williams, M. (1994) 'The natural physical alternative to cognitive theories of motor behavior: An invitation for interdisciplinary research in sports science?', *Journal of Sports Sciences*, 12: 495–528.

Davids, K., Williams, M., Button, C. and Court, M. (2001) 'An integrative modelling approach to the study of intentional movement behavior', in R. Singer, H. Hausenblas and C. Janelle (ed.), *Handbook of Sport Psychology* (2nd ed.), (pp. 144–73). New York: John Wiley.

Diedrich, F. and Warren, W. (1995) 'Why change gait? Dynamics of the walk–run transition', *Journal of Experimental Psychology: Human Perception and Performance*, 21: 183–202.

Esteves, P., Oliveira, R.d. and Araújo, D. (2011) 'Posture-related affordances guide attacks in basketball', *Psychology of Sport and Exercise*, 12: 639–44.

Fajen, B., Riley, M. and Turvey, M. (2009) 'Information, affordances and the control of action in sport', *International Journal of Sport Psychology*, 40: 79–107.

Gibson, J.J. (1979) *The Ecological Approach to Visual Perception*, Hillsdale, NJ: Lawrence Erlbaum Associates.

Handford, C., Davids, K., Bennett, S. and Button, C. (1997) 'Skill acquisition in sport: Some applications of an evolving practice ecology', *Journal of Sports Sciences*, 15: 621–40.

Kelso, J.S. (1995) *Dynamic Patterns: The Self-Organization of Brain and Behavior*, Cambridge, MA: MIT Press.

Kelso, J. and Engstrøm, D. (2006) *The Complementary Nature*, Cambridge, Ma: MIT Press.

Kugler, P.N. and Turvey, M.T. (1987) *Information, Natural Law, and the Self-Assembly of Rhythmic Movement*, Hillsdale, NJ: Lawrence Erlbaum Associates.

Kugler, P., Shaw, R., Vincente, K. and Kinsella-Shaw, J. (1990) 'Inquiry into intentional systems I: Issues in ecological physics', *Psychological Research*, 52: 98–121.

Lee, D.N. (1998) 'Guiding movement by coupling taus', *Ecological Psychology*, 10: 221–50.

McGarry, T., Anderson, D., Wallace, S., Hughes, M. and Franks, I. (2002) 'Sport competition as a dynamical self-organizing system', *Journal of Sports Sciences*, 20: 771–81.

Palut, Y. and Zanone, P.G. (2005) 'A dynamical analysis of tennis: Concepts and data', *Journal of Sports Sciences*, 23(10): 1021–32.

Passos, P., Araújo, D., Davids, K., Gouveia, L. and Serpa, S. (2006) 'Interpersonal dynamics in sport: The role of artificial neural networks and 3-D analysis', *Behavior Research Methods*, 38(4): 683–91.

Pepping, G.J. and Li, F.X. (2005) 'Effects of response task on reaction time and the detection of affordances', *Motor Control*, 9: 129–43.

Reed, E.S. (1996) *Encountering the World: Toward an Ecological Psychology*, Oxford: Oxford University Press.

Schmidt, R.C., O'Brien, B. and Sysko, R. (1999) 'Self-organization of between-persons cooperative tasks and possible applications to sport', *International Journal of Sport Psychology*, 30: 558–79.

Schöner, G., Zanone, P.G. and Kelso, J.A.S. (1992) 'Learning as change of coordination dynamics: Theory and experiment', *Journal of Motor Behaviour*, 24: 29–48.

Tuller, B., Case, P., Ding, M. and Kelso, J. (1994) 'The nonlinear dynamics of speech categorization', *Journal of Experimental Psychology: Human Perception and Performance*, 20: 3–16.

van der Kamp, J., Savelsbergh, G. and Davis, W. (1998) 'Body-scaled ratio as a control parameter for prehension in 5- to 9-year-old children', *Developmental Psychobiology*, 33: 351–61.

Warren, W. (2006) 'The dynamics of perception and action', *Psychological Review*, 113: 358–89.

Withagen, R. and Michaels, C. (2005) 'On ecological conceptualizations of perceptual systems and action systems', *Theory and Psychology*, 15: 603–20.

4

SELF-ORGANISATION AND CONSTRAINTS IN SPORTS PERFORMANCE

Paul S. Glazier[1] *and Matthew T. Robins*[2]

[1]INSTITUTE OF SPORT, EXERCISE AND ACTIVE LIVING, FOOTSCRAY PARK CAMPUS,
VICTORIA UNIVERSITY, MELBOURNE, AUSTRALIA

[2]CHICHESTER CENTRE OF APPLIED SPORT AND EXERCISE SCIENCE,
UNIVERSITY OF CHICHESTER, UK

Summary

A criticism often directed at sports performance analysis is that it is too focused on performance outcomes rather than the underlying processes and mechanisms that produce those outcomes. In recognition of these and other issues, dynamical systems theory has been promoted as a viable multidisciplinary theoretical framework for sports performance analysis because: (i) it has the potential to more effectively link behaviours to outcomes due to its process-oriented, rather than product-oriented, focus; (ii) the same principles and concepts govern pattern formation at all levels (i.e. intra- and inter-individual) of sports performance; and (iii) it provides an opportunity for sport physiologists and sport psychologists to play a more prominent role in sports performance analysis. In this chapter, we provide an overview of two of the main concepts of dynamical systems theory, namely self-organisation and constraints, and consider how these constructs might be applied to the analysis and explanation of sport performance at the individual and team levels.

Introduction

Over the last decade, sports performance analysis has emerged as an independent sub-discipline of sport science and an integral part of many applied sport science support programmes. In addition to using various information and communications technologies (e.g. video) to provide augmented information (e.g. visual feedback) about sports performance during competition and practice, a significant task for sports performance analysts has been to identify and measure key performance variables that are statistically associated with successful sports performance outcomes. However, these metrics, known variously in the literature as performance indicators or performance parameters (Hughes and Bartlett, 2002), have been criticised for promoting only a rudimentary understanding of sports performance and providing little information about the underlying techniques and behaviours that produce performance outcomes (McGarry, 2009; Glazier, 2010).

In recognition of these and other issues, Glazier (2010) outlined an alternative process-oriented approach to sports performance analysis based on the principles and concepts of dynamical systems theory. It was argued that the constraints-based framework advocated in that paper, which has previously been applied to other areas of sport and human movement science, such as strength and conditioning (e.g. Ives and Shelley, 2003), skill acquisition (e.g. Araújo *et al.*, 2004; Davids *et al.*, 2008), sport biomechanics (e.g. Glazier and Davids, 2009; Seifert and Chollet, 2008) and motor development (e.g. Heywood and Getchell, 2009), provides a suitable platform on which to base applied sports performance research and support work.

Glazier (2010) argued that this alternative approach to sports performance analysis offers the following benefits to researchers and practitioners: (i) it has the potential to more effectively link behaviours to outcomes due to its process-oriented, rather than product-oriented, focus (i.e. rather than simply *describing* performance outcomes in terms of key performance indicators and performance parameters, it seeks to *explain* the underlying mechanisms and processes causing those outcomes; see also Vilar *et al.*, 2012); (ii) the same principles and concepts (i.e. self-organisation and constraints) govern pattern formation at all levels of sports performance (i.e. they are equally applicable to the analysis of coordination and control within a single sports performer or among a group of sports performers); and (iii) it provides an opportunity for sport physiologists and sport psychologists to play a more prominent role in the performance analysis of sport, therefore, providing a more holistic understanding of sports performance.

In this chapter, we provide an overview of two of the main concepts of dynamical systems theory, namely self-organisation and constraints. Some consideration is then given to how these constructs might be applied to the analysis and explanation of sport performance at the individual and team levels. Further information regarding the application of dynamical systems theory to sports performance analysis, more generally, can be found in Chapters 5 and 6 of this book. Interested readers are also encouraged to consult the excellent monographs by Kugler and Turvey (1987), Thelen and Smith (1994), Kelso (1995) and Williams *et al.* (1999) for comprehensive overviews of dynamical systems theory as applied to the sport and human movement sciences.

Self-organisation

Despite being intuitively simple, the concept of self-organisation has proven to be notoriously difficult to define. A number of definitions have appeared in the literature over the years (see Anderson, 2002, for a summary) but one of the most popular was provided by Camazine *et al.* (2001). They defined self-organisation as:

> a process in which pattern at the global level of a system emerges solely from numerous interactions among the lower-level components of the system. Moreover, the rules specifying interactions among the system's components are executed using only local information, without reference to the global pattern.
>
> *(p. 8)*

In other words, self-organisation is a process whereby structure or pattern emerges in an open system (i.e. those systems that are capable of engaging in energy and matter transactions with the environment) without specification from an intelligent executive or external regulating agent. Camazine *et al.* (2001) provided a number of fascinating examples of self-organisation in nature, from the synchronised flashing of fireflies to the spiralling patterns of an aggregating slime mould.

The construct of self-organisation was first introduced to movement science during the 1980s in a series of landmark publications by Kugler, Kelso and Turvey (Kugler *et al.* 1980, 1982; Kugler, 1986; Kugler and Turvey, 1987). Kugler also edited a special issue of *Human Movement Science* in 1988 entitled 'Self-Organisation in Biological Work Spaces' (Vol. 7, Issue 2–4, pp. 91–407), which was dedicated to theoretical topics related to the then-new paradigm of self-organisation. In the early years, the concept of self-organisation was poorly understood and often misconstrued. Indeed, as Beek *et al.* (1995: 577) observed: '. . . the notion of self-organization is interpreted by some movement scientists as a kind of mystical ability, according to which movements come out of the blue. This is giving an incorrect ontological twist to the concept.' Readers are referred to Chapter 7 of Camazine *et al.* (2001) for a more extensive examination of some of the common misconceptions, in science and beyond, surrounding self-organisation. More recently, however, self-organisation has become firmly established as an overarching or guiding metaphor for investigating coordinated behaviours, although there is still much work to be done to develop it as a valid theoretical concept in the human movement domain (Robertson *et al.*, 1993; Newell and Jordan, 2007).

Self-organisation was originally introduced by Kugler *et al.* (1980, 1982) as part of a 'natural-physical' alternative to cognitive theories of motor behaviour following rejection of the symbol-based computer metaphor that had prevailed in movement science since the 1960s. According to Kugler *et al.* (1980, 1982), this recipient paradigm, which they borrowed from the theoretical sub-fields of homeokinetics (Soodak and Iberall, 1978), non-equilibrium thermodynamics (Nicolis and Prigogine, 1977) and synergetics (Haken, 1977), offered a principled solution to the problem originally formulated by Bernstein (1967) of how the many degrees of freedom residing at different levels of the movement system are harnessed during goal-directed action (see also Turvey, 1990). Instead of relying on anthropomorphic concepts such as programmes, plans and schemas to resolve this issue, Kugler *et al.* (1980: 6) argued that order and regularity in the human movement system emerge from 'the free interplay of forces and mutual influences among components tending toward equilibrium or steady states' – that is, they self-organise.

Although self-organisation occupies a central role in the evolution of physiological and biomechanical processes, it alone is insufficient. To guide and shape emergent pattern formation among degrees of freedom of the system, self-organising processes need to be juxtaposed with competing and cooperating internal and external constraints that pressurise the system into changes of organisational state (Kugler, 1986; Newell, 1986). This process is commonly referred to in the literature as 'self-organisation under constraint' (e.g. Williams *et al.* 1999; Araújo *et al.* 2004; Davids *et al.* 2008). In the next section, we provide an overview of the concept of constraints.

Constraints

The concept of constraints is central to many branches of science, including mathematics, physics and biology. Kugler *et al.* (1980: 9) highlighted the primacy of constraints in the human movement system by stating that:

> the order in biological and physiological processes is primarily owing to dynamics and that the constraints that arise, both anatomical and functional, serve only to channel and guide dynamics; it is not that actions are caused by constraints; it is, rather, that some actions are excluded by them.

Constraints can, therefore, be viewed as boundaries, limitations or design features that apply restrictions to the organisation of the degrees of freedom residing at the different levels of the movement system (Sparrow and Newell, 1998). Indeed, as Kugler (1986: 471) argued:

> the only sensible interpretation of a constraint is that it is an alternative description of the behaviour of the individual degrees of freedom [...] It is a reduced, less detailed description [...] Being less detailed it is less complex and therein lies its utility: in terms of control a constraint is simple and efficient because it makes the fullest use of the dynamical context without being a description of that context.

Although a number of different constraint models have been postulated in the literature over the years (see van der Kamp *et al.*, 1996), the most widely cited model was introduced by Newell (1986) and updated, more recently, by Newell and Jordan (2007). Inspired by the work of Kugler *et al.* (1980, 1982), Newell (1986) proposed that three types of constraints act to channel and shape emergent patterns of coordination and control underpinning human movement:

1. **Organismic constraints** are those constraints that reside within the boundaries of individual movement systems. They can be subdivided into structural and functional constraints. Structural constraints tend to be physical constraints that remain relatively constant over time and include: height, body mass and composition; genetic make-up; the anthropometric and inertial characteristics of the torso and limbs; the number of mechanical degrees of freedom and ranges of motion of articulating structures; the fast- and slow-twitch fibre composition; angle of pennation, cross-sectional area, and the activation and fatigue characteristics of skeletal muscle; and so on (e.g. Newell, 1984; Jensen, 1993; Carson and Riek, 1998; Shemmell *et al.*, 2004). Functional constraints that have a relatively faster rate of change, on the other hand, tend to vary quite considerably over time and are typically either physiological or psychological. Important functional constraints include: heart rate; lactate concentrations; glucocorticoid release; synaptic connections; anxiety; perception; motivation; and so on. Perhaps the most prominent and influential organismic constraint that can shape movement coordination is the intentions of the performer (Kelso, 1995).

2. **Environmental constraints** are those constraints that are external to the movement system. They tend to be global, non-specific constraints that pertain to the spatial and temporal layout of the surrounding world or the field of external forces that are continually acting on the movement system. Examples of environmental constraints include ambient light and temperature, altitude, acoustic information, ubiquitous gravitational forces and the reaction forces exerted by *terra firma* and other contact surfaces and apparatus. Sociocultural constraints, such as family support, peer pressure, societal expectations and cultural norms, can also be classified as environmental constraints (Clark, 1995). Newell (1986) originally made the distinction between environmental constraints that are general or ambient and those that are task specific. However, Newell and Jordan (2007) argued that it is much cleaner, in a definitional sense, not to force this distinction and they modified the definition of an environmental constraint to encompass any physical constraint beyond the boundaries of the organism. Any implements, tools or apparatus, which were originally categorised by Newell (1986) as being tasks constraints, are now classified as environmental constraints.

3. **Task constraints** are those constraints that are specific to the task being performed and are related to the goal of the task and the rules governing the task. McGinnis and Newell

(1982: 299) proposed that task constraints 'are not physical, rather they are implied constraints or requirements which must be met within some tolerance range in order for the movement to produce a successful action'. In sport, task constraints that explicitly specify limb and torso segment movements, or restrict them to within certain boundaries, are commonplace. For example, the successful performance or otherwise of many gymnastics skills is determined by whether or not a certain movement pattern can be executed, and in cricket, a bowler can use any action providing the elbow of the bowling arm is not extended beyond a pre-defined limit. Instructions issued by a coach or practitioner may also be viewed as a type, or subset, of task constraint (Davids *et al.*, 2008; Newell and Ranganathan, 2010).

A number of important points should be noted when attempting to apply Newell's model of constraints to analyses of human movement. First, the three categories of constraints only identify the source and not the actual nature of the constraints impinging on performance (Newell *et al.*, 1989). Second, as constraints can be interpreted differently by different performers, they need to be considered from the perspective of the performer rather than at a level of description that is external or independent of the performer (Newell, 1989). Third, although some constraints are clearly more influential than others in certain performance contexts, it is the *confluence* of *interacting* organismic, environmental and task constraints that channel and shape patterns of coordination, control and, ultimately, performance outcomes (Newell and Jordan, 2007). Fourth, small-scale changes in one of the three categories of constraints can have a large-scale impact on the ensuing pattern of coordination and control. By the same token, variations in two or three of the constraint categories can, in effect, cancel each other out and have very little impact on the resulting pattern of coordination and control (Newell, 1986). Fifth, the ensuing patterns of coordination and control that emerge from the confluence of constraints are putatively a reflection of 'self-organising optimality' (Newell, 1986) or 'constrained optimisation' (Maynard Smith, 1978), so even though the performance outcome might be suboptimal or unsuccessful with regard to some externally defined criterion, the pattern of coordination and control produced could be considered optimal in relation to the immediately imposed constraints. The concepts of self-organising optimality or constrained optimisation state that the behaviour of a system at any point in time will always be optimal for the specific confluence of constraints acting on the system. Some (e.g. Mazur, 1983) have argued that the usefulness of these explanatory concepts are limited, whereas others (e.g. Staddon and Hinson, 1983) have suggested that they allow a better understanding of the constraints within which optimisation occurs.

Implications for sports performance analysis

So far in this chapter, we have outlined how self-organising processes and constraints combine to channel and shape emergent pattern formation in single-agent neurobiological systems. In principle, these concepts also govern pattern formation in multi-agent neurobiological systems, although Newell's (1986) constraints model, to our knowledge, has yet to be applied formally in this context.

To date, most studies that have considered pattern formation in sports performance analysis have, following the recommendation of McGarry *et al.* (2002), applied concepts and tools of coordination dynamics, which have been derived from Haken's (1977) theory of synergetics. Briefly, this approach involves the identification of collective variables or '*order parameters*' that define stable and reproducible relationships among degrees of freedom and '*control parameters*' that move the system through its many different coordinative states or attractor states in dynamical systems parlance (see Jeka and Kelso, 1989, and Kelso *et al.*, 1993, for tutorial reviews). Although a number of order parameters have been proposed in the literature, such as linear and angular displacement and their derivatives, either between players or with respect to a specific location or object (e.g. target or obstacle) in the performance environment (e.g. Araújo, *et al.*, 2006; Hristovski *et al.*, 2006), relative phase has typically been promoted as the order parameter that best characterises coordination in a sports contest (e.g. Palut and Zanone, 2005; Lames, 2006; Walter *et al.*, 2007). Several control parameters have also been postulated in the literature, including oscillatory frequency, interpersonal distance and relative velocity (e.g. McGarry *et al.*, 1999; Passos *et al.*, 2008; Duarte *et al.*, 2010). Interestingly, control parameters may have no obvious informational link to the resultant movement pattern (i.e. they do not prescribe or specify movement patterns but rather usher the system through its organisational states).

A research strategy that has typically been invoked by investigators adopting a dynamical systems approach in sports performance analysis is the '*synergetic strategy*' (Kelso and Schöner, 1988). In this approach, the control parameter is allowed to vary, or is experimentally manipulated, through a broad range, and concurrent changes in the order parameter are monitored. At low control parameter values, order parameter dynamics typically remain consistent and stable, reflecting the adoption of an attractor state. As the control parameter is increased, order parameter dynamics can become unstable, leading to a non-equilibrium phase transition or bifurcation and the adoption of a new attractor state. This phenomena was first demonstrated in the now-classic experiments on bimanual rhythmic coordination by Kelso and colleagues in the 1980s (e.g. Kelso, 1984; Haken *et al.*, 1985) and have since been reported widely in studies of intra-limb, inter-limb and inter-individual coordination (e.g. Schmidt *et al.*, 1990; Kelso *et al.*, 1991; Kelso and Jeka, 1992). A number of studies examining symmetry-breaking behaviour in sub-phases (e.g. 1 v. 1 dyads) of sports contests have also reported similar results (e.g. Palut and Zanone, 2005; Bourbousson *et al.*, 2010).

However, there are a number of issues surrounding the application of the synergetic strategy and coordination dynamics, more generally, to sports performance analysis. First, as noted in the previous section, although control parameters might be considered the main constraint on performance, it is the *confluence* of *interacting* organismic, environmental and task constraints that ultimately determines pattern formation (Newell, 1986; Newell *et al.*, 1989; Newell and Jordan, 2007). Second, relative phase assumes that the movements of each degree of freedom are approximately sinusoidal and that they have a one-to-one frequency ratio. Although the effects of violating these assumptions have not been assessed in multi-agent systems, they have in single-agent systems, where it has been shown that anomalous results may be found where these conditions are not met (Peters *et al.*, 2003). To overcome this issue, additional processing using Hilbert Transforms have been recommended (e.g. Lames, 2006) but even this procedure has been shown to overestimate continuous relative phase (Varlet and Richardson, 2011). Third, the systematic scaling of control parameters has been a useful paradigm in research agendas attempting to empirically verify the existence of non-linearities in human movement but its application in sport is limited to a very narrow set of performance contexts, such as when an attacker and defender converge. Moreover, key issues that are of great important to practitioners, such as how collective behaviour changes with match location, environmental conditions, quality of opposition and match status, for example, cannot readily be accounted for using the synergetics approach. Fourth, some of the specialist terminology associated with the synergetic approach (e.g. order parameters, control parameters, non-equilibrium phase transition, bifurcation, critical fluctuations, hysteresis, etc.) is not readily comprehensible to the sports practitioner and, therefore, may limit its practical contribution to sport. The inability to effectively communicate research findings in an appropriate language has recently been identified as one of the reasons why sport science, to date, has only had a limited impact on practice (e.g. Bishop *et al.*, 2006; Meyers, 2006; Williams and Kendall, 2007). Owing to the highly applied nature of sports performance analysis, it is our opinion that a clear, concise and 'user-friendly' set of terms and definitions needs to be developed. We propose that the constraints-based framework advocated in this chapter could contribute to achieving this aim.

The constraints-based approach, originally outlined by Newell (1986) and advocated as a theoretical framework for sports performance analysis by Glazier (2010), may provide a less restrictive alternative to the synergetic approach. A key aspect of this approach is the monitoring of qualitative and quantitative changes in pattern formation among degrees of freedom with changing constraints. McGinnis and Newell (1982) outlined a framework based on '*topological dynamics*' that uses biomechanical measurements and control spaces for mapping movement to constraints (see also Newell and Jordan, 2007). Each control space frame of reference (i.e. configuration space, event space, state space and state–time space) describes different spatio-temporal properties of movement and provides a useful insight into the restrictive nature of the constraints impinging on the system. One of the virtues of this approach is that it describes both movement and imposing constraints in common terms. The graphical mapping of attractor states can also help visualise how intra- and inter-individual coordination patterns change under varying constraints, which is likely to be a useful tool for sports performance analysts when communicating with athletes and coaches.

Although this framework is presently difficult to implement at the within-individual level, particularly during competition, because markerless motion capture is still in its infancy and not widely available (see Mündermann *et al.*, 2006, for a recent review), recent advances in player tracking technology may make it a feasible proposition at the between-individual level in the near future. The increasing capacity of GPS and image-based systems (see recent reviews by Aughey, 2011, and Barris and Button, 2008, respectively) to generate the time-continuous kinematic datasets necessary to map movement trajectories and attractor states in different control spaces has great potential for enhancing understanding of how patterns of inter-personal coordination are shaped by changing constraints, particularly if physiological and psychological data can be collected concurrently using other interfaced biofeedback technologies (see Blumenstein *et al.*, 2002, and Edmonds and Tenenbaum, 2012, for reviews). We propose that the information yielded by this approach could be used to inform tactical decision making, direct technical development strategies and prescribe modifications to strength and conditioning programmes.

Concluding remarks

In this chapter, we have provided an overview of the self-organising processes and constraints that shape and guide pattern formation at both the within- and the between-individual levels of sports performance. In order to move self-organisation beyond a metaphor and further develop it as a valid theoretical concept in the area of sports performance analysis, more empirical research is required. Indeed, Newell and Jordan (2007) suggested that empirical examinations of the self-organisation metaphor in the human movement domain could be addressed, in part, by manipulating key constraints impinging on the system and examining any concomitant changes that may ensue in the qualitative and quantitative properties of movement. As discussed in this chapter, this approach may also prove to be a more accessible framework on which to base sports performance analysis. Although conceptually similar to the synergetic approach, this approach is mathematically less formal, is arguably more versatile in terms of the range of situations it can be applied to and uses terminology that is more understandable to athletes and coaches. Further developments in motion capture, player tracking and biofeedback technologies will greatly facilitate the application of this framework in both research and applied settings in the near future. This approach could also be instrumental in helping to establish firmer links between sport behaviour and performance outcome, as identified as a research priority by McGarry (2009) and Glazier (2010).

Acknowledgment

We thank Karl Newell for his feedback on an earlier version of this chapter.

References

Anderson, C. (2002) 'Self-organization in relation to several similar concepts: Are the boundaries to self-organization indistinct?', *Biological Bulletin*, 202: 247–55.

Araújo, D., Davids, K., Bennett, S.J., Button, C. and Chapman, G. (2004) 'Emergence of sport skills under constraints', in A.M. Williams and N.J. Hodges (eds), *Skill Acquisition in Sport Research, Theory and Practice* (pp. 409–33). London: Routledge.

Araújo, D., Davids, K. and Hristovski, R. (2006) 'The ecological dynamics of decision making in sport', *Psychology of Sport and Exercise*, 7: 653–76.

Aughey, R.J. (2011) 'Applications of GPS technologies to field sports', *International Journal of Sports Physiology and Performance*, 6: 295–310.

Barris, S. and Button, C. (2008) 'A review of vision-based motion analysis in sport', *Sports Medicine*, 38: 1025–43.

Beek, P.J., Peper, C.E. and Stegeman, D.F. (1995) 'Dynamical models of movement coordination', *Human Movement Science*, 14: 573–608.

Bernstein, N.A. (1967) *The Coordination and Regulation of Movements*, Oxford: Pergamon Press.

Bishop, D., Burnett, A., Farrow, D., Gabbett, T.W. and Newton, R. (2006) 'Sports-science roundtable: Does sports-science research influence practice?', *International Journal of Sports Physiology and Performance*, 1: 161–8.

Blumenstein, B., Bar-Eli, M. and Tenenbaum, G. (eds) (2002) *Brain and Body in Sport and Exercise: Biofeedback Applications in Performance Enhancement*, Chichester, East Sussex: Wiley.

Bourbousson, J., Sève, C. and McGarry, T. (2010) 'Space-time coordination dynamics in basketball: Part 1. Intra- and inter-couplings among dyads', *Journal of Sports Sciences*, 28: 339–47.

Camazine, S., Deneubourg, J.-L., Franks, N.R., Sneyd, J., Theraulaz, G. and Bonabeau, E. (2001) *Self-Organization in Biological Systems*, Princeton, NJ: Princeton University Press.

Carson, R.G. and Riek, S. (1998) 'Moving beyond phenomenology: Neuromuscular-skeletal constraints upon coordination dynamics', in J.P. Piek (ed.), *Motor Behavior and Human Skill: A Multidisciplinary Approach* (pp. 209–30). Champaign, IL: Human Kinetics.

Clark, J.E. (1995). 'On becoming skillful: patterns and constraints', *Research Quarterly for Exercise and Sport*, 66: 173–83.

Davids, K., Button, C. and Bennett, S. (2008) *Dynamics of Skill Acquisition: A Constraints-Led Approach*, Champaign, IL: Human Kinetics.

Duarte, R., Araújo, D., Gazimba, V., Fernandes, O., Folgado, H., Marmeleira, J. and Davids, K. (2010) 'The ecological dynamics of 1v1 sub-phases in association football', *The Open Sports Sciences Journal*, 3: 16–18.

Edmonds, W.A. and Tenenbaum, G. (eds) (2012) *Case Studies in Applied Psychophysiology: Neurofeedback and Biofeedback Treatments for Advances in Human Performance*, Chichester, East Sussex: Wiley.

Glazier, P.S. (2010) 'Game, set and match? Substantive issues and future directions in performance analysis', *Sports Medicine*, 40: 625–34.

Glazier, P.S. and Davids, K. (2009) 'Constraints on the complete optimization of human motion', *Sports Medicine*, 39: 15–28.

Haken, H. (1977) *Synergetics: An Introduction. Non-equilibrium Phase Transitions and Self-Organization in Physics, Chemistry and Biology*, New York: Springer Verlag.

Haken, H., Kelso, J.A.S. and Bunz, H. (1985) 'A theoretical model of phase transitions in human hand movements', *Biological Cybernetics*, 51: 347–56.

Heywood, K.M., and Getchell, N. (2009). *Life Span Motor Development* (5th ed.), Champaign, IL: Human Kinetics.

Hristovski, R., Davids, K., Araújo, D. and Button, C. (2006) 'How boxers decide to punch a target: Emergent behaviour in nonlinear dynamical movement systems', *Journal of Sports Science and Medicine*, 5: 60–73.

Hughes, M.D. and Bartlett, R.M. (2002) 'The use of performance indicators in performance analysis', *Journal of Sports Sciences*, 20: 739–54.

Ives, J.C. and Shelley, G.A. (2003) 'Psychophysics in functional strength and power training: Review and implementation framework', *Journal of Strength and Conditioning Research*, 17: 177–86.

Jeka, J.J. and Kelso, J.A.S. (1989) 'The dynamic pattern approach to coordinated behaviour: A tutorial review', in S.A. Wallace (ed.), *Perspectives on the Coordination of Movement* (pp. 3–45). Amsterdam: North-Holland.

Jensen, R.K. (1993) 'Human morphology: Its role in the mechanics of movement', *Journal of Biomechanics*, 26: 81–94.

Kelso, J.A.S. (1984) 'Phase transitions and critical behavior in human bimanual coordination', *American Journal of Physiology: Regulatory, Integrative and Comparative Physiology*, 246: R1000–4.

Kelso, J.A.S. (1995) *Dynamic Patterns: The Self-Organisation of Brain and Behavior*, Cambridge, MA: MIT Press.

Kelso, J.A.S. and Schöner, G. (1988) 'Self-organization of coordinative movement patterns', *Human Movement Science*, 7: 27–46.

Kelso, J.A.S. and Jeka, J.J. (1992) 'Symmetry breaking dynamics of human multilimb coordination', *Journal of Experimental Psychology: Human Perception and Performance*, 18: 645–68.

Kelso, J.A.S., Buchanan, J.J. and Wallace, S.A. (1991) 'Order parameters for the neural organization of single, multijoint limb movement patterns', *Experimental Brain Research*, 85: 432–44.

Kelso, J.A.S., Ding, M. and Schöner, G. (1993) 'Dynamic pattern formation: A primer', in L.B. Smith and E. Thelen (eds), *A Dynamic Systems Approach to Development: Application* (pp. 13–50). Cambridge, MA: MIT Press.

Kugler, P.N. (1986) 'A morphological perspective on the origin and evolution of movement patterns', in M.G. Wade and H.T.A. Whiting (eds), *Motor Development in Children: Aspects of Coordination and Control* (pp. 459–525). Dordrecht: Martinus Nijhoff.

Kugler, P.N. and Turvey, M.T. (1987) *Information, Natural Law, and the Self-Assembly of Rhythmic Movement*, Hillsdale, NJ: Erlbaum.

Kugler, P.N., Kelso, J.A.S. and Turvey, M.T. (1980) 'On the concept of coordinative structures as dissipative structures: I. Theoretical lines of convergence', in G.E. Stelmach and J. Requin (eds), *Tutorials in Motor Behavior* (pp. 3–47). Amsterdam: North-Holland.

Kugler, P.N., Kelso, J.A.S. and Turvey, M.T. (1982) 'On the control and coordination of naturally developing systems', in J.A.S. Kelso and J.E. Clark (eds), *The Development of Movement Control and Coordination* (pp. 5–78). New York: Wiley.

Lames, M. (2006) 'Modelling the interaction in game sports – Relative phase and moving correlations', *Journal of Sports Science and Medicine*, 5: 556–60.

Maynard Smith, J. (1978) 'Optimization theory in evolution', *Annual Review of Ecology and Systematics*, 9: 31–56.

Mazur, J.E. (1983) 'Optimization: A result or a mechanism?', *Science*, 221: 977.

McGarry, T. (2009) 'Applied and theoretical perspectives of performance analysis in sport: Scientific issues and challenges', *International Journal of Performance Analysis in Sport*, 9: 128–40.

McGarry, T., Khan, M.A. and Franks, I.M. (1999) 'On the presence and absence of behavioural traits in sport: An example from championship squash match-play', *Journal of Sports Sciences*, 17: 297–311.

McGarry, T., Anderson, D.I., Wallace, S.A., Hughes, M.D. and Franks, I.M. (2002) 'Sport competition as a dynamical self-organizing system', *Journal of Sports Sciences*, 20: 771–81.

McGinnis, P.M. and Newell, K.M. (1982) 'Topological dynamics: A framework for describing movement and its constraints', *Human Movement Science*, 1: 289–305.

Meyers, M.C. (2006) 'Enhancing sport performance: Merging sports science with coaching', *International Journal of Sports Science & Coaching*, 1: 89–100.

Mündermann, L., Corazza, S. and Andriacchi, T.P. (2006) 'The evolution of methods for the capture of human movement leading to markerless motion capture for biomechanical applications', *Journal of NeuroEngineering and Rehabilitation*, 3: 6.

Newell, K.M. (1984) 'Physical constraints to development of motor skills', in J.R. Thomas (ed.), *Motor Development During Childhood and Adolescence* (pp. 105–20). Minneapolis, MN: Burgess.

Newell, K.M. (1986) 'Constraints on the development of coordination', in M.G. Wade and H.T.A. Whiting (eds), *Motor Development in Children: Aspects of Coordination and Control* (pp. 341–60). Dordrecht: Martinus Nijhoff.

Newell, K.M. (1989) 'On task and theory specificity', *Journal of Motor Behavior*, 21: 92–6.

Newell, K.M. and Jordan, K. (2007) 'Task constraints and movement organization: A common language', in W.E. Davis and G.D. Broadhead (eds), *Ecological Task Analysis and Movement* (pp. 5–23). Champaign, IL: Human Kinetics.

Newell, K.M. and Ranganathan, R. (2010) 'Instructions as constraints in motor skill acquisition', in I. Renshaw, K. Davids and G.J.P. Savelsbergh (eds), *Motor Learning in Practice: A Constraints-Led Approach* (pp. 17–32). London: Routledge.

Newell, K.M., van Emmerik, R.E.A. and McDonald, P.V. (1989) 'Biomechanical constraints and action theory: Reaction to G.J. van Ingen Schenau (1989)', *Human Movement Science*, 8: 403–9.

Nicolis, G. and Prigogine, I. (1977) *Self-Organization and Nonequilibrium Systems: From Dissipative Structures to Order through Fluctuation*, New York: Wiley.

Palut, Y. and Zanone, P.-G. (2005) 'A dynamical analysis of tennis: Concepts and data', *Journal of Sports Sciences*, 23: 1021–32.

Passos, P., Araújo, D., Davids, K., Gouveia, L., Milho, J. and Serpa, S. (2008) 'Information-governing dynamics of attacker-defender interactions in youth rugby union', *Journal of Sports Sciences*, 26: 1421–9.

Peters, B.T., Haddad, J.M., Heiderscheit, B.C., van Emmerik, R.E.A. and Hamill, J. (2003) 'Limitations in the use and interpretation of continuous relative phase', *Journal of Biomechanics*, 36: 271–4.

Robertson, S.S., Cohen, A.H. and Mayer-Kress, G. (1993) 'Behavioral chaos: Beyond the metaphor', in L.B. Smith and E. Thelen (eds), *A Dynamic Systems Approach to Development: Applications* (pp. 119–50). Cambridge, MA: MIT Press.

Schmidt, R.C., Carello, C. and Turvey, M.T. (1990) 'Phase transitions and critical fluctuations in the visual coordination of rhythmic movements between people', *Journal of Experimental Psychology: Human Perception and Performance*, 16: 227–47.

Seifert, L. and Chollet, D. (2008) 'Inter-limb coordination and constraints in swimming: A review', in N.P. Beaulieu (ed.), *Physical Activity and Children: New Research* (pp. 65–93). New York: Nova Science Publishers.

Shemmell, J., Tresilian, J.R., Riek, S. and Carson, R.G. (2004) 'Musculoskeletal constraints on the acquisition of motor skills', in A.M. Williams and N.J. Hodges (eds), *Skill Acquisition in Sport Research, Theory and Practice* (pp. 390–408). London: Routledge.

Soodak, H. and Iberall, A. (1978) 'Homeokinetics: A physical science for complex systems', *Science*, 201: 579–582.

Sparrow, W.A. and Newell, K.M. (1998) 'Metabolic energy expenditure and regulation of movement economy', *Psychonomic Bulletin and Review*, 5(2): 173–96.

Staddon, J.E.R. and Hinson, J.M. (1983) 'Optimization: A result or a mechanism?', *Science*, 221: 976–7.

Thelen, E. and Smith, L.B. (1994) *A Dynamic Systems Approach to the Development of Cognition and Action*, Cambridge, MA: MIT Press.

Turvey, M.T. (1990). 'Coordination', *American Psychologist*, 45: 938–53.

van der Kamp, J., Vereijken, B. and Savelsbergh, G. (1996) 'Physical and informational constraints in the coordination and control of human movement', *Corpus, Psyche et Societas*, 3: 102–18.

Varlet, M. and Richardson, M.J. (2011) 'Computation of continuous relative phase and modulation of frequency of human movement', *Journal of Biomechanics*, 44: 1200–4.

Vilar, L., Araújo, D., Davids, K. and Button, C. (2012) 'The role of ecological dynamics in analysing performance in team sports', *Sports Medicine*, 42: 1–10.

Walter, F., Lames, M. and McGarry, T. (2007) 'Analysis of sports performance as a dynamical system by means of the relative phase', *International Journal of Computer Science in Sport*, 6: 35–41.

Williams, S.J. and Kendall, L. (2007) 'Perceptions of elite coaches and sports scientists of the research needs for elite coaching practice', *Journal of Sports Sciences*, 25: 1577–86.

Williams, A.M., Davids, K. and Williams, J.G. (1999) *Visual Perception and Action in Sport*, London: E & FN Spon.

5

SPORT COMPETITION AS A DYNAMICAL SELF-ORGANIZING SYSTEM

Coupled oscillator dynamics of players and teams underscores game rhythm behaviours of different sports

Tim McGarry

UNIVERSITY OF NEW BRUNSWICK, CANADA

Summary

This article traces development of research on sports behaviours in sports contests as complex self-organizing systems using principles of coupled oscillator dynamics. In short, relative phase analysis of kinematic data of players and teams are consistent with the idea that the collective behaviours that characterize different sports contests are the result of information-based interactions among coupled dyads. That different sports on different levels of analysis may be subsumed under a common description using coupled oscillators presents good reason for continued research in this regard for advancing understanding of sports behaviours. For a review of research investigations on sports behaviours as complex self-organizing systems not predicated on coupled oscillator dynamics, the reader is directed to other chapters of this handbook as appropriate.

Introduction

Visual inspection of sports performances points towards structured patterned behaviours for sports contests. Put simply, however, the behavioural patterns observed from visual perception have not been well demonstrated in data that supposedly describe them (McGarry, 2004). Sports performance data often get recorded using reductionist methods (e.g. the auditing of 'on-the-ball' sports behaviours in discrete sequential fashion of the type 'who-what-where-when') with the general intent of identifying meaningful associations between sports behaviours and sports outcomes (McGarry, 2009). This approach has yielded limited progress, however, and the implications for advancing understanding of sports performance and informing future sports practice should not be overlooked.

The idea of patterned behaviours in sports contests is described in the concept of signature behaviours. McGarry and Franks (1996) analysed shot selections and outcomes (winners and errors) of squash players for signature behaviours in view of predicting future performances from past observations using probability-based (Markov-chain) analysis. For the most part, the results demonstrated changing probabilities when players competed against different opponents, thus challenging the preconceived notion of signature behaviours, at least as measured using probability (percentage) behaviours, and questioning moreover the general accepted sports practice of applying information obtained from past observations in preparation of future performances (cf. scouting).

Should there be merit to scouting practice as supposed, then the 'who-what-where-when' system description used might be questioned instead. To the point, that sports behaviour data obtained for performance analysis might not be as patterned as otherwise thought opens the prospect of insufficient system description (McGarry and Franks, 1996). Perceptual experiences tend towards this viewpoint, which, if accepted, obliges a rethinking of data required for meaningful description of sports contests. On this reasoning, previous approaches investigating game behaviours using the reductionist method for providing system description were reconsidered and new thinking introduced considering sports games under the rubric of complex dynamical systems (McGarry *et al.*, 1996; Gréhaigne *et al.*, 1997).

Behavioural perturbations

In a keynote address to the First World Congress of Science and Racket Sports (1993), the insightful analogy of a dance couple was used to describe game behaviour produced in a badminton rally (Downey, 1993). This analogy suggests the badminton couple (dyad) as seeking to maintain behavioural synchrony in rallies while simultaneously looking for individual opportunities within rallies to disrupt synchrony at opportune times for advantage gain. (This same analogy applies equally well to combat sports such as fencing, boxing and other martial arts.) This observation prompted additional consideration, leading to the subsequent development and introduction by McGarry and Franks (1996) of 'perturbations' for sports contests, with illustrative examples offered from squash, soccer and rugby football, underscoring the generality of this description for sports contests. As noted in McGarry and Franks (1996), if the notion of perturbations in sports contests is accepted, then these behaviours would be considered key descriptors of sports performance, indicating that not all behaviours should be considered of equal importance (cf. probability analysis). Again, this consideration necessitated a rethinking of previous reductionist approaches to investigating sports behaviours, leading, ultimately, to a proposed new description for sports contests from that produced hitherto (McGarry *et al.*, 2002).

The concept of perturbations for sports contests is important in that perturbations mark the boundaries of behavioural change, thereby serving as signposts for identifying different coordination behaviours at different instants. Visual observation presents a good means for detecting perturbation behaviours in sports performance on two counts. First, introduction of the dance-couple analogy for badminton dyad behaviours was itself observation based and, second, the method of using visual observation in other social contexts was successful when investigating behavioural synchrony in mother–infant dyads (Bernieri *et al.*, 1988). For these reasons, McGarry *et al.* (1996) used human observers as the measurement instrument when examining sports (squash) contest behaviours for evidence of perturbations. Both experts and non-experts were tasked separately with identifying behavioural perturbations, if any, from video records comprising 60 squash rallies selected at random from highest-level tournament competition. More specifically, the observers were tasked with identifying those instants (shots) in any given rally perceived as changing (perturbing) squash dyad behaviours between periods of 'stability' and 'instability'. In general, good agreement between independent observers was reported, giving strong validation for the concept of behavioural perturbations in sports (squash) contests. Furthermore, in some rallies, multiple perturbations were identified, indicating repeat transitions between bouts of stable and unstable squash dyad behaviours. Additional evidence regarding the presence of these behavioural perturbations together with kinematic data interpreted in context of dynamical self-organizing systems was reported in McGarry *et al.* (1999). Behavioural perturbations in sports contests have also been reported from visual observations for football (Hughes *et al.*, 1998) and tennis (Jörg and Lames, 2009), offering additional support to the generality of this system description for different sports as proposed by McGarry and Franks (1996).

Complex systems

The basic premise of complex systems is that function (behaviour) results from self-organizing interactions among the system parts by virtue of information exchanges. System function is considered self-organizing in that regularity of behaviour is not preordained by means of instruction by some outside agency but instead produced from within. The collective behaviours observed for schools of fish, flocks of birds, societies of ants and African termite colonies offer some examples of complex systems. The general thesis presented here is that the collective behaviours of players in sports competition may likewise be explained by complex systems principles.

Take the nesting behaviours of African termites as an example. According to Kugler and Turvey (1987), these insects build nests by collective self-organizing behaviours as follows. Individual termites initially acquire nesting material that they later drop on a random basis. Together with the nesting material, however, the termites leave pheromone (scent) deposits, which increase the likelihood of attracting additional drops of nesting material from other termites. Further drops of nesting material are likewise accompanied by additional deposits of pheromones, with increasing pheromone gradients (information fields) increasing the likelihood of yet more nesting material, and so on. In this way, a number of pillars of nesting material are built in close proximity to each other, which subsequently connect by arches to form the base for the next layer, and the process repeats. Thus, individual structures are constructed by self-organizing interactions among termites according to physical principles (information exchanges) that govern system behaviours without design specification. This common description of nesting behaviours produces unique results, with buildings that are nonetheless recognizable (patterned), and, moreover, affords an understanding of system behaviour that otherwise may well be obscured by reductionist methods. The possibility is that sports performances may benefit from similar considerations, although this analogy of African termites for sports contests, introduced by McGarry and Franks (1996) and McGarry *et al.* (1996), should not be taken as literal. Sports players should not be considered as depositing pheromones at various positions on the fields of play, so developing increasing information fields (or gradients) and increasing likelihoods of additional behavioural actions at certain locations. Not yet anyway.

Coupled pendulums

Pendulums exhibit cyclical behaviours as they pass periodically by reason of gravity through some nadir on transit between two opposing zeniths. Regarding coordination, Huygens reported 'sympathy' in the behaviours of two pendulums when swung separately but suspended from a common frame – for additional context on the importance of this finding in respect to the 'coordination problem' for producing movement behaviours, see Meijer (2001). This result demonstrates self-organized behaviour by means of common information exchanges between pendulums – that is, unified behaviour is produced courtesy of mutual influences of each pendulum on the other. Once more, then, the answer to the 'coordination problem' is found from within the system and not from outside as a result of intelligent design by some external agent (Turvey, 1990). The specific thesis presented here is that the coordinated behaviours observed in sports contests are likewise attributed to mutual influences among players, a non-prescribed emerging result of ongoing information exchanges between players, rather than an intended consequence of outside intelligence.

Coordination

In time, the self-organization of coupled pendulums settles into one of two possible coordination patterns, in-phase and anti-phase. In-phase represents the same positions of the two pendulums in their respective cycles at the same time, and anti-phase represents the positions of both pendulums with one displaced a half cycle from the other at any instant. Thus, the two pendulums will reach the same zeniths at the same times for in-phase and opposing zeniths at the same times for anti-phase, while passing through their nadir at the same time for both phase relations. For completeness, other values of relative phase between in-phase and anti-phase remain possible for the two pendulums too, in the formal sense at least, if not sustained in practice.

These observations on coupled pendulums are considered important for coordinated actions of animals and humans. For example, a series of linked pendulums offers a sound basis for modelling animal gait (see Kugler and Turvey, 1987, for accounts of quadrupedal gaits for various animals). Also, the same accounting of coordination on the basis of coupled pendulums applies at different levels of analysis. Take quadruped gait for consideration – at one level, the couplings of pendulums (e.g. joints: ankle, knee and shoulder/hip) produces coordination within a limb (i.e. leg) and at another level the couplings of pendulums (e.g. legs) produces various coordination patterns recognized as different quadruped gaits (i.e. walk, trot or canter, and gallop). That the same principles of coupled pendulums (oscillators) explain the varied coordination behaviours of quadrupeds at different levels of consideration makes a compelling argument for complex dynamical self-organizing systems as an underlying basis for their coordination.

To demonstrate the proposed importance of this approach for explaining coordinated behaviours of sports contests, we turn first to some well-known 'finger waggling' experiments by Kelso and colleagues (e.g. Kelso *et al.*, 1981; Kelso, 1984; Haken *et al.*, 1985). Here, changing coordination stabilities of anti-phase and in-phase were reported, as well as phase transitions from anti-phase to in-phase as a result of anti-phase destabilization when the cycling frequencies of two index fingers oscillating (flexing–extending) in the transverse plane were increased towards and beyond 'critical' values. In introducing dynamical systems theory for human rhythmic coordination, Haken *et al.* (1985) developed a formal description for these dynamic coordination results using two coupled oscillators (pendulums). This description was subsequently extended to encompass other rhythmic movement behaviours – for example, the coordination of multiple joints (Kelso *et al.*, 1991) as well as multiple limbs (Schöner *et al.*, 1990; Kelso and Jeka, 1992). This same accounting was later applied successfully to the coordination behaviours produced by two persons in a leg-swinging coordination task (Schmidt *et al.*, 1990). Thus, dynamical principles of self-organizing systems for coordinated rhythmic behaviours apply equally well both within and between persons (see Schmidt *et al.*, 2011, for further details on aspects of social motor coordination dynamics).

Sports contests

In this section, the coordinated behaviours produced in sports contests are the proposed result of self-organizing interactions among coupled oscillators – that is, players and/or teams (McGarry *et al.*, 2002). From the dance-couple analogy, the suggestion of coupled oscillators for explaining sports contest behaviours emanated from developing considerations by McGarry and Franks regarding squash contest behaviours in the context of self-organizing coordination dynamics (see McGarry and Franks, 1996; McGarry *et al.*, 1996, 1999). This reasoning was advanced by McGarry *et al.* (2002) on the same principles to encompass the different and varied game rhythms that characterize many different sports, from the to-and-fro behaviours of individual (1 vs 1) sports like squash, tennis and badminton to the ebb-and-flow behaviours of team (many vs many) sports such as basketball, soccer and hockey. In the following sections, research investigations that have examined various sports as self-organizing on the basis of dynamical systems principles, and specifically on the basis of coupled oscillator dynamics, are reported.

Individual sports: squash, tennis and badminton

To win points and games in squash contests, both players look to gain control of the space–time dynamics of their interactions by seeking ownership of the T-position located approximately centre court. In pursuit of this game objective, both players manoeuvre the other from the T by means of shot selections, while at the same time themselves moving towards the T to await the next shot in the rally sequence. Since players trade shots in turn within squash rallies, as one player leaves the T to make the next shot and returns to the T after doing so, the other player exhibits similar behaviour in alternating sequence. Thus, both players demonstrate oscillating movement trajectories to and from the T in anti-phase sequence as shots are traded. As before, the requirement for information exchange among coupled oscillators for producing self-organizing behaviours is present in the squash dyad, with visual information, playing strategies, habitual behaviours and the like offering possibilities for information-based couplings. These considerations led McGarry *et al.* (1999) to investigate the coordinated behaviours of squash dyads as a self-organizing dynamical system.

Reporting on the presence of behavioural perturbations in squash rallies, McGarry *et al.* (1999) also analysed the changing radial distances from the T of both squash players on four separate squash rallies. Visual inspection of the kinematic data demonstrated anti-phase coordination of the squash dyads, as expected on the reasoning described above, with short-lasting fluctuations from anti-phase observed on occasion. No correspondences between the behavioural perturbations identified by independent observers and these intermittent phase disturbances from anti-phase could be established however and further research on understanding the information basis for identifying behavioural perturbations in sports contests using human perception is required.

Following important research in tennis as a dynamical system reported by Palut and Zanone (2005), McGarry and Walter (2012) re-examined the movement behaviours of squash dyads using formal analytic calculations of relative phase. The kinematic variables subjected to relative phase analysis were displacements from the T and their rates of change (velocities) for each of the lateral (side-to-side), longitudinal (front-to-back) and radial directions. The six combinations for the reporting of relative phase produced understandably varying results, with bi-modal phase attractions observed in both lateral and longitudinal directions for both displacement and velocity metrics, albeit with different phase attractions for the different kinematic metrics used. In contrast, single anti-phase attraction in the radial direction was reported for both displacement and velocity. Part of these phase results using displacement data reported in McGarry and Walter (2012) were also reported in McGarry (2006).

As with the findings reported by Palut and Zanone (2005) from the lateral velocities of tennis players trading baseline shots, bi-modal phase attractions in the lateral directions were observed for the squash dyads. Also, as with the results of Palut and Zanone (2005), transitions between in-phase and anti-phase coordination was attributed to the squash players switching shot types between straight (line) and cross-court shots. Specifically, line shots produced anti-phase and cross-court shots in-phase coordination as the players moved in the opposite and same directions, respectively. Similarly, bi-modal phase attractions for the squash dyads were reported for the longitudinal directions on the same reasoning – that being the shot exchange combinations between short and long shots being responsible for the transitions between in-phase and anti-phase. These results demonstrate that additional information is obtained from analysing movement kinematics in both lateral and longitudinal directions instead of using a single direction (radial), which, necessarily, results in some loss of information. Regardless, the various combinations of kinematic metrics and directions produced results consistent with dynamical system behaviours, be it single anti-phase behaviour or bi-modal phasing with intermittent transitions, depending on the measures used.

As stated already, information-based coupling is key in accounting for squash dyad behaviours as self-organizing. This requirement for information exchange was assessed by McGarry and Walter (2007) by analysing relative phase for different combinations of squash dyads. Take the squash dyads of AB and CD, for instance, where A, B, C and D represent different players observed in two separate contests (i.e. AB for one contest, CD for the other). If the reported phase attractions for AB and CD result from information-based coupling, as hypothesized, then AB and CD would be predicted to demonstrate stronger phase attractions than the other synthetic combinations of AC, AD, BC and BD, whereby any phase attractions would be attributed to chance associations by way of two separate oscillators (squash players) operating independent of the other. This prediction was upheld in results reported by McGarry and Walter (2007), producing good evidence for the reasoned argument that the coupling behaviours of squash dyads are indeed information based, as expected given the common principal means for information exchange between the two players – the ball.

From individual sports to team sports

The suggestion that space–time kinematics of the squash dyad subscribes to dynamical self-organizing principles was expanded to include many different types of sports contest (McGarry *et al.*, 2002). First, these authors suggested a common description for the racket sports of squash, tennis (including table-tennis) and badminton, as the players in these sports all demonstrate oscillating movements. For squash, as noted, the locus of oscillation for both players (the T) is shared, whereas in tennis and badminton each player oscillates about his (her) own locus. In squash, a player looks to control space–time dynamics by moving his (her) opponent around the shared playing surface with shot selections. In tennis and badminton, a player does likewise but this time only in respect to the half-court of the opponent. The different game characteristics determine that the locus of oscillation for the tennis player is the centre of his (her) own baseline, or thereabouts, whereas for the badminton player it is the centre of his (her) defending half-court, or thereabouts. These differences notwithstanding, the racket sports conform to a common system description, at least in principle – that being a self-organizing system predicated on information-based coupled oscillator dynamics.

The same consideration of coupled oscillator dynamics for the racket sports extends to doubles play. For distinction, we used the term intra-couplings to reference the interactions of two players comprising a playing double, and inter-couplings in reference to the interactions between two players from opposing doubles, as well as between opposing doubles themselves. Once again, the thesis is that individual players demonstrate oscillating movements about some locus with information-based interactions among playing dyads providing the basis for self-organized coordinated behaviours. Note that the same description applies for the playing doubles – that being a playing dyad comprising the playing doubles. Thus, the playing doubles likewise demonstrate oscillating movements about some locus with information exchanges between the two doubles again producing self-organizing outcomes.

At this juncture, the concept of changing locus of oscillations should be introduced. In singles tennis, a player will tend to oscillate about the mid-baseline, as suggested previously. However, sometimes a player will follow-up an attacking shot from the baseline by approaching the net. Alternatively, a player may be drawn towards the vicinity of the net in response to a drop shot from the opponent. Both examples might or might not constitute behavioural perturbations depending on whether or not the tennis rally is destabilized. Both examples constitute a 'transition' however if, as oftentimes happens, the approaching player thereafter occupies the new mid-position a short distance in front of the net for the remainder of the rally, or until forced back to the baseline some time later in reply, say, to a lob shot from the opponent. (Here, the term 'transition' refers to a change in locus of oscillation and not necessarily a change in relative phasing in the dyad.) Thus, two possible loci of oscillations for the single tennis player exist, with occasional transitions between them depending on game context (see Figure 5.1). Similarly, in badminton doubles play, a double will generally adopt a lateral (side-to-side) or longitudinal (front-to-back) playing formation within a given instant of a given rally, with intermittent transitions sometimes observed between these two formations depending on game circumstances (see Figure 5.2).

Similar considerations of coupled oscillator dynamics from singles play to doubles play were extended to include other team sports, such as basketball, hockey and soccer. First, however, we should note the different natures of individual sports like squash, tennis and badminton (includ-

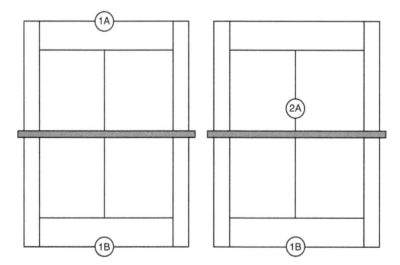

Figure 5.1 Representation of two loci of oscillations (1 and 2) for two tennis players (A and B) and a transition between them. The baseline locus (1) represents baseline shot exchanges between players (left panel). The net locus (2) indicates transition of A from 1 to 2, perhaps the result of a follow-up of an approach shot from A or a response to a drop shot from B (right panel)

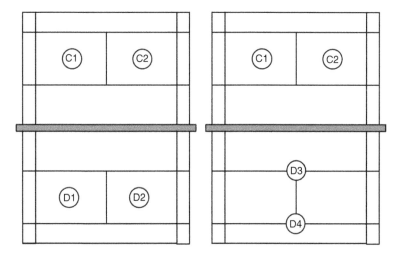

Figure 5.2 Representation of four loci of oscillations (1 through 4) for two badminton doubles players (C and D) and a transition between them. Badminton doubles occupy lateral formation (left panel). One badminton double (C) occupies a lateral formation and the other double (D) a longitudinal formation (right panel). The doubles may transit between lateral and longitudinal formations and hence loci of oscillations depending on game context

ing doubles play), where possession is traded in equal fashion, from these types of team sports, where possession is exchanged in unequal measure. Nonetheless, some common underpinnings for game behaviours are suggested in the structured to-and-fro of individual sports and the less structured, but structured nonetheless, ebb-and-flow rhythms of team sports that character-ize these different sports. As before, these proposed underpinnings are attributed to coupled oscillator dynamics, with the collective game behaviours of team sports now considered the result of couplings among many dyads on many levels, from player dyads through partial-team dyads (comprising two or more players per team) to the team dyad. The next section describes research on team sports as dynamical systems.

Team sports: basketball, football and futsal

The notion that team sport behaviours subscribe to dynamical self-organizing principles at different levels of analysis, a result of coupled interactions of dyads from players to teams, was investigated in the analysis of basketball game behaviours by Bourbousson and colleagues. These authors recorded the movement kinematics of all players and consequently reported relative phase analysis for all combinations of playing dyads in both lateral (side-to-side) and longitudinal (basket-to-basket) directions (Bourbousson *et al.*, 2010a). The results demonstrated in-phase attractions of playing dyads in both directions with stronger associations observed in the longitudinal direction. In-phase attractions within playing dyads were furthermore influ-enced by their make-up, with dyads containing opposing players matched on playing posi-tion reporting the strongest phase attractions, a finding attributed to the individual defensive marking strategies used by both teams. Also, anti-phase coordination behaviour in the lateral direction was reported for playing dyads comprising the wing players from the same teams, an indication of tactical game behaviour with both players working in tandem to decrease width when defending and to increase width when attacking.

Individual player kinematic data were combined to obtain geometric mean coordinates for investigating behavioural interactions of the teams (Bourbousson *et al.*, 2010b). These data were subjected to investigation using relative phase metrics with similar results of in-phase attractions between teams in both directions, as expected. In-phase attractions were again stronger in the longitudinal direction than the lateral direction, and stronger also between teams than between players. This finding is consistent with statistical considerations, with the aggregating (or averaging) of data serving, in effect, to reduce variability in the time series data. Similar results were reported by Lames *et al.* (2010) in their analysis of football game behaviour by means of relative phase. Kinematic data of all players obtained from video records of the 2006 FIFA World Championship final between France and Italy were recorded and relative phase obtained from the centroid data (geometric mean) of both teams. Strong in-phase attractions were reported for both directions, although, unlike the basketball results, marginal stronger attractions were reported in the lateral (sideways) direction as opposed to the longitudinal (forward–backward) direction. This finding may well reflect the behavioural characteristics of these different sports, with more direct play in the longitudinal direction attributed to basketball game behaviour and more probing of opponent defensive structure in the lateral direction in football. This said, the results indicated remarkably strong in-phase attractions between the two teams in both directions, and relative phase investigation of playing interactions between partial-team dyads, specifically the midfield lines of both teams identified as comprising four players per team, as well as between a couple of select attacker–defender playing dyads from players of opposing teams, indicated that these findings extended throughout all levels of analysis.

Frencken *et al.* (2011) also examined football playing behaviours at the team level, this time from small-sided (5 vs 5) game practice (for 11 vs 11 data, see Frencken *et al.*, 2008). Again, these authors investigated interacting behaviours between teams using centroid data as well as using measures of surface area. The distance between team centroids was interpreted as an indication of game 'pressure', with shorter distances taken as representing higher pressure applied by one or both teams. The surface area bounded by the team configuration perimeter was used to indicate player (or team) dispersion, with higher values indicating greater distribution of players in one or both directions. These authors did not undertake relative phase calculations. However, visual inspection of data nonetheless demonstrated strong in-phase attraction between teams for both centroid measures whereas the relation between surface area measures was less clear.

Research into team sports as dynamical self-organizing systems was extended by Travassos and colleagues by including ball kinematics in their investigation of futsal game behaviour (Travassos *et al.*, 2011, in press). Futsal is a FIFA-regulated football game comprising two teams of five players (four outfield players plus goalkeeper) and is played indoors on a hard-surface court delimited by lines. The ball is smaller than a regular football with less bounce and the combination of playing surface, ball characteristics and rules of the game are held by some to emphasize technical skills. In futsal competition, a common game strategy is for the trailing team, when in possession of the ball, to substitute the goalkeeper for an extra outfield player. Similar game tactics are also observed in football and ice hockey. Travassos *et al.* investigated futsal behaviour in game practice conditions using this game strategy, a condition referenced hereafter as 5-vs-4+GK.

As with previous investigations into dynamical interactions of team sports, the movement trajectories of players were recorded in two-dimensional space and relative phase analysed in both lateral and longitudinal directions. Unlike previous investigations, however, Travassos *et al.* also recorded ball trajectories. These data enabled the investigation of ball dynamics in game behaviour, which must contain key information given its centrality to game objectives (McGarry, 2009). Relative phase analysis of 5-vs-4+GK futsal game practice reported different strengths of phase attraction for different playing dyads, with general findings of strong in-phase attractions between defenders and ball as well as with each other, and weaker in-phase attractions for the attackers and ball and for attackers themselves. Thus, the defending and attacking dyads produced different coordination dynamics, indicating different playing patterns by way of the different team objectives of defending and attacking the goal, respectively, as well as due to unequal numbers of outfield players between teams (Travassos *et al.*, 2011). As expected, these results were replicated at the level of team interactions too, with increased in-phase attractions furthermore noted for the lateral direction than for the longitudinal one (cf. Lames *et al.*, 2010).

Interactions between players, teams and ball were also subjected to investigation using two separate coordinate systems – those being Cartesian coordinates (x, y), as with previous research, and polar coordinates (angle, radius), referenced to the centre of the single goal being attacked and defended (Travassos *et al.*, in press). In-phase relations between the defending team and ball were stronger than the attacking team and ball for both coordinate systems, with the strongest phase attractions produced using angles indicating ball position in respect to goal location as a key informational constraint for coordinated game behaviour. These results were attributed to the defending team establishing associations with ball and attacking team positions in the context of the goal line. The attacking team, for their part, tended to explore the defending team dynamics by probing for open and opening spaces, and hence possible scoring opportunities, through ball exchanges (passes) primarily in the lateral direction. As noted in Travassos *et al.* (in press), the relative phase results may be explained by the defending players guarding space in front of goal using zonal defence, thereby positioning themselves with respect to the dynamics of the ball and, to a lesser extent, the attacking players always in reference of the goal being defended. In other words, the defenders position themselves to align on the intercept path between the ball and attacker and the centre of goal. This explanation is consistent with the stronger in-phase attractions reported between defending team and ball in the lateral direction, because changes in ball position in this direction as compared with the longitudinal direction would generally produce increased changes in the angle of ball with respect to the centre goal line. As such, increased attention from the defending team to ball displacements in the lateral direction may be expected, with possibly differing amounts of attention paid by defenders to changes in the longitudinal direction of ball and attackers, depending on whether the ball and attackers are moving to or from goal.

Some final considerations

The general tenet of coordinated behaviours emerging in sports contests as a result of self-organization among coupled oscillators on the basis of shared information exchanges is predicated on universal theoretical principles of open complex dynamical systems. These principles are held as applying across different systems on varying levels of analysis and time scales (Kelso, 1995). That this reasoning should apply to sports contests, then, appears sound in principle, to this author at least, and is furthermore supported by increasing data, but generalizations should nonetheless remain tentative unless and until additional evidence is gathered. For example, each sport is unique, as is each contest within a given sport, and present generalizations from small data samples applied across many different factors (e.g. age, sex, level, sport, small-sided vs full-sided games, practice vs competition, etc.) might be questioned – the argument for universal properties of dynamical systems notwithstanding. Further research is required to address and ultimately resolve these concerns in future.

Concluding remarks

This article has presented gathering evidence in support of dynamical self-organizing principles underpinning game rhythm behaviours in sports practice and sports competition, from research on both individual sports (e.g. squash and tennis) and team sports (e.g. basketball, football and futsal). Coordinated game behaviours are held as self-organizing and resulting from information-based interactions of coupled oscillators (i.e. players and teams). This consideration for sports performance is attractive and, perhaps, compelling in the sense that it permits description of varied game behaviours for different sports by means of common principles. It furthermore accounts for the different game behaviours that characterize these different sports, as well as the unique behaviours that typify individual sports contests. Moreover, this same description applies for different levels of analysis, from displacement to velocity metrics and from radial direction to lateral and longitudinal directions, from player dyads to partial-team dyads to team dyads, from player interactions with the ball to team interactions with the ball, and from Cartesian coordinates to polar coordinates. These findings are interpreted as lending increasing weight to the notion that sports behaviours subscribe to universal principles of complex dynamical systems predicated on information exchanges between coupled oscillators.

References

Bernieri, F.J., Reznick, J.S. and Rosenthal, R. (1988) 'Synchrony, pseudosynchrony, and dissynchrony: Measuring the entrainment process in mother–infant dyads', *Journal of Personality and Social Psychology*, 54: 243–53.

Bourbousson, J., Sève, C. and McGarry, T. (2010a) 'Space-time coordination dynamics in basketball: Part 1. Intra- and inter-couplings among player dyads', *Journal of Sports Sciences*, 28(3): 339–47.

Bourbousson, J., Sève, C. and McGarry, T. (2010b) 'Space-time coordination dynamics in basketball: Part 2. The interaction between the two teams', *Journal of Sports Sciences*, 28(3): 349–58.

Downey, J. (1993) 'Match analysis of badminton', Keynote presentation to the 1st World Congress of Science and Racket Sports, Liverpool, UK, July.

Frencken, W., De Poel, H., Visscher, C. and Lemminck, K. (2012) 'Variability of inter-team distances associated with match events in elite-standard soccer', *Journal of Sports Sciences*, 30, 1207–13.

Frencken, W., Lemmink, K., Dellemann, N. and Visscher, C. (2011) 'Oscillations of centroid position and surface area of soccer teams in small-sided games', *European Journal of Sport Science*, 11(4): 215–23.

Gréhaigne, J.-F, Bouthier, D. and David, B. (1997) 'Dynamic-system analysis of opponent relationships in collective actions in soccer', *Journal of Sports Sciences*, 15: 137–49.

Haken, H., Kelso, J.A.S. and Bunz, H.A. (1985) 'Theoretical model of phase transitions in human hand movements', *Biological Cybernetics*, 51: 347–56.

Hughes, M., Dawkins, N., David, R. and Mills, J. (1998) 'The perturbation effect and goal opportunities in soccer', *Journal of Sports Sciences*, 16: 20.

Jörg, D. and Lames, M. (2009) 'Perturbationen im Tennis – Beobachtbarkeit und Stabilität', in M. Lames, C. Augste, O. Cordes, Ch. Dreckmann, K. Görsdorf and M. Siegle (eds), *Gegenstand und Anwendungsfelder der Sportinformatik* (pp. 86–96). Hamburg: Czwalina.

Kelso, J.A.S. (1984) 'Phase transitions and critical behavior in human bimanual coordination', *American Journal of Physiology: Regulatory, Integrative and Comparative Physiology*, 15: R1000–4.

Kelso, J.A.S. (1995) *Dynamic Patterns. The Self-Organization of Brain and Behaviour*, Cambridge, MA: Bradford Books, MIT Press.

Kelso, J.A.S. and Jeka, J.J. (1992) 'Symmetry breaking dynamics of human multilimb coordination', *Journal of Experimental Psychology: Human Perception and Performance*, 18: 645–68.

Kelso, J.A.S., Holt, K.G., Rubin, P. and Kugler, P.N. (1981) 'Patterns of human interlimb coordination emerge from the properties of non-linear, limit cycle oscillatory processes: Theory and data', *Journal of Motor Behaviour*, 13: 226–61.

Kelso, J.A.S., Buchanan, J.J. and Wallace, S.A. (1991) 'Order parameters for the neural organization of single, multijoint limb movement patterns', *Experimental Brain Research*, 85: 432–44.

Kugler, P.N. and Turvey, M.T. (1987) *Information, Natural Law, and the Self-Assembly of Rhythmic Movement*, Hillsdale, NJ: Lawrence Erlbaum Associates.

Lames, M., Ertmer, J. and Walter, F. (2010) 'Oscillations in football – order and disorder in spatial interactions between the two teams', *International Journal of Sports Psychology*, 41(4, Supplement): 85.

McGarry, T. (2004) 'Searching for patterns in sports contests', in S. Butenko, J. Gil-Lafuente and P.M. Pardalos (eds), *Economics, Management, and Optimization in Sports* (pp. 203–23). Berlin: Springer-Verlag.

McGarry, T. (2006) 'Identifying patterns in squash contests using dynamical analysis and human perception', *International Journal of Performance Analysis in Sport*, 6(2): 134–47.

McGarry, T. (2009) 'Applied and theoretical perspectives of performance analysis in sport: Scientific issues and challenges', *International Journal of Performance Analysis in Sport*, 9(1): 128–40.

McGarry, T. and Franks, I.M. (1996) 'In search of invariant athletic behaviour in competitive sport systems: An example from championship squash match-play', *Journal of Sports Sciences*, 14: 445–56.

McGarry, T. and Walter, F. (2007) 'On the detection of space-time patterns in squash using dynamical analysis', *International Journal of Computer Science in Sport*, 6(2): 42–9.

McGarry, T. and Walter, F. (2012) 'Sport competition as a dynamical self-organizing system: Example from the movement coordination kinematics of squash players', *International Journal of Motor Learning and Sport Performance*, 2: 59–67.

McGarry, T., Khan, M.A. and Franks, I.M. (1996) 'Analyzing championship squash match-play: In search of a system description', in S. Haake (ed.), *The Engineering of Sport* (pp. 263–9). Rotterdam: Balkema.

McGarry, T., Khan, M.A. and Franks, I.M. (1999) 'On the presence and absence of behavioural traits in sport: An example from championship squash match-play', *Journal of Sports Science*, 17: 298–311.

McGarry, T., Anderson, D.I., Wallace, S.A., Hughes, M. and Franks, I.M. (2002) 'Sport competition as a dynamical self-organizing system', *Journal of Sports Sciences*, 20: 771–81.

Meijer O.G. (2001) 'An introduction to the history of movement science', in M.L. Latash and V. Zatsiorsky (eds), *Classics in Movement Science* (pp. 1–57). Champaign, IL: Human Kinetics.

Palut, Y. and Zanone, P.S. (2005) 'A dynamical analysis of tennis players' motion: Concepts and data', *Journal of Sports Science*, 23: 1021–32.

Schmidt, R.C., Carello, C. and Turvey, M.T. (1990) 'Phase transitions and critical fluctuations in the visual coordination of rhythmic movements between people', *Journal of Experimental Psychology: Human Performance and Perception*, 16: 227–47.

Schmidt, R.C., Fitzpatrick, P., Caron, R. and Mergeche, J. (2011) 'Understanding social motor coordination', *Human Movement Science*, 30(5): 834–45.

Schöner, G., Jiang, W.Y. and Kelso, J.A.S. (1990) 'A synergetic theory of quadrupedal gaits and gait transitions', *Journal of Theoretical Biology*, 142: 359–91.

Travassos, B., Araújo, D., Vilar, L. and McGarry, T. (2011) 'Interpersonal coordination and ball dynamics in futsal (indoor football)', *Human Movement Science*, 30: 1245–59.

Travassos, B., Araújo, D., Duarte, R. and McGarry, T. (in press) 'Spatiotemporal coordination patterns in futsal (indoor football) are guided by informational game constraints', *Human Movement Science*. http://dx.doi.org/10.1016/j.humov.2011.10.004.

Turvey, M.T. (1990) 'Coordination', *American Psychologist*, 45: 938–53.

6

DYADIC SYSTEMS AS DYNAMIC SYSTEMS IN INDIVIDUAL AND TEAM SPORTS

Pedro Passos[1], Duarte Araújo[1] and Keith Davids[2]

[1]TECHNICAL UNIVERSITY OF LISBON, PORTUGAL

[2]QUEENSLAND UNIVERSITY OF TECHNOLOGY, AUSTRALIA

Summary

This chapter describes research on the behaviours of attacker–defender dyads in sports contests from the perspective of ecological dynamics. The main challenge for researchers is to find coordination variables for dyadic systems that accurately describe the mutual interactions between opposing performers that occur in competitive performance environments. In sports, proximity of opponents and teammates means that a significant amount of co-adaptive behaviours can be observed. Ecological dynamics predicts that these interpersonal interactions in competitive performance environments are shaped by self-organizing processes.

A dynamical approach to studying co-adaptive behaviours of performers in sport requires researchers to measure players' performance continuously, aiming to describe not only 'what', 'when' and 'where' events occur, but also 'how' specific patterns of performer interactions might emerge. The coordinative variables used to describe players' interactions capture different states of coordination that lead to distinct performance outcomes – for instance, when the balance between an attacker–defender sub-system remains or when that balance is broken with clear advantage to one performer over the other. Research evidence has revealed movement variability as a key platform for dyadic system interactions in sports, consistent with the existence of self-organizing processes.

Introduction

Experimental research on the behaviours of attacker–defender dyads in individual and team sports has developed significantly during the last decade. Examples include the work of: McGarry *et al.* (1999) in squash; Palut and Zanone (2005) in tennis; Lagarde *et al.* (2006) in boxing; Araújo *et al.* (2003) in sailing; Passos *et al.* (2008, 2009) in rugby union; Araújo *et al.* (2002), Cordovil *et al.* (2009) and Bourbousson *et al.* (2010) in basketball; and Headrick *et al.* (2012) and

Lopes *et al.* (2012) in soccer. In the following sections, we consider the findings of this body of work in different performance contexts. The first section introduces the issue of representative design, the next section addresses research on individual sports and the last section reviews findings of studies on team sports.

Representative design

The concept of *representative experimental design* proposed by Brunswik (1952, 1956) focuses on the participant–environment interaction and 'refers to the arrangement of conditions of an experiment so that they represent the behavioural setting to which the results are intended to apply' (Araújo *et al.*, 2007: 72; Hammond and Stewart, 2001). Thus, Brunswik argued that removing natural variability in experimental task conditions which participants otherwise encounter in performance settings is to remove the proper subject matter of research. In sport then, representative design implies that experimental task constraints need to faithfully represent the task constraints of a specific performance environment (Pinder *et al.*, 2011). These ideas suggest that in experimental settings participants must cope with the same multiple, noisy, messy situations that occur in specific performance environments (Araújo *et al.*, 2007), as removing these naturally-existing phenomena in order to gain greater 'control' in experimental conditions (internal validity), consistent with reductionism, leads to artificial constraints in experimental design (Davids *et al.*, in press). In this view, a good way to extend understanding is to faithfully represent the dynamic circumstances that naturally occur in specific performance environments in experimental settings. Without representative design, the behaviours that emerge may not be functional for performance in sports contexts (Dicks *et al.*, 2008; Davids *et al.*, in press; Pinder *et al.*, 2011). Thus, a significant challenge inherent to experimental design is to develop task constraints that are representative of specific environments. In sport performance analysis, a key issue therefore is to consider how affordances (opportunities for action) and/or behaviours in an empirical study correspond to those affordances that exist in a competitive performance setting.

The notion of task representativeness is predicated on what a particular experimental task *affords* a participant. An affordance requires that a performer regulates his/her activity according to information concerning both an object and/or an event (e.g. ball, opponent, pass, etc.) (Araújo *et al.*, 2007). Hence, affordances, behaviour and, consequently, the representativeness of the experimental task are likely to vary, being shaped by continuous interacting participant, task and environmental constraints (Kugler *et al.*, 1982; Newell, 1986). Different sources of perceptual information allow different possibilities for action (i.e. affordances) (Fajen *et al.*, 2009) and representing the information available for action is an important challenge for researchers in considering experimental design (Araújo *et al.*, 2007). For example, an important question concerns the use of static or dynamic tasks. According to Pinder and colleagues, static task constraints in sport science experiments typically lack functionality and are not representative of performance requirements in dynamic competitive environments (Pinder *et al.*, 2011). Constraints manipulation, however, is a powerful research approach in which to design experimental dynamic tasks that afford the individual the same possibilities of action that he/she will encounter in performance environments.

Standard vs in situ experimental task designs

Traditionally, experimental designs tend to emphasize static and 'decomposed' tasks which are intended to provide controlled simulations of performance environments. In these experiments, participants are typically required to perform only a simple action to represent more complex actions (e.g. button press or joystick to represent movements such as a tackle or pass, etc.). In some studies, participants make verbal reports only on what they would do in a given task context. For example, from video analysis of penalty kicks in soccer, a goalkeeper might be tasked with predicting the direction a penalty shot will be directed at. This type of experimental design is adopted in order to exert greater control over the variables under analysis. This standard experimental design is perceived to maximize control of manipulation of independent variables to observe changes in dependent variables. For instance, if the aim is to measure the distance from a defender that an attacker might start performing evasive manoeuvres to avoid being tackled in rugby union, a contact heavy bag might be used to represent the presence of the defender in simulation. Under these experimental conditions, it is possible to record the distance at which the attacker (ball carrier) begins to perform evasive manoeuvres and, also, what sort of action might emerge. Additionally, to measure the influence of the initial conditions during attacking performance, experimenters can manipulate the initial starting distances between the participant (i.e. the ball carrier) and the defender (i.e. the static tackling bag).

The perceived advantage of this type of experimental design is that researchers can accurately measure the influence of independent variables on dependent variables. A clear limitation, however, is that any relationship that might emerge between variables (e.g. the initial starting distance and the distance that the ball carrier begins to perform evasive manoeuvres) is only representative for this specific task. Generalization of the results, therefore, can be problematic. When performance conditions are made more natural, such as replacing the static tackling bag with an active defender who can actually tackle the ball carrier, investigators are altering the possibilities for action. Using artificial task constraints, such as a defensive bag, provides affordances that differ from those that are available for the ball carrier in practice and competitive environments. Of course, an important reason is that a tackling bag does not move or change direction towards the ball carrier, like a defender to make a tackle. The affordances available in a ball carrier–tackling bag simulation interaction are thus different from the affordances that emerge in a ball carrier–defender interaction on-field. This example demonstrates the standard approach to experimental design that is not representative of competitive performance contexts.

Contrary to standard experimental approaches, and supported by the theoretical framework of ecological dynamics, *in situ* experimental designs promote the representative design of tasks that maintain the coupling of information and action in participants. Key concepts such as constraints and affordances are useful for designing an experimental task that contains constraints that represent performance environments, allowing description of stability and/or variability that characterizes different states of performance. Indeed, the performance stability/variability balance is a key issue since it allows characterization of the state of coordination among system components in sports, such as players in a dyad. When an attacker–defender system is stable, the implication is that neither player is providing a strong perturbing influence on the system. Increased variability in behaviours of a dyadic system, however, signifies that one of the components (i.e. the attacker or the defender) is attempting to gain an advantageous position to achieve a task goal, such as score a goal/try or regain ball possession. These fluctuations in dyadic system behaviours can be identified by recording coordinative variables that accurately capture system dynamics.

To recap, an important advantage of an ecological dynamics approach, which emphasizes representative task design of *in situ* experiments, is that the results can be extended to understanding performance in real-world contexts. Performance is studied as it emerges and, typically, there are no attempts to control precisely the performance variables under analysis – for example, through prescriptive task instructions. Instead, use of general instructions allows behaviours to emerge through interpersonal interactions of participants. Going beyond the level of emergent behaviours to a more predictive level, however, is challenging in that researchers can manipulate variables that might alter the affordances available to the performer (player). The concept of 'action fidelity' introduced by Stoffregen and colleagues (Stoffregen *et al.*, 2003) has proved useful in confronting this challenge. In this approach, Araújo *et al.* (2007) have suggested the need to measure action fidelity variables, such as the time that it takes to complete a task, among other variables that capture states of coordination among system components. Similar values and patterns between 'laboratory' and 'field' indicate task representativeness and suggest the same possibilities of action in both settings. It is worth noting that the coordinative variables presented next exemplify some possible measures of action fidelity.

Dyadic behaviour analysis in individual sports

Squash

The study of McGarry and colleagues (1999) attempted to formally describe the dynamics of squash dyads in competitive settings, concluding that the interactive behaviour of opponent players within a dyad can be usefully described as a dynamical system. These authors captured the performance of both players in the dyad from video camera using a hand-held stylus and graphics tablet to track their movements. Performance data were analysed statistically with correlation coefficients that reported a single state (anti-phase), with periods of instability introduced by way of perturbations characterizing the behaviour of the dyadic system as a dynamical system. This research approach opened a window onto one of the most challenging issues in sport sciences: understanding the balance between stability and instability in performance behaviour.

Tennis

Similar to the research of McGarry *et al.*, Palut and Zanone (2005) described the interactive behaviours of tennis players as coupled oscillators, signifying that the players' interactions on court achieved two different states of coordination: synchronized movements in the same direction (in-phase mode) and in opposite directions (anti-phase mode). In their study, the authors successfully used relative phase as a collective variable that accurately described how the players' movements were coordinated on court, and also when they transited from one mode of coordination to another. State transitions were observed, accompanied by enhanced fluctuations in the collective variable, and again the stability–instability balance was revealed as a paramount issue in analysing behaviours of interactive dyads in sports.

Boxing

A study by Lagarde and colleagues investigated the behaviours of boxers as a dyadic system (Lagarde *et al.*, 2006). Data collection during performance was achieved with videogrammetry using a digital video camera that recorded the boxers' motions at 50 Hz. The boxers' bidimensional coordinates were extracted semi-automatically using video-markers and a head motion measure used to describe interpersonal coordination. The data revealed that, despite the 'random' motions of the boxers, the mean value of head radial distance (i.e. the distance of each head in the boxing dyad to the mean point between heads) fluctuated between periods of contraction and expansion. Using a symbolic configuration scheme that captured the macro configurations of the boxer–boxer dyadic system, the authors concluded that preferred modes of interaction depended on the rates of change of head radial distance. Moreover, the results demonstrated that particular configurations of interactive behaviour between performers were achieved based on head velocity of boxers from instant to instant. This observation was supported across a wide set of combined individual actions, leading the authors to suggest the existence of system degeneracy (Lagarde *et al.*, 2006). Degeneracy is a key property in the complexity sciences and recognizes that systems can use different solutions for achieving the same performance outcomes (Edelman and Gally, 2001). In the study of complex dyadic systems in sport, degeneracy signifies that, due to the need for continuous adaptive behaviours by performers, different forms of interactive behaviours can achieve the same performance outcomes (Lagarde *et al.*, 2006).

Sailing

In sailing, a sport with different task constraints to previous research, Araújo *et al.* (2003) analysed the behaviours of two competing boats during the racing start in a regatta. Due to wind shift tendencies in both intensity and direction, and the positioning of opponent boats during the start period, each crew needed to perform continuous adaptive manoeuvres, aiming to achieve the most advantageous position at the instant of starting. In this research, the authors investigated the angle between the wind direction and the starting line, with the intention of analysing how this system parameter influenced the decision-making behaviours of competing sailors (Araújo *et al.*, 2003). The data revealed preferred zones for starting the regatta close to the extremities of the starting line and zones of high instability in the middle of the starting line. Moreover, Araújo and colleagues provided a formal mathematical description of the boats' dynamical behaviours using the model of Tuller *et al.* (1994). This modelling allowed Araújo *et al.* (2003) to characterize the extremities of the starting line as attractors, or preferred states of behaviour in the start of a sailing regatta.

Dyadic behaviour analysis in team sports

Basketball

The behaviours of competing players in dyadic systems have also been investigated in team sports performance. Araújo and colleagues (2002) proposed the distance of an attacker and defender to the basket (i.e. the medium point of the attacker and defender to the basket) as a coordinative variable that accurately describes dyadic system behaviours in 1 v 1 basketball. They also proposed interpersonal distance between attacker and defender as a system parameter that, when achieving a critical value, can move the dyadic system towards a specific performance outcome (see also Schmidt *et al.*, 1999) – for instance, an interception of the ball by the defender or a shot at basket by the attacker. The aim of that study was to investigate whether the distance of the dyadic system to the basket became destabilized as interpersonal distance between the attacker and defender decreased. In other words, they sought to understand whether the balance of the attacker–defender dyad was disturbed or broken at specific critical values of interpersonal distance in respect of basket location. The data revealed that the coordinative variable was able to accurately describe different states of the dyadic system – for example, when the defender displayed advantage as judged from being able to maintain dyadic system stability by counterbalancing the attacker's movements. The data also showed a new system state when the attacker managed to dribble past the defender to move closer to the basket, a system change attributed to symmetry breaking in the attacker–defender relations. The authors identified this abrupt change in the balance of a dyadic system balance as a 'phase transition', a general feature of dynamical systems.

The work of Cordovil and colleagues aimed to analyse the influence of task constraints on the symmetry of attacker–defender dyads in basketball (Cordovil *et al.*, 2009). They sought to understand whether the attacker–defender–basket configuration could be disturbed, or even broken, under the influence of common task constraints. In the first experiment, different performance instructions labelled as neutral, conservative and risk taking were given to the attacking players. Interpersonal distances between the attacker and defender were used as a collective variable to investigate dyadic behaviour. Positive values of interpersonal distance signified the defender as closest to the basket and negative values, the attacker. Thus, when the coordinative variable changed from positive to negative, a symmetry-breaking process had occurred with the attacker now acquiring an advantageous position for scoring. The data revealed that conservative instructions led the attackers to increase variability of their running-line trajectories and they took more time to cross the mid-line of the court when dribbling. In other words, the use of different performance instructions changed the attacker–defender balance in dyadic systems, as revealed in the different variability of the attackers' running-line trajectories. The results also revealed, however, that the three distinct instructional constraints did not influence the frequency of symmetry-breaking occurrences.

In the second experiment of Cordovil *et al.* (2009), the authors created dyads consisting of different height relations, aiming to analyse whether this individual structural constraint influenced dyadic system behaviours. Contrary to the findings of the first experiment, the data revealed significant differences in the frequency of symmetry-breaking occurrences when the attackers were shorter than the defenders. Also, the time to cross the court mid-line when dribbling the ball was significantly less for shorter attackers, as compared with dyads comprising the same height relations or when attackers were taller than defenders (Cordovil *et al.*, 2009). These findings implied that the height relation between performers in basketball is a task constraint that can influence the balance in dyadic systems.

Staying with basketball, Bourbousson and colleagues (2010) used lateral and longitudinal players' movement displacements trajectories to analyse interpersonal patterns of coordination. Regarding the attacking–defending dyads, the data revealed strong in-phase attractions in the basket-to-basket (longitudinal) direction. On the contrary, weaker interpersonal coordination was observed within defending and attacking dyads in both longitudinal and lateral directions. In contrast with the preceding results, however, anti-phase coordination in the lateral direction only was reported for dyads comprising wing players from the same team. These varying interpersonal coordination patterns are consistent with the game demands of supporting teammates' actions in pursuit of team objectives. This research demonstrated relative phase as a powerful collective variable that accurately captures different modes of interpersonal coordination between different dyads.

Soccer

Similar to the studies in sailing and basketball, Headrick *et al.* (2012) analysed the influence of task constraints on behaviour in attacker–defender dyads in soccer. In this study, the authors investigated whether proximity to goal influenced the dynamics of dyadic system behaviours. The task involved a typical 1 v 1 sub-phase of soccer performed in three different locations on the pitch: i) attacking the goal (i.e. edge of the defender's penalty area; ii) in midfield; and iii) leaving the goal being attacked (i.e. edge of the defender/ball dribbler's penalty area). Players' performance was recorded using single video camera at 25 Hz and their bi-dimensional coordinates were extracted manually using TACTO 8.0 software (Fernandes and Caixinha, 2003). The variables under analysis included the distances of both defender and attacker to the ball. Results revealed significant differences in dyadic system behaviours at different pitch locations. Closer to the goal (i.e. at the edge of the defender's penalty area), the defender-to-ball distance stabilized at greater values than when the attacker–defender interactions occurred further from the goal. In other pitch locations, the defender-to-ball distance stabilized at lower values. The results showed how playing performance was highly constrained by on-field location where the dyadic system interactions occurred. The defender displayed more conservative behaviours closer to goal, whereupon poor decision making could lead to an advantageous situation for the attacker (a possible phase transition) with little prospect of recovery. The study of Headrick and colleagues showed how the behaviours of players in a dyad differed, based on key task constraints as reference points such as distance to goal, highlighting the importance of understanding the player–environment relationship in sports performance analysis.

Following the same line of experimental logic in manipulating task constraints to understand their effects on dyadic system behaviours, Lopes *et al.* (2012) investigated the dynamic interactions of goalkeeper and penalty taker in soccer. For reasons expressed previously, a major concern of Lopes *et al.* was to preserve the representativeness of the experimental task design. One way to achieve this goal was through providing instructional constraints that induced variability in the decisions and actions emerging from the interactions between penalty taker and goalkeeper. Thus, aiming to analyse the influence of specific task-related instructional constraints on action strategies and performance outcomes, the behaviours of both players were constrained under five different conditions: i) no specific instructions for penalty taker or goalkeeper; ii) the penalty taker had to choose one of the goal areas to place the ball prior to the run-up, combined with a free strategy for the goalkeeper; iii) the penalty taker had to choose the shot direction during the run-up, combined with a free strategy for the goal keeper; iv) no specific instructions for the penalty taker, combined with instructions for the goalkeeper to stay still as long as possible; and v) no specific instructions for the penalty taker, combined with the goalkeeper being free to move side to side on the goal line. Players' performance was video-recorded at 25 Hz using a single camera, and their bi-dimensional coordinates were extracted manually using TACTO 8.0 software (Fernandes and Caixinha, 2003).

In a descriptive analysis of the dyadic system under investigation, the coordinative variables selected were movement speed and goal line angles for both penalty taker and goalkeeper. Similar to previous research described in this chapter, the coordinative variables revealed different dyadic system states and sudden transitions between states. Similar to the results obtained by Cordovil and colleagues (2009) in basketball, the different instructional constraints led to differences in the dyadic behaviours of the penalty taker and goalkeeper when competing. However, no differences in performance outcomes emerging from the interactions were observed, implicating and reinforcing the view of system degeneracy as a common feature of dyadic systems in sports.

Rugby union

The existence of mutual behavioural dependency between attacker and defender drives dyadic systems to explore different solutions for achieving the same performance outcomes. The work of Passos *et al.* (2009) in 1 v 1 sub-phases of rugby union near the try line highlighted a coordinative variable that accurately described the interactive behaviours between attackers and defenders. That coordinative variable was angle calculated with a vector from defender to attacker referenced to a horizontal line parallel to the try line. Similar to previous research, the coordinative

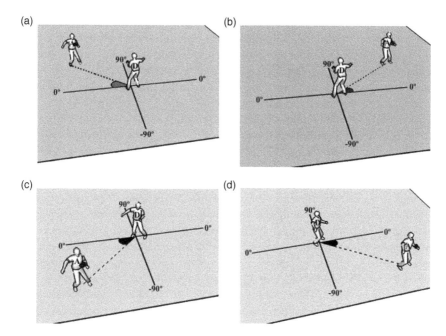

Figure 6.1 Coordinative variable used in 1v1 in rugby union: (a) and (b) Coordinative variable with positive values signifies that the ball carrier doesnot pass the defender; player A represents the ball carrier; player D represents the defender; (c) and (d) Coordinative variable with negative values signifies that the ball carrier already passed the defender; player A represents the ball carrier; player D represents the defender

variable in rugby union also characterized two different states of the attacker–defender system, as well as transitions between those states. Positive angles signified the defender was the closest player to the try line, a zero-crossing identified the transitional moment that the attacker drew level with the defender, and negative angles signalled emergence of a new system, whereupon the attacker had moved past the defender to become closest to the try line (Figure 6.1).

This coordinative variable allows description of the interactive behaviours of attackers and defenders in rugby union, nevertheless it does not explain why this dyadic system transitioned from an advantage to the defender to that of the attacker. For that purpose, Passos *et al.* (2008) suggested two candidate system parameters: interpersonal distance between attacker and defender, as before, and relative velocity of the players. Results revealed that these two system parameters acted in a 'nested' way. Specifically, decreasing interpersonal distance values attracted the attacker–defender system to a critical region whereupon players' behaviours become mutually dependent, and within that critical region the influence of relative velocity between players had a powerful effect, serving to move the dyadic system to one of the two preferred states. Put simply, if relative velocity in the critical region was increasing, the attacker was advantaged, and if it was decreasing, the advantage was with the defender.

Concluding remarks

In the first part of this chapter, the concept of representative design was introduced (Brunswick, 1952, 1956) and a constraints-based approach for investigating sports behaviours advocated. It was suggested that experimental task designs manipulate task constraints specific to each sport, thereby replicating the affordances available to players in competitive performance settings. In fact, the implication of this proposition goes beyond results transfer from experiment to performance environment, as argued here, and extends more generally to consideration of design in training and learning programmes in sports practice (Araújo *et al.*, 2007).

The studies reported in this chapter have strived to meet the requirement of representative design and document some of the research in dyadic system behaviours in sport over the past decade. They have in common the need for identifying coordinative variables that describe the interactive behaviours of performers, rather than describing the behaviour of each player as a single entity divorced from the other. The use of coordinative variables allows identification of stable states in dyadic systems, such as when a defender maintains an advantage over an attacker. These coordinative variables also describe when the attacker–defender balance is broken and a new stable state emerges, a phenomenon called phase transition. These same variables have also identified intra-system variability in support of the notion of system degeneracy, explaining how players' interactions display different solutions for achieving the same performance outcome. In the aim of advancing understanding of phase transitions in dyadic systems, some studies have gone beyond coordinative variables and suggested candidate variables as system parameters. Successful examples include the studies of Araújo *et al.* (2003) in sailing and Passos *et al.* (2008) in rugby union. These investigations have thus far indicated interpersonal distances, velocities and angles as important system parameters of dyadic system behaviour. The results presented in this chapter offer continuing evidence in support of the notion of competitive sports performance as self-organizing processes based on the theoretical framework of ecological dynamics.

References

Araújo, D., Davids, K., Sainhas, J. and Fernandes, O. (2002) 'Emergent decision-making in sport: A constraints-led approach', Paper presented at the International Congress of Movement, Attention and Perception, Poitiers, France, June.

Araújo, D., Davids, K., Rocha, L., Serpa, S. and Fernandes, O. (2003) 'Decision making in sport as phase transitions', *International Journal of Computer Science in Sport*, 2(2): 87–8.

Araújo, D., Davids, K. and Passos, P. (2007) 'Ecological validity, representative design, and correspondence between experimental task constraints and behavioral setting: Comment on Rogers, Kadar, and Costall (2005)', *Ecological Psychology*, 19(1): 69–78.

Bourbousson, J., Sève, C. and McGarry, T. (2010) 'Space-time coordination dynamics in basketball: Part 1. Intra- and inter-couplings among player dyads', *Journal of Sports Sciences*, 28(3): 339–47.

Brunswik, E. (1952) *Conceptual Framework of Psychology*, Chicago, IL: University of Chicago Press.

Brunswik, E. (1956) *Perception and the Representative Design of Psychological Experiments* (2nd ed.), Berkeley, CA: University of California Press.

Cordovil, R., Araujo, D., Davids, K., Gouveia, L., Barreiros, J., Fernandes, O. and Serpa, S. (2009) 'The influence of instructions and body-scaling as constraints on decision-making processes in team sports', *European Journal of Sport Science*, 9(3): 169–79.

Davids, K., Araújo, D., Hristovski, R., Passos, P. and Chow, J.-Y. (in press) 'Ecological dynamics and motor learning design in sport', in A.M.W.N. Hodges (ed.), *Skill Acquisition in Sport: Research, Theory and Practice* (2nd ed.). London: Routledge.

Dicks, M., Davids, K. and Araújo, D. (2008) 'Ecological psychology and task representativeness: Implications for the design of perceptual-motor training programmes in sport', in Y. Hong and R. Bartlett (eds), *The Routledge Handbook of Biomechanics and Human Movement Science* (pp. 129–39). London: Routledge.

Edelman, G.M. and Gally, J.A. (2001) 'Degeneracy and complexity in biological systems', *Proceedings of National Academy of Science, USA*, 98(24): 13763–8.

Fajen, B.R., Riley, M.A. and Turvey, M.T. (2009) 'Information, affordances, and the control of action in sport', *International Journal of Sport Psychology*, 40(1): 79–107.

Fernandes, O. and Caixinha, P. (2003) 'A new method in time-motion analysis in soccer training and competition', Paper presented at the the 5th World Congress of Science and Football, Lisbon, Portugal, May.

Hammond, K. and Stewart, T. (2001) *The Essential Brunswik: Beginnings, Explications, Applications*, New York: Oxford University Press.

Headrick, J., Davids, K., Renshaw, I., Araújo, D., Passos, P. and Fernandes, O. (2012) 'Proximity-to-goal as a constraint on patterns of behaviour in attacker-defender dyads in team games', *Journal of Sports Sciences*, 30(3): 247–53.

Kugler, P., Kelso, J.S. and Turvey, M.T. (1982) 'On the control and co-ordination of naturally developing systems', in J.S. Kelso and J. Clark (eds), *The Development of Movement Control and Co-ordination*, (pp. 5–78). New York: Wiley.

Lagarde, J., DeGuzman, G.C., Oullier, O. and Kelso, J.A.S. (2006) 'Interpersonal interactions during boxing: Data and model', *Journal of Sport and Exercise Psychology*, 28: S108–S108.

Lopes, J.E., Araújo, D., Duarte, R., Davids, K. and Fernandes, O. (2012) 'Instructional constraints on movement and performance of players in the penalty kick', *International Journal of Performance Analysis in Sport*, 12: 311–45.

McGarry, T., Khan, M.A. and Franks, I.M. (1999) 'On the presence and absence of behavioural traits in sport: An example from championship squash match-play', *Journal of Sports Sciences*, 17(4): 297–311.

Newell, K.M. (1986) 'Constraints on the development of coordination', in M.W.H.T.A. Whiting (ed.), *Motor Development in Children: Aspects of Coordination and Control* (pp. 341–60). Dordrecht, Netherlands: Martinus Nijhoff.

Palut, Y. and Zanone, P.G. (2005) 'A dynamical analysis of tennis: Concepts and data', *Journal of Sports Sciences*, 23(10): 1021–32.

Passos, P., Araújo, D., Davids, K., Gouveia, L., Milho, J. and Serpa, S. (2008) 'Information-governing dynamics of attacker-defender interactions in youth rugby union', *Journal of Sports Sciences*, 26(13): 1421–9.

Passos, P., Araújo, D., Davids, K., Gouveia, L., Serpa, S., Milho, J. and Fonseca, S. (2009) 'Interpersonal pattern dynamics and adaptive behavior in multiagent neurobiological systems: conceptual model and data', *Journal of Motor Behavior*, 41(5): 445–59.

Pinder, R.A., Davids, K., Renshaw, I. and Araújo, D. (2011) 'Representative learning design and functionality of research and practice in sport', *Journal of Sport and Exercise Psychology*, 33(1): 146–55.

Schmidt, R.C., O'Brien, B. and Sysko, R. (1999) 'Self-organization of between-persons cooperative tasks and possible applications to sport', *International Journal of Sport Psychology*, 30: 558–79.

Stoffregen, T.A., Bardy, B.G., Smart, L.J. and Pagulayan, R.J. (2003) 'On the nature and evaluation of fidelity in virtual environments', in L.J. Hettinger and M.W. Haas (eds), *Virtual and Adaptive Environments: Applications, Implications, and Human Performance Issues* (pp. 111–28). Mahwah, NJ: Lawrence Erlbaum Associates, Inc.

Tuller, B., Case, P., Ding, M. and Kelso, J.A. (1994) 'The nonlinear dynamics of speech categorization', *Journal of Experimental Psychology: Human Perception and Performance*, 20(1): 3–16.

7

COMPLEX SYSTEMS IN TEAM SPORTS

Felix Lebed

KAYE ACADEMIC COLLEGE OF EDUCATION, ISRAEL

Summary

This chapter examines the cardinal approaches to analysing performance in team sports and challenges a number of prevailing attitudes, relating to: (a) performance as reactive behaviour following interactions with teammates and opponents; (b) competitive play as instrumentally aimed behaviour; (c) performance analysis as a cybernetic system intending to provide feedback to the 'coach-player-team' units; (d) playing performance 'as is' without consideration of internal and external (environmental) contexts; and (e) a sports team as a playing domain without viewing it as a managed unit within the entire sports institution hierarchy. Review of research reports together with author perceptions on complexity features of sport performance leads to the view of team playing as a result of self-organization in a complex system. Suggestions for improving the scholarly foundations of performance analysis for future research are offered.

Introduction

The win-focus of team sports is supported by many professional processes, one of which is performance analysis. As can be seen from research reports (Hughes, 2004; Nevill *et al.*, 2008; O'Donoghue 2010; Reilly *et al.*, 1997), performance analysis has at least three origins: (1) applied performance analysis used by coaches for real-time and/or post-game analysis and consequent adjustments; (2) cybernetic systems theory, which emphasizes the importance of feedback for controlling a system; and (3) classical scientific method as reflected mainly through behaviouristic psychology, according to which only measured – or at least quantified – parameters of human behaviour should be the focus of analysis. The first source has provided the applied aspect of performance analysis. The second one structured the notion of multiple feedback mediated by performance analysis and is an integral part of pedagogical control in team management. According to this schema, the recorded, selected, and computed data is directed to both the functioning of sports institutions and scholarly research aiming to discover general regularities of performance (Figure 7.1). The third source provided a methodology for conducting performance analysis.

The view of playing athletes and teams as complex systems, which has developed since the 1990s and especially in the last decade, has somewhat altered the picture by challenging the

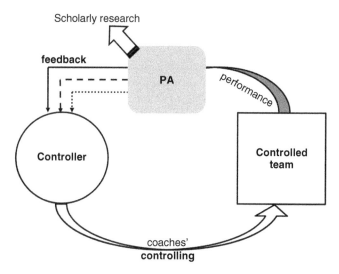

Figure 7.1 Schema of cybernetic control based on multiple feedback mediated by performance analysis (PA) in team sports

principles adopted by performance analysis. The challenges relate to both the principles of system control and the use of the Cartesian scientific method, which is built on the axiom of an inherent connection between cause and consequence, which laid the basis for the reactive input → output (stimulus → response) methodology of behaviourism.

This chapter consists of three sections. The first discusses the complexity scientific approach to human systems in general and teams in sports in particular. Here, a team is expressed by two qualities: first, a domain playing competitive games and, second, a unit within a managed hierarchy of other complex systems in a sports institution. The next section considers a playing team as reflected in the functional complexity of team sports. Such complexity must be related to unique features of human playing before connection to extrinsic and intrinsic factors and agents that will influence a team as a complex system, In the last section, the team as a managed unit reflects a structural complexity of team sports. Each level of the sports system (athletes, coaches, managers, staff) has its own complexity, and each must be managed in concert, like an orchestra.

Complexity as a principle for a proactive approach to team performance

Complexity and proactive behaviour

Classical systems theory evaluates managing efficacy along a loop: planning → preparation → performance → feedback → planning, etc. (Carling *et al.*, 2005). However, this schema has a problem in that performance analysis in team sports does not always play a role in a multi-channel feedback system. Complexity theory explains this phenomenon through one of the main characteristics of live systems. For the most part, these are self-organized dynamics and 'growth-from-within' (Dimitrov, 2005: 23) and both these features are based on a series of special characteristics (Bar-Yam, 1997; Cilliers, 2005; Gershenson and Heylighen, 2005; Richardson *et al.*, 2007; Wolfram 2002). These characteristics are as follows: (1) complex systems consist of a very large number of elements (levels), each of which can be simple; (2) the elements interact dynamically by exchanging flows of energy or information; (3) the interactions are non-linear, and distributed throughout a network; (4) the network consists of many direct and indirect feedback loops; (5) complex systems are open systems – they exchange energy or information with their environment and operate in conditions far from equilibrium; (6) complex systems have a memory which is not located in a specific place but distributed throughout the system; (7) the behaviour of the system is determined by the nature of the interactions and not by the contents of the components – the notion of emergence is used to describe this aspect; (8) all the dynamics of complex systems are expressed purposefully by behaviours that are directed to the most powerful attractor at a given time; (9) complex systems are adaptive, they are flexible enough to be disturbed by environment constraints, and they are susceptible to destruction by internal and external perturbations in the environment; and (10) self-organization is one of the most important cornerstones of complex systems.

One of the most relevant considerations for performance analysis features of complex systems is their unpredictability, which is expressed in a lack of generally expected connections between system input and output. Weak input can result in strong output and, conversely, imposed input may be followed by a weak and/or late response (Gershenson and Heylighen, 2005; Morrison, 2002). Such inadequate responses are caused by a very large number of both external factors and agents influencing complex systems and network intra-connections that compose intrinsic flows. These peculiarities indicate that complex behaviour cannot be comprehended by a rational approach based on the Cartesian world outlook, mainly reductionism, analysis, determinism, and rationality (Cilliers, 2005; Wolfram, 2002). Stated simply, this outlook means that a known impulse leads (or should lead) to a predictable effect, suggesting an implied law of managing behaviour, as if the controlling level of a system (manager, coach, etc.) has the right to expect a predictable response from the levels it controls. And if this response is not obtained, then the implication is that something is wrong in the regulating or managing act because, in the Cartesian world, the 'right' stimulus must always lead to the 'right' response.

Viewed methodologically, 'right' and 'unright' (i.e. unexpected) responding of complex systems can be presented through a counter-position of behavioural reactiveness and proactiveness. This counter-position would seem to be expressed, in its shortest form, through the question of primacy of human purpose versus the primacy of the environment as the main cause of an action strategy. The link to a proactive understanding of behavioural causality can be found in the works of early functionalists. Carr (1925) was first to consider motive as a stimulus and then as a primary cause of activity. Maslow's (1943) view of human motivation continued in this direction and led to purposeful consciousness and then to proactive behaviour. Psychological self-determination theory (Deci and Ryan, 1985; Ryan and Deci, 2000) can also be analysed as a reactive–proactive counterpoint because it presents this dichotomy through the opposing positions of extrinsic (forced) and intrinsic (freely chosen) motivation.

In the modern psychological version of action theory adapted to sports, Nitsch (2009) proposed that the entire world of multilevel intrinsic motivations of a person should be taken into account. Nitsch's views can be expanded to encompass a number of functional theories in psychology and sociology that offer a systems approach to the complicated phenomena of life, humans, and society. Some of these theories are the antithesis of behaviourism, popular during most of the twentieth century (Vygotsky, 1978; Parsons 1978). They equate reactivity of behaviour to an individual's proactivity that results from intrinsic dynamics. Returning to Nitsch (2009), one can view social components in this proactiveness. His behavioural model (Nitsch, 2009: 173) includes four levels of person–environment interrelations – physical, biological, mental, and social. According to these views, the social environment creates a person (an actor) by prolonged influence, and this actor determines his aims and 'reads' current environmental conditions through a 'subjective situation definition' (Nitsch, 2009: 170–1).

Basic features of a sports team as a complex system

Viewing sports contests through the complexity prism necessarily entails seeing each side as a domain having 'grown-from-within' self-dynamics that are independent of environment. This in turn leads to the claim that sports contests have a high probability of proactive performance, which can be examined mainly by new forms of performance analysis. Such a claim needs to establish one thing: is a sports team a complex system?

Because of its finite number of system elements and the strong limits on their functioning, a team lacks important complex system qualities, such as a large number of levels and flows and unpredictable freedom of behaviour. But this simplicity may be more apparent than real. First, complexity sciences offer a fundamental notion about the emergence of complex behaviours by simple parts (Cilliers, 1998; Wolfram, 2002). Second, being a system, a sports team can be included in a special subset of 'family' (Bar-Yam, 1997: 4), which is an example of a complex system characterized by the following qualities: 'It is a set of individuals. Each individual has a relationship with the other individuals. There is an interplay between the relationship and the qualities of the individual. And the family has to interact with the outside world.'

The case of the family is an illustration of emergent complexity (Bar-Yam, 1997: 5), which is a function of the collective behaviour of simple parts. One may claim that the small number of team levels and the established constraints of strategies do not restrict the emergent behaviour of the whole system for the following reasons. First, ball playing itself has its own complexity caused by specific features of this kind of human activity, by the obligatory presence of a human attitude towards an activity as play and by an emotional state of enjoyment caused by this activity. Second, each one of the levels (athletes) is a complex system exhibiting emergent unpredictable qualities on both the perceptive-motor and the mental sides of behaviour. And third, a mutually active conflict of opposing sides is a primary condition and main pattern of acting in a competitive game. The simultaneous struggle by both sides for a play thing makes the play of each athlete an emergent, uncertain, and unpredictable behaviour based on relative knowledge about every future moment of the contest.

When claiming that the playing team as a whole is a complex system, one has to analyse its features by means of problematic questions of complexity, the first of them being that, in such a situation, performance analysis can no longer be identified with the notion of feedback only. The complexity vision suggested here means seeing team performance both inside and outside of the 'coach–team' cybernetic loop (Figure 7.2). As demonstrated in Figure 7.2, many intrinsic and extrinsic factors have an influence, leaving footprints on performance, weakening the coach's control, and thus making the term feedback unessential. (For a review of intrinsic factors, see Lebed, 2009.) The extrinsic factors have been divided into four kinds (or two pairs) of environment: social–physical and supporting–menacing. The following example illustrates how social factors influence performance. From an analysis of 286 penalty kicks from various soccer games, Bar-Eli *et al.* (2007) reported that the goalkeeper chose to jump to the side they anticipated the kick would go on 93.7 per cent of trials, despite statistical indications that staying in the centre of the goal offered the best goalkeeping strategy. In other words, the goalkeeper's action of producing the norm of jumping to protect the goal is a product of social expectations, with teammates, coaches, and fans accepting that the goalkeeper has to jump to safely close one side of the goal. Thus, the norms and values of a given socium influence the choice of purposes

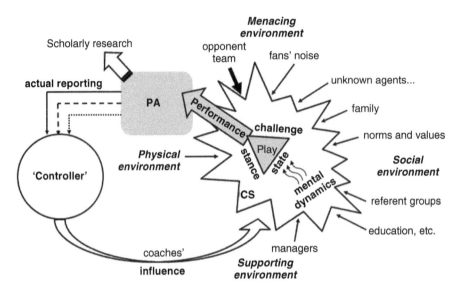

Figure 7.2 Place and role of performance analysis (PA) in 'control' of an emergent behaviour of a complex system that is a competing team

in the earliest stage of performance. They can correspond or not correspond with personal norms and values, but they influence and alter behaviour.

Only a few factors can be separately registered, recorded, and computed during performance analysis. At the same time, the need to relate to many forces perturbing a complex system (the competing team) has to be taken into account for comprehension of performance. In every game, in every competition, a team of players is influenced by an incomparable diversity of intrinsic and extrinsic factors and exhibits special, unmatchable indications of successful performance. In this sense, Socrates was right in that 'you cannot step twice into the same stream' (Fowler, 1921).

Because of space limitations, the discussion cannot cover all schematic factors that influence a team as a complex system. For additional information on these factors, the reader is referred to Lebed and Bar-Eli (in press). Two main factors will be analysed within the framework of functional complexity here: the complexity of playing itself and the complexity view of the opposing side in a competitive game. The first will be discussed because it has not been addressed within performance analysis; the second, because it is important for introducing complexity sciences into the field.

The functional complexity of competitive game playing

Complexity of playing as a background of team performance

Attention dealing with the complexity of human activity has focused mainly on the functioning of complex systems in conditions of uncertainty that border on chaos and seek the attractor. Emergent behaviour of complex systems is always aimed at less uncertainty. But the case of playing humans is special because the playing itself has its own complexity. The following analysis offers interpretation in which game playing can be perceived as a special skilful activity, an amusing mental state, and a spirited, playful attitude to real activity.

Complexity (uncertainty) of a process and the result of playing

The main thesis here proposes that the potentially playful side of reality can emerge only in a situation of uncertainty of both process and result. This approach is echoed in Huizinga's (1955: 8) requirement of uncertainty – 'play turns to seriousness and seriousness to play' – as an obligatory feature of play. A detailed analysis of the affinity between play and uncertainty is also given by Moore (1975), who used the term indeterminacy, and Turner (1983), who referred to liminality of play. It would seem that, in the philosophy of sport, this issue can be expressed in Esposito's (1974) concept of possibility and Kretchmar's (1975) concept of test. Kretchmar explains the situation of test by the unsteadiness between what he calls impregnability and vulnerability.

These approaches concur that the uncertainty created in a play activity by the possibility of both success and failure is what makes physical play and games pleasing. The challenge is adrenalized by possible crashes, uncertain duration of play, and ambiguous results, and is characteristic of all kinds of playing. All of the above focus attention on the issue of games playing which, to be played, must be uncertain and unpredictable. In games, this quality of activity is achieved by rules that introduce constraints for players – for example, complicated conditions for scoring a goal which demand the skills of a virtuoso, high physical effort, and more or less forceful counteraction of an opponent. The scholarly side of performance analysis in team sports usually does not relate to this properly playful side of performance. At the same time, one can recognize references to the subject in publications that separate data taken in games where playing itself displays different faces – for instance, balanced and unbalanced games (Gómez *et al.*, 2008; Sampaio *et al.*, 2010), games with different match status (Lago, 2009), levels of competition (Sampaio *et al.*, 2004), and variations of play parameters depending on the pace of the games (Volossovitch *et al.*, 2010).

Complexity (uncertainty) of a player's mental state

Using the longitudinal Socratic axiological tradition, one can consider every uncertain situation as satisfying or good for one person and at the same time not satisfying or bad for another. Extreme cases of various contingencies, such as military combat or mortal fighting, can cause joy and pleasure resulting from uncertainty, fear, and threat, or such activities can cause a mental state of fright, paralysis, and aversion. Many philosophical and psychological sources describe play in terms of good (e.g. happiness and amusement), although it can be illustrated that it is more complicated. The mental state of being totally involved in the good of playing is discussed by Csikszentmihalyi (1975, 1997) as a notion of being in the flow. While the flow is defined as a peak experience entailing inspiration and control of the situation, this approach was developed and changed by Csikszentmihalyi during 25 years of experience. In the first publication dedicated to flow, six elements of flow experience as the mental state of playing were distinguished – a merging of action and awareness, a centring of attention on a limited stimulus field, a loss of self-consciousness during play, control of actions and environment, unambiguous feedback on a person's actions, and the autotelic nature of actions (Csikszentmihalyi, 1975: 38–48). In a later version of flow, a distinction was made between the states of control and flow (Csikszentmihalyi, 1997: 31). This later interpretation of flow opens the opportunity to consider flow as a mental state of inspired loss of self-consciousness during play. According to Csikszentmihalyi, the mental state of play is subjective and depends on the level of uncertainty in a given situation. If the task given to a player is too hard, the mental state tends to anxiety, whereas if it is too easy, the mental state veers towards boredom. In both cases, play as a mental state does not exist.

Complexity (uncertainty) of a player's attitude towards a playful activity

One can note that the uncertainty of playing is not demarcated only by vagueness about the opponent, conflict duration, result, or current mental state. Play of any kind, even non-competitive, is uncertain because of its double message. Huizinga (1955: 13) noted this phenomenon 'standing quite consciously outside "ordinary" life as being "not serious"' and thus having, in our opinion, a double message. On the other hand, Bateson's (1955) double or meta message for 'this is play', regarding the fighting-playing of cubs, could, according to Handelman (1990: 71), 'be rewritten and rendered as "This is uncertainty".' These notions are developed and transformed into a significant dilemma in modern sports philosophy through a discussion of play as an activity versus a stance or an attitude towards the activity. Since the 1970s, a series of sports philosophers have considered play as a kind of attitude towards reality. Schneider (2001) criticized views of Suits (1988) and Meier (1989), who both discussed the issue of autotelicity–instrumentality of play as a kind of activity. Suits (2004) sharply scrutinized Schneider's view of play as a stance of mind, but, in fact, accepted some of her positions. All advocates of this view argue that any kind of human activity can become play, and this is dependent only on the human stance towards it (Garvey, 1991; Rieber, 1996; Roochnik, 1975). The mechanism of taking such a stance of mind towards the external reality in which one is involved is the temporary relocation, making-believe, or transcendentness of an activity.

It appears then that team sports can constitute a clear instance of both presence and absence of the stance of play in athletes. It is absent when an atmosphere of 'must' and hard work is disseminated within a team by the coaches and leading athletes. Being within a frame of 'must', athletes work hard until the end of the game, but their performance is different from true playing, as suggested in the observation that 'the best player can do this playfully, that is, an easy joyful expression of herself' (Howe, 2007: 54).

Taking the above elements together, one can propose three uncertain origins for the complexity of play. Play occurs when a possible failure in the activity creates a challenge and an intrigue, the latter of which influences motivation and forms the mental play-state and play attitude towards a game. This is the case analysed by Suits (2004) as an action and a mode of action together. Finally, if only one side of this 'challenge–state–stance' triangle (Figure 7.2) is removed, play does not occur.

Implications of the above description for performance analysis can be suggested. One of the leaders of modern sports philosophy, Kretchmar, speaks of unbalanced fixed-time games or parts of games in which certain moments of a game cease to be interesting (i.e. they cease to be play) because one of the competing sides has an obvious advantage (Kretchmar, 2005). One interpretation of this approach can be that such uninteresting periods of games lack uncertainty. Thus, the performance demonstrated during such periods is not true. It is a weak indication of a team's ability to compete in balanced games and to provide performances during long-term competition composed of a series of games. If this philosophical discussion of the essence of playing itself can be applied, one might suggest that unbalanced games and periods of games be excluded from performance analysis.

Team performance in direct competition with opponents from a complex viewpoint

Complexity views could influence performance analysis in team games, first of all, in the interpretation of the nature of the opponents' counteractions. Certainly an opponent is the most influential factor in terms of performance duration and outcome. Three approaches to the issue can be distinguished from the methodological viewpoint of complexity: the dynamical systems approach, the ecological approach, and the complex systems contest approach.

The first approach to competitive playing through a dynamical systems vision was developed during the first decade of this millennium (Lames, 1998; McGarry *et al.*, 2002). From the unanimity of ideas presented in most of the publications on the subject, one can generalize a list of main characteristics. First, the game itself is a dynamical system (Glazier, 2010; Lames, 2006; Lames and McGarry, 2007; McGarry *et al.*, 2002). Second, both sides (opponents) constitute components of the dynamical system (e.g. players and/or teams) that oscillate in tandem as they interact during a game (Bourbousson *et al.*, 2010; McGarry and Franks, 2007). Third, any of the components can push the system into a zone of instability or, in other terminology, to a phase of non-equilibrium. Here, 'perturbation' is a key category symbolizing a critical moment in the process of destabilization (Hughes *et al.*, 1998; McGarry and Franks, 1995; Reed and Hughes, 2006). Based on these key points, one has to interpret goal scoring as a destruction of the system caused by a previous perturbation. This approach seems an important attempt to perceive competing sides in individual and team sports through a complexity prism. However, it can be evaluated ambivalently. So, the notion of human competitive playing at the level of coupled oscillation within a system makes the approach reactive, in my view, as the order parameter describing the coupling behaviours plays a passive reactive role, with its dynamics emerging only to save the balance of the system. Such a dynamical systems perspective applies for brain–motor control (Haken *et al.*, 1985; Kelso, 1995), but it is not enough for a complexity vision at the level of playing human persons having free will and his/her own emergent dynamics. Another essential problem for this approach, in my assessment, concerns relation to the environment, which is an important element for understanding complexity in general and complexity of competitive play in particular. If both competing sides are levels of the same system game, then what is the environment of such a system? For additional considerations and debate on these points, the reader is referred to Lebed (2003, 2006, 2007) and McGarry and Franks (2007).

Despite using dynamical systems rhetoric, the ecological approach to sports performance analysis especially emphasizes the issue of environment, a rather ambiguous concept in the preceding approach. The view discussed here (Araújo *et al.*, 2006; Araújo and Davids, 2009) is based mostly on the Gibsonian version of ecological psychology (Gibson, 1979). In short, this approach claims that humans in action are in systematic perception–action relations with the environment, with conditions and constraints affecting decision making and acting. At the same time, this doctrine claims that an action is always a function of three interacting constraining factors: environment, task, and organism (Newell, 1986). From a complexity point of view, this relation does not contradict the main principles of complex systems emergent behaviour (Dimitrov, 2005; Varela *et al.*, 1974), that of self-dynamics, coupled interaction with the environment, and growth-from-within. However, the notion of self-constraints (individual constraints) may be associated negatively with the self-dynamics usually connected to creation and not only adaptation. Regarding self-constraints, Glazier and Davids (2009) raise Newell's notion of 'organismic constraints' to the level of 'specific individual constraints', but it is still not enough in comparison to the principle of proactiveness provided by other scholars for socially created persons acting within an environment (Nitsch, 2009; Vygotsky, 1978). Finally, because of its adaptive tone on one hand and the vision of a playing subject as an independent system on the other, the ecological psychology approach to complexity vision of competitive playing may be situated in the middle of the reactiveness–proactiveness scale, and this makes it a rather balanced approach between traditional and complex methodologies of human performance research in team sports.

When comparing both dynamical systems and ecological approaches with the complex systems' contest model suggested by Lebed (2006, 2007, 2008), we see that the latter approach has adopted some of the important elements from each and has left out those that seemed debatable (Figure 7.3). Specifically, the dynamical systems approach enriched the proposed model of two contesting complex systems by the notion of perturbation. The importance of perturbations that lead to scoring in a game is widely comprehended as a main tool of performance analysis of team play (Reed and Hughes, 2006). But the principle of mutual proactiveness of both complex systems demands a broadening of our understanding of perturbation to include not only offensive acts (Hughes *et al.*, 1998) but defensive activity as well. The defence-created perturbation is a most powerful weapon for destroying attacks. The efficacy of defence perturbations was illustrated by Holland's 'total football' back in the 1970s: 'The game . . . was about space and how you controlled it: make the pitch big when you have the ball . . . make it small when you do not and it becomes far more difficult for the opposition to keep it' (Wilson, 2008: 218). The total control of space in defence, when, at least, two players surround an attacker possessing a ball, is a brief example of proactiveness creating perturbations in defence. The ecological psychology contribution to competing complex systems (teams) creates a central place for environmental factors and, as such, forms a relation with this model. In the complex systems' contest view, each team in a contest is part of a menacing environment for the other team. However, as we have seen, not all environmental influences are constraints and menaces; some of them are supports instead. Thus we take one more step and claim that the playing team is backed by supporting forces because it is included in an entire hierarchy of higher-level complex systems of a sports institution. In this way, we come to the notion of structural complexity in team sports.

Structural complexity of competitive game playing

Epigraphs have not been attached to each part of this chapter, but an appropriate one for this section would be: '. . . new properties emerge at every level of organization, which are not predictable from lower levels in principle' (Kelso and Engstrøm, 2006: 80).

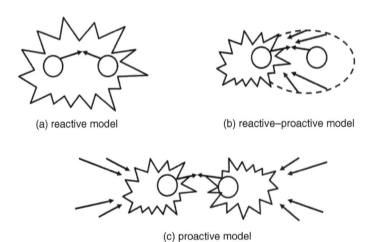

(a) reactive model

(b) reactive–proactive model

(c) proactive model

Figure 7.3   Three approaches to a complexity vision of competition in team sports: (a) player coupled oscillations within a dynamical system 'game'; (b) a team's 'ecological' systematic interaction with environmental constraints, one of which is an opponent; and (c) mutually proactive contest of two complex systems surrounded by environmental supports and constraints

Our analysis of complex systems in the field of team sports investigates the following basic notions (Lebed, 2005, 2006, 2007). First, a player (i.e. a single athlete and/or a team) and a sports institution are complex systems acting in institutionalized games. Second, the complex systems in team sports should be comprehended as a three-level hierarchy – athlete, team, and sports institution, which can be functionally interpreted as skilful and/or powerful movements, playing, and control and managing processes. Third, this hierarchy is expressed not only by levels of human organization, but also by synergetic interaction (flows) between levels. Each of the levels is supported and regulated by a higher one, providing needed flows of energy and/or information.

This case demands a special definition, 'a hybrid complex system' (Bar-Yam, 1997). It is hybrid because it acts both by its own internal self-organization and by external control by virtue of it being within a hierarchy. The hierarchical structure represents a command control, whereas self-organization indicates emergence of a network structure. The hybrid systems approach promotes an additional form of complex regulation. Because the internal self-organization must be synergized with the external control, one has to use a new approach that we call *regulation of equifinality*. By this we mean a professional intervention utilizing soft control that directs the self-organization of a human complex system from the outside and causes it to achieve a mutually agreed target in its own way.

The competition of athletes joined within a team creates a level of complexity that necessitates supervision by professional managing, coaching, and physical training, supervision that is carried out by a coach designated for this role by the sports institution. In elite team sports, the high level of complexity is higher yet. Therefore, this function is performed by a coaching team and managing staff, each of which incidentally has its own complexity, dynamics, and hierarchy. Thus, studies of complexity in team sports and performance analysis must relate to the entire hybrid complex system, which consists of a hierarchical connection of five sub-systems as follows: (1) the athlete as a bodily movement dynamical system. Motion and biomechanical performance analysis are tools for professional diagnostics on this level; (2) the athlete as a person, both playing with and against others and having a rich world of internal mentally and socially related dynamics. Notational quantitative and qualitative analysis, as well as psychological diagnostics, are the tools on this level; (3) the team as a domain. Notational quantitative and qualitative analysis, and socio-psychological diagnostics, serve as tools for this level; (4) the coaching team. Coach behaviour analysis, socio-psychological dynamics, and self-reports can be tools for professional diagnostics on this level; (5) the sports institution represented by the managing team and staff. This level is usually excluded from the field of performance analysis. In light of the model of structural complexity in team games suggested here, however, this issue should be a topic for future research.

Concluding remarks

Complex human systems are usually managed by ignoring their infinite openness towards diverse environments, intrinsic drives, and the variable relationships between the two. In this way, one is often surprised by inadequate reactions and behaviours of subalterns. In the frame of traditional systems theory, unexpected or inadequate feedback or responses cannot be accepted as normal. Hence, the axiomatic predictability of controlled behaviour stands as an obstacle to the complexity approach, which holds that unexpected responses are possible and even reflect a normal state of complex system functioning. The complexity sciences treat the unexpected as independent. This approach challenges the traditional scientific vision as well as traditional performance analysis. This chapter presented an attempt to reconceptualize this vision and offered three main conclusions.

First, the parameters of playing provided by performance analysis are not exactly feedback or responses to coaches that reflect the quality and intensity of preparation. These parameters are output that conceal extensive information and are only linked tangentially to a controlled system's input. This is because a team as a complex system has its own dynamics created both by playing against an opponent and by additional (non-playing) social, motivational, and other stressor influences. Note that a team's self-dynamics are quite independent from the environment. This independence characterizes a complex system's emergent behaviour and is also a cause of a team's possible grown-from-within proactive activity. As indicated through the term and process of perturbation, the episodes of clearly diagnosed proactive activity might be an essential display of successful performance.

Second, playing has its own complexity expressed through uncertainty and unpredictability. Understood in this way, complexity makes it possible to distinguish between just competing and truly playing. The latter is not obligatory during a match and this demands answers from performance analysis procedures. As a first step in this direction, these procedures should exclude from its computations and analysis clearly unbalanced games and parts of games where playing itself, as it can be understood from Kretchmar (2005), simply does not occur.

And third, the sports team is a unit within a sports institution. It cannot escape the influence of managing dynamics coming down from higher levels of the institute's hierarchy. Thus complex, all-enveloping performance analysis must include the managing and coaching level's performances as they are connected to and influence a team's competitive playing. Complex diagnostics, real-time notational analysis, and pre- and post-time quantitative and qualitative analysis (Franks, 1997; O'Donoghue, 2010) might give a fuller picture and bring more adequate answers in future about a team's performance as viewed through the complexity approach to playing in team sports.

References

Araújo, D. and Davids, K. (2009) 'Ecological approaches to cognition and action in sport and exercise: Ask not only what you do, but where you do it', *International Journal of Sport Psychology*, 40(1): 5–37.

Araújo, D., Davids, K., and Hristovski, R. (2006) 'The ecological dynamics of decision making in sport', *Psychology of Sport and Exercise*, 7: 653–76.

Bar-Eli, M., Azar, O.H., Ritov, I., and Keidar-Levin, Y. (2007) 'Action bias among soccer goalkeepers: The case of penalty kicks', *Journal of Economic Psychology*, 28: 606–21.

Bar-Yam, Y. (1997) *Dynamics of Complex Systems*, Reading, MA.: Addison-Wesley.

Bateson, G. (1955) 'A theory of play and fantasy', in J.C. Harris and R.J. Park (1983, eds), *Play, Games and Sports in Cultural Contexts* (pp. 313–26). Champaign. IL: Human Kinetics.

Bourbousson, J., Sève, C., and McGarry, T. (2010) 'Space-time coordination dynamics in basketball: Part 2. The interaction between the two teams', *Journal of Sports Sciences*, 28(3): 349–58.

Carling C., Williams, A.M., and Reilly, T. (2005) *Handbook of Soccer Match Analysis. A Systematic Approach to Improving Performance*, London: Routledge.

Carr, H. (1925) *Psychology*, New York: Longmans, Green, and Co.

Cilliers, P. (1998) *Complexity and Post Modernism: Understanding Complex Systems*, London: Routledge.

Cilliers, P. (2005) 'Knowing complex systems', in K.A. Richardson (ed.), *Managing Organizational Complexity: Philosophy, Theory, and Application. A Volume in Managing the Complex* (pp. 7–19). Greenwich, CT: Information Age Publishers.

Csikszentmihalyi, M. (1975) *Beyond Boredom and Anxiety*, San Francisco: Jossey-Bass Publishers.

Csikszentmihalyi, M. (1997) *Finding Flow. The Psychology of Engagement with Everyday Life*, New York: Basic Books, Harper Collins Publishers.

Deci, E.L. and Ryan, R.M. (1985) *Intrinsic Motivation and Self-Determination in Human Behaviour*, New York: Plenum.

Dimitrov, V. (2005) *A New Kind of Social Science. Study of Self-Organization of Human Dynamics*, Morrisville: Lulu Press.

Esposito, J.L. (1974) 'Play and possibility', in W.J. Morgan and K.V. Meier (1995, eds), *Philosophic Inquiry in Sport* (2nd ed.), (pp. 114–19). Champaign, IL: Human Kinetics.

Fowler, H.N. (1921) 'Translation of Plato', Cratylus, 402a, in *Plato in Twelve Volumes*, Vol. 12, Cambridge, MA: Harvard University Press.

Franks, I.M. (1997) 'Use of feedback by coaches and players', in T. Reilly, J. Bangsbo, and M. Hughes (eds), *Science and Football 3* (pp. 267–8). London: E & FN Spon.

Garvey, C. (1991) *Play* (2nd ed.), London: Fontana Press.

Gershenson, C. and Heylighen, F. (2005) 'How can we think complex?', in K.A. Richardson (ed.), *Managing Organizational Complexity: Philosophy, Theory, and Application. A Volume in Managing the Complex* (pp. 47–61). Greenwich, Connecticut: Information Age Publishers.

Gibson, J.J. (1979) *The Ecological Approach to Visual Perception*, Boston: Houghton Mifflin.

Glazier, P. (2010) 'Game, set and match? Substantive issues and future directions in performance analysis', *Sports Medicine*, 40(8): 625–34.

Glazier, P. and Davids, K. (2009) 'Constraints on the complete optimization of human motion', *Sports Medicine*, 39(1): 15–29.

Gómez, M.A., Alberto-Lorenzo, A., Sampaio, J., Ibáñez, S.J., and Ortega, E. (2008) 'Game-related statistics that discriminated winning and losing teams from the Spanish men's professional basketball teams', *Collegium Antropologicum*, 32(2): 451–6.

Haken, H., Kelso, J.A.S. and Bunz, H. (1985) 'A theoretical model of phase transitions in human hand movements', *Biological Cybernetics*, 51: 347–56.

Handelman, D. (1990) *Models and Mirrors: Toward an Anthropology of Public Events*, Cambridge: Cambridge University Press.

Howe, L.A. (2007) 'Play, performance, and the docile athlete', *Sport, Ethics and Philosophy*, 1(1): 47–57.

Hughes, M. (2004) 'Notational analysis: A mathematical perspective', *International Journal of Performance Analysis in Sport*, 4(2): 97–139.

Hughes, M., Dawkins, N., David, D., and Mills, J. (1998) 'The perturbation effect and goal opportunities in soccer', *Journal of Sport Sciences*, 16: 20.

Huizinga, J. (1955) *Homo ludens. A Study of Play-Element in Culture*, Boston: The Beacon Press.

Kelso, J.A.S. (1995) *Dynamic Patterns: The Self-Regulation of Brain and Behaviour*, Cambridge, MA: Bradford Books/MIT Press.

Kelso, J.A.S. and Engstrøm, D.A. (2006) *The Complementary Nature*, Cambridge, MA: MIT Press.

Kretchmar, R.S. (1975) 'From test to contest: An analysis of two kinds of counterpoint in sport', in W.J. Morgan and K.V. Meier (1995, eds), *Philosophic Inquiry in Sport* (2nd ed.), (pp. 120–33). Champaign. IL: Human Kinetics.

Kretchmar, R.S. (2005) 'Game flaws', *Journal of the Philosophy of Sport*, XXXII: 36–48.

Lago, C. (2009) 'The influence of match location, quality of opposition, and match status on possession strategies in professional association football', *Journal of Sports Sciences*, i: 1–7.

Lames, M. (1998) 'Leistungsfähigkeit, leistung und erfolg – ein beitrag zur theorie der sportspiele', *Sportwissenschaft*, 28: 137–52.

Lames, M. (2006) 'Modeling the interaction in game sports – relative phase and moving correlations', *Journal of Sports Science and Medicine*, 5: 556–60.

Lames, M. and McGarry, T. (2007) 'On the search for reliable performance indicators in game sports', *International Journal of Performance Analysis in Sport*, 7: 62–79.

Lebed, F. (2003) 'Is game a self-organizing system? (Criticism of some theoretical views on performance analysis by Tim McGarry and his colleagues)', presented at the 8th Annual Congress of the European College of Sport Science, Salzburg, Austria, July.

Lebed, F. (2005) *"Formula" of Game Playing: Comprehensive Theory, Teaching and Sport Coaching*, Volgograd, Russia: Volgograd State University Press.

Lebed, F. (2006) 'System approach to games and competitive playing', *European Journal of Sports Sciences*, 6(1): 33–42.

Lebed, F. (2007) 'A dolphin only looks like a fish: Players' behaviour analysis is not enough for game understanding in light of the system approach', *European Journal of Sports Sciences*, 7(1): 55–62.

Lebed, F. (2008) 'The logical model of team sporting game as a conflict of independent complex systems', Presentation on 2nd International Congress of Complex Systems in Sport and 10th European Workshop on Ecological Psychology, Madeira, 4–8 November.

Lebed, F. (2009) 'An interdisciplinary glance at the latent sides of performance in games', in A. Hokelman, K. Witte and P. O'Donoghue (eds), *Current Trends in Performance Analysis: World Congress of Performance Analysis of Sport VIII* (pp. 172–8). Aachen: Shaker Verlag.

Lebed, F. and Bar-Eli, M. (in press) *Complexity and Control in Team Sports*, London: Routledge.

Maslow, A.H. (1943) 'A theory of human motivation', *Psychological review*, 50: 370–96.

McGarry, T. and Franks, I.M. (1995) 'Modelling competitive squash performance from quantitative analysis', *Human Performance*, 8(2): 113–29.

McGarry, T. and Franks, I.M. (2007) 'System approach to games and competitive playing: Reply to Lebed', *European Journal of Sport Science*, 7(1): 47–53.

McGarry, T., Anderson, D.I., Wallace, S.A., Hughes, M., and Franks, I.M. (2002) 'Sport competition as a dynamical self-organizing system', *Journal of Sport Sciences*, 20: 771–81.

Meier, K.V. (1989) 'Triad trickery: Playing with sport and games', in W.J. Morgan and K.V. Meier (eds), *Philosophic Inquiry in Sport* (2nd ed.), (pp. 23–35). Champaign. IL: Human Kinetics.

Moore, S.F. (1975) 'Epilogue: Uncertainties in situations, indeterminacies in culture', in S.F. Moore and B. Myerhoff (eds), *Symbol and Politics in Communal Ideology* (pp. 210–39). Ithaca: NY, Cornell University Press.

Morrison, K. (2002) *School Leadership and Complexity Theory*, London, New York: Routledge.

Nevill, A.M., Atkinson, G., and Hughes, M. (2008) 'Twenty-five years of sport performance research in Journal of Sport Sciences', *Journal of Sports Sciences*, 26(4): 413–26.

Newell, K.M. (1986) 'Constraints on the development of coordination', in M. Wade and T.H.A. Whiting (eds), *Motor Development in Children: Aspects of Coordination and Control* (pp. 341–60). Dordrecht, Netherlands: Martinus Nijhoff.

Nitsch, J.R. (2009) 'Ecological approaches to sport activity: A commentary from an action-theoretical point of view', *International Journal of Sport Psychology*, 40: 152–76.

O'Donoghue, P. (2010) *Research Methods for Sport Performance Analysis*, London: Routledge.

Parsons, T. (1978) *Action Theory and the Human Condition*, New York: Free Press.

Reed, D. and Hughes, M. (2006) 'An exploration of team sport as a dynamical system', *International Journal of Performance Analysis in Sport*, 6(2): 114–25.

Reilly, T. Bangsbo, J., and Hughes, M. (1997) *Science and Football 3*, London: E & FN Spon.

Richardson, K.A., Cillers, P., and Lassack, M. (2007) *Complexity Thinking: A Middle Way for Analysts*, available at www.kurtrichardson.com.

Rieber, L.P. (1996) 'Seriously considered play: Designing interactive learning environments based on the blending of microworlds, simulations, and games', *Educational Technology Research and Development*, 44(2): 43–58.

Roochnik, D.L. (1975) 'Play and sport', *Journal of the Philosophy of Sport*, II: 36–44.

Ryan, R.M. and Deci, E.L. (2000) 'Self-determination theory and the facilitation of intrinsic motivation, social development, and well-being', *American Psychologist*, 55(1): 68–78.

Sampaio, J. Godoy, S.I., and Feu, S. (2004) 'Discriminative power of basketball game-related statistics by level of competition and sex', *Perceptual and Motor Skills*, 99(3): 1231–8.

Sampaio, J., Lago, C., Casais, L., and Leite, N. (2010) 'Effects of starting score-line, game location, and quality of opposition in basketball quarter score', *European Journal of Sports Sciences*, 10(6): 391–6.

Schneider, A.J. (2001) 'Fruits, apples, and category mistakes: On sports, games, and play', *Journal of Philosophy of Sport*, XXVIII: 151–9.

Suits, B. (1988) 'Tricky triad: Games, play, and sport', in W.J. Morgan and K.V. Meuer (1995, eds), *Philosophic Inquiry in Sport* (2nd ed.), (pp. 16–22). Champaign, IL: Human Kinetics.

Suits, B. (2004) 'Venn and the art of category maintenance', *Journal of Philosophy of Sport*, XXXI: 1–14.

Turner, V.W. (1983) 'Liminal to liminoid in play, flow, and ritual: An essay in comparative symbology', in J.C. Harris and P.J. Park (eds), *Play, Games and Sports in Cultural Contexts* (pp. 123–64). Champaign, IL: Human Kinetics.

Varela, F.J., Maturana, H.R., and Uribe, R. (1974) 'Autopoiesis: The organization of living systems, its characterization, and a model', *BioSystems*, 5: 187–96.

Volossovitch, A., Dumangane, M., and Rosati, N. (2010) 'The influence of the pace of match on the dynamic of handball game', *International Journal of Sport Psychology*, Special issue: 117–18.

Vygotsky, L.S. (1978) *Mind in Society – the Development of Higher Psychological Process*, Cambridge, MA: Harvard University Press.

Wilson, J. (2008) 'Total football', in *Inverting the Pyramid. The History of Football Tactics* (Chapter 12, pp. 218–34). London: Orion.

Wolfram, S. (2002) *A New Kind of Science*, Champaign, IL: Wolfram Media, Inc.

SECTION II

Measurement and evaluation in sports performance analysis

8

TACTICAL PERFORMANCE ANALYSIS IN INVASION GAMES

Perspectives from a dynamic system approach with examples from soccer

Koen Lemmink[1] and Wouter Frencken[1,2]

[1]UNIVERSITY MEDICAL CENTRE GRONINGEN, THE NETHERLANDS

[2]FOOTBALL CLUB GRONINGEN, THE NETHERLANDS

Summary

Performance analysis in invasion games like soccer, basketball, handball, rugby and field hockey requires objective recording and examination of behavioural events of one or more players during training or competition. The primary goal of performance analysis is to provide information to coaches and players about player and/or team performance in order to plan subsequent practices to improve performance or to support preparation for the next match. Performance analysis is most often used to create a permanent record of actions of players within a match through hand-based or computerized systems, often using video technology. Sophisticated data sets offer opportunities for analysing spatio-temporal patterns and network structures. However, these analyses have certain limitations, especially from a tactical point of view. For example, spatial information of the actions of players, if present at all, lacks accuracy and, due to a single camera viewpoint, only on-the-ball actions of individual players are monitored systematically.

Technological innovations, such as tracking based on synchronized multiple video cameras and Global Positioning System technology, have led to new possibilities for match and training analysis in ball team sports. Positional player data (up to 1000 Hz) are collected in the context of different ball team sports, such as soccer for example. These data are typically used to calculate distance, speed and acceleration/deceleration profiles of individual players. These analyses do not capture the game dynamics and complexity of a soccer match, however, and new approaches of the game are required for tactical analyses.

Dynamical systems theory offers a framework for analysing player and team interactions and its analytical tools and methods are ideal for coping with high spatial-temporal resolution data. For example, on an individual level it allows for analysis of symmetry-breaking processes in player dyads, whereas on the team level offensive and defensive spaces or other geometrical configurations confined by the players can be investigated. In this chapter, an over-view of several examples of recent research and new ideas on geometrical configurations in 1 v 1, small-sided games and real matches in soccer are presented. Future directions and practical impli-cations for tactical training and match preparation are considered.

Introduction

Tactical performance in games like soccer, basketball, handball, rugby and field hockey addresses the quality of actions of individual players or teams in space and time during training or match-play. In other words, to analyse tactical performance, information is required on 'what', 'how', 'where' and 'when'. Tactical behaviour is constrained by personal characteristics, such as physi-cal and technical capacities of players, task details, such as number of players, pitch size dimen-sions or scoring on two goals in small-sided games, and situational variables, such as home versus away matches. The primary goal of tactical performance analysis is to provide information to coaches and players about player and/or team performance in order to plan subsequent practices to improve performance or to support preparation for the next match (Maslovat and Franks, 2008; Carling et al., 2009).

Notational analyses have dominated the scientific literature on tactical performance analyses over the last couple of decades (Hughes and Franks, 2004). Notational analysis is a method to create a permanent record of on-the-ball actions of players ('what' and 'how') within a game through hand-based or computerized systems, often nowadays using video technology. Basic systems simply classify the type of actions of the players. More sophisticated systems gather information on global position of the actions on the field ('where') and sequence/time of actions ('when'), which allows spatial and temporal analysis. Other systems have tried to define actions (e.g. passes, in terms of success or unsuccess or to rate the quality on a three or five-point scale). Next to real-time or day-after use of a single training session or match, notational systems can be used to analyse a series of matches during tournaments such as the European or World Championships and continental competitions such as the Champions League or Euro league, as well as national competitions. Large amounts of sophisticated notational data open up new approaches. Temporal (T-pattern) analysis can find (hidden) patterns of play using sequences of actions in relation to success, for example, winning or losing a game, creating goal scoring opportunities or playing level (Borrie et al., 2002). Social network approaches or neural network approaches can shed light on how interpersonal interactions lead to coordi-nated patterns of plays that are related to successful performance outcomes (Duch et al., 2010; Passos et al., 2011). These approaches seem promising in expanding knowledge on tactical performance.

Although these notational systems have improved over time, they have certain limitations, especially from a tactical point of view (Lemmink and Frencken, 2009). First, due to a single camera viewpoint, only on-the-ball actions are monitored systematically. However, it can be argued that the behaviour of an individual player during training or a match is brought about by interactions with teammates and opponents. Second, spatial and temporal information of notational systems lack sufficient accuracy to analyse in-depth tactical performance.

In recent years, (semi)-automatic tracking methods based on video or GPS-like technolo-gies have been developed to collect spatio-temporal information (i.e. positional data over time) from all players during training or matches (Carling et al., 2008, 2009). These methods provide a new means to calculate players' physical demands (i.e. distance covered, speed profiles, accel-eration/deceleration patterns and directional changes). Once high-quality ball positional data become available, it also opens up new ways of analysing tactical performance during training or matches. The main advantage of these new methods is that accurate spatio-temporal information ('where and when') of all players is available. Configurations of the players on the field reflect the interaction between the players and the ball. As play progresses, spatio-temporal patterns emerge from the dynamics of the game.

The dynamical systems approach has shown to be useful for understanding spatio-temporal patters in individual and team sports (Frencken and Lemmink, 2008; Gréhaigne *et al.*, 1997; McGarry *et al.*, 1999, 2002; McGarry, 2005; Palut and Zanone, 2005; Reed and Hughes, 2006). The core of this theory is that the behaviour of a system is brought about by interactions of many subsystems. The dependent variable, or collective variable, describes the state of the system at any instant. Finding the collective variables that capture the dynamics of a system is an important scientific challenge.

Ball team sports like basketball, handball, field hockey, rugby or soccer are complex, primarily due to the invasive nature and the number of players. Gréhaigne *et al.* (1997) and McGarry *et al.* (2002) proposed that interactions between soccer players give rise to team behaviour and may be described as a dynamical system. As suggested earlier, positional information of players over time reflects interactions between players. So, positional data of players have the potential to describe the dynamics of training and matches.

Analyses have primarily focused on collective variables in discrete 1 v 1 training or match situations. Araújo *et al.* (2004) analysed 1 v 1 situations in basketball. They calculated the median point of the distance between the players to the goal area and the interpersonal distance between attacker and defender, with the former being the collective variable and the latter being a control parameter. Results showed that the attacker fluctuates the direction of attack in front of the defender and the defender countermoves in order to maintain stability. From these data, Araújo *et al.* (2004) concluded that features of dynamical systems were established in a 1 v 1 attacker–defender dyad in basketball. Recently, this finding was confirmed in studies by Bourbousson *et al.* (2010a), from intra- and inter-couplings among player dyads in basketball, and Passos *et al.* (2006) and Passos *et al.* (2008), using interpersonal distance and relative velocity in attacker–defender dyads in rugby.

Invasion games include more than discrete short-term 1 v 1 situations. To explore tactical behaviour of interacting players or tactical strategies of teams, there is a need for collective variables that capture the dynamics of ball team sports during real match-play or small-sided games in training, as representation of match sub-phases of full-sized matches (Davids *et al.*, 2007; Lemmink and Frencken, 2010). Frencken and Lemmink (2008) and Frencken *et al.* (2011b) showed that centroid positions in longitudinal and lateral direction and surface areas of two soccer teams during small-sided soccer games (4 v 4) provide a sound basis for collective variables that capture the dynamics of attacking and defending in soccer at team level.

The potential of centroid positions to describe the rhythmic flow of attacking and defending was also shown for an 11-a-side soccer match (Lames *et al.*, 2010) and specific game situations in basketball (Bourbousson *et al.*, 2010b). These findings are in line with general aims of the game, as such patterns reflect the goal of the two teams moving up and down the field to arrive in scoring positions or prevent that from happening (Gréhaigne *et al.*, 1997). From a dynamical system perspective, research is needed to explore if variability in inter-team distance (i.e. distance between teams' centroid positions) reflect perturbations that precede critical game events.

Data collection

In this section, we address technological innovations that have resulted in advancing (semi) automatic tracking systems. This means that positional data of training and matches is becoming available rapidly in different ball team sports, especially soccer. Up to date, three different tracking technologies can be distinguished: (semi-)automatic video tracking, Global Positioning Systems (GPS) and electronic tracking. Each of these technologies comes with its own pros and cons. Recently, other technologies for player tracking have been proposed, including the use of infrared-textile (Silva *et al.*, 2011) or pressure-sensitive floors.

Video-based systems, such as ProZone®, AMISCO Pro® or SportVU, generally require the installation of multiple cameras covering the whole playing surface. Extensive calibration procedures ensure overlap between camera images, which in turn allows for calculation of player positions from the camera viewpoints. An operator is required to improve tracking accuracy and real-time availability of data is restricted. Differential or non-differential GPS-based tracking systems (e.g. GPSports) make use of satellites to calculate player positions. Players need to wear a vest or belt containing a sensor that communicates with orbiting satellites. Its use is limited to outdoor activities only because of poor indoor signal reception. In outdoor conditions, signal reception is seriously influenced by satellite positions and weather conditions. Yet, it is the most affordable tracking technology at this moment.

Electronic tracking systems operate in a similar way to GPS. However, tracking takes place in a confined volume with local receivers surrounding the playing surface. Electronic tracking systems, such as the local position measurement (LPM) system (Figure 8.1), require tagging players electronically by way of a vest that contains antennae and a transponder to track players' movements by means of radio frequency signals. However, electronic aids and other equipment for players necessary for tracking purposes are not allowed in official soccer games currently, thus restricting applicability to training settings. When evaluating physical performances of athletes from kinematic data, the advantages and disadvantages of tracking systems are well documented (e.g. Barris and Button, 2008; Carling *et al.*, 2008; Dobson and Keogh, 2007), but this same information is lacking concerning evaluation of tactical performance.

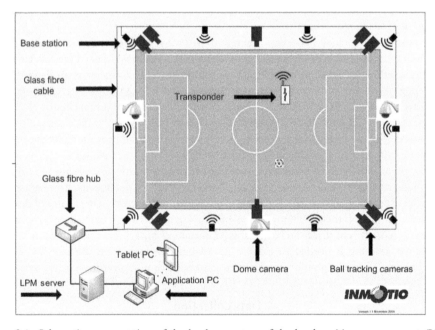

Figure 8.1 Schematic representation of the hardware setup of the local position measurement (LPM) system

Beyond the advantages and disadvantages of the different technologies, the quality of data provided is important in evaluating performance, and validity and reliability play a prominent role in this regard. In terms of the former, differences are observed across technologies (e.g. Edgecomb and Norton, 2006; Randers *et al.*, 2010). Most frequently, tracking technologies are validated by players that walk or run predetermined distances. The distances covered measured by a tracking system are subsequently compared to the actual distances that serve as the 'gold standard'. The scientific evidence generally indicates high degrees of agreement between the gold standard and the tracking system, regardless of the technology (e.g. MacLeod *et al.*, 2009; Di Salvo *et al.*, 2006; Frencken *et al.*, 2010; Varley *et al.*, 2012). However, when systems are compared with each other, significant differences are observed for a series of variables, including total distance covered. This observation holds for comparisons of video systems and GPS systems (Randers *et al.*, 2010) and also when GPS systems are compared to video systems (Edgecomb and Norton, 2006; Randers *et al.*, 2010). This finding leads to the notion of systematic errors, indicating that these systems cannot be used interchangeably. Because of limited availability of electronic tracking systems, similar comparisons have not yet been completed with the possibility of systematic error also present when contrasted against other measurement systems.

Limited data are available on the reliability of the various technologies. Hand-based video tracking systems tend to demonstrate good values of inter- and intra-user reliability in collecting positional data (e.g. Serrano and Fernandes, 2011). Likewise, high levels of absolute and relative reliability were observed for a computerized video tracking system (Di Salvo *et al.*, 2006). However, less convincing results are present for GPS devices, as considerable differences are observed between devices of the same technology, although differences tend to be smaller when new and high-frequency GPS devices of 10 Hz are concerned (Varley *et al.*, 2012). No reliability data are available yet for electronic systems.

Two other important aspects of tracking systems need to be addressed. First, accuracy of measurement is reported seldom. Second, tracking systems have difficulty in measuring players' positions at high running speeds (Coutts and Duffield, 2010). The relatively low sampling frequency of frequently used devices has been identified as a primary cause of this difficulty (Frencken *et al.*, 2010). For example, Global Positioning System units' sampling frequency varies from 1 to 10 Hz, whereas semi-automatic video tracking varies between 15 and 25 Hz and electronic systems generally start at 25 Hz or higher. Sampling frequency refers to the temporal resolution, whereas accuracy more generally speaking refers to the spatial resolution of a system. In order to provide meaningful answers to a wide variety of research questions or practically orientated issues, both temporal and spatial resolution of tracking systems need to be considered.

For evaluation of tactics or patterns of play, it can be argued that both the temporal and the spatial resolution of positional data need to be high. Most likely, in specific game situations like free kicks, a few centimetres may determine the correct or incorrect relative position of the player. Furthermore, as tactics are strongly related to position of the ball in the field, it is clear the ball position needs to be incorporated in data collection and data analysis. To date, various technologies are unable to accurately track ball position and, as such, no evidence has been provided on ball position. Currently, the only way to collect ball data is after a time-consuming post-processing procedure. While accurate ball data are not yet available, first attempts in tactical game analysis have nonetheless been realized.

Game analysis

Analysis of tactics and tactical aspects of soccer can take place at different levels. Individual player level may imply the 1 v 1 opposition relationship between an attacker and defender, say, or the cooperation between two attackers or two defenders. The next level involves subunits of a team that can be represented by small-sided games, like 4 v 4 or 7 v 7. The final level in soccer is 11 v 11 and comprises a full-sized match. Examples of each of these levels follow.

As discussed before, Araújo et al. (2004) examined positional data of an attacker and defender in basketball-specific exercises. They revealed symmetry-breaking processes, measured by distances between players and distances to the basket. It was demonstrated that, prior to the moment the attacker moves towards the basket, the attacker interacts with the defender to explore options by making small forward and backward movements. One may assume, by means of visual inspection, that these movements are of oscillatory nature. Dynamical systems theory offers tools for analysing this type of data by means of phase relations. In this respect, it has been suggested that a player with a lead phase relation has an advantage over the player with the lag phase relation (McGarry et al., 2002) and, as such, it may be taken as a measure of dominance (Palut and Zanone, 2005).

Extending this concept to soccer, it was hypothesized that a lead phase relation of the attacker would increase the chance to score (McGarry et al., 2002; Frencken and Lemmink, 2008). This idea led to an experiment in which ten young, male elite soccer players (17.3 years ± 0.7) participated in three small-sided soccer games (four-a-side, plus goalkeepers) of eight minutes on a 28×36 m pitch. Positional data were collected at 45 Hz per player by means of an electronic tracking system, the local position measurement (LPM) system. From the positional data, accelerations were calculated for each player. Next, all acceleration data of all players were cross-correlated over a moving 2.5 s time window. In addition, time delays were calculated between acceleration profiles for all players (NBody Software, UMCG, University of Groningen. To illustrate for an attacker–defender dyad, if the positive correlation between the acceleration profiles at any given instant is high, it means that players were moving at the same time such that there is minimal delay between the time series. Consequently, a large delay in the time series indicates one of the players waiting and reacting to the movements of the other player. In addition to these analyses, all goals and goal-scoring opportunities in the small-sided games were identified. They were defined as any successful or unsuccessful shot on goal by the attacker. Goals and goal-scoring opportunities were categorized as 1 v 1 situations, slow-build regular attacks, counterattacks and long shots. The attacker was the player that attempted to score, whereas the defender was the closest opponent of that particular attacker. All player couplings were investigated through visual inspection.

In total, 66 goal-scoring opportunities were notated, of which 19 resulted in a goal. Data showed that, for 65 per cent of the goals and goal-scoring opportunities, the attacker is dominant and holds initiative, with no difference observed between goals and goal-scoring opportunities. In addition, it was found that the percentage frequency of attacking initiative decreased with the type of attack from 100 per cent for 1 v 1 situations to 33% for, long-distance shots; see Figure 8.2). From this, we can take that attackers most frequently take initiative prior to goal-scoring opportunities. The absence of small differences between goals and goal-scoring opportunities, however, indicates that whether or not a goal is scored depends on additional factors (e.g. technical ability, goalkeeper's ability and/or chance).

The task for the attacker in the various types of attack influenced the attacking initiative required. In 1 v 1 situations, the attacker must take initiative more so than in long-distance shots, say, demonstrating that positional data expressed by relative phase can be used to evaluate the degrees of dominance of attackers over defenders. In this case, the focus was on specific events related to goals and goal-scoring opportunities. However, many more 1 v 1 situations happen during matches. Future research must indicate to what extent positional data can contribute in evaluating dominance of players in all kinds of game situations. Also, interactions

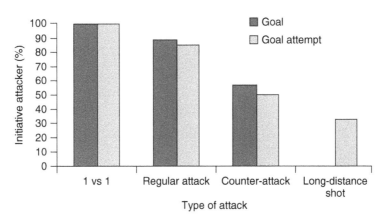

Figure 8.2 Dominance of the attacker over the defender. Data expressed as percentages

of players that may be less prominent to the naked eye can also be subjected meaningfully to dynamic analysis. For example, the central defender of the defending team may walk backwards toward his own goal when the central defender of the attacking team advances up the field while holding the ball. As such, they both move in the same direction and their movements are related. This dependency can be quantified using the methods proposed here.

The next level of analysis concerns clusters of players. One possible representation can be small-sided games. Taking all players of one team into account facilitates new types of analyses – for example, examining the interactive behaviour between teams. Often, the positional data of outfield players of one team are combined for this purpose. This leads to new types of parameters per team, such as the area of the field covered by a team, the geometrical centre of a team (i.e. centroid position; Figure 8.3) and the stretch index (see Bourbousson *et al.*, 2010b, and Frencken *et al.*, 2011b for detailed calculations). These measures are thought to reflect the rhythmic flow of attacking and defending in soccer. To illustrate, the centroid position is the average x–y position of all outfield players of one team. If the centroid position is calculated for both teams at each instant and the two teams represented by two dots then the rhythmic flow between teams attacking and defending may be visualized. In Figure 8.4, exemplar longitudinal data of both centroids are demonstrated in a small-sided game. It can be seen that both teams move up and down the pitch simultaneously, supported by high positive correlations between the centroid positions of both teams (Frencken *et al.*, 2011b). The same is true for the lateral motion of the centroids of both teams (not shown), although correlations were slightly lower compared to the longitudinal component. These findings are consistent for multiple small-sided games. Strong positive correlations indicated the predominant interaction between centroid positions as in-phase. In addition, specific patterns between centroids related to game events demonstrated the centroids swapped (crossed) positions prior to half of the goals and goal-scoring opportunities. That means the centroid of the attacking team moved past the centroid of the defending team, in similar fashion to the basketball example reported by Araújo *et al.* (2004). As such, the collective motion of one team relative to the other could be an important performance indicator of tactical game behaviour.

Similar to centroid position, the stretch index and surface area are measures of team interaction. Players of the team in possession open up space and increase interpersonal distances, whereas, in contrast, the team not in possession ties up space and decreases interpersonal distances. If the ball changes teams then so does the dispersion characteristics. Therefore, an anti-phase relation could be expected for these player dispersion measures, although

K. Lemmink and W. Frencken

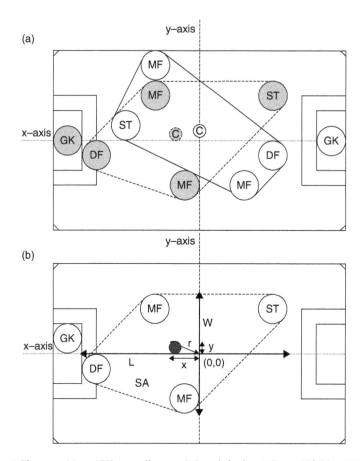

Figure 8.3 a) Player positions (GK = goalkeeper, DF = defender, MF = midfielder, ST = striker) and relation of centroid (c) and surface area (black and dashed line) measures for the two teams; b) calculation of measures for centroid position (black dot, r = radial distance, x = x-distance, y = y-distance) and surface area (L = length, W = width, SA = surface area)

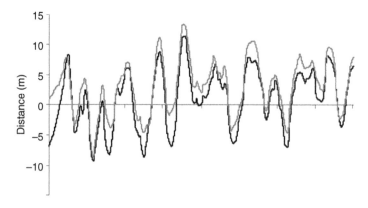

Figure 8.4 Exemplar time series data of centroid positions in a four-minute small-sided soccer game. Black and grey lines distinguish between teams

scientific evidence is not widely available in this respect and needs further inquiry (Frencken *et al.*, 2011b). Results thus far, however, have demonstrated that relative measures can be developed to describe the status of the system and give valuable information on tactically relevant concepts based on measures like centroid positions and player dispersion. Also, longitudinal and lateral inter-team distances can be considered and expressed in absolute instead of relative terms. That is, the absolute differences between the longitudinal or lateral components of the centroid positions of both teams, as well as surface area, could prove valuable measures of performance in future.

Analogous to analysis of interactive behaviour of teams in small-sided games, full-sized matches (11 v 11) can be evaluated. The reason for this is that, from a tactical perspective, it is unclear to what extent small-sided games reflect full-sized matches. Because players act under different constraints when playing small-sided and full-sized games, it might be expected that interaction patterns differ as well. Bearing this in mind, an additional step can be taken in terms of analysis. Based on the evidence currently available in the context of different team sports (e.g. Bourbousson *et al.*, 2010b; Frencken *et al.*, 2011b; Lames *et al.*, 2010), it appears that full-sized matches adhere to and exhibit traits of dynamical systems. If this is the case, then critical game periods can be established mathematically and predictions can be made based on dynamical systems theory. From this perspective, if centroid positions of two teams reflect the rhythmic flow of attacking and defending, and if this is a tactically relevant construct, then critical tactical game periods could be extracted from the positional data of the teams. Such critical game periods can possibly be identified by calculating variability of inter-team distances, especially given evidence currently available from small-sided games in which cross-over patterns were observed prior to goals and goal-scoring opportunities.

A similar approach was applied to one half of a women's soccer game (Frencken *et al.*, 2011a). The assumption was that teams' interactive behaviour could be described through the distance between the centroid positions and that sudden changes in this measure would be indicative of specific match events, like goal-scoring opportunities. For this purpose, positional data of an elite female soccer match were collected at 45 Hz with the local position measurement (LPM) system. For both teams, the centroid positions were determined from the average coordinate data of the outfield players. Subsequently, inter-team distance (ITD) was calculated in longitudinal (ITDX) and lateral (ITDY) direction and variability obtained from standard deviation over a moving 2.5 s window. This time window was considered reasonable for players to react to changing game conditions following consultation with five professional licensed soccer coaches. Critical periods in game dynamics were marked if variability exceeded a sample-based criterion value equal to three standard deviations of the variability signal. Time stamps of the extracted critical game periods were mapped to match events using qualitative video analysis. A similar approach was taken by Frencken *et al.* (2012).

Results reported 60 critical game periods, of which 24 and 36 were based on high variability of ITDX and ITDY, respectively. Video analysis of the 24 critical game periods extracted from ITDX were predominantly associated with forward passes (n = 5) and dead-ball situations, like throw-ins and free kicks (n = 8). It was unclear from game event observation what the trigger was for the high variability of the remainder of the critical game events. Likewise, the critical game periods extracted from ITDY were predominantly associated with dead-ball situations (n = 13) and sideways passing (n = 26). Because some free kicks were lateral passes over longer distance, these events were categorized in both dead-ball situations and sideways passing.

The results of Frencken *et al.* (2011a) did not replicate those of small-sided games (Frencken *et al.*, 2011b). As such, it appears that, in full-sized games, periods of high ITD variability do not precede goals and goal-scoring opportunities as with small-sided games. One explanation could be that the equal contribution of all players to the centroid positions causes variability to dissipate somewhat in full-sized games as compared with small-sided games. Because in small sided-games only four players per team contribute to centroid calculations, their influence on centroid position is greater compared to full-sized games. Therefore, the development of a mechanism that includes 'active' players in game situations may be appropriate. An alternative explanation is that the dynamics in small-sided games are indeed different from those of full-sized matches. If so, this would be important because small-sided games are frequently used for tactical training purposes for full-sized matches. Further research is needed to explore these ideas in future.

Future directions

Some important issues have to be addressed before practical implications for training can be determined. First, there is a strong need to capture the dynamics of interpersonal interactions during match-play in ball team sports in relation to successful performance (i.e. critical moments in the game). Some promising variables have been suggested and explored (e.g. relative phase of player positions or speeds at the player dyad level and variability of inter-team distance for team dynamics). Yet more research is needed to confirm these initial findings. Second, to advance tactical behaviour practice of players, there is a need to find out if the dynamics of different types of training (e.g. 1 v 1, 2 v 1, small-sided games, etc.) are reflected in full-sized matches. An interesting issue concerns whether and how task constraints like number of players or environmental constraints such as pitch size affect team dynamics. Third, personal constraints (e.g. physical, technical and psychological characteristics) should also be incorporated in analysis of tactical behaviour in small-sided games or real matches. For example, fatigue may influence distance between player dyads at the end of a match, or technical players may need less space and time to control the ball and/or dribble past a defender. Also, psychological mechanisms (e.g. perception of others, social relations, etc.) may influence player interactions during match-play and should be given due consideration in future.

Concluding remarks

New technologies like semi-automatic tracking methods based on video or GPS-like technologies, allow for high-frequency position data collection on a regular basis during training and matches. These data sets permit physiological analysis, allowing assessment of physiological load of individual players in terms of distance, speed, acceleration, deceleration and directional changes, not only in relation to performance but also in regard to injury risk (prevention) and rehabilitation programmes (treatment). Position data with high temporal–spatial resolution of different players also permits analysis of interactions of players ('where and when'). A dynamical system approach seems a promising framework to study these complex interactions between players and teams in ball team sports. This approach may lead to new insights into the interactions of players within different ball team sports.

To facilitate research in tactical performance analysis, an integrated approach is called for. Coaches and trainers should work on a structural basis with scientists from different disciplines (e.g. sport scientists, sport psychologists and statisticians). From a coaching perspective, it is important to unravel tactical aspects, such as applying pressure, transition play between attack and defence, passing opportunities and so on, and define guidelines for training as well as developing tactical strategies for real match-play. From a science perspective, it is important to continue to search for collective variables that describe the dynamics of players during training and match-play. These perspectives should be combined to understand and improve tactical behaviour of players in ball team sports, including handball, basketball, rugby, field hockey and soccer.

References

Araújo, D., Davids, K., Bennett, S.J., Button, C. and Chapman, G. (2004) 'Emergence of sport skills under constraints', in A.M. Williams and N.J. Hodges (eds), *Skill Acquisition in Sport: Research, Theory and Practice* (pp. 409–33). London: Routledge.

Barris, S. and Button, C. (2008) 'A review of vision-based motion analysis in sport', *Sports Medicine*, 38: 1025–43.

Bourbousson, J., Sève, C. and McGarry, T. (2010a) 'Space-time coordination dynamics in basketball: Part 1. Intra- and inter-couplings among player dyads', *Journal of Sports Sciences*, 28: 339–47.

Bourbousson, J., Sève, C. and McGarry, T. (2010b) 'Space-time coordination dynamics in basketball: Part 2. The interaction between the two teams', *Journal of Sports Sciences*, 28: 349–58.

Borrie, A., Jonsson, G.K. and Magnusson, M.S. (2002) 'Temporal pattern analysis and its applicability in sport: An explanation and exemplar data', *Journal of Sports Sciences*, 20: 845–52.

Carling, C., Bloomfield, J., Nelsen, L. and Reilly, T. (2008) 'The role of motion analysis in elite soccer: Contemporary performance measurement techniques and work rate data', *Sports Medicine*, 38: 839–62.

Carling, C., Reilly, T. and Williams, A.M. (2009) *Performance Assessment for Field Sports; Match Analysis* (Chapter 4, pp. 70–102), London: Routledge.

Coutts, A.J. and Duffield, R. (2010) 'Validity and reliability of GPS devices for measuring movement demands of team sports', *Journal of Science and Medicine in Sport*, 13(1): 133–5.

Davids, K., Araújo, D., Button, C. and Renshaw, I. (2007) 'Degenerate brains, indeterminate behavior and representative tasks: Implications for experimental design in sport psychology research', in G. Tenenbaum and B. Eklund (eds), *Handbook of Sport Psychology* (pp. 224–44). Hoboken, NJ: John Wiley.

Di Salvo, V., Collins, A., McNeill, B. and Cardinale, M. (2006) 'Validation of Prozone: A new video-based performance analysis system', *International Journal of Performance Analysis in Sport*, 6(1): 108–19.

Dobson, B.P. and Keogh, J.W.L. (2007) 'Methodological issues for the application of time-motion analysis research', *Strength and Conditioning Journal*, 29: 48–55.

Duch, J., Waitzman, J.S. and Amaral, L.A.N. (2010) 'Quantifying the performance of individual players in a team activity', *PLoS ONE*, 5(6): e10937. doi:10.1371/journal.pone.0010937.

Edgecomb, S.J. and Norton, K.I. (2006) 'Comparison of global positioning and computer-based tracking systems for measuring player movement distance during Australian football', *Journal of Science and Medicine in Sport*, 9: 25–32.

Frencken, W.G.P. and Lemmink, K.A.P.M. (2008) 'Team kinematics of small-sided soccer games: A systematic approach', in T. Reilly and F. Korkusuz (eds), *Science and Football VI* (pp. 161–6). London: Routledge.

Frencken, W.G.P., Lemmink, K.A.P.M. and Delleman, N.J. (2010) 'Soccer-specific accuracy and validity of the local position measurement (LPM) system', *Journal of Science and Medicine in Sport*, 13: 641–5.

Frencken, W.G.P., De Poel, H.J. and Lemmink, K.A.P.M. (2011a) 'Analysis of game dynamics and related game events in 11v11 soccer', presentation at the 7th World Congress on Science and Football, 102, Nagoya, Japan, May.

Frencken, W.G.P., Lemmink, K.A.P.M., Delleman, N.J. and Visscher, C. (2011b) 'Oscillations of centroid position and surface area of soccer teams in small sided games', *European Journal of Sport Science*, 11(2): 215–23.

Frencken, W.G.P., De Poel, H.J., Visscher, C. and Lemmink, K.A.P.M. (2012) 'Variability of inter team distance associated to game events in elite soccer', *Journal of Sports Sciences*, 30(12): 1207–13.

Gréhaigne, J.F., Bouthier, D. and David, B. (1997) 'Dynamic-system analysis of opponent relationships in collective actions in soccer', *Journal of Sports Sciences*, 15: 137–49.

Hughes, M. and Franks, I.M. (2004) 'Notational analysis – a review of literature', in M. Hughes and I.M. Franks (eds), *Notational Analysis of Sport. Systems for Better Coaching and Performance in Sport* (pp. 59–106). London: Routledge.

Lames, M., Ertmer, J. and Walter, F. (2010) 'Oscillations in football – order and disorder in spatial interactions between the two teams', *International Journal of Sport Psychology*, 41(4): 85.

Lemmink, K.A.P.M. and Frencken, W.G.P. (2009) 'Physiological and tactical match analyses in ball team sports; New perspectives', in A. Lorenzo, S.J. Ibáñez and E. Ortega (eds), *Aportaciones téoricas y practices para el baloncesto del futuro*, Seville: Wanceulen Editorial Deportiva.

Lemmink, K.A.P.M. and Frencken, W.G.P. (2010) 'Analyses of tactical patterns in ball team sports: From 1 vs. 1 to small sided games', *International Journal of Sport Psychology*, 41(4): 88.

MacLeod, H., Morris, J., Nevill, A. and Sunderland, C. (2009) 'The validity of a non-differential Global Positioning System for assessing player movement patterns in field hockey', *Journal of Sports Sciences*, 27(2): 121–8.

Maslovat, D. and Franks, I.M. (2008) 'The need for feedback', in M. Hughes and I.M. Franks (eds), *The Essentials of Performance Analysis: An Introduction* (pp. 1–7). London: Routledge.

McGarry, T. (2005) 'Soccer as a dynamical system: Some theoretical considerations', in T. Reilly and D. Araújo (eds), *Science and Football V* (pp. 561–70). London: Routledge.

McGarry, T., Khan, M.A. and Franks, I.M. (1999) 'On the presence and absence of behavioural traits in sport: An example from championship squash match-play', *Journal of Sports Sciences*, 17: 297–311.

McGarry, T., Anderson, D.I., Wallace, S.A., Hughes, M.D. and Franks, I.M. (2002) 'Sport competition as a dynamical self-organizing system', *Journal of Sports Sciences*, 20: 771–81.

Palut, Y. and Zanone, P. G. (2005) 'A dynamical analysis of tennis: Concepts and data', *Journal of Sports Sciences*, 23: 1021–32.

Passos, P., Araújo, D., Davids, K., Gouveia, L. and Serpa, S. (2006) 'Interpersonal dynamics in sport: The role of artificial neural networks and 3-D analysis', *Behavior Research Methods*, 38(4): 683–91.

Passos, P., Araújo, D., Davids, K., Gouveia, L., Milho, J. and Serpa, S. (2008) 'Information-governing dynamics of attacker-defender interactions in youth rugby union', *Journal of Sports Sciences*, 26: 1421–9.

Passos, P., Davids, K., Araújo, D., Paz, N., Minguéns, J. and Mendes, J. (2011) 'Networks as a novel tool for studying team ball sports as complex social system', *Journal of Science and Medicine in Sport*, 14: 170–6.

Randers, M.B., Mujika, I., Hewitt, A., Santisteban, J., Bischoff, R., Solano, R., Zubillaga, A., Peltola, E., Krustrup, P. and Mohr, M. (2010) 'Application of four different football match analysis systems: A comparative study', *Journal of Sports Sciences*, 28(2): 171–82.

Reed, D. and Hughes, M. (2006) 'An exploration of team sport as a dynamical system', *International Journal of Performance Analysis in Sport*, 6(2): 114–25.

Serrano, J. and Fernandes, O. (2011) 'Reliability of a new method to analyse and to quantify athletes' displacement', *Portuguese Journal of Sport Sciences*, 11(2): 935–6.

Silva, J., Araújo, D., Duarte, R., Parola, A., Lima, J. and Nabais, F. (2011) 'A tracking system using markers for association football', presentation at the World Congress of Science and Football 7, Nagoya, Japan, May.

Varley, M.C., Fairweather, I.H. and Aughey, R.J. (2012) 'Validity and reliability of GPS for measuring instantaneous velocity during acceleration, deceleration, and constant motion', *Journal of Sports Sciences*, 30(2): 121–7.

9

COLLECTIVE VARIABLES FOR ANALYSING PERFORMANCE IN TEAM SPORTS

Jean-Francis Gréhaigne[1] *and Paul Godbout*[2]

[1]UNIVERSITY OF FRANCHE-COMTÉ, FRANCE

[2]LAVAL UNIVERSITY, CANADA

Summary

In team sports, decision making requires, on the part of each player and the coach, an as-much-as-possible rational knowledge of elements of the sport and of events that occur during game play. The internal logic of team sports is presented as a basis for appreciating different analysis approaches. Two main categories of analyses are considered: static and dynamic, the second one being sub-divided into dynamic representational pictures, statistics of game play, and numerical performance indicators. Given the collective connotation of performance analysis considered in the chapter, configurations of play are seen as a central element to be used in the observation of game play and subsequent collective decision making.

Introduction

Analysing performance in team sports

In team sports, each player and the coach need as much information as possible about the unfolding of game play in order to make appropriate decisions. Therefore, one task is to collect objective data relating to players and their behaviours. It thus becomes logical to look for observation and assessment tools that make it possible to reflect on one's own team or on the opposing team. Planning performance assessment in team sport requires careful thinking about the parameters to be observed, the observational methods that ought to be used to collect the data, the way these data will be analysed, and finally the way the assessment results will be presented and used.

It is the coaches' and/or the players' duty to deepen their own knowledge acquired though experience. Indeed, this experienced knowledge is never enough for one to possess all fundamentals of the sport. They must therefore improve this knowledge by taking time to systematically observe matches, game play, and the players. The pursued objective is to analyse elements that best define the 'rapport de forces' in play and to draw significant elements that may be used to develop models that can be, at the same time, simple and as reliable as possible. In previous publications, we translated this concept as 'rapport of strength' or 'force ratio'. After long discussions with Anglophone colleagues, however, it seems better to keep the French term and explain what it means. For a definition, see the section on 'rapport de forces' of this chapter. Observational data make it possible to assess more precisely, for a given player and/or the team, game-play actions in order to:

- better understand the roles and level of integration of various players within the team;
- develop a typology or classification of individual and collective behaviours by making comparisons over several competition situations;
- obtain measurements that will make comparisons possible between players or for the same player over time;
- determine directions of the evolution of game play and that of players over time;
- elaborate play models, taking better account of observed performance/learning levels.

Intent and learning context of performance analysis

In team sports, performance may refer to the end result or product of a play action or of a whole match. It may also refer to the process of play action. For a discussion on the facets of performance assessment in team sports, one may consult Gréhaigne *et al.* (1997) or Nadeau *et al.* (2008b). In the present chapter, the term performance will refer to what a player does or what a group of players do during game play when defending their territory and/or attacking the adverse territory.

Discussing the nature of team sports and the consequences for performance assessment, Gréhaigne *et al.* (1997: 501) recognized defensive and offensive aspects to both attack and defence. Each of these aspects of game play may in turn be broken down into myriads of particular variables depending on the information sought by observers or by the players themselves.

Performance assessment may be conducted by a scout looking for interesting prospects, or by a coach attempting to improve the performance of the team or that of particular players. While a scout's assessment will likely be summative, leading to an acceptance or rejection decision, assessments conducted under the supervision of a coach may serve either a formative or a summative purpose. Also, the coaching approach may be coach-centred or player-centred. In a coach-centred approach, such as direct coaching, the purpose of the assessment will be to verify whether the player performs appropriately (that is the way he/she was told to do). In a player-centred approach, such as constructivism, the purpose of the assessment will be to provide the player(s) with a picture of what was accomplished and it will be up to the player(s) to reflect on that information under the guidance of the coach.

Finally, particularly but not exclusively in a constructivist approach, performance data collected during a match may involve three categories of observers: (a) the coach (or some neutral external observer), (b) teammates not involved in game play, and (c) players directly involved in the match (Gréhaigne *et al.*, 2005: 110).

In this chapter, we will focus on the following aspects of performance analysis in team sports:

- the discussion will be limited to invasion team sports (Gréhaigne *et al.*, 2005: 5);
- collective variables will be referred to in relation to the process aspect of performance;
- the discussion will apply to coaching, although many analysis tools could be used in a teaching environment as well.

Primary rules and logic of invasion team sports

Collective sports refer to sports that involve opposite teams where players interact directly and simultaneously with one another in view of achieving an objective. This objective calls for members of a team to facilitate the movements of a ball, or of some similar element, according to a given set of rules, in order to score points. The rules of a game are established in order to provide a structure that manages game play and guide practitioners' actions. These rules, called primary or fundamental, provide the foundations for the organization of game play. These constraints limit and regulate players' actions; they put restrictions on game play, without pre-scribing, allowing players to try out a variety of answers to problems encountered during game play. For instance, in soccer, the rule states that one cannot touch the ball with one's hands (except for the goalkeeper and for a player in charge of the throw-in), rather than stating that one must play the ball with one's feet. These primary rules concern: (a) scoring, in relation to specificities of the targets, (b) attackers' and defenders' rights or constraints with regards to their movement on the field, and (c) the degree of freedom of actions on the ball which favours, or not, the continuity of movements.

In addition, agreements or secondary rules make it possible to normalize or facilitate the evolution of game play. They differ from constraints in the fact that they may be modified without jeopardizing the essence of the game. Both primary and secondary rules impose play organization rules on the functioning of the confrontation system.

The 'rapport de forces'

In invasion games, the logic of the play has its source in the opposition relationship that gener-ates, during each sequence of play, a dynamics of moving from one target to the other. We call this opposition relationship the *rapport de forces*. It refers to the 'antagonist links existing between several players or groups of players confronted by virtue of certain rules of a game that deter-mine a pattern of interaction' (Gréhaigne *et al.*, 1997: 516). At all times, the possession of the ball can change and, then, the direction of play switches. This fact imposes on both teams an organization where location, movement, and replacement (general movement generated by the opposition of two teams on the pitch, between two targets) are responses to this reversibility of play. Each player must consider the general movement, keeping in mind a possible reversal of game play. Indeed, for each player, any defensive movement stays organically linked to the counter-attack play that it potentially contains; inversely, any offensive movement stays organi-cally linked to the defensive falling back that may eventually prove to be necessary. We will call such an organization a double-impact organization, where the basic challenge for each player is to cooperate with partners in order to oppose more effectively the opponents while either attacking (keeping one's defence in mind) or defending (getting ready to attack).

Organizational levels of play

The potential for reversibility of the general movement at any instant, in both dimensions (depth and width), is a major characteristic of the internal logic of team sports. One must bear this fact in mind. Team organization in response to the reversibility of play implies, for each team, a collec-tive frame of reference of which all players must remain aware. At the same time, everyone must be capable of initiatives that one's teammates can decode in order to react appropriately or, better still, anticipate. This double dimension of a collective frame of reference within a team strongly linked to individual initiative is fundamental in team sports; this fact is often overlooked.

The *rapport de forces* may be associated with the '*match* organizational level' (Gréhaigne and Godbout, 1995: 493); it is then interpreted as two teams facing one another. But in fact, during the game, the team opposition relationship breaks down into smaller opposition relationships, as shown in Figure 9.1.

The opposition setting that momentarily involves some of the players generates a particular shape of play representing the '*partial forefront* organizational level' (see Figure 9.1). At any moment of the match, this partial forefront contains a third-level opposition unit that links the ball holder and his/her direct opponent. We call this the '*primary* organizational level' (Gréhaigne, 1992). Figure 9.1 illustrates these last two organizational levels, whereas the drawing of the whole field would represent the '*match* organizational level'. Thus the *rapport de forces* may be looked at as involving two teams, two sub-groups of players, or eventually two specific players. The continuity of opposition influences the opponents' moves not only at the one-to-one level, but at the partial forefront level and at the match level as well. These simultaneous, interlocked opposition settings constitute the context of play (Deleplace, 1979). They evolve in reciprocal relationship in response to the evolution of any part of the system.

At any specific moment, according to the evolution of play, this reciprocal relationship offers, for example, a specific problem to attackers but, at the same time, contains pertinent solutions for action:

- to continue the action at the one-to-one level;
- to pursue the attack with the help of partners in the partial forefront; or
- to change the general movement by transforming its shape, its orientation, or even both.

Thus, besides the potential for reversibility mentioned earlier, the continual reciprocal relationship between the three organizational levels constitutes the second major characteristic of the logic of team sports (Deleplace, 1966).

As one can see, the general dynamics of team sports can be expressed as a '*rapport de forces*' where, in a sense, two networks of forces are confronted one to the other. This fact implies the consideration of a second frame of analysis, that of the '*team* organizational level' (Gréhaigne and Godbout, 1995: 494).

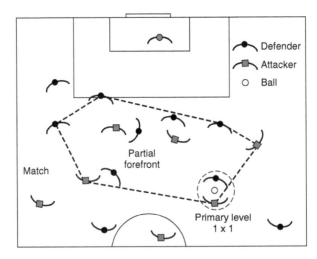

Figure 9.1 Partial forefront organizational level and primary organizational level (adapted from Gréhaigne *et al.*, 1999b)

The team competency network

At the '*team* organizational level', the numerous interrelations between players, within the team, make up what one might call a 'competency network' (Gréhaigne, 1992). Although based on each player's recognized strengths and weaknesses with reference to the practice of the sport, and also on the group's dynamism, the competency network is more a dynamical concept than a static one. It refers to the player's game-related conducts in general that one can identify in connection with the *rapport de forces*, or with each player's status, within the team. Such conducts vary depending upon players, moments, external factors, and the particular team sport involved. During play, in connection with conducts, the notion of 'role' is essential for analysing the competency network. In this case, 'role' refers to conducts and that conveys (a) what a player thinks he or she ought to do, given the way he or she experiences the *rapport de forces* or competency network within the team, and (b) how the player manages his or her resources in this system of constraints.

The function within the team, chosen by the player, or assigned by the coach or by the team, is another indicator of the player's position in the team's dynamism. At the interface of the player's logic, the team's logic, and the internal logic of the sport involved, the player's function in this competency network often is a reliable indicator of the reciprocal relationships between a player and the team. Contrary to what one might think at times, cooperation in team sports, as in other aspects of life, goes far beyond simple goodwill and an easy-going way of looking at sport. For the best possible use of the competency network, there is a need for both efforts and restraints on the part of all players.

Match analysis approaches

Due to the complexity of the environment, temporal and spatial characteristics of players' locations and movements, as well as those of the ball, game play must be analysed in a very systematic way if one wishes to obtain dependable, reliable, and useful information. This kind of analysis necessarily takes into account lasting elements, such as the playing surface, but also other variables which are controlled by players, such as the ball, play organization rules, tactics, etc. (Gréhaigne and Godbout, 1995).

Problems with analysis of performance in team sports are those related to the assessment of any complex system: that is (a) the intervening elements are not only numerous but also interacting, (b) the 'rapport de forces' plays an important role and it may vary in different opposition situations or even during one given situation, and (c) the members of a given team are interdependent.

Performance analyses reported in the literature reflect two main measurement strategies or observational points of view. On the one hand, the observation may be based on a frozen picture of game play at any given instant, drawing one's attention to the players' location on the field and the location of the ball, with respect to various phases of game play. Such an approach may be considered as static. On the other hand, the observation may focus on the evolution of game play with respect to players' location, direction of movements, and speed of movement, given momentary configurations of play. Such an approach may be classified as dynamic.

For the sake of illustration in this chapter, the approaches presented will be used in reference to soccer but they could as well be used for European handball, basketball, field hockey, and other invasion team sports.

Static approach to observation of game play

The simplest observational approach that can be used consists of considering, on the one hand, the defensive zone and, on the other hand, the offensive zone. If one divides each zone, one obtains four observation areas: (a) defensive; (b) pre-defensive; (c) pre-offensive; and (d) offensive, as shown in Figure 9.2. One could also consider the central corridor of the pitch and two bordering corridors on each side. This would make it possible to note play actions conducted in the 'attacked goal/defended goal' axis (central corridor [c3 in Figure 9.2]) and others carried in the median corridors (c2 and c4) or in the peripheral corridors (c1 and c5). A third type of grid might consider the direct play-space with a vertical target, as in soccer or handball, for instance. The direct play-space is then defined as the surface area of the pitch from where the ball can be shot directly at the target. Due to the verticality of the target, the apparent target area varies according to the shooting angle. In Figure 9.2, the direct play-space is delimited by four dotted lines.

An important feature of these tools is that they give some idea on the players' placement on the pitch, which illustrates different configurations of play. This type of information can be very useful to coaches and players in the evolution of a team's play and performance. For their part, the notions of 'centre of gravity' and 'effective place on the pitch' illustrate the way a coach can use static observational data of game play. For examples, readers may consult Bourbousson *et al.* (2010), Gréhaigne (1992), Gréhaigne *et al.* (1996) and Winkler (1988).

If one considers a given configuration of play as the one illustrated in Figure 9.2, one can summarize it using the notion of effective play-space (Gréhaigne, 1989; Gréhaigne *et al.*, 1999a; Mérand, 1977). The effective play-space (EP-S) may be defined as the polygonal area that one obtains by drawing a line that links all involved players located at the periphery of the play at a given instant (see dotted black line in Figure 9.2). The ball can be in different positions in relation to the effective play-space: located in a central position, in the middle of the effective play-space, at the rear of the effective play-space, in a flank position either on the left or on the right periphery of the pitch, ahead or at the rear of the effective play-space. In the example illustrated in Figure 9.2, the ball is located at the rear of the EP-S, in the central corridor (c3), in the pre-defensive area (b).

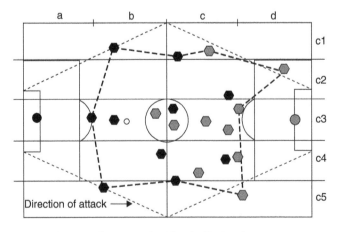

Figure 9.2 Various areas of a static observational grid and effective play-space

Considering the respective positioning of attackers and defenders, one may also determine an offensive effective play-space (OEP-S) and a defensive effective play-space (DEP-S). One obtains, then, two more or less interpenetrated polygonal surfaces (for an illustration, see Gréhaigne *et al.*, 2010b, Figures 3 and 4). The relationship between these two opposing areas and their respective evolutions in time may enlighten us on changes in the balance of the opposition relationship during matches.

Several studies have been conducted using the EP-S construct: Duprat (2005) on the topological aspect of the recovery of the ball in the defence area; Gréhaigne (2007) on the study of configurations of play; Meunier (2005) on the analysis of prototypic configurations of play in basketball; Zerai (2011) on the learning condition with verbalization on the action project and on the pertinence of choices in configurations of play during game play in handball.

For all their worth, static observational data remain particularly interesting inasmuch as they may be considered in a transitional mode, from one instant to the other. In so doing, they transform into dynamic observational data, considering not only the space aspect of performance but its time aspect as well.

Dynamic approach to the observation of game play

Contrary to the static analysis of performance in team sports, dynamic observational data provide information relative to the unfolding of game play, taking into account the passage of time. Collected data may take the form of (a) representational pictures, concerned with the evolution of the configurations of play or defined parts of configuration of play, or (b) numerical data presented as statistics of game play or as numerical indicators.

Dynamic representational pictures

During a match or over several matches, the different configurations of play can be analysed with respect to 'defence in block' plays or 'defence in pursuit' plays. We shall consider that the defence is in 'block' when it is positioned between the ball holder, the attackers, and its own goal. We shall consider that the defence is in 'pursuit' when it is positioned behind the ball holder and the attackers with reference to its goal (Gréhaigne, 1990; Gréhaigne and Godbout, 1995).

Two other analytical concepts are based on the different locations of the ball in relation to the effective play-space at the origin of the ball movement. In the rear-ball play (kick-and-run play), the origin of ball movement is always at the rear with respect to the future receiver of the ball. Play usually starts with the recovery of the ball until its loss to the opposition for whatever reason. In the forward-ball play (pretty pass play), at some point during the movement of the ball, it travels backward towards a supporting player. The transformation of the movement of the ball is the consequence of a defensive organization that creates great difficulty for the offensive team to move the ball forward. With respect to the effective play-space, one can see a diversification of the movement of the ball.

To better understand the evolution of configurations of play, it is also possible to study shapes and distortions of OEP-S and DEP-S. The main distortions are the respective contractions or expansions of the offensive or defensive effective play-space. As illustrated in Figure 9.3, a contraction of game play illustrates the presence of several players on a small surface; for its part, an expansion represents the distribution of several players over a large area. For a more elaborate discussion and illustrations in basketball, readers may consult Gréhaigne *et al.* (2010b).

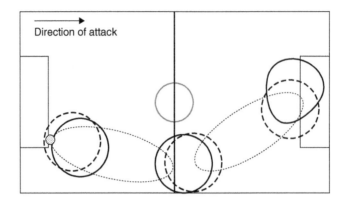

Figure 9.3 A succession of contraction/expansion phases in soccer (adapted from Gréhaigne *et al.*, 2011)

Transitions between two play states always contain potentially noticeable information on the evolution of game play. Describing dynamical states makes it possible to better understand, for one given instant, how players move. Each of them occupies one location but it is evolving since all players display different instantaneous speed and direction of movements, as shown, for instance, in Gréhaigne *et al.* (2010b: 37, Figures 10 and 11). Then, the evolution of a dynamic system can only be modelled as a discontinuous evolution through time.

To obtain a comprehensive representation of the opposition rapport, as illustrated in Figure 9.4, five observational criteria may be simultaneously considered: (a) location of the EP-S on the field, (b) location and circulation of the ball, (c) respective locations of OEP-S and DEP-S, (d) the type of defence (in block or in pursuit), and (e) the compressed or extended state of the EP-S.

Different dynamic representational pictures of game play have been studied in soccer (Ali and Farrally, 1990; Dugrand, 1989; Frencken *et al.*, 2011; Lemoine *et al.*, 2005), basketball (Bourbousson *et al.*, 2010), and Gaelic football (Bradley and O'Donoghue, 2011). For instance, in soccer, studying attack sequences in the offensive half of the field, Ali (1988) and Ali and Farrally (1990) identified seven types of attacking patterns and analysed their final actions prior to a shot at goal. They found that attacks along the length of the wing (e.g. at the periphery) were more successful than those in the central corridor. Also, the analysis showed that there were significant relationships between final actions and patterns of plays.

Studying 188 situations of play that led to a shot at goal or a goal, Gréhaigne *et al.* (2010a) isolated eight configurations of play that occur most frequently with novice players. A closer analysis of these 4 vs 4 games showed that short attacks with few ball exchanges, and the position on the field where ball possession originated, appeared to determine the form of attack adopted thereafter. These game play configurations are called 'prototypic configurations' (Caty and Gréhaigne, 2006), in the sense that they represent fundamental configurations of game play for a given team sport. In a similar study conducted with ice hockey, Moniotte *et al.* (2011) identified 13 prototypic configurations of play.

Statistics of game play

Although they are the oldest form of observational data, statistics drawn from game play remain largely used nowadays, not only by sport journalists but also by researchers. In 1981, Morris presented one of the first studies on the analysis of play with the objective of obtaining precise

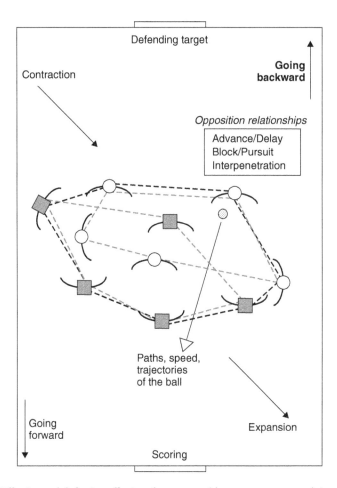

Figure 9.4 Offensive and defensive effective play-spaces with respect to space and time

statistical data. The author considered the number of played balls per match and the continuity of game play. After studying ten international matches, Morris showed that, in a typical match, one could expect 2000 played balls (roughly equally divided between the first half and the second half of the match) and approximately 100 periods of intense activity.

Nowadays, team sport performance researchers rarely make use of statistics for descriptive purposes only; they rather use statistics in correlational or in comparative studies, trying to establish a relationship between various events observed during game play and victory or defeat. Examples of comparative studies are those conducted by: Lago-Ballesteros and Lago-Peñas (2010), involving 18 variables and comparing, for each, the four top, 12 middle and four bottom teams of the Spanish soccer league; Lorenzo *et al.* (2010), involving 18 variables and comparing, for each, winning and losing basketball teams; and Ortega *et al.* (2009), using no less than 28 variables and comparing, for each, winning and losing rugby teams in the Six Nations tournament. Examples of correlational studies are those conducted by Tenga *et al.* (2010) in soccer and by Vaz *et al.* (2010) in rugby.

Although a series of statistics, either raw or transformed, have been considered in several team sports in an attempt to identify suitable predictors of performance, possessions, goals, and shots at goal remain, understandably, among the variables most consistently investigated (e.g. Hughes and Franks, 2005; Jones *et al.*, 2004; Lago and Martin, 2007; Lago-Ballesteros and Lago-Peñas, 2010; O'Shaughnessy, 2006; Sampaio *et al.*, 2010; Tenga *et al.*, 2010).

One particular team sport performance assessment instrument has been developed in the last 15 years (Gréhaigne *et al.*, 1997). The team sport assessment procedure (TSAP) calls for the systematic observation of six specific events: received ball (RB), conquered ball (CB), neutral ball (NB), offensive ball (OB), successful shot (SS), and lost ball (LB). Although statistics can be calculated for individual players, it is possible to compute the sum of each statistic to determine the collective performance of the team. Adaptations of the procedure for ice hockey have been reported in recent years (Nadeau *et al.*, 2008a, 2008b).

Numerical performance indicators

In order to better appreciate team performance, a coach may wish to compute indices combining particular statistics.

The conservation index

The conservation index consists of computing the ratio between lost balls and played balls (LB/ RB + CB). The index values vary from 0 (for no lost ball) and 1 (when the number of lost balls is equal to the number of played balls).

The defensive index

The defensive index considers the number of conquered balls and the number of lost balls; it is equal to CB/LB. It shows the players' capacity to recover the ball (offensive aspect of defence) and their capacity not to lose it (defensive aspect of offence). The index values vary from 0 (when there was no conquered ball) to a value higher than 1 (when the number of conquered balls exceeds the number of lost balls).

Other indices

Depending upon the coach's need for information, other indices may also be computed. Combining various TSAP statistics makes it possible to compute (a) the team's volume of play (RB + CB), indicative of the general involvement of the players in the game, (b) the efficiency index ([CB + OB + SS]/[10 + LB]), and (c) the performance score ([volume of play/2] + [efficiency index × 10]). Such indices provide an overview of the players' or the team's performance but coaches may prefer to work with the primary statistics of the assessment procedure and focus on specific weak elements that need to be improved. In the same line of thought, Thomas *et al.* (2009) have proposed the use of performance scores in soccer, based on the effect of the pass, the dribble, the first touch, and individual defensive tactics.

Using configurations of play for collective decision making

In a broad sense, a configuration is a list or a schema providing the nature and the main characteristics of all elements of a given system. As alluded to before, the notion of configuration of play, in team sports, refers to the relative positioning of players in both teams in relation to the possession and the location of the ball (or any object fought for) and in relation to the various players' movement. At times, it is also referred to as pattern of play (Ali and Farrally, 1990), situation of play (McPherson, 1993), or display (McMorris and Graydon, 1997). During the game, players need to study the shift from one configuration of play to another in order to better understand the evolution of the play. For instance, in soccer, if attackers who have circulated the ball at the centre of the pitch realize that the defenders have spread themselves width wise, they may elect to go on with an attack depth wise in order to get closer to the goal. In basketball, once they realize that they face a zone defence, attackers could choose to shoot from the periphery. Another choice could be to pass the ball to a player located behind the defenders in the front part of the actual play-space (the specific area where players are effectively engaged in the action).

During the game, a configuration of play evolves from a state 1 to a state 2, and so on, to a state n, as long as the ball remains in play. There are two ways of looking at this. First, as in a picture, the configuration of play may be defined by the positions of the players at a moment M (Gréhaigne *et al.*, 1997; Gréhaigne, 2007). This would lead to a static two-dimensional study of the spatial distribution of attackers and defenders and of the position of the ball. Considering then several successive configurations of play (like a series of pictures), one could determine the reasons for attackers' and defenders' choices of action.

However, another way of considering the problem in a more dynamic manner consists of defining the micro-state of the attack/defence system on the basis of location, direction, and possible speed of all players and the ball involved in the confrontation system at this moment. Then each micro-state is determined by a distribution of the players and the ball on the pitch with regard to their respective locations, orientations, and speeds of displacement (Gréhaigne *et al.*, 1997). Considering such dynamic configurations of play represents a more elaborate answer for describing the reality of the game.

In connection with perceptual and decisional skills, the construct of configuration of play appears crucial because it makes it possible for the players to optimize their activity during play in movement. In this case, one can hypothesize that:

> the perceptual learning consists in extracting configuration schemata from pertinent and typical clues whose covariance or co-presence, in a given situation, makes it possible to reduce the time of analysis and of evolution of the informational context through the choice of favoured indicators that are predictive of the global situation. [. . .] [This allows] the identification of spatial structures likely to reveal the surprising capacity of our nervous system for detecting constants and regularities. This confronts us with the problem of identifying the criteria that determine the choice, among the possible directions that the organizational process can take, of those that will be selected and stabilized.
>
> *(Paillard, 1987: 1422)*

One can think that, in order to detect pertinent clues in a given configuration of play, a novice needs to be guided with precise landmarks. These precise and simple reference elements are probable indicators of the evolution of the situation of play and they make it possible for the novice to ignore many parameters that are useless for dealing adequately with the configuration of play. Configurations of the game vary since players' actions bring in purposeful or random changes. Dealing adequately with a configuration of play means that a player makes a pertinent analysis of its characteristics and potential and takes an appropriate decision. However, there may be more than one pertinent analysis applicable to a configuration of play. As the opposition evolves, new relations are created between elements of the game, and others are destroyed, thus the production of endless instantaneous balance states. From the point of view of the player's activity, all these relations that constitute the whole set of configurations are not equally interesting. Some are not at stake and the player can ignore them; others must be recognized because they are the ones that will prompt the production of an adequate response in the shortest possible time. This subject has been also discussed by Carling *et al.* (2009).

Concluding remarks

In invasion games four elements are at play at the same time: opposition to opponents, cooperation with partners, attack on the adverse camp, and defence of one's own camp. In this opposition relationship, while ensuring the defence of its own camp, the team must coordinate its actions in order to recapture, conserve, and move the ball so as to bring it into the scoring zone and effectively score. Inversely, while attempting to move the ball towards the goal and effectively score, each team must coordinate its action to avoid loss of the ball to the hands of the opponents and face a possible counter-attack. Thus, choices must be made depending upon likely costs and benefits, and players must manage varying courses and trajectories of teammates, of opponents, and of the ball in conditions of decisional urgency. As decision making is constantly influenced by teammates' and opponents' movements, performance analysis in team sports must rely on representational pictures of transitions between successive configurations of play. In so doing, performance analysis brings in a qualitative dimension to notational analysis.

References

Ali, A.H. (1988) 'Statistical analysis of tactical movement patterns in association football', in T. Reilly, A. Lees, K. Davids and W.J. Murphy (eds), *Science and Football* (pp. 302–8). London: E. & F.N. Spon.

Ali, A.H. and Farrally, M. (1990) 'An analysis of patterns of play in soccer', *Science & Football*, 3: 37–44.

Bourbousson, J., Sève, C., and McGarry, T. (2010) 'Space-time coordination patterns in basketball: Part 2. The interaction between the two teams', *Journal of Sports Sciences*, 28: 349–58.

Bradley, J. and O'Donoghue, P. (2011) 'Counterattacks in elite Gaelic football competition', *International Journal of Performance Analysis in Sport*, 11: 159–70.

Carling, C., Reilly, T., and Williams, A.M. (2009) *Performance Assessment for Field Sports*, London: Routledge.

Caty, D. and Gréhaigne, J.F. (2006) 'Modélisations de l'attaque et didactique des sports collectifs en EPS [Modelling of the attack and didactics of team sports in physical education]', *e Journal de la Recherche sur l'Intervention en Éducation Physique et Sport*, 8: 70–80. IUFM de Franche-Comté.

Deleplace, R. (1966) *Le rugby [Rugby]*, Paris: Colin-Bourrelier.

Deleplace, R. (1979) *Rugby de mouvement-Rugby total [Rugby in Movement – Total Rugby]*, Paris: Éducation Physique et Sports.

Dugrand, M. (1989) *Le football: de la transparence à la complexité [Soccer: From Transparency to Complexity]*, Paris: PUF.

Duprat, E. (2005) 'Approche technologique de la récupération du ballon lors de la phase défensive en football, contribution à l'élaboration de contenus de formations innovants [Technological approach to the recuperation of the ball during defence in soccer, contribution to the development of innovative teacher-teaching contents]', unpublished doctoral dissertation, Cachan, France: École Normale Supérieure.

Frencken, W., Lemmink, K., Delleman, N., and Visscher, C. (2011) 'Oscillations of centroid position and surface area of soccer teams in small-sided games', *European Journal of Sport Science*, 11: 215–23.

Glazier, P.S. (2010) 'Game, set and match? Substantive issues and future directions in performance analysis', *Sports Medicine*, 40: 625–34.

Gréhaigne, J.F. (1989) 'Football de mouvement. Vers une approche systémique du jeu [Soccer in movement. Towards a systemic approach of the game]', unpublished doctoral dissertation, Dijon, France: Université de Bourgogne.

Gréhaigne, J.F. (1990) 'Analyse des mouvements collectifs précédant un but en football [Analysis of collective movements preceding a goal in soccer]', *Science et Motricité*, 12: 41–53.

Gréhaigne, J.F. (1992) *L'organisation du jeu en football* [The Organization of Game Play in Soccer], Paris: ACTIO.

Gréhaigne, J.F. (2007) *Configurations du jeu, débat d'idées et apprentissage des sports collectifs* [Configurations of Play, Debate of Ideas and Team-Sport Learning], Besançon: Presses de l'Université de Franche-Comté.

Gréhaigne, J.F. and Godbout, P. (1995) 'Tactical knowledge in team sports from a constructivist and cognitivist perspective', *Quest*, 47: 490–505.

Gréhaigne, J.F., Bouthier, D., and David, B. (1996) 'A method to analyse attacking moves in soccer', in T. Reilly, J. Bangsbo and M. Hughes (eds), *Sciences and Football III* (pp. 258–64). London, UK: E. & F.N. Spon.

Gréhaigne, J.F., Godbout, P., and Bouthier, D. (1997) 'Performance assessment in team sports', *Journal of Teaching in Physical Education*, 16: 500–16.

Gréhaigne, J.F., Billard, M., and Laroche, J.Y. (1999a) *L'enseignement des jeux sportifs collectifs à l'école. Conception, construction, évaluation* [Teaching Collective Sport Games in School, Conception, Construction, Assessment], Bruxelles: De Boeck.

Gréhaigne, J.F., Godbout, P. and Bouthier, D. (1999b) 'The foundations of tactics and strategy in team sports', *Journal of Teaching in Physical Education*, 18: 159–74.

Gréhaigne, J.F., Richard, J.F., and Griffin, L. (2005) *Teaching and Learning Team Sports and Games*, New York: Routledge Falmer.

Gréhaigne, J.F., Caty, D., and Godbout, P. (2010a) 'Modelling ball circulation in invasion team sports: A way to promote learning games through understanding', *Physical Education and Sport Pedagogy*, 15: 257–70.

Gréhaigne, J.F., Godbout, P., and Zerai, Z. (2010b) 'Using complex system analysis to model team ball sports', *International Journal of Physical Education*, 47(4): 28–40.

Gréhaigne, J.F., Godbout, P., and Zerai, Z. (2011) 'How the "rapport de forces" evolves in a soccer match: The dynamics of collective decisions in a complex system', *Revista de Psicología del Deporte*, 20: 747–64.

Hughes, M. and Franks, I. (2005) 'Analysis of passing sequences, shots and goals in soccer', *Journal of Sports Sciences*, 23: 509–14.

Jones, P.D., James, N., and Mellalieu, S.D. (2004) 'Possession as a performance indicator in soccer', *International Journal of Performance Analysis in Sport*, 4(1): 98–102.

Lago, C. and Martin, R. (2007) 'Determinants of possession of the ball in soccer', *Journal of Sports Sciences*, 25: 969–74.

Lago-Ballesteros, J. and Lago-Peñas, C. (2010) 'Performance in team sports: Identifying the keys to success in soccer', *Journal of Human Kinetics*, 25: 85–91.

Lemoine, A., Jullien, H., and Ahmaidi, S. (2005) 'Technical and tactical analysis of one-touch playing in soccer – Study of the production of information', *International Journal of Performance Analysis in Sport*, 5: 83–103.

Lorenzo, A., Gómez, M.A., Ortega, E., Ibáñez, S.J., and Sampaio, J. (2010) 'Game related statistics which discriminate between winning and losing under-16 male basketball games', *Journal of Sports Science and Medicine*, 9: 664–8.

McMorris, T. and Graydon, J. (1997) 'The contribution of the research literature to the understanding of decision making in team games', *Journal of Human Movement Studies*, 33: 69–90.

McPherson, S.L. (1993) 'The influence of player experience on problem solving during batting preparation in baseball', *Journal of Sport & Exercise Psychology*, 15: 304–25.

Mérand, R. (1977) *L'éducateur face à la haute performance* [The Educator Faced with Performance], Paris: Sport et Plein air.

Meunier, J.-N. (2005) 'Analyse des configurations de jeu prototypiques en basket-ball au collège [Analysis of prototypic configurations of play in basketball at the high school level]', unpublished Master's thesis, Besançon, France: Université de Franche-Comté.

Moniotte, J., Nadeau, L., and Fortier, K. (2011) 'Configurations de jeu d'équipes de hockey sur glace de niveau Pee Wee et Bantam [Ice hockey teams' configurations of play at Pee Wee and Bantam levels]', *e Journal de la Recherche sur l'Intervention en Éducation Physique et Sport*, 24: 31–52.

Morris, D. (1981) *The Soccer Tribe*, London: Jonathan Cape.

Nadeau, L., Godbout, P., and Richard, J.-F. (2008a) 'Assessment of ice hockey performance in real-game conditions', *European Journal of Sport Science*, 8: 379–88.

Nadeau, L., Richard, J.-F., and Godbout, P. (2008b) 'The validity and reliability of a performance assessment procedure in ice hockey', *Physical Education and Sport Pedagogy*, 13: 65–83.

Ortega, E., Villarejo, D., and Palao, J. (2009) 'Differences in game statistics between winning and losing rugby teams in the Six Nations Tournament', *Journal of Sports Science and Medicine*, 8: 523–52.

O'Shaughnessy, D.M. (2006) 'Possession versus position: Strategic evaluation in AFL', *Journal of Sports Science and Medicine*, 5: 533–40.

Paillard, J. (1987) 'Système nerveux et fonctions d'organisation [Nervous system and organization functions]', in J. Piaget, J.P. Bronckart and P. Mounoud (eds), *La Psychologie* (pp. 1378–441). Paris: Gallimard, Encyclopédie de la Pléïade.

Sampaio, J., Lago, C., and Drinkwater, E. (2010) 'Explanations for the United States of America's dominance in basketball at the Beijing Olympic Games (2008)', *Journal of Sports Sciences*, 28: 147–52.

Tenga, A., Holme, I., Tore Ronglan, L., and Bahr, R. (2010) 'Effect of playing tactics on goal scoring in Norwegian professional soccer', *Journal of Sports Sciences*, 28: 237–44.

Thomas, C., Fellingham, G., and Vehrs, P. (2009) 'Development of a notational analysis system for selected soccer skills of a women's college team', *Measurement in Physical Education and Exercise Science*, 13: 108–21.

Vaz, L., Rooyen, M., and Sampaio, J. (2010) 'Rugby game-related statistics that discriminate between winning and losing teams in IRB and Super twelve close games', *Journal of Sports Science and Medicine*, 9: 51–5.

Winkler, W. (1988) 'A new approach to the video analysis of tactical aspects of soccer', in T. Reilly, A. Lees, K. Davids, and W.J. Murphy (eds), *Science and Football* (pp. 368–72). London: E. & F.N. Spon.

Zerai, Z. (2011) 'Apprentissage du handball chez les jeunes filles Tunisiennes et Françaises; apport de la verbalisation [Handball learning in Tunisian and French young girls: Contribution of verbalization]', unpublished doctoral dissertation, Besançon, France: Université de Franche-Comté.

10

PERFORMANCE INDICATORS IN GAME SPORTS

Jaime Sampaio and Nuno Leite

UNIVERSITY OF TRÁS-OS-MONTES E ALTO DOURO, PORTUGAL

Summary

Performance indicators are a selection or combination of action variables that describe some or all aspects of sports performance (Hughes and Bartlett, 2002). They are demonstrated to be valid measures of performance, possessing the metric properties of an objective measurement procedure, a known scale of measurement and a valid way of interpretation (O'Donoghue, 2010). Performance analysts and coaches use them in order to describe or compare positive or negative aspects of performance within or between competitions. This chapter covers theoretical background on performance indicators and describes possible processes of improving validity. A review of several applied research studies addressing procedures for normalizing performance indicators is presented. Also, there is a brief discussion of how some recent studies are addressing some of the issues outlined in this chapter for several game sports (see Table 10.1, Appendix).

Sports performance and the performance indicators

Performance analysis is used to help sports organizations align activities with short-, mid- and long-term strategic objectives. In pursuit of this aim, there is a clear need to develop and implement the use of adequate performance measures. It is a fact that substantial amounts of data are gathered and analysed within these organizations; however, most of the time there is no certainty that these measures are linked with success factors and the process consumes too many resources for such limited usefulness. This issue demonstrates the need for valid indicators of sports performance.

The term performance indicator is not another designation for 'variable' because not all variables are valid measures of important aspects of sports performance, whereas performance indicators are, by definition (O'Donoghue, 2010). Performance indicators are single or combined action variables that describe some or all aspects of sports performance (Hughes and Bartlett, 2002). Therefore, they represent valid measures of performance and possess the metric properties of an objective measurement procedure, a known scale of measurement and a valid means of interpretation (O'Donoghue, 2010). From a theoretical and applied perspective, a performance indicator should help explain the game outcome and thus advance understanding, providing for meaningful understandings of game behaviour that are also useful in sports practice (McGarry, 2009). Naturally, performance indicators may be associated with the process of performance only and not necessarily with regard to outcomes. For example, the style of play, whether net play in tennis or directness of possession in soccer, may not ultimately be associated with player ranking or match outcome. There may be successful baseline players as well as net players in all areas of the world tennis rankings, just as there may be teams with slow build-up style and teams with direct counter-attacking styles in all areas of the FIFA world soccer rankings.

The framework presented in Figure 10.1 requires data processing if valid performance indicators are to be used in sports performance profiling. The substantial amount of data currently gathered by sports organizations needs to be transformed to performance indicators, with the aim of producing measures linked to performance processes. Performance indicators may be single or combined variables adequately normalized within and/or between sports contests to ensure that they can be compared. Particularly in game sports, they should also be able to capture global or partial aspects of complex, dynamic and non-linear properties of performance. Therefore, potential sources of variability and the criteria used to address validity should be considered carefully. Following this process, performance indicators may be suitable for use in profiling (see Figure 10.1).

There are several characteristics that seem to describe adequately the nature of game sports and, consequently, can be attended when performance is to be studied (Davids *et al.*, 2003; Glazier, 2010; Lames and MacGarry, 2007). Performance is complex in that interactions between players and opponents allow for emergent behaviour to occur. Performance is also dynamic, meaning that all interactions are time dependent and, finally, performance is non-linear because the output is almost never directly proportional to its input. Having these concepts in mind, theoretically, performance indicators should be able to capture global or partial aspects of these complex, dynamic and non-linear properties as required. However, these are non-simple tasks and require continuing development from scientific research in forthcoming years. Nevertheless, available research in performance analysis is already substantial and, importantly, has allowed knowledge of performance in sports to improve significantly.

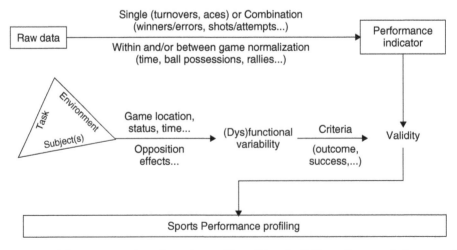

Figure 10.1 Adequate processing of raw data enables valid and reliable performance indicators to be established that can later be used in sports performance profiling

Several approaches have been followed to explore the validity of performance indicators, such as expert opinion (Hraste *et al.*, 2008; Trninic *et al.*, 2000), expert–novice paradigms (Araújo *et al.*, 2005), contrast between winners and losers (Ibáñez *et al.*, 2003; Ortega *et al.*, 2007) and contrast between successful and unsuccessful performances (Ibáñez *et al.*, 2008; Koh *et al.*, 2011). The main goals here are to associate behaviours (actions) in lawful ways with outcomes (e.g. point/goal scored, game won, etc.). However, the meaningful drawing of inferences from sports behaviour to sports outcomes remains an open challenge for sports scientists (McGarry, 2009).

In general, quality of data can be described in terms of objectivity, reliability and validity. Sports scientists often have to deal with noisy data; thus, these concepts play a vital role in research and have motivated the development of a substantial body of methodological literature, reported in both journal articles (Atkinson and Nevill, 1998; Hopkins, 2000; Jeukendrup and Currell, 2008) and books (Berg and Latin, 2007; Morrow *et al.*, 2011; Thomas *et al.*, 2011). These references are able to clarify basic concepts and techniques, addressing all the main problems when dealing with data gathering and analysis. Performance analysis in sports is furthermore the unique focus of literature that, for example, addresses the statistical procedures to measure data reliability (Hughes and Bartlett, 2002; Hughes and Franks, 2004, 2008; O'Donoghue, 2010). The use of adequate operational definitions and the validity of performance indicators are related to reliability of data collection in performance analysis and therefore have a strong impact (O'Donoghue, 2007).

Research in sports performance analysis using performance indicators aims to document performance behaviour. In this regard, performance analysis systems should attend to the fact that performance in many sports is variable and, therefore, performance indicators should be analysed under the influence of several constraints. These constraints can exist as a characteristic of an individual (height, weight, speed, strength), as an element of the environment (weather, surface, importance of the competition, quality of opposition, location, match status) or as part of the task that the individual or the team is trying to perform (executing a pass, zone defence in basketball) (Davids *et al.*, 2003; Newell, 1986). Consequently, sports behaviour emerges under the interaction of these constraints and variability is an essential feature for understanding how to operate efficiently in a variety of performing contexts. For example, available research in performance analysis has recognized opposition effects as one of the most important factors of variability (McGarry and Franks, 1994; O'Donoghue, 2009) and, particularly, how performance indicator values can be evaluated against the corresponding values for the opponent within a game (Hughes and Bartlett, 2002). In sum, it seems clear that most performance indicators are context- and time-dependent and therefore unreliable (Lames and MacGarry, 2007), unless adequate procedures are taken.

Normalizing the performance indicators

In performance analysis, the data are collected using mainly ratio (e.g. duration of ball possession measured in seconds) or nominal scales (e.g. categorizations of football passes as successful or unsuccessful). Afterwards, the data may be normalized according to adequate game criterions to allow for meaningful within- and between-game comparisons (Kubatko *et al.*, 2007; Sampaio and Janeira, 2003). The resulting performance indicators, expressed as non-dimensional ratios, have the advantage of being independent units of analysis (Hughes, 2004). For example, basketball game-related statistics are useful for analysing performance, but may lack validity when performance needs to be analysed across a season due to game rhythm contamination (i.e. the presence of faster- and slower-paced games throughout the season). For example, the performance of a team that makes 35 field goals in an 80-possession game is different to the performance of another team that makes 35 field goals in a 90-possession game, other things being equal. These facts point to the imperative for normalizing the data using adequate criterions according to game specificities (Sampaio and Janeira, 2003). Usually, these criterions would be score, time and innings dependent (Hughes and Franks, 2004, 2008). Several examples can be found using ball possessions in basketball or football (Hughes and Franks, 2005; Kubatko *et al.*, 2007; Sampaio and Janeira, 2003) or time in rugby union (Eaves *et al.*, 2005), but, surprisingly, the available research is not as systematized as might be expected.

Using criteria to improve validity

Available research has used several criteria to approach validity of performance indicators. One of the most common is the contrast between game outcomes (winning, losing and drawing teams) and has been carried out in several sports, such as basketball (Gomez *et al.*, 2008a, 2008b; Ibáñez *et al.*, 2003; Lorenzo *et al.*, 2010; Ortega *et al.*, 2007; Sampaio and Janeira, 2003; Toro *et al.*, 2007), football (Lago-Peñas *et al.*, 2010, 2011a, 2011b), rugby (Jones *et al.*, 2004; Vaz *et al.*, 2010) and water polo (Escalante *et al.*, 2011; Lupo *et al.*, 2011; Platanou, 2004). In general, research with these aims has tested these hypotheses either by identifying differences between group scores using univariate parametric/non-parametric techniques or by identifying relationships using bivariate or multiple regression models. However, performance in game sports often requires analysis of several sets of (dependent) variables simultaneously and, therefore, the use of statistical procedures such as MANOVA, principal components analysis, discriminant analysis, clustering systems or artificial neural networks and other non-linear procedures may be appropriate (Bracewell, 2003; Puterman and Wittman, 2009). For example, most of the available research hypothesizes predictive variables for discriminating different outcomes. For example, higher values in basketball defensive rebounding (Gomez *et al.*, 2008b), football crosses (Lago-Peñas *et al.*, 2010) or water polo goalkeeper-blocked shots (Escalante *et al.*, 2011) are traits of winning teams and, therefore, performance indicators that coaches might want to monitor closely.

It has been suggested that contrasting performances of winners and losers can only provide a measure of team success at a given instant because successful teams can lose some games and unsuccessful teams can win some games (Ibáñez *et al.*, 2008; Madrigal and James, 1999). Therefore, other authors have tried to measure the team's season-long success by contrasting performances from higher and lower classification ranks (Ibáñez *et al.*, 2008; Oberstone, 2009; Rampinini *et al.*, 2009). Oftentimes the selected cut-off points for ranking (discriminating) teams for classification purposes are quite arbitrary. For example, research undertaken in the English Football Premier League has divided the clubs into three groups: higher rank – the UEFA Champions League-qualified teams; lower rank – the teams relegated to the lower-division Championship; and middle rank – the remaining teams (Oberstone, 2009). Conversely, research in basketball divided the teams into higher and lower ranks according to their qualification (or not) to the playoff series (Ibáñez *et al.*, 2008). Although these cut-off points might represent natural divisions, they frequently might lack accuracy. In the previous examples, a football team might be performing as well as the qualified teams for the UEFA Champions League and, yet, are assigned to a lower-ranked group. Two basketball teams can have similar performances across the season, and even might end with the same number of wins, but only one of them reaches playoff qualification. In order to classify these cases more accurately, some research used clustering techniques performed with either a single or a combined group of variables. In volleyball, for example, a cluster analysis was used to group national teams that participated in a World Cup into competitive levels using a combined group of variables, such as: points at the end of competition, ratio of total number of points won and lost, ratio of sets won and lost, and the percentage of sets won (Marcelino *et al.*, 2011). The authors predefined three clusters that were labelled as 'high quality', which included the first four ranked teams, 'intermediate quality', which included the fifth, sixth and seventh ranked teams, and 'low quality', which included the five lowest-ranked teams. Afterwards, only high- and low-quality teams were compared for the purposes of maximizing contrasts in the statistical analysis.

There are occasions when clustering may helping improve validity of the performance indicators. In high-scoring sports such as basketball, volleyball or rugby, the contrast between winners and losers can be analysed according to game score differences. In general, research has considered *a priori* two (balanced and unbalanced) or three (close, balanced and unbalanced) groups for analysis. The results seem to demonstrate that the importance of performance indicators changes with game score differences. For example, basketball free-throw shooting and volleyball effectiveness of attack are important performance indicators, particularly when the differences in score are tightest (Drikos and Vagenas, 2011; Sampaio and Janeira, 2003). In squash, the percentage of rally time spent in the T area differentiates better the less-balanced confrontations (Vučković *et al.*, 2009).

Data reduction is a useful technique for processing data gathered in performance analysis. The main goal here is to identify from a smaller data set fewer performance indicators that might be used to provide accurate feedback to coaches and players, thereby avoiding presentation of redundant information (O'Donoghue, 2008). In football, Gómez *et al.* (2012) analysed 36 variables related to game actions that occurred in several pitch locations. The authors performed factor analysis in a database of 1,900 games from the Spanish Professional Football League and the principal components method reduced the data to a representative smaller set of four factors: Factor 1 – turnovers in zone 5.2 and crosses in zone 4; Factor 2 – goals and shots in zone 5.1, turnovers in zone 4 and ball recover in zone 2; Factor 3 – goals and shots in zone 5.2; and Factor 4 – turnovers in zone 5.1 (Gómez *et al.*, 2012). As expected in a highly unpredictable game like football, the obtained model only accounted for 22.3 per cent of total variance. The models obtained in less unpredictable games, as, for example, basketball or tennis, seem more representative. With similar goals, Sampaio *et al.* (2010) analysed a database containing 5,309 records from 198 basketball players and factor analysis reduced 11 variables to five factors (free throws, two and three-point field goals, passes and errors), accounting for 82 per cent of total variance. O'Donoghue (2008) gathered data from 24 variables by analysing 146 completed tennis matches from the women's singles events. Factor analysis reduced the data to eight factors while accounting for 72.7 per cent of variance (serving to the left on first serve; winning points; serving to the right to the advantage court; service speed; serving to the left on second serve to adversary court; service faults; unforced errors; serving to the left on second serve to deuce criteria). These data reduction techniques can be seen as a first step towards identifying factors that may act as performance indicators. Afterwards, these performance indicators can be contrasted, for example, according to quality of opposition or game outcome (Gómez *et al.*, 2012; Sampaio *et al.*, 2010).

Game time is an important source of variability of performance indicators, although research is generally scarce on this topic. 'Early success' models (Isoahola and Blanchard, 1986) suggested that strong initial performances may increase psychological momentum, increasing the prospect of winning outcomes, although it would appear that the latter moments of game time may be the most important determining feature (Bar-Eli and Tenenbaum, 1988a, 1988b). Thus, consensus is not yet reached regarding the hierarchical importance of game periods. Nevertheless, there is sufficient evidence to support the idea that some game periods are more important for game outcome than others. It is difficult to understand this effect in isolation of other considerations, however. For example, basketball teams' field goal percentages may be lower in the last five minutes of the game due to interaction with a favourable score more so than to game time itself. Game time is usually included in time motion analysis research, probably more with the intention of identifying periods of increased fatigue, in each game half, for example (Rampinini *et al.*, 2007, 2009) or each 15-minute period of a football game (Mohr *et al.*, 2003). Curiously, research has not yet explored in depth the dynamics of performance indicators. Possibly, the initial and final periods of games require analysis of different performance indicators or, at least, need to be considered using different normative values. For example, basketball free-throw performance indicators acquire much higher importance in the final moments of balanced games, where the game is yet to be decided and the frequency of fouling increases (Kozar *et al.*, 1994). Therefore, all information about performing on the free throw under uncertain game outcomes is probably obscured when data are averaged on total game time.

Performance indicators often exhibit substantial within-game variability but results may be different when it comes to variability between games. In game sports, the available research on seasonal variations is often centred on anthropometric and physiological variables (Drinkwater *et al.*, 2005; Metaxas *et al.*, 2006), with tenuous differences identified during the season and across seasons. Research on seasonal variation of performance indicators, in contrast, is scarce. Sampaio *et al.* (2010) undertook such investigation using professional basketball players' game-related statistics according to team quality and playing time. Seasonal variation was analysed over eight-month periods in a sample of 5,309 records from 198 players, and analysis was performed on stronger, intermediate and weaker teams and, also, on more and less important players. Although there were several team quality and playing time effects, no differences were found within season periods. Therefore, the results seem to suggest that those performance indicators are stable enough for use across the season.

Concluding remarks

The framework presented in Table 10.1 summarizes this chapter using examples from recent literature. The substantial amounts of data that are currently gathered by sports organizations need to be transformed to performance indicators that serve as valid performance metrics. Performance indicators may be single or combined variables adequately normalized within and/or between games to ensure that they can be compared. Particularly in game sports, they should also be able to capture global or partial aspects of complex, dynamic and non-linear properties of performance. Therefore, the potential sources of variability and the criteria used to address validity should be considered carefully. Only then might the performance indicators be viewed as appropriate for use in the profiling of sports performance.

Appendix

Table 10.1 Overview of recent studies carried out in different sports for approaching the validity of performance indicators

Study	Sport	Criteria	Normalization/variability	Statistics
Csataljay et al. (2009)	Basketball	Winners/losers	Clustered game final differences	Wilcoxon signed ranks
Lorenzo et al. (2010)	Basketball	Winners/losers	Ball possessions Clustered score final differences	Repeated measures ANOVA Discriminant analysis
Sampaio et al. (2010)	Basketball	Within-season variation	Ball possessions	Factor analysis Mixed linear model
Ziv et al. (2010)	Basketball	Team rankings	Clustered team quality and player duration on court	Factor analysis Stepwise multiple regressions
Ashker (2011)	Boxing	Winners/losers	—	Factorial ANOVA
Lago-Peñas et al. (2010)	Football	Wins/draws/losses	—	Kruskall–Wallis Discriminant analysis
Oberstone (2009)	Football	Teams' championship rankings	—	Linear multiple regression ANOVA
Taylor et al. (2010)	Football	Wins/draws/losses	Location Time	Log-linear modelling
Turner and Sayers (2010)	Football	Positive/non-positive outcomes	—	Chi-squared Correlations Two-way ANOVA
Waldron and Worsfold (2010)	Football	Elite/non-elite	—	Mann–Whitney U
Meletakos et al. (2011)	Handball	World Championships	—	MANOVA
Vaz et al. (2011)	Rugby	Winners/losers	Clustered set final differences	Repeated measures ANOVA Discriminant analysis
Vaz et al. (2010)	Rugby	Winners/losers	Clustered set final differences	Repeated measures ANOVA Discriminant analysis
Lim et al. (2009)	Rugby	Wins/draws/losses Point difference in scores	—	Linear regression Correlations ANOVA

Reference	Sport	Comparison	Context	Statistical method
Vučković et al. (2009)	Squash	Winners/losers	Playing standards Match closeness	Three-way ANOVA
Sindik and Kondri (2011)	Table tennis	Winners/losers Efficiency indexes	—	Multiple regression Correlations
Reid et al. (2010)	Tennis	Player rankings	—	Stepwise regression
Costa et al. (2011)	Volleyball	Success of the attack	—	Multinomial logistic regression
Drikos and Vagenas (2011)	Volleyball	Winners/losers	Clustered set final differences	MANOVA Discriminant analysis
Marcelino et al. (2011)	Volleyball	Winners/losers	Clustered team quality and set final differences	Multinomial logistic regression
Patsiaouras et al. (2010)	Volleyball	Team rankings	—	Kruskall–Wallis Mann–Whitney U
Lupo et al. (2011)	Water polo	Winners/losers	—	Two-way ANOVA
Lupo et al.(2010)	Water polo	Elite/sub-elite	—	MANOVA

References

Araújo, D., Davids, K. and Serpa, S. (2005) 'An ecological approach to expertise effects in decision-making in a simulated sailing regatta', *Psychology of Sport and Exercise*, 6(6): 671–92.

Ashker, S.E. (2011) 'Technical and tactical aspects that differentiate winning and losing performances in boxing', *International Journal of Performance Analysis in Sport*, 11(2): 356–64.

Atkinson, G. and Nevill, A.M. (1998) 'Statistical methods for assessing measurement error (reliability) in variables relevant to sports medicine', *Sports Medicine*, 26(4): 217–38.

Bar-Eli, M. and Tenenbaum, G. (1988a) 'The interaction of individual psychological crisis and time phases in basketball', *Perceptual and Motor Skills*, 66(2): 523–30.

Bar-Eli, M. and Tenenbaum, G. (1988b) 'Time phases and the individual psychological crisis in sports competition: Theory and research findings', *Journal of Sports Sciences*, 6(2): 141–9.

Berg, K. and Latin, R. (2007) *Essentials of Research Methods in Health, Physical Education, Exercise Science, and Recreation* (3rd ed.), Baltimore: Lippincott Williams & Wilkins.

Bracewell, P.J. (2003) 'Monitoring meaningful rugby ratings', *Journal of Sports Sciences*, 21(8): 611–20.

Costa, G., Ferreira, N., Junqueira, G., Afonso, J. and Mesquita, I. (2011) 'Determinants of attack tactics in youth male elite volleyball', *International Journal of Performance Analysis in Sport*, 11(1): 96–104.

Csataljay, G., O'Donoghue, P., Hughes, M. and Dancs, H. (2009) 'Performance indicators that distinguish winning and losing teams in basketball', *International Journal of Performance Analysis in Sport*, 9(1): 60–6.

Davids, K., Glazier, P., Araújo, D. and Bartlett, R. (2003) 'Movement systems as dynamical systems: The functional role of variability and its implications for sports medicine', *Sports Medicine*, 33(4): 245–60.

Drikos, S. and Vagenas, G. (2011) 'Multivariate assessment of selected performance indicators in relation to the type and result of a typical set in men's elite volleyball', *International Journal of Performance Analysis in Sport*, 11(1): 85–95.

Drinkwater, E.J., Hopkins, W.G., McKenna, M.J., Hunt, P.H. and Pyne, D.B. (2005) 'Characterizing changes in fitness of basketball players within and between seasons', *International Journal of Performance Analysis in Sport*, 5(3): 107–25.

Eaves, S.J., Hughes, M.D. and Lamb, K.L. (2005) 'The consequences of the introduction of professional playing status on game action variables in international Northern Hemisphere rugby union football', *International Journal of Performance Analysis in Sport*, 5(2): 58–86.

Escalante, Y., Saavedra, J.M., Mansilla, M. and Tella, V. (2011) 'Discriminatory power of water polo game-related statistics at the 2008 Olympic Games', *Journal of Sports Sciences*, 29(3): 291–8.

Glazier, P.S. (2010) 'Game, set and match? Substantive issues and future directions in performance analysis', *Sports Medicine*, 40(8): 625–34.

Gómez, M., Gómez-López, M., Lago, C. and Sampaio, J. (2012) 'Effects of game location and final outcome on game-related statistics in each zone of the pitch in professional football', *European Journal of Sport Science*, 12(5): 393–8.

Gomez, M.A., Lorenzo, A., Barakat, R., Ortega, E. and Palao, J.M. (2008a) 'Differences in game-related statistics of basketball performance by game location for men's winning and losing teams', *Perceptual and Motor Skills*, 106(1): 43–50.

Gomez, M.A., Lorenzo, A., Sampaio, J., Ibáñez, S.J. and Ortega, E. (2008b) 'Game-related statistics that discriminated winning and losing teams from the Spanish men's professional basketball teams', *Collegium Antropologicum*, 32(2): 451–6.

Hopkins, W. G. (2000) 'Measures of reliability in sports medicine and science', *Sports Medicine*, 30(1): 1–15.

Hraste, M., Dizdar, D. and Trninic, V. (2008) 'Experts' opinion about system of the performance evaluation criteria weighted per positons in the water polo game', *Collegium Antropologicum*, 32(3): 851–61.

Hughes, M. (2004) 'Notational analysis – a mathematical perspective', *International Journal of Performance Analysis in Sport*, 4(2): 97–139.

Hughes, M. and Franks, I. (2004) *Notational Analysis of Sport* (2nd ed.), London: Routledge.

Hughes, M. and Franks, I. (2005) 'Analysis of passing sequences, shots and goals in soccer', *Journal of Sports Sciences*, 23(5): 509–14.

Hughes, M. and Franks, I. (2008) *The Essentials of Performance Analysis: An Introduction*, London: Routledge.

Hughes, M.D. and Bartlett, R.M. (2002) 'The use of performance indicators in performance analysis', *Journal of Sports Sciences*, 20: 739–54.

Ibáñez, S.J., Sampaio, J., Saenz-Lopez, P., Gimenez, J. and Janeira, M.A. (2003) 'Game statistics discriminating the final outcome of Junior World Basketball Championship matches (Portugal 1999)', *Journal of Human Movement Studies*, 45(1): 1–19.

Ibáñez, S.J., Sampaio, J., Feu, S., Lorenzo, A., Gomez, M.A. and Ortega, E. (2008) 'Basketball game-related statistics that discriminate between teams' season-long success', *European Journal of Sport Science*, 8(6): 369–72.

Isoahola, S.E. and Blanchard, W.J. (1986) 'Psychological momentum and competitive sport performance – a field-study', *Perceptual and Motor Skills*, 62(3): 763–8.

Jeukendrup, A.E. and Currell, K. (2008) 'Validity, reliability and sensitivity of measures of sporting performance', *Sports Medicine*, 38(4): 297–316.

Jones, N., Mellalieu, S. and James, N. (2004) 'Team performance indicators as a function of winning and losing in rugby union', *International Journal of Performance Analysis in Sport*, 4(1): 61–71.

Koh, K., Wang, J. and Mallett, C. (2011) 'Discriminating factors between successful and unsuccessful teams: A case study in elite youth Olympic basketball games', *Journal of Quantitative Analysis in Sports*, 7(3): 1–13.

Kozar, B., Vaughn, R.E., Whitfield, K.E., Lord, R.H. and Dye, B. (1994) 'Importance of free-throws at various stages of basketball games', *Perceptual and Motor Skills*, 78(1): 243–8.

Kubatko, J., Oliver, D., Pelton, K. and Rosenbaum, D. (2007) 'A starting point for analyzing basketball statistics', *Journal of Quantitative Analysis in Sports*, 3(3): 1–22.

Lago-Peñas, C., Lago-Ballesteros, J., Dellal, A. and Gomez, M. (2010) 'Game-related statistics that discriminated winning, drawing and losing teams from the Spanish soccer league', *Journal of Sports Science and Medicine*, 9(2): 288–93.

Lago-Peñas, C., Lago-Ballesteros, J. and Rey, E. (2011a) 'Differences in performance indicators between winning and losing teams in the UEFA Champions League', *Journal of Human Kinetics*, 27: 137–48.

Lago-Peñas, C., Rey, E., Lago-Ballesteros, J., Casais, L. and Dominguez, E. (2011b) 'The influence of a congested calendar on physical performance in elite soccer', *Journal of Strength and Conditioning Research*, 25(8): 2111–17.

Lames, M. and MacGarry, T. (2007) 'On the search for reliable performance indicators in game sports', *International Journal of Performance Analysis in Sport*, 7: 62–79.

Lim, E., Lay, B., Dawson, B., Wallman, K. and Anderson, S. (2009) 'Development of a player impact ranking matrix in Super 14 rugby union', *International Journal of Performance Analysis in Sport*, 9(3): 354–67.

Lorenzo, A., Gomez, M.A., Ortega, E., Ibáñez, S.J. and Sampaio, J. (2010) 'Game related statistics which discriminate between winning and losing under-16 male basketball games', *Journal of Sports Science and Medicine*, 9(4): 664–8.

Lupo, C., Tessitore, A., Minganti, C. and Capranica, L. (2010) 'Notational analysis of elite and sub-elite water polo matches', *Journal of Strength and Conditioning Research*, 24(1): 223–9.

Lupo, C., Tessitore, A., Minganti, C., King, B., Cortis, C. and Capranica, L. (2011) 'Notational analysis of American women's collegiate water polo matches', *Journal of Strength and Conditioning Research*, 25(3): 753–7.

Madrigal, R. and James, J. (1999) 'Team quality and the home advantage', *Journal of Sport Behavior*, 22(3): 381–98.

Marcelino, R., Mesquita, I. and Sampaio, J. (2011) 'Effects of quality of opposition and match status on technical and tactical performances in elite volleyball', *Journal of Sports Sciences*, 29(7): 733–41.

McGarry, T. (2009) 'Applied and theoretical perspectives of performance analysis in sport: Scientific issues and challenges', *International Journal of Performance Analysis in Sport*, 9(1): 128–40.

McGarry, T. and Franks, I. M. (1994) 'A stochastic approach to predicting competition squash match play', *Journal of Sports Sciences*, 12(6): 573–84.

Meletakos, P., Vagenas, G. and Bayios, I. (2011) 'A multivariate assessment of offensive performance indicators in men's handball: Trends and differences in the World Championships', *International Journal of Performance Analysis in Sport*, 11(2): 284–94.

Metaxas, T., Sendelides, T., Koutlianos, N. and Mandroukas, K. (2006) 'Seasonal variation of aerobic performance in soccer players according to positional role', *The Journal of Sports Medicine and Physical Fitness*, 46(4): 520–5.

Mohr, M., Krustrup, P. and Bangsbo, J. (2003) 'Match performance of high-standard soccer players with special reference to development of fatigue', *Journal of Sports Sciences*, 21(7): 519–28.

Morrow, J., Jackson, A., Disch, J. and Mood, D. (2011) *Measurement And Evaluation In Human Performance* (4th ed.), Champaign, IL: Human Kinetics.

Newell, K. (1986) 'Constraints on the development of coordination', in M. Wade and H. Whiting (eds), *Motor Development in Children: Aspects of Coordination and Control* (pp. 341–60). Dordrecht, Germany: Martinus Nijhoff.

Oberstone, J. (2009) 'Differentiating the top English Premier League football clubs from the rest of the pack: Identifying the keys to success', *Journal of Quantitative Analysis in Sports*, 5(3): 1–27.

O'Donoghue, P. (2007) 'Reliability issues in performance analysis', *International Journal of Performance Analysis in Sport*, 7(1): 35–48.

O'Donoghue, P. (2008) 'Principal components analysis in the selection of key performance indicators in sport', *International Journal of Performance Analysis in Sport*, 8(3): 145–55.

O'Donoghue, P. (2009) 'Interacting performances theory', *International Journal of Performance Analysis in Sport*, 9(1): 26–46.

O'Donoghue, P. (2010) *Research Methods for Sports Performance Analysis*, London: Routledge.

Ortega, E., Palao, J.M., Gomez, M.A., Lorenzo, A. and Cardenas, D. (2007) 'Analysis of the efficacy of possessions in boys' 16-and-under basketball teams: Differences between winning and losing teams', *Perceptual and Motor Skills*, 104(3): 961–4.

Patsiaouras, A., Moustakidis, A., Charitonidis, K. and Kokaridas, D. (2010) 'Volleyball technical skills as winning and qualification factors during the Olympic Games 2008', *International Journal of Performance Analysis in Sport*, 10(2): 115–20.

Platanou, T. (2004) 'Analysis of the "extra man offence" in water polo: A comparison between winning and losing teams and players of different playing position', *Journal of Human Movement Studies*, 46(3): 205–11.

Puterman, M. and Wittman, S. (2009) 'Match play: Using statistical methods to categorize PGA Tour players' careers', *Journal of Quantitative Analysis in Sports*, 5(1): 1–63.

Rampinini, E., Coutts, A.J., Castagna, C., Sassi, R. and Impellizzeri, F.M. (2007) 'Variation in top level soccer match performance', *International Journal of Sports Medicine*, 28(12): 1018–24.

Rampinini, E., Impellizzeri, F.M., Castagna, C., Coutts, A.J. and Wisløff, U. (2009) 'Technical performance during soccer matches of the Italian Serie A league: Effect of fatigue and competitive level', *Journal of Science and Medicine in Sport*, 12(1): 227–33.

Reid, M., McMurtrie, D. and Crespo, M. (2010) 'The relationship between match statistics and top 100 ranking in professional men's tennis', *International Journal of Performance Analysis in Sport*, 10(2): 131–8.

Sampaio, J. and Janeira, M. (2003) 'Statistical analyses of basketball team performance: Understanding teams' wins and losses according to a different index of ball possessions', *International Journal of Performance Analysis in Sport*, 3(1): 40–9.

Sampaio, J., Drinkwater, E.J. and Leite, N.M. (2010) 'Effects of season period, team quality, and playing time on basketball players' game-related statistics', *European Journal of Sport Science*, 10(2): 141–9.

Sindik, J. and Kondri, M. (2011) 'Correlation between the result efficiency indexes and success in table tennis', *International Journal of Performance Analysis in Sport*, 11(2): 267–83.

Taylor, J.B., Mellalieu, S.D., James, N. and Barter, P. (2010) 'Situation variable effects and tactical performance in professional association football', *International Journal of Performance Analysis in Sport*, 10(3): 255–69.

Thomas, J., Nelson, J. and Silverman, S. (2011) *Research Methods in Physical Activity* (6th ed.), Champaign, IL: Human Kinetics.

Toro, E.O., Ruano, M.A.G., Calvo, A.L. and Zafra, A.O. (2007) 'Differences in the performance indicators of winning and losing women's basketball teams during home/away games', *Revista De Psicologia Del Deporte*, 16(1): 41–54.

Trninic, S., Dizdar, D. and Dezman, B. (2000) 'Empirical verification of the weighted system of criteria for the elite basketball players quality evaluation', *Collegium Antropologicum*, 24(2): 443–65.

Turner, B.J. and Sayers, M.G.L. (2010) 'The influence of transition speed on event outcomes in a high performance football team', *International Journal of Performance Analysis in Sport*, 10(3): 207–20.

Vaz, L., Van Rooyen, M. and Sampaio, J. (2010) 'Rugby game-related statistics that discriminate between winning and losing teams in IRB and Super twelve close games', *Journal of Sports Science and Medicine*, 9(1): 51–5.

Vaz, L., Mouchet, A., Carreras, D. and Morente, H. (2011) 'The importance of rugby game-related statistics to discriminate winners and losers at the elite level competitions in close and balanced games', *International Journal of Performance Analysis in Sport*, 11(1): 130–41.

Vučković G., Perš, J., James, N. and Hughes, M. (2009) 'Tactical use of the T area in squash by players of differing standard', *Journal of Sports Sciences*, 27(8): 863–71.

Waldron, M. and Worsfold, P. (2010) 'Differences in the game specific skills of elite and sub-elite youth football players: Implications for talent identification', *International Journal of Performance Analysis in Sport*, 10(1): 9–24.

Ziv, G., Lidor, R. and Arnon, M. (2010) 'Predicting team rankings in basketball: The questionable use of on-court performance statistics', *International Journal of Performance Analysis in Sport*, 10(2): 103–14.

11

SPORTS PERFORMANCE PROFILING

Peter O'Donoghue

CARDIFF METROPOLITAN UNIVERSITY, UK

Summary

The term profile has been used in performance analysis of sport to date and this chapter will serve to ensure the word 'profiling' is used correctly, as it is in other disciplines such as management and psychology. This chapter explains what a profile is and what a profile is not. It is a collection of related variables brought together to represent an athlete; for example, a fitness profile or a psychological profile. In sports performance, a profile can be used to represent typical performance based on multiple match data. However, a profile can also be used to represent an individual performance. The variables included within sports performance profiles are typically performance indicators. When a profile is produced for a team or athlete, it is necessary to represent the variability in performance indicator values showing where the team or athlete is consistent or inconsistent. This chapter reports on the techniques of James *et al.* (2005) and O'Donoghue (2005) and the different ways they represent average performance and spread of performances. However, these techniques average different types of performance in a way that conceals important information. For example, one may wish to know how a team or individual performs against different classes of opponent. This issue is addressed in the method of Cullinane and O'Donoghue (2011), which accounts for opposition effect when interpreting performances, leading to the generation of profiles that include sections for different types of matches. The three techniques outlined in this chapter use the same example for purposes of illustration and comparison.

Introduction

The word 'profile' has different meanings in different contexts. For example, a profile of a human head, a building or a mountain is a side view of the outline of the head, building or mountain, illustrating distinctive features. Other geographical uses of the word 'profile' include vertical cross-sections of soil or rock. A profile of a famous person is a short biographical article or documentary about the person. In computer systems, a profile is computer-readable text allowing a user's operating environment to be set up when they log on to the computer system. In many areas of scientific research and professional practice, the word 'profile' is used to represent a set of data that exhibit significant properties. For example, the profile of a manager can be characterised by a set of characteristics which should have optimal values (Quinn *et al.*, 1996). These characteristics are displayed on a radar chart (similar to Figure 11.1 in this chapter), allowing the manager to be portrayed in terms of relevant roles. This is the way in which the word is used in sports science. A profile is a collection of variables that characterise a person, organisation or some other entity. For example, a fitness profile for an athlete might contain a collection of anthropometric measurements and fitness test scores (McIntyre and Hall, 2005; Sedano *et al.*, 2009). The purpose of the fitness profile is to represent all of the different components of fitness that are relevant to the particular sport. Similarly, in sport psychology, profiles are used to represent a collection of variables that make up some overall construct or psychological profile (Butler, 1992; Dale and Wrisberg, 1996; Martens *et al.*, 1990; Gucciardi and Gordon, 2009). For example, the profile of mood states is comprised of self-report measures for anger, confusion, depression, fatigue, tension and vigour (McNair *et al.*, 1971). Sports performance profiling methods have included psychological, physical and technical variables. One such method uses radar charts to allow direct comparison of an athlete's profile with an ideal profile for the athlete's role (Doyle and Parfitt, 1996). The variables used in such profiles should be valid and reliable, though the reliability of a profile as a whole should also be investigated (Gleeson *et al.*, 2005). Performance profiles have helped athlete awareness of areas they need to improve and general monitoring of performance (Weston *et al.*, 2011). This in turn has helped goal setting and increased the athlete's motivation to improve.

There are other terms that are used in the current chapter, such as performance, performer and performance indicator. Profiles of sports performance can represent different types of performance. For example, we may wish to analyse an individual match to identify areas requiring attention. Alternatively, we may be characterising the typical performance of a team or individual using data from multiple performances against a range of opponents. Therefore, the word 'performance' can be used to refer to an abstract typical performance as well as an observed particular performance. The word 'performer' is used to represent a team or individual whose performance in sport is being profiled. The profile comprises a set of variables that together characterise the overall performance. These variables are typically performance indicators that are valid and reliable variables for different aspects of the performance. (For a review on performance indicators and their qualities, see Chapter 10.) Performance indicators in sports performance have similar characteristics to performance indicators in engineering disciplines (Bevan, 1995). The term 'performance indicator' is not another name for 'variable' but is a term for a variable or variables that are demonstrated to be valid measures of important aspects of performance, and which possess the metric properties of having an objective measurement procedure, a known scale of measurement and a valid means of interpretation (O'Donoghue, 2010: 21).

Sports performance variables are not stable characteristics of performers in the way anthropometric variables are (O'Donoghue, 2004; Gregson *et al.*, 2010). For example, various factors such as venue (Brown *et al.*, 2002; Carron *et al.*, 2005), importance of the match (Hale, 2004) and score-line within the match (O'Donoghue and Tenga, 2001; Bloomfield *et al.*, 2004a, 2004b; Shaw and O'Donoghue, 2004; Redwood-Brown, 2008) influence performance, with the largest source of variability in sports performance resulting from quality of opposition (McGarry and Franks, 1994). Therefore, Hughes *et al.* (2001) developed a technique to determine a typical value for a performance variable using multiple match data. Essentially, the technique determined how many matches were required for the mean value of the performance indicator to stabilise within a given percentage (e.g. 10 per cent) of the mean for the number of matches from which data were available. Hughes *et al.* (2001) referred to this as a 'profiling' technique, using the word 'profiling' in a manner inconsistent with the common description provided above. There are five specific objections to using the word 'profiling' to describe the technique developed by Hughes *et al.* (2001). These objections are: (1) The technique is applied to a single performance variable without the possibility of bringing a collection of performance variables together into a performance profile; (2) The technique forces stabilisation of variables in situations where unstable and inconsistent performance exists and needs to be recognised; (3) Stabilisation is based on percentage error, which expresses differences in values as a percentage of the mean of available values. This approach risks division by zero and the possibility of negative percentage errors being calculated with interval scale variables; (4) As matches are added, the percentage error of the evolving mean is calculated using the mean of the data available. This is a sample mean and is subject to sampling error, which has not been addressed (see O'Donoghue and Ponting, 2005); and (5) It is not necessary for multiple match data to be used to produce a profile of a performance. Profiles can be produced for performers where typical performance data from multiple matches is necessary; however, individual match analysis is also important in its own right.

It is the first criticism that is of primary concern, hence the technique of Hughes *et al.* (2001) will not be considered further in this review on profiling technique. Instead only those profiling techniques that characterise performance using a set of relevant performance indicators will hereafter be addressed.

Four main profiling techniques used in performance analysis of sport are those of James *et al.* (2005), O'Donoghue (2005), O'Donoghue *et al.* (2008) and O'Donoghue and Cullinane (2011). These techniques can be used to produce a profile of an individual performance, as well as the typical performance of a performer, and data from the 2010 and 2011 Australian and US Open tennis tournaments are used to compare them. These tournaments were chosen because they used the same Rebound Ace surface since 2010. The 23 matches completed by Novak Djokovic and the 25 matches completed by Roger Federer during these tournaments are used to illustrate different uses of these profiling techniques.

Performance profiles using confidence intervals of medians

The technique

The technique of James *et al.* (2005) represents a performance as a collection of all relevant performance indicators. The technique determines the median and 95 per cent confidence interval for the median for each performance indicator based on a set of performances. The locations of the lower and upper limits of a 95 per cent confidence interval for the median are $np \pm z_{\alpha/2}\sqrt{np(1-p)}$ where n is the number of performances, p is 0.5 because the quantile of interest is the median and $z_{\alpha/2}$ is 1.96. James *et al.* (2005) illustrated the technique using performances of rugby union players from a season of 22 matches. The use of 95 per cent confidence intervals gives the technique two advantages over previous methods. First, the technique recognises that typical performance is produced from a sample of performances and subject to sampling error. Second, the 95 per cent confidence intervals allow performers to be compared to identify those performance indicators where they significantly differ and those performance indicators where any differences could be due to sampling error.

A performer profile

The technique can be used to display a typical profile of a performer, compare the typical profiles of different performers and compare the typical profiles of the same performer under different match conditions, such as home games and away games. The medians and 95 per cent confidence intervals of the medians can be presented in tabular or graphical form. Table 11.1

compares typical profiles of Novak Djokovic and Roger Federer. The 95 per cent confidence intervals for the players overlap for each performance indicator. The reason for using a table to present these profiles is because the 13 performance indicators use different units (some percentages and some speeds in km.hour^{-1}) and different ranges of numerical values. The line graph representation used by James et al. (2005) to illustrate the medians of event frequencies was effective. However, for the performance indicators in the tennis example used here, graphical presentation would make it difficult to compare the percentage of service points that are aces or that are double faults between the two players. This is because the medians of these variables are less than 10 per cent, while median values of mean first service speed exceed 180 km.hour^{-1}.

There are a number of issues that can be discussed in relation to this profiling technique. First, the technique represents typical performance without representing the spread of values about that typical performance. The 95 per cent confidence interval is a confidence interval for the median such that the probability of the true median value being within that confidence interval is 95 per cent. The spread of values for the performer is not represented by this. A second issue is that the 95 per cent confidence interval for the median might be viewed as too stringent to detect differences in technical effectiveness indicators between players of similar world rankings. The matches are played against a range of opponents of differing tactical styles and different technical abilities. For example, Roger Federer played against opponents ranked between 3 and 109 in the 2010 US Open. Even when 20 performances were used to produce a profile, the percentiles used to calculate the lower and upper limits of the 95 per cent confidence interval are 45.6 per cent and 54.4 per cent. Inherently unstable data, such as those in sports performance, can render differences between performers to be non-significant. Consider the percentage of points won when a second serve is required; 52.8 per cent for Djokovic and 60.5 per cent for Federer. A set of 310 player performances from these tournaments can be used to create norms, revealing that Federer's performance when a second serve was required exceeded that of over 85 per cent of players, while Djokovic's performance in this situation was in the 5 per cent banding from 55 to 60 per cent. These norms can be used to show a meaningful difference between the two players when assessed against a large set of men's singles performances from relevant tournaments.

Table 11.1 Performance profiles for Novak Djokovic and Roger Federer for their matches in the 2010 and 2011 Australian and US Opens

Performance indicator	Novak Djokovic (n = 23)		Roger Federer (n = 25)	
	Median	95% Confidence interval	Median	95% Confidence interval
%First serves in	66.7	65.5–68.6	63.7	61.0–65.5
%Won when first serve in	74.7	68.9–75.6	77.4	74.0–82.8
%Won when second serve required	52.8	46.6–61.6	60.5	52.5–64.1
%Aces	5.0	4.0–7.7	8.9	7.3–10.7
%Double faults	2.8	1.4–4.8	1.7	1.0–2.3
%Unforced errors	13.6	12.2–18.2	17.9	15.1–19.1
%Winners	17.6	13.0–20.3	20.4	18.1–22.8
%Net points	13.2	8.8–15.5	16.0	13.6–19.6
%Net points won	66.0	61.9–71.1	68.4	66.7–72.5
%Break points won	44.4	38.7–54.1	46.2	41.7–50.0
%Points won when receiving	45.8	39.3–48.0	44.2	39.9–44.9
Mean first serve speed (km.h^{-1})	184.0	180.8–187.2	188.0	185.6–189.0
Mean second serve speed (km.h^{-1})	152.0	148.9–155.1	153.0	151.3–153.6

Interpreting performance indicators using quantiles

The technique

At the same time that James *et al.* (2005) produced a profiling technique based on confidence intervals, O'Donoghue (2005) produced a profiling technique that used quantiles. Quantiles include percentiles and are often used to interpret variables in sports psychology (Martens *et al.*, 1990), fitness (Hoffman, 2006; ACSM, 2010), health (Hulens *et al.*, 2001) and educational performance. For example, the percentiles for body mass index (BMI) of 20-year-old males are 99 values for BMI that partition the population of 20-year-old males into 100 groups containing 1 per cent of that population. The thirtieth percentile for BMI is that value at which 30 per cent of the 20-year-old male population have BMIs lower than that value. Other types of quantiles include quartiles, deciles and vigintiles (O'Donoghue, 2012: 59). O'Donoghue's (2005) technique used quantiles to evaluate performance indicators in sports performance. This is done by determining the quantile for each performance indicator and plotting it on a radar chart that is a performance profile comprising all relevant performance indicators, as shown in Figure 11.1.

Individual performances

The technique is not suitable for interpreting an individual performance because opposition effect is not addressed. For example, if a tennis player plays a match against the world number 1, the player's performance indicator values may be low and will map onto low percentiles. Similarly, if the player plays against an opponent ranked outside the world's top 1,000, performance indicators will be higher and will map onto higher percentiles.

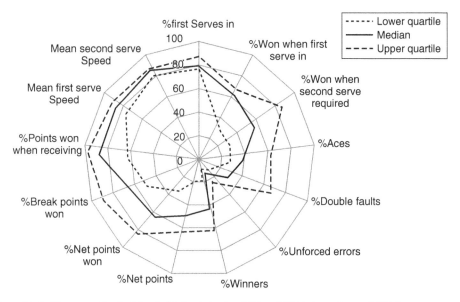

Figure 11.1   Player profile for Novak Djokovic in the 2010 and 2011 Australian and US Opens

A performer profile

The technique is used to produce a profile of a performer that represents the performer's typical performance as well as the spread of performances about that typical performance. This is done by using a representative set of performances by the performer against a full range of opponents and determining measures of location and dispersion for each performance indicator. The technique can be used with medians and lower and upper quartiles where the player's performances show a skewed distribution or with the mean+0.67 standard deviation for each performance indicator. The reason for using mean+0.67 standard deviations is that this range of values covers 50 per cent of values in normally distributed data, which is the same as the inter-quartile range. A range of values from one standard deviation below the mean to one standard deviation above the mean would cover 68.3 per cent of values in normally distributed performances.

The technique demonstrates where some performance indicators have high values while others are low or average. A key property of the technique is that it recognises that a performer may have consistent values for some performance indicators and inconsistent values for other performance indicators. The degree of consistency of a performance indicator for a given performer is something that coaches and opponents need to be aware of, and so this profiling technique, by design, does not force performance indicator values to stabilise. Figure 11.1 is a profile of Novak Djokovic's 23 performances at the Australian and US Opens in 2010 and 2011. Vigintile norms were determined from 310 performances within the two tournaments, thereby allowing the median, lower and upper quartiles of each performance indicator to be associated within a 5 per cent band. The midpoint of the band (2.5 per cent, 7.5 per cent, 12.5 per cent ... 97.5 per cent) is plotted on the radar chart in Figure 11.1. The performance profile shows Djokovic's typical performance within the relevant population of tennis performance, using medians. The player has relatively high values (greater than the values observed in 80 per cent of the performances at the Australian and US Opens) for the percentage of points won when receiving serve, mean first serve speed, mean second serve speed and the percentage of service points where the first serve is in. Furthermore, he makes a relatively low percentage of unforced errors. The inter-quartile range represents the spread of performances about the median. This is interpreted by relating the variability within Djokovic's performances to the variability that exists in men's singles tennis in general. In other words, if Djokovic's inter-quartile range for a variable is similar to the inter-quartile range for men's singles tennis in general, then there is a similar variability within his performances and the performances between different male players. His most consistent areas were the percentage of service points where the first serve was in and the mean speed of his second serve. The inter-quartile range for each of these performance indicators was equivalent to 10 per cent or less of the spread of performances observed at the tournaments. The most inconsistent areas were the percentage of points won when he required a second serve and the percentage of points won when he went to the net. He had an inter-quartile range of 50 per cent or higher for each of these performance indicators. Therefore, the spread of values for these two performance indicators was greater than or equal to that of the wider population of different players.

A criticism of Figure 11.1 is that performance indicator values are replaced by quantiles. There are performance indicators in many sports that are sufficiently well established that coaches and scientists have a good knowledge of what are high, average and low values. Therefore, an alternative representation to the radar chart is a table that shows actual values for the median, lower and upper quartiles (or mean+0.67standard deviation) for each performance indicator, as well as the quantiles that these map onto.

Interpreting performance indicators using norms for different types of matches

The use of quantiles to interpret performances is suitable for producing a profile of a performer based on a representative set of matches against a full range of opponents (O'Donoghue, 2005). However, the technique is not recommended for the interpretation of individual performances because performance indicator values and their corresponding quantiles will often be influenced by the quality of opposition. This risks misinterpreting a performance against a higher-ranked opponent as below standard simply because low performance indicator values map onto corresponding low quantiles. Therefore, a further profiling technique was proposed to use separate norms for different types of matches (O'Donoghue, 2006). The different types of matches could include matches against opponents of similar strength, matches against opponents of lower strength and matches against opponents of higher strength. The technique is essentially the same as that of O'Donoghue (2005), except the population of performances used to produce the quantiles is divided into different types of matches. Therefore, a performance against a higher-ranked opponent will be evaluated using quantile norms for this type of match. The technique has been applied using quartiles (O'Donoghue, 2008) and deciles (O'Donoghue *et al.*, 2008). In British National Superleague netball, teams were classified as being in the top half of the league or in the bottom half of the league (O'Donoghue *et al.*, 2008). This meant that there were four different types of performance (Top v Top, Top v Bottom, Bottom v Top and Bottom v Bottom). Therefore, separate norms were produced for these four different types of matches. The approach was also illustrated in women's singles tennis at Grand Slam tournaments using three groups of players (O'Donoghue, 2008). Group A contained players ranked in the world's top 20, Group B contained players ranked 21 to 75 in the world, while Group C contained players ranked outside the world's top 75. This meant that there were nine different types of performance; A v A, A v B, A v C, B v A, B v B, B v C, C v A, C v B and C v C. This technique was not only used to evaluate individual performances accounting for the quality of the opponent, but it also allowed trends in performances within tournaments to be monitored. Performance indicator values might decrease during successive rounds of a tournament simply because the quality of opponent increases as a player progresses from the first round to the final. The use of norms based on the quality of the player and the opponent in each round allows a more meaningful comparison to be made between performances. The technique is not used to profile performers' typical performances, however, and O'Donoghue's (2005) technique using unified norms would be recommended for this purpose, while separate norms would be used to evaluate individual performances.

Regression-based interpretation of performance indicators

The technique

The technique of O'Donoghue *et al.* (2008) interprets performances using norms for the particular type of match being evaluated. Most importantly, the technique uses different norms depending on the quality or rankings of the performers involved. As noted, the technique has been applied in British Superleague netball between 2005 and 2008 where there was justification for assuming two broad strengths of team (O'Donoghue *et al.*, 2008); there were four teams at the upper half of the league with a noticeable gap to the four teams in the lower half of the league. Cullinane and O'Donoghue (2011) investigated performances of a semi-professional rugby league team and noticed that performance indicator values changed gradually as opposition quality increased or decreased, rather than producing a 'plateauing' effect assumed by O'Donoghue *et al.* (2008). An important disadvantage of O'Donoghue's (2008) approach in tennis is that the same decile norms are used to represent performances against any opponent ranked between 21 and 75 in the world. This risks an evaluation overestimating a performance against the world number 75 and underestimating a performance against the world number 21.

This issue motivated Cullinane (2011) to develop a profiling technique that used a finer-grain approach to addressing opposition quality. This technique is made up of the following steps:

1. Determine an indicator of performer quality – for example, the league position of a team or a world ranking of an individual performer.
2. Use recent and relevant performance data to produce models for performance indicators in terms of relative quality of the performers that contest matches. The relative quality of the match is a function of the difference between the quality indicators for the performers involved.
3. The performances used to produce the models of performance indicators are also used to determine the spread of performance indicator values about the expected performances.
4. Use these models to interpret performance indicator values in future performances. This is done by comparing the observed performance indicator values with the expected values determined using the models. A residual value is the difference between the observed and the expected value for a performance indicator. The residual value can be interpreted using the known spread of historical values, giving a percentage evaluation score that addresses opposition quality

Readers should note the use of the plural (models instead of model) in the steps above. This is because the use of a regression equation and the known distribution of residuals alone do not produce a performance profile. When dealing with a single performance indicator, the technique simply provides a means of interpreting that individual performance indicator addressing opposition quality. It is when the technique is applied to multiple performance indicators producing percentage evaluation scores for the full set of relevant performance indicators that a performance profile is produced.

This technique has several advantages over O'Donoghue *et al.*'s (2008) technique that assumed broad groupings of performers with respect to quality. First, smoother and more realistic relationships between performance indicators and relative quality are represented. Second, the technique is a flexible and general technique that can be used with different types of relationship between performance indicators and relative quality. For example, curvilinear models can be supported as well as linear models. Third, the residual values do not have to be normally distributed or homogeneous. Where other distributions are evidenced from the previous case data used to create the models, these other distributions can be applied when interpreting performance indicator values. Fourth, the percentage evaluation score is not a broad decile or quartile band that a performance is judged to fit within, but is on a continuous scale. The percentage evaluation score represents the percentage of matches between performers of the given qualities where the performance indicator value would be expected to be lower than the value observed.

This chapter discusses how the technique can be used to produce profiles for individual performances as well as for performers. There is another use of the technique, which is to evaluate trends in performance addressing opposition quality (O'Donoghue and Cullinane, 2011).

A performance profile

The technique should only be used where there is evidence of a relationship between the relative quality of the performers and the performance indicators. Of the 13 performance indicators used in the Australian and US Open men's singles tennis data, the percentage of points won when the first serve was in (S1) and the percentage of points won when a second serve was required (S2) had a positive linear relationship with relative quality. Relative quality, RQ, was defined as the difference between the quality ratings, R_X and R_Y, of the two players, X and Y, contesting a match. The 52-week world ranking, $Rank_X$, of player X was transformed into a quality rating, R_X, using the method described by Klaassen and Magnus (2001), as shown in equation (11.1).

$$R_X = 8 - \log_2(Rank_X) \tag{11.1}$$

R_X is an estimate of the round in the tournament a player could be expected to reach based on his ranking for singles. For example, the world number 1 would be expected to win the tournament ($R_X = 8$), while the world number 2 would be expected to reach the final ($R_X = 7$), the world number 4 would be expected to reach the semi-final ($R_X = 6$), the world number 128 would be expected to reach the first round ($R_X = 1$) and the world number 512 would be expected to reach the penultimate qualifying round ($R_X = -1$).

   Given that one player's serving performance is another player's receiving performance, the percentage of receiving points won when the opponent's first serve was in (R1) and the percentage of receiving points won when the opponent required a second serve were also correlated with relative quality. Once regression models for the expected values of S1, S2, R1 and R2 in terms of RQ are created, it is possible to evaluate a performance. This is done using the following steps:

1.   Determine the expected value for a performance indicator based on the relative quality of the players involved in the match. For example, the model of S1 is S1 = 1.723RQ + 70.566.
2.   Determine the residual value, which is the difference between the observed and expected values for the performance indicator.
3.   Divide this residual by the standard deviation of the residuals in the data used to create the model to give a z-score (if the residuals are normally distributed). For example, the standard deviation for the residuals of S1 in men's singles at the Australian and US Open's is 8.184.
4.   Using the standard normal distribution (or an alternative distribution if necessary), determine the area of the probability distribution for the residuals for z-scores less than that calculated in step 3.
5.   Multiply the probability determined in step 4 by 100 to achieve a percentage evaluation score.

The percentage evaluation score addresses the relative quality of the two players, thus allowing relative performance to be assessed. An absolute assessment is still possible if the original performance indicators are used instead of the relative evaluation scores. A crude evaluation could use the average of the four performance indicators to represent absolute performance and the mean of the four percentage evaluation scores to represent relative quality. Consider the sequence of performances for Novak Djokovic shown in Table 11.2. The best performance

Table 11.2 Performance indicator values and their corresponding evaluation scores using O'Donoghue and Cullinane's (2011) technique

Djokovic rank	Opponent name	Rank	S1 Value	S1 %ES	S2 Value	S2 %ES	R1 Value	R1 %ES	R2 Value	R2 %ES
Australian Open 2010										
3	Gimeno Traver	74	75.8	37.0	57.1	51.1	29.1	15.5	66.7	83.9
3	Chiundelli	58	74.7	34.6	32.6	0.7	42.1	74.1	57.8	54.9
3	Istomin	103	73.3	23.1	45.2	9.9	60.6	99.7	74.1	95.4
3	Kubot	86	80.4	57.2	69.6	90.0	31.9	23.7	69.0	88.4
3	Tsonga	10	67.0	21.2	48.9	35.4	31.8	46.8	52.5	48.8
US Open 2010										
3	Troicki	47	66.7	9.5	50.0	27.1	30.6	24.2	58.3	59.1
3	Petzscher	52	76.8	45.9	59.4	63.2	31.3	26.3	50.0	25.6
3	Blake	108	68.9	9.9	70.0	89.8	35.8	38.0	45.8	10.5
3	Fish	21	78.8	66.3	45.8	19.5	41.0	79.5	53.1	44.9
3	Monfils	19	68.9	22.3	50.0	34.3	47.5	95.1	58.3	66.8
3	Federer	2	68.1	42.9	63.2	92.9	26.2	39.2	53.9	68.7
3	Nadal	1	64.2	32.9	45.8	43.2	26.7	49.8	43.2	32.2
Australian Open 2011										
3	Granolars	42	75.0	39.8	68.2	90.3	32.3	32.4	76.5	98.3
3	Dodig	81	74.7	31.0	64.3	77.2	32.1	25.1	53.2	33.6
3	Almagro	14	85.7	91.7	47.4	27.1	39.1	76.3	56.3	61.3
3	Berdych	6	82.3	88.9	41.4	15.0	29.4	41.5	64.4	90.8
3	Federer	2	73.3	67.5	41.0	20.5	28.6	50.7	52.4	62.8
3	Murray	5	70.0	41.2	60.0	82.4	36.2	74.9	68.6	96.4
US Open 2011										
1	Berlocq	74	67.6	4.7	63.2	65.6	62.2	99.7	77.3	96.7
1	Davydenko	39	75.0	28.4	65.6	78.9	44.1	75.0	54.5	35.6
1	Dolgoporov	23	75.4	35.7	52.8	34.1	20.5	2.0	58.2	55.0
1	Federer	3	82.9	88.1	55.2	61.8	33.0	54.0	43.8	18.2
1	Nadal	2	65.5	20.3	44.2	22.8	47.9	98.0	57.8	73.8

in absolute terms was against Berlocq, who was ranked 74 in the world. The worst performance in absolute terms was the four-set loss to Rafael Nadal in the final of the 2010 US Open. This absolute view of the performance indicators fails to account for Nadal being ranked world number 1 at the time. The worst performance in relative terms was against Troicki in an early round of the 2010 US Open. Although this was a win, the models of S1, S2, R1 and R2 suggest that Djokovic should have won more comfortably against this opponent. The best performance in relative terms was the victory over Andy Murray in the 2011 Australian Open final. In particular, winning 68.6 per cent of points where Murray had a second serve (R2) is a higher percentage than would be expected in 96.4 per cent of matches where the players involved had the same relative quality as Djokovic and Murray.

A performer profile

Although this technique was originally developed to address opposition quality when evaluating sports performance in individual matches, it also has an advantage when used to produce a profile of a performer. A disadvantage of O'Donoghue's (2005) technique using quantiles is that two players' typical profiles could be created using matches against different ranges of opposition. Players ranked in the world's top four are more likely to play opponents ranked in the world's top four than players ranked outside the world's top 50 would be. This is because higher-ranked players tend to progress further in tournaments than lower-ranked players. This could lead to profiles for higher-ranked players being based on median values from matches against higher-ranked opponents than the average player would be expected to play.

The percentage evaluation scores for a series of matches used to create a profile have the advantage of addressing the quality of the opponent within each match. This means that a typical performance profile based on evaluation scores rather than the original performance indicator values will address the balance of opponents in the matches used.

Future work

The regression based technique of O'Donoghue and Cullinane (2011) is suitable for performance indicators whose values increase or decrease as relative quality increases. However, there are many performance indicators where optimal values are better − the percentage of points where the first serve is in during a tennis performance is an example. If this value is too low, the player will have too many points emanating from a second serve, which has been shown to be less effective than when the first serve is in (O'Donoghue and Ingram, 2001). If the percentage of points where the first serve is in is too high, it could be because the serve is easier to return. For example, the serve is in because it is not placed close enough to the lines or because it is not played fast enough. Research is needed to develop a means of identifying optimal values of such performance indicators and a means of evaluating these, such that optimal values are graded better than values that are too high or too low.

A second area for future research is to weight recent performances more highly than earlier performances when producing performer profiles based on multiple performances. Mosteller (1979) proposed weighting the most recent matches within a profile more heavily than earlier matches with matches eventually being excluded from the data used to produce the profile when they were deemed to be no longer current. This could be a potential extension to all of the performance profiling techniques described in this chapter.

Concluding remarks

This chapter has described four profiling techniques used in performance analysis of sport. What all four have in common is that the profiles contain a set of performance indicators that together characterise performance in the given sport. James *et al.* (2005) used 95 per cent confidence intervals of the median. O'Donoghue (2005) used norms so that typical performances could be evaluated using quantiles in the same way that variables are evaluated in other disciplines. O'Donoghue *et al.* (2008) addressed opposition quality by using separate norms for different types of matches. This can be considered a coarse-grain approach because it is assumed that there are broad classes of matches. The most recent profiling technique is that of Cullinane and O'Donoghue (2011), which applies a more fine-grain approach, assuming gradual change in expected performance indicator values as the quality of opposition changes.

References

ACSM (2010) *ACSM's Health-Related Physical Fitness Assessment Manual, 3rd Edition*, Philadelphia, PA: Wolters Kluwer/Lippincott Williams and Wilkins.

Bevan, N. (1995) 'Measuring usability as quality of use', *Software Quality Journal*, 4: 115–30.

Bloomfield, J.R., Polman, R.C.J. and O'Donoghue, P.G. (2004a) 'Effects of score-line on work-rate in midfield and forward players in FA Premier League Soccer', *Journal of Sports Sciences*, 23: 191–2.

Bloomfield, J.R., Polman, R.C.J. and O'Donoghue, P.G. (2004b) 'Effects of score-line on match performance in FA Premier League Soccer', *Journal of Sports Sciences*, 23: 192–3.

Brown, T.D. Jr., Van Raalte, J.L., Brewer, B.W., Winter, C.R. and Cornelius, A.E. (2002) 'World Cup soccer home advantage', *Journal of Sport Behaviour*, 25: 134–44.

Butler, R. (1992) 'The performance profile: Theory and application', *The Sport Psychologist*, 6: 253–64.

Carron, A.V., Loughead, T.M. and Bray, S.R. (2005) 'The home advantage in sport competitions: Courneya and Carron's (1992) conceptual framework a decade later', *Journal of Sports Sciences*, 23: 395–407.

Cullinane, A. (2011) 'Addressing opposition quality in rugby league performance', unpublished M.Sc. thesis, University of Wales Institute, Cardiff.

Cullinane, A. and O'Donoghue, P.G. (2011) 'Addressing opposition quality in rugby league performance', poster presented at the World Congress of Science and Football, Nagoya, Japan, May.

Dale, G.A and Wrisberg, C.A (1996) 'The use of a performance profiling technique in a team setting: Getting the athletes and coach on the "same page"', *Sport Psychologist*, 10: 261–77.

Doyle, J.M. and Parfitt, G. (1996) 'Performance profiling and predictive validity', *Journal of Applied Sport Psychology*, 8: 160–70.

Gleeson, N., Parfitt, G., Doyle, J. and Rees, D. (2005) 'Reproducibility and efficacy of the performance profile technique', *Journal of Exercise Science and Fitness*, 3(2): 66–73.

Gregson, W., Drust, B, Atkinson, G. and Salvo, V.D. (2010) 'Match-to-match variability of high-speed activities in Premier League Soccer', *International Journal of Sports Medicine*, 31: 237–42.

Gucciardi, D.F. and Gordon, S. (2009) 'Revisiting the performance profile technique: Theoretical underpinnings and application', *The Sport Psychologist*, 23: 93–117.

Hale, S. (2004) 'Work-rate of Welsh National League players in training matches and competitive matches', in P.G. O'Donoghue and M.D. Hughes (eds), *Performance Analysis of Sport VI* (pp. 35–44), Cardiff, UK: CPA, UWIC Press.

Hoffman, J. (2006) *Norms for Fitness, Performance and Health*, Champaign, IL: Human Kinetics Publishers.

Hughes, M., Evans, S. and Wells, J. (2001) 'Establishing normative profiles in performance analysis', *International Journal of Performance Analysis of Sport*, 1: 4–27.

Hulens, M., Beunen, G., Claessens, A.L., Lefevre, J., Thomis, M., Philippaerts, R., Borms, J., Vrijens, J., Lysens, R. and Vansant, G. (2001) 'Trends in BMI among Belgian children, adolescents and adults from 1969 to 1996', *International Journal of Obesity*, 25: 395–9.

James, N., Mellalieu, S.D. and Jones, N.M.P. (2005) 'The development of position specific performance indicators in professional rugby union', *Journal of Sports Sciences*, 23: 63–72.

Klaassen, F.J.G.M. and Magnus, J.R. (2001) 'Are points in tennis independent and identically distributed?

Evidence from a dynamic binary panel data model', *Journal of the American Statistical Association*, 96: 500–9.

Martens, R., Vealey, R.S. and Burton, D. (1990) *Competitive Anxiety in Sport*, Champaign, IL: Human Kinetics.

McGarry, T. and Franks, I.M. (1994) 'A stochastic approach to predicting competition squash match-play' *Journal of Sports Sciences*, 12: 573–84.

McIntyre, M.C. and Hall, M. (2005) 'Physiological profile in relation to playing position of elite college Gaelic footballers', *British Journal of Sports Medicine*, 39: 264–6.

McNair, D.M., Lorr, M. and Droppleman, L. (1971) *Manual for the Profile of Mood States*, San Diego, CA: Educational and Industrial Testing Service.

Mosteller, F. (1979) 'A resistant analysis of 1971 and 1972 professional football', in J. Goldstein (ed.), *Sports, Games and Play* (pp. 371–401). Hillsdale, NJ: Lawrence Erlbaum Associates.

O'Donoghue, P.G. (2004) 'Sources of variability in time-motion data; measurement error and within player variability in work-rate', *International Journal of Performance Analysis of Sport*, 4(2): 42–9.

O'Donoghue, P.G. (2005) 'Normative profiles of sports performance', *International Journal of Performance Analysis of Sport*, 5(1): 104–19,

O'Donoghue, P.G. (2006) 'Performance indicators for possession and shooting in international netball', in H. Dancs, M. Hughes and P.G. O'Donoghue (eds), *Performance Analysis of Sport 7* (pp. 483–503). Cardiff, UK: CPA, UWIC Press.

O'Donoghue, P.G. (2008) 'Performance norms and opposition effects in Grand Slam women's singles tennis', presentation at European College of Sports Science, Lisbon, Portugal, July.

O'Donoghue, P.G. (2010) *Research Methods for Sports Performance Analysis*, London: Routledge.

O'Donoghue, P.G. (2012) *Statistics for Sport and Exercise Science: An Introduction*, London: Routledge.

O'Donoghue, P.G. and Ingram, B. (2001) 'A notational analysis of elite tennis strategy', *Journal of Sports Sciences*, 19: 107–15.

O'Donoghue, P.G. and Tenga. A. (2001) 'The effect of scoreline on work rate in elite soccer', *Journal of Sports Sciences*, 19: 25–6.

O'Donoghue, P.G. and Ponting, R. (2005) 'Equations for the number of matches required for stable performance profiles', *International Journal of Computer Science in Sport*, 4(2): 48–55.

O'Donoghue, P.G. and Cullinane, A. (2011) 'A regression-based approach to interpreting sports performance', *International Journal of Performance Analysis in Sport*, 11: 295–307.

O'Donoghue, P.G., Mayes, A., Edwards, K.M. and Garland, J. (2008) 'Performance norms for British National Super League netball', *International Journal of Sports Science and Coaching*, 3: 501–11.

Quinn, R.E., Faerman, S.R., Thompson, M.P. and McGrath, M.R. (1996) *Becoming a Master Manager: A Competency Framework* (2nd ed.), New York: Wiley.

Redwood-Brown, A. (2008) 'Passing patterns before and after goal scoring in FA Premier League soccer', *International Journal of Performance Analysis of Sport*, 8(3): 172–82.

Sedano, S., Vaeyens, R., Philippaerts, R.M., Redondo, J.C. and Cuadrado, G. (2009) 'Anthropometric and anaerobic fitness profile of elite and non-elite female soccer players', *Journal of Sports Medicine and Physical Fitness*, 49: 387–94.

Shaw, J. and O'Donoghue, P.G. (2004) 'The effect of score-line on work rate in amateur soccer', in P.G. O'Donoghue and M. Hughes (eds), *Performance Analysis of Sport 6* (pp. 84–91), Cardiff, UK: CPA Press, UWIC.

Weston, N., Greenlees, I. and Thelwell, R. (2011) 'Athlete perceptions of the impacts of performance profiling', *International Journal of Sport and Exercise Psychology*, 9(2): 173–88.

12
SCORING/JUDGING APPLICATIONS

Anthony (Tony) N. Kirkbride

CSIR SPORTS TECHNOLOGY, SOUTH AFRICA

Summary

The evolution of sports scoring and judging systems is driven by a need to accurately assess sports excellence. Sports performance analysis is constantly striving to migrate from a subjective assessment of performance to a more objective appraisal. Generally, expert judges and referees are engaged in assessing events, actions and movements that occur in their field of observation. These observations are, by and large, subjective in nature. Consequently, modern scoring and judging systems have developed in an attempt to address this limitation and provide a consistent framework within which reliable assessments of performance can be undertaken. As levels of competition become ever closer, the margins separating performances are decreasing, often necessitating the use of technology to adjudicate some occurrences. This area is often catalysed by the development of innovative and engaging broadcast technologies, which subsequently find redeployment as an integral part of the adjudication process.

Generally, scoring and judging systems are designed specifically to minimise bias, be fair and equitable, reduce errors in observation and improve decision making and communication. Nevertheless, some challenges remain and a review of the current developments in this critical area of competition was undertaken by examining relevant peer-reviewed journals which included a technology scan. The chapter concludes with an assessment of future trends in scoring/judging systems and provides a summary of the salient points of this section.

Introduction

The term sportsmanship can be defined in terms of the aspiration of fair play; competition is relished more when there is an equitable chance to gain victory. Ill-conceived and ill-designed tournaments, in which the top seeds eliminate each other in the early rounds, are generally disparaged. However, in the English FA Cup, the lack of seeding in this particular knockout tournament has injected a degree of romance, with potentially exciting draws that would be impossible in a seeded competition. The objective is for the best athlete or team to win and this should not be unduly influenced by the tournament design or scoring/judging system (Appleton, 1995; Clarke *et al.*, 2009; Pollard and Pollard, 2010). The well-known idiom it's not cricket is often used to imply the unacceptable. The saying originates from the fundamental sportsmanship principle of fair play or gentlemanly conduct historically applied to a cricket player's obligation. It derives from a time when instant television replays were non-existent and, consequently, there was an unwritten onus on the batsman to *walk* (i.e. the act of giving himself or herself out prior to a decision by an umpire). The general trend, at least at the elite international level, is for the batsman to stand his/her ground and rely on the technology available to the umpire to make the correct judgement. Errors can be made in the umpire's analysis and decision-making process and the batsman is hoping for a decision in his favour. Batsmen can stand their ground aiming to deceive the umpire, even when blatantly aware of their obligation. In close decisions, typically in cases of uncertainty and where there is an absence of evidence, the batsman is always *given the benefit of doubt*. In many sports, players can deliberately attempt to deceive, the more theatrical footballers by diving, particularly in the penalty area (known as embellishing in ice hockey). Soccer players feign injury to draw free kicks/penalties and rugby players have faked blood injuries to gain substitutions. While the debate continues at pace regarding sportsmanship, sport in general strives for fairness.

Soccer, rugby and cricket are three of the most popular spectator and participation sports worldwide and considered the least subjective when deciding a winner when compared to, for example, boxing, ice skating or martial arts. The aim of these ball sports is to score more goals, points or runs than the opposition. The primary objective is so simple and yet why would judging play such an important role? These sports are played in accordance with, and reference to, the notion of the 'spirit' of the game and 'letter' of the laws. In cricketing parlance, the 'spirit' of the game refers to the way the game should be played and incorporates ideas such as fair play or gentlemanly conduct. In the early days of football (circa 1800s), there was self-regulation of rule infringements of players by the offending captain and, as competition increased, so did professionalism, and this led to external regulation and the appointment of neutral umpires and referees (Colwell, 2000). In the modern game, one referee and two assistant referees are the most common in soccer and rugby; cricket generally has two umpires and can have additional technical support from so-called Third Umpires and TV Umpires, depending on the nature of the tournament. Referees permit the game to flow by interpreting the laws in the 'spirit' of the game. If they were to apply the 'letter' of the law, then every minor infringement could potentially stop the game. Consequently, referees are constantly making subjective judgements and this level of discretion can have a profound influence on the outcome of games. Controversy usually surrounds referees perceived not to be enforcing laws or, conversely, applying the letter of the law too rigidly. Many laws do not permit room for misinterpretation and are relatively straightforward (e.g. goals, throw-ins). However, where a decision or judgement is made on an opinion, this is much more problematical and controversial. As TV coverage of these sports increases, so does the ability to review, interrogate and scrutinise (in increasingly fine detail) umpire and referee decisions. This is where adjudication mistakes are exposed and where proposals are made and debated to reduce inconsistencies. Many sports codes openly welcome aids to assist scoring and judging, while others are more reticent. In an attempt to minimise human intervention in scoring and judging of sports, automated image processing and sensor processing technologies are also finding some applications and these areas are arousing researchers' interests. Nevertheless, the majority of sports currently rely on human cognition, and concepts that influence our human perception are outlined in the following section.

Challenges

Almost a third of all sports registered with the International Olympic Committee (IOC) rely on a system of human judging to partially or fully assess performance (Wolframm, 2010).

Unfortunately, many researchers and commentators have raised doubts about judging bias, both natural and nationalistic (Balmer *et al.*, 2005; Emerson *et al.*, 2009; Hawson *et al.*, 2010; Zitzewitz, 2006, 2010). Emerson *et al.* (2009) claimed to have found one occasion where the medal standings could have been changed as a result of unbiased judging.

So, what is the process of judging and just how do we perceive? The ability of *not* being able to perceive things that are in plain sight has coined the term *inattentional blindness*. One of the best-known examples, and one frequently shown to students of performance analysis, is the 'Invisible Gorilla Test'. This was conducted by Simon and Chabris (source: en.wikipedia.org/wiki/Inattentional_blindness). Subjects were asked to watch a short video in which two competing teams wearing two different coloured T-shirts were passing a basketball around. In the original test, the subjects were asked either to count the number of passes made by one team or to keep a tally of the number of times the ball was passed either by bounce or by an aerial pass. In the famous video experiment, a person is seen to enter the field of play and walk around the basketball court for approximately 30 seconds, wearing a gorilla suit, before walking off screen. After watching the video, the subjects were asked to recount if they noticed anything unusual take place. A subsequent review of the data indicated that, in most groups tested, 50 per cent of the subjects failed to see the gorilla. One solution to this problem, in scoring and adjudication applications, is to utilise a video review to minimise potential inattentional blindness.

Observation, by its very nature, is subjective. What one person 'sees' or 'perceives' is never identical to what another person sees. Performance appraisal of aesthetic sports, such as ice skating, dressage or gymnastics, is almost entirely 'in the eye of the beholder'. We assume and take for granted that judges are impartial, fair and do their job to the best of their abilities. However, the scoring system can be flawed or the appraisal process can have some inherent, built-in biases. No two people think alike. How people construct their own subjective reality is a separate branch of psychology and is influenced by our individual knowledge, experiences and thought processes. In making a judgement, the brain runs though a sequence of processes. Initially, the first step involves perception of the situation or, in the case of sport, this could be the execution of movement. Second, our minds place this event in context; it is given meaning, which is characterised using a mental process that relies heavily on stored prior knowledge and past experiences. This occurs within a framework of what is known about classifying performance. Lastly, the classified executed movement is augmented with additional information, such as relevant past memories, circumstantial information, venue, team or athlete reputation. One particular recognised bias is the so-called 'halo effect' (see en.wikipedia.org/wiki/Halo_effect). This is a cognitive bias where perceived traits influence interpretation of events due to expectations. You could say, 'an athlete's reputation precedes them!' In the scoring/judging process, errors can creep in at any of the three stages outlined previously. Perhaps a judge's view is obscured at the time of an event. For instance, in boxing, the judge's view could be hindered by the position of the referee. Even if the event was observed equally by two judges, they may disagree on a number of aspects and be inconsistent in awarding or deducting points. This problem can be further compounded if these two judges are aware of both their individual scores. In this instance, a conformity bias effect may kick in and the two judges may adapt and align their scores. This could be considered a form of peer pressure and is a normative human characteristic of psychological behaviour. In dressage and gymnastics, bias has been detected when scoring/judging is done later in the competition (Ansorge and Scheer, 1988), with higher scores being reserved for gymnasts, or riders and horses that enter later in the draws; Wolframm (2010b) termed this order bias. Ice dancing is particularly prone to patriotic or nationalistic bias (Zitzewitz, 2006, 2010), where scores awarded are influenced by the country the athlete is representing. This effect has also been observed in other sports, including dressage and gymnastics

(Popović, 2000), as well as the Eurovision Song Contest (Wolframm, 2010a). As a consequence of all these tendencies to bias, the first step in striving to improve the scoring and judging of sports is to be aware of these pitfalls when designing and implementing objective performance analysis systems for competition. The ultimate objective is fairness by excluding prejudice and to be achievable through accurate recall, consistent observation and scoring.

Current trends

In the preceding section, some common pitfalls in scoring and judging aesthetic sports were outlined. The current trend to reduce controversy and improve fairness in performance appraisal is to reduce the variability whilst increasing the accuracy of modern scoring/judging systems.

The driver for judging reform is often a perceived or real injustice that robs one athlete of a potential victory on the basis of bias detected in the scoring process. In the recent past, this has galvanised a number of sports, including ice skating and boxing, to review and amend their scoring/judging systems. The next section highlights the different approaches adopted by each of these codes in order to improve the reliability of adjudication so that the resultant process is robust and improves the probability of a fair outcome. It is beyond the scope of this chapter to catalogue the development of scoring systems in these two codes. The examples provide insight into modern approaches to solving a long-standing problem and could be equally applicable to other sports codes.

Ice skating

A highly controversial ice skating judging scandal at the 2002 Winter Olympics in Salt Lake City was the catalyst for speeding up adjudication reform in the sport. In the 2002 Games, the single panel of nine international judges utilised a 6.0 grading scale and deducted points for errors, mistakes or problems in execution. In the pairs figure skating competition, a firestorm of controversy broke out when the Russian pair of Yelena Berezhnaya and Anton Sikharulidze was awarded the gold medal over the Canadian pair of Jamie Salé and David Pelletier. The subsequent investigation into the judges' scoring revealed that the French judge alleged that she had been pressured, by the head of the French skating organisation, to vote for the Russian pair, regardless of how the others performed (Swift, 2002). A subsequent investigation into the controversy by the world's governing body and the IOC led to the award of a second gold medal to the Canadians.

The replacement international judging system (IJS) started at the fundamental level, by reviewing the decision process used to appoint judges. To reduce nationalistic bias, the International Skating Union (ISU) decided to appoint the judges directly rather than permit the national federations to do so. Furthermore, in an attempt to make collusion more difficult, the judging pool was increased from 9 to 14 and now currently consists of two panels, a judging panel and a new technical panel. The technical panel comprises of a technical specialist (also known as the caller), assistant technical specialist, technical controller, data operator and video replay operator. In the new system, all 14 scores would be publically reported, but only 9 would be used in computing the results. This means which scores were counted and which judge gave which score was not to be revealed, thus making any future determination of nationalistic bias impossible. Two more reforms were introduced: first, the technical merit and artistic impression scores were to be replaced with a system similar to that used in diving and gymnastics in which elements are assigned a predetermined score or degree of difficulty, known as Base Value

(BV), which is linked to a Scale of Values (SOV) calculated by a group of skating experts. It is the responsibility of the judges to grade the quality of execution, taking cognisance of the BV and SOV. Second, scores were to be aggregated and the trimmed mean or average of the middle five scores out of nine determined. For example, a salchow has a BV of 0.4, while a quadruple salchow has a BV of 8.5 in the SOV. The panel of judges must evaluate each technical element identified by the caller in the routine and assign a Grade of Execution (GOE, from +3 to −3). Consequently, judges have seven grades of execution from which to choose and these can either add or subtract from the score. These seven grades are also listed in the SOV. As an example:

- Salchow – BV = 0.4, and the possible GOEs are: −0.3, −0.2, −0.1, 0, +0.3, +0.6, +1.
- Quadruple salchow – BV = 8.5, and the possible GOEs are: −3, −2, −1, 0, +1, +2, +3.

The trimmed mean is determined when an equal number of the highest and lowest judges' scores are excluded from the calculation and the average of the remaining grades is determined. For example, assuming a panel of nine judges and the assigned GOEs for a quadruple salchow are as follows: −2, 1, 1, 1, 1, 2, 2, −1, 2, the two highest (2, 2) and the two lowest (−2, −1) grades are removed from the grouping. The average of the remaining numbers is calculated (1+1+1+1+2 = 6; 6÷5 = 1.2). The panel's score for each element is then calculated by adding the trimmed mean (1.2) to the technical element's base value (8.5) for a total (9.7). The panel's scores for all the elements are added together to create a Total Element Score (TES). The next part of the adjudication process is to calculate the Programme Component Scores (PCS). The overall presentation and technical mastery is assessed on a scale of zero to ten and represents their overall skating ability and performance level and on five different components. These are:

- skating skills
- transitions/linking footwork
- performance/execution
- choreography/composition, and
- interpretation.

(Ice dancing is also graded on timing.)

The TES is then added to the five Programme Component Scores and any adjustments are applied to determine the Total Segment Score (TSS). Some examples of possible deductions include penalties incurred due to falls, time violations, music violations, illegal element violations and costume or prop violations. The final score or competition score is the total of the combined TSS, to produce the final competition ranking. More detailed information on the current system is available from the IJS Handbook (2010). The results of this modification are that the skaters earn points on what they successfully achieve and not what they attempt. Generally, modern ice skaters strive to undertake the most difficult elements for which the maximum grades of execution are available.

Boxing

Boxing is awash with controversial decisions in both the amateur (Olympic) and the professional codes of this contact sport. Knocking an opponent to the canvass in an amateur bout has no influence on the scoring/judging system, whereas in a professional bout, it counts for significantly more. Why should this inconsistency prevail? What is the rationale for the two different scoring/judging systems in essentially the same sport? Once again, the impetus for review and change in the scoring/judging systems can be traced back to controversial decisions, in both codes.

Firstly, let's examine the scoring system in the Olympics prior to 1988. In essence, the scoring was simple. Five judges scored the bout, a point was scored each time the white part of the glove landed on the front of the head/torso and each judge tallied the score on his card as the bout progressed. Controversy erupted when Roy Jones Jnr was robbed of the gold medal by a South Korean fighter, Park Si-Hun, despite pummelling Park for three rounds and landing 86 punches to Park's 32 (www.royjonesjr.com/biography). A subsequent official IOC investigation revealed that three of the judges were wined and dined by South Korean officials and all three who voted against Jones were suspended. The incident led to the IOC insisting on the development of a new scoring system.

1992 new scoring system

1. Five judges score the bout.
2. One point is scored if the white part of the glove lands on the front part of the head/torso, if point (3) is satisfied.
3. Each judge has two electronic buttons, one for each of the contestants. Three out of five of the judges must press the button within one second for the boxer to receive a point.

Bouts are scheduled for four, two-minute rounds. No points are awarded or deducted for a knockdown in Olympic boxing. Consequently, the introduction of this system has led to a radical change in fighting style (IOC, 2005). Competitors no longer strive to knock out an opponent. The aim has shifted to scoring as many points as possible through correct blows to the head and torso. The introduction of electronic scoring was an attempt to make officiating more objective. Interestingly, a series of studies by Coalter *et al.* (1998) and Mullan and O'Donoghue (2001) failed to improve on the accuracy of the scoring system and found that a minority (less than one third) of actual scoring punches are scored. Judges focussing on counting blows may lead to secondary errors, such as inattentional blindness, and may outweigh the aim of the new system. Furthermore, when there is a flurry of blows being traded, the time taken for the judge to review and process the information may be outside the one-second window, even for highly experienced judges (Brown, 2008).

Scoring a professional bout is an inherently subjective process. A prize fight is judged on four basic criteria, namely:

1. Clean punching
2. Effective aggressiveness
3. Ring generalship
4. Defence.

Unless the bout ends in a knockout or other stoppage, the winner is decided on the basis of the score cards submitted by three judges. The boxing rounds, of varying duration and number depending upon the competition, are scored on a ten-point must system in which the boxer winning the round is awarded the maximum permissible, namely ten. Consequently, his or her opponent will receive nine (or lower). Knockdowns count and usually result in the deduction of an extra point from the opponent's score. The abovementioned basic criteria are relatively self explanatory, with perhaps the exception of ring generalship, which is the ability of a fighter to control the pace and style of a fight. This basket of measures is subjective and consequently creates the necessary conditions under which boxing results, based on judges' decisions, are too readily challenged. Furthermore, each criterion should have equal weighting (25 per cent); however, clean punches tend to count more than the other three areas. Interestingly, boxing broadcasters often keep a tally of the punch statistics, but this data is not currently used by the judges to objectively assess performance. Judges cannot see each other's scores and cannot modify scores assigned from previous rounds. One of the most controversial results occurred on 13 March 1999 when heavyweight champions Lennox Lewis and Evander Holyfield fought to a draw. Many observers felt that Lewis had outperformed Holyfield, and one judge's results, in particular, drew much of the attention (Lee *et al.*, 2002). Eugenia Williams became the focus of speculation that the result of the contest was 'fixed' and an official investigation was prompted.

The match was watched by the three judges, using the same basket of measures described previously and following the common and well-developed ten-point scoring system. Table 12.1 shows the variability in scoring for each round and reproduces the score cards for the official judges and well-respected media commentators and pundits.

The first point of note is that there is variability in all the judges' scores over the bout. The most consistent scoring, however, was between the first three unofficial scorers, who returned precisely the same scores over each round. Nevertheless, focussing on the official scorers, it is important to review the variability in their scores and compare these to the unofficial scorers, since this is the prime source of controversy expressed in the media. On the basis of what we know, how can the discrepancies in the score cards be explained?

The scoring system itself can create an imbalance when the final scores are calculated. If boxer (A) wins five rounds by a 'definite' margin and his opponent (B) seven rounds by a close margin, then boxer (B) wins on the ten-point must system with a 115–113 score. The armchair fan or even boxing commentator is not rigorously completing and submitting a score card at the end of each round, instead, preferring to make judgements on general impressions made

Table 12.1 Scorecards for the 1999 Holyfield–Lewis Prize Fight

Scorer	Individual scores for the following rounds												Total
	1	2	3	4	5	6	7	8	9	10	11	12	
Officials													
Williams (USA)	L	L	H	H	H	L	L	H	H	H	H	L	115–113
O'Connell (UK)	L	L	H	L	L	H	E	H	H	E	H	L	115–115
Christodoulu (RSA)	L	L	H	L	L	L	L	H	H	H	E	L	113–116
Media and others													
HBO-Lederman	L	L	H	L	L	L	L	L	H	H	L	L	111–117
Sportsticker	L	L	H	L	L	L	L	L	H	H	L	L	111–117
Boxing Times	L	L	H	L	L	L	L	L	H	H	L	L	111–117
Sportsline	L	L	H	L	L	H	L	L	L	H	L	L	111–117
Associated Press	L	L	H	H	L	L	L	L	L	H	L	L	111–117
ESPN	L	L	L	L	L	L	L	L	L	H	L	L	109–119
Boxing Monthly	L	L	H	E	L	E	L	H	H	H	H	L	115–115

Note

H and L denote rounds in favour of Holyfield and Lewis, respectively, and E denotes even rounds (tie). All non-even rounds were scored 10–9 in favour of the fighter indicated.

over multiple rounds. Therefore, such impressions can be unduly influenced by fight statistics and slow-motion replays produced by the broadcasters and not available to the official judges. Furthermore, aggression and ring generalship are very subjective measures of performance, unlike clean punches and defence, which have slightly higher degrees of objectivity. Lewis won the rematch, by a decision.

In challenging bias in boxing or even corruption or incompetence in judging, it is first necessary to determine the variability of scoring that can lead to judges arriving at different conclusions after watching the same bout. The simple fact that they differ in opinion is not necessarily an indication of foul play. People always see things in slightly different ways and it is important to recognise the inherent variability in boxing scoring so that the sport can minimise its scoring controversies.

The role of technology in assisting the referee and umpire

The role of a referee or umpire is to make impartial and accurate judgements on both the spirit and the law of the sport. In some codes, such as soccer, they are the sole authority and their decision is final; in others, such as cricket, they can consult off-field umpires, who have access to a vast array of technology tools and can amend their decision according to the supplementary information available. Generally, referees and umpires are the on-field authority responsible for making discretionary decisions and enforcing the rules. Soccer referees make many hundreds of decisions per game and in the 2010 FIFA World Cup, 8 per cent of the decision events were inaccurate (Solomon *et al.*, 2011). Cricket umpires make fewer decisions, but, in terms of percentage correct, are much more accurate. There are many options available to sports governing bodies to improve the accuracy of decision making in sport. Some opt for additional human intervention and others rely more on technology intervention.

In soccer, the accuracy of decision making has been found to be a function of the distance the referee is away from the infringement or action (De Oliveira *et al.*, 2011). In their study of the 2002 under-20 Brazilian Championship, they indicated the optimum distance to achieve the maximum (80.6 per cent) correct decisions was 20.1 to 25 m. (Coincidently, in cricket, this is the approximate distance the facing umpire stands away from the facing batsman.) In order to minimise errors due to incorrect positioning of referees on the field, FIFA (1982) established a diagonal system of match control so that the referee and his or her assistants work in harmony to provide optimal adjudication cover on the pitch and can use communication devices to maintain contact (Mignerat and Audebrand, 2010). Furthermore, the experience level of the referee and crowd noise both influence the decision-making process. Home-team advantage is recognised and acknowledged in a wide variety of sports. Nevill *et al.* (2002) observed in their analysis a distinct bias when awarding fewer fouls to the home team. Gender bias has also been reported in handball (Souchon *et al.*, 2009). However, bias in soccer is inherently difficult to quantify and much additional work is required in this area to determine the potential causal mechanism and its magnitude (Lucey and Power, 2009).

Prior to the introduction of referral technology in cricket, umpires operated at ±93 per cent correct decisions on average. With the introduction of the Umpire Decision Review System by the International Cricket Council (ICC), accuracy went up to 98 per cent (PTI, 2011).[1] Rugby union and league use 'video refs' to make judgements on a number of rule infringements. In rugby league, the Television Match Official (TMO) is frequently called upon to review the grounding of the ball in try situations. In the view of many spectators, both in the stadium watching replays on big screen TVs and those viewing the broadcast at home, this anticipation of the result adds a new dimension to the game. Depending on the sport, the video ref can only adjudicate on certain aspects. For instance, in rugby, he/she is not permitted to adjudicate on forward passes, since the reliability of these calls varies on the camera angle and is not dependable.

Today, television replays are the *de facto* norm during live sports broadcasts. The instant replay of an action almost immediately post-event has become an integral part of the broadcasters' content package. This provides the armchair viewer the ability to review the decisions of on-field umpires and referees and quickly form their own opinions and conclusions. Since researchers have observed, with only ±80 per cent and ±93 per cent of correct decisions being made in soccer and cricket, respectively, the door was open for spectator criticism of an official's performance during telecasts. Some sports codes permit the use of video review in official in-game adjudication and others specifically exclude it. The role of the video referee varies between sports and very little consistency exists. However, in many sports, video evidence is almost universally admissible post-match – for example, in cases of misconduct, disciplinary sanctions or other match infringements by players or spectators.

Basketball was one of the pioneering sports to opt for video review and its first recorded use was in the 2002–3 season to determine whether the Lakers player Samaki Walker scored a field goal in Game 4 of the NBA 2002 Western Conference Finals. The video replay showed the ball was still in his hand as the match clock expired.

The ability to show videos in slow motion or from multiple angles provide the TV viewer with much more information for decision support than was available to the referee or umpire. In cricket, normal video cameras placed perpendicular to the wicket are capable of more accurately determining close dismissals via run-out than the unaided eye. Hence, cricket fans watching at home are capable of increasing the probability of a correct umpiring call than on-field officials. Historically, when the broadcast feed was relayed into the stadium's big TV screens, the images frequently caused frustration in the crowd when poor decisions were exposed. Consequently, in cricket, controversial decisions referred to the Third Umpire are not permitted to be shown on stadium screens until the final decision has been made.

From these simple beginnings, the video replay has evolved immensely, with high-speed (>1000 fps) cameras, thermal imaging, frame-by-frame analysis, graphical overlays, ball-trajectory tracking and such like finding application in a diverse range of sports.

In their quest to obtain the highest percentage accuracy of decision making, the ICC has driven the introduction of the Umpire Decision Review System (UDRS) over a period of years. It is now a cornerstone of all international matches, although not mandatory. It incorporates high-speed video cameras, audio analysis from stump microphones, approved ball-tracking technologies and thermal imaging. The UDRS (2011) is a complex process and a full explanation is available on-line from the ICC. In essence, each team is currently permitted two unsuccessful review requests per innings. The fielding team can challenge and dispute an umpire's not out call and the batting team an *out* call. The decision is then referred to an off-field, TV or Third Umpire for review. Subsequently, a number of options are available in the post-event analysis, by either verifying the first decision or correcting it. In cases where there is no clear reason on review to overturn an umpire's on-field call, then the original decision stands. Cricket is a game that can easily accommodate interruptions to play to permit the verification of decisions. Soccer, on the other hand, is a much more dynamic and fast-paced sport and, consequently, the governing body is reluctant to interfere during play and is currently resisting the introduction of the video replay in adjudication. However, one particular area of controversy and worthy of FIFA's high-level investigation is that of *goal-line technology*. The objective is to assist the referee in determining when the ball has crossed the goal-line. It appears FIFA are currently hesitant to introduce technology that interferes with the very fabric of the game, since their opinion is that the human element is an integral part of the sport. There are currently a number of proposals being evaluated by FIFA (up to March 2012), which include image processing (Hawk-Eye, Hawk-Eye Innovations, Basingstoke, UK) and sensors (Cairos, Cairos Technologies AG, Munich, Germany). Supporters of the proposed solutions contend that striving to obtain the correct decisions, in critical games during competition, outweighs the arguments regarding non-uniformity of rules and competitions. Due to the costs involved, the use of video tools in adjudication is generally reserved for use at the elite and professional levels.

In tennis, errors in line calls by chair umpires in the 2004 US Open stimulated the introduction of Hawk-Eye technology (en.wikipedia.org/wiki/Hawk-Eye#Tennis). By 2007, the system was used as an officiating aid on centre court with each player permitted access to the technology to challenge calls until they have made three incorrect challenges within the current set. The accuracy of the system is subject to much debate; however, it remains an engaging technology and one whose application is increasing worldwide.

On the horizon

The simplest of performance review processes in scoring and judging applications is the video replay. However, this tool is still to find universal acceptance in all sports. Other, more sophisticated approaches have been proposed that tend to focus on solving specific challenges in certain sports. In the majority of video review cases, human intervention interprets and then makes an informed decision based on the observed and reviewed content. Major research focus is shifting towards automated image processing in order to classify specific actions. Researchers are looking into real-time analysis of in-game events, such as goal-mouth incidents (Assfalg *et al.*, 2003; Wan *et al.*, 2003) to automatically identify and annotate match events and actions. Although object tracking shows some promising results, the proposed systems are a long way from the accuracy and reliability necessary for adjudication purposes (Chen *et al.*, 2009). In soccer, for the determination of off-side play, Maruenda (2009) has proposed that neither human nor machine is capable of error-free judging when determining an off-side position and, in his opinion, the rule should be scrapped.

The patent area in sports scoring and adjudication is exceptionally strong and a wide range of technologies have been proposed. These range from real-time sensors for determining when a basket is scored in basketball (Klein, 2009) to sensors on cricket wickets to determine whether the bails have been dislodged from the stumps (Eichstädt, 2003) and the ubiquitous ball tracking (Holthouse and van de Greindt, 2009). In taekwondo, the subjective nature of the scoring led to the development of a wearable vest (SensorHogu) that incorporates piezoelectric sensors that monitor the amount of force delivered to a body protector (Chi *et al.*, 2004). In the area of computer-augmented systems, Reilly *et al.* (2009) have proposed a general-purpose taxonomy system aimed at assisting researchers and designers to clarify these systems with respect to both form and function.

Due to the problems highlighted previously in the scoring of boxing, this sport has not avoided the researchers' attention (Hahn *et al.*, 2010). In an attempt to develop a system that outperforms the current system of judging, boxing has also witnessed the application of sensors that detect impact in an attempt to automate the scoring. Unfortunately, one of the system's current limitations is its inability to differentiate between valid scoring and non-scoring hits (Krajewski *et al.*, 2011).

Cricket has seen the further refinement of the Snikometer, a technology utilised by broadcasters that uses the audio component from the stump microphone to indicate when the ball had hit either the bat/pad or glove. Further refinement of the audio signal was proposed as the basis to develop an intelligent cricket decision-making system (Ting and Chilukuri, 2009). It

149

was proposed that the umpiring decision could be automated through audio analysis alone; however, poor accuracy limits its application. Nevertheless, it can be used very effectively in conjunction with video-based evidence.

One of the most entertaining and novel proposals is that of audience participation in scoring and judging. Van Beusekom *et al.* (2004) proposed that, by monitoring an audience's response to performance (i.e. clapping, cheering and waving), a fun and entertaining system could be developed that ranks athletes using a system that captures the audience's expressions and calculates an associated score. As an interesting concept, it has merit, but a number of serious drawbacks would limit its applicability in elite level sport (e.g. audience response along partisan lines or national pride, spectators not familiar with the rules or making inputs based on 'gut feel').

Concluding remarks

This chapter has provided an overview of the common problems encountered in scoring and judging of sport. The often subjective nature of the process of adjudication has been described and the most common approaches to improve reliability and reduce bias outlined. Two sports in particular, boxing and ice skating, were chosen as exemplars to highlight the challenges faced in both scoring and judging competitive sport. The role of adjudication in umpiring and refereeing was also described, as well as a technology scan of the aids currently on the horizon aimed at improving the decision-making process.

Note

1 Historically, the ICC published the percentage correct decisions by each umpire on the Elite and International Panel of Umpires on their web site. The publication of this sensitive data in the open press has now ceased. However, performance analysts working with elite level teams often gather this type of information to support the development of their team's tactical match plans.

References

Ansorge, C.J. and Scheer, J.K. (1988) 'International bias detected in judging gymnastics competition at the 1984 Olympic Games', *Research Quarterly for Exercise and Sport*, 59: 103–7.

Appleton, D.R. (1995) 'May the best man win', *The Statistician*, 44(4): 529–38.

Assfalg, J., Bertini, M., Colombo, C., Bimbo, A.D. and Nunziati, W. (2003) 'Semantic annotation of soccer videos: Automatic highlights identification', *Computer Vision and Image Understanding*, 92(2–3): 285–305.

Balmer, N.J., Nevill, A.M. and Lane, A.M. (2005) 'Do judges enhance home advantage in European championship boxing?', *Journal of Sports Sciences*, 23(4): 409–16.

Brown, B. (2008) 'Olympic boxing ruined: Scandal and rule changes have stripped Olympic boxing of former glory', http://bobby-brown.suite101.com/olympic-boxing-ruined-a64539 (accessed 26 October 2011).

Chen, H.-T., Tien, M.-C., Che, Y.-W., Tsai, W.-J. and Lee, S.-Y. (2009) 'Physics-based ball tracking and 3D trajectory reconstruction with applications to shooting location estimation in basketball video', *Journal of Visual Communication and Image Recognition*, 20: 204–16.

Chi, E.H., Song, J. and Corbin, G. (2004) '"Killer App" of wearable computing: Wireless force sensing body protectors for martial arts', paper presented at the ACM International Conference on Human Factors in Computing Systems, Vienna, Austria, April.

Clarke, S.R., Norman, J.M. and Stride, C.B. (2009) 'Criteria for a tournament: The World Professional Snooker Championship', *Journal of the Operational Research Society*, 60: 1670–3.

Coalter, A., Ingram, B., McCrory, P. MBE, O'Donoghue, P.G. and Scott, M. (1998) 'A comparison of alternative operation schemes for the computerised scoring system for amateur boxing', *Journal of Sports Sciences*, 16: 16–7.

Colwell, S. (2000) 'The "letter" and the "spirit": Football laws and refereeing in the twenty-first century', *Soccer and Society*, 1 (1): 201–14.

De Oliveira, M.C., Orbetelli, R. and De Barros Neto, T.L. (2011) 'Call accuracy and distance from the play: A study with Brazilian soccer referees', *International Journal of Exercise Science*, 4(1): 30–8.

Emerson, J.W, Seltzer, M. and Lin, D. (2009) 'Assessing judging bias: An example from the 2000 Olympic Games. Letter to the editor', *The American Statistician*, 63(4): 406.

Eichstädt, J.-L. (2003) *Patent Cooperation Treaty Application*, PCT/ZA2002/000162.

FIFA (1982) *Fédération Internationale de Football Association. FIFA H andbook: 1981–82*, 149, Zurich: FIFA.

Hahn, A.G., Helmer, R.J.N., Kelly, T., Partridge, K., Krajewski, A., Blanchonette, I., Barker, J., Bruch, H., Brydon, M., Hooke, N. and Andreass, B. (2010) 'Development of an automated scoring system for amateur boxing', *Procedia Engineering*, 2(2): 3095–101.

Hawson, L.A., McLean, A.N. and McGreevy, P.D. (2010) 'Variability of scores in the 2008 Olympic dressage competition and implications for horse training and welfare', *Journal of Veterinary Behaviour*, 5: 170–6.

Holthouse, S. and van de Greindt, I. (2009) 'Tracking balls in sports', *European Patent Application*, EP2 025 372 A2.

IJS Handbook (2010) www.usfsa.org/content/2010-11%20IJS%20Handbook.pdf (accessed 26 October 2011).

IOC (2005) *Olympic Programme Commission*, Report on 117th IOC Session, www.olympic.org/Documents/Reports/EN/en_report_1153.pdf (accessed 26 October 2011).

Klein, W.M. (2009) *Real-Time Wireless Sensor Scoring*, US Patent 2009/0191988.

Krajewski, A., Helmer. R.J.N. and Lucas, S.R. (2011) 'Signal processing for valid score determination in amateur boxing', *Procedia Engineering*, 13: 481–6.

Lee, H.K.H., Cork, D.L. and Algranti, D.J. (2002) 'Did Lennox Lewis beat Evander Holyfield? Methods for analysing small sample interrater agreement problems', *Journal of the Royal Statistical Society. Series D (The Statistician)*, 51(2): 129–46.

Lucey, B.M. and Power, D.A. (2009) 'Do soccer referees display home bias?', available at SSRN: http://ssrn.com/abstract=552223 (accessed 26 October 2011).

Maruenda, F.B. (2009) 'An offside position in football cannot be detected in zero milliseconds', available from Nature Precedings: http://hdl.handle.net/10101/npre.2009.3835.1 (accessed 26 October 2011).

Mignerat, M. and Audebrand. L.K. (2010) 'Towards the adoption of e-refereeing and e-ticketing in elite soccer championships: An institutional perspective', *ICIS 2010 Proceedings. Paper 114*, http://aisel.aisnet.org/icis2010_submissions/114 (accessed 26 October 2011).

Mullan, A. and O'Donoghue, P.G. (2001) 'An alternative computerised scoring system for amateur boxing', in M. Hughes and I.M. Franks (eds), *Proceedings of the World Congress of Performance Analysis, Sports Science and Computers (PASS.COM)* (pp. 359–64). Cardiff: CPA Press, UWIC.

Nevill, A.M., Balmer, N.J. and Williams, A.M. (2002) 'The influence of crowd noise and experience upon refereeing decisions in football', *Psychology of Sport and Exercise*, 3: 261–72.

Pollard, Geoff and Pollard, Graham (2010) 'The efficiency of tennis doubles scoring systems', *Journal of Sports Science and Medicine*, 9: 393–7.

Popović, R. (2000) 'International bias detected in judging rhythmic gymnastics competition at Sydney 2000 Olympic Games', *Facta Universitatis (Series: Physical Education and Sport)*, 1: 1–13.

PTI (2011) 'Press Trust of India. ICC believes DRS is improving accuracy of umpiring decisions', *TheSports Campus*, http://articles.timesofindia.indiatimes.com/2011-09-04/top-stories/30112421_1_drs-ball-tracking-technology-number-of-correct-decisions (accessed 10 September 2012).

Reilly, S., Barron, P., Cahill, V., Moran. K. and Haahr. M. (2009) 'A general-purpose taxonomy of computer-augmented sports systems', *Digital Sport for Performance Enhancement and Competitive Evolution: Intelligent Gaming Technologies*, IGI Global, 2009: 19–35, www.igi-global.com/chapter/digital-sport-performance-enhancement-competitive/8532 (accessed 26 October 2011).

Solomon, A.V., Paik, C., Alhauli, A. and Phan, T. (2011) 'A decision support system for the professional soccer referee in time-sensitive operations', *Systems and Information Engineering Design Symposium (SIEDS)*, IEEE, 35–40.

Souchon, N., Cabagno, G., Rascle, O., Traclet, A., Dosseville, F. and Maio, G.R. (2009) 'Referees' decision making about transgressions: The influence of player gender at the highest national level', *Psychology of Women Quarterly*, 33(4): 445–52.

Swift, E.M. (2002) 'Thorny issue', *Sports Illustrated Web Vault*, http://sportsillustrated.cnn.com/vault/article/magazine/MAG1024982/index.htm (accessed 26 October 2011).

Ting, S. and Chilukuri, M.V. (2009) 'Novel pattern recognition technique for an intelligent cricket decision making system', paper presented at the 12th MTC-International Instrumentation and Measurement Technology Conference', Singapore, May.

UDRS (2011) 'The Umpire Decision Review System', http://static.icc-cricket.com/ugc/documents/DOC_39EFCA4C7A2F335D543EF937F162F837_1257924398353_687.pdf (accessed 10 September 2012)..

Van Beusekom, M., Bignert, J. and Taşar. Ő. (2004) 'SoMo: An automated sound and motion sensitive audience voting system', in *CHI '04: CHI '04 Extended Abstracts on Human Factors in Computing Systems*, Vienna, 24–29 April, 1680–4.

Wan, K., Yan, X., Yu, X. and Xu, C. (2003) 'Real-time goal-mouth detection in MPEG soccer video', paper presented at the 11th Annual ACM International Conference on Multimedia, Berkeley, Ca, November.

Wolframm, I. (2010a) 'Natural bias, the hidden controversy in judging sports', www.eurodressage.com/equestrian/2010/11/04/natural-bias-hidden-controversy-judging-sports (accessed 26 October 2011).

Wolframm, I. (2010b) 'Judging systems in the firing line at the 2010 Global Dressage Forum', www.eurodressage.com/equestrian/2010/10/29/judging-system-firing-line-2010-global-dressage-forum (accessed 26 October 2011).

Zitzewitz, E. (2006) 'Nationalism in winter sports judging and its lessons for organisational decision making', *Journal of Economics and Management Strategy*, 15(1): 67–99.

Zitzewitz, E (2010) 'Does transparency really increase corruption? Evidence from the "reform" of figure skating judging', www.dartmouth.edu/~ericz/transparency.pdf (accessed 29 March 2011).

SECTION III

Sports performance analysis in professional contexts

13

PERFORMANCE ANALYSIS, FEEDBACK AND COMMUNICATION IN COACHING

Peter O'Donoghue and Anna Mayes

CARDIFF METROPOLITAN UNIVERSITY, UK

Summary

Sports performances are complex and dynamic situations that yield a potentially large volume of quantitative and qualitative information. Coaches need to identify and act on the most critical information to help players improve. The role of performance analysis within the coaching process is to produce quantitative information allowing areas requiring attention to be quickly identified. This allows coaches to focus on those areas requiring attention and to select video sequences to discuss with players through interactive use of video analysis systems. Coaches and players can then engage in detailed analysis of video sequences, identifying why and how performance can improve and to make decisions about training to enhance performance. The use of information by coaches and how it is communicated to players has evolved as performance analysis technology has developed in recent years.

Introduction

Coaching is the main application area of performance analysis. Several models of performance analysis within coaching have been proposed over the years, including the feedback models of Lees (2008), Irwin *et al.* (2005), Franks (1997), Winkler (1988), O'Donoghue (2006) and Mayes *et al.* (2009). Performance analysis processes used in coaching depend on a number of factors, including the nature of the sport, the level of the athletes and access to technology. This chapter will cover the typical model used with video feedback technology in formal games, as well as a typical model used in technique-intensive sports. With video feedback being provided over the internet, the chapter will also cover the use of internet video streaming within the coaching process and its potential for remote analysis.

Rationale for performance analysis support

Providing feedback is an essential part of the coaching process if athletes are to improve (Maslovat and Franks, 2008). Athletes receive sensory feedback from experiencing the sport, including sight, sound, tactile and proprioceptive information. Augmented feedback (or extrinsic feedback) is additional information provided to help athletes improve. Augmented feedback can be provided by a coach who observes and analyses the performances of athletes. However, there are limitations to the accuracy with which coaches can recall critical events within the performance (Maslovat and Franks, 2008). Franks and Miller (1986) found that international level soccer coaches recalled less than 45 per cent of critical events during a match. Coach education has changed over the period since, with continuous professional development enhancing the quality of coaching. When Laird and Waters (2008) repeated the study of Franks and Miller on UEFA-qualified coaches, the coaches recalled 59 per cent of critical events. While this is an improvement, there is still a large number of critical events that are not being accurately recalled by coaches. A further issue is the possibility of biased observation by coaches or emotions influencing the accuracy of their evaluations (Maslovat and Franks, 2008). Therefore, the augmented feedback provided by coaches should be supported by performance analysis.

The information provided to coaches and players by performance analysis support can be broadly classified as quantitative and qualitative. The quantitative information provided in game sports includes match statistics, which can be presented as tables, charts or special-purpose diagrams of the playing surface, showing the location of events. These statistics can help identify areas of performance that require more detailed attention during analysis. Event frequencies on their own can provide some indication of how a team played. Where event outcomes are also included, areas where performance can improve can be rapidly identified. For example, if the number of points won and lost in a tennis match is displayed for points where different types of serve are used, then any serve type that leads to a relatively low proportion of points won can be targeted for more detailed analysis. Similarly, different types and length of pass made in a team game can be assessed based on the percentages that are successfully received by a teammate. This not only allows areas requiring attention to be recognised, but also allows areas where players and teams are performing well to be identified.

Once the match statistics have been assessed, video analysis packages can be used to interactively view video sequences of events based on criteria of interest. For example, if the statistics have deemed that a player wins fewer points when using a slice serve to advantage service court than when using other serves, then the coach can very quickly view video sequences of points lost when the player used the slice serve to the advantage service court. This qualitative viewing of the events by coaches allows more detailed qualitative analysis to be done, identifying how events were performed and why they may not have been performed as well as other events. This can also allow the coach to identify how players and teams may be able to improve performance in these areas and devise training activities to help enhance performance. Once the coach has viewed candidate video sequences for event types of interest, key clips for discussion with players can be selected. Coaches and players can then view these key sequences, engaging in detailed conversations about performance while viewing relevant video sequences. In this sense, performance analysis support involves analysts analysing what problems exist, with coaches and players doing more in-depth analysis of how and why problems occurred and how to enhance performance. The role of the analyst in tagging the match video, providing match statistics and a means of interactively viewing video sequences is important in helping coaches and players focus on the aspects of play most requiring attention. The discussions between players and coaches and decisions made about preparation have been facilitated by performance analysis support.

Performance analysis within coaching

Information needs

There are some general principles that should be observed when providing performance analysis support to coaches and athletes. First, the system used should be dictated by the information needs of the coaching processes that the system serves. Coaches make decisions based on aspects of performance that are important to the style of play used. Those performance indicators that genuinely represent these aspects of performance should be the highest priorities of the analysis system. Once the information needs of coaches and players are understood, the raw event data required to produce this information can be determined. The system can then be developed to allow the event data to be recorded and performance indicators to be produced in the most efficient way. Regardless of whether manual methods are being used or computer technology is being used, the system should be developed in a user-friendly way to ease the task of data collection and provision of feedback.

Reliability

O'Donoghue and Longville (2004) argued for the importance of reliability in performance analysis support work. This is because important decisions about team and player preparation are made using the information. O'Donoghue and Longville (2004) proposed the use of consistency checking to improve the reliability of data collected using performance analysis systems prior to the processing of performance indicators and selection of related video clips. For example, a point in tennis may be recorded with details of who served, the number of shots played, whether the point ended on a winner or an error and who won the point. If the serving player won the point with a winner or lost the point with an error, then there must have been an odd number of shots played. If, on the other hand, the serving player won the point through an opponent error or lost the point through an opponent winner, then there must have been an even number of shots played. These conditions can be tested by systems highlighting data entry errors that can be corrected relatively quickly after the match. This consistency checking and correction process should not be viewed as 'cheating' by the analyst; it should be viewed as part of the method of data collection, which is not completed until the various consistency checking tasks have been completed.

Models of performance analysis support

Models for technique-intensive sports

The importance of technique varies between sports. Lees (2008) classified skills as event skills, major skills and minor skills. Event skills are skills that are themselves the sports performance of interest – for example, the high jump. Major skills are not complete sporting events in their own right but are dominant within the given sporting event. For example, hurdle clearance would be a major skill within the 400 m hurdles. Minor skills are important but do not dominate the sporting performance of interest – for example, kicking a football in a game of soccer. This section is concerned with models of performance analysis support for technique-intensive sports that involve major skills or event skills.

Two similar models are discussed: Lees (2008) described a two-phase approach to the use of qualitative biomechanics in sports performance, while Irwin *et al.* (2005) describe a process where coaches work with biomechanists to improve the performance of athletes. Lees (2008) described a model of two broad phases. In the first phase, detailed observation is undertaken to diagnose faults in technique. The second stage is a remediation stage, where performance is enhanced through instruction.

Irwin *et al.*'s (2005) conceptual model of technique and performance describes how coaches develop skills in athletes with the aid of biomechanical support. This model recognises sources of biomechanical and coaching knowledge and consists of five phases:

1. development of a mindset of technique (conceptual understanding of technical aspects of the skill)
2. understanding the fundamental components of the technique
3. replication of the spatio-temporal characteristics of the technique
4. developing training drills
5. development of technique.

Both the models of Lees (2008) and Irwin *et al.* (2005) make use of abstract models of technique that make the processes of fault identification and performance enhancement more manageable. Hierarchical models show how an overall performance outcome, such as long jump distance, is determined from key technical variables which themselves are determined from other technical variables (Hay and Reid, 1988). There are also sequential models that represent a skill as a sequence of phases presented in chronological order (Lees, 2008).

These models have an important role to play because the identification of faults and development of training drills require an accurate technical understanding of the skill. Coaching is informed about biomechanical aspects of technique through the 'coaching-biomechanics interface' (Kerwin and Irwin, 2008). This enhances the coach's knowledge about the underlying principles of movement and how they apply to key aspects of the skill being considered. It gives a better understanding of those aspects of technique that are most associated with successful performance of the skill.

Models of technique can be used in experimentation with athletes. For example, Kerwin and Irwin (2008) described how quantitative biomechanics was used to determine the optimal block setting to give an Olympic sprint athlete a more effective sprint start. Models can also be used in simulation studies to investigate the potential effects on outcome of minor changes in different parts of the technique. Due to the nature of the equipment involved and the data being analysed, these uses of biomechanical models require close cooperation between coaches and biomechanists.

Franks' model

The most widely used model of the coaching process in performance analysis literature is that of Franks *et al.* (1983). This simple model was presented as a flowchart of activity, with athletes performing and coaches observing with performance analysis support. The coach's evaluation of performance from observation is qualitative and subjective. The role of performance analysis in the coaching process is to provide additional feedback based on a more systematic and objective analysis. The information produced by performance analysis includes quantitative information. Franks *et al.*'s model of the coaching process has been widely used in academia and in sports practice, with organisations such as the National Coaching Foundation (NCF) in the UK adopting it. Some variants of the model have elaborated some activities to show different stages of data processing between video recording of a match and providing feedback to players (Franks, 1997).

Magill (2001) classified feedback as being sensory or augmented. Players receive sensory feedback from their own experience of competing in sport. This sensory feedback includes visual, audio, proprioceptive and tactile data. Augmented feedback is additional feedback provided to players in the form of video sequences, images, quantitative results and qualitative findings about performance. Franks (1997) showed some excellent examples of statistical and graphical outputs from performance analysis that have good visual impact and communicate important aspects to players and coaches. As technology has developed over the years, there has been greater scope to provide even more sophisticated graphical information, using systems such as Dartfish (Dartfish, Fribourg, Switzerland), Hawk-Eye (Hawk-Eye Innovations, Basingstoke, UK), Prozone (Prozone Sports Ltd, Leeds, UK), Amisco (Amisco, Nice, France) and Catapult (Catapult Sports, South Melbourne, Victoria, Australia). Performance analysis has a role in the provision of augmented feedback, which is particularly important to help athletes improve (Franks, 1997). This augmented information provides additional perspectives on the performance that the athletes would not have access to from their own experiences of competing in the sport. Augmented feedback includes information about the outcome and process of performing events during competition or training. Consider a given stroke in tennis: outcome indicators are concerned with the effectiveness of the stroke in terms of winners, errors or getting the ball back into the opponent's court. Process indicators are concerned with the way in which the stroke was played, going into detail of the technique used. Knowledge of results (outcomes) can identify broad areas that require attention, with knowledge of performance helping detailed decisions about why problems have occurred and how they may be addressed.

Any information used must be capable of being evaluated by the coach and players. It is essential to have some understanding of what high, low and average values are. There are several ways in which this can be done. Franks (1997) showed how data from recent performances could be used to develop baseline measures for a performer or team. This baseline information could then be used when evaluating performances in a tournament situation. Hughes and Bartlett (2002) introduced the term 'performance indicators' within performance analysis of sport. They proposed three alternative ways of using performance indicators: (a) to compare performance with that of an opponent, (b) to compare with values for a peer group of performers, or (c) in isolation. The first two of these are means of evaluating performances. Comparison with peer group performances has been developed further through the use of norms for matches against different qualities of opposition (O'Donoghue, 2006; O'Donoghue *et al.*, 2008; O'Donoghue and Cullinane, 2011).

Winkler's model

There are a number of models of performance analysis process that have been used in coaching, with individual models being influenced by the type of sport and resources available. One of the earliest models for feedback and control in professional soccer was presented by Winkler (1988). This model represented observational analysis activity within the coaching process, a cycle of activity involving systematic observation of matches and training, evaluation of the data gathered and providing feedback to the squad. An important point made by Winkler was that there should be clear aims and purpose to any observation done. This is an aspect of performance analysis that has been consistent in further models that have been developed. According to Winkler, systematic game analysis is only possible if:

- the aims of observation are clearly defined
- observation methods include the use of technical aids (video and computer equipment)

- there is a viable means of analysis of observation
- results are presented in the form of video sequences, figures, graphs and tables
- results are interpreted and stored for later reference.

Performance analysis within the Norwegian FA

The Norwegian national football squads were among the first international soccer squads to introduce performance analysis (match analysis) into the coaching process. The approach was distinguished from other match analysis processes used in soccer since then because the information produced was the information required to analyse the effectiveness of the style of play used by Norwegian squads (Olsen and Larsen, 1997). This is a direct style of play aiming to penetrate the opposing defence and capitalise, especially when the opposing defence is unbalanced. The system used by the Norwegian FA bridged the gap between research and practice, and the match analysis support was developed during a three-phase programme. First, the system was developed for analysing individual matches. The second step introduced match event databases, while the third step provided interactive video feedback. This is commonplace today, with many commercial systems such as Sportscode and Focus providing such features. However, in the mid-1990s, this was highly innovative and allowed Norway to maximise its limited playing population (Olsen and Larsen, 1997). During this period, it is notable that Norway qualified for the 1994 World Cup ahead of two of Europe's leading soccer nations (Holland and England) and, in the 1998 World Cup, they defeated Brazil during the pool stage and qualified for the second round.

Interactive video feedback systems

The emergence of multimedia computer technology has been exploited by performance analysis of sport. The MAVIS (Match Analysis Video Integrated System) was an early prototype developed in the Borland Delphi programming language (O'Donoghue *et al.*, 1995, 1996). Commercial packages have been developed since and used extensively in coaching in many sports. Packages such as Sportscode (SportsTec, Warriewood, Australia) and Focus X2 (Elite Sports Analysis, Fife, UK) are generic packages that can be tailored to record and analyse details of the specific events in a given sport. These systems integrate the video information with a database of recorded events (O'Donoghue, 2006; Hughes, 2008) so that users can inspect matrices of events and outcomes and set criteria for video sequences to be displayed. There are many different ways video can be used to enhance performance, including instructional and motivational feedback, video profiles of key opponents and videos focussing on a single area of technique (O'Donoghue, 2006).

Research into the effectiveness of feedback produced using interactive video analysis systems cannot be controlled like laboratory experiments. There are many variables outside the control of researchers that impact on sports performance. This has discouraged many researchers from investigating the effectiveness of performance analysis support for athletes. However, there are some studies and experience reports that have provided evidence that performance analysis support can be effective. Brown and Hughes (1995) used athlete diaries to record details of training that might influence performance in squash. Murray *et al.* (1998) provided further evidence that the provision of feedback to elite and non-elite squash players might be responsible for an improvement in performance observed. Factors such as quality of opposition have an effect on performance. Therefore, studies of performance within knockout tournaments may see performance indicator values decline, simply because the quality of opposition increases as a team progresses through the tournament (Martin *et al.*, 2004).

There are various models of the coaching process and how feedback is provided to players within a cycle of preparation and competition (Winkler, 1988; Franks *et al.*, 1983; Hughes, 2008). These models describe how audio-visual aids and commercial computerised systems are used within the process of analysing a performance and preparing feedback for players. Gasston (2004) reported that such models often failed to recognise the need to fit performance analysis and feedback activities within the players' schedules of training, competition, recovery, medical support, eating and sleeping. This is especially true in sports where there may be competition on a daily basis during tournaments, such as netball.

Jenkins *et al.* (2007) used the Focus X2 package to provide instructional and motivational feedback to a university netball squad over a series of eight matches. This study showed some areas where feedback was effective in aiding coach decision making, team preparation and subsequent team performance. There were other areas that remained unchanged and some where performance deteriorated. The study showed how an injury keeping a key player out of the squad for the last four matches could affect performance indicator values. One of the main findings of the work of Jenkins *et al.* (2007) was that areas requiring attention that had been identified by performance analysis were often not dealt with in training because they were problems that would require a long-term solution. Shorter-term tactical aspects could be addressed more effectively within match-to-match cycles. A further finding was that some aspects of the game needed to be practised regularly, even where performance analysis did not identify problems with them. This is particularly true of fundamental aspects of the game that are encountered regularly by players during competition.

Internet technology

There have been major technological advances in recent years (Lieberman *et al.*, 2002) that have not only made the process of performance analysis support more efficient, but have also changed the way in which feedback can be provided. Video sequences can now be provided by internet streaming for players to view at times and locations convenient to them. Systems such as Replay (Replay Analysis Limited, London, UK) and Team Performance Exchange (Team Performance Exchange, Best, Netherlands) allow video sequences to be accessed securely by players prior to training sessions. This allows squads to make better use of training time as feedback and discussion about areas of previous performance can be done on-line in the days before the next squad training session. This technology is especially useful for travelling athletes (such as tennis players on the ATP or WTA tours) or teams of players who live in different areas. Mayes *et al.* (2009) described how the use of performance analysis video streaming has enhanced the coaching process. A greater volume of video feedback has been provided to players through internet streaming than would have been possible before this type of system was used. Figure 13.1 shows the model used by Mayes *et al.* (2009).

Research and action (decision making) are often done separately by different groups of individuals: researchers and policy makers. Some research findings may never be used to inform decisions, some research is used indirectly and other research studies may be commissioned by policy makers in order to obtain independent evidence to inform decisions. The term 'action research' represents a cycle of action and research within a real-world situation. Action research can be done on a range of scales, from the reflective practice of individual professionals (Schön, 1983) to a very large scale for entire organisational change (Zuber-Skerritt, 1996). The role of performance analysis within a coaching context is essentially one that follows four key stages of action research: observing, reflecting, planning and acting. Figure 13.1 shows a modified version of a model of performance analysis activity within the coaching process (Mayes *et al.*,

2009). When a match is played, it is observed, with match events being entered into a match analysis system live. Match statistics are produced and performance indicator values are compared to norms for the level of opposition faced in the match (O'Donoghue *et al.*, 2008), allowing areas requiring attention to be identified. Commercial match analysis packages have password-protected internet sites for relevant video sequences to be uploaded and viewed by the squad. This helps the squad discuss and reflect on the performance prior to the next training session. Coaches can plan training sessions to specifically address areas where the squad needs to improve. The action taken in training and subsequent match performance can then be evaluated. This activity is repeated in a cyclical fashion throughout the season in a process of gradually improving the quality of performance. The most important aspect of the model of Mayes *et al.* (2009) is that it is an athlete-centred model, where the intention is to make every player a better player through a coaching process in which different forms of information flow between coaches and players in both directions.

The underlying paradigm of action research is critical theory, which has been described by Cohen *et al.* (2007: 26–32). The four stages of description, information, confrontation and reconstruction used in critical reflection (Smyth, 1989) are relevant to the way performance analysts work in practice. The performance analyst working with a squad will analyse squad performance, providing a description of the current situation. Analysis of sports performance data identifies areas of the squad's performance that can improve. This empowers the squad and challenges the status quo of the squad's situation within the sport, threatening the interests of dominant squads. The confrontation stage is also relevant to performance analysis in practice as

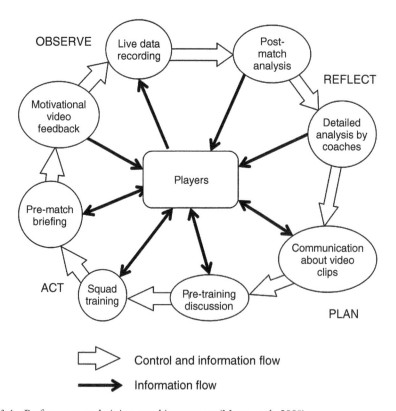

Figure 13.1 Performance analysis in a coaching context (Mayes *et al.*, 2009)

the squad is determining ways in which it can improve. The reconstruction stage is where decisions are made about squad preparation to specifically improve performance. The effectiveness of decisions made and action taken is evaluated during analysis of training and subsequent competition. Critical theory has a transforming intention and seeks to ensure the catalytic validity of research, meaning that the research can be an agent of change. This is a role of performance analysis as well as the wider coaching process.

Concluding remarks

This chapter has reiterated the rationale for performance analysis support in coaching that has been made by Franks and Miller (1986) and Laird and Waters (2008) previously. There are general principles of performance analysis support in coaching that apply irrespective of the particular coaching process that is used. There are a variety of coaching processes that typically work in a cycle of diagnosing problems and developing solutions. In game sports, where tactical information is paramount, the models have evolved with technological developments in performance analysis. Similarly, in technique-intensive sports, different models have been proposed where qualitative biomechanics is being used (Lees, 2008) and where quantitative biomechanics support is being provided (Irwin *et al.*, 2005; Kerwin and Irwin, 2008).

References

Brown, D. and Hughes, M. (1995) 'The effectiveness of quantitative and qualitative feedback on performance in squash', in T. Reilly, M. Hughes and A. Lees (eds), *Science and Racket Sport* (pp. 232–7). London: E & FN Spon.

Cohen, L., Manion, L. and Morrison, K. (2007) *Research Methods in Education* (6th ed.), London: Routledge.

Franks, I.M. (1997) 'Use of feedback by coaches and players', in T. Reilly, J. Bangsbo and M. Hughes (eds), *Science and Football 3* (pp. 267–78). London: E & FN Spon.

Franks, I.M. and Miller, G. (1986) 'Eyewitness testimony in sport', *Journal of Sport Behaviour*, 9: 39–45.

Franks, I.M., Goodman, D. and Miller, G. (1983) 'Analysis of performance: Qualitative or quantitative', *Science Periodical of Research and Technology in Sport*, March: 1–8.

Gasston, V. (2004) 'Performance analysis during an elite netball tournament: Experiences and recommendations', in P.G. O'Donoghue and M. Hughes (eds), *Performance Analysis of Sport 6* (pp. 8–14). Cardiff: CPA Press, UWIC.

Hay, J.G. and Reid, J.G. (1988) *Anatomy, Mechanics and Human Motion*, Englewood Cliffs, NJ: Prentice Hall.

Hughes, M. (2008) 'Notational analysis for coaches', in R.L. Jones, M. Hughes and K. Kingston (eds), *An Introduction to Sports Coaching: From Science and Theory to Practice* (pp. 103–13). London: Routledge.

Hughes, M. and Bartlett, R. (2002) 'The use of performance indicators in performance analysis', *Journal of Sports Sciences*, 20: 739–54.

Irwin, G., Hanton, S. and Kerwin, D.G. (2005) 'The conceptual process of progression development in artistic gymnastics', *Journal of Sports Sciences*, 23: 1089–99.

Jenkins, R.E., Morgan, L. and O'Donoghue, P.G. (2007) 'A case study into the effectiveness of computerized match analysis and motivational videos within the coaching of a league netball team', *International Journal of Performance Analysis of Sport*, 7(2): 59–80.

Kerwin, D.G. and Irwin, G. (2008) 'Biomechanics for coaches', in R.L. Jones, M.D. Hughes and K. Kingston, K. (eds), *An Introduction to Sports Coaching: From Science and Theory to Practice* (pp. 87–100). London: Routledge.

Laird, P. and Waters, L. (2008) 'Eye-witness recollection of sports coaches', *International Journal of Performance Analysis of Sport*, 8(1): 76–84.

Lees, A. (2008) 'Qualitative biomechanical analysis of technique', in M. Hughes and I.M. Franks (eds), *The Essentials of Performance Analysis: An Introduction* (pp. 162–79). London: Routledge.

Liebermann, D., Katz, L., Hughes, M.D., Bartlett, R.M., McClements, J. and Franks, I.M. (2002) 'Advances in the application of information technology to sports performance', *Journal of Sports Sciences*, 20: 755–69.

Magill, R.A. (2001) *Motor Learning: Concepts and Applications* (6th international ed.), Singapore: McGraw-Hill.

Martin, D., Cassidy, D. and O'Donoghue, P.G. (2004) 'The effectiveness of performance analysis in elite Gaelic football', paper presented at the World Congress of Performance Analysis of Sport 6, June.

Maslovat, D. and Franks, I.M. (2008) 'The need for feedback', in M. Hughes and I.M. Franks (eds), *The Essentials of Performance Analysis: An Introduction* (pp. 1–7). London: Routledge.

Mayes, A., O'Donoghue, P.G., Garland, J. and Davidson, A. (2009) 'The use of performance analysis and internet video streaming during elite netball preparation', poster presented at the 3rd International Workshop of the International Society of Performance Analysis of Sport, Lincoln, UK, April.

Murray, S., Maylor, D. and Hughes, M. (1998) 'A preliminary investigation into the provision of computerised analysis feedback to elite squash players', in A. Lees, I. Maynard, M. Hughes and T. Reilly (eds), *Science and Racket Sports II* (pp. 235–40). London: E & FN Spon.

O'Donoghue, P.G. (2006) 'The use of feedback videos in sport', in H. Dancs, M. Hughes and P.G. O'Donoghue (eds), *Performance Analysis of Sport 7* (pp. 126–37). Cardiff: CPA Press, UWIC.

O'Donoghue, P.G. and Longville, J. (2004) 'Reliability testing and the use of statistics in performance analysis support: A case study from an international netball tournament', in P.G. O'Donoghue and M. Hughes (eds), *Performance Analysis of Sport 6* (pp. 1–7), Cardiff: CPA Press, UWIC.

O'Donoghue, P.G. and Cullinane, A. (2011) 'A regression-based approach to interpreting sports performance', *International Journal of Performance Analysis in Sport*, 11: 295–307.

O'Donoghue, P.G., Robinson, J. and Murphy, M.H. (1995) 'An object oriented intelligent notational analysis multimedia database system', paper presented at the Object Oriented Information Systems Conference, Dublin, Ireland, December.

O'Donoghue, P.G., Robinson, J. and Murphy, M.H. (1996) 'MAVIS: A multimedia match analysis system to support immediate video feedback for coaching', in M. Hughes (ed.), *Notational Analysis of Sport III* (pp. 276–85). Cardiff: CPA Press, UWIC.

O'Donoghue, P.G., Mayes, A., Edwards, K.M. and Garland, J. (2008) 'Performance norms for British National Super League netball', *International Journal of Sports Science and Coaching*, 3: 501–11.

Olsen, E. and Larsen, O. (1997) 'Use of match analysis by coaches', in T. Reilly, J. Bangsbo and M. Hughes (eds), *Science and Football 3* (pp. 209–20). London: E & FN Spon.

Schön, D.A. (1983) *The Reflective Practitioner. How Professionals Think in Action*, London: Temple Smith.

Smyth, J. (1989) 'Developing and sustaining critical reflection in teacher education', *Journal of Teacher Education*, 40(2): 2–9.

Winkler, W. (1988) 'A new approach to the video analysis of tactical aspects of soccer', in T. Reilly, A. Lees, K. Davids and W. Murphy (eds), *Science and Football* (pp. 368–72). London: E & FN Spon.

Zuber-Skerritt, O. (1996) 'Emancipatory action research for organisation change and management development', in O. Zuber-Skerritt (ed.), *New Directions in Action Research* (pp. 83–105). London: Falmer.

14

COACH BEHAVIOUR

Peter O'Donoghue and Anna Mayes

CARDIFF METROPOLITAN UNIVERSITY, UK

Summary

There are different coaching styles that are appropriate with different types of athletes. The factors that influence coaching style include the type of sport, gender, age and level of the athletes. Coaches also use different styles between training sessions and competitive matches. Different behaviour analysis systems have been proposed, including the Arizona State University Observation Instrument (ASUOI), which can be used with a single variable or two variables. Using a limited number of variables and combining behaviour classes can improve reliability. However, some coaches may want more detailed information when reflecting on their behaviour. Therefore, other more complex systems use as many as seven variables (Harries-Jenkins and Hughes, 1995). There is a trade-off between reliability and detail of coach behaviour analysis systems. In scientific research, simpler instruments such as the ASUOI have been used due to the levels of reliability achieved. The more complex systems are preferred in coach education and reflective practice.

Introduction

'Coaching process' is an all-embracing term incorporating planning, delivery and management (Lyle, 2002). Successful coaching depends on the knowledge of the coach, the 'coachability' of the athletes, the ability of the coach in planning and designing training schedules, and decision making of the coach, as well as the behaviour of the coach during instructional sessions and competition. This chapter covers coach behaviour and how it is analysed in scientific research as well as within reflective practice by coaches. This will cover observational analysis methods and their application to the study of coach behaviour. Some systems record instructional behaviours of coaches (Lacy and Darst, 1984), while others analyse athletes' time performing different tasks (Smith *et al.*, 2005), as well as coach–athlete interactions (Hastie, 1999). There are limitations to observational methods and some aspects of coaching delivery should be investigated using other methods. For example, Strean (1998) suggested using interpretive interviews to allow a more substantial understanding, while Culver and Trudel (2006) used semi-structured interviews.

The rationale for analysing coaching behaviour is similar to that of teaching style. An understanding of successful coaching styles can be beneficial to aspiring coaches, and evaluation of coach behaviour can identify areas for improvement. Research in education is much more developed than research in coaching. Therefore, research in teaching behaviour has been a foundation for research in coach behaviour. More (2008) described the historical development of observational analysis in teaching and coaching. The purpose of this chapter is to provide an up-to-date review of analysis of coach behaviour and suggest areas for future research efforts.

Performance analysis can be used within coach development programmes to assist coaches to develop appropriate coaching styles. Those aspects of coaching that can be directly observed can be recorded and analysed in detail. These aspects are behaviour during instructional sessions and behaviour during competition. The coach can reflect on their performance the same way as players can reflect on their performances, using a combination of quantitative, qualitative and video information.

Coaching styles

Coaching delivery involves a range of behaviours, activities, interactions and processes (Lyle, 2002). Lyle (2002) stated that there are four main styles of coaching demonstrated during delivery: authoritarian, autocratic, democratic and person-centred. Sherman *et al.* (2000) found that athletes from male, female and mixed sports preferred to participate in a democratic rather than authoritarian environment, receiving positive feedback, training and instruction. However, there is no one coaching style that will lead to success in all coaching environments and effective coaching requires flexible behaviour to adapt to different situations (Cratty, 1983). The use of these four broad behaviours varies from coach to coach. The style of coaching can be characterised by the vocabulary being used by a coach (Lyle, 2002) and even varies between sessions delivered by the same coach (Donnelly and O'Donoghue, 2008; Bowley *et al.*, 2012). This is similar to the range of behaviour styles used in teaching (Mosston and Ashworth, 2002).

Coaching style is influenced by a number of factors, including individual coach philosophy (Abraham and Collins, 1998; Jones *et al.*, 2002), the type of sport (Massey *et al.*, 2002) as well as the gender (Lacy and Goldston, 1990; Millard, 1996), age group (Lacy and Darst, 1985; Miller, 1992) and level of athlete (Erle, 1981; Serpa *et al.*, 1991; Jones *et al.*, 1995). Coaching behaviour differs between training sessions and competition (Chaumeton and Duda, 1988; Wandzilak *et al.*, 1988). Typically there will be a greater use of silent monitoring during competition than during training. Trudel *et al.* (1996) found that ice hockey coaches spent 51 per cent of matches observing without any interaction with the players and that there was little instruction given during competition.

Coach behaviour analysis systems

Early instruments

The study of coach behaviour has developed from more established research into teaching styles within educational contexts (More, 2008). One of the first instruments used to analyse instructional behaviour was the Flanders Interaction Analysis System (FIAS), which was designed to analyse verbal behaviours of teachers (Flanders, 1960). Three different aspects of teacher–pupil communication are analysed using FIAS: teacher talk, pupil talk and silence/confusion. Modified versions of FIAS were developed for use in physical education and may be considered more relevant to coaching (Dougherty, 1970; Cheffers, 1972). Prior to the development of systematic observational techniques for coaching, coaching effectiveness was measured indirectly using self-report forms (Kahan, 1999). Early observation instruments for coaching typically used tick box forms to record instances of behavioural categories (Abraham and Collins, 1998). Tharp and Gallimore (1976) developed the Coaching Behaviour Recording Form (CBRF) to observe coaching behaviours. Their case study of a basketball coach found that half of all behaviours were instructional and that there was a 2:1 ratio for the use of scolding/re-instruction to praise.

The Coaching Behaviour Assessment System (CBAS) was developed by Smith *et al.* (1978) to examine youth baseball coaches' behaviours. The CBAS analysed 12 behavioural categories, which were divided into reactive and spontaneous behaviours. Reactive behaviours were recognised as immediate responses to player or team mistakes or effort, while spontaneous behaviours did not respond to observation of preceding events.

The Arizona State University Observation Instrument

Lacy and Darst (1984, 1985, 1989) developed the Arizona State University Observation Instrument (ASUOI), which is comprised of two variables: behaviour type and use of an athlete's first name by the coach. Behaviour type is a categorical variable of 14 named behaviours:

- Pre-instruction
- Concurrent instruction
- Post-instruction
- Questioning
- Positive modelling
- Negative modelling
- Hustle
- Praise
- Scold
- Management
- Humour
- Talking to assistant
- Silent monitoring
- Uncodable.

The use of the first name of an athlete is a dichotomous variable that is used as a modifier of the recorded behaviour. The ASUOI has been the most popular instrument used in scientific research into coach behaviour, with research spanning from 1984 to the publication of the current handbook (Lacy and Darst, 1984; Harry and O'Donoghue, 2012). The ASUOI is a recognised standard for the analysis of coach behaviour and has been used to analyse the behaviour of strength and conditioning coaches (Massey *et al.*, 2002), coach behaviour during ice-hockey games (Trudel *et al.*, 1996) and the behaviour of coaches of youth soccer squads (Cushion and Jones, 2001; Smith and Cushion, 2006). Both manual and computerised versions of the method have been used, with recent research implementing the ASUOI using the Focus X2 package (Elite Sports Analysis, Fife, UK). The Focus X2 implementation of the ASUOI has been used in the analysis of netball coaching (Donnelly and O'Donoghue, 2008; Harry and O'Donoghue, 2012), youth soccer coaching (Bowley *et al.*, 2012) and physical education teaching (Paisey and O'Donoghue, 2008). The use of such interactive video analysis packages improves reliability as video recordings of coach behaviour can be analysed diligently, pausing where necessary and replaying video sequences to help choose the behaviour name that best fits the observed instance. There are other systems that are similar to the ASUOI, such as the Revised Coaching

Behaviour Recording Form, which uses 12 behavioural categories (Côté *et al.*, 1995; Durand-Bush, 1996; Bloom *et al.*, 1999).

Computerised Coaching Analysis System

The CCAS (Computerised Coaching Analysis System) has been used for the analysis of coaching behaviour (Franks *et al.*, 1988) and has provided a quantitative breakdown of coach behaviour (Harries-Jenkins and Hughes, 1995). CCAS uses seven variables to characterise coach behaviour:

- Behaviour (verbal commentary, demonstration or reconstruction)
- Audience (individual, team or group)
- Content (skill related or non-skill related)
- Aspect of player behaviour (effort, organisation, behaviour or other)
- Type (positive, negative or neutral)
- Appropriateness (appropriate or inappropriate)
- Style (interrogative, evaluative, descriptive, affective and prescriptive).

Mayes and O'Donoghue (2006) implemented CCAS in the Focus X2 system, allowing interactive quantitative and video feedback to be provided. More (2008) also used Focus X2 to implement an interactive video analysis system for coach behaviour. More's system used four variables:

- Focus (instruction, feedback on correct performance and feedback on incorrect performance)
- Timing (during performance, post-performance or stopped/freeze)
- Delivery (whether or not demonstration was used)
- Emphasis (key factors or non-key factors).

The Coach Analysis Instrument (CAI) is part of the CCAS (Johnson and Franks, 1991) and produces detailed quantitative information about coach behaviour profile, allowing reflection on the content of practice sessions and the performance needs of the athletes. Partridge and Franks (1996) made recommendations for improvement of the CAI and consequently it was updated to the CAI II system.

Split-screen systems

Brown and O'Donoghue (2008) used the Dartfish package (Dartfish, Fribourg, Switzerland) to develop a split-screen analysis system for coach behaviour. A 60-minute netball coaching session was filmed using two cameras, with one focussing on the coach and the other recording a wider view of coach and athlete behaviour. The coach wore a microphone and radio transmitter (Sennheiser electronic GmbH & Co. KG, Hannover, Germany) so that the coach's voice was recorded clearly, even though the cameras were located on a balcony overlooking the coaching session. The two video recordings were integrated within Dartfish using the split-screen facility so that the two views were presented side by side. The 60-minute split-screen video used a single sound source, which was the coach's voice as picked up by the remote microphone. This video was tagged using a coach behaviour system developed in Dartfish.

The coach was able to look at tables that cross-tabulated different pairs of variables, consider frequencies and look at video sequences of events of interest. The coach provided feedback on the information produced and how it could be helpful to her reflective practice. The coach did not find the quantitative information to be useful because there were no norms for coach behaviour to compare it to. The approach could be enhanced if the coach tagged her own behaviour because she would recall what she was thinking during the periods of silent monitoring that preceded periods of intervention and communication. This knowledge of the coach's thoughts would help interpretation of communication events. The benefit of the split-screen view was that the coach was able to see her own body language while also being able to see athlete behaviour before, during and after coach instructions.

The system made the coach aware of subtle aspects of body language. Where coach evaluation is assisted by a mentor, the ability to review and discuss video sequences was considered beneficial. While the quantitative information was not seen as directly important to reflective practice, the importance of having a tagged video allowing interactive and efficient viewing of relevant video sequences was recognised.

Brown and O'Donoghue (2008) reported that filming the session, analysing the video and producing the results and video products took 12 hours of computer time, including five hours where the operator was actively using the Dartfish system and two hours where the operator used a video editing package to complete the highlights video. Such effort needs to be justified and the system is probably best used periodically rather than on a weekly basis.

Qualitative and mixed methods

In areas of sports science where observational techniques are used, the methods are not limited to quantitative data and analysis. The analysis of coach behaviour can also be analysed using qualitative observational analysis (Smith *et al.*, 1983; Morgan *et al.*, 2005) and mixed method approaches (Potrac *et al.*, 2007a, 2007b). In some mixed methods research, the ASUOI can be used to analyse coach behaviour showing 'what' the coach did, while qualitative observation can be used to analyse 'why' the coach used the given style of coaching. For example, Paisey and O'Donoghue (2008) supported the ASUOI with detailed field notes made during qualitative observation of videos of physical education teaching. These field notes considered teacher behaviour, pupil behaviour and the interaction between the teacher and pupils. Donnelly and O'Donoghue (2008) used qualitative methods in a different way to support the ASUOI. They presented quantitative results to an experienced coach and then conducted an interview with the coach to seek explanations for the behaviour observed. Potrac *et al.* (2007b) also used qualitative research to assess coaches' interpretation of their role, their priorities and the philosophy underpinning their practice.

Reliability and validity

There is a trade-off between the level of detail of an observational system and the reliability with which the system can be operated. The ASUOI uses two variables and CCAS uses seven variables. This can make the ASUOI more reliable than CCAS when they are implemented using similar apparatus (manual forms or computerised systems). The reliability of the ASUOI varies from study to study and depends on the way in which the instrument is implemented, the definition of the behaviours and the experience and training of the observers. One investigation reported agreement on 85 per cent of the recorded behaviour instances (Siedentop, 1991), while others found lower levels of reliability. Paisey and O'Donoghue (2008) reported kappa values of 0.628 for behaviour type and 0.422 for use of the first name, which are interpreted as good and moderate strengths of agreement, respectively. Similarly, Donnelly and O'Donoghue

(2008) reported kappa values of 0.720 for behaviour type and 0.498 for use of the first name, which are also interpreted as good and moderate strengths of agreement, respectively.

Franks *et al.* (1988) found that different dimensions of behaviour had differing levels of reliability. Smith *et al.* (1977) found that trained observers could use a coach behaviour analysis system sufficiently reliably. Smith *et al.* (2005) used Gamebreaker (SportsTec, Warriewood, Australia) to analyse coach behaviour and focussed on the two out of five behavioural classes that they demonstrated could be observed reliably.

More complex systems give greater scope for disagreement between independent operators within reliability studies (Mayes and O'Donoghue, 2006). Consider the coach comment 'why was this group the only group to complete the task without an error?' This could be entered as negative feedback to the team or as positive feedback to a group. A further issue is that many of the named behaviours in coaching analysis systems are not independent. There will be many occasions where an observer could classify observed behaviour in more than one way. These kinds of situation were quite common and would limit the reliability of observation.

There are also challenges to the validity of analysis methods for coach behaviour. Fletcher (2006) suggested that the invasive nature of a video camera could affect the behaviours of the athletes and coaches. A further challenge to quantitative systems is that they may over-simplify coach behaviour. Gaining a balance between the need for objective reliable information about coach behaviour and the need to understand the complex nature of coach behaviour is a difficulty for researchers in the area. However, quantitative coach behaviour analysis systems can be used effectively in applied settings along with complementary qualitative techniques.

Application areas

Research

There are two main application areas of coach behaviour analysis: the first is developing scientific knowledge about coaching and the other is within coach education and development. These two application areas place different emphases on measurement issues, complexity of data and use of video information. In scientific research, the video footage of coach behaviour is used during data collection. The video is indexed with behaviours performed by the coach and these behaviours are used in subsequent analysis. There are examples of case study research reporting on the behaviour of an individual coach (Bloom *et al.*, 1999), but it is more typical for scientific research to report on the average member of the sample of coaches who participated in the study (Cushion and Jones, 2001; Smith and Cushion, 2006). The results included in research papers are tabular or graphical summaries of quantitative data without supporting video sequences. For the study to be replicable, the behaviours need to be defined and the level of reliability must be measured and reported. Many scientific studies use the ASUOI, where there are only two dependent variables (behaviour and whether the first name of the athlete is used by the coach). This makes the research manageable in terms of stating hypotheses and reporting results, as well as improving the reliability of the observation method. Coach behaviour has been assessed in many sports, including basketball (Bloom *et al.*, 1999), soccer (Miller, 1992; Potrac *et al.*, 2007a, 2007b), tennis (Claxton, 1988) and weight training (Massey *et al.*, 2002). Coach behaviour research has included case studies of individual coaches (Bloom *et al.*, 1999; Tharp and Gallimore, 1976) and comparison of successful and unsuccessful coaches (Claxton, 1988), youth coaches (Smith *et al.*, 1978; Lacy and Goldston, 1990; Miller, 1992) and elite-level coaches (Potrac *et al.*, 2007a) as well as gender effects on coach behaviour (Miller, 1992).

Analysis of coach behaviour has become an established area of research (Van der Mars, 1989; Kahan, 1999; Potrac *et al.*, 2007a; Gilbert and Trudel, 2004; More, 2008). An important area of research is comparing the behaviours of successful and less successful coaches. Successful coaches use more questioning and post-instruction than their less successful counterparts (Lacy and Darst, 1984).

Earlier in this chapter, we identified various factors that influence the coaching style used, including the type of sport, level of the athletes, age group of the athletes and the type of session being conducted. Published results give an indication of the styles used in different scenarios. For example, in competition, there is a greater use of silent monitoring than there is during instructional sessions. This is obvious to many in coaching but the real contribution of coach behaviour analysis is the description of how much silent monitoring is used in each situation by successful coaches. Understanding that there is a greater use of silent monitoring in competition than during instructional sessions is not enough. Another research finding is that there is less post-instruction in physical education teaching than in coaching contexts (Paisey and O'Donoghue, 2008).

Variability of coach behaviour has been recognised within and between coaches. There is no 'ideal' model of coaching (Kidman, 2001), suggesting coaching styles are situational to the team or athlete at a specific time. Such situations can be affected by both a coach's and an athlete's behaviour and there is a need for different approaches in different contexts (Cross, 1999). Research has revealed that there is greater variability in higher-level coaches' behaviour than in the behaviour of their lower-level counterparts. This has been found in both netball (Donnelly and O'Donoghue, 2008) and soccer (Bowley *et al.*, 2012) and may result from higher-level coaches being more reactive to situations, while lower-level coaches may apply a similar style in different situations.

Coach development and reflection

Pedagogic literature reveals that instructional behaviour can be modified through systematic analysis (Borg, 1972; Werner and Rink, 1989; Grant *et al.*, 1990). In coach education applications, coaching behaviour data is analysed on an individual basis and video sequences are used extensively when reflecting on coaching performance. Reliability does not have to be as high as when used in scientific research because the information is not being generalised beyond the particular coach. Furthermore, any quantitative results are supported by the actual video sequences. This allows the coaches and their mentors to interactively use coach behaviour analysis systems to view behaviours where quantitative patterns highlight areas of interest. Any modification of behaviour will be based on an in-depth analysis of the video sequences, rather than on the quantitative results for a session. The relaxed reliability requirements allow multiple modifiers for behaviour to be used to enrich the analysis. These may include focus, timing, delivery and emphasis of comments (More, 2008) or the seven variables used in the CCAS (Franks *et al.*, 1988). Methods of analysing instructional behaviour should still be objective, reliable and valid (Rink, 1993) but to a lesser extent perhaps than in scientific research.

Reflective practice by coaches should use video analysis of coaching behaviour (Farres, 2004). More and Franks (1996) used CAI along with audio and video recordings of coach behaviour and reflective logs within an intervention to help coach development. When such systems are used to provide feedback to coaches, the direct evidence to support recommendations made can be effective (More and Franks, 1996). The advantage of using video is that it assists the coach to recall events during coaching sessions they are reflecting on (Gilbert and Trudel, 2001).

Future work

There are three areas for future research that are proposed here: behaviour of successful coaches, the development of norms for coach behaviour and temporal analysis of coaching behaviour. There is previous research that has compared the behaviours of successful and unsuccessful coaches (Lacy and Darst, 1984). However, when one considers the nature of different sports and the variety of different age groups, gender and levels of athletes, it is clear that more research is needed in this area. These studies are time-consuming and need to be well planned. If the sample size for each coach group was 15 and the number of sessions observed to gain a typical behaviour pattern for each coach was 10 sessions of at least 60 minutes, then 150 hours of video footage would need to be analysed. This is clearly not advisable within an undergraduate degree project where the time commitment required would be excessive.

Norms are used in many areas of education and health and they permit values to be interpreted using the relevant population. The ASUOI is an established instrument such that norms should be developed for coach behaviour in different levels of different sports. When one considers the variety of different training sessions where different coaching styles may be required, the programme of research needed to provide norms for coaching behaviours based on all influencing factors is substantial.

It is surprising to the authors that there has been little research into temporal aspects of coach behaviour considering how long the ASUOI has been available to researchers and practitioners. The quantitative results presented in research to date have been static in nature: frequency profiles, percentage session times and mean durations of behaviour instances. Temporal analysis would give an indication of the orderings of events and cycles of behaviours that may occur during sessions. Uncovering such patterns may reveal interesting new knowledge about the behaviour of successful coaches. One study that has attempted such an analysis shows some temporal patterns in netball coaching (Harry and O'Donoghue, 2012). Much more research of this type is needed in other sports.

Concluding remarks

Performance analysis techniques can be applied to the behaviour of coaches just as they can be applied to the behaviour of players and teams. This chapter has surveyed the research that has been done on coach behaviour and the methods used. Analysis of coach behaviour can be applied in both scientific research and the reflective practice of coaches. In both types of work, the analysis can be enhanced when quantitative coaching behaviour information is combined with complementary qualitative research.

References

Abraham, A. and Collins, D. (1998) 'Examining and extending research in coach development', *Quest*, 50: 59–79.
Bloom, G., Crumpton, R. and Anderson, J. (1999) 'A systematic observation study of the teaching behaviours of an expert basketball coach', *The Sport Psychologist*, 13: 157–70.
Borg, W.R. (1972) 'The minicourse as a vehicle for changing teacher behaviour: A three-year follow-up', *Journal of Educational Psychology*, 63(6): 572–9.
Brown, E. and O'Donoghue, P.G. (2008) 'A split screen system to analyse coach behaviour: A case report of coaching practice', *International Journal of Computer Science in Sport*, 7(1): 4–17.
Bowley, C. Bodden, W. and O'Donoghue, P.G. (2012) 'Behaviour of academy soccer coaches during training sessions', Book of Abstracts, World Congress of Performance Analysis of Sport IX, Worcester, UK, 25–28 July.

Chaumeton, N. and Duda, J. (1988) 'Is it how you play the game or whether you win or lose? The effect of competitive level and situation on coaching behaviors', *Journal of Sport Behavior*, 11: 157–74.

Cheffers, J.T.F. (1972) 'The validation of an instrument designed to expand the Flanders system of interaction analysis to describe non-verbal interaction, different varieties of teacher behaviour and pupil response', unpublished doctoral dissertation, Temple University, Philadelphia.

Claxton, B. (1988) 'A systematic observation of more and less successful high school tennis coaches', *Journal of Teaching in Physical Education*, 7: 302–10.

Côté, J., Trudel, P., Baria, A. and Russell, S.J. (1995) 'The coaching model: A grounded assessment of expert gymnastic coach's knowledge', *Journal of Sport and Exercise Psychology*, 17: 1–17.

Cratty, B.J. (1983) *Psychology in Contemporary Sport*, Englewood Cliffs, NJ: Prentice-Hall.

Cross, N. (1999) 'Individualization of training programmes', in N. Cross and J. Lyle (eds), *The Coaching Process: Principles and Practice for Sport* (pp. 174–91). Oxford: Butterworth Heinemann.

Culver, D. and Trudel, P. (2006) 'Cultivating coaches' communities of practice – Developing the potential for learning through interactions', in R. Jones (ed.), *Re-Conceptualizing the Coaching Role and How to Teach it: New Ways of Thinking About Practice* (pp. 97–112). London: Routledge.

Cushion, C.J. and Jones, R.L. (2001) 'A systematic observation of professional top-level youth soccer coaches', *Journal of Sport Behaviour*, 24: 354–65.

Donnelly, C. and O'Donoghue, P.G. (2008) 'Behaviour of netball coaches of different levels', poster presentation at the World Congress of Performance Analysis of Sport VIII, Magdeburg, Germany, September.

Dougherty, N.J. (1970) 'A comparison of command, task and individual program styles of teaching in the development of physical fitness and motor skills', unpublished doctoral dissertation, Temple University, Philadelphia.

Durand-Bush, N. (1996) 'Training blood sweat and tears', in J.H. Salmela (ed.), *Great Job, Coach! Getting the Edge from Proven Winners*, Ottawa, On: Potentium.

Erle, F.J. (1981) 'Leadership in competitive and recreational sport', unpublished Master's thesis, University of Western Ontario, London, Canada.

Farres, L. (2004) 'Becoming a better coach through reflective practice' *BC Coach's Perspective*, 6: 10–1.

Flanders, N. (1960) *Interaction Analysis in the Classroom: A Manual for Observers*, Minneapolis: University of Minnesota Press.

Fletcher, S. (2006) 'The final hour: coach/athlete interactions, immediately, prior to performance in basketball', unpublished Ph.D. thesis, Victoria University, Canada.

Franks, I.M., Johnson, R.B. and Sinclair, G.D. (1988) 'The development of a computerised coaching analysis system for recording behaviour in sporting environments', *Teaching Physical Education*, 8: 23–32.

Gilbert, W. and Trudel, P. (2001) 'Learning to coach through experience: Reflection in model youth sport coaches', *Journal of Teaching in Physical Education*, 21: 16–34.

Gilbert, W.D. and Trudel, P. (2004) 'Role of the coach: How model youth team sport coaches frame their roles', *Journal of Sports Sciences*, 24(6): 549–64.

Grant, B.C., Ballard, K.D. and Glynn, T.L. (1990) 'Teacher feedback intervention, motor-on-task behaviour, and successful task performance', *Journal of Teaching in Physical Education*, 29(3): 26–9.

Harries-Jenkins, E. and Hughes, M. (1995) 'A computerised analysis of female coaching behaviour with male and female athletes', in T. Reilly, A. Lees and M. Hughes (eds), *Science and Racket Sports* (pp. 238–43). London: E & FN Spon.

Harry, L. and O'Donoghue, P.G. (2012) 'Temporal aspects of coach behaviour', poster presented at the World Congress of Performance Analysis of Sport IX, Worcester, UK, July.

Hastie, P.A. (1999) 'An instrument for recording coach's comments and instructions during time-outs', *Journal of Sport Behaviour*, 22(4): 467–78.

Johnson, R.B. and Franks, I.M. (1991) 'Measuring the reliability of a computer aided systematic observation instrument', *Canadian Journal of Sport Science*, 16: 45–57.

Jones, D.F., Housner, L.D. and Kornspan, A.S. (1995) 'A comparative analysis of expert and novice basketball coaches' practice planning', *Applied Research in Coaching Athletics Annual*, 10: 201–26.

Jones, R.L., Armour, K.M. and Potrac, P. (2002) 'Understanding the coaching process: A framework for social analysis', *Quest*, 54(1): 186–99.

Kahan, D. (1999) 'Coaching behaviour: A review of the systematic observation research literature', *Applied Research in Coaching and Athletics Annual*, 14: 17–58.

Kidman, L. (2001) *Developing Decision Makers: An Empowerment Approach to Coaching*, Christchurch: Innovative.

Lacy, A.C. and Darst, P.W. (1984) 'Evolution of a systematic observation system: The ASU coaching observation instrument', *Journal of Teaching in Physical Education*, 3: 59–66.

Lacy, A.C. and Darst, P.W. (1985) 'Systematic observation of behaviour of winning high school head football coaches', *Journal of Teaching in Physical Education*, 4: 256–70.

Lacy, A.C. and Darst, P.W. (1989) 'The Arizona State University Observation Instrument (ASUOI)', in P.W. Darst, D.B. Zakrajsek and V.H. Mancini (eds), *Analysing Physical Education and Sport Instruction* (2nd ed.), (pp. 369–77). Champaign, IL: Human Kinetics.

Lacy, A.C. and Goldston, P.D. (1990) 'Behaviour analysis of male and female coaches in high school girls' basketball', *Journal of Sport Behaviour*, 13(1): 29–39.

Lyle, J. (2002) *Sports Coaching Concepts: A Framework for Coaches' Behaviour*, London: Routledge.

Massey, C., Maneval, L., Phillips, J., Vincent, J., White, G. and Zoeller, B. (2002) 'An analysis of teaching and coaching behaviours of elite strength and conditioning coaches', *Journal of Strength and Conditioning Research*, 16: 456–60.

Mayes, A. and O'Donoghue, P.G. (2006) 'Computerised analysis and feedback relating to coach behaviour', in H. Dancs, M. Hughes and P.G. O'Donoghue (eds), *Performance Analysis of Sport 7* (pp. 288–92). Cardiff: CPA UWIC Press.

Millard, L. (1996) 'Differences in coaching behaviours of male and female high school soccer coaches', *Journal of Sport Behaviour*, 19(1): 19–31.

Miller, A.W. (1992) 'Systematic observation behaviour similarities of various youth sport soccer coaches', *Physical Educator*, 449: 136–43.

More, K. (2008) 'Notational analysis of coaching', in M. Hughes and I.M. Franks (eds), *The Essentials of Performance Analysis: An Introduction* (pp. 264–76). London: Routledge.

More, K.G. and Franks, I.M. (1996) 'Analysis and modification of verbal coaching behaviour: The usefulness of a data driven intervention strategy', *Journal of Sport Sciences*, 14: 523–43.

Morgan, K., Sproule, J., Wiegand, D. and Carpenter, P. (2005) 'Teaching styles, motivational climate and pupils' cognitive and affective responses in physical education', *European Physical Education Review*, 11(3): 257–86.

Mosston, M. and Ashworth, S. (2002) *Teaching Physical Education* (5th ed.), Columbus, OH: Merrill Publishing Co.

Paisey, T. and O'Donoghue, P.G. (2008) 'Physical education teacher behaviour: A quantitative and qualitative investigation', poster presented at the World Congress of Performance Analysis of Sport VIII, Magdeburg, Germany, September.

Partridge, D. and Franks, I.M. (1996) 'Analysing and modifying coaching behaviours by means of computer-aided observation', *The Physical Educator*, Winter: 8–23.

Potrac, P., Jones, R. and Cushion, C. (2007a) 'Understanding power and the coach's role in professional English soccer: A preliminary investigation of coach behaviour', *Soccer and Society*, 8: 33–49.

Potrac, P., Jones, R. and Armour, K. (2007b) 'It's all about getting respect: The coaching behaviours of an expert English soccer coach' *Sport, Education and Society*, 7(2): 183–202.

Rink, J. (1993) *Teaching Physical Education for Learning*, St. Louis: Mosby.

Serpa, S., Patco, V. and Santos, F. (1991) 'Leadership patterns in handball international competition', *International Journal of Sport Psychology*, 22: 78–89.

Sherman, C., Fuller, R. and Speed, H. (2000) 'Gender comparisons of preferred coaching behaviours in Australian sports', *Journal of Sport Behaviour*, 23: 389–406.

Siedentop, D. (1991) *Developing Teaching Skills in Physical Education*, Boston, MA: Houghton-Mifflin.

Smith, M., and Cushion, C.J. (2006) 'An investigation of the in-game behaviours of professional, top-level youth soccer coaches', *Journal of Sports Sciences*, 24(2): 355–66.

Smith, R.E., Smoll, F.L. and Hunt, E.B. (1977) 'A system for the behavioural analysis of athletic coaches' *Research Quarterly*, 48: 401–7.

Smith, R.E., Smoll, F.L. and Curtis, B. (1978) 'Coaching behaviours in little league baseball', in F.L. Smoll and R.E. Smith (eds), *Psychological Perspectives in Youth Sports* (pp. 173–201). Washington, DC: Hemisphere.

Smith, R.E., Zane, N.S., Smoll, F.L. and Coppel, D.B. (1983) 'Behavioural assessment in youth sports: Coaching behaviours and children's attitudes', *Medicine and Science in Sports and Exercise*, 15: 208–14.

Smith, T., Hammond, J. and Gilleard, W. (2005) 'The use of performance analysis technology to monitor the coaching environment in soccer', *International Journal of Performance Analysis in Sport*, 5(3): 126–38.

Strean, W. (1998) 'Possibilities for qualitative research in sport psychology', *The Sport Psychologist*, 12: 333–45.

Tharp, R.G. and Gallimore, R. (1976) 'What a coach can teach a teacher', *Psychology Today*, 9: 75–8.

Trudel, P., Côté, J. and Bernard, D. (1996) 'Systematic observation of youth ice hockey coaches during games', *Journal of Sport Behaviour*, 19: 50–65.

Van der Mars, H. (1989) 'Systematic observation: An introduction', in P.W. Darst, D.B. Zakrajsek and V.H. Mancini (eds), *Analysing Physical Education and Sport Instruction* (2nd ed.), (pp. 3–18). Champaign, IL: Human Kinetics.

Wandzilak, T., Ansorge C.J. and Potter, G. (1988) 'Comparison between selected practice and game behaviours of youth sport soccer coaches', *Journal of Sport Behaviour*, 11: 78–88.

Werner, P. and Rink, R. (1989) 'Case studies of teacher effectiveness in second grade physical education', *Journal of Teaching in Physical Education*, 8: 280–97.

15

SPORTS PERFORMANCE ANALYSIS FOR HIGH PERFORMANCE MANAGERS

Huw Wiltshire

CARDIFF METROPOLITAN UNIVERSITY, UK

Summary

This chapter will discuss the fundamental need for sports performance analysis for high performance managers. In doing so, it will explore the nature of the performance environment and the need for performance management systems that convert multi-disciplinary performance analysis data into an inter-disciplinary end product that can be used by coaches and athletes. This remains a major challenge for performance managers who require strategies to compress unwieldy data sets into meaningful individual and group performance feedback. Finally, the section proposes an integrated model of performance management and analysis that can be applied to design, implement and measure the effectiveness of a performance review.

Introductory concepts

High performance (HP) sport is primarily concerned with winning and change; HP managers must affect the latter to either start or maintain the former. Performance must be managed coherently and analysed in an accurate and formative manner in order to highlight a meaningful direction for both coach and athlete that can deliver world-class performance under pressure. Performance involves a behavioural and an outcome dimension and is dynamic and multi-dimensional in nature; it is a concept that is open to judgemental and evaluative processes (Sonnentag, 2002) and constantly evolves.

A HP manager needs to lead, enable and develop people, squads, systems and structures in order to optimise performance and, through meaningful performance management and analysis, nurture self-sufficient and self-aware athletes. Jones *et al.* (2009: 140) indicated that 'the performance environment the organisation creates is just as important as the people performing in it'. HP managers must create environments that facilitate:

- agreement (on critical targets and needs)
- alignment (between and within all tiers of a HP environment)

- accountability (for organisational, team and individual targets)
- adjustment (the ability to initiate, and communicate, context-specific change effectively).

HP managers are invariably tasked with monitoring performance trends and improvements across all tiers of an elite sports environment, and it is vital that they possess the capability to synthesise wide-ranging and often unwieldy data sets into key markers that impact upon performance, either directly or indirectly. The measurement outputs and objectivity of performance analysis has the potential to accelerate coach–athlete learning and positive change. As an HP manager, one can often facilitate change without actually being able to control the rate at which it occurs. However, it is imperative to avoid analysis for analysis sake; if the data we generate does not impact upon performance, why are we measuring it in the first place? For a HP manager, sport performance management and analysis are not models but rather applied processes that are undertaken with a clear outcome or target in mind. This chapter will discuss the need for performance management systems that clearly define the framework for multi-disciplinary performance analysis. A system framework can be used to define success markers across a variety of disciplines, develop squads on and away from the competition arena, create visual databases and translate multi-disciplinary data into an inter-disciplinary end product, for both athletes and coaches. Finally, the issue of how to design, implement and measure the effectiveness of a performance review will be explored.

Within elite sport, Gilson *et al.* (2001) defined Peak Performance Organisation (PPO) theory, which explains how to organise for sustained peak performance. The latter is defined as constantly exceeding organisational best in pursuit of the organisation's purpose. For most HP managers, this is a realistic target, although not necessarily indicative of a high performance level. Scott (2009) defined a model of high performance management that is athlete-centred, coach-led and scientifically and medically supported. Whilst clear and logical in nature, the fundamental criticism of the model centres on the second tier, in the sense that a high performance sports environment invariably seeks to nurture self-sufficient and self-aware athletes, which contradicts the ethos of a coach-led environment: an ongoing relationship management tension in high performance sport. A more balanced and accurate definition of high performance sport encompasses performance that is consistently higher than that of the majority of peer organisations in the same sector, and over a prolonged time period (Jones *et al.*, 2009). This definition differentiates high performance from peak performance and suggests that the former is consistent and sustainable, and is relative to, and affected by, the performance of other organisations. Jones *et al.* (2009) attempted to define a performance environment model where high performance is perceived to be both inevitable and sustainable (Figure 15.1).

This model disaggregates into leadership, performance enablers and people factors, represented within three areas, and organisational climate, represented by four aspects containing achievement, well-being, innovation and internal processes. The practical merit of the model reflects its capacity to assess existing strengths and weaknesses of any HP environment and, consequently, highlights strategies for potential improvement. It may also represent a means of objectively assessing predictors of organisational performance. Fletcher and Arnold (2011) are conceptually aligned to the model in the way they discuss four main areas in performance leadership and management in elite sport:

- vision (strategic)
- operations
- people (capability)
- culture (values and behaviours).

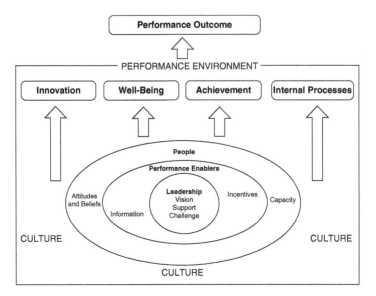

Figure 15.1 A performance environment model (Jones *et al.*, 2009)

Hoye *et al.* (2006) designed a nine-point model of performance management by adapting the four basic aspects of Kaplan and Norton's (1992) balanced scorecard. The advantage of their model relates to the fact that it is broad and inclusive, and geared to sport. However, it would need to be adapted in a context-specific manner to a functional HP environment. Smither and London (2009) viewed performance management as a process that contributes to the effective management of individuals and teams in order to achieve high levels of organisational performance. It is a process that establishes shared understanding and should be strategic and integrated in nature, in order to provide an accurate and informed direction for raising performance standards. Performance management can disaggregate into three main processes: setting the objectives; managing performance to objectives; and measuring performance against objectives (Winstanley and Stuart-Smith, 1996). All objectives should be benchmarked externally, in an ongoing fashion, but a HP manager should avoid an over-reliance on measuring performance to the potential detriment of managing performance.

HP managers must deal with the perennial problem of change gaps (the ability to innovate and change in a challenging environment) by applying key principles: establishing and deploying the right managers and analysts; refreshing and communicating strategic approaches to analysis and management; managing analysis process skills; improving performance; and managing and applying evolving knowledge (adapted from Paladino, 2011). Fundamental questions for a HP manager include: What types of data exist within the elite sporting environments? Does a positive relationship exist between performance analysis and enhanced sports performance? Does current application of performance management and analysis reflect a multi-disciplinary approach? Can multi-disciplinary data translate into an inter-disciplinary end product that impacts upon performance? How are these data used? What are meaningful performance trends? How can we evidence performance progression? A fundamental requirement for a performance management approach in sport is the joint preservation and support for individualism and teamwork. Moreover, it cannot be a one-dimensional mechanism for 'policing' performance, but instead should embrace ethical principles, such as respect for the individual, procedural fairness and transparency of decision making.

Ostensibly, HP sports environments require strategies for integrated, dynamic multi- and inter-disciplinary performance analysis feedback that aims to directly impact upon performance. O'Donoghue (2010: 8) provided a compelling justification by asserting that 'rather than assuming that supporting a coach with feedback based on (*match*) analysis will enhance performance, we need evidence to support this theory'. What precisely must be managed and analysed? O'Donoghue (2010) highlighted performance analysis as an area of sport and exercise science concerned with actual sports performance rather than self-reports by athletes or laboratory experiments. The main reason for doing performance analysis is to develop an understanding of sports that informs decision making by those seeking to enhance sports performance. O'Donoghue's (2010) definition emphasised the fact that successful sports performance is multi-disciplinary in nature and never a result of a single cause and effect. For a HP manager, performance analysis defines essential truths and provides a reality check for the talent development environment; the HP manager must use meaningful data to ensure ongoing talent identification and development occurs, as opposed to the common error of talent selection.

High performance management systems

HP environments potentially benefit from a bespoke performance management system (PMS) that allows all key stakeholders to manage, monitor, plan and evaluate performance and, as a consequence, obtain an accurate holistic view of both performance and development. Integrated automated performance alerts and data analysis can be used to provide training direction and performance enhancement. The PMS must align closely to a detailed performance plan that optimises outputs and generates solution-based recommendations to deliver improved performance and development standards. The system shown in Figure 15.2 constitutes a realistic framework for multi-disciplinary performance analysis.

This high performance management system (HPMS) is in keeping with Cleveland *et al.*'s (1989) view that performance management systems can serve six broad purposes: strategic

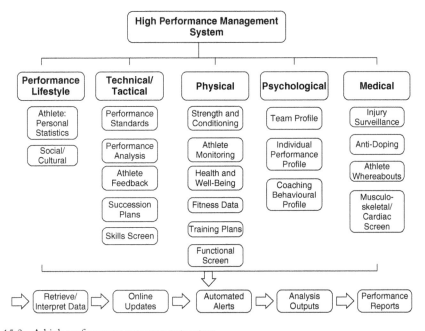

Figure 15.2 A high performance management system

purpose (linking the organisation's goals with the individual's goals); administrative purpose (a source of valid evidence that can accelerate accurate and informed decision making); communication; development; organisational maintenance; and documentation. The process also emphasises the types of data that will need to be collected and analysed. From an output perspective, the HPMS can take several data sets and convert them into a fusion of meaningful inter-disciplinary targets for athletes and coaches. This type of system potentially provides transparency, accountability and clarity, whilst promoting quality assurance for quality improvement (Q_a to Q_i) in order to elevate performance standards. The key to its success is the way in which data are entered and then structured to enable efficient processing. Therefore, each stakeholder should have a dedicated data manager; this role will ultimately determine the reliability of the data and overall effectiveness of the system. Definition of HPMS capability relates to the optimisation of data use to increase throughput and minimise contention, enabling the largest possible workload to be processed; in doing so, it will need to effectively combine feedback and feed forward information, whilst complying with the Data Protection Act (Department of Health, 1998). The HP manager as a data controller must adhere to eight data protection principles. Moreover, as a data processor, it is the service provider's responsibility to ensure that the personal information is kept secure and adheres to specifications for a personal information management system (e.g. BSI, 2009). The functional capacity of a HPMS relates to the filters to data mine (the ability to compress large, unwieldy data sets into simple features that provide meaningful knowledge) information into key performance and development questions or to monitor key trends (e.g. athlete loads against injury rates via GPS data). The advantages of a HPMS can be numerous: shared data; reduced redundancy; fewer inconsistencies in data; enforcement of performance standards; security restrictions (data protection provides integrity to the system); ability to balance perennial conflicting requirements; and improved monitoring through automated alerts. Ultimately, a good performance management and analysis tool is not just a control mechanism but a learning system that effectively communicates and informs. Hoye *et al.* (2006) highlighted the importance of applying a dashboard of critical indicators or key success factors that accurately reflect an organisation's mission and goals.

A HPMS must be compelling and user-friendly, functionally and cognitively interactive and constitute a viable means of facilitating person-to-person dialogue. It is essentially a knowledge management and sharing system that should embody three levels of knowledge flow (from tangible to intangible) with regard to performance analysis outputs: the transfer of tangible resources (team and individual performance indicators); the transfer of activity plans (performance plans and targets); and the transfer of material prototypes (innovative amalgamation of coded data with other multi-disciplinary outputs) (Carroll *et al.*, 2003). For a HP manager, knowledge management can entail collective learning, learning how to learn and idea facilitation (Lin and Chen, 2009).

If the start point for any high performance sport is winning, a HP manager must initially have a completely accurate picture of win–loss ratios for all relevant tiers and squads for an annual, four-yearly, decade or more longitudinal period. In 19 FIFA World Cup football tournaments and 97 games, Brazil, as the number one-ranked side over that period, exhibit a 78 per cent win ratio (FIFA, 2010), but a HP manager must still explore whether this constitutes consistency of performance or under-achievement. In terms of broad performance indicators, analysis of three IRB Rugby World Cup tournaments indicate that, in a 12-year period (three tournaments) within the pool stages, there was a 21 per cent decrease in the overall number of tries scored; this pattern was magnified at the knockout stages with a 33 per cent drop. A similar pattern emerges when analysing the last four FIFA Football World Cups; a 12-year period has seen a 15 per cent decrease in the total number of goals scored. The issue for the HP manager is to ask the right question in attempting to understand the trend; are these patterns a result of improved defence, weaker attacking play, rule changes, more conservative coaching philosophy, financial pressure or a combination of all of these variables? Examination of both the Tri Nations and Six Nations competitions over the last ten years shows that there has been a steady reduction in the number or tries being scored in each competition. In brief, there were around 60–70 per cent more tries being scored at the beginning of the decade than at the end. The possible reasons for this decrease in tries could be the result of many diverse factors or relatively few. For example, a reduction in the number of kicks from hand (2009 saw 60 per game; 2010 averaged 37) or a change in type of kick made. Further factors included rucks and mauls, increasing by over 40 per cent, with passes elevated by 35 per cent (IRB, 2010). A HP manager must examine whether this trend has application to other tiers of the performance environment. A common but nevertheless key conceptual issue to address for many HP managers relates to successful elite age-grade performance not translating to the senior elite environment.

The HPMS has the potential to alleviate a practical problem of athlete support services working in an incoherent and disjointed manner. The system can clarify the challenge facing athlete support staff in aiming for sustained performance excellence. Relative success hinges on the fact that a 'climate of cooperation and collaboration needs to be actively fostered in what is potentially an environment that fosters competition and conflict' (Reid *et al.*, 2004: 205). Proactive multi-disciplinary teams (M-DTs) have impacted on sport but their existence raises a number of practical questions: What are the outputs and deliverables? Are they an incidental bi-product of larger budgets, imitation or the need for more individualised athlete support? Are the backroom staff isolated or integrated within the environment? Do the elements function within silos? What constitutes the key elements of a M-DT? In elite sport, M-DTs embody professional practice that constitutes ongoing decision-making and athlete management. Within elite sports environments, conflict can be personal, idiosyncratic, a function of the group dynamic or specific to the sport. Conflict may take the shape of interpersonal, to individual-group conflict (one individual's needs differ from the group), to conflict between groups. With the ever-expanding M-DTs, HP managers have to manage structural risk factors, such as the coach's perception of the efficacy of each service, competition for resources (in partially accountable environments), implicit or explicit pressure (discrediting an alternative approach in an effort to justify one's own), task interdependence and jurisdictional ambiguity (Reid *et al.*, 2004). Integrated performance management data must provide empirical evidence that highlights the value of the many components within an elite sporting environment and balances the perceived value of each.

The mode of performance analysis feedback is key. Learning from dynamic representations is improved when learners are able to control the pacing of the presentation because new information can be integrated into existing knowledge structures at a rate that reflects the capabilities and needs of the learner. Three levels of interactivity exist: the control of the information delivery; manipulation of the content; and control of the representation (Kalyuga, 2007). A HPMS should reflect such functional interactivity.

O'Donoghue (2010) identified three key purposes of performance analysis that underpin the type of data sets generated: technique analysis, technical effectiveness and tactical evaluation. The three approaches form the performance analysis base for the HPMS. Performance analysis data on team and individual levels can be monitored against pre-determined performance targets within attacking success and defensive completion rates. Bracewell *et al.* (2003) argued that performance could be condensed into contextual ratings on a game-by-game basis from match data using a combination of dimension reduction techniques and an adaptation of multivariate control methodology. A performance screening process must be monitored for trends relating to medical (cardiac and musculo-skeletal), physical (functional and biomechanical) and psychological aspects. Analysing training loads against the extent of injury can generate trends that form the basis for a very specific model for injury prevention.

In terms of capability development, HP managers focus on succession planning for coaches, athletes and athlete support staff. The HPMS will include evaluation data relating to high performance coaches and based on athlete questionnaire, coach observation and summary reports (Mallett and Côté, 2006).

The HPMS will also synthesise data into individual psychological and performance profiles: a collection of related variables brought together to represent an athlete. From a group or squad perspective, a sports performance profile can be used to represent a typical performance based on multiple match data. Where a typical profile is produced for a team or an athlete, it is also necessary to represent the variability in performance indicator values, showing where the team or athlete is consistent or inconsistent. A team profile helps an athlete to apply their role understanding back into a team or squad context. Athletes can assess their group against seven characteristics of high-performing teams: performance; empowerment; relationships; flexibility; output; recognition; and morale (Blanchard, 2006).

Individual assessment of athletes via real and lapsed time training and competition monitoring is central to high performance management and analysis. Application of a Global Positioning System (GPS) will provide objective data on athlete workloads via quantitative measurement of activity profiles. Real-time measurement of athlete movements is vital to the process of performance analysis. GPS measures specific workloads in terms of total distance, heart rate and velocity per game, half, quarter or smaller unit. In contact sports, 10 Hz GPS units that possess accelerometers, gyroscopes, and magnetometers and heart rate measures enable impact forces to be assessed. Synchronising such data with coded computerised performance analysis constitutes a vital form of formative, inter-disciplinary performance feedback that has huge relevance for coach and athlete; a type of data that prevents barrier-impact from negating performance progression.

A constant challenge involves the need to compress unwieldy multi-disciplinary data sets into meaningful individual and group performance feedback. One potential solution is a performance analysis dashboard that equates to an all-embracing fusion of key performance data trends. Few (2006) suggested that 'a dashboard's success as a medium of communication is a product of design, a result of a display that speaks clearly and immediately'. A dashboard must be tailored specifically to the requirements of a given person, group or function. The condensing of salient information to one screen enhances what Few (2006) referred to as the 'simultaneity of vision': viewing all data together facilitates comparative analysis and possible recognition of key trends. A dashboard approach may also enhance an organisation's ability to arrive at accurate, informed and rapid decisions by integrating data from all of its constituent parts on to a single, centralised platform in order to obtain an accurate, holistic view of performance. However, any HPMS will need to be sensitive to the potential barriers to successful implementation of performance management and analysis within a high performance environment: inability to prioritise; silo mentality; self-interest; ex-athlete mentality; complicated, uninspiring and non-innovative performance management and analysis; overcoming simple tools that create complex results; resistance, or lack of desire, to change; and a lack of shared values (Cameron and Green, 2009).

Performance reviews: integrating performance management and analysis

In many respects, integrated performance management and analysis is a direct antidote to the five dysfunctions of a team (Lencioni, 2002): inattention to results; avoidance of accountability;

lack of commitment; fear of conflict; and absence of trust. Figure 15.3 highlights the transition from the outer ring of how to manage performance via the middle ring of what needs to be managed and analysed, to the inner ring of how to analyse and impact directly on athlete and squad (including the management team of coaches).

This model has additional value in the sense that it can be applied to form the basis for a performance review that should embody: a people-centred approach; an ethos based on sustained excellence; the recognition of the need to provide leadership during and post review; and totally transparent integrity (i.e. implementation of a completely ethical and professional process). A performance review should gather data according to three main themes:

1. Structure – which relates to how elite performance is implemented, specifically the key objectives and management of the programme.
2. Process – how elite performance is delivered; service provision, philosophies and personnel capability.
3. Outcome – the manner in which elite performance is evaluated for effectiveness.

The objectives of a review could incorporate: a critical assessment of the existing governance, management, structure and performance standards of elite performance; and solution-based recommendations to deliver improved performance standards, a comprehensive governance framework and management structure for elite sport that addresses the needs of affiliate organisations and stakeholders. These recommendations may include adjustments to existing governance systems and/or integration of activities and operations; identification of potential impediments to reform and strategies to overcome those impediments; and a plan to implement the recommendations. Data collection will primarily involve two types:

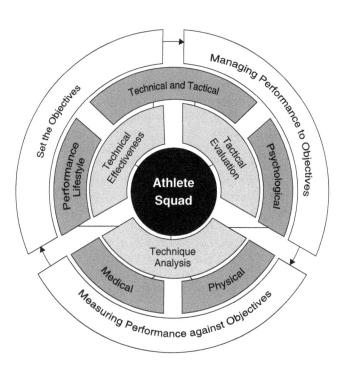

Figure 15.3   An integrated model of performance management and analysis

1. Secondary data – data which already exist and which were collected for some other (primary) purpose but which can be used a second time in the current project (previous high performance strategic and analysis reports).
2. Primary data – qualitative and quantitative data consisting of original information that comes from people and includes information gathered from surveys, focus groups, independent observations and questionnaire results.

Interviewing key stakeholders will be integral to successful completion of the review process, and focus questions would include: Is the performance environment fit for purpose? Can the current athlete demands deliver consistency of performance? What changes need to be made to the performance environment, and why? How do we ensure improved standards of performance? What actually matters?

Broad outcomes for the review will link to defining management frameworks that align to principles of outcome-driven investment and data outputs that measure the effectiveness of the organisation. This could incorporate a new best-practice high performance structure or model and a plan that highlights the main strategic imperatives to move elite performance forward. The specific performance plan might include some key targets to improve a performance environment: capability development (right people with the right skills); redefined structures and systems; strategic leadership; behavioural congruence; application and transference of knowledge and understanding; world-class physical and human resources; outcome-driven investment; athlete welfare; talent development environment; coach development; multi-disciplinary athlete support provision; commitment to long-term applied research and development; and a sustainable continuing professional development culture. This framework for the review outputs can be used to assess an elite performance environment in terms of a balance of competencies in performance, coach education, sports science, commercial and operational management plans, and overall performance management and analysis. The latter impacts upon the overall management quality of the eight concurrent lines of capability within any performance environment: training; equipment; personnel; information; organisation; infrastructure; logistics; and values. Future improvements in elite sports performance will rely on improved technology and coaching. The latter relies on coaches being better developed scientifically and on the use of better technical analysis systems. Compressing large, unwieldy multi-disciplinary data sets into simple inter-disciplinary outputs that provide meaningful knowledge will assist the change process in elite sport by answering key performance questions and monitoring key trends.

The integrated model of performance management and analysis can help to facilitate: individual long- and short-term targets; squad threshold bands to review performance and for squad selection; use of threshold bands longitudinally to monitor performance over time; and age-related thresholds for talent identification and development purposes. These areas demand that HP managers work to a set of clear general priorities: to provide clear direction; to be simple and focused; to clarify roles; to be outcome-orientated; and to prioritise in areas that make the greatest difference. Such an approach will help support a HP manager to produce evidence that performance analysis enhances sports performance; this will demand that the manager critically evaluates the multi-disciplinary nature of performance analysis and how this translates into formative feedback as an accelerator in performance analysis and management. Coherent performance management and analysis underpins and promotes competitive success of an elite sport, which can be critically important for a number of reasons: it helps attract high-profile sport to a given country; it may be the single most important financial factor underpinning the high performance environment; it can be fundamental to the creation of a sense of national identity and pride; it encourages a nation to be more active and improves concomitant health-related fitness levels; and it develops a positive image to market a country's products overseas.

Concluding remarks

In conclusion, there will be an increasing demand for HP managers to apply performance analysis to answer cutting-edge performance issues via a research and development strategy: sports behaviours and sports outcomes; relative significance of contextual sports behaviours (McGarry, 2009); team interactions and game behaviour; principal component analysis; and real-time interventions (O'Donoghue, 2009). Ultimately, the main focus for any HP manager is winning performance and, as such, the most fundamentally important question will remain: Tactically, are we performing the right skill and, technically, are we performing the skill right (O'Donoghue, 2011)? Converting the multi-disciplinary reality into an inter-disciplinary end product that can be used by coaches and athletes remains a major challenge, which can be overcome by applying a HPMS and an integrated model of performance management and analysis.

References

Blanchard, K. (2006) *Leading at a Higher Level*, Upper Saddle River, NJ: Prentice-Hall, FT Press.

Bracewell, P., Meyer, D. and Ganesh, S. (2003) 'Creating and monitoring meaningful individual rugby ratings', *Research Letters in the Information and Mathematical Sciences*, 4: 19–22.

BSI (2009) *BS 10012:2009: Data Protection. Specification for a Personal Information Management System*, London: ICT Publications.

Cameron, E. and Green, M. (2009) *Making Sense of Change Management*, 2nd ed., London: Kogan Page.

Carroll, J.M, Choo, C.W., Dunlap, D.R. and Isenhour, P.L. (2003) 'Knowledge management support for teachers', *Educational Technology, Research and Development*, 51(4): 42–64.

Cleveland, J., Murphy, K. and Williams, R. (1989) 'Multiple uses of performance appraisal: Prevalence and correlates', *Journal of Applied Psychology*, 74: 130–5.

Department of Health (1998) *Data Protection Act*, London: Government Legislation.

Few, S. (2006) *Information Dashboard Design: The Effective Visual Communication of Data*, Sebastopol, CA: O'Reilly Media Inc.

FIFA (2010) *World Cup South Africa: Technical Report and Statistics*, Switzerland: FIFA.

Fletcher, D. and Arnold, A. (2011) 'A qualitative study of performance leadership and management in elite sport', *Journal of Applied Sport Psychology*, 23(2): 223–42.

Gilson, C., Pratt, M., Roberts, K. and Weymes, E. (2001) *Peak Performance*, London: Harper-Collins.

Hoye, R., Smith, A., Westerbeek, H., Stewart, B. and Nicholson, M. (2006) *Sport Management: Principles and Applications*, Oxford: Elsevier.

IRB (2010) *Tri Nations 2010: Statistical Review and Match Analysis*, Dublin: IRB.

Jones, G., Gittins, M. and Hardy L. (2009) 'Creating an environment where high performance is inevitable and sustainable: The High Performance Environment Model', *Annual Review of High Performance Coaching & Consulting*, 1: 139–49.

Kalyuga, S. (2007) 'Expertise reversal effect and its implication for learner-tailored instruction', *Educational Psychology Review*, 19(4): 509–39.

Kaplan, R. and Norton, D. (1992) 'The balanced scorecard: Measures that drive performance', *Harvard Business Review*, January–February: 71–79.

Lencioni, P.M. (2002) *The Five Dysfunctions of a Team: A Leadership Fable*, California: Jossey-Bass.

Lin, C. and Chen, M. (2009) 'Factors affecting teachers' knowledge sharing behaviors and motivation: System functions that work', *eLAC*, 1–8.

Mallet, C. and Côté, J. (2006) 'Beyond winning and losing: Guidelines for evaluating high performance coaches', *The Sport Psychologist*, 20: 213–21.

McGarry, T. (2009) 'Applied and theoretical perspectives of performance analysis in sport: Scientific issues and challenges', *International Journal of Performance Analysis of Sport*, 9(1): 128–40.

O'Donoghue, P. (2009) 'Interacting Performances Theory', *International Journal of Performance Analysis of Sport*, 9(1): 26–46.

O'Donoghue, P.G. (2010) *Research Methods for Sports Performance Analysis*, London: Routledge.

O'Donoghue, P.G. (2011) Personal communication.

Paladino, B. (2011) *Innovative Corporate Performance Management*, Hoboken, NJ: John Wiley & Sons.

Reid, C., Stewart, E. and Thorne, G., (2004) 'Multi-disciplinary sports science teams in elite sport: Comprehensive servicing or conflict and confusion', *The Sport Psychologist*, 18: 204–17.

Scott, S. (2009) 'High performance planning: Managing an effective high performance program', *Coaches Plan*, 16(3): 18–19.

Smither, J.W.L. and London, M. (2009) *Performance Management: Putting Research into Action*, San Francisco, CA: Jossey-Bass.

Sonnentag, S. (2002) *Psychological Management of Individual Performance*, Chichester, UK: John Wiley & Sons.

Winstanley, D and Stuart-Smith, K. (1996) 'Policing performance: The ethics of performance management', *Personnel Review*, 25(6): 66–84.

16

MEDIA APPLICATIONS OF PERFORMANCE ANALYSIS

Anthony (Tony) N. Kirkbride

CSIR SPORTS TECHNOLOGY, PRETORIA, SOUTH AFRICA

Summary

The media applications of performance analysis have led to the development of the armchair fan or spectator into a savvy consumer of sports performance analysis data. As the print and television media have utilised statistics and graphics to enhance the enjoyment of their broadcast content, the concomitant availability of match and individual data has led to an enlightened viewer. This new domain of 'infotainment' occurs at the nexus where information is blended with entertainment. Traditionally, sports newspapers, radio and TV media typically provided low-level data in match reporting, such as the score as a function of match time. In modern sports broadcasting, this simple data set is now amplified with complex statistics and real-time, in-game data to provide unrivalled information sets for both decision support by coaches and infotainment. Statistics have always played a role in sports performance monitoring, to evaluate either an individual's performance or that of a team. Leading the way are undoubtedly the bat games of baseball and cricket, which capture and record ever-increasing amounts of facts and figures. Such accurate and comprehensive data sets are easily accessible, which is leading to an increased interest in modelling and simulation of games. Commercially available statistics – for example, from Castrol Index (www.castrolfootball.com) or Wisden Cricketers' Almanack (www.wisden.com) – can be used very effectively by a diverse consumer group, ranging from the progressive coach to the sports gambler. A representative illustration was provided by Michael Lewis in the bestselling book *Moneyball,* in which Billy Beane's interpretation of players' baseball statistics changed the fortunes of the Oakland Athletic team. When this type of 'raw' information is augmented with the addition of bespoke video data from commercial notational analysis systems, such as Amisco™ (Amisco France, Nice, France) or Prozone™ (Prozone Sports Ltd, Leeds, UK), the resultant enlarged data sets provide a sound basis for decision support.

Introduction

Previous chapters in this handbook have primarily devoted attention to the role sports performance analysis plays in providing meaningful advice to athletes, players, coaches and managers. Such feedback is predominantly focused on improving sports performance, but it can have secondary or tertiary applications; for instance, to inform the armchair fan or improve the health or well-being of an athlete. This chapter will focus on the commercial applications of performance analysis data – in particular, how such data is represented in the media. Explosive growth in both the amount and the complexity of performance-related data in the open press has been observed recently. This chapter is dedicated to providing an overview of the current state of data reporting in both the traditional press/TV media and the so-called new media of internet and mobile devices. It is not intended to be an exhaustive review or catalogue of newspaper clippings and graphics, rather a representative sample of the current state of media applications of performance analysis.

The term 'infotainment' has been coined to describe the nexus between sport (as entertainment) and information (often in the form of low-level statistics and/or raw data). At this early juncture, it is important to highlight the difference between performance analysis data used in the professional context and that used as the basis for infotainment. Although some similarities may exist between the gathering and reporting of such data, a clear distinction must be made in terms of the confidence that should be afforded to each context. Although real-time data, often appearing in eye-catching graphics during play, may add to the spectators' enjoyment of the broadcast, its accuracy can be readily challenged. Potential measurement errors can creep in due to the speed of real-time event coding, which are usually quickly and easily identified and remedied in any post-match analysis. Nevertheless, such statistics are often used as the basis of debate and comment, at half- or full-time, by in-studio commentators and guests. These pundits frequently use generalisations and rely on the unscientific interpretation of (sometimes erroneous) low-level performance analysis data to provide their match insights. This type of match analysis data must only be used with extreme caution and its accuracy and precision must always be verified prior to any reliance being placed on it. Data from subscription sources is by and large more accurate (since it is generally subject to more stringent verification checks) than data produced at venues for TV graphics. Whatever system is relied upon, performance analysts have an obligation to verify any media data before placing any weight on its validity.

Historically, media in the form of newspapers, television, radio, books and magazines were the primary source of the general public's access to low-level performance data. Typical examples would be the score as a function of time, or perhaps percentage ball possession for each team. This information would be used as the source of playground banter by children or perhaps more in-depth scholarly discussions at universities or company offices. Contemporary new media outlets, such as the internet, smart phones, tablet computers and the like, are awash with content-rich performance analysis data of staggering complexity. For instance, take time to examine the comprehensiveness of the soccer match data and reports from games in the 2010 FIFA World Cup™ held in South Africa (www.fifa.com). Today, sports fans are becoming savvy consumers of performance analysis data through regular exposure to a plethora of such information. The ever-increasing sports knowledge of the armchair fan has an empowering effect on all sports. The publication of modern sports performance analysis data, particularly in new media, coupled with social media development (such as Facebook and Twitter) has led to the ability of fans to readily challenge coaches' and managers' decisions and to express their concerns directly to team management and owners. Dedicated sports radio stations, such as the UK's talkSPORT (www.talksport.co.uk), permit in-depth analysis and dialogue on a wide variety of sports-related topics, particularly focused on match analysis.

The explosion of match statistics and data has also led to the phenomenal growth of 'Fantasy Leagues' and sports ranking systems. What started out life as journalistic reporting of match events in a daily newspaper has now led to supporters having unprecedented real-time access to information from a wide variety of on-line sources. Consequently, coaches and team mangers are increasingly responding by providing, to a greater extent, details of match strategies and tactics, particularly post-match, and often in defence of their results.

Statistics, and their subsequent analysis, are playing an increasingly important role in sports performance monitoring. Historically, baseball and cricket led the way since the slower pace of these games permitted highly accurate, real-time data capture and coaching scrutiny. The increasing availability of such exact and comprehensive data sets is now leading to a renewal and resurgence of interest in modelling and simulation of games – for instance, to optimise team selection or, in the case of cricket, the team's batting order.

Science plays an important role in developing novel products and services capable of delivering high-quality performance analysis data that underpins more accurate decision support. One emerging example in cricket is the ability to apply modern statistical techniques to large data sets and utilise this data for decision support. For example, to maximise the probability of a team winning, the batting order in the second innings of limited-over games can be modified (as the game is in progress) by taking account of the score as a function of time and the availability of resources.

Today, the internet has revolutionised the way we access information. The performance analysis data it holds provides an outstanding starting repository for sports scientists and performance analysts, with the proviso to verify the accurateness and precision of its content prior to exploitation.

Classification of media applications

The approach

There are two possible approaches to classifying media applications of performance analysis: the first is by media type (i.e. print, radio, TV, on-line) and the second by sports type. Since this is a handbook dedicated to sports performance analysis, the taxonomy according to sport type is used. Consequently, examples have been chosen for sports that receive the most column inches or satellite/terrestrial TV coverage time. It must be stressed that the media applications for the sports illustrated below can generally be applied to related sports. As an example, *shots on target* as a function of total number of shots on goal is an applicable statistical ratio used to compare teams' attacking proficiency in soccer, hockey, handball or polo. Therefore, the section on soccer could potentially be applicable and of equal value to similar sporting codes.

The objective of providing match data and performance analysis statistics are two-fold. First, to keep abreast of the match status (i.e. score or elapsed time) and, second, to elucidate various *key performance indicators* (KPIs). It is not the intention of this chapter to discuss in detail sports performance profiling; this has been covered elsewhere. Nevertheless, match commentators often use platitudes, such as 'rugby is a game of possession', that lead to the TV broadcaster generating statistics and graphics to report on possession. Furthermore, as statistics become available, such as each team's percentage ball possession of the play, this regularly receives a secondary treatment. For instance, the area in which possession was lost/gained is then subsequently analysed and reported on. Consequently, as performance analysts, we begin to see the complexity of the information increase, but unfortunately it often is linked to a decrease in data accuracy.

It could be argued that TV spectators are bombarded with match statistics and data (push), whereas, conversely, internet-based fans only access data when required (pull). Both types of approaches can suffer from the same problem. That is, the data may not be representative of KPIs determined by rigorous scientific investigation, but rather more aligned to the broadcaster's requirement to enhance its viewers' enjoyment of their programming. In the case of Formula 1™ motor racing coverage, high-definition TV cameras augmented with real-time telemetry provide monitoring of the cars' track status, engine revolutions and speed, giving unprecedented and engaging TV content aimed at ensuring a captive audience. Furthermore, the telemetry data supplied by Formula 1's Management's Technical Facility is also fed to the F1™ web site (www.formula1.com) for distribution to desktop and laptop computers. There are also mobile applications for multiple platforms for live timing, weather and wind speed and lap data. None of this data, however, should be classified as a KPI, rather as an appealing media application of hi-tech performance analysis.

Classifying sports codes

The primary objectives of mass media are to entertain and inform via mass communication; consequently, each media type competes to portray performance analysis results in an increasingly engaging manner. Their aim is to maintain viewers, listeners and readership in a progressively competitive market vying for market share and coverage. In mass media terms, those outlets with the highest followings attract higher advertising revenue and are thus considered more successful. Sports codes also compete for column inches or bandwidth and in this chapter the sports selected contribute the largest proportion of the media coverage observed at the time of writing.

In classifying sports codes, a distinction has been made between invasive, net and wall sports, and striking and fielding sports. This chapter focuses on the media's portrayal of the dominant sports codes in each of these domains.

Invasive team games

Generally, invasive team games share a common objective and similar characteristics – that is, to score points/goals by successfully moving a game object (usually a ball) into a demarcated area or zone. Typical examples include football, rugby and hockey. Such sports have language to express both attacking and defending strategies, as well as clearly defined zones on the field of play. Irrespective of the sport, these games share many common characteristics (passing, interception, shooting) and often performance analysis approaches are easily adaptable from one sport to another, although the descriptive language may often vary between codes – for example, tackling in one sport may be referred to as checking in another. A resemblance also exists in the various roles of players in the team, particularly with respect to offensive and defensive players and their KPIs, which are often similarly reported (e.g. shots on target, missed tackles). Consequently, the media applications of performance analysis for invasive sports are easily translatable between invasive sports codes.

Soccer

Undoubtedly, 'the beautiful game' is the largest spectator sport in the world. Pelé, one of the legends of the sport, coined the colloquial phrase in his autobiography *My Life and the Beautiful Game* and it is a descriptor now often endorsed by the sport's controlling body, the Fédération Internationale de Football Association (FIFA). The game's simplicity and range of derivatives and variations, such as five-a-side, help maintain a strong following. Traditional newspapers are currently attempting to display complex 2-D and 3-D graphics of passing sequences leading to goal-scoring incidents. These would probably be more suited to the visual world of TV; nevertheless, they portray a media outlet keen to retain and grow their readership with more engaging presentations of performance analysis-type data.

The simplest performance analysis report of match data is the final score. Almost all newspapers that contain a sports section dedicate a small area or column to only providing final result tables. Sometimes, the score at half-time is included for comparison and shown in brackets. This simple data set can sometimes be augmented with events, times of goals and goal scorers. Generally, newspapers are a good resource for fixtures, results and league tables, and they are certainly improving the quantity of performance analysis data in press. Conversely, new media applications contain abundant performance analysis statistics, generally acquired on a subscription basis from a single centralised source, such as Opta (www.optasports.com) or Press Association Sport (www.pressassociation.com).

Newspapers, television, internet and mobile generally digest sports metadata on such a subscription basis. The information utilised is commonly delivered as an XML feed (Extensible Markup Language) and varies in complexity depending on the level of the client's subscription. Basic packages will contain fixtures, results and tables. Standard data packages augment this to include information such as time of goal, scorer, line-ups, referee, red/yellow cards, attendance and the like. Premium subscription packages typically enrich this data and include shots on/off target, possession (percentages), number of corners, throw-ins, saves, off-sides, etc. (see, for example, Table 16.1). Subscription services are specialists in collating, packaging and distributing performance analysis data in compelling ways to enhance match insights for a wide variety of applications. Football fans are migrating away from newspaper sports content and now follow the action on the go. Consequently, iPhone®, iPad® and Android™ applications developed to exploit the mobile web are increasing in growth.

Figure 16.1 is an example from FIFA's web site of line-up graphics indicating player name and possession. Often the placement of the shirts will give an indication of the tactical formation of play. Since the graphic was accessed post–match, additional information, such as yellow (and red) cards, has been added, along with substitutions.

An important characteristic of soccer is the accuracy and complexity of passing. These performance statistics are reported extensively by FIFA, breaking them down into short, medium

Table 16.1 Internet match statistics for 2010 FIFA World Cup South Africa™ (sourced from www.fifa.com for match 64, Final, 11 July 2011)

Netherlands (NED)	Statistics	Spain (ESP)
13	Shots	18
5	Shots on goal	6
0	Goals scored	1
28	Foul committed	19
18	Fouls suffered	28
6	Corner kicks	8
18	Free kicks shots (scored)	23
0/0	Penalty kicks (goals/shots)	0/0
7	Off-sides	6
0	Own goals	0
7	Yellow cards	5
1	Second yellow and red card	0
0	Red cards	0
36	Actual playing time	48
43%	Possession	57%

Source: www.fifa.com/worldcup/archive/southafrica2010/statistics/matches/round=249721/match= 300061509/index.html (accessed 11 October 2011, used with permission).

Figure 16.1   Illustration of performance analysis data from 2010 FIFA World Cup™ illustrating player line-up for match 64, the final (used with permission)

and long passes (Figure 16.2). However, no operational definition could be accessed to provide a more accurate explanation of these terms.

An intriguing graphic is the ball possession heat map, which aims to indicate, in the form of a gravity map, where most of the possession took place (Figure 16.3). For each team, the deeper

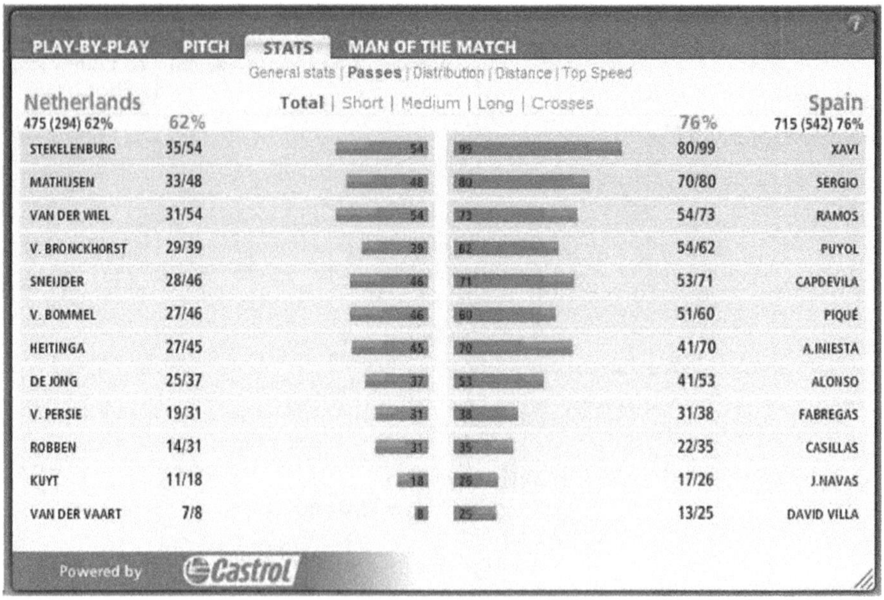

PLAY-BY-PLAY	PITCH	**STATS**	MAN OF THE MATCH			
		General stats | **Passes** | Distribution | Distance | Top Speed				
Netherlands		Total | Short | Medium | Long | Crosses			**Spain**
475 (294) 62%	62%			76%		715 (542) 76%
STEKELENBURG	35/54	54	99	80/99		XAVI
MATHIJSEN	33/48	48	80	70/80		SERGIO
VAN DER WIEL	31/54	54	73	54/73		RAMOS
V. BRONCKHORST	29/39	39	62	54/62		PUYOL
SNEIJDER	28/46	46	71	53/71		CAPDEVILA
V. BOMMEL	27/46	46	60	51/60		PIQUÉ
HEITINGA	27/45	45	70	41/70		A.INIESTA
DE JONG	25/37	37	53	41/53		ALONSO
V. PERSIE	19/31	31	38	31/38		FABREGAS
ROBBEN	14/31	31	35	22/35		CASILLAS
KUYT	11/18	18	26	17/26		J.NAVAS
VAN DER VAART	7/8	8	25	13/25		DAVID VILLA

Powered by *Castrol*

Figure 16.2   Illustration of performance analysis data from 2010 FIFA World Cup™ showing pass retention ratios (used with permission)

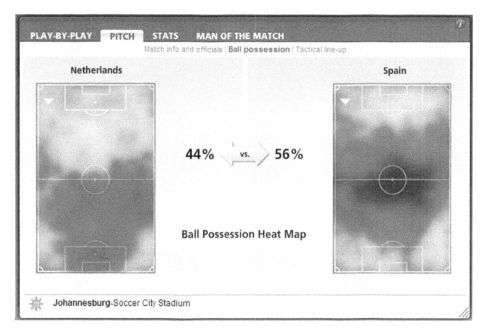

Figure 16.3 Illustration of performance analysis data from 2010 FIFA World Cup™ showing ball possession heat maps (used with permission)

the red (grey) colouration, the greater the percentage ball possession in that specific area. Such
graphics are normally produced through image analysis and post-processing multi-angle video
of the match. Amisco™ and Prozone™ are notable companies currently generating this type of
data for provision to both sport and media clients.

Since much of the data is in XML format, it is easily ported to a variety of devices and
applications. Whether they are pre-match statistics, live in-game data or post-match analysis, the aim is to provide compelling match insights to an increasingly demanding audience.
Recently, live match data is being ported to specialist web sites, such as FourFourTwo.com
(http://fourfourtwo.com/statszone/), that cater for the fan with a more-than-passing interest in
match analysis. See the examples of match line-up and player statistics in Figures 16.4 and 16.5,
respectively (accessed via iPhone® application).

One of the most comprehensive and insightful of the current internet-based performance
analysis offerings in soccer is located at www.whoscored.com. With Facebook and Twitter
links, the site provides access to an extraordinary array of complex statistics that would not be
out of place in a professional team environment, and available at no subscription cost. Pre-
match statistics, live in-game data and post-match analysis are all accessible, as well as an active
blog that provides an entertaining array of insights into the modern game.

The example chosen and illustrated in Figure 16.6 is the 'clumsiest/cleanest tackling XI' and
is a measure of effectiveness in tackling compiled just two months into the 2011–12 Premier
League season. There are 20 teams in the English Premier League and more than 13 are represented in the analysis. The analysis extracts the best and worst tackling to compile a starting XI
(excluding goalkeeper) to provide an interesting snapshot at contact. Stoke lead the way with
three appearances, two in the cleanest tackling and one in the clumsiest. Wolves and Swansea

Figure 16.4 Performance analysis data originally from Opta and ported to FourFourTwo.com (match line-up) (used with permission)

Figure 16.5 Performance analysis data originally from Opta and ported to FourFourTwo.com (player statistics) (used with permission)

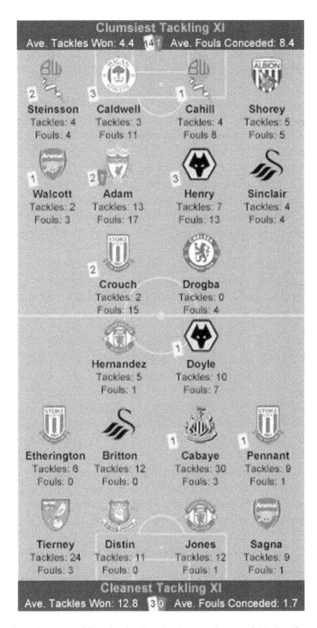

Figure 16.6 Clumsiest/cleanest tackling in the Premier League (accessed 11 October 2011 from www. whoscored.com/Blog/v0nk3_z_zkqbnkre-xvfba/Show/The-Cleanest-vs-Clumsiest-Premier-League-Tacklers; used with permission)

contribute a player to each category and Bolton Wanderers exhibit a tendency to commit more fouls than tackles, especially in a defensive position.

Furthermore, analysis of the Clean XI reveals that, for the period under analysis, the combined total of tackles was 128, approximately 13 for each player, who only conceded a total of 17 fouls (Doyle contributed 7). This excellence in tackling is reflected with a relatively clean disciplinary record: only three players were cautioned (yellow carded) and none sent off.

Conversely, the Clumsiest XI, who appear to be rather over-exuberant in contact when judged by the match officials, win only a third of their tackles and they concede five times as many fouls. Seven players were booked (amassing 14 yellow cards) and one sent off.

In this handbook, it is challenging to provide examples of TV graphics since these are subject to copyright and are not necessarily in the general public domain, since they are often country-specific, as compared to blogs and internet sites. Nevertheless, similarities exist in the depiction of internet graphics and those of TV. Some TV companies choose to collect their own in-game statistics, which are subsequently used in conjunction with broadcast graphic engines (such as VizRT, utilised by Alston Elliot, www.aelgraphics.co.uk/ae.html), or the engines digest XML content on a subscription basis from Opta and PA Sports.

Data visualisation using 3-D graphics engines and event re-rendering using tools such as LibroVision™ are becoming commonplace as sports broadcasters strive to produce increasingly engaging content. The result is annotated analysis of plays that inform through clarification and visualisation of in-game events and actions. For an example, refer to www.vizrt.com/news/article12795.ece.

The future of performance analysis in soccer is encouraging. Accurate match insights based on increasingly precise data, faster 3-D render times and graphics engines will see XML streams provide an increasing amount of material to feed the media's almost insatiable craving for content.

Rugby union

Rugby is a football sport with two distinct derivatives: rugby league and rugby union (Midgley, 1983). In both codes, the objective of the game is to win by scoring more points than the opposition in a set amount of time. There are several ways in which to score points and a full description can be easily accessed on-line via Wikipedia (en.wikipedia.org) or in rule books (www.irb.com). This section refers to the union code. The field of play is rectangular and has limits to its maximum dimensions, the football is oval and there are two assistant referees (known as touch judges) and one on-field referee. Each team consists of 15 players and a possible seven substitutes. A match consists of two 40-minute halves and each team has eight forwards (positions 1 to 8) and seven backs (positions 9 to 15). Performance analysis data is usually presented in the form of a team's percentage possession and territory. Table 16.2 shows data from the 2011 Rugby World Cup quarter-final match between South Africa and Australia. Prior to each game in the tournament, the International Rugby Board (IRB, 2011) publishes a comprehensive data sheet of the key facts and figures for both teams when competing in head-to-head situations. In 73 previous encounters, South Africa had won 41 and one match was drawn (a winning ratio of 41/73 = 56.2 per cent).

The match statistics taken in isolation portray a dominant performance by South Africa over Australia; however, the scoreboard reveals a different story. Despite South Africa having attacking possession of the ball for four times longer than Australia (12'30" compared to 3'30") and 76 per cent territorial advantage and winning 19/22 (86 per cent) of the lineouts, this was not good enough to secure the win. Such results suggest that generalisations, such as 'rugby is a game of possession', implying that teams with more possession generally win games, need to be applied with caution. Possession *per se* is not necessarily a performance indicator of success. Previous Rugby World Cups, in the recent past, have been won by teams with experience; this is reflected in success being highly correlated with test caps. However, in 2011, South Africa fielded a team with 836 caps and was beaten by a team with 523 caps (Ackford, 2011).

In this match encounter, the team with the least possession and territory won the match. Success, in this instance, can be ascribed to good defence and this can be seen in the high tackle

Table 16.2 Internet match statistics for 2011 IRB Rugby World Cup™ (sourced from www.rugbyworld-cup.com for quarter-final – 9 October 2011)

South Africa (RSA)	Statistics	Australia (AUS)
9	Score	11
56%	Ball possession	44%
76%	Territory	24%
12'30"	Time in opposition 22	3'31"
0	Tries	1
0 (0)	Conversions (missed)	0 (1)
2 (2)	Penalties (missed)	2 (0)
1 (1)	Drop goals (missed)	0 (0)
7/0	Scrums (won/lost)	13/1
14/0	Lineouts (won/lost)	8/5
5	Turnovers won (ruck + maul)	9
53 (11)	Tackles (missed)	147 (13)
1	Clean line breaks	1
11	Handling errors	9
4	Penalties conceded	6
0	Yellow cards	0
0	Red cards	0

Source: www.rwc2011.irb.com/rugbytracker/match=11229/statistics.html(used with permission)

count for Australia (147) compared to South Africa (53). This specific match caused a high degree of refereeing controversy since many analysts and commentators (Rich, 2011) were highly critical of Bryce Lawrence's handling of the match. Subsequent analysis attempted to show that South Africa had 131 rucks compared to Australia's 44 and, consequently, for every opportunity for South Africa to contest and slow the ball down, Australia had three to do so (Tucker and Dugas, 2011). Media analysis of this specific match highlighted the simple fact that teams that win matches do not necessarily have possession and territorial advantage. Indeed, the 2011 Rugby World Cup was won 8–7 by New Zealand with less possession (45 per cent) and territory (45 per cent) than their opponents, France (source www.rwc2011.irb.com/rug-bytracker/match=11235/index.html).

Basketball

Basketball is a fast paced, non-contact, court-based sport that is played in over 200 countries and is particularly popular in North America (Griffiths, 2010). The objective is to attain more points than the opposition team and this is achieved by scoring 'baskets' in an allotted time. Two or three points can be scored by successfully throwing or shooting a ball from different zones on the playing court. Two points are awarded if the player is relatively close to the basket and three points if the player is outside the three-point line. Once a basket is scored, possession changes to the other team. Since basketball is characterised by relatively high scores, possession changes regularly during play. If, at the end of normal play, the scores are tied, then additional time (overtime) is played. Play is usually in either four quarters or two halves and the length varies according to the playing rules of specific competitions. The two teams usually consist of five on-court players and five substitutes each. Time is actual playing time and the match clock stops whilst play is inactive, which leads to games taking much longer to complete than the allotted time. Often, teams monitor real-time statistics and have a dedicated analyst who provides match insights for coaching decision support.

The main components of the sport are shooting, rebounding, passing, blocking and dribbling. Many terms are self-explanatory; rebounding is the ability of either the defensive or the offensive team to successfully gain possession after a missed field goal and plays a major role in the sport. Players and team statistics are generally reported as a function of these defining aspects of the sport. Typical examples include field goal attempts (FGA), offensive rebounds per game (OREB), defensive rebounds per game (DREB), percentage passing accuracy, free throws made (FTM), field goals made (FGM) and three-point field goals made (3FGM).

There is a wide variety of media sources of statistics available for this sport. The amount of raw data and analysis, both freely available and on subscription, is phenomenal. One of the most recognised sources of freely available data is the National Basketball Association (www.nba.com). Their home web page provides a portal to a comprehensive database of on-line statistics dating back to the 2004–5 season. This data can be filtered by 'Leaders in Category', 'Year and Season', 'Player Options', 'Filter Options' and'Splits'. This internet site provides a comprehensive data set for analysis and not only reports on performance indicators, such as free throw percentages, but also reports on the actual numbers so that the weight that can be attached to the result can also be considered. Data is presented in tabular format with the aid of filters and sort functions to manipulate the data for interpretation, direct comparisons and ranking purposes.

Media statistics, particularly on the internet, can be sorted and ranked with ease. Caution must be applied – for instance, scoring is an important aspect of basketball and, consequently, accuracy is an important component of shooting (Table 16.3). Although Kevin Durant had the highest points per game (PTS) average over 17 matches, his shooting accuracy was lower than that of Dirk Nowitzki. Of particular note is the variation in the percentage success rate for field throws. Compare Durant at 83.8 per cent to that of Nowitzki at 94.1 per cent over comparative average attempt ranges (8.2–9.8 compared to 8.3–8.9, respectively).

Since the NBA data can be filtered and sorted, a subsequent sort on FG% high–low yields the result shown in Table 16.4 for the same season.

Table 16.3 2010–11 post-season scoring leaders: points per game – all teams (NBA)

Player name, Team name	GP	MPG	PTS	FGM–FGA	FG%	3PM–3PA	3P%	FTM–FTA	FT%
1 Kevin Durant, OKC	17	42.5	28.6	9.1–20.3	0.449	2.2–6.4	0.339	8.2–9.8	0.838
2 Dirk Nowitzki, DAL	21	39.3	27.7	9.1–18.9	0.485	1.1–2.4	0.460	8.3–8.9	0.941
3 Derrick Rose, CHI	16	40.6	27.1	9.3–23.5	0.396	1.6–6.3	0.248	6.9–8.4	0.828
4 Dwight Howard, ORL	6	42.9	27.0	8.5–13.5	0.630	0.0–0.2	0.000	10.0–14.7	0.682
5 Carmelo Anthony, NYK	4	38.9	26.0	8.2–22.0	0.375	2.2–6.5	0.346	7.2–8.5	0.853

Key: GP – Games Played; MPG – Minutes Per Game; PTS – Points; FGM – Field Goals Made; FGA – Field Goals Attempted; FG% – Field Goals Percentage; 3PM – Three Points Made; 3PA – Three Points Attempted; 3P% – Three Points Percentage; FTM – Field Throws Made; FTA – Field Throws Attempted; FT% – Field Throws Percentage.
The NBA Statistics are used with permission from NBA Properties, Inc. All Rights Reserved.

Table 16.4 2010–11 post-season scoring leaders: field goal % – all teams (NBA)

Player name, Team name	GP	MPG	PTS	FGM–FGA	FG%	3PM–3PA	3P%	FTM–FTA	FT%
1 Rasual Butler, CHI	3	2.2	1.0	0.3–0.3	1.000	0.3–0.3	1.000	0.0–0.0	0.000
2 Patrick Ewing Jr., NOH	2	1.0	1.5	0.5–0.5	1.000	0.5–0.5	1.000	0.0–0.0	0.000
3 T.J. Ford, IND	2	6.8	3.5	1.5–1.5	1.000	0.5–0.5	1.000	0.0–0.0	0.000
4 Royal Ivey, OKC	2	3.1	3.0	1.0–1.0	1.000	1.0–1.0	1.000	0.0–0.0	0.000
5 Chris Johnson, POR	4	4.7	1.0	0.2–0.2	1.000	0.0–0.0	0.000	0.5–0.5	1.000

Key: GP – Games Played; MPG – Minutes Per Game; PTS – Points; FGM – Field Goals Made; FGA – Field Goals Attempted; FG% – Field Goals Percentage; 3PM – Three Points Made; 3PA – Three Points Attempted; 3P% – Three Points Percentage; FTM – Field Throws Made; FTA – Field Throws Attempted; FT% – Field Throws Percentage. The NBA Statistics are used with permission from NBA Properties, Inc. All Rights Reserved.

Table 16.4 shows those players with a 100 per cent field goal scoring record for the 2010–11 season. Viewed in isolation, these players could be considered the 'cream-of-the-crop' since their ability to score baskets on every shot attempt is unrivalled. However, the data when sorted takes no account of the number of games played (very low), minutes per game (very low) or points scored (very low). In basketball, as in other sports, it is important to place absolute figures in context when reporting performance data. Without additional reference information, statistics, particularly in the form of percentages, can be misleading.

The statistical data generated in match analysis is used as a basis for team selection and to optimise the strategies and tactics employed by team management. Reliance on NBA and in-house generated statistics is therefore important in developing winning teams. The NBA data reported is an excellent measure of trends within seasons and from season to season. However, in order to develop effective offensive and defensive strategies, team managers and coaches need access to much more detailed information and this is often the responsibility of the performance analyst in the team. One of the analyst's roles is to provide spatial or positional information to augment the general passing or shooting accuracy on court. In doing so, teams can identify areas on court where an individual's shooting accuracy is increased or decreased and zonal or man-to-man marking can be used to limit players exploiting these areas. Basketball is a game of efficiency and any improvements in scoring per possession can have a big effect on the match outcome. In Table 16.3, for example, only minor improvements to the FG% can have a major positive influence on the average score per match for an individual player.

Net and wall games

There are many varieties of competitive net and wall games with an equal assortment of scoring systems, but which are generally characterised by players trading shots to score points. Games are played within demarcated areas and the objective is to gain more points than an opponent through forcing an error during play either by the shot not being returned or by it going out of play. Usually the object is introduced into play by the 'service' and the game's rules dictate what constitutes fair and foul play in this area. Once in play, court coverage, shot selection and shot execution are key components of winning points. Generally, net and wall games are played by individuals, but derivatives exist to accommodate pairs and teams. Typical examples include squash, racquetball, tennis, badminton, volleyball and table tennis. World-wide, by far the largest media coverage is given to tennis. Therefore, this section will focus on this specific code.

The definitive web site for performance analysis data in tennis is the ATP (Association of Tennis Professionals). The ATP (www.atpworldtour.com) ranking began in 1973 and remains the official ranking system for men's professional tennis. However, it should be noted that the world governing body for the sport is the International Tennis Federation (www.itftennis.com).

The richness of the ATP match data is complemented by the presentation style of the graphics. Whereas the ITF hosts the more technical and scientific aspects of the diversity found in this sport, the more tactical and statistical information content is provided by the ATP. The ATP is an excellent repository of historical data on completed matches and provides a real-time stream of live match data and analysis. On subscription, access to official live streaming video on-demand is provided by the ATP (www.tennistv.com). Currently, over 1,600 live matches annually are streamed from 52 ATP World Tournaments and 41 Women's Tennis Association tournaments.

The ATP 2011 Shanghai Rolex Masters Final was held in China between David Ferrer and Andy Murray. Their head-to-head record is shown in Table 16.5. They are almost equivalent in world rankings and in head-to-head matches the slight favourite is Andy Murray (five wins to three over David Ferrer).

The match statistics from the final of the 2011 Shanghai Rolex Masters (16 October 2011) are presented in Table 16.6. The statistics support the dominant role Andy Murray played in the match. The final score was 7–5, 6–4. In addition to statistical information, many web sites provide graphics to indicate positions on the courts where specific events happened. For instance, the Australian Open web site (www.australianopen.com) provides schematic illustrations of where the first and second serves were successful and unsuccessful. Such tactical information is of benefit to coaches and players when undertaking post-match analysis.

In 2007, the Australian Open was the first Grand Slam tournament to utilise image-processing technology to challenge line calls. A commercial system, known as Hawk-Eye (Hawk-Eye

Table 16.5 Head-to-head comparison for David Ferrer and Andy Murray (as of 11 October 2011), Shanghai Rolex Masters

David Ferrer	3–5	Andy Murray
5	Ranking	3
(02.04.1982) 29	Age	(15.05.1987) 24
Javea, Spain	Birthplace	Dunblane, Scotland
Valencia, Spain	Residence	London, England
5' 9" (175 cm)	Height	6' 3" (190 cm)
160 lbs (73 kg)	Weight	185 lbs (84 kg)
Right-handed	Plays	Right-handed
2000	Turned Pro	2005
51/15	YTD Win/Loss	54/11
2	YTD Titles	5
11	Career Titles	21
$11,783,292	Career Prize Money	$18,495,016

(Used with permission)

Table 16.6 Match statistics provided by ATP for the Shanghai Rolex Masters Final (16 October 2011)

	David Ferrer	Andy Murray
Service Statistics		
Aces	1	7
Double Faults	4	4
First Serve	44%	63%
First Serve Points Won	24/35 (69%)	32/37 (86%)
Second Serve Points Won	20/45 (44%)	9/22 (41%)
Break Points Saved	5/9 (56%)	2/4 (50%)
Service Games Played	11	11
Return Statistics		
First Return Points Won	5/37 (14%)	11/35 (31%)
Second Return Points Won	13/22 (59%)	25/45 (56%)
Break Points Won	2/4 (50%)	4/9 (44%)
Return Games Played	11	11
Points Statistics		
Total Service Points Won	44/80 (55%)	41/59 (69%)
Total Return Points Won	18/59 (31%)	36/80 (45%)
Total Points Won	62/139 (45%)	77/139 (55%)

(Used with permission)

Innovations, Basingstoke, UK), was used to track the trajectory of the ball and to display this information in a graphic visualisation to assist adjudication of line calls. Many questions have been raised regarding the system's accuracy and the developer's reluctance to share data on accuracy, precision and reliability (Collins and Evans, 2008). In a direct response to Collins and Evans, Hawk-Eye Innovations published a press release describing the testing and evaluation protocol used by the International Tennis Federation that led to its accreditation as an aid to officiating in tennis (Hawk-Eye, 2008). Thus Hawk-Eye remains a valid tool good enough for match adjudication, analysis and reporting. The data generated from its triangulation of moving objects can be used for a wide variety of purposes, and in its early years of development this has mainly been to aid adjudication.

Another internet-based technology used at the 2007 Australian Open was IBM's Point-Tracker system. This system provided a schematic, visual representation of the match in progress (or previous match data). The observer's viewpoint could be modified and the court viewed from a wide variety of perspectives. Additionally, filters could be applied to show only shots of specific interest – for instance, first or second serves. In the forthcoming 2012 Australian Open, the system will be known as IBM Slam Tracker and will 'push' point-by-point scoring information to the internet in real time. The main functionality will be the real-time scoreboard of ongoing matches; however, the 'View match stats' button will bring up match and serve statistics. As with other sports, the collection and publication of live performance data is prone to measurement and reporting errors. Elite-level tennis is a fast-paced sport; nevertheless, high-level reporting, such as the match score (e.g. number of sets), is not considered problematical. However, counting the specific number of backhand/forehand shots in a rally to determine style of net play is much more difficult and prone to errors. As previously stated, performance analysts and researchers can use statistics published in the open press, but reliability is always a cause for concern. O'Donoghue (2007) reported that there was a systematic bias of 1.95 more net points being web-reported on average for each player when comparing his results to that from the US Open internet site (www.usopen.org [2006]). O'Donoghue suggested that this could be attributed to the operational definition used to define a net point. This type of study clearly articulates the need for separate reliability studies to be undertaken before any reliance should be placed on the data. O'Donoghue argued that precise operational definitions *per se* do not guarantee good reliability; neither does their absence guarantee poor reliability.

Striking and fielding games

In sports where the ball-in-play time is a low percentage of the total playing time, such as in striking and fielding games, these codes are generally characterised by a significantly high number of performance statistics. This can be attributed to two different aspects of these sports. First, there is sufficient time for the analysts to compile, and report on, a large collection of performance-related statistics and, second, the sports themselves can be distilled into their component parts, which can usually be easily represented statistically. This chapter focuses on two sports that receive visually stunning media coverage in terms of the performance analysis data reported. Golf and cricket are popular spectator sports that consume vast amounts of statistical data (cricket, in particular, is on a par with baseball in this regard). Television audiences are treated to complex, visually appealing graphics that inform the viewer, often to the level of distraction. For spectators with access to Wi-Fi, tournaments and match video and statistics of these sports are disseminated to bespoke applications on mobile phones and tablets (see, for example, iPhone ® applications: ECB Cricket, CricInfo mobi or USGA-US Open [downloadable from iTunes®]). Live video streaming may be country specific due to broadcast rights issues – however, live scoring, latest news feeds, photographs and biographies of players are readily available.

Golf

Much debate surrounds the early beginnings of this sport, with many conflicting origins. From golf's adoption in 1754 to the modern era, the rules of golf are set by the Royal and Ancient Golf Club of St Andrews, Scotland. One of the most influential national governing bodies of the sport is the United States Golf Association. Together, these two organisations control and revise the codes of play in consultation with other countries, particularly as they relate to international competitions. The objective is simple; to master the game is much more demanding. Golf is a precision sport in which players use a variety of clubs to hit balls into a series of holes on a dedicated golf course. The winner is the golfer who takes the least number of strokes or shots to complete the course (usually multiples of 18 holes). There is a variety of basic forms of golf, the two principal ones being match play and stroke play. In either scoring system, the fundamental performance analysis principles apply. Golf consists of a collection of different shot types. Consequently, it is relatively straightforward to monitor each aspect of the game using statistics; each individual's statistics can then be compared to other players' in order to gain an understanding of their strong and weak points. In essence, this can be broken down into the drive, the approach, the short game and the putt.

In golf, the lack of valid performance indicators has hampered credible scientific performance analysis. Generally, performance analysis has been limited to descriptive statistics of shots, one of the most popular of which is known as green(s) in regulation (GIR). This is an official statistic of the Professional Golfers' Association (PGA) Tour and describes a shot that is touching the putting surface and the number of strokes taken is at least two less than par. Others include driving distance and average putts per green (James, 2007). Recently, Lamb *et al.* (2011)

presented the ISOPAR method, which uses the ball location on the green and the number of shots to hole out to describe the difficulty of the hole. Using ISOPAR values, this group was able to determine shot quality as a performance indicator. Although much work still needs to be done to determine meaningful performance indicators, it will not be long before these new measures form part of the basket of statistics reported in the media.

The PGA Tour web site classifies golf statistics into six main domains, excluding the money listings and results in the form of points and rankings. The numbers in brackets below represent the total number of statistics reported in these areas. These are:

- off the tee (47)
- approach to the green (99)
- around the green (29)
- putting (89)
- scoring (99)
- streaks (21).

Greens in regulation (GIR) can be found in the section 'approach to the green'. At the time of access, the percentage of time a player made the green in regulation is shown in Table 16.7. Chad Campbell slid down the table from position 2 to 4 as his percentage dropped to 71.13. It was not possible to access his specific GIR percentage from the previous week, but, if we assume it was approximately 71.4, then this reduction represents only a drop in −0.38 per cent, which equates to only four shots in 1,746 holes (1,242/1,746 compared to 1,246/1,746). Boo Weekley heads the table with 71.68 per cent, indicating an outstanding drive and approach game. Table 16.8 shows the percentage of putts made from within ten feet of the hole.

In essence, a general rule of thumb is that nine out of ten putts will be made at this level of golf if the ball is within ten feet of the hole. Boo Weekley's average is 8.4 out of ten and he is tied at position 185 in the rankings with Harrison Frazar. Statistics such as these provide insights to the strong and weak areas of the game and are often a good starting point for coaching interventions.

Table 16.7 2011 PGA Tour greens in regulation percentage (up to 23 October 2011)

Rank this week	Rank last week	Player	Rounds	%	Greens hit	# Holes
1	1	Boo Weekley	66	71.68	800	1116
2	3	Heath Slocum	89	71.40	1131	1584
3	5	Joe Durant	71	71.26	885	1242
4	2	Chad Campbell	99	71.13	1242	1746
5	4	John Sneden	94	70.86	1199	1692

(Used with permission)

Table 16.8 2011 PGA Tour putting inside ten feet (up to 23 October 2011)

Rank this week	Rank last week	Player	Rounds	%	Attempts	Putts made
1	1	Bryce Molder	82	90.37	1267	1145
2	2	Fredrik Jacobson	92	90.18	1242	1120
3	5	Jerry Kelly	85	89.89	1226	1102
T185	181	Harrison Frazar	58	84.10	805	677
T185	182	Boo Weekley	66	84.10	1113	936

(Used with permission)

One of the more fascinating set of statistics is ball speed, which can be found in the section 'off the tee' (www.pgatour.com/r/stats/filter/?4). Doppler radar is used to determine the flight trajectory of golf balls in the more prestigious and televised tournaments. The company responsible for the system's development, EDH, uses its in-house developed phased array antenna called FlightScope® (EDH Holdings South Africa (Pty) Ltd., Stellenbosch, South Africa), a 3D Doppler tracking system that monitors a series of variables, including (but not limited to):

- club head speed
- club vertical angle of attack
- club horizontal attack angle
- club face angle
- ball spin rate
- hang time.

Data from FlightScope® (or similar) are available in real time during competition via TV and the internet (Figure 16.7) and also post-tournament on a range of web sites. FlightScope® is a commercial product that runs on a PC and recently the X2 version has been launched, which is compatible with Android ™, iPad ®, iPhone ® and iPod Touch ®. Its main application in the media is to provide engaging statistics that are captured and reported by the PGA and others.

Table 16.9 illustrates the peak speeds of the golf ball at launch (mph) on par 4 and 5 tee shots where a valid radar measurement was taken. For current golf club and ball designs and materials, the current maximum launch speed is in the order of 190 mph.

The PGA encourages performance analysts and scientists to undertake research into golf and, on application, will consider making data from SHOTLink (www.shotlink.com) avail-

Figure 16.7   Example of FlightScope® schematic data (used with permission)

Table 16.9 2011 PGA Tour ball speed (up to 23 October 2011)

Rank this week	Rank last week	Player	Rounds	Avg.	Fastest speed	Slowest speed
1	1	JB Holmes	57	185.01	190.79	171.60
2	2	Bubba Watson	85	182.90	190.50	165.12
3	3	Gary Woodland	93	179.27	188.60	150.21
4	4	Robert Garrigus	83	178.98	186.12	161.70
5	5	Jhonattan Vegas	84	178.96	185.52	164.51

Notes
All speeds in miles per hour (used with permission).

able to academia. As a starting point, the PGA made available a small sub-set of data in a semi-colon delimited text file to enable potential researchers the opportunity to view the data sets available. There are 37 different variables presented in the data file, which can be accessed at www.pgatour.com/stats/academicdata/institutions. SHOTLink was developed in partnership with IBM to catalogue and save statistical data for historical purposes (Deason, 2006). Today, around 350 people per tournament are employed with laser rangefinders, GPS and Doppler radar (Trackman®) to provide immense amounts of data. The primary consumer is the players, but its secondary use is to provide engaging statistics for the broadcast and on-line media. In 2011, a new 'strokes gained-putting' statistic was introduced after an academic study of the SHOTLink data by Fearing (2012) and Broadie (2011). Since its announcement in May 2011, this new statistic has been welcomed as one of the more accurate and meaningful ways to represent putting efficiency. Historically, 'putts per round' was used as the definitive measure; however, one drawback of this measurement was that it could be skewed by chipping close to a hole after missing the green. 'Strokes gained-putting' takes into account putting proficiency from various distances and calculates the players' performance on every green – the number of strokes needed to hole out – against the performance of other players for each round. The objective is to remove biases towards specific styles of play in order to elucidate how the best players maintain their advantage. Academia now has access to detailed golf data that is opening up unprecedented possibilities for analysis. It will not be long before this work trickles down into the media domain and we begin to see statistics in the open press and on TV that define what makes a good golfer.

Cricket

Cricket and baseball are the two most popular fielding games and their origins, at least in print, can be traced back to the eighteenth century. These types of games are characterised as outdoor sports in which one team hits a ball and the other retrieves it. Whilst one team attempts to maximise their score (via runs or bases), the opposition's role is to catch, field and bowl the ball with the intent of minimising their score. Cricket is a sport mainly played in the former British colonies and baseball in the USA, Cuba and Japan. Since both codes have been played for relatively long periods, both have amassed vast amounts of statistical information. The study of baseball statistics has coined the term 'Sabermetrics', derived from the acronym SABR – Society for American Baseball Research, and defined as the search for objective knowledge about baseball. There is no equivalent counterpart in cricket analysis.

The definitive web-based information resource for cricket is arguably Cricinfo (www.espncricinfo.com). The oldest match in their archive is from the English domestic season on 24 and 25 June 1772. Hampshire XI beat England by 53 runs (Hampshire XI 146 and 79; England 109 and 63). The record keeping was poor. It is noted in the general match comments that:

- Hampshire XI first innings: bowlers' runs conceded do not balance
- England first innings: bowlers' runs conceded do not balance
- Hampshire XI second innings: bowlers' runs conceded do not balance
- England second innings: bowlers' runs conceded do not balance.

A typical modern cricket scorecard is shown in Table 16.10. From the very humble beginnings of cricket, where scorers only kept a tally of runs per player, the modern game now provides the richest array of data imaginable. For in-game decision support, the fielding captain often just needs to glance at the scoreboard to obtain the information outlined in Tables 16.10 and 16.11. In the dressing room, or similar vantage point, the performance analyst will have a much greater array of complex stats at his/her fingertips, which can provide match insights to the coaching staff and team management. This includes partnership tables, over-by-over comparisons,

Table 16.10 Scorecard for India innings, 5th one day international (ODI), Eden Gardens, 25 October 2011

India innings (50 overs maximum)		R	M	B	4s	6s	SR
AM Rahane	c †Kieswetter b Bresnan	42	80	61	6	0	68.85
G Gambhir	b Finn	38	70	46	4	0	82.60
V Kohli	b Finn	0	5	5	0	0	0.00
MK Tiwary	c †Kieswetter b Meaker	24	41	30	4	0	80.00
SK Raina	run out (Bopara)	38	82	46	5	0	82.60
MS Dhoni*†	not out	75	103	69	3	4	108.69
RA Jadeja	c Bell b Patel	21	27	21	2	0	100.00
R Ashwin	c Bairstow b Patel	7	8	10	0	0	70.00
P Kumar	c Bairstow b Patel	16	17	12	1	1	133.33
R Vinay Kumar	not out	0	3	0	0	0	—
Extras	(b 2, w 8)	10					
Total	(8 wickets; 50 overs; 222 mins)	271(5.42 runs per over)					

Did not bat: VR Aaron
Fall of wickets: 1–80 (Gambhir, 17.1 ov), 2–80 (Kohli, 17.6 ov), 3–80 (Rahane, 18.4 ov), 4–123 (Tiwary, 27.2 ov), 5–162 (Raina, 36.5 ov), 6–206 (Jadeja, 43.4 ov), 7–215 (Ashwin, 45.4 ov), 8–259 (Kumar, 49.2 ov)
Source: www.espncricinfo.com/india-v-england-2011/engine/match/521222.html (used with permission)

Table 16.11 England's bowling statistics for India innings, 5th ODI, Eden Gardens, 25 October 2011

Bowling	Overs	Maidens	Runs	Wickets	Econ.	Misc
TT Bresnan	9	0	36	1	4.00	
ST Finn	10	2	47	2	4.70	(1w)
SC Meaker	10	0	65	1	6.50	(3w)
SR Patel	9	0	57	3	6.33	
GP Swan	8	0	45	0	5.62	
RS Bopara	4	1	19	0	4.75	

Econ = runs/overs
(Used with permission)

Hawk-Eye data, cumulative runs scored as a function of over (known colloquially as Worms) and runs per over as a function of over (known colloquially as Manhattans).

From Figure 16.8, such data visualisations clearly indicate a problem of losing wickets for the England team around the twentieth over. Up until this point, they appeared on track to win the match comfortably since they were well ahead of the run rate and projected score. More importantly, since there was an inflection of the India 'Worm' curve in the last few overs, maintaining the same average run rate to the fiftieth over would see England win the match. This scenario changed at the fifth wicket of Bairstow. With few batting resources left and an increasing run rate required to win, the three quick wickets around the thirty-sixth over sealed England's fate.

The most engaging cricket graphics for both web and TV consumption are those produced by Hawk-Eye (www.hawkeyeinnovations.co.uk). Using video cameras to track the trajectory of the ball, Hawk-Eye displays a record of its most statistically likely path as a moving image. In tennis and cricket, it has found acceptance as part of the adjudication process. In cricket, it can be referred to the third umpire for leg before wicket (lbw) appeals. The data sets can be refined to display pitch maps showing where the ball pitched on the wicket, as well as the number of runs scored (via colour coding the dots; Figure 16.9). The same flight path can be used to display so-called beehives – that is, the position of the ball when it went past the stumps. More and more derivatives are becoming available, giving broadcasters the power to tailor the presentation to their style of production.

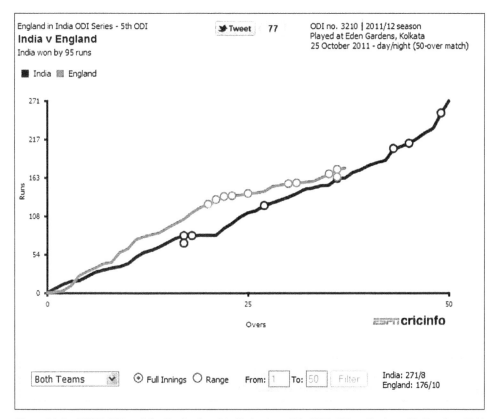

Figure 16.8   ESPN 'Worm' for England and India innings, 5th ODI, Eden Gardens, 25 October 2011 (used with permission)

India 271/8 (50 ov)
England 176 (37.0 ov)
India won by 95 runs

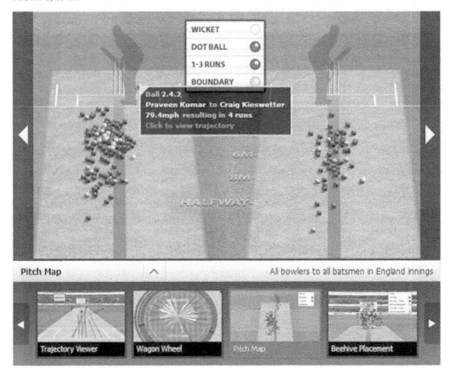

Figure 16.9 Schematic illustration of Hawk–Eye data visualisation from England v India 5th ODI, Eden Gardens, 25 October 2011 (used with permission)

For the armchair fan, comprehensive cricket statistics can be easily accessed from a broad spectrum of sources, dedicated radio stations, annual publications, iPhone® apps, web-based portals, TV and print. For the analyst, these data sets are augmented with video-based notational analysis products, such as Optiplay and Dartfish, to more accurately track trends over time and identify strengths and weaknesses in technique, tactics and strategy.

Concluding remarks

This chapter focuses on the media applications of performance analysis and presents a modern perspective on sports data capture and visualisation in mass communication. An overview has been presented that represents a snapshot of the most popular sports and mass media outlets which best reflect current performance analysis trends in mass media.

Generally, the most comprehensive performance analysis data is available on the internet (pull) via a comprehensive array of web-based sports repositories. Arguably, television (push) provides the most visual impact, with high definition, 3-D type animations, such as Hawk-Eye and FlightScope®, being used to generate content-rich, engaging graphics for infotainment. Whatever the source of media-based performance analysis data, caution should be exercised before placing any reliance on the data.

As a general rule, sports teams and individual athletes prefer to rely on their own analysis data, generated either in-house or under contract, as a basis for decision support and coaching intervention. In conclusion, performance analysis data in mass media is entertaining and grips the attention of the savvy audience; however, it should be no substitute for professional performance analysis data without first investigating its reliability.

References

Ackford, P. (2011) 'This World Cup in New Zealand has rewritten the rules and created new falsehoods', *Telegraph*, 12 October, www.telegraph.co.uk/sport/rugbyunion/rugby-world-cup/8822158/Paul-Ackford-this-World-Cup-in-New-Zealand-has-rewritten-the-rules-and-created-new-falsehoods. html (accessed 12 October 2011).

Broadie, M. (2011) 'Assessing golfer performance on the PGA Tour', Mark Broadie: Research, Colombia University, www.columbia.edu/~mnb2/broadie/research_golf.html (accessed 23 October 2011).

Collins, H. and Evans, R. (2008) 'You cannot be serious! Public understanding of technology with special reference to "Hawk-Eye"', *Public Understanding of Science*, 17: 3, www2.geog.ucl.ac.uk/~mdisney/teaching/1006/papers/collins_hawkeye.pdf (accessed 11 October 2011).

Deason, L. (2006) 'Shotlink: A statistical superstar', *PGA Tour*, 11 August, www.pgatour.com/story/9596346/ (accessed 23 October 2011).

Fearing, D., Acimovic, J. and Graves, S.C. (2010) 'How to catch a tiger: Understanding putting performance on the PGA Tour', *MIT Sloan Research Paper No 4768-10*, http://papers.ssrn.com/sol3/papers.cfm?abstract_id=1538300 (accessed 23 October 2011).

Griffiths, S. (2010) 'The Canadian who invented basketball', *BBC News*, 20 September, www.bbc.co.uk/news/world-us-canada-11348053 (accessed 11 October 2011).

Hawk-Eye (2008) *Cardiff University press release*, June, www.cardiff.ac.uk/news/mediacentre/mediar-eleases/y2008/2875.html (accessed 13 February 2012).

IRB (2011) 'Key facts and figures', IRB data extracted from Rugby Information Management System, www.irb.com/mm/document/tournament/mediazone/02/05/77/92/20111009rsavaus.pdf (accessed 11 October 2011).

James, N. (2007) 'The statistical analysis of golf performance', *International Journal of Sports Science and Coaching*, 2(1): 231–48.

Lamb, P., Stöckl, M. and Lames, M. (2011) 'Performance analysis in golf using the ISOPAR method', *International Journal of Performance Analysis in Sport*, 11(1): 184–96.

Lewis, M. (2003) *Moneyball: The Art of Winning an Unfair Game*, 1st ed., London: W.W. Norton & Co. Ltd.

Midgley, R. (1983) *Sports Laws*, 1st ed., London: The Diagram Group, J.M. Dent & Sons Ltd.

O'Donoghue, P. (2007) 'Reliability issues in performance analysis', *International Journal of Performance Analysis in Sport*, 7(1): 35–48.

Rich, G. (2011) 'Boks dominate but lose the game', *SuperSport*, 9 October, www.supersport.com/rugby/article.aspx?id=1072221 (accessed 23 October 2011).

Tucker, R. and Dugas, J. (2011) 'Rugby World Cup: New Zealand's drought ends and rugby's referee problem', *The Science of Sport*, 23 October, www.sportsscientists.com/2011/10/rugby-world-cup-ref-debate.html?utm_source=feedburner&utm_medium=email&utm_campaign=Feed%3A+blogspot%2FcJKs+%28The+Science+of+Sport%29 (accessed 23 October 2011).

SECTION IV

Other issues in sports performance analysis

17

TECHNICAL EFFECTIVENESS

José M. Palao[1] *and Juan Carlos Morante*[2]

[1]UNIVERSITY OF MURCIA, SPAIN

[2]UNIVERSITY OF LEÓN, SPAIN

Summary

The objective of this chapter is to describe the concepts, criteria, and ways to express effectiveness, as well as to provide examples of technical effectiveness in the different types of sports. The evaluation of technique effectiveness is influenced by the purpose of the evaluation, the characteristics of the technique, and the sport (e.g. purpose and structural aspects). From this conceptual basis, the criteria and ways to express effectiveness (i.e. types of calculations) are reviewed. After determining these aspects, examples of the ways that technical effectiveness is monitored in the different types of sport are presented.

Concepts and definitions of efficacy and technique

Technique is the ability to use certain movements or actions. In sport, the concept of technique involves the movements executed by athletes in their sport practice (training or competition). In the specialized literature, there are many definitions or concepts of technique, as well as misconceptions about this term (see Lees, 2002). However, most of these definitions were influenced by the perspective or the context of the author(s) that wrote the definitions (e.g. mechanical perspective, applied perspective, specific sport, etc.). The way in which technique is defined influences the way sport and performance evaluation are understood. The definition of technique that we are going to use as a reference will be the following: technique is the 'proper pattern of movements to do a specific sport skill' (adapted from Antón, 1998). With regard to effectiveness, it is defined as the power to produce an effect (decided, decisive, or desired effect). In other words, a movement is effective if the execution achieves the objective(s) of the movement (e.g. accuracy, scoring, power, projecting the body as far or as high as possible, etc.).

In certain sports, the idea of a proper pattern of movements involves only movement execution (e.g. athletics) but in other sports it involves perception, decision making, and movement execution (e.g. basketball). Regardless of its application, it is important to re-emphasize that the concept of technique involves perception, decision making, execution, and evaluation. The application of technique by an athlete involves intention, which is a tactic, because the technique is adapted to accomplish a purpose. Therefore, a proper analysis of the technique efficacy involves the integration of the different perspectives of analysis (e.g. biomechanical and notational analysis) (Bartlett, 2001).

In order to properly establish the efficacy of the sport technique, the aspects that characterize and define it must be considered (adapted from Morante and Izquierdo, 2008): a) it is conditioned by sport rules; b) it seeks efficiency; c) it seeks economy; d) it follows a model; and e) it requires adaptation.

The execution of a sport technique is influenced by sport rules. The regulations state the conditions of the sport and the purpose for implementing the technique (e.g. time, distance, points, goals, etc.). In order to properly understand how these aspects affect technique and its efficacy, it is necessary to know the purpose and goals of the sport, the sport's structural aspects, and the repertoire of technical skills in the given sport. According to these criteria, the different sports can be grouped according to their purposes and goals (see Table 17.1). Therefore, the set of movements executed in a sport technique in order to achieve performance in that technique is unique to each sport (Bompa, 1990).

Sport techniques attempt to take advantage of athletes' functional and motor abilities to resolve the situations that sport competition create. The concept of efficiency can vary even within a sport. For example, the same concepts cannot be applied to establish the efficiency of running in a sprint race as in a fast-break in basketball (Brechue, 2011). The economy of the application of the technique refers to how to manage resources in the best possible way to be effective (i.e. energy cost, time, concentration, etc.). Therefore, this concept refers to the relationship between technical efficiency and the cost involved in its execution. For example, the same concept cannot be applied to establish the economy of running for a marathoner as for a football player (Brechue, 2011; Kyröläinen *et al.*, 2001).

Table 17.1 Type of sport according to its purposes and goals (adapted from Thorpe *et al.*, 1984)

Type	Definition	Examples
Precision and accuracy sports	Sports where the athlete tries to put the projectile or object close to a designated area.	Archery, shooting (pistol, rifle, etc.), golf, bowling, billiards, curling, etc.
Batting and field sports	Sports where the athlete tries to hit the ball and score runs by advancing through the field.	Baseball, softball, cricket, etc.
Net and/or wall sports	Sports where the athlete tries to put the ball or shuttlecock in the opponent's court, making it difficult or impossible for the opponent to return it over the net or by playing on one or more walls.	Tennis, table tennis, badminton, volleyball, beach volleyball, squash, paddle, etc.
Invasion sports	Sports where athletes try to put the ball or object in the opposing team's goal.	Football, basketball, team handball, rugby, ice hockey, water polo, etc.
Combat sports	Sports where the athlete attempts to throw and/or contact parts of the opponent, etc.	Judo, fencing, boxing, etc.
Aesthetic or evaluation sports	Sports where the athlete is evaluated for the way that he/she performs his/her movements (e.g. timing, form, execution, expression, etc.).	Gymnastics, rhythmic gymnastics, diving, synchronized swimming, figure skating, etc.
Results or position sports	Sports where the athlete tries to go as fast, far, or high as possible.	Athletics, swimming, cycling, triathlon, sailing, etc.
Mixed sports	Sports where the athlete performs a combination of disciplines that involve different purposes	Nordic combined, modern pentathlon, equestrian events, etc.

Further, the structural characteristics of the human body establish the possible movements that can be made by the athlete. From the application of mechanical principles, sport characteristics, and the context of the movement execution, the ideal pattern or model of movement execution can be determined. Sport technique involves an integrated intervention of the processes of perception, decision making, execution, and evaluation. Through this process, the athlete attempts to respond optimally to the situation that he or she faces. The success of the technique involves the proper execution of the different stages of this process (perceiving the situation, making a decision about the movement execution, carrying out the movements, and analysing the execution). The analysis of the efficacy of the athlete's technique involves understanding the aspects of this process and the aspects that affect technique efficacy (Bartlett, 2001).

Criteria to establish technique effectiveness

Technique effectiveness can be established in relation to reference criteria. Any evaluation of efficiency is based on the comparison of the performance with an ideal technical model or concept. This ideal model establishes how an athlete's technical execution or outcome should be carried out for all the parameters of the movement (adapted from Morante, 2004). This ideal model is established in relation to aspects that characterize each sport technique: efficiency, economy, models of execution, need for adaptation, and outcome. These aspects are not given the same importance in all types of sport.

To establish the technical reference or model with regard to efficiency, the mechanical parameters of the execution must be considered. Using biomechanical principles, the way the movement should be done to be effective can be established. Parameters such as speed of movement, angle, body position, movements executed, times, etc. are used to establish the level of technique effectiveness. An example of parameters used to establish efficacy is the study of the trajectory of the centre of mass in a long jump from the speed components and jump angle (McGinnis, 2005). To establish the effectiveness of the technique from the perspective of economy, the physiological parameters of movement execution are generally considered to establish the energy efficiency and mechanical efficacy. Examples of parameters that are used for this include heart rate, thresholds, muscle tension, oxygen consumption, etc. A specific example would be establishing which running technique is most effective from the oxygen consumption that each one requires (Fletcher *et al.*, 2009).

The efficacy of the technique can be also established in relation to a specific model. This is common in aesthetic sports, where the sport's rules establish the movements according to standardized aesthetic criteria. Examples of parameters that are used to establish the efficacy include amplitude, rhythm, flow, body alignment, posture, position, etc. A specific example would involve establishing the judge's scoring of a back handspring in relation to the alignment of a gymnast's legs during a floor exercise routine (e.g. according to the rules of the Federation Internationale de Gymnastique). This way of establishing the efficacy of the execution is commonly used by coaches when they analyse their athlete in training and competition and compare the athlete's technique executions with the theoretical model of execution that they have in their minds.

In sports where the success of the technique execution is related to the variability and uncertainty in the athlete's actions (to reduce the opponent's chances of anticipating the athlete's movements), the psycho-tactical criteria of the technique execution must be considered to establish its efficacy. Examples of parameters that are used here include cues, feints, speed of the movements, etc. A specific example would be establishing efficacy by using the number of cues that the position adopted by the setter when getting ready to set in volleyball gives the opponent (Hernández *et al.*, 2004).

The outcome of the movement execution provides a reference for the way the movement is done. This has traditionally been the criteria for establishing efficacy in sport. It involves establishing the performance level that is achieved by an athlete that changes in relation to the sport and the technique (e.g. distance jumped in the long jump, points scored, or free throws percentage). Examples of parameters that are used for this include winner–error ratios, success percentages, attempts, etc. A specific example would be to establish the efficacy using the number of turnovers, steals, field goal percentage, etc. of a basketball player in a game (Gómez *et al.*, 2009).

The ideal model can be absolute (a theoretical model or movement execution of reference, e.g. the movement execution used to achieve the world record) or relative (e.g. comparison of an athlete's accomplishment with his/her motor potential). When an absolute model is used, the evaluation is carried out by assessing whether the critical aspects of movement are executed properly, or by comparing a referent outcome from the same level of competition (e.g. average free-throw percentage). When a relative model is used, the evaluation is based on the optimal technique that allows the athlete to take advantage of all his/her capacities (Morante, 2004). An example would be to compare the athlete's running speed with the athlete's dribbling speed in a fast-break.

It must be kept in mind that, in some sports, some patterns should not be given consideration or should not be given the same importance as the rest because they evaluate an aspect that is not the aim of these sports (see Table 17.2). Additionally, some of these patterns are more appropriate for the analysis of the athlete's technical efficacy for coaching purposes, such as, for example, the degree of technique efficacy regarding an athlete's motor potential.

Ways to express technique effectiveness

The study of parameters to evaluate a technique's efficacy can be done from two perspectives: quantitatively and qualitatively. Quantitative analysis involves description through quantifiable data. An example would indicate the number of points scored, the angle and speed of release in a free throw, or the outcome of a long jump. Qualitative perspective refers to the efficiency with which a movement has been done according to the objectives set out (Carr, 2004; Hall,

Table 17.2 Type of sport and criteria to evaluate effectiveness

Criteria	Type of sport							
	Precision and accuracy	Batting and field	Net and/or wall	Invasion sport	Combat sport	Aesthetic or evaluation	Results or position	Mixed
Biomechanical parameters	✓	✓	✓	✓	✓	✓	✓	✓
Physiological parameters	✓	✓	✓	✓	✓	✓	✓	✓
Aesthetic						✓		✓
Psycho-tactical		✓	✓	✓	✓		✓	
Outcome	✓	✓	✓	✓	✓	✓	✓	✓

2003; Knudson and Morrison, 2002). Qualitative analysis involves the description of how the movement was done (e.g. outcome of the serve or reception in volleyball) or whether or not key aspects of the movement were carried out (e.g. correct or incorrect execution). Both perspectives are important in the description and analysis of sport technique.

Quantitative analysis involves the numerical description of motion using an interval scale (e.g. temperature) and/or ratio measurements (e.g. time). Qualitative analysis involves the description of motion using category systems, field formats, or rating scales (Anguera, 2003; Baumgartner *et al.*, 2003) that can be expressed using nominal (e.g. type of technique used) and ordinal scales (e.g. poor, medium, and good). The different types of scales permit different types of data analysis. With certain limitations, it is also possible to treat the qualitative data as quantitative data but it requires a transformation of the data (i.e. percentages or coefficients).

The most common ways to monitor efficacy are: occurrence, average, balance, totals, attempts, relative attempts, ratio, percentages, and coefficients:

- Occurrence (count): the number of times that a certain type of movement, action, or combination of actions occurred. For example, the total number of points or shots made by a player in a game.
- Average: the sum of the scores or measurements divided by the number of scores or measurements. For example, the average points per match are the sum of the points scored in all matches divided by the number of matches (e.g. 58.7 points).
- Balance: the difference between the number of occurrences of different actions or a combination of actions. For example, the difference between the points won and lost by a beach volleyball player.
- Total: the sum of the occurrences and/or balances. For example, the total number of positive actions and negative actions done by a player on offence and on defence.
- Attempts: the number of times a movement, action, or combination of actions is tried, regardless of whether the result is positive or negative. In some cases, this value will be the same as the occurrences. For example, the total number of free throws taken by a player.
- Relative attempts: the fraction relating the number of actions taken and the number of actions that have achieved the desired result. This value can be expressed in absolute values (e.g. four attempts to get three points) or in an equivalently reduced fraction (e.g. 1.30 attempts to get 1 point). This value can be calculated by game phase, match, competition, etc.
- Ratio: the relationship between two values. It is the fraction between the number of actions that have achieved the desired result and the number of attempts made. This value can be expressed in absolute values (e.g. three points out of four attempts, 3:4) or in an equivalently reduced fraction (e.g. 1 point in side-out from 1.30 tries, 1:1.30). This value can be calculated by game phase, match, competition, etc.
- Percentages: the measurement expressed in terms of values of 100. It is the result of multiplying the number of actions that have achieved the desired result by 100 and then dividing by the number of attempts made. For example, the success percentage of a player's free-throw attempts.
- Coefficients: the sum of attempts by category multiplied by the value of the category and divided by total attempts. This value expresses efficacy in values between 0 and the highest value of the category. For example, in volleyball, a spike coefficient of 2.35, where error has a value of zero, allowing maximum opponent attack options has a value of 1, limiting the opponent's attack options has a value of 2, not allowing the opponent any attack options has a value of 3, and a point has a value of 4.

Once the technical effectiveness is measured, it is necessary to normalize the data and have reference values to interpret the data (Bartlett, 2001). Data normalization involves expressing the data in values relative to reference values, and it is necessary to properly analyse technical efficacy. After that, it is necessary to have norms or profiles to compare the measurements done in relation to a reference, a group, or a population. The most common way to monitor efficacy is by using percentiles and/or percentile ranks. This type of value serves as a reference point for analysing the data (standard score):

- Percentiles: the value below which a certain percentage of observations fall. The twenty-fifth percentile is the value (or score) below which 25 per cent of the measurements may be found. The percentile is used to report scores from norm-referenced tests or reference values. The twenty-fifth percentile is also known as the first quartile (Q1), the fiftieth percentile as the median or second quartile (Q2), and the seventy-fifth percentile as the third quartile (Q3). For example, these values allow us to have a reference of the athlete's performances. If in a competition an athlete scores at the seventy-fifth percentile, he/she scores greater than 75 per cent of the scores in this competition.
- Percentile ranks: the relative position of the athlete's performance in a group or database that scored below a given value. These values allow us to rank the performances of the athlete. For example, if an athlete scores 58 points in a competition, he/she ranks in the eighteenth percentile of this competition.

Examples of technical effectiveness by type of sport

The goals, purposes, and rules of the different sports establish the technique repertory and what is considered correct regarding technical effectiveness. However, it must be taken into consideration that not all the actions produced in a sport pursue the same goals. For example, in an invasion sport such as football, the actions executed by the goalkeeper are different from a field player and, for both of these players, the actions and goals change if they are on offence or on defence. Therefore, it must be kept in mind that the following examples are general and attempt to provide a global perspective of the criteria used to measure technical efficacy in the different type of sport, and its use must be put into context.

An overview of the different ways of calculating technical effectiveness in different sports types is given in Table 17.3.

Precision and accuracy sports

In precision and accuracy sports (e.g. archery, shooting, golf, etc.), efficacy is measured as the ability of the athlete to put the projectile or object close to a designated area. The usual outcome measure is the shooting accuracy relative to the target or the shot taken to reach the target. In archery or shooting sports, the different parts of the target give different points to the athlete. The final score is the number of points attained by the athlete. In golf, the outcome is measured by the number of shots used to put the ball in the hole in relation to a standard (par). From a mechanical perspective, the efficacy of the skills is related to the way the projectile or object is thrown, the angle of the release, the speed of the release, etc. (McGinnis, 2005). However, research has shown that the aspect that differentiates bad shots from good shots in performance athletes is the range of variability in the mechanical execution (Edelmann-Nusser *et al.*, 2006; Horsak and Heller, 2011) as well as the moment of execution (relationship between trigger time and cardiac cycle) (Konttinen *et al.*, 2003).

Table 17.3 Different ways of calculating technical effectiveness by type of sport (according to their purposes and goals)

Type of sport	Sport	Examples of types of efficacy measurements
Precision and accuracy	Archery, shooting, golf, etc.	Accuracy, points, distance to target, number of shots to reach the target in relation to a standard (par for the hole), percentage of variability between movement executions, etc.
Batting and field	Baseball, softball, etc.	Batters: batting average, walks per plate appearance, doubles plus triples per at bat, home runs per at bat, on-base percentage, on-base plus slugging, slugging average, etc.
		Pitchers: walks allowed per nine innings, earned-run average, home runs allowed per nine innings, strikeouts per nine innings, earned run average, etc.
Net and/or wall	Tennis, table tennis, volleyball, etc.	Percentage of shots won or errors, effect of the shot (point, error, or continuity), efficacy coefficient (point, error, or continuity), etc.
Invasion	Soccer, basketball, rugby, etc.	Number of ball contacts, percentage of duels won, successful passes, shot attempts and successful shots, balance, etc.
Combat	Judo, fencing, boxing, etc.	Points, number of techniques (e.g. punching, kicking) or manoeuvres executed, the way that they are done, penalties, etc.
Aesthetic or evaluation	Gymnastics, diving, figure skating, etc.	Technical-merit score, the ability of the athlete to use both dominant and non-dominant sides of the body, etc.
Results or position	Athletics, swimming, cycling, triathlon, sailing, etc.	Time, distance, points, index, etc.

Batting and fielding games

In batting and field sports (e.g. baseball, softball, cricket, etc.), efficacy is measured as the ability of the athlete to hit the ball and score runs by advancing through the field or by preventing this (offence or defence, respectively). This type of sport, especially baseball, has a long tradition of evaluating players' efficacy. Monitoring players, with regard to batting, running, pitching, and playing in the field, is part of the game (e.g. batting average, at bats per home run, walks allowed per nine innings, etc.). The efficacy evaluation is done in relation to the outcome. Performance sport analysts have developed methods to study the players' and teams' actions. An example of these methods is the Data Envelopment Analysis (DEA), popularized by Charnes *et al.* (1978), which evaluates the relative performance by peer comparison. Using these methods, one can study players' performance (Bradbury, 2009; Chen and Johnson, 2010), the economic impact on a team (Dennis *et al.*, 2009; Jane *et al.*, 2010), or the recovery after an injury (Namdari *et al.*, 2011).

Net/wall sports

In net and/or wall sports (e.g. tennis, table tennis, badminton, volleyball, beach volleyball, etc.), efficacy is measured as the ability of the athlete to put the ball or shuttlecock in the opponent's court, making it difficult or impossible for the opponent to return it over the net, or by playing on one or more walls. This type of sport traditionally collects information about the efficacy of a player's execution from the perspective of outcome (point, error, or continuity). In this type of sport, it is common for the competition's organizing committee to put together a report of the players' actions (e.g. number of points, errors, and actions of continuity, etc.). Performance sport analysts use percentages, coefficients, indexes, etc. to study the performance of players and teams (Marcelino *et al.*, 2008; Palao, 2008; Pfeiffer *et al.*, 2010; Reid *et al.*, 2010; Sindik and Kondri, 2011). The characteristics of the sport influence the aspects that are important and that determine efficacy. For example, in tennis, where the net is low, the serve is the critical action affecting the final outcome (O'Donoghue, 2001; Reid *et al.*, 2010). However, in volleyball or beach volleyball, where the net is higher, actions close to the net (i.e. the spike and block) are the ones that are critical to the final outcome (Eom and Schutz, 1992; Giatsis and Panagiotis, 2008; Marcelino *et al.*, 2008; Palao *et al.*, 2004).

Invasion games

In invasion sports (e.g. football, basketball, team handball, rugby, ice hockey, water polo, etc.), efficacy is measured as the ability of the athlete to put the ball or object in the opposing team's goal, or the actions that allow or prevent that (offence or defence, respectively). The study of technical performance has been carried out on ball actions (e.g. heading, ground duels, passing, ball touches) (Dellal *et al.*, 2010, 2011; Rampinini *et al.*, 2009). Evaluation of the efficacy has been measured by collecting the number of ball contacts, the percentage of duels won, successful passes, shot attempts, and successful shots, etc. (Carling *et al.*, 2009; Lago-Ballesteros and Lago-Peñas, 2010; Olsen and Larsen, 1997; Ortega *et al.*, 2009). Due to the characteristics of this type of sport, efficacy has been measured in relation to goals/points scored, offence, and defence (Hughes and Franks, 2005; Lago-Ballesteros and Lago-Peñas, 2010; Wright *et al.*, 2011), playing positions (Sampaio *et al.*, 2008), set plays (penalty, corner, etc.) (López-Botella and Palao, 2007), home advantage (Pollard, 2008), and fatigue (Carling *et al.*, 2008; Carling and Dupont, 2011).

Combat sports

In combat sports (e.g. judo, fencing, boxing, etc.), efficacy is measured as an athlete's ability to throw and/or contact parts of the opponent, etc. The outcome is measured by the number of times the goals are achieved (e.g. contacting the opponent's body or properly executing a technique). The outcome is measured in relation to the points, number of different types of techniques (e.g. punching, kicking) or manoeuvres executed, the way that they are done, penalties incurred, etc. (Ashker, 2011; Franchini and Sterkowicz, 2003). Studies about athletes' technique efficacy have measured the ability of the athlete to use both dominant and non-dominant sides of the body (Čular *et al.*, 2010), the variability in the techniques (Adam, 2007), and the number of different techniques used (Fatma and Özden, 2009; Kajmović *et al.*, 2011; Kapo *et al.*, 2008; Sterkowicz-Przybycień, 2010).

Aesthetic evaluation sports

In aesthetic or evaluation sports (e.g. gymnastics, rhythmic gymnastics, diving, synchronized swimming, figure skating, etc.), efficacy is measured as the ability of the athlete to perform standardized movements (e.g. timing, form, positioning, expression, etc.). Technical efficacy is established using the technical merit score and the judging criteria established by the sport rules (Alentejano *et al.*, 2008). In the bibliography review carried out, few studies have been found that assess technique efficacy in this type of sport. Most of the information found is related to the mechanical study of the movements executed in these sports. Studies about gymnastics skills and skill level demonstrated the importance of the ability of the athlete to use both dominant and non-dominant sides of the body (Bozanica and Miletica, 2011; Jastrjembskaia and Titov, 1999).

Timed/position sports

In results-dependent or position sports (e.g. athletics, swimming, cycling, triathlon, sailing, etc.), efficacy is measured as the ability to go as fast, far, or high as possible. Studying efficacy in this type of sport usually uses the outcome (e.g. time, distance, position, etc.); technical effectiveness can also be studied by assessing the efficacy or economy of the execution from a mechanical and physiological perspective. An example of efficacy in cycling is the pedalling effectiveness index (Mornieux *et al.*, 2008). Regarding the study of economy, examples include bike fit or skiing position (Bini *et al.*, 2011; García-López *et al.*, 2009) or the manner of technical execution (Leskinen *et al.*, 2009; Støren *et al.*, 2011).

Concluding remarks

To establish technique efficacy, the first step is to know the purpose, context, and characteristics of the movement, etc. The second step is to determine how the efficacy of the technique is going to be established (i.e. in relation to which aspects [efficiency, economy, models of movement execution, need for adaptation, and outcome]). The outcome criteria is the most common criterion used, although the aspects to be considered vary in relation to the type of sport, the skills used, the purpose of the analysis. The third step is to determine the ways in which technique effectiveness is going to be expressed (occurrence, average, balance, totals, attempts, relative attempts, ratios, percentages, efficacy, or coefficients). Once the technical effectiveness is measured (fourth step), it is necessary to normalize the data and have reference values to interpret the data.

The different types of sport have different purposes, and even the different actions that the athletes have to do within a sport can have different purposes. The last part of this chapter reviewed examples of how technical effectiveness is measured in the different types of sport, from a general perspective. There are significant differences in the standardization, normalization, and information that is available about the efficacy evaluation in the different types of sport. There is a need to standardize measurement protocols as well as normalized reference values for technical effectiveness (Bartlett, 2001). Normative profiles are needed for males and females at different levels of competition, different age groups, etc. This criterion is necessary in order to contextualize and properly interpret technique efficacy (O'Donoghue, 2005).

References

Adam, M. (2007) 'Effectiveness of techniques performed by outstanding judo competitors', *Research Yearbook*, 13(2): 216–20.
Alentejano, T., Marshall, D., and Bell, G. (2008) 'A time-motion analysis of elite solo synchronized swimming', *International Journal of Sports Physiology and Performance*, 3(1): 31–40.
Anguera, M.T. (2003) 'Observational methods (general)', in R. Fernández-Ballesteros (ed.), *Encyclopedia of Psychological Assessment*, Vol. 2 (pp. 632–7). London: Sage.
Antón, J. (1998) *Táctica Grupal Defensiva. Concepto, estructura y metodología [Group Tactics. Concept, Structure, and Methodology]*, Madrid: Gymnos.

Ashker, S. (2011) 'Technical and tactical aspects that differentiate winning and losing performances in boxing', *International Journal of Performance Analysis in Sport*, 11(2): 356–64.

Bartlett, R. (2001) 'Performance analysis: Can bringing together biomechanics and notational analysis benefit coaches?', *International Journal of Performance Analysis in Sport*, 1(1): 122–6.

Baumgartner, T.A, Jackson, A.S., Mahar, M.T., and Rowe, D.A. (2003) *Measurement for Evaluation in Physical Education and Exercise Science*, 7th ed., New York: McGraw Hill.

Bini, R., Hume, P.A., and Croft, J.L. (2011) 'Effects of bicycle saddle height on knee injury risk and cycling performance', *Sports Medicine*, 41: 463–76.

Bompa, T.O. (1990) *Theory and Methodology of Training: The Key to Athletic Performance*, Iowa City, IA: Kendall-Hunt.

Bozanica, A. and Miletica, A. (2011) 'Differences between the sexes in technical mastery of rhythmic gymnastics', *Journal of Sports Sciences*, 29(4): 337–43.

Bradbury, J. (2009) 'Peak athletic performance and ageing: Evidence from baseball', *Journal of Sports Sciences*, 27(6): 599–610.

Brechue, W.F. (2011) 'Structure-function relationships that determine sprint performance and running speed in sport', *International Journal of Applied Sports Sciences*, 23(2): 313–50.

Carling, C. and Dupont, G. (2011) 'Are declines in physical performance associated with a reduction in skill-related performance during professional soccer match-play?', *Journal of Sports Sciences*, 29(1): 63–71.

Carling, C., Bloomfield, J., Nelsen, L., and Reilly, T. (2008) 'The role of motion analysis in elite soccer: Contemporary performance measurement techniques and work rate data', *Sports Medicine*, 38: 839–62.

Carling, C., Reilly T., and Williams, A. (2009) *Performance Assessment for Field Sports: Physiological, Psychological and Match Notational Assessment in Practice*, London: Routledge.

Carr, G. (2004) *Sport Mechanics for Coaches*, 2nd ed., Champaign, ll: Human Kinetics.

Charnes, A., Cooper, W.W., and Rhodes, E. (1978) 'Measuring the efficiency of decision making units', *European Journal of Operational Research*, 2: 429–44.

Chen, W. and Johnson, A. (2010) 'The dynamics of performance space of Major League Baseball pitchers 1871–2006', *Annals of Operations Research*, 181(1): 287–302.

Čular, D., Miletić, D., and Miletić, A. (2010) 'Influence of dominant and non-dominant body side on specific performance in taekwondo', *Kinesiology*, 42(2): 184–93.

Dellal, A., Wong, D.P., Moalla, W., and Chamari, K. (2010) 'Physical and technical activity of soccer players in the French first league with special reference to their playing position', *International Sport Med Journal*, 11: 278–90.

Dellal, A., Chamari, K., Wong, D.P., Ahmaidi, S., Keller, D., Barros, R., Bisciotti, G.N., and Carling, C. (2011) 'Comparison of physical and technical performance in European soccer match-play: FA Premier League and La Liga', *European Journal of Sport Science*, 11(1): 51–9.

Dennis, S.A., Nelson, S., and Beneda, N. (2009) 'Player salaries and team performance in Major League Baseball', *Review of Business Research*, 9(4): 174–82.

Edelmann-Nusser, J., Heller, M., Hofmann, M., and Ganter, N. (2006) 'On-target trajectories and the final pull in archery', *European Journal of Sport Science*, 6(4): 213–22.

Eom, H. and Schutz, R. (1992) 'Statistical analyses of volleyball team performance', *Research Quarterly for Exercise and Sport*, 63(1): 11–18.

Fatma, A. and Özden, T. (2009) 'Video analysis of techniques in 17th Men World Taekwondo Championship in 2005', *Ovidius University Annals, Series Physical Education and Sport/Science, Movement and Health*, 9(2): 117–21.

Fletcher, J.R., Esau, S.P., and MacIntosh, B.R. (2009) 'Economy of running: Beyond the measurement of oxygen uptake', *Journal of Applied Physiology*, 107(6): 1918–22.

Franchini, E. and Sterkowicz, S. (2003) 'Tactics and techniques in high level judo competition (1995–2001): Considerations about weight category and gender', *Revista Mackenzie de Educação Física e Esporte*, 2(2): 125–38.

García-López, J., Díez-Leal, S., Rodríguez-Marroyo, J.A., Larrazabal, J., de Galdeano, I.G., and Villa J.G. (2009) 'Eficiencia mecánica de pedaleo en ciclistas de diferente nivel competitivo [Mechanical efficiency of pedalling in cyclists of different competitive levels]', *Biomecánica*, 17(2): 9–20.

Giatsis, G. and Panagiotis, Z. (2008) 'Statistical analysis of men's FIVB beach volleyball team performance', *International Journal of Performance Analysis in Sport*, 8(1): 31–43.

Gómez, M.A., Lorenzo, A., Ortega, E., Sampaio, J., and Ibáñez, S.J. (2009) 'Game related statistics discriminating between starters and nonstarters players in Women's National Basketball Association League (WNBA)', *Journal of Sports Science and Medicine*, 8(2): 278–83.

Hall, S.J. (2003) *Basic Biomechanics*, 4th ed., Dubuque, IA: McGraw Hill Higher Education.

Hernández, E., Ureña, A., Martínez, M., and Oña, A. (2004) 'Kinematic analysis of volleyball setting cues that affect anticipation in blocking', *Journal of Human Movement Studies*, 47(4): 285–301.

Horsak, B. and Heller, M. (2011) 'A three-dimensional analysis of finger and bow string movements during the release in archery', *Journal of Applied Biomechanics*, 27(2): 151–60.

Hughes, M.D. and Franks, I.M. (2005) 'Possession length and goal-scoring in soccer', *Journal of Sport Sciences*, 23: 509–14.

Jane, W., Kong, W., and Wang, Y. (2010) 'Individual efficiency and club performance: A panel analysis of professional baseball', *Managerial and Decision Economics*, 31(5): 363–72.

Jastrjembskaia, N. and Titov, Y. (1999) *Rhythmic Gymnastics*, Champaign, IL: Human Kinetics.

Kajmović, H., Rađo, I., Crnogorac, B., and Mekić, A. (2011) 'Notational analysis of the State championship of Bosnia and Herzegovina and Balkans championship in judo for male competitors', *Homo Sporticus*, 13(2): 23–6.

Kapo, S., Kajmovic, H., Cutuk, H., and Beriša, S. (2008) 'The level of use of technical and tactical elements in boxing based on the analysis of the 15th B&H Individual Boxing Championship' *Homo Sporticus*, 10(2): 15–20.

Knudson, D. and Morrison, C. (2002) *Qualitative Analysis of Human Movement*, Champaign, IL: Human Kinetics.

Konttinen, N., Mets, T., Lyytinen, H., and Paananen, M. (2003) 'Timing of triggering in relation to the cardiac cycle in non-elite rifle shooters', *Research Quarterly for Exercise and Sport*, 74(4): 395–400.

KyrÖläinen, H., Belli, A., and Komi P.V. (2001) 'Biomechanical factors affecting running economy' *Medicine and Science in Sports and Exercise*, 33(8): 1330–7.

Lago-Ballesteros, J. and Lago-Peñas, C. (2010) 'Performance in team sports: Identifying the keys to success in soccer', *Journal of Human Kinetics*, 25: 85–91.

Lees, A. (2002) 'Technique analysis in sports: A critical review', *Journal of Sports Sciences*, 20: 813–28.

Leskinen, A., Hakkinen, K., Virmavirta, M., Isolehto, J., and Kyrolainen, H. (2009) 'Comparison of running kinematics between elite and national-standard 1500-m runners', *Sports Biomechanics*, 8(1): 1–9.

López-Botella, M. and Palao, J.M. (2007) 'Relationship between laterality of foot strike and shot zone on penalty efficacy in specialist penalty takers', *International Journal of Performance Analysis of Sport*, 7(3): 26–36.

Marcelino, R., Mesquita, I., and Afonso, J. (2008) 'The weight of terminal actions in volleyball. Contributions of the spike, serve and block for the teams' rankings in the World League 2005', *International Journal of Performance Analysis in Sport*, 8(2): 1–7.

McGinnis, P. (2005) *Biomechanics of Sport and Exercise*, 2nd ed., Champaign, IL: Human Kinetics.

Morante, J.C. (2004) 'La valoración de la eficacia técnica en el deporte [Evaluation of the technique efficacy in sport]', *Rendimiento Deportivo.com (e)*, 9, www.rendimientodeportivo.com/N009/Artic044.htm (accessed 5 September 2006).

Morante, J.C. and Izquierdo, M. (2008) 'Técnica deportiva, modelos técnicos y estilo personal [Sport technique, technical models and personal style]', in M. Izquierdo (ed.), *Biomecánica y bases neuromusculares de la actividad física y el deporte* (pp. 91–106). Madrid: Panamericana.

Mornieux, G., Stapelfeldt, B., Gollhofer, A., and Belli, A. (2008) 'Effects of pedal type and pull-up action during cycling', *International Journal of Sports Medicine*, 29(10): 817–22.

Namdari, S., Baldwin, K., Ahn, A., Huffman, G., and Sennett, B.J. (2011) 'Performance after rotator cuff tear and operative treatment: A case-control study of major league baseball pitchers', *Journal of Athletic Training*, 46(3): 296–302.

O'Donoghue, P. (2001) 'Performance models of ladies' and men's singles tennis at the Australian Open', *International Journal of Performance Analysis in Sport*, 2(1): 73–84.

O'Donoghue, P.G. (2005) 'Normative profiles of sports performance', *International Journal of Performance Analysis of Sport*, 5(1): 104–19.

Olsen, E. and Larsen, O. (1997) 'Use of match analysis by coaches', in J. Bangsbo, T. Reilly and M. Hughes (eds), *Science and Football III* (pp. 209–20). London: Taylor and Francis.

Ortega, E., Villarejo, D., and Palao, J.M. (2009) 'Differences in game statistics in the Six Nations tournament between winning and losing rugby teams', *Journal of Sports Science and Medicine*, 8(3): 523–7.

Palao, J.M. (2008) 'Options for analysis of the volleyball score sheet', *International Journal of Performance Analysis in Sport*, 8(2): 26–43.

Palao, J.M., Santos, J.A., and Ureña, A. (2004) 'Effect of team level on skill performance in volleyball', *International Journal of Performance Analysis of Sport*, 4(2): 50–60.

Pfeiffer, M., Hui, Z., and Hohmann, A. (2010) 'A Markov chain model of elite table tennis competition', *International Journal of Sports Science and Coaching*, 5(2): 205–22.

Pollard, R. (2008) 'Home advantage in football: A current review of an unsolved puzzle', *The Open Sports Sciences Journal*, 1: 12–4.

Rampinini, E., Impellizzeri, F.M., Castagna, C., Coutts, A.J., and Wisloff, U. (2009) 'Technical performance during soccer matches of the Italian Series A League: Effect of fatigue and competitive level', *Journal of Science and Medicine in Sport*, 12: 227–33.

Reid, M., McMurtrie, D., and Crespo, M. (2010) 'The relationship between match statistics and top 100 ranking in professional men's tennis', *International Journal of Performance Analysis in Sport*, 10(2): 131–8.

Sampaio, J., Ibáñez, S., Gomez, M., Lorenzo, A., and Ortega, E. (2008) 'Game location influences basketball players' performance across playing positions', *International Journal of Sport Psychology*, 39(3): 205–16.

Sindik, J. and Kondri, M. (2011) 'Correlation between the result efficiency indexes and success in table tennis', *International Journal of Performance Analysis in Sport*, 11(2): 267–83.

Sterkowicz-Przybycień, K.K. (2010) 'Technical diversification, body composition and somatotype of both heavy and light Polish ju-jitsukas of high level', *Science and Sports*, 25(4): 194–200.

Støren, Ø., Helgerud, J., and Hoff, J. (2011) 'Running stride peak forces inversely determine running economy in elite runners', *Journal of Strength and Conditioning Research*, 25(1): 117–23.

Thorpe, R., Bunker, T., and Almond, L. (1984) 'A change in focus for the teaching of game', in J. Tolleneer and R. Renson (eds), *Olympic Scientific Congress Proceedings*, 6 (pp. 163–9). Champaign: IL: Human Kinetics.

Wright, C., Atkins, S., Polman, R., Jones, B., and Lee, S. (2011) 'Factors associated with goals and goal scoring opportunities in professional soccer', *International Journal of Performance Analysis in Sport*, 11(3): 438–49.

18

NEURAL NETWORKS FOR ANALYSING SPORTS TECHNIQUES

Peter Lamb[1] and Roger Bartlett[2]

[1]TECHNISCHEN UNIVERSITÄT MÜNCHEN, GERMANY

[2]UNIVERSITY OF OTAGO, NEW ZEALAND

Summary

The coordination of many components of the movement system involved with most sports actions makes technique analysis a difficult endeavour. Usually discrete biomechanical variables are created in order to simplify the process. However, with converging acceptance among many researchers that coordination emerges by means of a self-organising interaction with all of the relevant constraints, the importance of an analysis tool for making these complex interactions discoverable becomes apparent. Artificial neural networks are able, through an iterative training process, to learn complex patterns, which make them attractive for analysing sports techniques. This chapter introduces self-organising maps (SOMs), a specific type of artificial neural network (ANN), as a potential tool for technique analysts, mainly because of the ability to provide a simple visualisation of the SOM output which represents the original complex movement pattern. A simple example to demonstrate SOMs is provided, followed by an overview of several techniques for visualising the output layer. Finally, a review of recent literature using SOMs for technique analysis is presented. Our outlook on the use of SOMs in technique analysis involves practitioners using them to focus on the coordination pattern itself, rather than narrowing the scope of the analysis to a few predefined key events in the action or in fact simply by judging the performance outcome.

Introduction

Technique analysis is concerned with understanding both the most effective way movements are made as well as their effect on performance (Lees, 2002). By understanding these concepts, a performance analyst should be able to advise the athlete so that the technique used reduces risk of injury, improves performance or both. The main components of technique analysis, according to Lees (2002), are the identification of faults in performance and the remediation or intervention to alleviate the performance symptoms associated with such faults. These components will be referred to throughout this chapter.

The process of diagnosing faults is certainly not unanimously agreed upon. In qualitative analysis, the performance analyst often visually inspects the movement and decides on components of the movements which have negative effects on performance. These are the components which should be modified in accordance with biomechanical principles (Knudson and Morrison, 2002). The faults the analyst chooses, however, subjectively depend on past experiences and the knowledge of the analyst. Furthermore, it has been suggested that visual observation, on which analysts may rely, is particularly vulnerable to being over-influenced by the motion of distal segments, thus threatening the validity of the analysis. The reason the motion of distal segments weighs so heavily in visual analysis is probably because these segments move through a greater range of motion than proximal segments and they usually achieve high velocities at the moment of release or contact, depending on the action (Hodges *et al.*, 2007; Lamb *et al.*, 2010).

Quantitative techniques are not without their limitations and have often been misused by performance analysts to convey to the coach very specific information (such as a joint angular velocity) at a specific instant in the movement (such as the top of the backswing in golf). The information relayed to the athlete is far too specific for the athlete to make use of, and information from a discrete instance in the movement has little use in explaining the movement as a whole. The transition from beginning to end of any phase of the movement should be at least as important to the analyst as any arbitrarily chosen event during the movement. A more appropriate approach has been to view the movement as a 'movement pattern', which is more conducive to qualitative analyses.

Research on the organisation and control of coordinated movement has led to the discovery of several key characteristics of human movement (we refer the reader to Kelso, 1995, and Davids *et al.*, 2006). Particularly relevant to performance analysis of sports techniques is the inherent, functional role of variability and the self-organising emergence of ordered behaviour. These insights come from dynamical systems theory and the mathematics of complex systems and are rooted in the view that coordinated movement collectively represents the unordered behaviour of the sub-components of the movement system. These theoretical insights have typically been off limits to performance analysts because of the limited practical applications put forth by researchers. However, relatively recently, many qualitative methods for performance analysis of sports techniques have become available, which have made the insights into coordination available to performance analysts. For example, the time-series coupling of moving segments is central to modern systems perspectives on human movement. These couplings can be observed, for example, with the use of angle–angle diagrams, phase plane portraits (Bartlett, 2007), continuous relative phase (Hamill *et al.*, 2000) and cross-correlation functions (e.g. Bartlett and Bussey, 2012). Unfortunately, in studying joint coordination, these techniques are limited to the coordination of only two joint angles for angle–angle diagrams, two joint angles and their angular velocities for phase planes and continuous relative phase, and two joint angles or two joint angular velocities for cross-correlation functions.

Artificial neural networks (ANNs) represent an attractive method for analysing human movement because of their non-linear characteristics. As a beneficial side effect, ANNs thrive on data and, considering the large data sets representing biomechanical variables performance analysts are faced with analysing, ANNs seem particularly useful. This chapter will introduce ANNs and outline their application in performance analysis of sports techniques.

Artificial neural networks

Artificial neural networks are adaptive, non-linear systems that are loosely modelled on the human brain. They have been applied for two main purposes in sport science: prediction and classification.

Networks used for prediction typically involve a feed-forward design, in which a set of input variables is used to predict an output variable. These types of networks, although fairly commonly used in sport science, have relatively little to contribute specifically to analysing sports *techniques*. Feed-forward networks have been used to model training and predict performance (Edelmann-Nusser *et al.*, 2002), and have also been used to model biomechanical data and predict the outcome of movement patterns (Yan and Li, 2000). The usefulness, however, is limited to identifying the contribution of the input variables to the variability in the outcome. Feed-forward networks cannot tell the performance analyst about the structure of the movement pattern. For this reason, supervised networks will not be discussed further in this chapter, but remain relevant for other disciplines within sport science.

For classification, ANNs learn to identify features in input patterns. This means that, without the user defining the outcome, certain patterns may be discovered. In performance analysis, certain movement patterns hidden within the kinematic and kinetic data may be discovered. This technique has been particularly useful because it can be used in qualitative analyses and is robust to the biases associated with visual observation.

Self-organising networks

Kohonen's self-organising map (SOM; Kohonen, 2001) is a specific type of ANN useful for visualising and clustering data, and is by far the most common type of ANN used in technique analysis. The real strength of SOMs lies in their ability to compress redundant, high-dimensional information into a simple, low-dimensional mapping, while retaining the original topological relationships within the data. The actions studied using SOMs include javelin (Bauer and Schöllhorn, 1997) and discus throwing (Schöllhorn and Bauer, 1998), basketball shooting (Lamb *et al.*, 2010; Memmert and Perl, 2009), golf shots (Lamb *et al.*, 2011a), soccer kicking (Lees and Barton, 2005), as well as gait (Barton *et al.*, 2006, 2007; Lamb *et al.*, 2011b).

The Kohonen algorithm

The output of a SOM is commonly visualised as a layer of grid nodes, each with an associated weight vector connected to a layer of input nodes (see Figure 18.1). The dimensionality of the weight vectors is the same as the dimensionality of the input data set. For example, an input may represent a single time frame for any number of kinematic variables representing a movement. The dimensionality of the input vectors (and weight vectors) is equal to the number of kinematic variables used for training. The number of nodes is typically fewer than the number of inputs, thereby reducing the data and forcing them into clusters of similar data.

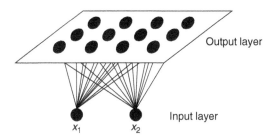

Figure 18.1 Model of the SOM input and output layers

A brief description of the SOM algorithm is provided below (for a more detailed description, see Negnevitsky, 2002):

Initialisation. Map dimensions, training parameters and initial values for the weight vectors are chosen (often based on the principal components of the input data set).

Find best-matching node. For each input vector, the node whose weight vector has the shortest Euclidean distance to the respective input is identified and declared the 'best-matching node' (this is called a competitive learning strategy). The Euclidean distance between the input vector ($x = \xi_1,...,\xi_p$) and weight vector ($y = \eta_1,..., \eta_p$) is shown by

$$d_E(x,y) = \sqrt{(\xi_1 - \eta_1)^2 + (\xi_2 - \eta_2)^2 + ... + (\xi_p - \eta_p)^2}$$, where p is the number of variables.

Adjust weight vectors. The weight vectors are adjusted during an iterative training process to model the input distribution. The weight vector of the best-matching node is adjusted the most, while nodes close to the best-matching node (see output layer in Figure 18.1) are adjusted less, as their proximity decreases. The neighbourhood relation determines the magnitude of these adjustments and is the feature which preserves the topology of the input data set and, therefore, allows the nodes to 'self-organise'.

Example

Before going further, a brief example will be made to clarify how SOMs retain a link between the input data set and the output. Feed-forward networks, on the other hand, usually adjust training parameters based on the training data, which earns them the moniker 'black box'. In this example, we use the coordination of three sine waves with the possibility of each wave being $y = \sin x$, which we will call A, or $y = -\sin x$, which we will call B. This gives eight (2^3) possible coordination patterns: AAA, AAB, ABA, ABB, BBB, BBA, BAB and BAA. The coordination of these waves is considered three-dimensional, as there are three variables. Although a seemingly abstract example, AA and BB represent in-phase coordination, while AB and BA represent anti-phase coordination, which are important coordination phases in technique analysis.

The data were represented as an [800 3] matrix and were used to train a SOM. Notice that there are 800 inputs, each consisting of three dimensions. The original time series for AAA and AAB are shown in Figure 18.2a and c. Default parameters from the 'somtoolbox' for MATLAB® were used for the example (Vesanto *et al.*, 2000).

A visualisation, called a U-matrix, of the output is shown in Figure 18.2b, d and e. The U-matrix shows not only the geometrical configuration of the nodes on the output map (grid space) but also the similarity between the weight vectors of the nodes (weight space). Dark areas on the U-matrix represent similar information (short Euclidean distance between neighbouring nodes), while lighter-coloured areas represent dissimilar information (large Euclidean distance between neighbouring nodes). To enhance the visualisation, the Euclidean distance between neighbouring nodes is shown on the z-axis. This makes the U-matrix a visualisation of both grid space and weight space – an important distinction that will be clear later.

The trained network can be simulated with a subset of the input so as to learn about the organisation of the output. This is done by identifying, for any input, its best-matching node in the output. To visualise the change in coordination within the input, the corresponding consecutive best-matching nodes on the output can be connected with a trajectory. Accordingly, the U-matrices in Figure 18.2 should be read as follows: the start of the pattern t_1, in which the values of the three variables are [0 0 0], is best represented by nodes in the middle of the U-matrix. As the pattern progresses to the respective maximum and minimum of each wave

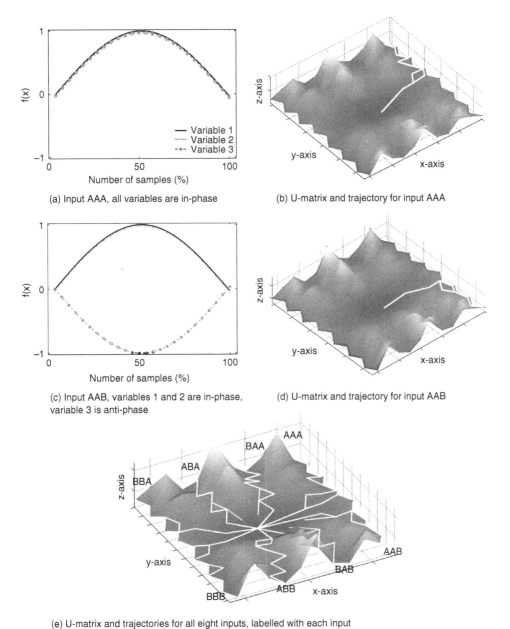

(a) Input AAA, all variables are in-phase

(b) U-matrix and trajectory for input AAA

(c) Input AAB, variables 1 and 2 are in-phase, variable 3 is anti-phase

(d) U-matrix and trajectory for input AAB

(e) U-matrix and trajectories for all eight inputs, labelled with each input

Figure 18.2   Two example input patterns (AAA and AAB) are shown in a) and c). Their respective best-matching node trajectories shown on U-matrices are shown in b) and d). All eight best-matching node trajectories are shown on the U-matrix in e). Each trajectory is labelled with the corresponding input

(t_{50}), for example, input AAB has values [1 1 −1], the trajectory on the U-matrix moves to the appropriate valley at the edges of the map (shown by dark areas and representing low values on the z-axis) and returns to the centre of the U-matrix at t_{100} when the values are, once again, [0 0 0]. Each of the eight valleys represents the eight different combinations of maxima and minima in the input data set of our example. The contours of the U-matrix reveal the gradual change in coordination of the three variables with time.

This simple example may seem trivial but one can surely imagine that, as the dimensionality of the data set grows and the subtlety of the coordination increases, the task of visualising the coordination becomes far from trivial. The next section reviews some of the studies of sports techniques which have used SOMs.

SOMs in technique analysis

In a study by Bauer and Schöllhorn (1997), the kinematics of a decathlete and a specialist javelin thrower were shown on an 11×11 grid visualisation. The kinematic data were represented by 34 variables and 53 throws, each consisting of 51 normalised time samples. This gives a training set of [2703 34]. The visualisation was used to compare the throws to one reference throw by the specialist (see Figure 18.3a). The Euclidean distances from the reference throw were calculated and used as input into a cluster analysis. The cluster analysis revealed that the specialist thrower was most similar to the reference throw, which was not surprising since the reference throw was performed by the specialist (see Figure 18.3b). More interestingly, however, was the variability between and within sessions by the decathlete.

The SOM trajectories were much more similar within sessions than between sessions, suggesting high day-to-day variability compared to within-day variability, even for elite throwers. This finding was strong evidence that coaches and athletes should not strive for an invariant optimal throwing technique; rather they should find ways to increase the functionality of movement variability (Müller and Sternad, 2004). The Bauer and Schöllhorn study was important because it used SOMs, a new technique in biomechanics, to deny the existence of an optimal movement pattern – something which many biomechanists at the time were trying to define.

One point of criticism on the visualisation of the output map in Figure 18.3a is that it does not accurately reflect the similarity in weight vectors of the nodes. The visualisation, which only shows the geometric orientation of the nodes in the output, gives the impression that the similarity between the weight vectors associated with each node is evenly distributed. In fairness, the authors did not draw much attention to the visualisation, rather to the clustering of similar trials.

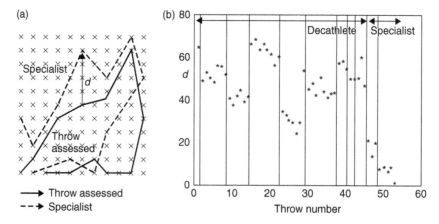

Figure 18.3   a) The grid space visualisation, and b) the throw clustering, adapted from Bauer and Schöllhorn (1997)

Lees and Barton (2005) used SOMs to classify soccer kicking techniques among right- and left-footed players. Six soccer players performed several trials of kicking a soccer ball into an open goalmouth. Three different maps were created: one map trained with all trials, one map trained with just right-footed kicking trials and one map created with just left-footed kicking trials. Like Bauer and Schöllhorn (1997), the best-matching node trajectory on a grid space visualisation was used for a qualitative analysis of the movement patterns. The authors stated that the map trajectories separated left- and right-footed kicking trials, which was deemed a non-trivial problem using just angular joint kinematics. The map trained with all trials definitely showed a qualitative difference between trajectories of right- and left-footed kicking trials. On the maps trained with either right- or left-legged kicking trials, there were qualitative differences between performers, showing evidence of inter-individual differences in soccer kicking. This is thought to add to the validity of the SOM as a tool to assess movement patterning and supports the argument that neither optimal nor invariant movement patterns exist in sport techniques.

Recently, Lamb *et al.* (2010) looked at the performance of basketball shots by four professional basketball players. The shots performed were: free throw, three-point shot and the hook shot. The authors hypothesised that the free throw shot would be more similar to the three-point shot than either would be to the hook shot. Ten trials of each shot were performed by each player and ten kinematic joint angles were used to train one SOM. The sequence of best-matching node trajectories was used for analysis with two additions: instead of grid space, the trajectories were superimposed on a U-matrix and a hit histogram was used to show any long 'jumps' between best-matching nodes (Figure 18.4).

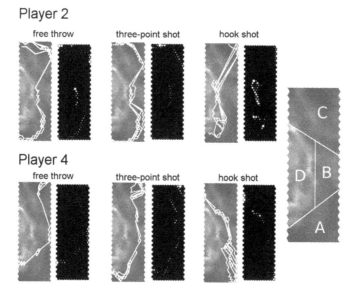

Figure 18.4 U-matrix and hit histogram visualisations for two players in Lamb *et al.* (2010). The left figure for each shot type shows the best-matching node trajectory in white on the U-matrix; to the right of the U-matrices are the hit histograms, which show the 'jumps' between best-matching nodes. The size of the white areas on the hit histograms represents the frequency of hits for each node – as frequency increases, size increases. The labelled U-matrix on the right identifies the phases of the movement: A – Preparation, B – Extension, C – Release and D – unique coordination. Adapted from Lamb *et al.* (2010)

The study showed that, for two of the players, the free-throw shot and three-point shot were more similar to each other than was either to the hook shot. However, for the other two players, the three-point shot and the hook shot were more similar to each other than was either to the free throw. This was an unexpected finding, which the authors speculated could be because of the jumping kinematics involved in the hook shot for the latter two players. The three-point is usually performed as a jump shot so that the point of ball release is high, making it difficult for opponents to block. The hook shot is also a shot played in a way so that the ball release is protected from the defender. The subtle differences in the kinematics of the proximal and inferior joints (ankle, knee, hip joint angles) separated the techniques of two of the players from the other two. These differences were not discernible from visual observation of the movement. This study provided more evidence that qualitative techniques such as SOMs could expose new characteristics in data sets representing movement patterns.

Lamb *et al.* (2011a) performed a study looking at the coordination involved with performing the golf chip shot to various target distances (4 m, 8 m, 12 m, 16 m, 20 m, 24 m). Six kinematic joint angles (hip, torso, spine, right and left shoulder, and club shaft) and their angular velocities were used, as well as the *x, y, z* linear displacement and velocity of the head as input. Because of the relationship between inter- and intra-individual variability, four SOMs were trained on the data for each respective player. Had a single SOM been trained on data for all players, the authors argued that the variability between trials would have been masked by the variability between players. The trajectories of the best-matching nodes were shown on U-matrices to visualise changes in coordination (see Figure 18.5a).

Even though the ranges of joint angles were normalised, the authors found changes in coordination for all players at different target distances. To emphasise, the changes in coordination were not attributable to scaling the range of motion as target distance increased or decreased. The stability of coordination at the target distances tested was also assessed using a second SOM

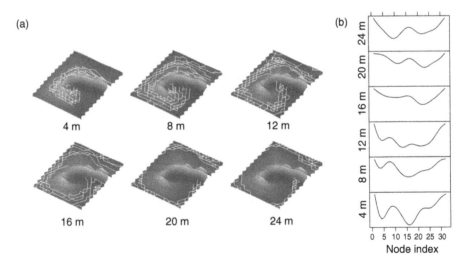

Figure 18.5 a) The best-matching node trajectories shown on U-matrices for golf chip shots performed by one player from various distances from Lamb *et al.* (2011a). b) Attractor diagram of coordination stability for the same player as in a). The attractor diagrams are a representation of the movement as a whole. Reprinted from Lamb, P., Bartlett, R. and Robins, A. (2011) 'Artificial neural networks for analyzing inter-limb coordination: The golf chip shot', *Human Movement Science, 30*: 1129–43, with permission from Elsevier

trained on the trajectories of the first SOMs (see Figure 18.5b). Several other studies have used a second SOM and will be discussed next.

Second SOM analyses

All the studies mentioned above used the best-matching node trajectory to visualise the change in coordination of input variables throughout the movement. Data in similar regions on the map, therefore, represent similar coordinative states during the movement – usually known as phases of the movement (Bartlett, 2007; Lees, 2002). Various methods have been used to classify the movement patterns as a whole.

Lamb *et al.* (2010) used a second SOM to show the relationship between the different basketball shots performed by each of the four players. The authors referred to the original SOM as the phase SOM (Figure 18.4) and the second as the trial SOM (see Figure 18.6). The output of the trial SOM was visualised on a grid for which, because of its smaller size, the distances between all nodes could be calculated fairly accurately and plotted. On that output, the assignment of each shot to a best-matching node was shown, giving a simpler representation of the similarity between the player's shots. The type of shot was identified with text and the frequency of each type of shot represented by a single node was shown with varying text size.

Returning to the golf study by Lamb *et al.* (2011a), the second SOM was used to classify the similarity of coordination patterns as well as their frequency (Figure 18.5). In this case, the second SOM was created differently from the basketball study. For relevance in motor control studies using the coordination dynamics framework, the original SOM trajectories were used as an order parameter, or collective variable. The second SOM showed stability of coordination at each of the chipping distances (Figure 18.5b). In this sense, stability refers to the player's ten-

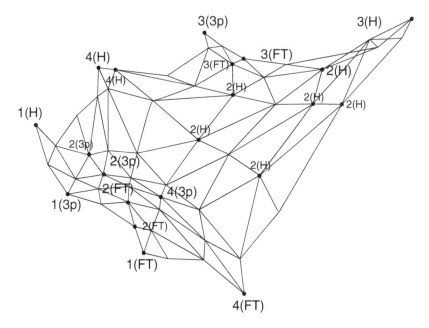

Figure 18.6 Second SOM representing the similarity of different basketball shot types by each of the players in Lamb *et al.* (2010). FT = free throw; H = hook shot; 3p = three-point shot. For example, Player 1's hook shot is abbreviated as 1(H). Adapted from Lamb *et al.* (2010)

dency to recruit similar movement patterns for similar shot types. Non-linear phase transitions were shown for three of the players between what the authors termed 'short distance' and 'long distance' movement patterns for chipping. Certain distances displayed instability, which might be targeted in practice sessions by the performance analyst as a weakness in movement patterning. Furthermore, the theoretical framework of coordination dynamics has been typically limited to researchers studying low-dimensional rhythmic movements (Obhi, 2004); however, the SOM trajectory as a low-dimensional representation of high-dimensional coordination may represent an opportunity for those studying discrete multi-dimensional movements to benefit from the theoretical understanding of movement coordination (Davids and Glazier, 2010).

Concluding remarks

Self-organising maps allow the analyst to look at one (or many) movement pattern(s) and make comparisons to movement patterns which occur at different parameter values (e.g. target distances) or movement patterns performed by other athletes. Coordination variability is easily seen using the trajectory of consecutive best-matching nodes. Determining variables and phases in the movement in which unexpected variability occurs is essentially what fault diagnosis in technique analysis is all about. One major difference between the SOM approach and conventional techniques is that, when using conventional techniques, the performance analyst is looking for a narrow set of faults, whereas, in light of recent work using SOMs, when using SOMs the analyst may have to be willing to explore unknown aspects of the movement. Using SOMs may require a re-evaluation of what technique faults are. In the past, a segment out of place would represent a flaw in the movement and the technique would be adjusted so that the segment moved in an acceptable range. However, the ability to look at high-dimensional coordination may reveal that one segment out of place does not pose a problem for the movement because other joints compensate for it. This is an opinion that performance analysts and coaches have held for a long time but they have not had the analytical tools to observe high-dimensional coordination.

A new component that may be added to the process of technique analysis might involve finding a good way of understanding how movement patterns differ between athletes and how they relate to success. The redundancy of the movement patterns involved in performing sports techniques has puzzled performance analysts for a long time. Indeed, it is puzzling to think of how two elite athletes can perform an action so differently while both achieving success (e.g. Bauer and Schöllhorn, 1997; Lamb *et al.*, 2010). The use of SOMs may provide a broad, objective view of the movement so that task- and individual-specific variability can be understood. When should actions look the same (e.g. impact position of professional golfers) and when can they look different (e.g. top of backswing for professional golfers)?

SOMs also provide the performance analyst with new tools for identifying strengths and weaknesses in an athlete's technique and, therefore, a basis for remediation. If an athlete displays instability at certain parameter values (e.g. shooting distance, fatigue level, shot type), an observation that only SOMs have been able to provide so far, the athlete might have new cues for training, although not necessarily specifically aimed at changing technique. Instead, the analyst might look at ways of building up stability in those movement patterns. The role of dealing with and controlling variability may find a more prominent role in technique analysis than in the past. This may provide a better opportunity for improving performance (or reducing the risk of injury) than trying to achieve a desired movement pattern.

The next step in technique analysis might be to look at the structure of the movement in a new way and to try to force the movement pattern through different levels of stability. This would have implications for skill acquisition (at many developmental levels) as well as technique analysis. The path to reliable and stable technique, resilient to the pressure of competition, may be to manipulate indirectly an athlete's movement pattern repertoire. If so, SOMs represent a qualitative technique for determining how to manipulate and measure an athlete's coordination stability. With continued use, and advances in visualisation and processing time, we expect that SOMs will provide a valuable tool for the analyst to continue the growing trend promoted by cognitive scientists (e.g. Riley *et al.*, 2012), motor control theorists (e.g. Latash, 2008) and biomechanists (e.g. Bartlett *et al.*, 2007; Glazier *et al.*, 2006) to include understandings from motor control, concepts from dynamical systems theory and the considerations of functional role of variability in practice.

References

Bartlett, R.M. (2007) *Introduction to Sports Biomechanics: Analysing Human Movement Patterns*, 2nd ed., London: Routledge.

Bartlett, R.M. and Bussey, M. (2012) *Sports biomechanics: Reducing injury risk and improving performance*, 2nd ed., London: Routledge.

Bartlett, R.M., Wheat, J. and Robins, M. (2007) 'Is movement variability important for sports biomechanists?', *Sports Biomechanics*, 6(2): 224–43.

Barton, G., Lees, A., Lisboa, P. and Attfield, S. (2006) 'Visualisation of gait data with Kohonen self-organising neural maps', *Gait and Posture*, 24: 46–53.

Barton, G., Lisboa, P., Lees, A. and Attfield, S. (2007) 'Gait quality assessment using self-organising artificial neural networks', *Gait and Posture*, 25: 374–9.

Bauer, H. and Schöllhorn, W.I. (1997) 'Self-organizing maps for the analysis of complex movement patterns', *Neural Processing Letters*, 5: 193–7.

Davids, K. and Glazier, P.S. (2010) 'Deconstructing neurobiological coordination: The role of the biomechanics-motor control nexus', *Exercise and Sports Sciences Reviews*, 38: 86–90.

Davids, K., Bennett, S.J. and Newell, K.M. (2006) *Movement System Variability*, Champaign, IL: Human Kinetics.

Edelmann-Nusser, J., Hohmann, A. and Henneberg, B. (2002) 'Modeling and prediction of competitive performance in swimming upon neural networks', *European Journal of Sport Science*, 2: 1–10.

Glazier, P.S., Wheat, J.S., Pease, D.L. and Bartlett, R.M. (2006) 'The interface of motor control and biomechanics: Dynamic systems theory and the functional role of movement variability', in K. Davids, S. Bennett and K. Newell (eds), *Movement System Variability* (pp. 49–69). Champaign, IL: Human Kinetics.

Hamill, J., Haddad, J.M. and McDermott, W.J. (2000) 'Issues in quantifying variability from a dynamical systems perspective', *Journal of Applied Biomechanics*, 16: 407–18.

Hodges, N.J., Williams, M.A., Hayes, S.J. and Breslin, G. (2007) 'What is modelled during observational learning?', *Journal of Sports Sciences*, 25: 531–45.

Kelso, J.A.S. (1995) *Dynamic Patterns: The Self-Organization of Brain and Behaviour*, Cambridge, MA: MIT Press.

Knudson, D.V. and Morrison, C.S. (2002) *Qualitative Analysis of Human Movement*, 2nd ed., Champaign, IL: Human Kinetics.

Kohonen, T. (2001) *Self-Organizing Maps*, 3rd ed., Berlin: Springer-Verlag.

Lamb, P.F., Bartlett, R.M. and Robins, A. (2010) 'Self-organising maps: An objective method for clustering complex human movement', *International Journal of Computer Science in Sport*, 9: 20–9.

Lamb, P.F., Bartlett, R.M. and Robins, A. (2011a) 'Artificial neural networks for analyzing inter-limb coordination: The golf chip shot', *Human Movement Science*, 30: 1129–43.

Lamb, P.F., Mündermann, A., Bartlett, R.M. and Robins, A. (2011b) 'Visualizing changes in lower body coordination with different types of foot orthoses using self-organizing maps (SOM)', *Gait and Posture*, 34: 485–9.

Latash, M.L. (2008) 'Motor control: The heart of kinesiology', *Quest*, 60: 19–30.

Lees, A. (2002) 'Technique analysis in sports: A critical review', *Journal of Sports Sciences,* 20: 813–24.

Lees, A. and Barton, G. (2005) 'A characterisation of technique in the soccer kick using a Kohonen neural network analysis', in T. Reilly, J. Cabri and D. Araújo (eds), *Science and Football V: The Proceedings of the Fifth World Congress on Science and Football* (pp. 83–8), London: Routledge.

Memmert, D. and Perl, J. (2009) 'Analysis and simulation of creativity learning by means of artificial neural networks', *Human Movement Science*, 28: 263–82.

Müller, H. and Sternad, D. (2004) 'Decomposition of variability in the execution of goal-oriented tasks: Three components of skill improvement', *Journal of Experimental Psychology: Human Perception and Performance*, 30: 212–33.

Negnevitsky, M. (2002) *Artificial Intelligence: A Guide to Intelligent Systems*, 1st ed., Harlow, UK: Pearson Education Limited.

Obhi, S.S. (2004) 'Bimanual coordination: An unbalanced field of research', *Motor Control*, 8: 111–20.

Riley, M.A., Schockley, K. and Van Orden, G. (2012) 'Learning from the body about the mind', *Topics in Cognitive Science*, 4: 21–34.

Schöllhorn, W.I. and Bauer, H.U. (1998) 'Identifying individual movement styles in high performance sports by means of self-organizing Kohonen maps', in H.J. Riehle and M. Vieten (eds), *XVI ISBS '98 Konstanz* (pp. 574–7). Konstanz: Konstanz University Press.

Vesanto, J., Himberg, J., Alhoniemi, E. and Parkankangas, J. (2000) *SOM Toolbox for MATLAB 5* (Tech. Rep. No. A57), Helsinki, Finland: Helsinki University of Technology (HUT). Available at www.cis.hut.fi/projects/somtoolbox/.

Yan, B. and Li, M. (2000) 'Shot put technique using an ANN AMT model', in Y. Hong and D. Johns (eds), *XVIII ISBS 2000 Hong Kong* (pp. 580–4). Hong Kong: The Chinese University of Hong Kong.

19

NEURAL NETWORKS FOR ANALYSING SPORTS GAMES

Jürgen Perl[1], Markus Tilp[2], Arnold Baca[3] and Daniel Memmert[4]

[1]UNIVERSITY OF MAINZ, GERMANY

[2]UNIVERSITY OF GRAZ, AUSTRIA

[3]UNIVERSITY OF VIENNA, AUSTRIA

[4]GERMAN SPORT UNIVERSITY COLOGNE, GERMANY

Summary

Two interlinked challenging tasks characterize the problem of analysing sports games: recording complex process game data and transforming them into useful information. These days, a significant part of the first task can be carried out using automatic position recording, thus placing increased emphasis on the second task; tracking a soccer game at 25 frames per second results in about 135,000 frames per game, which sums to about 6 million x-y coordinate data per game. Nevertheless, an experienced coach can filter significant information from these data and recognize patterns of player constellations in the playing processes. Neural networks using self-organizing maps (SOMs; see Kohonen, 1995) can recognize patterns in large data sets too and hence net-based data analysis can support the coach's work. The first ideas of net-based analysis of sports games date back a few years, with recent advances in automatic position recording lending increased attention to complex games like soccer, handball, or basketball. Following a brief introduction to net-based game analysis, the chapter introduces the basics of net-based handling of process data and reports three instances detailing conceptual and methodical approaches of current research projects investigating handball, basketball, and soccer, respectively.

Introduction

The complexity of game processes is a challenging aspect of game analysis and conventional methods make it difficult to produce more than simple results, like frequencies of actions for comparison purposes. Even automatic position recordings are used typically for calculation of kinematic data, such as position distributions of players, distances covered, and work rate (e.g. time spent walking, jogging, running, and sprinting). In contrast, self-organizing neural networks, like the dynamically controlled network DyCoN (Perl, 2001), are useful for game analysis by recognizing movement patterns, including the behavioural processes of tactical groups like offence or defence. First approaches of net-based game analysis began in the late 1990s with the idea of using pattern recognition abilities of SOMs for identifying static patterns (e.g.

237

constellations of volleyball players: Perl and Lames, 2000; Jäger *et al.*, 2007) and dynamic patterns (e.g. position sequences of squash players: Perl, 2001; McGarry and Perl, 2004).

While studies in volleyball (Perl and Lames, 2000; Jäger *et al.*, 2007) and handball (Pfeiffer and Perl, 2006) focussed on pattern frequencies and distributions as statistical characterizations of a game or a team, the squash study and later some volleyball studies started to analyse the dynamic process patterns of the players and teams under the aspect of technical or tactical behaviour. Problems recording position data, until recent times, restricted these investigations to games with relatively small numbers of players. In 2005, first approaches in automatic position recording yielded accessible data for dynamic analysis of volleyball. In soccer, a first research project dealing with net-based constellation analyses was conducted successfully (Leser, 2006), encouraging development for increasing research activities in this field. Since 2006 then, a specific focus of net-based game analysis has been on soccer (Perl, 2008; Grunz *et al.*, 2009; Memmert and Perl, 2009a, 2009b; Grunz *et al.*, 2012), although other complex team games, such as handball and basketball, have also been the subject of net-based process analyses.

In the following sections, research approaches are introduced, dealing with handball, basketball, and soccer, thereby offering different aspects of data recording technologies, data pre-processing, pattern recognition and analysis, as well as data post-processing. The next section presents a brief introduction of concepts and methods of net-based pattern analysis with particular attention on aspects of data reduction and the transfer of data to information.

The general approach: net-based constellation analysis

To optimize the abilities of a pattern-recognizing neural network, the data must be reduced to pattern-containing fragments. In case of position data, this means that constellations of players on the playground (i.e. field of play) are usable for situational patterns. However, there are a huge number of constellations during a game, making it necessary to map them to formations by separating their centroid (i.e. the 'centre of gravity' of the players' positions). If the same constellation of players appears on different positions on the playground, it is mapped to the same formation, storing the centroid information for position-oriented analyses. This reduces the huge number of constellations to a small number of formations, which can easily be learned and, again, reduced to characteristic types by a network. The automatically generated game protocol for each point in time contains the formation, the formation type, and the centroid. Together with manually added information about activities and success, it enables a wide range of analyses, from process animation to tactical concepts, to statistical analysis.

In Figure 19.1, a trained network is presented as a matrix of coloured (presented white through black) squares, where each colour stands for a formation type. Different neurons of equal colour represent variant formations of the same type. Representing those variants by just one characteristic type reduces the number of significantly different items to about ten, which has the advantage of enabling statistical analyses on reasonable distributions. On a more dynamical level of analysis, sequences of position data can be fed to the trained network. In so doing, each data set marks its corresponding neuron, mapping the original process to a neuron-trajectory of the time-depending formation series.

Figure 19.1 shows how it works. The position data sets of the game activate corresponding neurons of the network, starting with the one with the black mark. The process then runs through some light grey neurons followed by some middle grey and some dark grey ones, and so on. Reduced to the significant types represented by the corresponding colours, the trajectories become much simpler in representing the specific behaviours of the corresponding tactical group (see the small embedded graphic on top left). By switching from formations to forma-

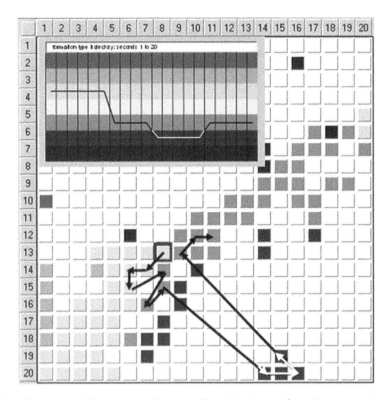

Figure 19.1   Trajectory of formations on the net and its reduction to a formation–type trajectory

tion types, the formation trajectories are smoothed and allow easier comparisons between each other. Note that all specific information is nevertheless retained for use if needed for special analyses.

In a second step, those patterns of processes like the embedded one of Figure 19.1 can be used for training a second-level network, the input of which are vectors of formation-type numbers derived from the type trajectories. This method has already proved successful in several cases of motion analysis. As one example for handling game processes, the trajectory from Figure 19.1 represents the type sequence 5,5,5,5,5,5,5,3,3,3,3,2,2,2,2,2,3,3,3,3,3, which, for example, could characterize a particular tactical manoeuvre, like preparing an attack phase (note that this same sequence can be represented in condensed phase sequence as 5,3,2,3). As described in more detail in the following section, the second-level network would find those tactical patterns and compare their frequencies and distributions with those of opposing teams. Even infrequent and possibly creative patterns can be found using advanced network approaches (Memmert and Perl, 2009a, 2009b).

Handball: movement and action sequence analysis

Notational analysis of complex sport games like soccer, basketball, or team handball has gained a lot of interest in the last few decades. Scientific challenges remaining in the analysis of such complex sports games are: (1) identifying team tactics; (2) discriminating between successful and unsuccessful player/team behaviours; (3) anticipating player/team behaviours; and (4) determining the physical demands on players/teams during a game. Unfortunately, most of the analyses in complex sport games are still based on the counting of single elementary actions, such as passes or shots. A typical shortcoming of this method is the loss of important information regarding the game context and the player interactions, which makes it difficult, if not impossible, to meet the challenges stated. Therefore, a major motivation for the project on team handball reported here is analysis of action sequences, instead of the single actions themselves (see Figure 19.2).

Specifically, our approach goes beyond simply counting single actions and assesses the combination of position and action information in order to understand complex interactions in sport games. To meet the four challenges listed, a significant amount of action sequences and the physical demands in team handball were analysed. Specifically, a unique combination of an easy-to-handle and affordable multiple camera system, a semi-automatic position tracking and event recognition system, and a database for recording single actions and action sequences was developed. In addition, a novel system for analysing action sequences using a two-level neural network was established, going beyond reporting elementary statistics, as described next.

Analysis of action sequences

Similar to previous work (Koch and Tilp, 2009a, 2009b), video analysis enabled the basic structure of sport games to be determined, including information about frequency of observed techniques and their success probability. Using six to eight cameras, information about action position for each video frame can be obtained (Mauthner *et al.*, 2007) and movement paths of athletes recorded with an accuracy of about 1.5 per cent error. In a next step, neural networks were used to evaluate action sequences. This approach has already been used successfully in other similar tasks (Perl, 2002; Jäger *et al.*, 2007).

For network training, each neuron in the network initially contains a vector of position data representing a specific type of playing constellation. For example, (x1, y1, ..., x7, y7) could be such a vector of x-y coordinates of all handball players in a team. Neighboured neurons can build clusters of similar constellation types, representing specific states or phases of the game

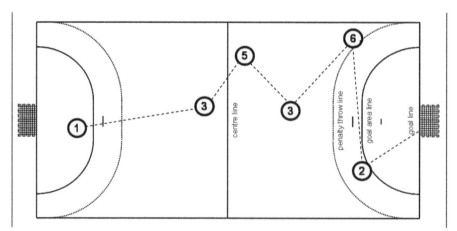

Figure 19.2 Simplified action sequence of a counter-attacking situation in team handball. Each circle represents an acting player (with number) and simultaneously its single elementary action (including position). The dashed lines represent the path of the ball. The temporal combination of the single actions together constitutes the action sequence

process, such as offence or defence formations. Mapping the time series of position data to the corresponding neurons of the net and connecting the neurons by edges results in a two-dimensional trajectory as a simplified representation of the game process (Figure 19.1). In the next step, by connecting the respective meaning to the clusters, like specific defence or offence constellations, the complex game process can be reduced to a one-dimensional phase diagram of the corresponding constellation types. Together with semi-automatic position recording from video, which is used for estimating physical demand, the whole process of data recording, evaluating, and phase analysis can be done semi-automatically.

Furthermore, the phase diagrams themselves build patterns, which, by means of a second-level network, can be analysed for similarity, main types, interaction, success, and even creativity. This two-level approach has been used successfully in a project dealing with basketball free throws, where intra-individual stability as well as inter-individual similarities of throws have been identified (Schmidt *et al.*, 2009; Schmidt, 2012). Using the methods and results from basketball, specific parts of the process trajectories can be identified by neurons in the second-level network as representing types of tactical activities. Following initial training of the first- and second-level networks, and an initial semantic interpretation of the neurons by experts, the automatic recording and analysis of the game is now covered.

The sequence of position data on the first-level net is transformed to a trajectory of constellation types. This master trajectory is subdivided into pieces of equal length, which are tested on the second-level net, resulting in corresponding neurons that classify the respective semantic information. The sequences of resulting time codes, positions, constellation, and semantics can then be transferred to the database. Together with the action classifications, this represents a complete record of the game. Thus, specific action sequences with increased frequencies related to team tactics can be detected and related to game outcome. The recorded action sequences in the database also allow prediction of team/individual behaviour in similar, future game situations.

Statistical methods of cluster and pattern analysis are often preferred over artificial intelligence approaches, like neural networks, because of their simple reproducibility. However, cluster or pattern type detection by means of statistical methods normally needs pre-information, whereas the network approach does not. In the following section, both approaches are compared with each other.

Basketball: tactical patterns in basketball – statistical vs. net-based analysis

In a joint research project carried out in 2010 and 2011 between the Departments of Biomechanics/Kinesiology and Applied Computer Science (University of Vienna, Austria), the Institute of Cognitive and Team/Racket Sport Research (German Sport University Cologne), and the National Institute of Physical Education (INEFC; Barcelona, Spain), different approaches were applied in order to identify patterns from position data in basketball. The positions of the players from two semi-professional basketball teams were measured with the Ubisense tracking system (Ubisense Real Time Location System, Ubisense, Cambridge, UK). This system provides positional information based on time difference of arrival and angle of arrival data of radio frequency signals. Six base stations were mounted in the corners and in the middle of the sidewalls of a gymnasium at a height of about 5 m. Small-sized active (signal emitting) tags were attached to the players atop of their heads (see Figure 19.3). Position data of the players were thus obtained with an average frequency of about 5 Hz and an accuracy of about 10–15 cm. In addition, the players and the ball were recorded using standard video cameras placed into the four corners of the gymnasium.

Altogether, a complete basketball match, including 67 attacks of two different types (set plays and fast breaks), was recorded. Based on the video recordings, each attack starting at the instant the ball crossed the midline was described as a sequence of distinguishable events (actions). These events were characterized by the laterality of play determined in three lanes (right, centre, left), as well as an interaction context defined as the dynamic positioning of the ball with regard to the positions of the players of both teams. In particular, ball position was categorized by its location with regard to the forward line, midline, and rear lines of both attacking and defending teams.

T-pattern-analysis (Magnussen, 2000) was performed to detect patterns in action sequences during attacks. Two actions occurring in the same sequence in approximately the same time intervals repeatedly, more often than expected by chance, form a (minimal) T-pattern, with more complex T-patterns formed by sequences of simpler patterns identified using a hierarchical bottom-up procedure. A variety of complex and repeated temporal patterns in the data sets were found using this analysis.

To establish the procedure for identifying different types of offensive and defensive tactics automatically and, moreover, to detect two separate types of attack (i.e. set plays and fast breaks), a hierarchical set-up of special self-organizing maps was developed (Grunz *et al.*, 2012). In a pre-processing step, raw player position data of each basketball team were composed into a sequence of constellations. These constellations were then used to train a DyCoN (Perl, 2004). Following DyCoN learning, typical constellation prototypes became encoded by different neurons, with trajectories of neurons thus representing time-dependent processes of the basketball game. Using the sliding-window technique, these trajectories were taken as input for a second net, with each neuron in the second DyCoN encoding a movement of constellations.

After training, labelled data gained from the set plays and fast breaks were used to attach a soft-labelling to neurons on the second layer. This process enabled classification on the test data, which has shown average results, and more labelled data might be necessary in future to obtain better classification results. However, the neural-network approach was nonetheless

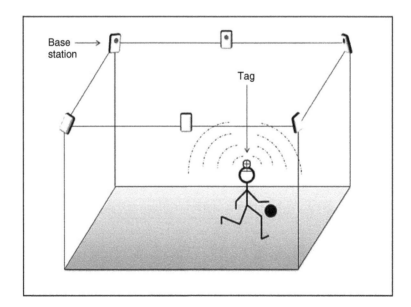

Figure 19.3 Schematic recording of basketball player-position data

successful in identifying types of constellations and in discriminating between different offensive and defensive tactics. Preferred tactics of the teams could be detected.

Both T-pattern-analysis and DyCoN analysis, then, were able to identify patterns from position data in basketball. T-patterns represent the tactical context of the events, resulting in high validity of the findings. While T-patterns were able to identify sequences of predefined categories, neural networks can identify constellations not foreseen previously. Applying a neural network approach, however, requires interpretation of the semantic meanings of clusters found in the respective nets by an expert. In the basketball project, a description of event sequences was obtained from video recordings, requiring manual data acquisition. However, in future investigations, this information might be derived directly from position data, given that a feasible solution can be found for assembling a tag into the basketball itself. The neural network approach was able to provide automated analysis of automated position data collected from the radio-wave based system.

Soccer: analysis and assessment of tactical performance

In this section, we present the problem of semantic assessment of game activities, which is particularly difficult in soccer because of the high complexity of game situations. In contrast with review articles about assessment of technical skills (e.g. Ali, 2011), assessment of tactical behaviour in team sports has not been paid much attention until recently (Memmert, 2010; Memmert and Roth, 2007). According to prevalent belief, however, a high level of tactical skills in soccer is important for effective player performances at the highest international levels.

The present standard is to assess tactical performance in soccer by means of game observation (Franks, 1985). Qualitative game observations are less objective and less systematic (less structured and less comprehensive), use subjective impressions of the observers, and take advantage of the experiences and know-how of experts (Leser, 2006). In contrast, quantitative game observations proceed in an objective fashion, using predefined observation schedules (e.g. category systems) to collect data. Subsequently, these data are evaluated and indices calculated to value the whole-player performances or individual performance components (Baca *et al.*, 2004; Leser and Baca, 2008; Memmert and Harvey, 2008). Both qualitative and quantitative observation methods imply a high expenditure of time for data evaluation (often several days) and objectivity between two observers is often lower than desired.

In recent years, progress in computer science has made it possible to provide position data and thus track player movements (Baca, 2008). In turn, a concept for automatic analyses and assessments of tactical behaviour based on position data using a net-based approach is now becoming possible for the first time. With this in mind, the first part of the soccer project was focussed on the recognition of tactical behaviour in games. An expert categorized the 2006 FIFA World Championship final based on video and position data. The categories were short and long game initiations, counter-attacks, and standard situations (e.g. throw-in, free kick, and corner kick). The identified tactical sequences were used for training and validation of the developed architecture of dynamical controlled neural networks (Grunz *et al.*, 2012). The method is analogue to that described previously for identifying fast breaks and set plays in basketball. Comparison of results gained from expert categorization to those from the architecture showed good average recognition rate for each category (see Table 19.1). Game opening and standard situations were identified with high probability by the neural network, although counter-attacks showed poor recognition rate due to high variability in the pattern.

The second part of the soccer project focussed on assessment of tactical performance using a software compound Neural Network Assessment System (NNAS). The NNAS uses a hierarchy

Table 19.1 Comparison of results based on a hierarchy of neural networks and an expert categorizing the 2006 FIFA World Championship data. High recognition rate is achieved in standard situations but the architecture was unable to detect all game initiations. Attacks and counter-attacks show high variability and poor recognition rate

Category	Experts	Net-based analysis	Recognition rate
Game initiation	131	110	84%
Throw–in	27	27	100%
Free kick	16	14	88%
Corner kick	12	12	100%
(Counter-)attacks	49	29	59%
Sum	235	192	86%

of DyCoNs as a basis and was developed in previous work by Grunz (VisuCat, pre-processing) and Perl (SOCCER, assessment/post-processing) (for details, see Perl and Memmert, 2011). The aim of NNAS is to develop and verify concepts and methods for assessing observable behaviour of soccer players and, especially, to automatically judge tactical performance. This is done by means of automated position tracking (players and ball) and artificial intelligence. Application of methods of artificial intelligence, in particular neural networks, can be helpful in describing, analysing, and evaluating game situations for objectively identifying tactical performance components in soccer. In addition, such computational analysis offers a dramatic time advantage concerning evaluation of position data (e.g. from 6–8 hours to 2 minutes, say). Small efforts in data acquisition enable accumulation of huge amounts of data, bringing new opportunities for theory construction and practical applications. For example, automatic assessment of tactical behaviour in time-limited soccer situations, such as during half-time, will be possible in future.

Data and procedure: Recent technical improvements allow complete capture of x-y position data of all 22 players and ball for the entire game duration (e.g. 90 minutes). With a sampling rate of 25 frames per second, 270,000 x-y-data per player and ball are produced in 90 minutes. Thus, when looking at all data, one gets 6,210,000 x-y-data (i.e. 23 x 270,000) for a game, give, or take. Transformation of position data into team formation data has been mastered so that transformation of respective semantic assessments works properly. Also, an automatic match protocol can be created and action type analyses conducted with the hierarchical structure of the analysis sequence being automated in usable software (see Figure 19.4). Otherwise a lot of work would be necessary when undertaking team formation analyses.

Categorization: To examine prototypical geometric patterns with NNAS and to recognize and typify team formations, a software tool was developed in the frame of a feasibility study for stochastic generation of geometric patterns. Thus, prototypical position data for specified player combinations and team formations were generated which function as a basis for pattern recognition tests. Tests with soccer data confirm this initial approach.

Validation: Results from net analysis can be compared with video-based expert analyses with the help of a software tool for automatic match evaluations. This automatic validation analysis can be conducted using different tolerance thresholds (e.g. recognition of the same action with time difference of 5 per cent). For validation of the trained nets, the results of the traditional game analysis ('gold standard') and the NNAS results were compared. The results showed high accordance with traditionally identified group tactics, with playmaking, set pieces (further differentiated into throw-ins, free kicks, and corner kicks), and shots on goal also identified in the hierarchical net-based approach.

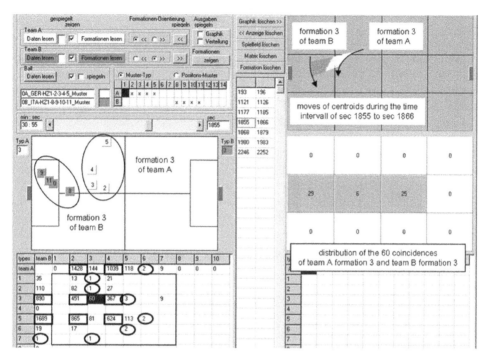

Figure 19.4 Screenshot from the team formation recognition software SOCCER. Top left: Selection screen for the data of both teams, including a scrollbar for revision of the entire game, the team formation overview screen, and the synoptic table, which lists the number of formations as well as the coincidence frequencies for the entire playing time. Bottom left: Frequently occurring team formations are framed by rectangles; infrequently occurring team formations are framed by ellipses. Clicking one of those entries shows the static distribution of those formation coincidences (right). It also activates a list of corresponding time sequences, which can be clicked (e.g. 1,855 to 1,866) to show the dynamical development (top right) and the current position of the formation on the playground (left). Top right: Simplified view of a team formation, the group's key aspects and the key aspects of the combination of the offensive and defensive groups

If validity of the NNAS tool can be ensured, it will be an important step towards identifying tactical performance components in team sports objectively. This would be of great benefit for sports practice, not only for talent selection in different youth sports (e.g. basketball, team handball, soccer, field hockey, tennis) but also in analysis of professional team sports. Apart from being aware of the components of sports performance and their interactions, the diagnostic possibilities of neural net analysis should also be considered. Diagnostics can be helpful in both sports practice (e.g. for sophisticated assessments of player performances) and science (e.g. for evaluation of sports teaching approaches). Information technology advances now provide a lot of data for many facets of sports, and fast automated systems for assessing tactical behaviour in game sports are desirable too. These demands have been met only to a limited extent in the past and high synergetic potential exists between the sports and computer sciences for tackling these issues in future (Balagué and Torrents, 2005; Memmert and Perl, 2009a, 2009b).

Concluding remarks

The net-based game analysis approach is a promising way of combining automatic position tracking with computer-based tactics assessment, oriented not just in statistical numbers but in the dynamical process patterns themselves. In turn, data reducing and condensing techniques enable handling of tactical patterns without losing key information for statistical analysis. Cooperation of artificial neural networks, T-pattern-analysis, and tools like the Neural Network Assessment System allows a fruitful combination of qualitative pattern recognition and quantitative statistical analysis.

Some open problems, however, have to be dealt with in future. One major technical problem is recording ball position, which up to now has had to be tracked manually. Also, qualitative judgements of situations like 'ball possession' or 'opening an attack' are difficult to detect by automatic programs and currently, therefore, have to be added manually too. It might be that more detailed analyses of the movements of players and ball in future work can find patterns indicating such qualitative situations. In this case, a combination of automatic video data tracking with automatic position data recording and pattern analysis offers a promising and attractive way of solving these problems.

References

Ali, A. (2011) 'Measuring soccer skill performance: A review', *Scandinavian Journal of Medicine Science in Sports*, 11: 170–83.

Baca, A. (2008) 'Tracking motion in sport – trends and limitations', in J. Hammond (ed.), *Proceedings of the 9th Australasian Conference on Mathematics and Computers in Sport* (pp. 1–7). MathSport (ANZIAM).

Baca, A., Baron, R., Leser, R., and Kain, H. (2004) 'A process oriented approach for match analysis in table tennis', in A. Lees, J.F. Kahn, and I.W. Maynard (eds), *Science and Racket Sports III* (pp. 214–19). London: Routledge.

Balagué, N. and Torrents, C. (2005) 'Thinking before computing: Changing perspectives in sport performance', *International Journal of Computer Science in Sport*, 4: 5–13.

Franks, I. (1985) 'Qualitative and quantitative analysis', *Coaching Review*, 8: 48–50.

Grunz, A., Memmert, D., and Perl, J. (2009) 'Analysis and imulation of actions in games by means of special self-organizing maps', *International Journal of Computer Science in Sport*, 8(1): 22–37.

Grunz, A., Perl, J., and Memmert, D. (2012) 'Tactical pattern recognition in soccer games by means of special self-organizing maps', *Human Movement Science*, 31(2): 334–43.

Jäger, J., Perl, J., and Schöllhorn, W. (2007) 'Analysis of players' configurations by means of artificial neural networks', *International Journal of Performance Analysis in Sport*, 7(3): 90–105.

Koch, C. and Tilp, M. (2009a) 'Beach volleyball techniques and tactics: A comparison of male and female playing characteristics', *International Journal of Fundamental and Applied Kinesiology*, 41(1): 51–8.

Koch, C. and Tilp, M. (2009b) 'Analysis of beach volleyball action sequences of female top athletes', *Journal of Human Sport and Exercise*, 4(3): 272–83.

Kohonen, T. (1995) *Self Organizing Maps*, Berlin: Springer.

Leser, R. (2006) 'Applied video and game analysis in professional soccer', in H. Dancs, M. Hughes, and P. O'Donoghue (eds), *Proceedings of the 7th World Congress of Performance Analysis of Sport* (pp. 20–9). Cardiff: CPA UWIC Press.

Leser, R. and Baca, A. (2008) 'Practice oriented match analyses in table tennis as coaching aid', in A. Lees, D. Carbello, and G. Torres (eds), *Science and Racket Sports IV* (pp. 214–9). London: Routledge.

Magnusson, M.S. (2000) 'Discovering hidden time patterns in behavior: T-patterns and their detection', *Behavior Research Methods, Instruments and Computers*, 32(1): 93–110.

Mauthner, T., Koch, C., Tilp, M., and Bischof, H. (2007) 'Visual tracking of athletes in beach volleyball using a single camera', *International Journal of Computer Science in Sports*, 6(2): 21–35.

McGarry, T. and Perl, J. (2004) 'Models of sports contests – Markov processes, dynamical systems and neural networks', in M. Hughes and I.M. Franks (eds), *Notational Analysis of Sport* (pp. 227–42). London: Routledge.

Memmert, D. (2010) 'Testing of tactical performance in youth elite soccer', *Journal of Sports Science and Medicine*, 9: 199–205.

Memmert, D. and Roth, K. (2007) 'The effects of non-specific and specific concepts on tactical creativity in team ball sports', *Journal of Sport Sciences*, 25: 1423–32.

Memmert, D. and Harvey, S. (2008) 'The Game Performance Assessment Instrument (GPAI): Some concerns and solutions for further development', *Journal of Teaching in Physical Education*, 27: 220–40.

Memmert, D. and Perl, J. (2009a) 'Analysis and simulation of creativity learning by means of artificial neural networks', *Human Movement Science*, 28: 263–82.

Memmert, D. and Perl, J. (2009b) 'Game creativity analysis by means of neural networks', *Journal of Sport Sciences*, 27: 139–49.

Perl, J. (2001) 'DyCoN: Ein dynamisch gesteuertes Neuronales Netz zur Modellierung und Analyse von Prozessen im Sport [A dynamically controlled neural network for modelling and analysis of processes in sport]', in J. Perl (ed.), *Sport and Informatik VIII* (pp. 85–98). Cologne: Strauß.

Perl, J. (2002) 'Game analysis and control by means of continuously learning networks', *International Journal of Performance Analysis in Sport*, 2(1): 21–35.

Perl, J. (2004) 'A neural network approach to movement pattern analysis', *Human Movement Science*, 23(5): 605–20.

Perl, J. (2008) 'Modelling', in P. Dabnichki and A. Baca (eds), *Computers in Sport* (pp. 121–60). Southampton, UK: Wit Press.

Perl, J. and Lames, M. (2000) 'Identifikation von Ballwechselverlaufstypen mit Neuronalen Netzen am Beispiel Volleyball [Identification of types of ball-rallies by means of neural networks, exemplarily for volleyball]', in W. Schmidt and A. Knollenberg (eds), *Sport – Spiel – Forschung: Gestern. Heute. Morgen* (pp. 211–15). Schriften der dvs 112, Hamburg: Czwalina.

Perl, J. and Memmert, D. (2011) 'Net-based game analysis by means of the software tool SOCCER', *International Journal of Computer Science in Sport*, 10(2): 77–84.

Pfeiffer, M. and Perl, J. (2006) 'Analysis of tactical structures in team handball by means of artificial neural networks', *International Journal of Computer Science in Sport*, 5(1): 4–14.

Schmidt, A. (2012) 'Movement pattern recognition in basketball free-throw shooting', *Human Movement Science*, 31, 360–82.

Schmidt, A., Fikus, M., and Perl, J. (2009) 'Typisierung von Basketball-Freiwürfen mit Hilfe Neuronaler Netze [Classification of basketball free throws by means of neural networks]', in M. Lames, C. Augste, O. Cordes, C. Dreckmann, K. Görsdorf, and M. Siegle (eds), *Schriften der Deutschen Vereinigung für Sportwissenschaft* (pp. 189–94). Hamburg: Czwalina.

20

STRATEGY AND TACTICS IN SPORTS PERFORMANCE

Angela Hibbs[1] and Peter O'Donoghue[2]

[1]NORTHUMBRIA UNIVERSITY, UK

[2]CARDIFF METROPOLITAN UNIVERSITY, UK

Summary

This chapter proposes a model of strategy and tactics in sport based on a survey of coaching literature in game sports. The nature of strategy and tactics in various contexts is discussed before considering strategy and tactics in sport. The model is described and supporting evidence for the model discussed. The model includes influence of game objectives, regulations, environmental factors, game state and the relative strengths and weaknesses of performers with respect to opponents. The role of decision making and how strategy and tactics manifest themselves in observable behaviour are also addressed.

Introduction

Humans make tactical and strategic decisions in all areas of their lives and there is evidence of this in observable behaviour. This means that there are general theories of strategy and tactics from many contexts that may be relevant in sports performance. As such, this chapter briefly examines strategy in business and military contexts, identifying the general factors that influence strategy, tactics and subsequent action. Of prime importance is the objective of any undertaking and often there are many different ways in which individuals or organisations can set about achieving them. The strategy chosen and activities planned must be conducted within constraints, such as legal constraints, limitations of resources and environmental factors. The strategy chosen will also make the best use of talent and other resources available. Many of these issues are transferable to sport where athletes have long-, medium- and short-term objectives, must compete within the regulations of their sports and must perform in an optimal way given their relative strengths and weaknesses with respect to the opponents.

One of the purposes of performance analysis is the analysis of strategy and tactics. This has traditionally been done by analysing patterns of play and making inferences about tactical decisions made by players and coaches that cannot be observed directly. Unfortunately, theoretical models of strategy and tactics in sport for explaining the results of these investigations are missing. Therefore, a purpose of this chapter is to propose a general theoretical model of strategy and tactics in sports performance that is evidenced by previously developed research in coaching theory and practice. The chapter commences with discussion of strategy and tactics in non-sports contexts, comparing these to the nature of strategy and tactics in sport. The model of strategy and tactics in sport is then shown, followed by a discussion of supporting evidence.

Strategy and tactics in non-sports contexts

General decision making

What clothes did you decide to wear today? How did you travel to your place of work today? What did you eat for lunch today? Now ask yourself what the other alternatives were in each case and why you made the decisions you did. This should show that we make decisions every time we act, having weighed up the advantages and disadvantages of different alternative actions that could be taken. Whilst being aware of some disadvantages to the actions eventually taken, you will probably have justified the actions based on their advantages or greater disadvantages of the alternative options. The choice of clothing may have considered how the weather might change and the probability of different weather conditions occurring. Each opportunity or risk is considered with the probability of different events occurring. Some decisions, such as travel arrangements and accommodation for a weekend break, require more consideration than other decisions that have to be made in situations that arise more rapidly. For example, when driving, we are often faced with a choice of lanes where the queue in one lane may be longer and moving more slowly than the queue in another lane. However, the shorter, faster-moving queue may completely stop if a vehicle ahead needs to turn off the road by crossing lanes of on-coming traffic. Such choices of lanes are not planned before taking the journey but decisions are made as such situations are encountered. These examples of planning a weekend break and making decisions while driving illustrate the contrast between strategy and tactics. Strategy is typically planned in advance of action, considering a great deal of available information. Tactical decision making, on the other hand, involves more moment-to-moment decisions made under time pressure as situations arise.

Military strategy

Military strategy has been studied and developed over thousands of years. There are multiple translations of Sun Wu's *Art of War*, which is thought to have originated in around 500 BC and covers tactical aspects of warfare. Military strategy is an immense area of decision making that is beyond the scope of this chapter. However, there are some interesting aspects of military strategy that are relevant to sport. One similarity between sport and military contexts of strategy is the hierarchy of situations where strategic and tactical decisions have to be taken. Military campaigns may include many engagements, which are made up of phases and which, in turn, are made up of individual incidents. Similar hierarchies can be seen in sport, with campaigns such as seasons or tournaments, individual matches, matches being made up of different periods and individual set play and open play events occurring within these periods.

The role of communication through chains of command is vitally important in any undertaking by organisations of large numbers of people, such as military forces. Misinterpretation of instructions and information as they are passed though different levels of command can lead to catastrophe, such as the charge of the Light Brigade at the battle of Balaclava in 1854. Coaches are less remote to the on-field action in sport than generals would be to a battlefield in the nineteenth century, but there is still a need for clear, unambiguous instruction.

Unorthodox military tactics have the advantage of being unexpected by opposing forces but also come with risks of being untried and untested. At the battle of Trafalgar in 1805, Admiral

Lord Nelson's fleet attacked the opposing line of French and Spanish ships from a perpendicular direction, rather than moving past the opposing line in an orthodox parallel direction. This high-risk strategy was used because it gave an opportunity for a decisive victory. Unorthodox tactics have also proved successful in sport – for example, Muhammad Ali conserved energy during his successful world heavyweight boxing challenge against George Foreman in 1974 by leaning against the ropes and covering up, a strategy that has been termed 'rope-a-dope'. Unorthodox attacking strategies in rugby union have the advantages of surprise, deception and not being as easy to counter as routine expected attacks (Van Heerden, 1968). Other common factors that are considered in strategy and tactics in sport and military contexts are strategic objectives, resources, capabilities, geographical environmental, climate, logistics and practical considerations, conventions and laws.

A difference between military and sports contexts is the use of information. In sport, opposing teams can be analysed using public information about their competitions, including statistics and full-match video recordings. However, covert observation of closed opposition training sessions would be frowned upon in many sports. By contrast, intelligence services go to great efforts to obtain and analyse secret data about opposing forces. For example, the US Navy had knowledge of Japanese intentions prior to the battle of Midway in 1942 as a result of successfully decoding Japanese radio signals.

Strategy for business

Strengths, weaknesses, opportunities and threats (SWOT) analysis was originally developed for business contexts but the general technique applies in many fields (Hill and Westbrook, 1997). Strengths and weaknesses are considered to be internal factors of an enterprise, while opportunities and threats come from external sources. Internal factors include personnel, finance and manufacturing capability. External factors include legislation, market conditions, economic environment, technological advances and social changes. The approach of SWOT analysis involves matching strengths to opportunities while converting (or mitigating) weaknesses and threats. There are many similarities between sport and business when it comes to the analysis of strengths, weaknesses, opportunities and threats. However, a key difference is that, while business enterprises may avoid areas where they have difficulty competing, in some sports it is not possible to completely withdraw from a match to play alternative matches where there is a better chance of success.

Model of strategy and tactics in sport

Figure 20.1 shows the model of strategy and tactics proposed. This model is based on a survey of coaching literature in different sports, as well as other sources of evidence to support different aspects of the model. Evidence was drawn from textbooks for various sports that included the words 'strategy' or 'tactics' within the title. The performer may have general strengths and weaknesses but these need to be related to the given opponent because a relative weakness against one opponent might be a relative strength against another. An important aspect of this model is the knowledge that performers have about their opponents. There may be relative strengths and weaknesses that are not considered when making tactical decisions simply because of a lack of knowledge about the opponent. As a match is played, the experience of observing and competing against an opponent may increase a performer's knowledge about him or her.

In any game, performers attempt to achieve their objectives playing within the constraints of the regulations of the sport. Over time, strategies and tactics have been devised to maximise the

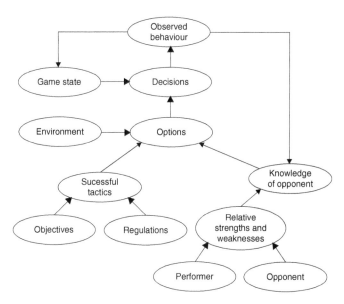

Figure 20.1 Model of tactics and strategy

chance of success in different situations. These tactics need to be tailored depending on various considerations, including environmental conditions and the relative strengths and weaknesses of performers and their opponents. In most situations, there is a choice of actions that can be taken by the performer. Some actions may be rehearsed moves, while others may be improvised plays. The various actions will offer different opportunities and risks, as well as differing chances of success and failure. The degree of success and failure (e.g. benefit–cost pay-off), as well as the probability of success and failure, need to be considered when deciding on an option. Strategic and tactical decisions are mental processes that cannot be directly observed. However, patterns of observed behaviour can be used to make inferences about the decisions that have been taken. For example, if a soccer team uses a slow build-up style rather than a direct fast-breaking style, then the team probably decided to adopt this tactic. If a tennis player goes to the net on an above-average percentage of points, it is probably because the player decided to adopt a strategy of attacking the net when possible.

Evidence supporting the model

Strengths and weaknesses of performers

Doubles tennis players have been classified variously as poachers/quick movers, hard hitters, precision players and all-court players (Cayer, 2004). These different types of players all have strengths and weaknesses when serving, when the partner is serving, when receiving and when the partner is receiving. There are different abilities, including physical, tactical, technical and psychological, that may constitute strengths and weaknesses for particular players and opponents. Ultimately, sports players require a collection of strengths, as illustrated in the view of Holzman and Lewin 1973: 70) on Bill Russell's basketball defence: 'He had the physical equipment. He had the mind. He had the knowledge. He had the ability to quickly analyse and react. He was the perfect blend of what it takes to play sound, fundamental defence.' In similar vein, Navin (2008) listed a collection of abilities necessary for maintaining ball possession in netball, including the ability to scan and recognise important cues, being alert to intentions of teammates, well-timed movements and good passing technique. Netball players likewise were identified as requiring a set of abilities for applying zonal defence, including excellent movement skills, peripheral vision and the ability to intercept.

Strengths and weaknesses of players are considered in the development of tactics, as the following examples demonstrate:

1. Physical ability. In soccer, for example, physical abilities are considered when choosing tactics because some tactics involve higher physical demands than others (Daniel, 2003; Prestigiacomo, 2003). In rugby union, the positions in which players should be included in the team also depend on physical attributes, including physique, strength, speed, quickness of reaction and anticipation (Van Heerden, 1968).
2. Technical ability. Shot types in basketball, for instance, are characterised by the technical abilities of players (Holzman and Lewin, 1973). Also, technical abilities and tactics are linked in soccer, as a sound technical base is necessary if players are to carry out a given tactical plan (Daniel, 2003). For example, players need to be aware of their own technical abilities when selecting passing tactics in soccer (Hughes, 1998).
3. Tactical awareness. In soccer, tactical awareness has been identified as an ability that dictates what defensive tactic a team may use, be it 'man-to-man', zonal or a combined defence (Daniel, 2003). Similarly, awareness of surroundings in field hockey has been reported to help players in possession of the ball make better tactical choices when passing and players receiving the ball move to the best position to receive it (Mitchell-Taverner, 2005: 19).
4. Psychological traits. Psychological skills are important in the performance of many skills as well as broader plays in team sports. In volleyball, they are important to passing accuracy and anxiety management (Herbert, 1991). Psychological traits identified as important in soccer include concentration, determination, conviction and motivation (Prestigiacomo, 2003).

As well as analysing strengths and weaknesses of individual players, it is also important to analyse collective strengths and weaknesses of teams. Soccer teams need to play cohesively when defending, with players working in coordinated fashion to maintain appropriate width and depth of defence (Bangsbo and Peitersen, 2002). Prestigiacomo (2003) included group harmony and unity of intent as collective strengths of a team, while identifying selfishness by individuals as a weakness for the team. In field hockey, strengths and weaknesses of the defensive unit should be considered when selecting tactics to defend against penalty corners (Mitchell-Taverner, 2005).

Opposition effects

Tactics are also based on the strengths and weaknesses of opponents. Soccer coaching literature acknowledges the need to study the opposition to avoid underestimation by establishing what opponents are good at and how they perform such plays (Prestigiacomo, 2003). However, not only should opponents be considered at a strategic level before a match commences, but moment-to-moment tactical decisions by players during matches must also account for opposition effects. For example, when defending in soccer, tracking opponents and timing tackles depend on the speed of teammates, the area of the pitch and the type of opponent on the ball (Hughes, 1998). From basketball coaching literature, consideration of opposition effects was articulated by Holzman and Lewin (1973: 82) thus:

How close you play an opponent depends on him . . . it is a good idea to determine a shooter's range and play him accordingly . . . determining everyone's strength, then act accordingly. If the man you play is not a good outside shooter, you can float until he gets the ball in close. If the man is a playmaker, you must play him closer. If he is an excellent shooter, play as tightly as possible and attempt to discourage getting the ball to him.

Knowledge of opponents

Tactical decisions are not so much made based on the relative strengths and weaknesses of a performer and the opposition but the perceived relative strengths and weaknesses (O'Donoghue, 2009a). Indeed, the relative strengths and weaknesses of a performer with respect to a given opponent may not be fully understood, particularly at lower levels of sports performance. For example, university-level performers have reported that they know little about the opponents in intervarsity competition prior to matches (O'Donoghue, 2009b). Thus, preparation is tailored to the strengths and weaknesses of the performer without necessarily addressing the unknown strengths and weaknesses of forthcoming opponents. Knowledge about opponents, however, changes over the course of a match as performers become more aware of opposition performance, allowing the relative strengths and weaknesses of opponents to influence tactical decisions later in the game. This can occur in many individual and team games, particularly those when coaches are able to intervene between match periods, in sports such as netball and basketball. Strategies and tactics are therefore made using appropriate knowledge of opponent strengths and weaknesses, as well as appropriate self-knowledge (McGee, 2007). Decisions made in women's tennis, for example, are influenced by problem-solving ability and knowledge of opponents (Antoun, 2007).

Relative strengths and weaknesses of performers

The style of play used by a field hockey team depends on the strengths and weaknesses of the team and their opponents (Mitchell-Taverner, 2005). The same holds for basketball, where the relative strengths and weaknesses of competing teams include physical and technical components. Good examples when considering strengths and weaknesses of a team and opponent for both offensive and defensive tactical skills in basketball are described in McGee (2007), who reported that the entire game plan should be based on the relative abilities (strengths and weaknesses) of the two teams, as perceived. A further example from basketball offered by Holzman and Lewin (1973: 134) shows how the same team may adopt different offensive tactics against different opponents:

> For example, the Boston Celtics, normally a fast breaking team, may find it advisable to play control ball simply to slow down an opponent. Or a deliberate team, such as the Chicago Bulls, might be faced with a situation where the opponent is slowing things down. As a matter of strategy, or change of pace, the Bulls would want to start fast breaking to interrupt the other team's pattern.

Soccer is another sport where it is recognised that a coach needs knowledge of team qualities and opposition style in order to be able to make strategic decisions (Bangsbo and Peitersen, 2000). This is done at both a team and an individual level, with the tactical system evolving based on emerging strengths and weaknesses that become apparent during the match (Bangsbo and Peitersen, 2000). Optimal tactics in squash may also be based on the abilities of the opponent (McGarry, 2008) if advance knowledge of opponents' shot and winner–error profiles can be used to determine playing strategy.

Regulations and conventions

The main objective of a performer in any game is to win, which usually involves scoring more goals or points than the opponent. Some plays may be more productive for scoring than others – for example, 40 per cent (Hargreaves and Bate, 2010) to 50 per cent (Hughes, 1998) of goals in soccer come from set plays and so special preparation will be made to execute them. Performers and coaches need to devise ways of scoring goals and avoiding conceding goals within the rules specified for the sport. Therefore, there is an inherent link between rules of games and the tactical behaviours that emerge within sports. Indeed, as rules change in sports, performers will find new tactics to optimise performance under the new regulations, an observation confirmed by studies undertaken on rule changes in sport (Williams *et al.*, 2005; Eaves *et al.*, 2008; Williams, 2008). An example of a rule change that has had an effect on tactics in soccer is the rule restricting the goalkeeper to holding the ball for six seconds or less when the ball is in play (Bangsbo and Peitersen, 2004). Williams (2008) surveyed research on rule changes in many sports and discussed examples where rule changes resulted in changing styles of play. In many cases, the rule changes were intended to change the nature of play. However, even when the specific purpose of a rule change was to improve player safety, there are examples in rugby league, rugby union, ice hockey and American football where such rule changes have also changed the nature of play.

The first thing to understand about rules in sport is that they are frequently broken and match officials award free kicks, caution players and/or dismiss players when rule violations occur. Sports rules open the possibility of a 'professional foul', where a rule is intentionally violated by a player in some instances to help a team achieve its objective (Hargreaves and Bate, 2010). Consider the handball by Suarez of Uruguay against Ghana in the quarter-final knock-out match of the 2010 FIFA World Cup that prevented a goal for Ghana in the closing minutes of normal time. The rules of the game do not prevent a player from doing what Suarez did, and Suarez was consequently dismissed from the game. In addition, as a result of this infringement, Uruguay conceded a penalty kick (which Ghana failed to score from) and thereafter had to play extra time with only ten players. Uruguay proceeded to win the game and advance to the semi-final. The sequence of events described occurred within the laws of the game. Thus, unless the soccer authorities introduce a 'penalty goal' similar to the penalty try that exists in rugby union, situations will remain where, in some instances, committing a professional foul is the best tactical option for a player and team.

Successful tactics

Tactics are commonly used in different sports and are often shaped by the regulations of that sport. For example, in volleyball, the primary hitter system has evolved over time (Herbert, 1991). In basketball, defending teams pressurise the ball carrier as much as the rules permit to prevent penetration and to force and exploit errors by the opposing ball carrier (Holzman and Lewin, 1973). In martial arts, the best tactics to use in different situations are understood such that they should be taught early so that skills can be performed in their tactical context (Kozub and Kozub, 2004). The tactics that are successful in soccer are typically founded on principles of possession, support and communication in attack, as well as delay, concentration, mobility and balance in defence (Hargreaves and Bate, 2010). These tactics change as the game evolves, as described in Bangsbo and Peitersen (2000). When 4–2–4 formations were used, the 'Brazilian' system created numerical superiority in defence and offence and relied on physical and tactical abilities of the two midfield players. Indeed, some systems were influenced by the strengths of particular players within teams. For example, the 4–3–3 system played by Juventus in 1996 was successful due to the ability of Conte and Dechamps to play long balls and the ability of Del Piero and Vialli to make breaks. The 3–5–2 system used by Barcelona in 1994 relied on good player interactions, while the 3–4–3 system played by Ajax Amsterdam in 1995 required players to be versatile and defenders to be good at applying zonal and 'man-to-man' defending. Furthermore, different styles of play in soccer have been based on national characteristics; for example, there are Latin styles, South American styles, a British style, a Norwegian style and an African style (Bangsbo and Peitersen, 2000: 41–7). The Norwegian style, for instance, is a direct, fast-breaking style that is supported by evidence that a greater percentage of counter-attacks lead to goals than elaborate, slow-build attacks (Tenga *et al.*, 2010a).

Environmental factors

The weather, including its effects on the surface of a football pitch, should be considered when developing a strategy for a soccer match (Prestigiacomo, 2003). Tactics in tennis likewise can be influenced by both sun and wind, as illustrated in the following examples (Anderson, 2009). When the sun affects the server's toss-up, the receiving player may have opportunities to gain the upper hand with a strong return of serve. The position of the sun is also a factor in deciding which direction to play lobs and whether to attempt overhead shots and volleys. Also, approach shots can be played effectively with the wind, whereas drop shots are infrequently played in that same direction. The wind is also a factor in volleying and attempting winning shots.

Game state

Game state is a combination of score-line, numerical advantage, time remaining and how the game came to be in its current state (Mitchell-Taverner, 2005), with players and teams possibly changing tactics if the tactics used to that time have not been effective. For example, from basketball: 'We were outrebounded most of the time. We had to find other ways to get the ball' (Holzman and Lewin, 1973: 90). In volleyball, Herbert (1991) also acknowledged the need to allow players flexibility to change tactics on court if situations changed within the match. This type of tactical decision making might be improved if 'what-if' questions are considered by squads before matches take place (Mitchell-Taverner, 2005). In soccer, Tenga *et al.* (2010b) found that attacks are more effective against unbalanced defences than against balanced defences, indicating that teams in possession need to recognise the state of opposing defences from moment to moment and look to exploit unbalanced defences as they occur.

Opportunities and risks

Often in sport the tactics associated with the highest opportunities of success are also those with the greatest risk. By contrast, 'playing safe' usually limits opportunities for success. For example, Herbert (1991) discussed low-risk side-out offence in volleyball, explaining that tactics should be designed not only to maximise winning the side-out but also to reduce risk of error. Other examples of risk taking associated with opportunity in sport include the following:

1. In rugby union, a player in possession may bypass other teammates and make a long pass to a teammate on the wing, a successful pass opening the possibility of the wing player running through unopposed for a try. However, long passes are more prone to interception and therefore bring the prospect of a counter-attack and possible try scored by the opponent.
2. In cricket, many of the shots required to score four or six runs have greater risk than safer shots of the batsman being dispatched, by being either bowled out, caught by a fielder or run out.
3. In tennis, a player leading 40–0 during service may try the 'cannon ball' on second serve (Ashe, 1981). This decision risks serving a double fault but, if the serve is in, it may be a point-winning serve, either directly or indirectly.
4. In soccer, when a team is losing by a single goal with little time remaining in an important match, the goalkeeper may enter the opponents' penalty area when the team has a corner. This decision risks conceding a goal if the opponents regain the ball with the goalkeeper stranded; however at the same time the presence of the goalkeeper when the corner is taken serves as an additional attacker, increasing the chance of scoring an equalising goal.
5. In boxing, a 'haymaker' punch can knock out the opponent or otherwise cause substantial damage, leading to further punches resulting in the same outcome. However, this same punch leaves the boxer vulnerable to a counter–punch, leading to similar consequences as that intended for the opponent.

Some of the high risk 'all-or-nothing' plays listed above are often seen in score-line states where a performer is likely to lose the match if risks are not taken. The performer may still lose the match if risks are taken, but the opportunities associated with high-risk play give the chance of avoiding defeat and hence are considered a good, late (albeit somewhat desperate) option for the trailing contestant.

Rehearsed and improvised play

In team sports, there is a balance between rehearsed play and improvisation. Rehearsed play can be predictable or unpredictable and is possible when players have a shared understanding of the tactics used and their specific roles within them. These plays are not only communicated to squads during preparation but also practised. Transition from rehearsed play to spontaneous play is made under conditions where spontaneous play may create opportunities, with players knowing when to stick to rehearsed moves and when to play 'off the cuff' (Daniel, 2003). Spontaneous improvised play by soccer players in possession of the ball can cause difficulties for opposing defences as 'no system can handle the unexpected if it is allied with skill, speed of thought, and deception' (Daniel, 2003: 34).

Rehearsed and spontaneous plays occur in rugby union also. Indeed, tactical decisions are often evolutionary as the game progresses and opportunities become apparent (Herbert, 1991). Van Heerden (1968: 11) used words such as 'wizardry', 'magic', 'surprise', 'subtle' and 'cunning gambits' to describe how improvised play can lead to a try being scored, with opposing defences kept guessing, suggesting that coaches allow specialist players to make spontaneous plays and improvise when appropriate, rather than restricting all players to rehearsed moves, reasoning 'never stifle genius – opposition can cope with the obvious'.

Decision making

In brief, the relative strengths and weaknesses of performers and opponents, as well as environmental factors and the importance of a particular match, will influence strategic decisions made prior to the match. During the match, players will be faced with many situations where there is a choice of options. Each option will have its advantages and disadvantages. Players need to be able to make use of available information (Williams and Davids, 1998) and use situational probabilities in selecting a given option at a given time (Singer and Janelle, 1999).

Observed behaviour

When players follow a strategy, the observed behaviour allows analysts to make inferences about the strategy (O'Donoghue, 2010). Patterns of play at different levels of different sports have been analysed using objective data for many years to give an indication of tactics without seeking self-report data from coaches and players to confirm or otherwise the tactics used. The data gathered to infer tactics typically include the frequency profiles of events, the location of events within the playing area, the players involved and the timings and orderings of events (Yamanaka *et al.*, 2002; O'Donoghue and Liddle, 1998).

Concluding remarks

From surveying coaching texts, this chapter has proposed a general model of strategy and tactics in sport and presented supporting evidence. The model recognises accepted long-standing tactics that optimise the chances of success while playing within the regulations of that sport. Strategies and tactics for individual matches need to account also for the relative strengths and weaknesses of performers and opponents while also considering environmental factors. Together with advance strategies, moment-to-moment tactical decisions are made using available current information to decide on the best options available. Game state and evolving knowledge of the opponent's playing style, strengths and weaknesses are also considered during such decisions.

References

Anderson, K. (2009) *Coaching Tennis: Technical and Tactical Skills*, Champaign, IL: Human Kinetics.
Antoun, R. (2007) *Women's Tennis Tactics: Winning Today's Game*, Champaign, IL: Human Kinetics.
Ashe, A. (1981) *Arthur Ashe's Tennis Clinic*. London: Heinemann.
Bangsbo, J. and Peitersen, B. (2000) *Soccer Systems and Strategies*, Champaign, IL: Human Kinetics.
Bangsbo, J. and Peitersen, B. (2002) *Defensive Soccer Tactics: How to Stop Players and Teams from Scoring*, Champaign, IL: Human Kinetics.
Bangsbo, J. and Peitersen, B. (2004) *Offensive Soccer Tactics: How to Control Possession and Score More Goals*, Champaign, IL: Human Kinetics.
Cayer, L. (2004) *Doubles Tennis Tactics*, Champaign, IL: Human Kinetics.
Daniel, J. (2003) *The Complete Guide to Soccer Systems and Tactics*, Spring City, PA: Reedswain Publishing.
Eaves, S.J., Hughes, M.D. and Lamb, K.L. (2008) 'Assessing the impact of the season and rule changes on specific match and tactical variables in professional rugby league football in the United Kingdom', *International Journal of Performance Analysis in Sport*, 8(3): 104–18.
Hargreaves, A. and Bate, R. (2010) *Skills and Strategies for Soccer Coaching: The Complete Soccer Coaching Manual*, 2nd ed., Champaign, IL: Human Kinetics.
Herbert, M. (1991) *Insights and Strategies for Winning Volleyball*, Champaign, Il: Leisure Press.
Hill, T. and R. Westbrook (1997) 'SWOT analysis: It's time for a product recall', *Long Range Planning*, 30(1): 46–52.

Holzman, R. and Lewin, L. (1973) *Holzman's Basketball: Winning Strategy and Tactics*, New York: Macmillan.

Hughes, C. (1998) *The Football Association Coaching Book of Soccer Tactics and Skills*, Harpenden, Herts, UK: Queen Anne Press.

Kozub, F.M. and Kozub, M.L. (2004) 'Teaching combative sports through tactics: The tactical games approach can enhance the teaching of some martial arts by emphasizing their similarities to one another and to wrestling', *Journal of Physical Education, Recreation and Dance* (JOPERD), 75(8): 16.

McGarry, T. (2008) 'Probability analysis of notated events in sports contests: Skill and chance', in M. Hughes and I.M. Franks (eds), *The Essentials of Performance Analysis: An Introduction* (pp. 206–25). London: Routledge.

McGee, K. (2007) *Coaching Basketball: Technical and Tactical Skills*, Champaign, IL: Human Kinetics.

Mitchell-Taverner, C. (2005) *Field Hockey Technique and Tactics*, Champaign, IL: Human Kinetics.

Navin, A. (2008) *Crowood Sports Guides: Netball Skills, Techniques, Tactics*, Marlborough, UK: The Crowood Press.

O'Donoghue, P.G. (2009a) 'Interacting performances theory', *International Journal of Performance Analysis of Sport*, 9: 26–46.

O'Donoghue, P.G. (2009b) 'Explanations of interacting performances theory', keynote presentation at the 1st International Symposium of Sports Performance, Vila Real, Portugal, July.

O'Donoghue, P.G. (2010) *Research Methods for Sports Performance Analysis*, London: Routledge.

O'Donoghue, P.G. and Liddle, S.D. (1998) 'A match analysis of elite tennis strategy for ladies' singles on clay and grass surfaces', in A. Lees, I. Maynard, M. Hughes and T. Reilly (eds), *Science and Racket Sports II* (pp. 247–53). London: E & FN Spon.

Prestigiacomo, L. (2003) *Coaching Soccer: Match Strategy and Tactics*, Spring City, PA: Reedswain Publishing.

Singer, R.N. and Janelle, C.M. (1999) 'Determining sport expertise: From genes to supremes', *International Journal of Sport Psychology*, 30: 117–50.

Tenga, A., Holme, I., Ronglan, L.T. and Bahr, R. (2010a) 'Effect of playing tactics on goal scoring in Norwegian professional soccer', *Journal of Sports Sciences*, 28: 237–44.

Tenga, A., Holme, I., Ronglan, L.T. and Bahr, R. (2010b) 'Effect of playing tactics on achieving score-box possessions in a random series of team possessions from Norwegian professional soccer matches', *Journal of Sports Sciences*, 28: 245–55.

Van Heerden, I. (1968) *Tactical and Attacking Rugby*, London: Herbert Jenkins.

Williams, J.J. (2008) 'Rule changes in sport and the role of notation', in M. Hughes and I.M. Franks (eds), *Essentials of Performance Analysis of Sport: An Introduction* (pp. 226–42). London: Routledge.

Williams, A.M. and Davids, K. (1998) 'Visual search strategy, selective attention and expertise in soccer', *Research Quarterly for Exercise and Sport*, 69(2): 111–28.

Williams, J.J., Hughes, M., O'Donoghue, P. and Davies, G. (2005) 'The effect of rule changes on match and ball in play time in rugby union', *International Journal of Performance Analysis in Sport*, 5(3): 1–11.

Yamanaka, K., Nishikawa, T., Yamanaka, T. and Hughes, M. (2002) 'An analysis of the playing patterns of the Japan national team in the 1998 World Cup for soccer', in W. Spinks, T. Reilly and A. Murphy (eds), *Science and Football IV* (pp. 101–5). London: Routledge.

21

SITUATIONAL VARIABLES

Miguel-Ángel Gómez[1], Carlos Lago-Peñas[2] and Richard Pollard[3]

[1]POLYTECHNIC UNIVERSITY OF MADRID, SPAIN

[2]UNIVERSITY OF VIGO, PONTEVEDRA, SPAIN

[3]CALIFORNIA POLYTECHNIC STATE UNIVERSITY, SAN LUIS OBISPO, USA

Summary

Notational analysis in sport is used to investigate teams' and players' performance across different sports. Research in this area, especially when focussing on the determinants of success, has grown rapidly in the last few years. During this time, the role of a new concept, 'situational variables', has emerged. This term includes the different game/situational conditions that may influence performance at a behavioural level. These situational variables need to be analysed in depth to understand their influence in team sports. In order to do so, we have included the main situational conditions that may affect the team's or player's performance. These are game location, match status, quality of opposition, game quarter or game period and type of competition. We also address the importance of a combination of these situational variables and their interactive effects. Finally, we suggest directions for further research within this topic and how improved knowledge of situational variables can be used to refine the impact of notational analysis on sports performance.

Game location

Home advantage has been in existence since the dawn of professional sport in the late-nineteenth century and continues to play a significant role in determining the outcome of sporting events. This has been quantified annually since 1872 for the main professional team sports in North America and in England (Pollard and Pollard, 2005). General reviews of the home advantage phenomenon have been made by Courneya and Carron (1992) and Carron *et al.* (2005). A recent meta-analysis confirms that home advantage exists in a wide variety of sports, both individual and team, and at different levels of play (Jamieson, 2010). The benefits of playing at home appear to be greatest for football (soccer) and rugby. Table 21.1 shows the current home advantage in the five major sports leagues in the USA, as well as the Premier League for football in England. Home advantage was quantified as the proportion of all games that were won by the home team or, where ties are permitted, the proportion of all points. The advantage ranges in North America from 54.1 per cent in ice hockey to 62.7 per cent in soccer, with the Premier League in England also higher than the other sports and similar to the advantage found in the other main football leagues of Europe (Pollard and Gómez, 2009). Since a home advantage value of 60 per cent would mean that the home team is averaging 50 per cent more success than the away team, an objective analysis of performance clearly needs to take game location into account. This is not always done. For example, the algorithm from which FIFA calculates its world rankings does not incorporate game location, so that a home win is given the same weight as an away win (Pollard and Stefani, 2007). This is an extraordinary omission, given the prominence that home advantage has always received in football. Home advantage can be magnified or diminished by other factors. For example, it varies greatly between the domestic football leagues of Europe, with teams from Balkan countries having a much higher advantage, while it is lower in northern Europe (Pollard, 2006). Similarly, individual teams show considerable variation, with teams from isolated, ethnically distinct locations tending to see a greater home advantage than teams from large metropolitan areas (Pollard and Gómez, 2009). Crowd size and travel distance have also been shown to modify home advantage in a number of sports. In addition, analysis of team performance spanning or comparing different time periods needs to allow for the fact that home advantage has declined in most sports over the last two decades.

Turning to non-outcome measures of team performance, several authors have shown that, in football, shots, corners and other offensive performance measures follow a similar pattern to game outcome with regards to home advantage (Carmichael and Thomas, 2005; Poulter, 2007; Seckin and Pollard, 2008). However, similar effects for other measures, such as off-sides and fouls, were less convincing. Tactics and strategies in football have also been investigated, with significant differences found between home and away teams (Tenga et al., 2010; Tucker et al., 2005). In basketball, Gómez et al. (2010) found differences between home and away teams in performance indicators (fouls and turnover percentages) and defensive strategies used in Spanish men's basketball. Also, in volleyball, Marcelino et al. (2009b) found that numerical indicators for success at attack, serves, reception and set performance were higher for home teams.

There is sparse research with regards to home advantage at the individual player level. In international cricket, Indian spin bowlers such as Kumble and Harbhajan Singh have been shown to have bowling averages that are well over ten runs per wicket better at home than away, a huge difference (Pollard, 2005). In contrast, other elite bowlers worldwide were generally equally effective at home and away. In football, Poulter (2007) has shown that in the Premier League in England game location effects for goal scoring were greater for foreign-born players than for those that were native born.

In summary, there is sufficient evidence to conclude that the performance analyst needs to carefully consider and incorporate the effects of game location when assessing performance both of teams and of individual athletes.

Table 21.1 Home advantage in professional sports leagues for the most recent five seasons up to 1 January 2012

Sport	League	Location	Games played	Home advantage
Baseball	MLB	North America	12145	54.7%
Basketball	NBA	North America	6150	59.9%
American football	NFL	USA	1280	56.8%
Ice hockey	NHL	North America	6150	54.1%
Football (soccer)	MLS	North America	1176	62.7%
Football (soccer)	EPL	England	1900	61.8%

Match status

Performance accomplishments are a powerful source of efficacy expectations and such expectations determine the task-related effort that has to be expended (Bandura, 1977). In sport, the match status may be viewed as a measure of performance accomplishment and hence may influence the effort made by a player (O'Donoghue and Tenga, 2001). Match status is determined by whether a team or a player is winning, losing or drawing at the time a particular behaviour is recorded (Bloomfield *et al.*, 2005a, 2005b; Jones *et al.*, 2004; Taylor *et al.*, 2008). According to Bloomfield *et al.* (2005a), Lago and Martin (2007) and Taylor *et al.* (2008), the importance of this situational variable is reflected in changes in team and player's strategies in response to the score-line. For low-scoring team sports like soccer, there are just three major levels of match status to be considered during analysis (team winning, losing or drawing). However, for high-scoring team sports like volleyball, handball or basketball, final scores can be viewed as narrow, intermediate or large margins (Marcelino *et al.*, 2011).

Existing notational analysis has provided information on the effects of match status on player and team performance. For example, it has been demonstrated that soccer players perform less high-intensity activity when winning than when losing (Bloomfield *et al.*, 2005b; Castellano *et al.*, 2011; Lago *et al.*, 2010; Shaw and O'Donoghue, 2004). These results suggest that players do not always use their maximal physical capacity during the match. In fact, given that winning is a comfortable state for a team, it is possible that players assume a ball retention strategy, slowing down the game and resulting in lower speeds (Bloomfield *et al.*, 2005b). On the other hand, when losing, players try to reach their maximal activity in order to draw or win the match. Other studies have considered match status in relation to the tactical aspects of performance. The influence of this factor is reflected in changes in team strategies and tactics as a response to match situations (Taylor *et al.*, 2008). Teams often show a more defensive strategy when winning than when losing, and vice versa. For example, James *et al.* (2002) and Lago and Martin (2007) found that in soccer successful and unsuccessful teams had longer periods of possession in matches when they were losing than when they were winning. When ahead, teams decreased their possession, suggesting they preferred to play counter-attacking or direct play (that is, move the ball quickly to within scoring range, often using long passes downfield). However, when behind, they increased their possession, suggesting they preferred to control the game by dictating play. Moreover, Lago (2009) demonstrated that time spent in possession of the ball in different zones of the pitch (defensive third, middle third, attacking third) was influenced by match status: when teams were losing, possession of the ball was less in the defensive zone and more in the attacking zone than when winning or drawing.

In volleyball, it has been shown that match status has an effect on tactical indicators and this relationship interacted with quality of opposition (Marcelino *et al.*, 2011). In men's singles tennis, Scully and O'Donoghue (1999) found that some players reduce the percentage of points where they attack the net once they have achieved a break of serve. Finally, the relationship between match status and technical performances in team sports is still inconclusive. For example, in soccer, Taylor *et al.* (2008) found that playing at home and winning resulted in a decreased number of aerial challenges, dribbles, losses of control, passes, tackles and times tackled, whereas the frequency of these behaviours increased when playing at home and losing. However, the outcomes of most behaviours were not influenced by the situation variables. In the same way, in volleyball, it has been suggested that technical variables are not affected by situational variables (Eom and Schutz, 1992; Marcelino *et al.*, 2011). Further research is needed in order to clarify the effects of match status on technical performances.

Consideration should also be given to the fact that performance analysis has often tended to aggregate the performances of different players, of different teams and over different match situations. Study designs of this type may have limitations because these aggregated data sets potentially mask the factors that determine or contribute to each team's success or failure. It would therefore appear that case studies of performance over a sustained time period may represent a more fruitful approach to analysis, with comparisons between case studies offering specific insight into the characteristics of interest (e.g. Taylor *et al.*, 2008). In this context, the conclusions of prior studies might have to be re-assessed. For example, such a study might be one in which the overall percentage of time spent in different score-line situations was reported in the context of the total match statistics, rather than what individual players or specific teams did in the different score-line situations.

Quality of opposition

The opponent level has been considered from different methodological perspectives. For example, teams and players have been categorized as 'successful' and 'unsuccessful' according to their standings within a particular tournament (Grant *et al.*, 1999), or classified as 'strong' or 'weak' based on symmetric division of end-of-season classification (O'Donoghue *et al.*, 2008; Taylor *et al.*, 2008). Lago *et al.* (2010) defined the quality of opposition as the differences in the end-of-season ranking between opposing teams. Recently, team performance has been classified using cluster analysis procedures, which improve the classification by using more valid cut-off values (Sampaio *et al.*, 2010a Marcelino *et al.*, 2011).

In a previous section, we noted the importance of allowing for the effects of home advantage when assessing performance. Several studies have emphasized the need to adjust for team ability when quantifying the magnitude of home advantage for individual teams in sports such as football (Barnett and Hilditch, 1993; Clarke and Norman, 1995; Pollard and Gómez, 2009) and basketball (Pollard and Gómez, 2007). For example, when the calculation of home advantage is based on the results of games and hence points, a problem arises. If a strong team plays against a weak team, their difference in ability is likely to outweigh the relatively small effect of home advantage in influencing the result. The greater the difference in ability, the more likely the stronger team will be able to win both at home and away and hence mask the effect of home advantage. In comparisons of individual teams in European football and basketball leagues, team ability was quantified for each team each season as its winning percentage (Pollard and Gómez, 2009; Gómez and Pollard, 2011) and regression analysis used to adjust for the effect of team ability. For the performance analyst, the implication is that, when considering the effect of home advantage on performance, the quality of the opponent should also be taken into account.

Game period

The game period is also a situational variable of great importance in team sports, as suggested by research considering the critical moments of a game. Bar-Eli and Tracinsky (2000) established that, during such critical moments, players may create a state of psychological crisis that decreases their effective performance. The coach then needs to break up an opponent's momentum so that players can return to their previous performance levels during these critical periods of the game. In this way, Bar-Eli and Tenenbaum (1988) found that, during basketball and handball games, there were three psychologically meaningful phases of each half: a beginning, main and end phase. In particular, there is research identifying the end of a game (the last five minutes) as being the most critical (Bar-Eli and Tracinsky, 2000; Mechikoff *et al.*, 1990; Kozar *et al.*, 1993; Navarro *et al.*, 2009). According to these authors, during the last minutes of a game a decrease in players' quality of decision making may be expected. Recently, Navarro *et al.* (2009) identified 41 critical moments in basketball games and found that free throws and three-point field-goals discriminated between winning and losing teams. Thus, during these periods of the game, teams should try to be more effective in their ball possessions, selecting better field-goal positions or drawing fouls that allow going to the free-throw line.

There is also recent research addressing the importance of the starting periods of the game (Sampaio *et al.*, 2010a, 2010b). In particular, Sampaio *et al.* (2010b) studied the influence of game quarter in starting score-line in Spanish basketball. Their results showed that the influence of game location and quality of opposition on the starting score-line was stronger at the beginning of a game. The authors suggested that, at the beginning of a game (first quarter), the crowd effects and familiarity with the home facility were stronger than during the other game quarters. In the same way, Sampaio *et al.* (2010a) studied the dominance of the United States of America in basketball at the Beijing Olympic Games in 2008. Their results showed the importance of game periods, whereby the USA team performed better in assertive game indicators during the first half of the game. According to these authors, the importance of game period should be considered not only in the last phase of a game, but also at the beginning of a game when the performance of both individual players and of teams may be affected by this situational variable.

The importance of game period has been investigated in other team sports. In volleyball, Marcelino *et al.* (2009a) studied team performance according to game location and set number during the 2005 Men's Senior World League. Their results showed that home teams have more advantage at the beginning of the game (first set) and in the two last sets of the game (fourth and fifth sets), probably due to facility familiarity and crowd effects. Similarly, Jones (2007) showed that the strength of home advantage in basketball in the National Basketball Association (NBA) varied throughout the game and that it was strongest in the first quarter. In summary, these studies have shown that the performance of both players and teams are influenced by game periods, reflecting especially the importance of the beginning and the end of a game. Further research should control for this variable when analysing the interactions and effects of situational variables in performance analysis.

Type of competition

Another situational variable that has great importance in sports competition and in the performance of teams and players is the type of competition, especially differences between regular season and playoff games. Different strategies may be used when teams are playing to add points to their championship regular season standings, as opposed to when they are struggling directly with another team facing elimination from a playoff series. In the same way, this specific game context may lead to performance differences, for example, between a close playoff game and an early season game with little immediate significance (see Gómez *et al.*, 2008; Sampaio and Janeira, 2003).

In considering this variable, we have to take into account the influence of team sport characteristics. High-scoring team sports (e.g. volleyball or basketball) that are divided into game quarters or sets may be less affected by this situational variable because teams can modify their strategies and tactical behaviours several times during the game. In this context, coaches can play a special role in controlling the influence of this situational variable (Sampaio *et al.*, 2010b). In particular, basketball research has described differences in teams' and players' performances according to the type of competition. In regular season play, the game-related statistics that can influence the final outcome are field-goals and defensive rebounds (Sampaio and Janeira, 2003; Sampaio *et al.*, 2004). However, in specific game contexts such as close games, other game-related statistics such as fouls and free throws exhibit higher importance (Kozar *et al.*, 1993). On the other hand, studies that have used samples from the European Championships have identified the same game-related statistics associated with the winning teams (both defensive rebounds and field-goal percentage) (Dežman *et al.*, 2002; Trninić *et al.*, 2002). Analysing the Women's National Basketball League (WNBA, USA) during the 2004 season, Gómez *et al.* (2009) and Gómez *et al.* (2007) found differences between players' performances during the regular season and the playoff games. The authors suggested that the type of competition affects both the pace of the game and the playing styles. Conversely, some authors studied the teams' performances during the Spanish professional men's basketball league during the 2006–2007 regular season (Gómez *et al.*, 2010) and playoff games (Gómez *et al.*, 2006). Their results mainly reflected the different defensive systems used during each type of competition, where the playoff games involved more pressure defences and a more controlled game style. Therefore, according to these authors, the coaches' decisions have a great influence on this situational variable during a game played during a playoff series where a substitution or a called timeout has an immediate effect on players' performances. Conversely, the coaches' decisions during regular season games may be focussed on regulating and better preparing for the next round of games by using more substitutions, or by experimenting with new game tactics during a blowout game.

In contrast, the low-scoring team sports, such as football, may be more affected by this situational variable, probably because the coaches cannot stop the game so that opportunity for information transfer to players is reduced. Furthermore, when each type of competition is considered, the situational variable 'quality of opposition' should be considered because, for example, during a typical basketball playoff phase only the top eight best teams of the regular season might participate. The performance profiles of teams in such games would be different from those obtained during the regular season, where the best teams play against all the others in the league, with quality ranging from best to worst. In this case, the type of competition should be simultaneously studied with the quality of the opposition in order to incorporate and investigate any interactive effect.

Finally, the importance of international competitions for national teams, such as a World Cup or European Championships, was reflected by differences in players' and teams' performances in different team sports, such as basketball (Mexas *et al.*, 2005), football (Sainz de Baranda and López Riquelme, 2012; Sainz de Baranda *et al.*, 2008), handball (Rogulj *et al.*, 2004), rugby (Ortega *et al.*, 2009; Vaz *et al.*, 2010) and volleyball (Marcelino *et al.*, 2009a). These studies pointed out the influence of top elite competitions that influenced different game patterns, with special relevance given to coaches' and players' decision making during these games.

Interactive effects

Existing notational analysis has provided preliminary information on the effects of situational variables such as match location, match status, quality of the opponent and game period on sports performance at a behavioural level (Bloomfield *et al.*, 2005a, 2005b; Jones *et al.*, 2004; O'Donoghue and Tenga, 2001; Sasaki *et al.*, 1999). Nonetheless, with the exception of Lago and Martin (2007), Taylor *et al.* (2008), Lago (2009), Castellano *et al.* (2011) and Marcelino *et al.* (2011), previous research has examined situational variables independently, not accounting for the possibility of higher-order interactions (e.g. playing at home and losing). However, the examination of situational variables in isolation would appear to provide limited insight into the complex nature of team sports performance (McGarry and Franks, 2003; Reed and O'Donoghue, 2005). For example, in volleyball, it has been shown that teams took more risky decisions when scores were unbalanced and adopted safer tactical options when scores were balanced or there was a moderate advantage or disadvantage (Marcelino *et al.*, 2011). However, this tendency was affected by the quality of opposition, as more offensive strategies were adopted at the highest level (1st–4th) and safer strategies at the lowest level (8th–12th) when scores were balanced. In soccer, Lago (2009) demonstrated variations in ball possession as a function of match location and match status, with home teams having more possession when drawing than away teams. Taylor *et al.* (2008) showed that the frequency of on-the-ball behaviours (passes, shots, tackles, clearances, crosses, dribbles, losses of control and aerial challenges) performed by a professional soccer team was explained by the interaction between the variables of match location and match status. Lago *et al.* (2010) examined the effects of match location, quality of opposition and match status on distance covered at various speeds in elite soccer. As can be seen in Table 21.2, physical performance was influenced by the situational variables, either independently or interactively. These results emphasize the need for notational analysis and for coaches to consider the potential interactive effects of situational variables during the assessment of tactical, technical and physical performances.

One interesting factor that should be considered when investigating the interactive effects is the sample size for the study. This should certainly be increased in proportion to the number of situational variables whose effects are being studied, especially if interactions are to be included. However, there are few existing guidelines as to exactly how much larger the sample size should be. Hughes *et al.* (2001) established a method to decide the minimum number of games needed to profile the performance of players and teams. This approach has been used in studies investigating the isolated effects of several situational variables, but needs to be extended if interactions are to be incorporated. In a detailed discussion of sample size, Hopkins (2006) reiterated that, with more than one effect, a larger sample size is needed to constrain the overall chance of error. He also noted that the size of the increase in sample size needed to allow for interacting effects is hard to estimate. We therefore suggest that, when considering two or more effects and their interactions, care should be taken to avoid a situation in which the sample size is not large enough. In addition, the inclusion of possible confounding variables in the study design should be considered, to reduce the likelihood of error and increase the validity of the interpretation of the results.

Concluding remarks

In conclusion, previous studies have emphasized the importance of accounting for situational variables during the assessment of sport performance (Carling *et al.*, 2005). The importance of these factors is reflected in changes in the teams' and players' activities as a response to match situations. As Taylor and co-workers (2008) explained, the implications for match analysts and coaches for evaluating performance and developing relevant training drills are important. Existing recommendations suggest that the scouting of upcoming opposition should be carried out under circumstances that are reflective of the conditions under which the future match will occur. However, such procedures are unlikely to be practical due to time and resource constraints. Consequently, by establishing the impact of particular situational variables on performance, teams and players can be observed, when possible, with appropriate adjustments being made to analyses based on knowledge of such effects (Taylor *et al.*, 2008). Similarly, post-match assessments of the technical, tactical and physical aspects of performance can be made more objective by factoring in the effects of situational variables (Carling *et al.*, 2005; Kormelink and Seeverens, 1999). Finally, if a match analyst or coach has identified that the technical, physical or tactical aspects of performance are adversely influenced by specific situational variables, possible causes can be examined and match preparation focussed on reducing such effects.

Table 21.2 Simulated distance covered (m) at different speeds depending on match location, quality of opposition and match status

Match status	Quality of opposition	Home matches						Away matches					
		Total	0–11 km/h	11.1–14 km/h	14.1–19 km/h	19.1–23 km/h	>23 km/h	Total	0–11 km/h	11.1–14 km/h	14.1–19 km/h	19.1–23 km/h	>23 km/h
Winning 90 min	Strong	11140	7050	1744	1649	481	217	10856	6911	1584	1653	453	189
Winning 90 min	Weak	10824	6727	1662	1665	540	231	10540	6587	1501	1669	512	204
Losing 90 min	Strong	10856	6853	1678	1653	555	281	10641	6713	1518	1629	527	253
Losing 90 min	Weak	10540	6529	1596	1669	614	295	10325	6390	1435	1646	586	268

Source: Lago et al. (2010).

ᄀᄀᄀ

References

Bandura, A. (1977) *Social Learning Theory*, Englewood Cliffs, NJ: Prentice-Hall.

Bar-Eli, M. and Tenenbaum, G. (1988) 'Time phases and the individual psychological crisis in sports competition: Theory and research findings', *Journal of Sports Sciences*, 6: 141–9.

Bar-Eli, M. and Tracinsky, N. (2000) 'Criticality of game situations and decision making in basketball: an application of performance crisis perspective', *Psychology of Sport and Exercise*, 1: 27–39.

Barnett, V. and Hilditch, S. (1993) 'The effect of an artificial pitch surface on home team performance in football (soccer)', *Journal of the Royal Statistical Society, A*, 156: 39–50.

Bloomfield, J.R., Polman, R.C.J. and O'Donoghue, P.G. (2005a) 'Effects of score-line on intensity of play in midfield and forward players in the FA Premier League', *Journal of Sports Sciences*, 23: 191–2.

Bloomfield, J.R., Polman, R.C.J. and O'Donoghue, P.G. (2005b) 'Effects of score-line on team strategies in FA Premier League Soccer', *Journal of Sports Sciences*, 23: 192–3.

Carling, C., Williams, A.M. and Reilly, T. (2005) *Handbook of Soccer Match Analysis: A Systematic Approach to Improving Performance*, Abingdon, UK: Routledge.

Carmichael, F. and Thomas, D. (2005) 'Home-field effect and team performance', *Journal of Sports Economics*, 6: 264–81.

Carron, A.V., Loughhead, T.M. and Bray, S.R. (2005) 'The home advantage in sport competitions: Courneya and Carron's (1992) conceptual framework a decade later', *Journal of Sports Sciences*, 23: 385–407.

Castellano, J., Blanco-Villaseñor, A. and Álvarez, D. (2011) 'Contextual variables and time motion analysis in soccer', *International Journal of Sports Medicine*, 32: 415–21.

Clarke, S.R. and Norman, J.M. (1995) 'Home ground advantage of individual clubs in English professional soccer', *The Statistician*, 44: 509–21.

Courneya, K.S. and Carron, A.V. (1992) 'The home advantage in sports competitions: A literature review', *Journal of Sport & Exercise Psychology*, 14: 13–27.

Dežman, B. Erčulj, F. and Vučković, G. (2002) 'Differences between winning and losing basketball teams in playing efficiency', *Acta Kinesiologiae Universitatis Tartuensis*, 7: 71–4.

Eom, H. and Schutz, R. (1992) 'Transition play in team performance in volleyball. A log-linear analysis', *Research Quarterly for Exercise and Sport*, 63: 261–9.

Gómez, M.A. and Pollard, R. (2011) 'Reduced home advantage for basketball teams from capital cities in Europe', *European Journal of Sport Science*, 11: 143–8.

Gómez, M.A., Tsamourtzis, E. and Lorenzo, A. (2006) 'Defensive systems in basketball ball possessions', *International Journal of Performance Analysis in Sport*, 6: 98–107.

Gómez, M.A., Jiménez, S., Leite, N. and Sampaio, J. (2007) 'Differences in basketball game statistics between starters and nonstarters according to player position in women's basketball', *Iberian Congress on Basketball Research*, 4: 5–9.

Gómez, M.A., Lorenzo, A., Sampaio, J., Ibáñez, S.J. and Ortega, E. (2008) 'Game-related statistics that discriminated winning and losing teams from the Spanish men's professional basketball teams', *Collegium Antropologicum*, 32: 315–9.

Gómez, M.A., Lorenzo, A., Ortega, E., Sampaio, J. and Ibáñez, S.J. (2009) 'Game related statistics discriminating between starters and nonstarters players in women's National Basketball Relation League (WNBA)', *Journal of Sports Science and Medicine*, 8: 278–83.

Gómez, M.A., Lorenzo, A., Ibáñez, S.J., Ortega, E., Leite, N. and Sampaio, J. (2010) 'An analysis of defensive strategies used by home and away basketball teams', *Perceptual and Motor Skills*, 110: 159–66.

Grant, A.G., Williams, A.M. and Reilly, T. (1999) 'Analysis of the successful and unsuccessful teams in the 1998 World Cup', *Journal of Sports Sciences*, 17: 827.

Hopkins, W.G. (2006) 'Estimating sample size for magnitude-bases inferences', *Sportscience*, 10 : 63–70, available at www.sportsci.org/2006/wghss.htm (retrieved on 15 January 2012).

Hughes, M., Evans, S. and Wells, J. (2001) 'Establishing normative profiles in performance analysis', *International Journal of Performance Analysis in Sport*, 1: 1–26.

James, N., Mellalieu, S.D. and Holley, C. (2002) 'Analysis of strategies in soccer as a function of European and domestic competition', *International Journal of Performance Analysis in Sport*, 2: 85–103.

Jamieson, J.P. (2010) 'Home field advantage in athletics: A meta-analysis', *Journal of Applied Social Psychology*, 40: 1819–48.

Jones, M.B. (2007) 'Home advantage in the NBA as a game-long process', *Journal of Quantitative Analysis in Sport*, 3(4): article 2, available at www.bepress.com/jqas (retrieved on 15 January, 2012).

Jones, P.D., James, N. and Mellalieu, D. (2004) 'Possession as a performance indicator in soccer', *International Journal of Performance Analysis in Sport*, 4: 98–102.

Kormelink, H. and Seeverens, T. (1999) *Match Analysis and Game Preparation*, Spring City, PA: Reedswain.

Kozar, B., Whitfield, K.E., Lord, R.H. and Mechikoff, R.A. (1993) 'Timeouts before free-throws: Do the statistics support the strategy?', *Perceptual and Motor Skills*, 76: 47–50.

Lago, C. (2009) 'The influence of match location, quality of opposition, and match status on possession strategies in professional association football', *Journal of Sports Sciences*, 27: 1463–9.

Lago, C. and Martin, R. (2007) 'Determinants of possession of the ball in soccer', *Journal of Sports Sciences*, 125: 969–74.

Lago, C., Casais, L., Dominguez, E. and Sampaio, J. (2010) 'The effects of situational variables on distance covered at various speeds in elite soccer', *European Journal of Sport Science*, 10: 103–9.

Marcelino, R., Mesquita, I., Palao, J.M. and Sampaio, J. (2009a) 'Home advantage in high-level volleyball varies according to set number', *Journal of Sports Sciences and Medicine*, 8: 352–6.

Marcelino, R., Mesquita, I., Sampaio, J. and Anguera, M.A. (2009b) 'Análisis de la diferencia de jugar en casa en voleibol de alto rendimiento', *Revista de Psicología del Deporte*, 18: 181–96.

Marcelino, R., Mesquita, I. and Sampaio, J. (2011) 'Effects of quality of opposition and match status on technical and tactical performances in elite volleyball', *Journal of Sports Sciences*, 29: 733–41.

McGarry, T. and Franks, I. (2003) 'The science of match analysis', in T. Reilly and M. Williams (eds), *Science and Soccer* (pp. 265–75). London: Routledge.

Mechikoff, R.A., Kozar, B., Lord, R.H., Whitfield, K.E. and Brandenburg, J. (1990) 'Perceptions of basketball coaches', *The Basketball Bulletin*, Fall: 72–5.

Mexas, K., Tsiskaris, G., Kyriakou, D. and Garefis, A. (2005) 'Comparison of effectiveness of organised offenses between two different championships in high level basketball', *International Journal of Performance Analysis in Sport*, 5: 72–82.

Navarro, R.M., Lorenzo, A., Gómez, M.A. and Sampaio, J. (2009) 'Analysis of critical moments in the League ACB 2007–2008', *Revista de Psicología del Deporte*, 18 (suppl.): 391–5.

O'Donoghue, P. and Tenga, A. (2001) 'The effect of store-line on work rate in elite soccer', *Journal of Sports Sciences*, 19: 25–6.

O'Donoghue, P., Mayes, A., Edwards, K. and Garland, J. (2008) 'Performance norms for British National Super League Netball', *International Journal of Sports Science and Coaching*, 3: 501–11.

Ortega, E., Villarejo, D. and Palao, J.M. (2009) 'Differences in game statistics between winning and losing rugby teams in the Six Nations tournament', *Journal of Sports Science and Medicine*, 8: 523–7.

Pollard, R. (2005) 'Home advantage in cricket and its effect on Indian test players', *Research Bi-annual for Movement*, 21: 12–29.

Pollard, R. (2006) 'Worldwide regional variations in home advantage in association football', *Journal of Sports Sciences*, 24: 231–40.

Pollard, R. and Pollard, G. (2005) 'Long term trends in home advantage in professional team sports in North America and England (1876–2003)', *Journal of Sports Sciences*, 23: 337–50.

Pollard, R. and Gómez, M.A. (2007) 'Home advantage analysis in different basketball leagues according to team ability', *Iberian Congress on Basketball Research*, 4: 61–4.

Pollard, R. and Stefani, R. (2007) 'FIFA rankings', *Soccer Journal*, 52(4): 32–6.

Pollard, R. and Gómez, M.A. (2009) 'Home advantage in football in South-West Europe: Long-term trends, regional variation, and team differences', *European Journal of Sport Science*, 9: 341–52.

Poulter, D.R. (2007) 'Non-outcome measures underlying the home advantage effect for teams and individual players in the UEFA Champions League', in Y. Theodorakis, M. Goudas and A. Papaioannou (eds), *Book of Long Papers, 12th European Congress of Sport Psychology* (pp. 49–52). Halkidiki, Greece: FEPSAC.

Reed, D. and O'Donoghue, P. (2005) 'Development and application of computer-based prediction methods', *International Journal of Performance Analysis in Sport*, 5: 12–28.

Rogulj, N., Srhoj, V. and Srhoj, L. (2004) 'The contribution of collective attack tactics in differentiating handball store efficiency', *Collegium Antropologicum*, 28: 739–46.

Sainz de Baranda, P. and López-Riquelme, D. (2012) 'Analysis of corner-kicks in relation to match status in the 2006 World Cup', *European Journal of Sport Science*, 12(2): 121–9.

Sainz de Baranda, P., Ortega, E. and Palao, J.M. (2008) 'Analysis of goalkeepers' defence in the World Cup in Korea and Japan in 2002', *European Journal of Sport Science*, 8: 127–34.

Sampaio, J. and Janeira, M. (2003) 'Statistical analyses of basketball team performance: Understanding teams' wins and losses according to a different index of ball possessions', *International Journal of Performance Analysis in Sport*, 3(1): 40–9.

Sampaio, J., Ibáñez, S. and Feu, S. (2004) 'Discriminative power of basketball game-related statistics by level of competition and sex', *Perceptual and Motor Skills*, 99: 1231–8.

Sampaio, J., Lago, C. and Drinkwater, E.J. (2010a) 'Explanations for the United States of America's dominance in basketball at the Beijing Olympic Games (2008)', *Journal of Sports Sciences*, 28: 147–52.

Sampaio, J., Lago, C., Casais, L. and Leite, N. (2010b) 'Effects of starting score-line, game location and quality of opposition in basketball quarter score', *European Journal of Sport Sciences*, 10: 391–6.

Sasaki, Y., Nevill, A. and Reilly, T. (1999) 'Home advantage: A case study of Ipswich Town football club during the 1996–1997 season', *Journal of Sports Sciences*, 17: 831.

Scully, D. and O'Donoghue, P. (1999) 'The effect of score line on tennis strategy in Grand Slam men's singles', *Journal of Sports Sciences*, 17: 64–5.

Seckin, A. and Pollard, R. (2008) 'Home advantage in Turkish professional soccer', *Perceptual and Motor Skills*, 107: 51–4.

Shaw, J. and O'Donoghue, P. (2004) 'The effect of score line on work rate in amateur soccer', in P. O'Donoghue and M.D. Hughes (eds), *Performance Analysis of Sport VI* (pp. 84–91). Cardiff: CPA UWIC Press.

Taylor, J.B., Mellalieu, S.D., James, N. and Shearer, D. (2008) 'The influence of match location, quality of opposition and match status on technical performance in professional association football', *Journal of Sports Sciences*, 26: 885–95.

Tenga, A.P.C., Holme, I., Ronglan, L.T. and Bahr, R. (2010) 'Effects of match location on playing tactics for goal scoring in Norwegian professional soccer', *Journal of Sport Behavior*, 33: 89–108.

Trninić, S., Dizdar, D. and Lukšić, E. (2002) 'Differences between winning and defeated top quality basketball teams in final tournaments of European club championship', *Collegium Antropologicum*, 26: 521–31.

Tucker, W., Mellalieu, S.D., James, N. and Taylor, N.B. (2005) 'Game location effects in professional soccer', *International Journal of Analysis in Sport*, 5: 23–35.

Vaz, L., Van Rooyen, M. and Sampaio, J. (2010) 'Rugby game-related statistics that discriminate between winning and losing teams in IRB and Super Twelve close games', *Journal of Sports Science and Medicine*, 9: 51–5.

22

FROM GAME MOMENTUM TO CRITICALITY OF GAME SITUATIONS

António Paulo Ferreira

TECHNICAL UNIVERSITY OF LISBON, PORTUGAL

Summary

Despite the typical differences in sport games, it is possible to identify some invariant characteristics. The cooperation–opposition nature determines a conflict of interests between two opposite strategic fields that can cause disruptions to the natural flow of the match. Some investigators have studied these perturbation factors or critical incidents. However, there is a lack of a theoretical framework that includes the criticality of game situations as a well-identified research line in sport performance analysis. Assuming the interest in the concept and the models developed to understand it, this chapter aims to describe the main guidelines of these models. Some results obtained from the empirical research focused on criticality game situations will be described and finally a definition of the basic guidelines will be presented that characterizes the criticality of game situations as a research line and critical incidents as its investigation objects.

Introduction

The existence of critical incidents in sport games development is widely recognized by all participants, analysts and investigators. However, research efforts on criticality of game situations have not been framed in a theoretical context that can be distinguished in sport performance analysis. In many cases implicitly, there are some references to the phenomenon and to the mechanisms that underlie its existence. However, they are scattered over different approaches based on distinct theoretical frameworks, making its synthesis an increasingly difficult task (Cornelius *et al.*, 1997; Taylor and Demick 1994; Vallerand *et al.*, 1988).

The exploration of the momentum construct gave the first contribution towards understanding the criticality of game situations. First, and specially designed to answer some psychological questions, momentum was converted into a sport game concept and used by several investigators who tried to understand some mysteries of sport games development. Understanding the concept in a psychological dimension has had the merit of raising important questions and imposing a set of new issues. However, criticality of game situations does not have a conceptual framework that covers the entire spectrum of sport games. Some theoretical guidelines need to be clarified in order to support methodological tools and define ecological tracks. This chapter aims to achieve the following three interrelated goals:

1. To review the more relevant momentum models, exploring their contributions to understanding the criticality of game situations.
2. To sum up the most interesting results from the empirical research on these models.
3. And finally to define the main guidelines for understanding the criticality of game situations and, particularly, to define the concept of critical incidents in sports games.

The multidimensional model of momentum: more than a psychological construct

Given the reductionist focus of the momentum concept (Adler, 1981; Iso-Ahola and Mobily, 1980; Vallerand *et al.*, 1988), Taylor and Demick (1994) argued the need to clarify the construct. They supported momentum as more than a psychological concept, considering the important and interdependent roles of emotional, behavioural, social and environmental factors. Refusing the term *psychological momentum*, momentum was considered a multidimensional change of the individual's internal state, 'a positive or negative change in cognition, affect, physiology, and behaviour caused by an event or series of events that will result in a commensurate shift in performance and competitive outcome' (Taylor and Demick, 1994: 54). Based on this concept, the multidimensional model of momentum emerged as a set of steps linked in a logical sequence that is figuratively called the momentum chain (see Figure 22.1).

Understanding momentum in the light of this model, Taylor and Demick (1994) provided a conceptual improvement of the phenomenon's framework, contributing to a better comprehension of perturbations and critical incidents in sports games. This contribution can be divided

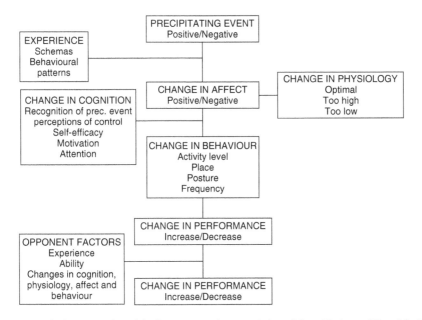

Figure 22.1 Multidimensional model of momentum in sports (adapted from Taylor and Demick, 1994)

into two basic domains: first, the introduction of a multidimensional view on the concept; and second, the search for the game precipitating events inside the real games context, which could be considered as the factual stimuli for the chain momentum development. In order to validate the model, Taylor and Demick tried to connect the first and the last steps of the chain (see Figure 22.1): the precipitating events and the performance changes.

Expert coaches of tennis and basketball were questioned in order to characterize the potential criticality in game occurrences. About 30 potential precipitating events were selected (32 in the case of tennis and 30 for basketball), which were then reduced to five categories for tennis and four categories for basketball (see Table 22.1). Two independent teams of analysts observed five matches from each sport game. Regarding tennis, momentum was observed as a consequence of one of the two following occurrences: a run of three or more points or a subsequent service break in a game. As for basketball, a significant change was considered when the team favoured by the precipitating event changed the game score in its favour by at least five points during the five minutes following the event's occurrence. When the basketball matches were decided in overtime, the five minutes of overtime duration were identified as a momentum episode, which favoured the team that won the match. Table 22.2 shows the descriptive results found by Taylor and Demick's (1994) study. Results revealed differences between these two sport games contexts. In tennis, winners and losers were distinguished by the amount of positive and negative events produced in their matches. Winners showed a tendency to produce more positive actions and losers demonstrated more negative behaviours. In tennis, it was clear that the positive occurrences related to the positive momentum were significantly higher for winners than for losers. In basketball, no differences were found for the proportional relationships between positive and negative events and the final outcome of the match.

Table 22.1 Precipitated events selected by tennis and basketball expert coaches (adapted from Taylor and Demick, 1994)

Tennis	Basketball
• Dramatic shot: dropshot, ace, overhead smash	• Starting player must leave game for a negative reason, such as injury, foul trouble, ejection
• Service break early in the set	• Scoring run of three straight baskets by one team
• Winning game after long deuce	• Timeout called by the opponent after a scoring run
• Making an unforced error at a crucial point	• Dramatic play: for example, slam dunk, three-point basket, fast-break, steal leading to basket, blocked shot, 'prayer' shot at the buzzer
• Not converting 15–40 or 0–40 opportunity	

Table 22.2 Descriptive results from Taylor and Demick's studies (adapted from Taylor and Demick, 1994)

Tennis	Basketball
• 30.4 precipitating events per match	• 12.8 precipitating events per match
• 45.0% 'dramatic shots'	• 43.1% 'dramatic plays'
• 18.0% unforced errors	• 35.2% scoring run from three or more consecutive ball possessions
• 16.0% service breaks	
• 15.0% not converting 15–40 or 0–40 break opportunity	• 13.7% an important player must leave the game
• 66.4% positive events; 33.6% negative events	• 7.8% timeout
• 77.2% three-point run; 22.8% service break	• 78.4% positive events; 21.6% negative events

Considering the timeout as a precipitating event, Salitsky (1995) investigated its influence on volleyball matches. The consecutive points scored and the points difference between teams before and after the timeout were both significantly different. Recently, Gómez *et al.* (2011) reported the effects of game timeouts on basketball teams' offensive and defensive performances. The same trend as volleyball was also found for basketball matches. Gómez *et al.* (2011) illustrate a higher post-timeout offensive and defensive performance and also an interaction between timeouts and the momentary score differences. Increased values were found on the momentary score difference when teams were losing and when they played in balanced situations. These values decreased when teams demonstrated a dominating behaviour against their opponents.

Although the multidimensional model of momentum emerged to solve a psychological problem, its validation process introduced new and interesting contributions for analysing the relationship between critical incidents and performance perturbations. However, the demonstration of the momentum chain is not yet sufficiently clarified. The performance shifts seen by a sequence of interdependent steps, caused by a particular game incident, are in fact to be confirmed (Kerick *et al.*, 2000; Mack and Stephens, 2000; Stanimirovic and Hanrahan, 2004). However, with their model, Taylor and Demick (1994) established a new construct concept for momentum. Even without having reached their goal, they showed that some game occurrences might be related to performance shifts, depending on the sports contexts and the specificity of performance.

The projected performance model: an alternative model to explain the momentum existence

Lack of a theoretical basis to support the momentum construct enabled the emergence of new alternatives to explain the phenomenon. The projected performance model is one of these proposals (Cornelius *et al.*, 1997), inspired by Tversky and Kahneman's (1974) work, which focused on biased heuristics of judgments under uncertainty circumstances. Cornelius *et al.* (1997) suggested that the athlete's or team's performance can be viewed as fluctuating around an average performance level. In this sense, momentum is reflected by a performance assessment taking into account its average level. As the authors clearly stated:

> if athletes' performances rise moderately above a mean level and they are defeating their opponent, this phenomenon may be labelled as a positive momentum. If performance drops moderately below their mean level and they are losing to their opponent, this phenomenon is likely to be labelled as a negative momentum. Thus, positive and negative momentum may be labels of performance to which competitors and observers attribute a spurious causal link to performance.
>
> *(Cornelius* et al.*, 1997: 482)*

As fluctuations occur around an average level, the performance could behave according to a Gaussian curve. The notions of positive and negative momentum are two performance areas situated at the opposite sides of this curve. When a momentum circumstance occurs, athletes and teams are exposed to a set of internal and external competition influences that are forcing them to return back to their average performance level. Thus, this is the reason why momentum tends to be a brief phenomenon; a particular episode corresponding to the extremes of the performance curve (see Figure 22.2).

Within this framework, the projected performance model incorporates two interesting phenomena: the negative facilitation and the positive inhibition. Previously mentioned by Silva

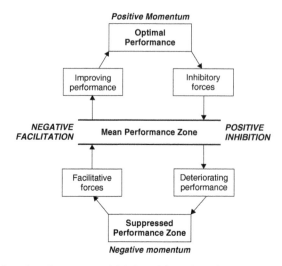

Figure 22.2   The projected performance model (adapted from Cornelius *et al.*, 1997)

et al. (1988), these are the sudden transitions between the two extremes of performance. When a positive momentum episode is occurring, a team or player is out-scoring the opponent, but suddenly, due to an amount of critical events, the performance decreases below the average to a suppressed performance level. It is called the positive inhibition phenomenon: a transition from positive momentum to a negative one. Inversely, the sudden increase in performance after performing poorly is also possible in many circumstances. This case is designated as the negative facilitation: a sudden transition from a negative to a positive momentum. Naturally, these are two faces of the same coin. Even as circumstantial and transitory phenomena, it means that they occur in opposite directions during the competition: when a team or athlete is experiencing a good momentum, on the opposite side there is a negative one.

The projected performance model proposes a new and different framework for momentum analysis and, consequently, for the critical game instances. Introducing the mean performance level as a reference, investigators, coaches and analysts need to know how it is possible to quantify the performance in order to understand the real meaning of deviations. In the spectrum of sport games, the relationship between quantification and qualification of performance is not linear, but it is possible and desirable in many of them. For sport games where the 'numbers' objectivity' could give important information about individual and team behaviours, the projected performance model can be an interesting framework to understand how players and teams behave, not only in a short-term analysis, but also during long-term performance. Although there is no relevant empirical experience using this model, it may offer an interesting contribution to the study of some issues around critical incidents and perturbations in sport games, particularly for those where score fluctuations may be sensitive to sudden changes in the players' and team's performance.

The incidental perspective of momentum (Burke *et al.*, 1997, 1999, 2003): a problem of individual perception

Inspired by the antecedents–consequences model (Vallerand *et al.*, 1988), Burke *et al.* (1997, 1999, 2003) studied momentum perception of sport games' precipitating events. They focused on performance alterations – positive or negative modifications – due to the wide range of events that can occur during a match or competition. Assuming that momentum can be identified throughout the relationship between events occurrence–game consequence, Burke *et al.* (1997, 1999, 2003) tried to redefine the momentum concept through an incidental approach. Using individual perception to certify the criticality of precipitating events, the authors determined the agreement levels among multiple observers. Simultaneously, they tried to identify the match episodes that supposedly could correspond to a momentum episode.

The inter-observer agreement levels never reached values above 50 per cent (Burke *et al.*, 1997, 2003). In basketball and tennis (Burke *et al.*, 1997), the inter-observer ratings agreed by less than 20 per cent. In a later study, this level reached 45 per cent, but using only two observers (Burke *et al.*, 2003). On the agreement levels of game momentum, the studies of Burke *et al.* (1997, 1999, 2003) revealed two interesting methodological aspects: first, a decrease in the number of matches observed and a reduction in the number of observers used in their studies; and second, the use of expert knowledge on the observation tasks. The observers' experience and their specific knowledge about the context observed were a decisive step in the decrease of the high inference recorded.

An important aspect of this methodological development is the opportunity to distinguish two different analysis levels around the momentum episodes. Through a micro-analysis, Burke *et al.* (1997, 1999, 2003) tried to define the starters, the interrupters and the prevalent events that make momentum such a special match occurrence. In addition, they made a general analysis, which can be called a macro-analysis, in order to support the general reasons why momentum happened. The general idea of 'good performance' predominates as the main reason for momentum starting and for momentum ending. As expected, the agreement ratings were higher in the macro-level analysis compared with the micro-level observation. Table 22.3 sums up the basketball events studied by Burke and colleagues (1999, 2003) in two of their studies.

Table 22.3 Occurrence percentages of the top five precipitating events recorded by Burke *et al.*'s studies of basketball matches

	Burke et al. (1999)	Burke et al. (2003)
Momentum's beginning	Three-points field goal – 26% Defensive stop – 24% Ball steal – 20% Fast-break – 14% Caused turn-over – 10%	Three-points field goal – 82.5% Caused turn-over – 62.5% Two-points lay-up – 50% Ball steal – 42.5% Two-points field goal-jump shot – 42.5%
During momentum	Caused turn-over – 72% Crowd noise – 66% Defensive stop – 60% Ball steal – 58% Scoring run – 24%	Caused turn-over – 95% Two-points lay-up – 92.5% Three-points field goal – 90% Ball steal – 87.5% Defensive stop – 85%
Momentum's end	Turn-over – 36% Missed shot– 30% Opponent timeout – 18% Committed foul– 10% End of the quarter or game – 10%	Opponent timeout – 55% Foul – 10% Opponent scoring – 45% Turn-over – 37.5% Opponent ball steal – 30%
Immediate performance	Momentum's team – 7.58 (+/−3.66) Non-momentum's team – 2.62 (+/−2.32)	Momentum's team – 7.38 (+/−5.17) Non-momentum's team – 2.70 (+/−3.25)

The design of the studies of Burke *et al.* (1997, 1999, 2003) was based on a qualitative approach to momentum. At its core, it is not an entirely different approach from the attempts developed by Taylor and Demick (1994) in order to validate the multidimensional model of momentum. Not focusing on the momentum foundations, Burke and colleagues developed a momentum concept based on the incidental occurrences during the sport game's dynamics. It is a behaviourist approach to momentum and is not particularly concerned with understanding its foundations. Defining momentum as a game episode, it would be possible to assume that there are many games inside the whole game. Therefore, it is basically a momentum perspective focusing on the game and its conditional factors.

The weighting system of game actions from McCutcheon (1997)

Contrasting with the subjectivity of individual perception to isolate game momentum, McCutcheon (1997) proposed a weighting system of game events. Based on a panel of coaches (60 per cent), athletes (30 per cent) and fans (10 per cent) from three different competitive contexts – American football, basketball and freestyle wrestling – McCutcheon (1997) translated the relative importance of different events on the global performance of teams or competitors. According to this proposal, momentum was quantified by the sum of sequential occurrences during the match. Through the McCutcheon technique, game momentum was characterized as a numerical parameter, which the author named *momentum scoring* (see Table 22.4).

Table 22.4 Scores for momentum in basketball, football and high-school wrestling (adapted from McCutcheon, 1997)

Basketball	Three-points field goal – *3 points*
	Two-points field goal – *1.9 points*
	Free throw – *1.2 points*
	Slam dunk – *0.9 points (in addition to the 1.9 points for a two-pointer)*
	Offensive rebound – *1.4 points*
	Steal or forced turnover in backcourt – *2 points*
	Points to team A if team B loses a starter – *1.5 points*
	7 consecutive momentum points establishes momentum
Football	First down – *1.7 points*
	First down that moves sticks 20 yards or more – *2.6 points*
	Field goal – *3.2 points*
	Touchdown – *6 points*
	Kick-off return that results in offence starting past its own 40-yard line – *2.6 points*
	Punt return that nets more than 15 yards – *2.1 points*
	Punt that nets 60 yards or more (60-yard punt into end zones nets 40 yards) – *2.7 points*
	Defence prevents first down on fourth down – *3.3 points*
	Turnover – *3.5 points*
	Safety – *3.4 points*
	9.2 consecutive momentum points establishes momentum
Wrestling	Pin – *6 points*
	Bonus points for pin recorded in first period – *1.9 points*
	Forfeit – *3.5 points*
	Disqualification – *3.9 points*
	Technical foul (15-point lead) – *4.4 points*
	Major decisions (8- to 14-point difference) – *3.5 points*
	Decision – *2.9 points*
	16 consecutive points establishes momentum

McCutcheon's (1997) main goal was to verify the momentum effect on immediate and long-term performances. The immediate momentum effect was defined by the *first five period* notion. It consisted of the sum produced by the first five events that occurred after momentum identification. The long-term momentum effect was considered as the events' sum, since the last event of the *first five periods* until the end of the match. Results demonstrated that, for basketball and American football, 60 per cent of the teams that first stabilized momentum during the match won in the final. For wrestling, this was observed in 84 per cent of cases. Regarding the momentum effect in short-term performance, no differences were found between winners and losers, in team sports or in wrestling. However, in long-term game analysis, winners and losers from both team sports demonstrated different performances after they stabilized momentum. Wrestlers did not show any distinction in this performance parameter.

Indeed, McCutcheon's proposal (1997) is a quantitative approach to operationalize momentum episodes. Momentum scoring supports the idea that different game events have different meanings during the game timeline. This is considered in the weighting system, in order to understand the relative importance of several events (see Table 22.4). However, the external and internal validity of this proposal are not sufficiently clarified. For instance, how do we explain the absence of rebound as an important event in basketball, particularly the defensive rebound? Actually, there is great consensus about the importance of rebounding in basketball game dynamics (Marques, 1995; Sampaio and Janeira, 2003; Sampaio *et al.*, 2006). Other questions may also be raised: What were the criteria for defining the events' weighting process? What was the scale used to define it? What were the questions posed to the panel of players, coaches and fans? These questions point out the weaknesses of the method. However, this criticism should not detract from the usefulness of and the interest in the method. It gives an important contribution towards understanding and overcoming the methodological problems of the momentum concept. On the one hand, trying to measure the construct highlights the objectivity of the concept using the 'power of the numbers'; on the other hand, it focuses the momentum concept in the game context through the critical incidents that can change the course of the match.

The binomial relationship of time–score: a criticality factor of game development

Burke *et al.*'s (1997, 1999, 2003) and McCutcheon's (1997) studies neglected one important question of match development: the incidents' time-framing. Two identical events can have different impacts on a match, depending on the timing of their occurrences. If the score evolution is added to the incidents' timeline, there is an indivisible set of game factors that follows the game's life from its beginning to its end.

Time–score relationship research has focused on the critical incidents that disturb the teams' balance and have a potential influence over the final game score. For instance, a goal scored in soccer at a given match moment or a free throw scored in the last minutes of a basketball match. Kozar *et al.* (1992) investigated the free throw's efficacy relationship with the supposed home-court advantage and with the timeouts called by coaches (Kozar *et al.*, 1993). Although the away teams show higher efficacy on free-throw shooting in the last minutes of the match than the home teams, the home advantage phenomenon is confirmed for college basketball in close matches (Kozar *et al.*, 1992). On the other hand, the authors showed that there are no influences on shooting efficacy for free throws made in the last five minutes of the match after a timeout is called. In this way, the authors tried to demystify a belief among coaches which considered that free-throw percentages would be reduced when a timeout was called immediately before the free-throw shot (Kozar *et al.*, 1993). A free throw can be considered a critical incident of the basketball game, not only because it is an important structural performance factor for teams (Kozar *et al.*, 1994), but also because, in the last minutes or seconds of a close basketball match, there are many psychological influences that may affect the shooter's performance.

The functional specificity of each sport game was defined as the best way to understand the relationship between the match time and the score evolution. While investigation in sport games with 'high scores' has centred on the last minutes of the game, or on the psychological consequences of score evolution, in sport games with 'low scores', the issue is usually the connection between game events and winning probabilities. In the context of racket sports, Iso-Ahola and Blanchard (1986) showed that 74.3 per cent of the winners of the second set, and consequently of their matches, were also the winners of the first set. Silva *et al.* (1988) corroborate the same trend. Weinberg *et al.* (1981) investigated the final outcomes from an archive of over 20,000 tennis matches. They found that 86 per cent of men and 91 per cent of women who had won the first set went on to win their matches. Richardson *et al.* (1988) monitored the balance level of the matches and isolated games 8, 10 and 11 of the first set and game 4 of the second set as the most significantly correlated with the final outcome of the match. In pool, Adams (1995) indicated the existence of the same tendency – in 70 per cent of the observed cases, the winner would win the opening game. However, focusing on this 'success breeds success' trend, Weinberg *et al.* (1983) have proved the so-called 'coming back to win the match' phenomenon. They studied a sample of 2,400 men's and women's basketball and volleyball matches, determining the frequency of occurrences in which a team that is losing at half-time reverses the outcome during the second half. Despite gender and basketball/volleyball differences, it was possible to confirm the existence of this kind of reverse outcome in such game circumstances. It seemed to be more frequent with males and in basketball than with women and in volleyball matches.

As a sport game that can be considered a 'low score' game, soccer has been the target of many investigations regarding goals scored and final outcome. Results show two opposite trends. On the one hand, the number of goals seems to increase at every 15 minutes of the match, with a peak during the last 75–90-minute period (Acar *et al.*, 2008; Dickson and Mummery, 1999; Gréhaigne, 1998; Jinshan *et al.*, 1993). In general, there is an increment of goals scored from the first half to the second half of the match (Yiannakos and Armatas, 2006). On the other hand, there is a relationship between scoring early or being the first scorer and the positive outcome reached by the scorer's team (Olsen and Larsen, 1997). As a 'low score' game which is played in an open space, it seems that it might be an advantage in order to reach a positive final outcome. Knowing that the relationship between goals scored and shots at goal is not linear, Hughes and Churchill (2005) studied the frequency of shots on goal during the course of the match. They broke the whole game down into sequential ten-minute episodes and identified a global increment of shots as the game proceeds to its end. However, this increase was not significantly evident for all consecutive episodes of ten minutes. There were three episodes with fewer frequent shots: the 0–10, 30–40 and 70–80 minute intervals. These episodes can be characterized as the 'game beginning', the immediate moment 'before the half-time' and the 'end of the game'. Analysts, coaches and fans clearly agree that these three game moments are the worst times for a team to concede a goal. It probably means that these are the game moments in which teams are more concerned with their conservative defensive actions than with creating offensive solutions to score.

Assuming that one team can disrupt the natural balance of their opponent and that the defending team needs to make an increased effort to re-balance positions when a perturbation occurs, Hughes *et al.* (1998a) and Hughes *et al.* (1998b) analysed how teams act in these circumstances. They defined a perturbation ratio – goals scored/perturbation – understanding perturbation as the several actions that can interrupt the normal rhythm imposed by teams. The authors distinguished winners and losers from the English Premier League and the best classified teams from the 1996 European Championship according to three perturbation factors: quality of pass, ability in 1 x 1 situations and loss of ball control. These three perturbation types obtained the best perturbation ratios and they were indicated as the potential causes for balance disruption between teams in the competitive soccer context.

Defining criticality of game situations and critical incident

In sport games, the match is developed under a conflict of interests where two strategic organizations fight to achieve antagonistic goals. Despite the differences in the formal structure and in specific functionality, this dialectic is an invariant characteristic of match development in sports games contexts. This investigation focused on the match changes, disturbances or shifts that can affect its final outcome and that could be designated to the study of criticality of game situations. Applied to sport games, momentum and critical incidents are similar concepts, which suggest the criticality properties of sport games. They suggest that some matches are played under a proper flow imposed by the tactics and rhythms adjusted by teams. The evolution of the cooperation–opposition process of the match will determine disruptions to this balance tendency. Inevitably, inside the natural match dynamics, there will be some balance instabilities (perturbation factors or precipitating events), some imbalance circumstances, such as players' errors or merits, or some instants where one team will outperform the other (Gréhaigne *et al.*, 1997). The proper rhythm of the match will be broken and probably this will have consequences on the final outcome of the match (Hodges *et al.*, 1998; McGarry *et al.*, 2002).

In order to compose a conceptual framework for criticality of game situations that can comprehend the spectrum of sport games, five theoretical issues can be highlighted:

1. It seems clear that criticality is a generic quality of the game. Critical incidents and perturbation factors or precipitating events are its specificities. The operationalization process of critical incidents and the selection of each perturbation type follow the criteria of contextual specificity that characterizes the particularity of each sport game.
2. Understanding the critical incidents as an investigation object, available research pointed out two forms to define it: an incidental form, in which the perturbation is itself the critical incident (see Hughes *et al.*, 1998a, 1998b); and an episodic form, in which it can be defined by temporal limits that characterize the beginning and end of the balance disruption. In the latter case, perturbation types could be presented in antecedence or in consequence of the critical incident (see Burke *et al.*, 1997, 1999, 2003).
3. Coaches, players or sport fans (i.e. those who should have specific knowledge of the game) could play a decisive role in the criteria defining critical incidents and perturbations. Sport game agents have a wealth of expertise and knowledge that should not be wasted by research.
4. The current outcome or the behaviours that are directly related with it can be the best measures to evaluate the impact of some critical incident on the game. If the relationship between teams is disrupted, even for a brief moment, the current score will reflect the different performances that they are achieving.
5. Criticality may be perceived from a multidimensional perspective (see Figure 22.3). It is desirable to classify the different characteristics in which critical incidents can be expressed

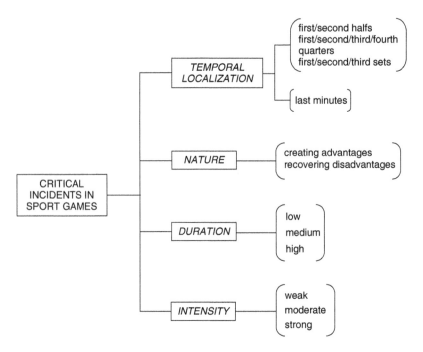

Figure 22.3   Taxonomic proposal for critical incidents in sport games

– their temporal localization, nature, duration and intensity can be considered distinctive qualities that characterize the critical incidents as investigation objects. In order to respect the sport game dynamics, critical game situation research should not neglect the multidimensionality understanding.

Concluding remarks

Given the need to place the study of sport games' criticality within a basic theoretical framework, this chapter has reviewed several momentum models and summarized their interesting contributions in order to understand the critical incidents and perturbations in matches. Taylor and Demick's (1994) multidimensional model of momentum was reviewed, highlighting the empirical studies they made to validate the model. The projected performance model was defined as an alternative proposal to describe the phenomenon. Focusing the momentum concept on the relationship between precipitating events and performance shifts, Burke *et al.* (1997, 1999, 2003) transformed it into an incidental perspective. However, the subjective perceptions about game criticality have opened up quantitative approaches to calculate it. Contrasting strengths and weaknesses, McCutcheon's (1997) momentum scoring was presented as an innovative way to differentiate the amount of events that can occur during a match. Finally, the time–score relationship was highlighted as a topic that has motivated many researchers to try to predict the best partial scores or the decisive moments in defining final outcome. In order to define sport games' criticality, critical incidents and perturbations, this chapter concluded with some theoretical guidelines to embrace criticality in the spectrum of sport games.

References

Acar, M., Yapicioglu, B., Arikan, N., Yalcin, S., Ates, N. and Ergun, M. (2008) 'Analysis of goal scored in the 2006 World Cup', in T. Reilly and F. Korkusuz, F. (eds), *Science and Football VI* (pp. 235–44). London: Routledge.

Adams, R. (1995) 'Momentum in the performance of professional tournament pocket billiards players', *International Journal of Sport Psychology*, 26: 580–7.

Adler, P. (1981) *Momentum: A Theory of Social Action*, Beverly Hills, CA: Sage Publications.

Burke, K., Edwards, C., Weigand, D. and Weinberg, R. (1997) 'Momentum in sport: A real or illusionary phenomenon for spectators', *International Journal of Sport Psychology*, 28: 79–96.

Burke, K., Burke, M. and Joyner, A. (1999) 'Perceptions of momentum in college and high school basketball: An exploratory, case study investigation', *Journal of Sport Behavior*, 22: 303–9.

Burke, K., Aoyagi, M., Joyner, A. and Burke, M. (2003) 'Spectator's perceptions of positive momentum while attending NCAA men's and women's basketball regular season contests: Exploring the antecedents-consequences model', *Athletic Insight: The Online Journal of Sport Psychology*, 5(3). Online. Available at www.athleticinsight.com (accessed 12 February 2005).

Cornelius, A., Silva III, J., Conroy, D. and Petersen, G. (1997) 'The projected performance model: Relating cognitive and performance antecedents of psychological momentum', *Perceptual and Motor Skills*, 84: 475–85.

Dickson, G. and Mummery, W. (1999) 'Goal scoring patterns over the course of a match: An analysis of the Australian National Soccer League', *Journal of Sports Sciences*, 17: 824.

Gómez, M., Jiménez, S., Navarro, R., Lago-Penas, C. and Sampaio, J. (2011) 'Effects of coaches' timeouts on basketball teams' offensive and defensive performances according to momentary differences in score and game period', *European Journal of Sport Sciences*, 11: 303–8.

Gréhaigne, J. (1998) 'Time distribution of goals in soccer: Some championships and the 1998 World Cup', in M. Hughes and F. Tavares (eds), *Notational Analysis of Sport IV* (pp. 41–50). Porto: FCDEF-UP.

Gréhaigne, J., Bouthier, D. and David, B. (1997) 'Dynamic-system analysis of opponent relationship in collective actions in soccer', *Journal of Sport Sciences*, 15: 137–49.

Hodges, N., McGarry, T. and Franks, I. (1998) 'A dynamical system's approach to the examination of sport behaviour', *Avante*, 4: 16–38.

Hughes, M. and Churchill, S. (2005) 'Attacking profiles of successful and unsuccessful teams in Copa America 2001', in T. Reilly, J. Cabri and D. Araújo (eds), *Science and Football V* (pp. 219–24). London: Routledge.

Hughes, M., Dawkins, N., David, R. and Mills, J. (1998a) 'The perturbation effect and goal opportunities in soccer', *Journal of Sport Sciences*, 16: 20.

Hughes, M., Landridge, C. and Dawkin, N. (1998b) 'Perturbation leading to shooting in soccer', in M. Hughes and F. Tavares (eds), *Notational Analysis of Sport IV* (pp. 23–32). Porto: FCDEF-UP.

Iso-Ahola, S. and Mobily, K. (1980) 'Psychological momentum: A phenomenon and an empirical (unobtrusive) validation of its influence in a competitive sport tournament', *Psychological Reports*, 46: 391–401.

Iso-Ahola, S. and Blanchard, W. (1986) 'Psychological momentum and competitive sport performance: A field study', *Perceptual and Motor Skills*, 62: 763–8.

Jinshan, X., Xiaoke, C., Yamanaka, K. and Matsumoto, M. (1993) 'Analysis of the goals in the 14th World Cup', in T. Reilly, J. Clarys and A. Stibble (eds), *Science and Football II* (pp. 203–5). London: E. and F.N. Spon.

Kerick, S., Iso-Ahola, S. and Hatfield, B. (2000) 'Psychological momentum in target shooting: Cortical, cognitive-affective, and behavioral responses', *Journal of Sport and Exercise Psychology*, 22: 1–20.

Kozar, B., Whitfield, K. and Lord, R. (1992) 'Free throw shooting in critical game situations: The home-court disadvantage', *Research Quarterly of Exercise and Sport*, March Supplement: A-79.

Kozar, B., Whitfield, K., Lord, R. and Mechikoff, R. (1993) 'Timeouts before free-throws: Do the statistics support the strategy?', *Perceptual and Motor Skills*, 76: 47–50.

Kozar, B., Vaughn, R., Whitfield, K., Lord, R. and Dye, B. (1994) 'Importance of free-throws at various stages of basketball games', *Perceptual and Motor Skills*, 78: 243–8.

Mack, M. and Stephens, D. (2000) 'An empirical test of Taylor and Demick's multidimensional model of momentum in sport', *Journal of Sport Behavior*, 23: 349–63.

Marques, F. (1995) 'Métodos de quantificação em desportos colectivos', *Revista Horizonte*, 65: 183–9.

McCutcheon, L. (1997) 'Does the establishment of momentum lead to athletic improvement?', *Perceptual and Motor Skills*, 85: 195–203.

McGarry, T., Anderson, D., Wallace, S., Hughes, M. and Franks, I. (2002) 'Sport competition as a dynamical self-organizing system', *Journal of Sport Sciences*, 20: 771–81.

Olsen, E. and Larsen, O. (1997) 'Use of match analysis by coaches', in T. Reilly, J. Bangsbo and M. Hughes (eds), *Science and Football III* (pp. 209–20). London: E. and F.N. Spon.

Richardson, P., Alder, W. and Hankes, D. (1988) 'Game, set, match: Psychological momentum in tennis' *The Sport Psychologist*, 2: 69–76.

Salitsky, P. (1995) 'Effects of time-outs on psychological momentum in intercollegiate women's volleyball', unpublished doctoral thesis, Temple University, Philadelphia.

Sampaio, J. and Janeira, M. (2003) 'Statistical analyses of basketball team performance: Understanding teams' wins and losses according to a different index of ball possessions', *International Journal of Performance Analysis in Sport*, 3: 40–9.

Sampaio, J., Janeira, M., Ibáñez, S. and Lorenzo, A. (2006) 'Discriminant analysis of game-related statistics between basketball guards, forwards and centers in three professional leagues', *European Journal of Sport Sciences*, 6: 173–8.

Silva III, J., Hardy, C. and Crace, R. (1988) 'Analysis of psychological momentum in intercollegiate tennis', *Journal of Sport and Exercise Psychology*, 10: 346–54.

Stanimirovic, R. and Hanrahan, S. (2004) 'Efficacy, affect and teams: Is momentum a misnomer?', *International Journal of Sport and Exercise Psychology*, 2: 43–62.

Taylor, J. and Demick, A. (1994) 'A multidimensional model of momentum in sport'. *Journal of Applied Sport Psychology*, 6: 51–70.

Tversky, A. and Kahneman, D. (1974) 'Judgment under uncertainty: Heuristics and biases', *Science*, 185: 1124–31.

Vallerand, R., Colavecchio, P. and Pelletier, L. (1988) 'Psychological momentum and performance inferences: A preliminary test of the antecedents-consequences psychological momentum model', *Journal of Sport and Exercise Psychology*, 10: 92–108.

Weinberg, R., Richardson, P. and Jackson, A. (1981) 'Effect of situation criticality on tennis performance of males and females', *International Journal of Sport Psychology*, 12: 253–9.

Weinberg, R., Richardson, P., Jackson, A. and Yukelson, D. (1983) 'Coming from behind to win: Sex differences in interacting sport teams', *International Journal of Sport Psychology*, 14: 79–84.

Yiannakos, A. and Armatas, V. (2006) 'Evaluation of the goal scoring patterns in European Championship in Portugal 2004', *International Journal of Performance Analysis in Sport*, 6: 178–88.

23
TIME-MOTION ANALYSIS

Christopher Carling[1,2] and Jonny Bloomfield[3]

[1]LOSC LILLE MÉTROPOLE FOOTBALL CLUB, FRANCE

[2]UNIVERSITY OF CENTRAL LANCASHIRE, UK

[3]SUPPORT 2 PERFORM, HIGH PERFORMANCE SOLUTIONS, UK

Summary

Time-motion analyses are used to indirectly quantify the physical efforts of athletes in training and competition. Information derived from analyses can be used to make objective decisions for structuring the conditioning elements of training and to optimise match preparation. Over recent years, time-motion analysis has grown in popularity, especially at elite levels, mainly due to major advances in computer and video technology and to greater recognition by applied practitioners of its benefits in supplying objective information on physical performance. Indeed, research on physical performance over the last decade has led to the emergence of a comprehensive mass of knowledge on competitive activity profiles across a wide range of sports. While contemporary techniques provide efficient means for the collection and analysis of large amounts of data, scientific validation must have been conducted to ensure information derived from these methods is both accurate and reliable. The number of techniques used to collect data in matches are limited as the rules and regulations in certain sports restrict these approaches and a lack of interchangeability for data derived from different systems suggests the need for a single, internationally accepted 'gold-standard' approach. Finally, while the cost of computer and video technology has significantly reduced over the last decade, many of these systems remain expensive and are therefore inaccessible to practitioners at lower levels of the game. Future developments in time-motion analysis are shifting towards the development of miniaturised systems that analyse physical performance data in real-time, allowing objective split-second evaluation and decision making at any moment during performance. The development of intelligent systems is also underway to aid the fitness conditioning process by suggesting pertinent strategies and interventions for optimising training and preparation on the basis of data derived from motion analyses of play.

Introduction

Time-motion analysis has been used extensively since the 1970s to indirectly quantify the physical demands of many sports. Locomotor activities are coded and classified according to the intensity of movements performed by the athlete. Data can be translated into distances covered or the frequency of time spent in a variety of movement activities. The activity profile may be placed on a time-base so that exercise-to-rest ratios or low-to-high intensity exercise ratios can be calculated to accurately represent the specific demands of the sport and provide objective guidelines for optimising the conditioning elements of training programmes (Reilly, 2007). Indeed, an increased understanding of the specific demands imposed upon sports performers by match-play and training not only provides opportunities for the development of appropriate controlled fitness training regimes but can also inform match-to-match recovery programmes. This may lead to enhanced athletic ability and enable players to maintain high performance levels throughout the duration of games and across the entire season. Information can also be interfaced with physiological measures, such as heart rate, leading to increased opportunities for monitoring the strain and workload inherent to different sports and potentially reducing the risk of injury or ill health (Macleod *et al.*, 2009), especially when recovery between successive matches is short. Finally, motion analysis data can also assist in monitoring the physical progression of players – for example, across age groups or from sub-elite to elite levels of competition.

In this chapter, different techniques commonly used to collect time-motion data in match-play and training are visited. These include manual systems and the computer and video tracking technologies currently employed at elite levels. Examples of published data from the accumulated body of knowledge on physical performance in contemporary competition across many sports are also provided. These include discussion of general characteristics of performance, position-specific demands and the occurrence of fatigue in competition.

Motion analysis systems and techniques

Manual motion analysis

Up until the last two decades or so, manual coding systems were generally employed for the time-motion analysis of athletic performance. Early efforts involved simply tracing soccer player movements on a scaled plan of the playing surface to estimate distances covered and were subject to large inaccuracies. Subsequently, two definitive studies using manual coding techniques to collect data on physical performance in professional soccer were conducted by Bangsbo *et al.* (1991) and Reilly and Thomas (1976). Reilly and Thomas employed a subjective assessment of distances and exercise intensities recorded manually or onto an audiotape recorder. A learnt map of pitch markings was used in conjunction with visual cues around the pitch boundaries. Bangsbo and colleagues combined analysis of video recordings of soccer player movements in match-play with individual locomotor characteristics pre-established according to runs performed at different exercise intensities. The time for the player to pass pre-markers and known distances was used to quantify the speed for each activity of locomotion. Data collected using these manual methodologies were shown to be reliable and their use in contemporary motion analysis research, notably in soccer, is still frequent (Andersson *et al.*, 2010; Gabbett and Mulvey 2008; Mohr *et al.*, 2008).

More recent developments on these early techniques include the Noldus Observer behavioural analysis software and Sportstec's Trakperformance system. The Observer XT is an event–logging, video-based computer software used for the capture, analysis and presentation of observational data. An early version of this software was used extensively to analyse the wide range of motions, movements and specific playing activities observed in professional soccer (Bloomfield *et al.*, 2004, 2007). Trakperformance enables a single player to be mechanically followed throughout training or competition using a computer pen and tablet on a scaled version of the specific playing field or court. Ground markings and cues around the pitch are used as reference points for tracking the players. The miniaturised playing field is calibrated so that a given movement of the mouse or mouse-pen corresponds to the linear distance travelled by the player. Analysis of soccer match-play has shown this system to be accurate and real-time analysis is possible, although high levels of operator skill and experience are necessary (Edgecomb and Norton, 2006).

In general, data capture via manual coding methods is considerably labour-intensive and time-consuming, and analysis is limited to the analysis of a single player at a time. To a certain extent, the data collection process is subject to inaccuracies, notably when recording positional information. Moreover, these techniques do not allow accurate quantification of transitional changes between running speeds, such as acceleration and deceleration movements (James, 2006). However, manual analysis systems are convenient and relatively cheap, and an experienced observer can provide reliable and pertinent data sets for dissemination. They are within reach of standard coaches and can readily provide answers to many of the questions posed on physical performance, particularly at lower levels of the game. For additional information on the workings, strengths and limitations of manual coding processes, the reader is referred to Carling *et al.* (2005) and Hughes and Franks (2004).

Computerised motion analysis and portable electronic tracking devices

The numerous difficulties encountered in using early manual motion analysis techniques mentioned earlier led to the development in the mid-to-late 1990s of computer and video technologies enabling automatic or semi-automatic tracking of player movements during match-play. At present, a plethora of time-motion analysis systems exist and a non-exhaustive list of these technologies is presented in Table 23.1. For additional information on the workings of and strengths and weaknesses of these and other technologies, the reader is referred to three recent reviews (Barris and Button, 2008; Carling *et al.*, 2008, 2009). Presently, the scientific legitimacy of some commercially available tracking systems has not been adequately established, despite the need to comply with four basic quality control specifications: accuracy, reliability, objectivity and validity (Drust *et al.*, 2007). The lack of a single test protocol considered the 'gold standard' for testing the validity, reliability and objectivity of motion analysis systems may be one reason for this failure (Carling *et al.*, 2008). Nevertheless, two main categories of player tracking technology currently exist: computerised video-based tracking and portable electronic tracking devices worn by athletes. Examples of both of these categories are discussed in turn.

Computer and digital video-based analysis

The development of commercial video-based player tracking systems, notably AMISCO Pro (Sport-Universal, Nice, France) and Prozone 3 (Prozone Sports Ltd, Leeds, UK), initially revolutionised the analysis of physical performance in professional soccer and rugby competition in the late 1990s. These pioneer systems semi-automatically track the movements of all players simultaneously on digital video footage obtained from a permanently fixed set of cameras positioned strategically to cover the entire pitch. This video-based analysis provides an unobtrusive means of collecting competition-specific information on technical, tactical and physically performance. Analysis is done post-match, but often requires manual intervention to correct errors by an operator, mainly when interruptions in player tracking occur due to occlusions (Barris and Button, 2008). Players are frequently lost or cannot be tracked during situations where multiple players cluster in restricted playing areas (e.g. a scrum or lineout in rugby or a crowd of soccer players in the penalty area for a corner kick). Results are thus only available 12–24 hours

Table 23.1 Some examples of contemporary systems used for time–motion analysis of sports performance

Company/Institution	Country	System	Web site	Further reading
Digital video				
Cairos Technologies AG	Germany	VIS.TRACK	www.cairos.com	
Feedback Sport	New Zealand	Feedback Football	www.feedbacksport.com	
Lynx System Developers Inc	USA	Isolynx	www.finishlynx.com/isolynx	
Prozone Ltd	UK	ProZone 3	www.prozonesports.com	Di Salvo et al. (2009)
Spinsight Ltd	UK	Spinsight K2	www.spinsight.com	
Sport-Universal Process SA	France	AMISCO Pro	www.sport-universal.com	Randers et al. (2010)
STATS LLC	USA	SportVU	www.stats.com	
Tracab	Sweden	Tracab	www.tracab.com	
University of Campinas	Brazil	Dvideo	www.unicamp.br	Barros et al. (2007)
University of Ljubljana	Slovenia	Sagit/Squash	www.uni-lj.si	Vučković et al. (2010)
Venatrack	UK	Venatrack	www.venatrack.com	Redwood-Brown et al. (2012)
GPS				
Catapult Sports	Australia	Minimax	www.catapultsports.com	Castellano et al. 2011
Garmin Ltd	USA	Forerunner	www.garmin.com	Webber and Porter (2009)
GPSports	Australia	SPI Elite	www.gpsports.com	Macutkiewicz and Sunderland. (2011)
Real Track Football	Spain	Real Track Football	www.realtrackfutbol.com	Pino et al. (2007)
Electronic transponder				
CSIRO	Australia	WASP	www.csiro.au	Sathyan et al. (2011)
Inmotio Object Tracking BV	Netherlands	LPM Soccer 3D	www.inmotio.nl	Frencken et al. (2010)
Trakus Inc	USA	Trakus	www.trakus.com	
ZXY Sport Tracking AS	Norway	ZXY Sport Tracking	www.zxy.no	
Activity pedometer/accelerometer				
Orthocare Innovations, LLC	USA	StepWatch	www.orthocareinnovations.com	Feito et al. (2011)
PAL Technologies Ltd	UK	ActivPAL	www.paltech.plus.com	Harrington et al. (2011)
Manual systems				
Noldus Information Technology	Netherlands	Observer XT	www.noldus.com	Bloomfield et al.(2007)
Sportstec	Australia	TrakPerformance	www.sportstec.com	Edgecomband Norton (2006)

post-competition. However, independent testing of movement data produced by the Prozone system has shown high levels of accuracy, reliability and validity (Di Salvo *et al.*, 2009), thereby reassuring applied practitioners and academics of the scientific legitimacy of the system.

Recently, passive technologies such as Tracab (Tracab AB, Stockholm, Sweden) and Venatrack (Venatrack Ltd, Slough, UK) are providing information in real-time on competitive play through improvements in mathematical algorithms especially developed for movement tracking. The advantage of real-time analysis is the availability of objective performance-related data upon which coaching staff can base their half-time 'team talk' and make immediate decisions on tactical changes and/or substitutions over the course of a match. The video-tracking processes developed by Tracab AB are reportedly based on state-of-the-art image-processing technology and enhanced mathematical algorithms for guiding missiles in the military industry (see www.tracab.com). Venatrack monitors player movements on video at a frequency of 25 measures per second, with accuracy rates for player identification operating at 98 per cent and player position tracking at 98 per cent (Redwood-Brown *et al.*, 2012). A further development is the Spinsight K2 Camera System (Spinsight, Edinburgh, UK). This portable system reportedly provides real-time player tracking using a portable camera configuration with three video images being merged into one to provide a panoramic view of the match (see www.spinsight.com). In comparison to the aforementioned fixed multiple camera systems, the system is apparently transportable, enabling player performance to be monitored anywhere, thus avoiding potential operational problems when analysis of performance in training environments or away games is desired. This combined use of data derived from the same system is welcome as research has shown large discrepancies in information generated from concomitant analyses of play using semi-automated video analysis systems and global positioning technology (Harley *et al.*, 2011; Randers *et al.*, 2010).

Portable electronic tracking devices

In recent times, Global Positioning Systems (GPS) have impacted on the measurement of physical performance in daily training and competition (Coutts and Duffield, 2010). GPS have also been applied to detect fatigue in matches, identify periods of most intense play and identify activity profiles by position, competition level and sport (Aughey, 2011). Indeed, there is a growing body of knowledge examining the use of GPS for analysis in numerous sports, notably Australian rules football (Brewer *et al.*, 2010), cricket (Petersen *et al.*, 2011b), field hockey (Macutkiewicz and Sunderland, 2011), golf (Hayes *et al.*, 2009), rugby league (Waldron *et al.*, 2011) and union (Coughlan *et al.*, 2011), skiing (Brodie *et al.*, 2008), tennis (Duffield *et al.*, 2010) and soccer (Bucheit *et al.*, 2010). GPS receivers estimate their position on earth by triangulating their position based on the receive time for signals sent from satellites orbiting the earth. The units are worn in a harness on the athlete's back to avoid hindrance and to reduce interference with play. They are used to capture data on distances run and movement speeds and are also interfaced to provide physiological information on exercise intensity via heart-rate measures (see www.gpsports.com and www.catapultsports.com). The latest versions of these systems transmit live data to a laptop via wireless connection, enabling immediate analysis, evaluation and feedback. In addition, integrated tri-axis accelerometers can be used to record information on the frequency and intensity of accelerations and impacts, such as tackles and collisions. These events can be identified and incorporated in the analysis to provide an overall index of the physical stresses placed on the player.

While these systems are regularly used in friendly matches and youth competitions, they are generally limited in many sports to measuring and controlling work intensity in training as performers are equipped with electronic material which may be forbidden at professional and senior international level. The accuracy of GPS is influenced by several variables: the number of satellites and their geometrical arrangement relative to each other and the receiver, and the topography of the playing area surroundings. Large buildings notably can affect signal reception. In addition, despite the increased sampling rate of more recent models (>10 Hz), the efficacy of GPS technology to accurately and reliably quantify critical high-speed movements, accelerations and changes in direction at speed over short distances is still questionable at the time of writing this chapter (Jennings *et al.*, 2010). Similarly, contrasting evidence exists on whether the same GPS device should be used by the same player in order to avoid possible inter-unit measurement error (Castellano *et al.*, 2011; Duffield *et al.*, 2010).

The development of electronic tracking systems using small lightweight transponders worn by players provides alternative opportunities for real-time movement data acquisition and analysis. Systems such as the Local Positioning Measurement monitoring system (LPM) collect information on the movements and positions of every player and the ball up to several hundred times per second. Independent research has shown that the LPM system produces highly accurate position and speed data in static and dynamic conditions (Frencken *et al.*, 2010). The LPM system also permits the collection of heart-rate responses to exercise. However, usage is again generally restricted to training, friendly matches and youth competitions played on a single training pitch equipped with the system. Alternatively, it is worthwhile noting that time-motion information on physical performance can be captured at a relatively lower cost to GPS and/or electronic transponders using small accelerometer-based physical activity devices strapped to the athlete's ankle. For example, simple step activity monitors have been used to monitor and record the number of steps over set time intervals and subsequently determine the duration and intensity of work bouts performed in soccer match-play (Orendurff *et al.*, 2010).

Competitive activity profiles: general characteristics and position-specific demands

Within any evidence-based performance framework for sport, and especially at elite levels, knowledge of the physical requirements of play is necessary to aid in the design and application of optimal fitness training strategies in preparation for contemporary competition. Over the last four decades, motion analysis has helped identify the physical performance demands and fitness requirements for competition across many sports. It has aided in determining physical activity profiles across the playing positions respective to many sports, as well as in referees. Information from motion analysis enables objective and realistic decisions to be made for structuring the physical conditioning elements of training programmes. Questions commonly asked by coaching and conditioning personnel about the physical performance of their athletes in competition and training include:

* What are the general contemporary physical characteristics and position-specific demands in my sport?
* Can my players respond to these requirements and the demands directly imposed on them by opposition in competition?
* Are my players contributing physically to all aspects of the game: defence, attack, build-up play?
* Is physical performance in my players consistent throughout games and over the course of the season and have the demands of play evolved over recent seasons?
* Are competitive physical demands adequately replicated in the training we perform?

Irrespective of the sport, the overall work contribution in field sports can be expressed as the total distance covered in a game, since this feature generally determines the energy expenditure irrespective of the speed of movement (Reilly, 2007). Motion analyses have shown that the total distance run in competition varies greatly in relation to the sport. Elite junior male Australian rules footballers are shown to run up to 17 km (Veale *et al.*, 2007), whereas elite senior field hockey players cover around 7 km (Edgecomb and Norton, 2006) per match. Outfield male professional soccer players run on average 8–12 km (Reilly, 2007). In one-day cricket, a fast bowler has been shown to run approximately 16 km over the course of a match (Petersen *et al.*, 2009). In some sports, longitudinal measures of the total distance run have enabled analysis of the evolution of physical activity profiles over seasons. The overall physical demands in professional soccer (Carling *et al.*, 2008) and Australian rules football (Wisbey *et al.*, 2010) match-play notably have increased. In turn, this information has had important consequences for contemporary fitness training strategies.

In time-motion analyses of athletic performance, the total distance covered is generally broken down into discrete movement activities. These activities are coded according to their intensity, which is determined by the speed of actions. Choice of speed thresholds is often arbitrary among practitioners and sports science personnel and some examples of default speed zones for time-motion analysis of sports performance in match-play and training are presented in Table 23.2. Alternatively, speed thresholds used to categorise and quantify physical efforts can also be tailored in relation to the individual physiological capacity of the player (Abt and Lovell, 2009). Club personnel might want to evaluate the frequency of the types of movement or the time spent or distance covered in each category of movement. Traditionally, categories used are classed as standing, walking, jogging, cruising (striding) and sprinting.

In soccer, these categories of movement have been extended to include other activities such as skipping and shuffling (Bloomfield *et al.*, 2004). Additional game-related activities must also be taken into account in the analysis which contribute to overall energy expenditure. These include alterations in pace, unorthodox running modes (backwards and sideways movement) and rapid changes in direction. In Australian rules football, more than half of all sprints performed in competitive matches involved at least one change of direction, mostly within the 0–90 degrees arc and left or right (Dawson *et al.*, 2004). Contemporary Global Positioning Systems provide a means to quantify, in a single index, the amount of stress placed upon a player from actions such as accelerations, decelerations, changes of direction and impacts (McLellan *et al.*, 2011). Other game-related activities include challenging for possession and the execution

Table 23.2 Some examples of default speed zones for time-motion analysis of sports performance (km.hour^{-1})

System	Variable 1	Variable 2	Variable 3	Variable 4	Variable 5	Variable 6	Variable 7
Video-based							
Prozone 3	0.0–7.0	7.1–11.0	11.1–14.0	14.1–19.0	19.1–23.0	>23.0	—
Amisco Pro	0.0–7.0	7.1–11.0	11.1–14.0	14.1–19.0	19.1–23.0	>23.0	—
Tracab	0.0–2.0	2.1–7.3	7.4–14.5	14.6–20.0	>20.0	—	—
GPS							
Catapult	0.0–7.2	7.3–14.4	14.5–21.6	21.7–28.8	>28.8	—	—
GPSports	0.0–7.5	7.6–10.0	10.1–17.5	17.6–20.0	20.1–22.5	22.6–30.0	>30.0
RealTrack Football	0.0–3.0	3.1–6.0	6.1–9.0	9.1–15.0	>15.0	—	—
Electronic transponder							
ZXY Sport Tracking	0.0–5.0	5.1–10.0	10.1–15.0	15.1–25.0	>25.0	—	—

of game-specific skills with the ball. While a common feature of many sports is that only a small percentage of the total distance covered by players is in individual possession of the ball, analyses in professional soccer have shown that the majority (34.3 per cent) of the distance covered was performed at high speeds (>19.1 km.hour⁻¹) (Carling, 2010).

In most sports in which time-motion analyses are employed, activities at lower levels of intensity tend to dominate physical activity profiles. Indeed, in a recent detailed review of time-motion analyses in team sport events, it was shown that sprint-type activities generally constitute 1–10 per cent of the total distance covered (Girard *et al.*, 2011). Research by Spencer *et al.* (2004) on international field hockey players reported that the large majority of the total game time was spent in the low-intensity motions of walking, jogging and standing (46.5±8.1, 40.5±7.0 and 7.4±0.9 per cent, respectively). In comparison, the proportions of time spent in striding and sprinting were 4.1±1.1 and 1.5±0.6 per cent, respectively. Junior elite basketball players covered 7558±575 m per game, of which 1743±317, 1619±280 and 2477±339 m was performed at high, moderate and low intensities, respectively (Ben Abdelkrim *et al.*, 2010b). Data from Petersen *et al.* (2010) for an elite fast bowler playing in international Twenty20 cricket competition showed that around 9 per cent of movement was performed at high intensities (sprinting and striding).

In an earlier related review of literature, Spencer (2005) concluded that the mean distance and duration of sprinting actions in team sports was between 10–20 m and 2–3 s, respectively. Only on rare occasions do team sport players attain maximal speed in competition, and acceleration capacity over short distances is probably more important. High-intensity activity is often unpredictable and intense efforts sometimes follow each other after a short recovery period, resulting in dense phases of work. In general, intense efforts interspersed with brief recoveries (<60 s) are common during the majority of team and racket sports (Bishop *et al.*, 2011). Analyses of physical performance over short periods in professional soccer match-play also show that players transiently perform substantially higher amounts of high-intensity running than the game average (Carling and Dupont, 2011). Gabbett and Mulvey (2008) found that international female players performed repeated-sprint bouts (defined in their study as a minimum of three consecutive sprints, with recovery of less than 21 s between actions) approximately five times per game and that recovery between sprint efforts was generally active in nature (~93 per cent of the time). In intermittent-type sports, the capacity of players to perform high-intensity work repeatedly is therefore essential. Indeed, Krustrup *et al.* (2005) have reported a strong correlation between performance in a field test of intermittent recovery and competitive sprint activity in elite female soccer players.

Information on the frequency of repeated high-intensity efforts and time spent in recovery between discrete intense bouts of exercise is pertinent for designing high-intensity conditioning programmes. Data from motion analyses can also be used to a certain extent to determine the effects of physical conditioning interventions on work activity profiles in match-play. Work by Impellizzeri *et al.* (2006) in youth soccer players demonstrated significant improvements in high-intensity running performance during actual match-play after a period of aerobic interval training. However, there is a lack of information across elite sports on whether fitness training regimens in general provide a sufficient training stimulus to simulate the high-intensity needs specific to competition. While a study in cricket (Petersen *et al.*, 2011a) has shown this to be the case, the same trend was not observed in elite soccer (Gabbett and Mulvey, 2008) or field hockey (Gabbett, 2010).

Work activity profiles can vary across geographical locations and playing standards. For example, substantially greater distances were covered at high intensities in players belonging to the English Premier League compared to peers in the Spanish Liga (Dellal *et al.*, 2011). International-level male basketball players sprinted significantly more than national-level male basketball players (Ben Abdelkrim *et al.*, 2010a). In cricket, test-level fielders covered moderately greater (29–48%) distances in the higher-intensity movement categories (running, striding, and sprinting) than fielders in first-class competition (Petersen *et al.*, 2011b). In contrast, high-intensity activity profiles and fatigue patterns were similar between international and professional domestic soccer players (Bradley *et al.*, 2010). Similarly, high-intensity activity in professional soccer was unrelated to team success as players in lower-ranked teams in the English Premier League covered significantly greater distances compared to peers belonging to teams finishing in the top five positions (Di Salvo *et al.*, 2010). In addition, motion analyses have also demonstrated differences between different formats of the same sport. The shorter formats of cricket (Twenty 20 and one-day) were shown to be more 'physically intensive' per unit of time than multi-day cricket, but a greater overall physical load was the reported in the latter (Petersen *et al.*, 2010). Motion analysis of classical ballet and contemporary dance performance has shown the former to be associated with substantially higher levels of intensity (Wyon *et al.*, 2011). While other factors such as team formation, score line, opposition standard, environmental conditions, match congestion and stage across the season, player dismissals and substitutions, time spent in ball possession and time the ball is in play are also known to substantially affect competitive physical activity profiles, their discussion is beyond the scope of this chapter. For additional information, the reader is referred to work by Carling *et al.* (2005) and Carling *et al.* (2008).

The effect of playing position on the physical contributions of players must be taken into account when evaluating motion analysis data as marked differences are known to exist in the overall work pattern and intensity of various running activities performed in competition. Thus, there is a need for a criterion model for the tailoring of training programmes to suit the particular needs across individual positions. The total distance run by elite junior Australian rules football players ranged from 10,419 m to 16,691 m across playing positions (Veale *et al.*, 2007). Mean distances covered during professional rugby league match-play by hit-up forwards, wide-running forwards, adjustables and outside backs were 3,569 m, 5,561 m, 6,411 m and 6,819 m, respectively (Gabbett *et al.*, 2012). In an analysis of English Premier League soccer, position was shown to have a significant influence on time spent sprinting, running, shuffling, skipping and standing still (Bloomfield *et al.*, 2007). The total number of sprints and explosive and leading sprints performed according to playing position in the European Champions League and UEFA Cup competitions is shown in Table 23.3. In netball, centres have been shown to run significantly greater distances than the other playing positions, covering around 6 km per match compared to distances ranging from 2 to 4.6 km in other positions (O'Donoghue and Loughran, 1998). Fast bowlers in international cricket sprinted twice as often and covered over three times the distance sprinting, with much smaller work-to-recovery ratios in comparison to other positions (Petersen *et al.*, 2010). Finally, analysis of Super 12 rugby union play has shown that backs sprint more often and have a longer duration of each sprint, whereas forward players spent more time in overall work activities (Duthie *et al.*, 2005). Further detailed analyses of sprint patterns in rugby union players during competition showed that forwards commenced sprint actions from a standing start most frequently (41 per cent), whereas backs sprinted from

Table 23.3 Total number of sprints and explosive and leading sprints performed according to positional role in European Champions League and UEFA Cup competition (data from Di Salvo *et al.*, 2010)

	Central defenders	*Wide defenders*	*Central midfielders*	*Wide midfielders*	*Attackers*
Explosive sprints	4.5 ± 4.2	7.2 ± 5.5	6.3 ± 5.8	8.4 ± 6.3	7.2 ± 5.7
Leading sprints	12.8 ± 6.0	22.2 ± 8.5	17.3 ± 8.2	27.4 ± 9.5	22.8 ± 8.8
Total sprints	17.3 ± 8.7	29.5 ± 11.7	23.5 ± 12.2	35.8 ± 13.4	30.0 ± 1.0

standing (29 per cent), walking (29 per cent), jogging (29 per cent) and occasionally striding (13 per cent) starts (Duthie *et al.*, 2006).

Finally, physical activity profiles from time-motion analyses of competition have shown that a decline in exercise intensity is frequently inevitable over the course of competition and successive games, especially when these are played in a short time-frame. The profiling of a player's physical performance can highlight a susceptibility to fatigue, shown up as a drop-off in efforts towards the end of the first or second half of games or a need for a long recovery period after successive high-intensity actions. A fall in activity may also be observed towards the end of competition and after breaks in play. In professional soccer, a substantial drop in running performance was observed at the beginning of the second half and was linked to the players getting 'cold' in the half-time break (Mohr *et al.*, 2004). Work by Coutts *et al.* (2010) in Australian rules football has demonstrated significant reductions in the total distance covered in the second (−7.3 per cent), third (−5.5 per cent) and fourth (−10.7 per cent) quarters compared to the first quarter and high-intensity running (> 14.4 km.hour^{-1}) was substantially reduced after the first quarter. Activity profiles of elite-level female field hockey players during competition have shown that players undertake significantly less high-intensity exercise in the second half of the game, despite the continual substitution rule (MacLeod *et al.*, 2007). However, the total distance covered or that in sprinting in some sports is unaffected across playing halves, as observed in an analysis of professional futsal competition (Barbero-Alvarez *et al.*, 2008). Finally, fatigue may be evident as a prolonged recovery during the game itself. After the five-minute period during which the amount of high-intensity running peaked, performance was reduced by 50 per cent in the following five minutes compared with the game average in professional soccer players (Bradley *et al.*, 2009). In addition, the authors reported that transient declines in high-intensity running immediately after the most intense five-minute period were most evident in attackers and central defenders compared to other positional roles. These data show there is a need for countermeasures to fatigue in order to maintain physical performance throughout match-play. As well as physical conditioning interventions, other potentially useful means of preventing drops in and maintaining competitive physical performance include appropriate warm-up and nutritional interventions, post-match recovery treatment (e.g. cryotherapy, sports massage, compression tights) and the use of substitutions (Carling *et al.*, 2011).

Concluding remarks

A key step in the conditioning process for the contemporary team sport player is the monitoring of exercise intensity via time-motion analyses during competition and training. The events underpinning physical performance are recorded and analysed to quantify the physical efforts of the player. Technological advances in computer software and digital video techniques, as well as miniaturised portable tracking devices, have enabled accumulation of a substantial body of knowledge on the physical demands of play, despite the rules and regulations of certain sports restricting the use of some approaches during competition. Contemporary systems are now providing opportunities for real-time monitoring of physical activity, enabling split-second evaluation and objective decision making at any moment during performance.

References

Abt, G. and Lovell, R. (2009) 'The use of individualized speed and intensity thresholds for determining the distance run at high-intensity in professional soccer', *Journal of Sports Sciences*, 27: 893–8.

Andersson, H.A., Randers, M.B., Heiner-Møller, A., Krustrup, P. and Mohr, M. (2010) 'Elite female soccer players perform more high-intensity running when playing in international games compared with domestic league games', *Journal of Strength and Conditioning Research*, 24: 912–9.

Aughey, R.J. (2011) 'Applications of GPS technologies to field sports', *International Journal of Sports Physiology and Performance*, 6: 295–310.

Bangsbo, J., Nørregaard, L. and Thorsøe, F. (1991) 'Activity profile of competition soccer', *Canadian Journal of Sports Science*, 16: 110–16.

Barbero-Alvarez, J.C., Soto, V.M., Barbero-Alvarez, V. and Granda-Vera, J. (2008) 'Match analysis and heart rate of futsal players during competition', *Journal of Sports Sciences*, 26: 63–73.

Barris, S. and Button, C. (2008) 'A review of vision-based motion analysis in sport', *Sports Medicine*, 38: 1025–43.

Barros, R.M.L., Misuta, M.S., Menezes, R.P., Figueroa, P.J., Moura, F.A., Cunha, S.A., Anido, R. And Leite, N.J. (2007) 'Analysis of the distances covered by first division Brazilian soccer players obtained with an automatic tracking method', *Journal of Sports Science and Medicine*, 6: 233–42.

Ben Abdelkrim, N., Castagna, C., El Fazaa, S. and El Ati, J. (2010a) 'The effect of players' standard and tactical strategy on game demands in men's basketball', *Journal of Strength and Conditioning Research*, 24: 2652–62.

Ben Abdelkrim, N., Castagna, C., Jabri, I., Battikh, T., El Fazaa, S. and El Ati, J. (2010b) 'Activity profile and physiological requirements of junior elite basketball players in relation to aerobic-anaerobic fitness', *Journal of Strength and Conditioning Research*, 24: 2330–42.

Bishop, D., Girard, O. and Mendez-Villanueva, A. (2011) 'Repeated-sprint ability – Part II: recommendations for training', *Sports Medicine*, 41: 741–56.

Bloomfield, J., Polman, R.C.J. and O'Donoghue, P.G. (2004) 'The "Bloomfield Movement Classification": Motion analysis of individuals in team sports', *International Journal of Performance Analysis of Sport*, 4(2): 20–31.

Bloomfield, J., Polman, R.C.J. and O'Donoghue, P.G. (2007) 'Physical demands of different positions in FA Premier League soccer', *Journal of Sports Science and Medicine*, 6: 63–70.

Bradley, P.S., Sheldon, W., Wooster, B., Olsen, P., Boanas, P. and Krustrup, P. (2009) 'High-intensity running in English FA Premier League soccer matches', *Journal of Sports Sciences*, 27: 159–68.

Bradley P.S., Di Mascio, M., Peart, D., Olsen, P. and Sheldon, B. (2010) 'High-intensity activity profiles of elite soccer players at different performance levels', *Journal of Strength and Conditioning Research*, 24: 2343–51.

Brewer, C., Dawson, B., Heasman, J., Stewart, G. and Cormack, S. (2010) 'Movement pattern comparisons in elite (AFL) and sub-elite (WAFL) Australian football games using GPS', *Journal of Science and Medicine in Sport*, 13: 618–23.

Brodie, M., Walmsley, A. and Page, W. (2008) 'Fusion motion capture: A prototype system using inertial measurement units and GPS for the biomechanical analysis of ski racing', *Sports Technology*, 1: 17–28.

Buchheit, M., Mendez-Villanueva, A., Simpson, B.M. and Bourdon P.C. (2010) 'Match running performance and fitness in youth soccer', *International Journal of Sports Medicine*, 31: 818–25.

Carling, C. (2010) 'Analysis of physical activity profiles when running with the ball in a professional soccer team', *Journal of Sports Sciences*, 28: 319–28.

Carling, C. and Dupont, G. (2011) 'Are declines in physical performance associated with a reduction in skill-related performance during professional soccer match-play?', *Journal of Sports Sciences*, 21: 63–7.

Carling, C., Williams, A.M. and Reilly, T. (2005) *The Handbook of Soccer Match Analysis*, London: Routledge.

Carling, C., Bloomfield, J., Nelsen, L. and Reilly, T. (2008) 'The role of motion analysis in elite soccer: Contemporary performance measurement techniques and work-rate data', *Sports Medicine*, 38: 839–62.

Carling, C., Reilly, T. and Williams, A.M. (2009) *Performance Assessment for Field Sports*, London: Taylor and Francis.

Carling, C., Le Gall, F. and Dupont, G. (2011) 'Are physical performance and injury risk in a professional soccer team in match-play affected over a prolonged period of fixture congestion?', *International Journal of Sports Medicine*, 32: 1–7.

Castellano, J., Casamichana, D., Calleja-González, J., San Román, J. and Ostojic, S.M. (2011) 'Reliability and accuracy of 10 Hz GPS devices for short-distance exercise', *Journal of Sports Science and Medicine*, 10: 233–4.

Coughlan, G.F., Green, B.S., Pook, P.T., Toolan, E. and O'Connor, S.P. (2011) 'Physical game demands in elite rugby union: A Global Positioning System analysis and possible implications for rehabilitation', *Journal of Orthopaedic Sports Physical Therapy*, 41: 600–5.

Coutts, A.J. and Duffield, R. (2010) 'Validity and reliability of GPS devices for measuring movement demands of team sports', *Journal of Science and Medicine in Sport*, 13: 133–5.

Coutts, A.J., Quinn J., Hocking J., Castagna, C. and Rampinini, E. (2010) 'Match running performance in elite Australian Rules Football', *Journal of Science and Medicine in Sport*, 13: 543–8.

Dawson, B., Hopkinson, R., Appleby, B., Stewart, G. and Roberts, C. (2004) 'Comparison of training activities and game demands in the Australian Football League', *Journal of Science and Medicine in Sport*, 7: 292–301.

Dellal, A., Chamari, K., Wong, D.P., Ahmaidi, S., Keller, D., Barros, R., Bisciotti, G.N. and Carling, C. (2011) 'Comparison of physical and technical performance in European soccer match-play: FA Premier League and La Liga', *European Journal of Sport Science*, 11: 51–9.

Di Salvo, V., Gregson, W., Atkinson, G., Tordoff, P. and Drust, B. (2009) 'Analysis of high intensity activity in Premier League Soccer', *International Journal of Sports Medicine*, 3: 205–12.

Di Salvo, V., Baron, R., González-Haro, C., Gormasz, C., Pigozzi, F. and Bachl, N. (2010) 'Sprinting analysis of elite soccer players during European Champions League and UEFA Cup matches', *Journal of Sports Sciences*, 28: 1489–94.

Drust, B., Atkinson, G. and Reilly, T. (2007) 'Future perspectives in the evaluation of the physiological demands of soccer', *Sports Medicine*, 37: 783–805.

Duffield, R., Reid, M., Baker, J. and Spratford, W. (2010) 'Accuracy and reliability of GPS devices for measurement of movement patterns in confined spaces for court-based sports', *Journal of Science and Medicine in Sport*, 13: 523–5.

Duthie, G., Pyne, D. and Hooper, S. (2005) 'Time motion analysis of 2001 and 2002 super 12 rugby', *Journal of Sports Science*, 23: 523–30.

Duthie, G.M., Pyne, D.B., Marsh, D.J. and Hooper, S.L. (2006) 'Sprint patterns in rugby union players during competition', *Journal of Strength and Conditioning Research*, 20: 208–14.

Edgecomb, S.J. and Norton, K.I. (2006) 'Comparison of global positioning and computer-based tracking systems for measuring player movement distance during Australian Football', *Journal of Science and Medicine in Sport*, 9: 25–32.

Feito, Y., Bassett, D.R. and Thompson, D.L. (2011) 'Evaluation of activity monitors in controlled and free-living environments', *Medicine in Science and Sports and Exercise*, 43: 350–6.

Frencken, W.G., Lemmink, K.A. and Delleman, N.J. (2010) 'Soccer-specific accuracy and validity of the local position measurement (LPM) system', *Journal of Science and Medicine in Sport*, 13: 641–5.

Gabbett, T.J. (2010) 'GPS analysis of elite women's field hockey training and competition', *Journal of Strength and Conditioning Research*, 24: 1321–4.

Gabbett, T.J. and Mulvey, M.J. (2008) 'Time-motion analysis of small-sided training games and competition in elite women soccer players', *Journal of Strength and Conditioning Research*, 22: 543–52.

Gabbett, T.J., Jenkins D.G. and Abernethy, B. (2012) 'Physical demands of professional rugby league training and competition using microtechnology', *Journal of Science and Medicine in Sport*, 15: 80–6.

Girard, O., Mendez-Villanueva, A. and Bishop, D. (2011) 'Repeated-sprint ability – part I: factors contributing to fatigue', *Sports Medicine*, 41: 673–94.

Harley, J.A., Lovell, R.J., Barnes, C.A., Portas, M.D. and Weston, M. (2011) 'The interchangeability of Global Positioning System and semiautomated video-based performance data during elite soccer match play', *Journal of Strength and Conditioning Research*, 25: 2334–6.

Harrington, D.M., Welk, G.J. and Donnelly, A.E. (2011) 'Validation of MET estimates and step measurement using the ActivPAL physical activity logger', *Journal of Sports Sciences*, 29: 627–33.

Hayes, P.R., Van Paridon, K., French, D.N., Thomas, K. and Gordon, D.A. (2009) 'Development of a simulated round of golf', *International Journal of Sports Physiology and Performance*, 4: 506–16.

Hughes, M.D. and Franks, I.M. (2004) *Notational Analysis of Sport: Systems for Better Coaching and Performance*, London: E. and F.N. Spon.

Impellizzeri, F.M., Marcora, S.M., Castagna, C., Reilly, T., Sassi, A., Iaia, F.M. and Rampinini, E. (2006) 'Physiological and performance effects of generic versus specific aerobic training in soccer players', *International Journal of Sports Medicine*, 27: 483–92.

James, N. (2006) 'The role of notational analysis in soccer coaching', *International Journal of Sports Science and Coaching*, 1: 185–98.

Jennings, D., Cormack, S., Coutts, A.J., Boyd, L. and Auger, R.J. (2010) 'The validity and reliability of GPS units for measuring distance in team sport specific running patterns', *International Journal of Sports Physiology and Performance*, 5: 328–41.

Krustrup, P., Mohr, M., Ellingsgaard, H. and Bangsbo, J. (2005) 'Physical demands during an elite female soccer game: Importance of training status', *Medicine and Science in Sports and Exercise*, 37: 1242–8.

Macutkiewicz, D. and Sunderland, C. (2011) 'The use of GPS to evaluate activity profiles of elite women hockey players during match-play', *Journal of Sports Sciences*, 29: 967–73.

MacLeod, H., Bussell, C. and Sunderland, C. (2007) 'Time-motion analysis of elite women's field hockey, with particular reference to maximum intensity movement patterns', *International Journal of Performance Analysis in Sport*, 7(2): 1–12.

MacLeod, H., Morris, J., Nevill, A. and Sunderland, C. (2009) 'The validity of a non-differential Global Positioning System for assessing player movement patterns in field hockey', *Journal of Sports Sciences*, 27: 121–8.

McLellan, C.P., Lovell, D.I. and Gass, G.C. (2011) 'Biochemical and endocrine responses to impact and collision during elite Rugby League match play', *Journal of Strength and Conditioning Research*, 25: 1553–62.

Mohr, M., Krustrup, P., Nybo, L., Nielsen, J.J. and Bangsbo, J. (2004) 'Muscle temperature and sprint performance during soccer matches – beneficial effect of re-warm-up at half-time', *Scandinavian Journal of Medicine and Science in Sports*, 14: 156–62.

Mohr, M., Krustrup, P., Andersson, H., Kirkendal, D. and Bangsbo, J. (2008) 'Match activities of elite women soccer players at different performance levels', *Journal of Strength and Conditioning Research*, 22: 341–9.

O'Donoghue, P. and Loughran, B. (1998) 'Analysis of distance covered during intervarsity netball competition', *Proceedings of the IV World Congress of Notational Analysis of Sport*, University of Porto, Porto, Portugal, 75.

Orendurff, M.S., Walker, J.D., Jovanovic, M., Tulchin, K.L., Levy, M. and Hoffmann, D.K. (2010) 'Intensity and duration of intermittent exercise and recovery during a soccer match', *Journal of Strength and Conditioning Research*, 24: 2683–92.

Petersen, C.J., Pyne, D.B., Portus, M.R., Karppinen, S. and Dawson, B. (2009) 'Variability in movement patterns during One Day Internationals by a cricket fast bowler', *International Journal of Sports Physiology and Performance*, 4: 278–81.

Petersen, C.J., Pyne, D., Dawson, B., Portus, M. and Kellett, A. (2010) 'Movement patterns in cricket vary by both position and game format', *Journal of Sports Sciences*, 28: 45–52.

Petersen, C.J., Pyne, D., Dawson, B., Kellett, A.D. and Portus, M.R. (2011a) 'Comparison of training and game demands of national level cricketers', *Journal of Strength and Conditioning Research*, 25: 1306–11.

Petersen, C.J., Pyne, D.B., Portus, M.R. and Dawson, B.T. (2011b) 'Comparison of player movement patterns between 1-day and test cricket', *Journal of Strength and Conditioning Research*, 25: 1368–73.

Pino, P., Martinez-Santos, R., Moreno, I. and Padilla, C. (2007) 'Automatic analysis of football games using GPS on real time', *Journal of Sports Science and Medicine*, 10: 9.

Randers, M.B., Mujika, I., Hewitt, A., Santisteban, J., Bischoff, R., Solano, R., Zubillaga, A., Peltola, E., Krustrup, P. and Mohr, M. (2010) 'Application of four different football match analysis systems: A comparative study', *Journal of Sports Sciences*, 28: 171–82.

Redwood-Brown, A., Cranton, W. and Sunderland, C. (2012) 'Validation of a real-time video analysis system for soccer', *International Journal of Sports Medicine*, 33(8): 635–40.

Reilly, T. (2007) *Science of Training: Soccer*, London: Routledge.

Reilly, T. and Thomas, V. (1976) 'A motion analysis of work-rate in different positional roles in professional football match-play', *Journal of Human Movement Studies*, 2: 87–97.

Sathyan, T., Humphrey, D. and Hedley, M. (2011) 'WASP – a system and algorithms for accurate radio localization using low-cost hardware', *IEEE Transactions on Systems, Man and Cybernetics – Part C: Applications and Reviews,* 41: 211–22.

Spencer, M., Lawrence, S., Rechichi, C., Bishop, D., Dawson, B. and Goodman, C. (2004) 'Time-motion analysis of elite field hockey, with special reference to repeated-sprint activity', *Journal of Sports Science*, 22: 843–50.

Spencer, M., Bishop, D., Dawson, B. and Goodman, C. (2005) 'Physiological and metabolic responses of repeated-sprint activities: Specific to field-based team sports', *Sports Medicine*, 35: 1025–44.

Veale, J.P., Pearce, A.J. and John, S. (2007) 'Profile of position movement demands in elite junior Australian Rules Football', *Sixth World Congress on Science and Football, Book of Abstracts*, 16–20.

Vučković, G., Perš, J., James, N. and Hughes, M. (2010) 'Measurement error associated with the SAGIT/ Squash computer tracking software', *European Journal of Sport Science*, 10: 129–40.

Waldron, M., Twist, C., Highton, J., Worsfold, P. and Daniels, M. (2011) 'Movement and physiological match demands of elite rugby league using portable Global Positioning Systems', *Journal of Sports Sciences*, 29: 1223–30.

Webber, S.C. and Porter, M.M. (2009) 'Monitoring mobility in older adults using Global Positioning System (GPS) watches and accelerometers: A feasibility study', *Journal of Aging and Physical Activity*, 17: 455–67.

Wisbey, B., Montgomery, P.G., Pyne, D.B. and Rattray, B. (2010) 'Quantifying movement demands of AFL football using GPS tracking', *Journal of Science and Medicine in Sport*, 13: 531–6.

Wyon, M.A., Twitchett, E., Angioi, M., Clarke, F., Metsios, G. and Koutedakis, Y. (2011) 'Time motion and video analysis of classical ballet and contemporary dance performance', *International Journal of Sports Medicine*, 32: 851–5.

24

TACTICAL CREATIVITY

Daniel Memmert

GERMAN SPORT UNIVERSITY COLOGNE, GERMANY

Summary

This chapter discusses current models and paradigms of tactical creativity in sports to give a theoretical framework for performance analysis of creativity in sports. After definitions, different components of creativity and the role of different types of play/practice in developing creativity are listed. Then possible assessments to evaluate creative behaviour in team sports are described. Here, a detailed comparison between video tests and game test situations of creativity is presented. This chapter is enclosed by different factors (attention, motivation) which influence tactical creativity in team sports.

Introduction

One of the world's best soccer players, Lionel Messi, is able to make decisions in specific soccer situations which are unexpected and therefore less likely to be anticipated by his opponents. Creative solutions are of crucial importance in all team sports. By means of creative, unexpected solutions, basketball, soccer or team handball players are more likely to set up their teammates' shots on goal.

Since the work of Guilford (1967), the systematic scientific examination of creative processes has become an established part of psychology and has delivered important results in various contexts, such as science, literature, music, art, religion and politics (for an overview, see Runco, 2007). In sport sciences, the notion of creativity has come to play an important role in sport didactics, sport pedagogy, movement science, dancing science and sport psychology in the last few decades.

Without being able to delve into the history of creativity research in any more detail (overview by Runco, 2007), one must give special consideration to the work of Robert J. Sternberg. In his integration model 'investment approach to creativity: buy low, sell high' (Sternberg and Lubart, 1991, 1992, 1995), he succeeded in uniting different theoretical designs into one draft framework (see Figure 24.1). This includes the componential theory by Amabile (1983), the systems approach by Csikszentmihalyi (1988), the synectic model by Gordon (1961), as well as the 'triarchic theory of intelligence' by Sternberg (1985). Beyond this, it incorporated patterns of results from studies on personality (Barron, 1965), problem solving (Getzels and Csikszentmihalyi, 1976), creative styles (Kirton, 1976), as well as different environmental influences (Simonton, 1988).

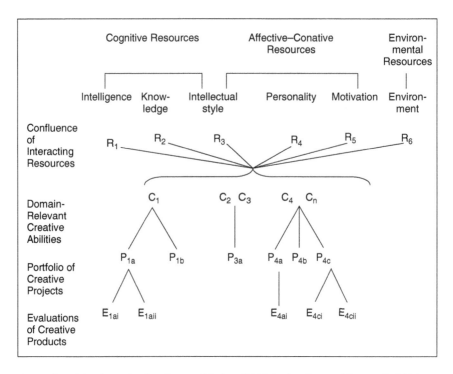

Figure 24.1 Creativity theory by Sternberg and Lubart (1991; in Amelang and Bartussek, 2006)

As shown in Figure 24.1, the authors distinguished four different levels in their model: interacting resources, domain-specific 'creative' abilities, a portfolio of 'creative' projects and assessments of the 'creative' products. Originally, the model aimed to depict the creative process from start (required resources and abilities) to finish (assessment of the product).

Sternberg and Lubart (1991) initially postulated six resources (R_{1-6}), which are assigned to the three areas of cognition (intelligence, knowledge), affective–conative factor (personality, motivation) and environment, in which 'intellectual styles' are regarded as a 'mixed resource' between the first two categories. Sternberg and Lubart (1991: 5) assumed that all resources are connected with each other in a complex way and depending on the given task in the generation of domain-specific creative solutions (level 2; C_{1-n}). In a first multivariate validation study ($N = 48$), the authors showed that the five resources – the environment factor was not taken into account – give a sufficiently exact prediction of the creative performances (as in the sum of scores from drawings, stories, scientific problem solving, etc.), with a multiple correlation coefficient of $R = .81$. The measurement of the cognitive and affective–conative resources was conducted by means of an extensive test battery (for more details, see Sternberg and Lubart, 1991), with fluctuations in the intercorrelations of the predictor variables of between .09 and .68.

The importance of tactical creativity in sports seems to be increasing due to coaches' ability to collect more and more information about their opponents. For example, by means of game observation and game analysis, it is possible to study the individual tactical behaviour of players (e.g. feints and defensive behaviour in one-on-one-situations), the tactical interaction of a group of players (specific combinations in the offensive or defensive) and the general game strategy of a team (e.g. using more counter-attacks, double-teaming players).

Definition of creativity

The fundamental point of the research group of Guilford was the separation of two different cognitive thinking processes, which were later picked up by team sport research, too (Memmert and Roth, 2007). While convergent thinking processes aim for so-called ideal solutions for problems, divergent thinking processes try to generate a variety of new and not necessarily self-evident solutions. For team and racket sports, two different cognitive thinking processes can be discriminated: tactical game intelligence and tactical creativity.

- **Tactical game intelligence (convergent tactical thinking):** in team and racket sports, tactical game intelligence is understood as the production of the best solution for specific individual, group or team tactic match situations.
- **Tactical creativity (divergent tactical thinking):** in team and racket sports, tactical creativity is understood as the generation of a variety of solutions in specific individual, group and team tactic situations which are surprising, seldom and/or original.

This classification also corresponds to the consensus of coaching textbooks in sports supporting the balance between planned behaviour and improvised creative behaviour (Reilly, 1996; Smith and Cushion, 2006).

For the operationalization of tactical creativity, three different characteristics are often used, namely *originality*, *flexibility* and *fluency*, which Guilford and his research group identified by means of factor analysis in 1967.

- **Originality:** the exceptionality of tactical solutions can be rated by experts.
- **Flexibility:** the variety of tactical solutions is determined by the diversity of actions/ answers of the test persons.
- **Fluency:** the number of tactical solutions that test persons generate for a specific match situation.

In differential psychology, there is a multitude of studies that are concerned with the correlation between divergent and convergent cognitive thinking performances (for a review, see Runco, 2007). For the explanation of variance between 20 and 30 per cent, there is a controversial discussion of different models. The threshold hypothesis assumes that high intelligence is not identical to according creativity but rather a prerequisite for high creativity. The first field studies in team sports support the current trend of psychological studies and therefore do not confirm the threshold model. New data, however, have identified positive correlations between both cognitions (between .36 and .71; see Memmert and Roth, 2007). A higher game intelligence indeed seems to go hand in hand with a higher creativity value. So far, there are almost no examinations which trace the development of tactical creativity in sports. A first cross-sectional study (peer group: 7, 10 and 13 years) suggests that children do not follow a linear development (Memmert, 2010b). Whilst there are significant improvements in tactical creativity from the age of seven until ten, there seems to be stagnation after that. Findings from neuroscience support these assumptions because both the absolute number of synapses and the density of synapses reach their maximum at this age (Bekhtereva *et al.*, 2001).

From a methodological point of view, there are generally two ways of training tactical intelligence and tactical creativity:

- **'Deliberate play':** the uninstructed and free operation in game-oriented, unstructured situations.
- **'Deliberate practice':** the instructionalized operation in routine-centred, structured situations with the aim of effectively improving specific individual performance criteria.

Evidence from children and youth sports provides a basis for a convergence of the two prevalent research programmes (expertise research, creativity research) that have not been discussed in the same context yet. Both results suggest that practical experiences and early play are important influences on the development of creativity in sports. In this case, specific experiences (such as deliberated practice) over a long period of time (ten-year rule) are necessary for the attainment of expertise (e.g. Helsen *et al.*, 1998; Kalinowski, 1985; Monsaas, 1985). At the same time, current theoretical approaches and empirical research regarding the development of creativity (Csikszentmihalyi, 1999; Kurtzberg and Amabile, 2001; Martindale, 1990; Milgram, 1990; Smith *et al.*, 1995; Sternberg and Lubart, 1995) support the view that gathering diversified and even non-specific experience (such as deliberated play) over years is an ideal medium for the development of creative thinking.

By means of an experimental field study (treatment: 18 real training sessions of youth players) in the sport of basketball, Greco *et al.* (2010) were able to show that a *deliberate play* training programme leads to greater improvements in both convergent and divergent tactical thinking than the training of a control group. Whilst the deliberate play group operated in relatively unstructured majority/minority situations (1×2, 2×3 and 3×4) or situations with a neutral player (1×1 +1, 2×2 +1, 3×3 +1 and 4×4 +1), the control group practised traditional, basketball-specific routines according to precise guidelines (Lumsden, 2001). Further empirical research is missing which shows that creativity is trainable in later stages of player's development (e.g. adult training scenarios).

Tactical creativity tasks

Whilst physical parameters such as distances covered or performed speeds are easy to analyse, tactical parameters or even creativity are much harder to evaluate in team sports. On the one hand, game observations are performed under field conditions and have therefore very high ecological validity (Leser, 2006). On the other hand, however, due to the high number of confounding variables (e.g. daily constitution of players, pitch conditions, opponent's influence), the internal validity is very low. Thus, the method of observation is the less common diagnostic instrument to assess the creative performance of players in team sports.

In psychology, usually test procedures are used in which all possible ideas and solutions which come to one's mind for a task must be named (for an overview, see Runco, 2007). For example, a subtest of the well-known divergent thinking test for pre-school and school children involves giving them a pen and a sheet with 24 ovals (Krampen, 1996) with the instruction to give their creativity free rein and draw in the ovals anything that comes to mind. The children's performances were judged using the three above-described observation criteria of originality, flexibility and fluency. Two independent expert coaches judged the unusualness and innovativeness of the solutions for each sheet. For flexibility, all suggested solutions were classified into 18 different categories (e.g. fruit, vegetables, animals, people, food, toys, vehicles, etc.). Fluency was measured by the number of ovals that a subject submitted per sheet.

The tests developed for the evaluation of tactical creativity in sports go in the same direction and can be classified into two different categories (see Table 24.1). These include ecologically valid game test situations and relatively high-standardized specific tactical creativity tasks.

Table 24.1 Description of sport-specific divergent thinking tests which evaluate tactical creativity in sport (from Memmert *et al.*, 2010)

Label	Task	Authors (examples)
Game test situation	This instrument contains a context-dependent, real-world setting that can directly provoke tactical tasks in ecologically valid situations. Participants' tactical behaviour is recorded on videotape and their tactical decisions are analysed by expert coders using a subsequent concept-oriented expert rating system (criteria: originality, flexibility).	Memmert (2006, 2007, 2010a); Memmert and Roth (2007)
Video test	In this decision task, participants watch sport-specific videos. The image is frozen after one minute. The participants have to imagine themselves as the acting player and name all opportunities that might possibly lead to a goal. The answers are evaluated according to the criteria of originality, flexibility and fluency.	Johnson and Raab (2003); Memmert (2010b)

Video test

Video tests capture the individual components of creative performance under standardized conditions. The test persons are given cognitive tasks with special demands and are asked to answer based on their best outcome. For example, in relatively high-standardized specific tactical creativity tests, athletes have to view brief video sequences of a sport game (e.g. basketball, soccer) in which, for example, attacking players play against defending players (see Figure 24.2b). At the end of each clip, the image was frozen for a period of time. The players had to imagine themselves as the player with the ball and had to name all opportunities that may possibly lead to a goal. The motor executions (e.g. pass with the non-dominant hand, indirect pass) could also be mentioned here. The experimenter noted the players' answers on a specially designed sheet which contained all appropriate tactical decisions. All participants had to view several (up to 30) sport-specific video scenes.

The above-described observation criteria of originality, flexibility and fluency are usually used for the athletes' performances (see Charles and Runco, 2001 for a similar procedure in general creativity measurements). For example, the assessments of the judges could be varied between 1 (= not creative at all) and 5 (= very creative) for each tactical decision and for each of the video situations, respectively. For *flexibility*, all possible tactical decisions in each situation could be categorized into different solution options (e.g. perform a one-on-one action, shoot at goal with jump throw, no-look-pass and pass with a feint). One point could be given for each larger category selected by a subject for the video sequence. The precise number of (appropriate) answers given by a subject for each video scene could finally be used for *fluency*.

By means of creative tests, also specific and isolated subcomponents of creativity can be measured, controlled and repeated. However, very often video tests fail practical relevance and the isolated attendance of creative demands does not ensure their appearance in more complex situations (Memmert, 2011).

Game test situations

Game test situations are able to study human behaviour in natural, complex and ecologically valid situations of team sports. They contain a context-dependent, real-world setting which can directly provoke creative behaviour in recurring comparable situations. This new idea has been extensively described by Memmert (2011) in a chapter of the *Encyclopedia of Creativity* (Runco and Pritzker, 2011).

Game test situations are simple forms of game play with clearly defined playing conditions and rules as well as specified numbers of players. The basic idea and the rules are determined so that a high number of specific tactical situations can be induced without standardizing the actions of the participating players (Memmert and Harvey, 2008). Therefore, the most essential properties of game sports survive (e.g. the interaction process between and the game goal of the different parties, as well as the game idea). Also, the tactical abilities of interest emerge more or less isolated and in an adequately high number so that the performance can be assessed. Game test situations involve different kinds of motor skills (e.g. hand, feet, hockey stick) in a system where players take turns (two rounds for each person). Therefore, positions and players/opponents can be systematically varied.

For example, in the game test situation 'making use of gaps', the pitch is separated into three different, smaller fields (see Figure 24.2a). There are two children in each of the outer fields and three in the central field. The pairs in the outer fields have to pass the ball to each other with their hands without entering the central field and without letting the defending team get ball possession. The defending team must avoid passes and is also not allowed to leave their field. The pitch is limited by gym mats on both sides and a rope above the central field. If the children do not find any gaps, they have to pass the ball to their team member.

Memmert (2007) used concept-oriented expert rating systems for the evaluation of the tactical creativity of players in game test situations (see Figure 24.2c). For example, the characterization of the tactical element 'making use of gaps' stands for the demand for spatial decision making in match situations in which gaps are used adequately. Therefore, it has to be assessed whether or not the children have found the optimum gap. The technical execution of the passes is not evaluated. Experts in a particular team game have to evaluate all the children's actions according to the above-mentioned characterizations. The assessment is based on a scale which has been validated by external experts and which the evaluators got to know by means of a multitude of exemplary video sequences.

For the future, game test situations seem to be particularly interesting for children and youth training (diagnostics of development and talent) and the evaluation of theories of training tactics.

A detailed comparison between video tests and game test situations

Table 24.2 gives an overview of specific possibilities and limits of both approaches (video tests vs. game test situations). All in all, the video tests are definitely less complex (e.g. stimuli, response options, etc.) than the game test situations. Distinct advantages of the video tests are the clear test situations in the video sequences so that almost no confounding variables (e.g. conditional or technical factors) appear. In contrast, the performances in game test situations are always confounded with partial performances of the test persons. For example, motor skills interact with tactical solutions. Of course, the technical skills of a player have an influence on the solution of tactical situations. This has to be avoided so that one does not unconsciously assess the observed motor performances of the test person but exclusively concentrates on the expected tactical actions of the player. The observation of motor actions for the assessment of tactical actions is technically possible in videos, too, but it is rarely used and applicable only to some extent. In game test situations, however, the motor–action coupling is given by nature.

At present, the interactivity with the medium of the huge screen is quite low for most of the published approaches; in contrast, the interaction between offensive and defensive players

Tactical creativity

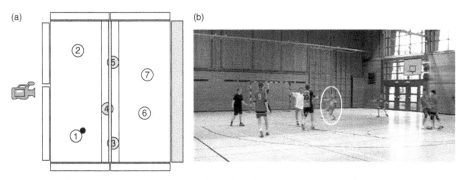

Originality of solutions to the situation (using gaps or passing)	Flexibility in the solutions to the situation (using gaps or passing)	Scaling	Anchor examples
Way above average (very unusual)	Two or more (different, original actions)	10	The subject demonstrated different, highly unusual solutions to situations. The gaps and passes found were absolutely unique.
Way above average (unusual)	Two or more (different, original actions)	9	The subject demonstrated different, unusual solutions to situations. Finding of gaps or passes were unique.
Above average (rare)	Two (different, original/rare actions)	8	The subject demonstrated different, still unusual solutions to situations. The gaps and passes found were very rare.
Average (rather rare)	Two (different, rare actions)	7	The subject demonstrated two different solutions to situations which were not unusual, but still very rare. The gaps and passes found were very surprising.
Average (quite rare)	Two (different, rare/new actions)	6	The subject demonstrated two different solutions to situations which were not unusual but rare. The gaps and passes found were surprising.
Just below average (still new)	One (rare action)	5	The subject demonstrated one solution to situations which was not the usual standard but which had already occurred. The gaps and passes found were still innovative.
Just below average (very little new)	One (new action)	4	The subject demonstrated one solution to situations which was not the usual standard, but which had already occurred often. The gaps and passes found were still innovative.
Below average (rather standard)	none	3	The subject generally offered standard solutions to situations which had been displayed often. The gaps and passes found were rarely innovative.
Way below average (almost all standard)	none	2	The subject almost exclusively offered standard solutions to situations which had all been displayed already. The gaps and passes found were very rarely innovative.
Way below average (only standard)	none	1	The subject only offered standard solutions to situations. The gaps and passes found were never new.

Figure 24.2 (a) Diagram of the game test situation 'making use of gaps' (pitch dimensions = 8 × 7 metres; width of the midsection = 1 metre; height of the line above the midsection = 1.50 metres; distance between video camera and pitch = 8 metres; Memmert, 2007, 2010); (b) video-test situation in team handball. Three defenders play against three offenders. The player in the middle, who cannot be seen during the test, would be the ideal solution in this match situation (Memmert and Furley, 2007); (c) Scaling for the evaluation of tactical creativity (Memmert and Roth, 2007)

Table 24.2 Advantages and disadvantages of different tests to measure tactical creativity: A detailed comparison between video tests and game test situations

	Video tests	Game test situations
Complexity	Low	High
Confounding variables (teammate, etc.)	Low	Middle to high
Motor–action coupling	Only middle	High
Interactivity	Low	High
Authenticity of situations	Low	High
Transferability in practice	Low	High
One-dimensional structure of tasks	Given	Nearly given
Density of relevant actions	High	Middle to high
Relative consistency of conditions	High	Middle
Experimental manipulations	High	Middle to high

as well as team members is always given in game test situations. The game test situations have a high authenticity regarding complex match situations, which is rather not the case for video tests due to their artificial set-up in a laboratory setting. Since they only assess isolated, partial performances, the results from the video tests can be transferred to practical exercise scenarios only to a certain extent. Game test situations, however, are of high practical relevance since the test persons operate in almost realistic field conditions.

Another advantage of video tests is that the selected video sequences can be chosen and adjusted to specific tactical decision performances. In game test situations, it is more difficult to provoke tactical actions of the test persons which then cause only one isolated tactical partial performance. For example, in the game test situation 'making use of gaps', running into space and asking for the ball is restricted by the fact that every player has their set position, which they must not leave. Another advantage of video tests is that, through tactical responses, the test persons are forced to react to many different comparable situations. This can only be set up adequately if the test persons operate in game test situations for a long period of time (ca. 15 minutes or more). By means of adequate, according video sequences, a high consistency and thus reliability of the examined material can be guaranteed. Due to the creation of natural conditions in game test situations, there will, despite a consistent formulation of tasks, always be a certain amount of variability, which can be optimized through an extension of the playing time in the game test situations (improvement of the reliability).

One advantage of video tests is that one can easily add further manipulation stimuli (e.g. inducing motivational focus or attention-directing instructions). Technically, this is possible for game test situations, too; however, it is harder to control. One variation is that the test persons must operate in different forms of motor actions (e.g. with hands, feet or hockey sticks) (Memmert and Roth, 2007).

Creativity and attention

Several studies from psychology compellingly demonstrated that attention plays an important role in the generation of creative thoughts (for a review, see Kasof, 1997). These results will be discussed next with a link to practical implications in sport.

A broad attention focus is necessary in order to perceive unexpected objects, such as unmarked teammates, which could potentially be the starting point for original solutions (Furley *et al.*, 2010; Memmert and Furley, 2007). Fewer instructions by the coaches imply an induction of a broad attention focus and lead to significantly better results in finding original and various solutions than for children who are constantly confronted with attention-directing instructions during training sessions (Memmert, 2007).

These findings support previous research on attention-narrowing environment stimulations (Dewing and Battye, 1971; Friedman *et al.*, 2003; Martindale, 1999; Mendelsohn, 1976; Mendelsohn and Griswold, 1964, 1966; for a review, see Kasof, 1997), which found that, with a narrow breadth of attention, not all stimuli and information that could lead to original and possibly unique solutions in a certain situation can be taken in and associated with one another. A wide breadth of attention, on the other hand, makes it possible to associate different stimuli that may initially appear to be irrelevant. Considered together, the findings highlight the fact that the attention-broadening programme can play a useful role in promoting the development of creativity in children. This programme appears to be particularly suitable for achieving a wide breadth of attention during game play. Martindale (1981: 372) explains this fact as follows:

> The more elements that a person can focus on simultaneously, the more likely it is that a creative idea will result. Why? Because the more elements that can be focused on, the more candidates there are for combination. Thus, with two elements – A and B – in the focus of attention, only one relationship – AB – can be discovered. With three elements – A, B, and C – there are three potential relationships – AB, AC, and BC – to be discovered. With four elements, there are six potential relationships, and so on.

In general, coaches have two options to influence the breadth of attention of their players: (1) direct, by means of instructions or (2) indirect, by inventing routines, exercises and game variations which provoke a broad attention focus of the players.

There are two aims of the training: one is the coach's help by naming different solutions to certain situations. More important, however, is that, through a reduction of instructions, the children are given the possibility to find unexpected, possibly better solutions on their own.

The perception and operation in many *different* team and sport game situations has a positive influence on the development of tactical creativity (Memmert and Roth, 2007). Movement biographies of professional ball sport players indicate that creative players, as opposed to less original ball sport players, (a) had the opportunity to try and practise various different sports in their childhood, (b) were able to experience movement in different team game-related situations, (c) operated in many relatively unstructured (complex) team game situations ('deliberate play') without instructions and (d) had participated over a long period of goal-oriented training in their main sports ('deliberate practice').

Important for the generation of original solutions is that children start to experience different ball sports at an early stage. In the frame of a variety of game forms, they learn to play with all sorts of balls by means of their hands, feet, tennis rackets or hockey sticks. This way, they are forced to think through different game situations in many different and new ways. Therefore, the training and fostering of tactical creativity by means of 'deliberate play' and 'deliberate practice' must be considered when coaching beginners and promoting talents.

Creativity and motivation

The amount of studies from psychology fascinatingly displays that instructions which provoke a *happy mood* can forward creative performances (for an overview, see Isen, 2000), stimulate the production of innovative ideas (Isen *et al.*, 1987) and further the generation of unusual free associations (Hirt *et al.*, 1997). In addition, to improve divergent performances, for example, it is sufficient for participants to be instructed, whilst working on established creativity tests, to press their hand against the table top from below (crook of arm) and not from above (straight arm; Friedman and Förster, 2000).

Different kinds of motivationally oriented theoretic models from social psychology explain why creative performances can directly be influenced by the simplest of instructions – for instance, manipulating emotional states of the participants ('regulatory focus theory', Higgins, 1997; 'theory of personality systems interactions', Kuhl, 2000). Higgins (1997) proposed two modes of self-regulation, in order to regulate pleasure and suffering (i.e. to direct behaviour towards promotion or prevention targets). More specifically, a focus on accomplishments and aspirations are labelled as promotion focus, and a focus on safety and responsibilities are called prevention focus. In addition, there is no a priori advantage of either motivational orientation in terms of performance. According to this approach, the performance on a given task may depend on the fit between people's regulatory focus (promotion or prevention) and people's chronic regulatory orientation (promotion or prevention; Higgins, 2000).

This idea of better performance and a more positive effect via regulatory fit has already received some empirical support in the domain of cognitive (e.g. Keller and Bless, 2006; Memmert *et al.*, 2010) and even motor tasks (Plessner *et al.*, 2009). Thus, such considerations seem to have the potential for optimizing divergent tactical performances by sport-specific motivational instructions (Memmert *et al.*, 2012). On the other hand, it is desirable that sports science can, in ecological settings, make a contribution to the further development of motivationally oriented theoretic models from social psychology.

Concluding remarks

The term tactical creativity has been used poorly in performance analysis of sports in recent years and this chapter plays an important role in explaining the impact of creativity in performance analysis as it is in other disciplines, such as creativity research and sports psychology. This chapter has been very specific in explaining how creativity is defined and how it can be used for performance analysis in sports. Therefore, the techniques of different creativity tasks (video tests, game test situations) which can produce reliable and valid creative performance values in sport were introduced. In addition, specific possibilities and limits of both procedures to determine the level of decision making were considered. The interaction of tactical creativity with attention and motivation was also discussed: theoretically, empirically and practically. This is important because attentional and motivational processes play a considerable role in tactical creativity training and diagnostics in sport.

References

Amabile, T.M. (1983) 'Social psychology of creativity: A componential conceptualization', *Journal of Personality and Social Psychology*, 45: 357–76.
Amelang, M. and Bartussek, D. (2006) *Differenzielle Psychologie und Persönlichkeitsforschung [Differential Psychology and Psychology of Personality]*, Stuttgart: Kohlhammer.
Barron, F. (1965) 'The psychology of creativity', in T.M. Newcomb (ed.), *New Directions in Psychology II*, New York: Rinehart.
Bekhtereva, N.P., Dan'ko, S.G., Starchenko, M.G., Pakhomov, S.V. and Medvedev, S.V. (2001) 'Study of the brain organization of creativity: III. Positron-emission tomography data', *Human Physiology*, 27: 390–7.
Charles, R. and Runco, M.A. (2001) 'Developmental trends in the evaluation and divergent thinking of children', *Creativity Research Journal*, 13: 417–37.

Csikszentmihalyi, M. (1988) 'Society, culture, and person: A systems view of creativity', in R.J. Sternberg (ed.), *The Nature of Creativity* (pp. 325–39). New York: Cambridge University Press.

Csikszentmihalyi, M. (1999) 'Creativity', in R.A. Wilson and F.C. Keil (eds), *The MIT Encyclopedia of the Cognitive Sciences* (pp. 205–6). Cambridge, MA: MIT Press.

Dewing, K. and Battye, G. (1971) 'Attention deployment and non-verbal fluency', *Journal of Personality and Social Psychology*, 17: 214–8.

Friedman, R.S. and Förster, J. (2000) 'The effects of approach and advoice motor actions on the elements of creative insight', *Journal of Personality and Social Psychology*, 79: 477–92.

Friedman, R.S., Fishbach, A., Förster, J. and Werth, L. (2003) 'Attentional priming effects on on creativity', *Creativity Research Journal*, 15: 277–86.

Furley, P., Memmert, D. and Heller, C. (2010) 'The dark side of visual awareness in sport – inattentional blindness in a real-world basketball task', *Attention, Perception, and Psychophysics*, 72: 1327–37.

Getzels, J.W. and Csikszentmihalyi, M. (1976) *The Creative Vision: A Longitudinal Study of Problem Finding in Art*, New York: Wiley.

Gordon, W. (1961) *Synectics: The Development of Creative Capacity,* New York: Harper and Row.

Greco, P., Memmert, D. and Morales, J.C.P. (2010) 'The effect of deliberate play on tactical performance in basketball', *Perceptual and Motor Skills*, 110: 849–56.

Guilford, J.P. (1967) *The Nature of Human Intelligence*, New York: McGraw Hill.

Helsen, W.F., Starkes, J.L. and Hodges, N.J. (1998) 'Team sports and the theory of deliberate practice', *Journal of Sport and Exercise Psychology*, 20: 12–34.

Higgins, E.T. (1997) 'Beyond pleasure and pain', *American Psychologist*, 52: 1280–300.

Higgins, E.T. (2000) 'Making a good decision. Value from fit', *American Psychologist*, 55: 1217–30.

Hirt, E.R., Levine, G.M., McDonald, H.E., Melton, R.J. and Martin, L.L. (1997) 'The role of mood in quantitative and qualitative aspects of performance: Single or multiple mechanisms?', *Journal of Experimental Social Psychology*, 33: 602–29.

Isen, A.M. (2000) 'Positive affect and decision making', in M. Lewis and J. Haviland-Jones (eds), *Handbook of Emotions*, 2nd ed. (pp. 417–35). New York: Guilford.

Isen, A.M., Daubman, K.A. and Nowicki, G.P. (1987) 'Positive affect facilitates creative problem solving', *Journal of Personality and Social Psychology*, 52: 1122–31.

Johnson, J.G. and Raab, M. (2003) 'Take the first: Option-generation and resulting choices', *Organizational Behavior and Human Decision Processes*, 91: 215–29.

Kalinowski, A.G. (1985) 'The development of Olympic swimmers', in B.S. Bloom (ed.), *Developing Talent in Young People* (pp. 139–92). New York: Ballantine.

Kasof, J. (1997) 'Creativity and breadth of attention', *Creativity Research Journal*, 10: 303–15.

Keller, J. and Bless, H. (2006) 'Regulatory fit and cognitive performance: The interactive effect of chronic and situationally induced self-regulatory mechanisms on test performance', *European Journal of Social Psychology*, 36: 393–405.

Kirton, M.J. (1976) 'Adaptors and innovators: A description and measure', *Journal of Applied Psychology*, 61: 622–9.

Krampen, G. (1996) *Kreativitätstest für Vorschul- und Schulkinder (KVS-P)* [*Divergent Thinking Test for Pre-School and School Children*], Göttingen: Hogrefe.

Kuhl, J. (2000) 'A functional–design approach to motivation and self–regulation: The dynamics of personality systems interactions', in M. Boekaerts, P.R. Pintrich and M. Zeidner (eds), *Handbook of Self–Regulation* (pp. 111–69). San Diego, CA: Academic Press.

Kurtzberg, T.R. and Amabile, T.M. (2001) 'From Guilford to creative synergy: Opening the black box of team-level creativity', *Creativity Research Journal*, 13(3, 4): 285–94.

Leser, R. (2006) 'Applied video and game analysis in professional soccer', paper presented at the World Congress of Performance Analysis of Sport VII, Hungary, Szombathely, September.

Lumsden, K. (2001) *Complete Book of Drills for Winning Basketball*, Paramus, NJ: Prentice Hall.

Martindale, C. (1981) *Cognition and Consciousness*, Homewood, IL: Dorsey.

Martindale, C. (1990) *The Clockwork Muse: The Predictability of Artistic Styles*, New York: Basic Books.

Martindale, C. (1999) 'The biological basis of creativity', in R.J. Sternberg (ed.), *Handbook of Creativity* (pp. 137–52). Cambridge: Cambridge University Press.

Memmert, D. (2006) 'Developing creative thinking in a gifted sport enrichment program and the crucial role of attention processes', *High Ability Studies*, 17: 101–15.

Memmert, D. (2007) 'Can creativity be improved by an attention-broadening training program? An exploratory study focusing on team sports', *Creativity Research Journal*, 19: 281–92.

Memmert, D. (2010a) 'Game test situations: Assessment of game creativity in ecological valid situations', *International Journal of Sport Psychology*, Supplement to Volume 41: 94–5.

Memmert, D. (2010b) 'Creativity, expertise, and attention: Exploring their development and their relationships', *Journal of Sport Science*, 29: 93–104.

Memmert, D. (2011) 'Sports and creativity', in M.A. Runco and S.R. Pritzker (eds), *Encyclopedia of Creativity*, 2nd ed. (pp. 373–8). San Diego: Academic Press.

Memmert, D. and Furley, P. (2007) '"I spy with my little eye!" – Breadth of attention, inattentional blindness, and tactical decision making in team sports', *Journal of Sport and Exercise Psychology*, 29: 365–81.

Memmert, D. and Roth, K. (2007) 'The effects of non-specific and specific concepts on tactical creativity in team ball sports', *Journal of Sport Science*, 25: 1423–32.

Memmert, D. and Harvey, S. (2008) 'The Game Performance Assessment Instrument (GPAI): Some concerns and solutions for further development', *Journal of Teaching in Physical Education*, 27: 220–40.

Memmert, D. and Harvey, S. (2010) 'Identification of non-specific tactical problems in invasion games', *Physical Education and Sport Pedagogy*, 15: 287–305.

Memmert, D., Baker, J. and Bertsch, C. (2010) 'Play and practice in the development of sport-specific creativity in team ball sports', *High Ability Studies*, 21: 3–18.

Memmert, D., Hüttermann, S. and Orliczek, J. (2012, forthcoming) 'Decide like Lionel Messi! The impact of regulatory focus on divergent thinking in sports', *Journal of Applied Social Psychology*.

Mendelsohn, G.A. (1976) 'Associative and attentional processes in creative performance', *Journal of Personality*, 44: 341–69.

Mendelsohn, G. and Griswold, B. (1964) 'Differential use of incidental stimuli in problem solving as a function of creativity', *Journal of Abnormal and Social Psychology*, 68: 431–6.

Mendelsohn, G. and Griswold, B. (1966) 'Assessed creative potential, vocabulary level, and sex as predictors of the use of incidental cues in verbal problem solving', *Journal of Personality and Social Psychology*, 4: 423–31.

Milgram, R.M. (1990) 'Creativity: An idea whose time has come and gone', in M.A. Runco and R.S. Albert (eds), *Theory of Creativity* (pp. 215–33). Newbury Park, CA: Sage.

Monsaas, J.A. (1985) 'Learning to be a world–class tennis player', in B.S. Bloom (ed.), *Developing Talent in Young People* (pp. 139–92). New York: Ballantine.

Plessner, H., Unkelbach, C., Memmert, D., Baltes, A. and Kolb, A. (2009) 'Regulatory fit as a determinant of sport performance', *Psychology of Sport and Exercise*, 10: 108–15.

Reilly, T. (1996) *Science and Soccer*, London: E and FN Spon.

Runco, M.A. (2007) *Creativity – Theories and Themes: Research, Development, and Practice*, Burlington, VT: Elsevier Academic Press.

Runco, M.A. and Pritzker, S.R. (2011) *Encyclopedia of Creativity*, San Diego: Academic Press.

Simonton, D.K. (1988) *Scientific Genius: A Psychology of Science*, Cambridge: Cambridge University Press.

Smith, M. and Cushion, C.J. (2006) 'An investigation of the in-game behaviours of professional, top level youth soccer coaches', *Journal of Sport Sciences*, 24(4): 355–66.

Smith, S.M., Ward, T.B. and Finke, R.A. (1995) *The Creative Cognition Approach*, Cambridge, MA: MIT Press.

Sternberg, R.J. (1985) *Beyond IQ*, New York: Cambridge University Press.

Sternberg, R.J. and Lubart, T.I. (1991) 'An investment theory of creativity and its development', *Human Development*, 34: 1–31.

Sternberg, R.J. and Lubart, T.I. (1992) 'Buy low and sell high: An investment approach to creativity', *Current Directions in Psychological Science*, 1: 1–5.

Sternberg, R.J. and Lubart, T.I. (1995) *Defying the Crowd*, New York: Free Press.

25

QUALITATIVE ASPECTS IN PERFORMANCE ANALYSIS

Germain Poizat[1], Carole Sève[2] and Jacques Saury[2]

[1] UNIVERSITY OF GENEVA, SWITZERLAND

[2] UNIVERSITY OF NANTES, FRANCE

Summary

Qualitative and quantitative research methods have distinctly different strengths and weaknesses. The purpose of this chapter is not to review the issues regarding the authenticity, trustworthiness or validity of qualitative data. The aim is instead to look closely at the contributions of qualitative approaches to performance analysis, with a particular focus on those studies that have sought to describe athletic performance from the inside. We also deal with a promising direction in this field: the articulation of descriptions of athletes' activity from the 'inside' (i.e. qualitative) and from the outside (i.e. quantitative and semi-quantitative).

What about qualitative research in performance analysis?

The term performance analysis is used to describe an approach that combines biomechanical analysis (e.g. analyses of technique, motor control, etc.) and notational analysis (e.g. match analysis) in order to provide coaches and athletes with an objective set of information on performance (Bartlett, 2001; Hughes, 2004; Hughes and Bartlett, 2002a; Hughes and Franks, 2004; Lees, 2002). Usually, this approach focuses on numerical indicators (i.e. quantifiable or countable) that target and capture diverse but specific dimensions of sports performances. These indicators are sub-categorized into general performance, tactical, technical, and biomechanical indicators, and they are defined according to the study objectives and the specificities of the sport under consideration (Hughes and Bartlett, 2002b). For example, these indicators may be players' movements on the playing field (e.g. McGarry *et al.*, 1999; Passos *et al.*, 2009), the duration of tennis rallies (O'Donoghue and Ingram, 2001), the release speeds in javelin throwing (Bartlett *et al.*, 1996) or the take-off velocity in the men's long jump (Lees *et al.*, 1994).

How does qualitative research contribute to performance analysis? This question is eminently reasonable, as it is raised in a research field that aims to analyse sports performance using essentially measurable and quantifiable indicators. Yet qualitative research has progressively infiltrated performance analysis, to such a point that it is sometimes difficult to distinguish qualitative studies from quantitative studies (O'Donoghue, 2010: 210–1). As an illustration, this approach has contributed to a way of studying sports biomechanics based on the qualitative analysis of movement patterns (e.g. Bartlett, 2007; Knudson and Morrison, 2002). Qualitative analysis in biomechanics describes and analyses movements non-numerically by seeing movements as 'patterns', while quantitative analysis describes and analyses movements numerically. The study of Lafont (2007) on the head position in tennis during the hitting phase is a good illustration of the qualitative research that can be conducted in the field of performance analysis. This shift from strictly quantitative analysis towards more qualitative methods can be explained principally by growth in the profession of movement or performance analysis. Although sports biomechanists mainly use a quantitative approach to analysing human movement patterns in sport, movement or performance analysts generally use qualitative or quasi-quantitative analysis (Bartlett, 2007). The practical value of qualitative and quasi-quantitative movement analysis lies in its effectiveness in helping coaches to identify good and bad techniques, to compare athletes' performances and/or to identify injurious techniques (Bartlett, 2001). However, despite the undeniable interest of the qualitative analysis of movement patterns, we have chosen to give special attention to qualitative research with a psychological orientation, which is less well known in performance analysis, although it also provides useful results in this field. This type of research seeks to give an account of the cognitive and experienced dimension of sports performance, based on the assumption that performance cannot be reduced to observable behaviour: it always comprises an important interpretable component that allows athletes to adapt to the changing characteristics of the competitive situation (e.g. Hauw *et al.*, 2003; Sève *et al.*, 2002).

In sport and exercise psychology, qualitative research is distinguished from quantitative research principally by the emphasis given to descriptions 'from the inside' of observed phenomena (e.g. Biddle *et al.*, 2001). Qualitative research (i.e. interpretive, naturalistic, ethnographic or phenomenological) tries to account for the athlete's subjective experience, thereby offering a detailed (or in-depth) description of how athletes make sense of their world (e.g. Dale, 1996). This type of study offers interesting opportunities for performance analysis as it is widely acknowledged that qualitative research is especially suited to (a) understanding the meaning of events and actions, (b) understanding their context, (c) identifying unanticipated phenomena, and (d) understanding the processes by which the events and actions take place (e.g. Stelter *et al.*, 2003). This type of research can, for example, identify the performance indicators taken into account by athletes even during competition. These subjective indicators may in some cases be inappropriate and thus lead to deterioration in performance (which justifies the continued use of classic methods in performance analysis). However, in other cases, these same indicators, even when partial, may be pertinent and sufficient for making decisions in dynamic and uncertain situations presenting with strong time constraints.

In this chapter, we present the results of several studies conducted within the theoretical and methodological framework of the *course-of-action* (e.g. Theureau, 2003). These studies provide insight into what descriptions from-the-inside can offer to performance analysis. The *course-of-action* framework seems to be particularly well suited for performance analysis for many reasons: (a) it reaches the subjective dimension of performance and identifies performance indicators from the point of view of the athletes; (b) it responds to both athletic and scientific needs and concerns; (c) the procedures for data collection function as a short-term aid to athletes and coaches; and (d) the results can help coaches to develop new training programmes.

Performance described from-the-inside: an illustration with the course-of-action methodology

The observational method used in studies conducted within the theoretical and methodological framework of the *course-of-action* differs from the dominant qualitative template in sport and exercise psychology, which is the combination of protocols for semi-structured interviews and content analysis (e.g. Côté *et al.*, 1995). It typically encompasses the intensive collection of observational data regarding actions and communications in real competitive situations, complemented by data from self-confrontation interviews.

The observational data are collected during the period of participative observation by the researchers, which is part of a long-term collaboration agreement with the athletes and coaches (therefore requiring ethnographic notes and collections of diverse traces of the activity: action plans; written preparations for the training sessions or competitive meets; transcriptions of significant events, etc.). They are also collected by audiovisual recordings of the behaviours and verbal exchanges of the athletes and coaches in situations of training or competition. Each intervention requires an ad hoc adaptation of the set-up (recording equipment may be portable or fixed, filming may be close-up or distant, distance transmission, etc.).

During the self-confrontation interview, the athlete is confronted with an audiovisual recording of his or her activity and is encouraged to describe and comment on the personally meaningful elements of this activity in the presence of the researcher (Theureau, 2003). The researcher tries to place the athlete in an attitude and mental state favourable to this description, using prompts concerning sensations (what sensations are you experiencing?), perceptions (what are you perceiving?), focalizations (what has your attention?), concerns (what are you trying to do here?), thoughts and interpretations (what are you thinking about?), and emotions (what emotions are you experiencing?). These prompts are not systematic but rather are made as needed to encourage the athlete in describing his or her activity. Their main purpose is to help the athlete to reconstitute his or her experience during the activity period under study while limiting attempts at justification. By guiding the interview with only a set of generic questions, the researcher does not a priori seek a particular content. The self-confrontation interview therefore differs from the semi-structured interview, which is conducted using a predetermined interview guide around a predetermined theme. This procedure of self-confrontation therefore increases the chance of successfully capturing the athlete's experience and discovering the hidden dimensions of performance (e.g. Dale, 1996).

In summary, the self-confrontation interview is a precise research protocol for gaining access to the athlete's experience. It can be used to identify the non-observable phenomena that are not spontaneously verbalizable by the athletes in other forms of interview or debriefing. This methodology has several advantages: (a) sports performance can be studied in real situations without the risk of penalizing the performance of the athletes; (b) researchers have access to the experiential dimension of performance, including athletes' concerns, intentions, sensations, emotions, expectations, and interpretations; and (c) changes in these dimensions over the course of the performance can also be determined. Other methodologies, such as the explicitation interview (e.g. Gouju *et al.*, 2007), may also be used to access the experience of athletes. However, the self-confrontation interview presents a major advantage for performance analysis: it is grounded in the objective evidence of performance – that is, the behavioural and contextual data from objective audiovisual recordings. This specificity is a strong argument in favour of the self-confrontation interview in the field of performance analysis. By confronting the participant with the traces of his or her activity, the self-confrontation interview allows a consensus to be built from the analysis of a concrete performance situation by an outside observer of the behaviour (whether a researcher or a coach) and the athlete who was engaged in the situation.

Another way of understanding performance

The purpose of this section is to show how a description from-the-inside provides a better understanding of performance. To do so, we will rely on the results of research conducted in collaboration with table tennis experts. These studies were all conducted within the theoretical and methodological framework of the *course-of-action* and have been published in peer-reviewed journals (e.g. Sève *et al.*, 2002, 2003, 2006; Sève and Poizat, 2005).

The first study was conducted in collaboration with the French Table Tennis Association and the French Ministry of Youth and Sports. The aim was to study the activity of expert table tennis players during competition with the goal of optimizing training procedures. The performance analysis from the player's point of view revealed two characteristic modes of involvement during matches: exploration and execution (e.g. Sève *et al.*, 2002, 2003). These modes expressed the two characteristic preoccupations of table tennis players: interpreting the interplay of one's own strengths and weaknesses with those of the opponent and scoring points. The players' activity during matches could thus be seen as an alternation of exploration and execution phases (Sève *et al.*, 2003). During the exploration phases, they carried out exploration activity to reduce their uncertainty about their opponent's actions and to orient future courses of action. During the execution phases, they looked for immediate opportunities to make winning plays. Prior to September 1, 2001, matches consisted of two or three winning sets of 21 points, with the players alternating the roles of server and receiver every five points. Since September 1, matches consist of three or four winning sets of 11 points, with players alternating the roles every two points. The results also showed that the players divided the 21-point set into three characteristic periods related to the successions of five serves: the beginning of the set (the first four successions of serves); the middle of the set (the following two successions); and the end of the set (the last two successions). They assumed that they could perform exploration actions at the beginning of a set without risking their chances of winning. They prolonged this period in an attempt to identify as many effective actions as possible to be used at the end of the match (Sève *et al.*, 2003). This exploration was abandoned when their opponent had already won two sets and the loss of a third set would mean the loss of the match (Sève *et al.*, 2003).

A second study focused on analysing the effect of a rule change on the players' activity organization (Sève and Poizat, 2005). In 2001, the International Table Tennis Federation implemented a new system for scoring points. Since this rule change, matches consist of three or four winning sets of 11 points, with players alternating the roles every two points. The analysis showed two principal results under the new scoring system: (a) a decrease in the duration of exploration phases compared with execution phases and (b) a new mode of engagement: deception. This mode expressed a new concern of table tennis players, which is to dissimulate any element that would help the opponent to be more effective. Although this concern was present under the old scoring system, it was much more important under the new system. The players felt it was much easier to hide their weaknesses from their opponent, since they were forced to limit the exploration phase. This concealment was accomplished by bluffing actions; that is to say, by making difficult shots that the players knew had little chance of succeeding but which, from their point of view, would impress the opponent. By bluffing, they attempted to disturb the construction of their opponent's interpretations about the balance of power. In addition, the players found that the early exploration actions posed a threat to winning, and they therefore placed greater emphasis on maximal effectiveness from the very beginning of play. They had thus shortened the exploration phase, which occurred only during the first set: as soon as the players identified the actions that disturbed their opponent, they reproduced them. For the lost matches, exploration did not occur beyond the second set. Even when they had identified only a small number of actions that perturbed their opponents, they did not continue to explore. Under the old system, the element that determined the shift from exploration to execution activity was the number of sets won by the opponent. The players abandoned their exploration when the loss of the current set would put the match at risk. Even when they were ahead of the opponent by a set, they continued their exploration activity at the beginning of sets so that the greatest number of effective actions could be employed in later sets and at the end of the match to increase their chances of winning. Under the new scoring system, the shift from exploration to execution seemed to have little relation to the number of sets won by the opponent. Their activity seemed circumscribed by the duration of a single set and not by the succession of several sets.

This type of qualitative study gives major attention to the actors' point of view, which makes it particularly interesting in the field of performance analysis. The originality of the results is partly due to the use of descriptive categories and analysis of experience that do not a priori reduce actors' activity to the usual categories of technical or tactical language or to classes of task analysis. For example, in the case of the from-the-inside studies in table tennis, the results revealed the importance of certain components of activity in table tennis competition (exploratory and dissimulating modes of engagement) that were not taken into account by coaches (Sève *et al.*, 2006). Thus, understanding the organization of athletes' activity is likely to complement or enhance match analysis. Indeed, knowing the distribution and alternation of the exploration, execution, and deception phases of a table tennis player can help make sense of objective indicators, such as the type of service, the shot selection, the execution shot, the shot distribution, and so on (e.g. Baca *et al.*, 2004; O'Donoghue, 2004), as well as of the observations following the change in the scoring system (e.g. Zhang and Hohmann, 2004). The alternating phases of exploration, execution, and deception indicate that making the same shot may not always have the same meaning for the player (especially if it is produced at the beginning or end of the set), which can be important to take account of in the interpretation of the data from notational analysis.

The contributions of descriptions from-the-inside are not limited to the context of sports games. Various studies using the theoretical and methodological framework of the *course-of-action* have also shown the benefits of this approach with regard to acrobatic performance (e.g. Hauw and Durand, 2008). Several studies in collaboration with trampolinists, for example, revealed the variations in athletes' involvement modes during move execution (e.g. Hauw *et al.*, 2003; Hauw and Durand, 2004). These studies also pointed to the substantial differences in how the trampolinists organized their performances. By taking into account their point of view, the analysis was able to show that the same move could be broken down into a variable number of meaningful phases (three to seven), depending on the athlete. The sequence of moves was organized by groupings (e.g. the first three, the middle two, the next three, and the last two) and was not a mere juxtaposition of moves. Moreover, the groupings were characterized by specific modes of involvement (pushing hard, seeking to reposition the body, calming down the exercise, etc.). Aerial freestyle skiing was also examined from-the-inside (Hauw *et al.*, 2008). The analysis revealed that the skiers organized performance into six sequences: (a) pick up speed in the descent; (b) manage the curve of the hill; (c) take off; (d) manage the exiting of the springboard; (e) perform rotation; and (f) organize the landing. From the skiers' perspective, each of these sequences provided the conditions for deploying the next sequence. This suggested that successful landing resulted more from the sequence chaining than from the final adjustment of the angular momentum at the time of contact with the landing hill. Thus, the athletes' ability to land on their feet could not be attributed to the final step in the leap, but rather to a gradual process that began at the very start of the leap. In conclusion, these studies have shown that a description from-the-inside even in non-game sports provides original insights into the intelligibility of performance by, for example, including athletes' kinaesthetic sensations.

Improvement of sports performance and training

These qualitative studies conducted within the theoretical and methodological framework of the *course-of-action* have a place in performance analysis, given their focus on the analysis and improvement of sports performance. The coaches and athletes who participated in this type of interview reported beneficial effects and greater insight into performance (e.g. Sève, 2006). We can distinguish three types of performance support: (a) 'immediate' support deriving from the data collection methods; (b) 'short-term' support from the researchers to both the athlete and coach; and (c) 'longer-term' support from the researchers to the broader community of coaches and coach educators.

The first type of support is immediate and arises from the characteristics of the data collection methods. The self-confrontation interviews give the athletes the opportunity to relive and describe their performance to a third party, a process which in itself has the salutary effect of helping them to better understand the processes of production and deterioration in their performance (e.g. Hauw and Durand, 2007; Sève *et al.*, 2006). This form of stimulated recall immediately enriches study participants' cognitive and reflective resources for training and competition (Gilbert and Trudel, 2001). Released from the constraints inherent to the competition situation, athletes can re-experience their activity and explain the grey areas of their performance. For example, table tennis players, as they describe their activity throughout the match during self-confrontation, may find that they have built interpretations about the opponent on the basis of a small number of observations and that these interpretations have led them to 'lock themselves' into irrelevant strategies (e.g. Sève *et al.*, 2005). Although they may experience a sense of dissatisfaction at the end of a match, the players are not always able to understand why they persisted in making ineffective strokes. In contrast, during the self-confrontation interview, they may realize that some of the choices they made in the match that they felt were ineffective were, in fact, rather effective. Reliving the whole game and describing it to someone else thus helps them to better understand how they interpret the opponent's game. Moreover, this process strengthens certain elements of knowledge that they may have started building during the game but were unable to stabilize at that time because of time pressure and the uninterrupted flow of action. In the case of the trampolining studies, the self-confrontation interviews gave the athletes the opportunity to more precisely link certain of their kinaesthetic sensations with decisions they had made about the sequencing of acrobatic moves and motor adjustments. In doing so, they were better able to perceive and understand how certain sensations and perceptions (e.g. the landing zone on the trampoline bed, sensations of speed or alignment) had prompted them to modify the sequence order and the degree of openness in body parts during the various phases of an acrobatic move. This greater understanding was matched by a greater awareness of the most commonly encountered periods of disturbance during performance (e.g. finding the best moment to begin the performance) (Hauw and Durand, 2007).

The second type of support is given over the short term in response to the pressing need for optimized training and optimal performance. This consists of providing a set of procedures for cognitively enriching competitive or training situations (through the equipment and materials used for analysis). The classic procedure is to give feedback to the athlete and coach while the experience is still hot, using the self-confrontation interview with the athlete as the basis. This interview gives the coach access to the interpretations, perceptions, emotions, etc. experienced by the athlete during performance. It also has the advantage of being indexed to a video recording of behaviour, which gives the coach the opportunity to compare his or her own analysis of the performance with the athlete's experience. The self-confrontation interview is thus likely to provide coaches with a better understanding of performance, as the inner experience of the athletes is added to the external observation. The interview also promotes the construction of consensus in the interpretations of coach (giving expert analysis of performance) and athletes (living the performance from the inside) about performance in concrete situations. Immediate feedback may also serve to elucidate certain training or competition situations with an enigmatic character and can be used to adapt training contents to the specificities of each athlete. By allowing an analysis from-the-inside, self-confrontation interviews help to identify each athlete's characteristics. Remedial steps are not exclusively defined by comparing what should have been done and what actually was done, but they also take into account experiential data. For example, athletes presenting the same behaviour do not necessarily have the same reasons for doing so: an analysis based on the individual athlete's experience may distinguish a very personal cause of a behaviour and thus better equip the coach to make an optimal intervention. Other, more complex support procedures can be envisaged, such as, for example, the use of cross self-confrontation (e.g. Clot *et al.*, 2002; Clot and Kostulski, 2011). The objective of this procedure would be to develop a rigorous approach to organizing reflective practices regarding collective activity, but from the point of view of the actors (i.e. self-confrontation interviews). Cross self-confrontation also confronts the athlete with his or her partner's or coach's activity in his or her presence. However, in this procedure, the researcher seeks to promote controversy between the players based on the assumption that these points of controversy will allow each actor to develop the power to act. This technique of crossed self-confrontation would be interesting to use to improve both training sessions and performance. For example, it might be used with partners to improve team performance or with an athlete and coach to improve team training.

The third type of support is longer term and has the aim of designing and delivering more elaborated 'guidance' or 'proposals' to meet mid- and long-term objectives (e.g. Sève *et al.*, 2006), once the entire analysis has been completed. For example, after the rule change in table tennis and given the difficulties encountered by the players, new forms of training were suggested to help develop skills using the resources offered by the new form of counting. Coaches developed new training procedures to develop skills of exploration and deception of the players (Sève and Poizat, 2005).

Future issues in performance analysis: mixed methods

To open a debate and suggest directions for future research in the field of performance analysis, we argue that it would be interesting to articulate our approach, which is focused on activity that is meaningful to the actor, with both biomechanical analysis and notational analysis. There can be tremendous value in combining descriptions from-the-inside and from-the-outside. We assume that the combination of qualitative description of the athlete's experience and (semi-)quantitative description of objective performance indicators would provide a better understanding of performance. To illustrate the usefulness of mixed methods (e.g. Tashakkori and Teddlie, 1998, 2003; Johnson and Onwuegbuzie, 2004), we will refer to studies in swimming, rowing and basketball. The first two studies were designed to articulate the description of athletes' experience with biomechanical indicators. The third study crossed a match analysis with the analysis of the experiences of basketball teammates.

Combination of biomechanical analysis and qualitative description of athletes' experience

An initial study by Gal-Petitfaux *et al.* (in press) analysed both athletes' experiences (i.e. from-the-inside) and biomechanical data (i.e. from-the-outside). The objective was to understand the activity of elite swimmers as they dealt with an underwater device as part of a biomechanical protocol to evaluate performance. Specifically, the authors sought to describe the athletes' propulsive experiences using the training device to assess its impact on the organization of swimming (Poizat *et al.*, 2010). The biomechanical analysis showed a pad effect in the interactions between the swimmers and the technology: the force applied to each pad by the swimmers was not constant, despite the instructions given for the biomechanical evaluation protocol (the athletes were instructed to swim each lap more quickly than the last but to maintain a constant speed during each lap). The experiential data confirmed this pad effect and provided some possible explanations. Indeed, the analysis of the swimmers' experiences revealed that the speed constraints had a significant impact on the way they approached the device and caused them to have several concerns (e.g. 'put their hands on every pad without missing any', 'place their hands correctly', and 'increase the arm-stroke rate to reach maximum speeds') and to organize their swim differently (e.g. 'raise their heads to look at the pads', 'press quickly on the first pads with rhythm', and 'press hard on the pads in the middle of the pool'). The results also highlighted discrepancies between the biomechanical data and the experiential data. These discrepancies occurred mainly when the swimmers had to use the device at fast speeds. As an example, one swimmer tried to press hard and fast on the first four pads and then maintain a constant speed: 'I'm not going to increase my speed linearly. I'll do four pads to start.' The analysis of the forces exerted by the swimmer's hands pointed to a discrepancy with this feeling: it revealed that the swimmer exerted strong forces on pads 7, 9, and 10, as well as 14 and 16. Although the swimmer felt the sensation of 'maintaining a constant speed' after the first four pads, he did not perceive the sensation of 'again exerting high forces on the pads' in the middle and the end of the 25 m swim. Following this study, several design proposals were made so that the device could be included in underwater training sessions. A more 'training friendly' device was designed to maintain swimmers' action organization and reasoning so as not to be at odds with swimmers' experience in natural conditions.

The second study tried to specify a single salient phenomenon in rowing experienced by a coxless pair crew during a race (Sève *et al.*, in press). The analysis of the athletes' experience revealed that one of the rowers had the sensation during the race of 'being pushed' by her partner and thus felt unable to fully carry out her movements. This phenomenon was particularly interesting for the coaches because, according to the pre-established roles, this rower, as the stroke rower, should have been imposing the stroke rhythm and her partner, as the bow rower, should have been following the rhythm set by the stroke rower. From the coaches' point of view, the stroke rower's perception reflected a problem in the coordination of the rowers' actions. The biomechanical analysis showed that this phenomenon could be explained principally by an amplitude differential between the two rowers. In terms of the richness of empirical detail, the combined analysis of the athletes' experience and the biomechanical parameters showed characteristics of the rowers' coordination that were compatible with their perceptions but unsuspected by them and their coaches. The rowers' describable and personally meaningful experiences were put into relationship with largely unconscious adjustments that could be measured using other methodologies, yielding new insights into certain facets of performance. For example, the stroke rower's perceptions of 'not being in synch', 'being pushed' by her partner, and 'not being able to complete her strokes' at certain moments of the race were syncretic descriptions of her experience. Although they served to identify and localize a critical incident from her point of view, they were uninformative as to their source. The sensation of 'being pushed' by her partner could in fact have been linked to several behavioural adjustments between the rowers that were not only meaningless for them, but also too subtle to be identified by the coaches by direct observation or by viewing the video recordings. When the biomechanical parameters were mapped to the syncretic perceptions of 'being pushed', it emerged that differences in stroke amplitude and the speed in the first and second parts of the recoveries had a notable impact on the global dynamics of the collective activity. This study also indicated another interest of indexing an objective performance analysis to a prior analysis of athletes' experience. The wide range of objective performance indicators makes it difficult to choose those that are most relevant. An initial analysis of athletes' experience makes it possible to formulate hypotheses that will guide the choice of the objective parameters relevant to exploring specific performance phenomena.

Combination of notational analysis and the qualitative description of athlete experience

A third study to articulate descriptions from-the-inside and from-the-outside is currently underway. It differs from the previous two in that it seeks to better understand how the collective performance of a basketball team is built by crossing a match analysis with an analysis of the teammates' experiences. Several *course-of-action* studies have been conducted to better understand how basketball teams coordinate (Bourbousson *et al.*, 2010, 2011). These studies have demonstrated, for example, that the coordination network of a basketball team is heterogeneous and based on local interactions that are constantly constructed and deconstructed in relation to the unfolding events of the situation. They also showed that the occurrence of many local coordinations at once do not compromise the viability of the overall team functioning. Such findings led the researchers to turn to the tools and methods of match analysis (e.g. McGarry, 2004) for corroboration. Two studies were conducted to analyse the spatiotemporal coordination of a basketball game in connection with the theory of dynamical systems (e.g. McGarry *et al.*, 1999; Passos *et al.*, 2009). The first study was an analysis of the match (Bourbousson *et al.*, 2010a), while the second focused on player dyads (Bourbousson *et al.*, 2010b). The results showed three types of dyads; those that did not maintain stable spatiotemporal coupling, those that maintained simple spatiotemporal coupling (a single stable interactive behaviour), and those that displayed complex spatiotemporal coupling (two alternating stable interactive behaviours). The results also indicated that, for players whose coordination showed some stability, the analysis was likely to distinguish phases of stability, destabilization, recovery of stability, and transition between two modes of coordination. Tools from dynamical approaches are very interesting in that they are able to pinpoint breaks in the dynamic coordination of certain players or in the dynamic interaction between two teams. A study is in fact currently underway to articulate a match analysis with an analysis of players' experience so that the data and interpretations resulting from the two methods can be mutually enriched. The tools used in match analysis reveal aspects of performance that athletes are unaware of and that are imperceptible to the researcher and thus indescribable (e.g. Hughes and Franks, 2004). These tools also have the advantage of enabling simple and rapid descriptions of players' interactive behaviours, even though these descriptions are only spatiotemporal. The results of this type of analysis can then guide the analysis of athletes' experience. Conversely, the analysis of experience gives 'experiential meaning' to match analysis because this last type of analysis provides little evidence about the processes underlying the production of collective behaviour (e.g. McGarry *et al.*, 2002). From this point of view, the analysis of athletes' experience provides guidance on which type of data should be collected to produce a meaningful description and subsequent understanding of game behaviour (e.g. McGarry, 2009). It also takes into account the context in which the behaviour is being produced, which is often overlooked when only objective data is analysed (e.g. McGarry and Franks, 2003).

Concluding remarks

To conclude, mixed methods are relevant in the field of performance analysis as a means to access phenomena that might be overlooked by a single analytic approach. Mixed methods are also able to provide interesting results for coaches and athletes, especially when problems or dysfunctions occur that cannot be clearly identified, as, for example, in the study of the two rowers.

References

Baca, A., Baron, R., Leser, R., and Kain, H. (2004) 'A process oriented approach for math analysis in table tennis', in A. Lees, J.-F. Kahn, and I.W. Maynard (eds), *Science and Racket Sports 3* (pp. 214–19). London: Routledge.

Bartlett, R.M. (2001) 'Performance analysis: Can bringing together biomechanics and notational analysis benefit coaches?', *International Journal of Performance Analysis in Sport*, 1(1): 122–6.

Bartlett, R.M. (2007) *Introduction to Sports Biomechanics: Analyzing Human Movement Patterns*, 2nd ed., Abingdon, UK: Routledge.

Bartlett, R.M., Müller, E., Lindinger, S., Brunner, F., and Morriss, C. (1996) 'Three-dimensional evaluation of the release parameters for javelin throwers of different skill levels', *Journal of Applied Biomechanics*, 12: 58–71.

Biddle, S.J.H., Markland, D., Gilbourne, D., Chatzisarantis, N.L.D., and Sparkes, A.C. (2001) 'Research methods in sport and exercise psychology: Quantitative and qualitative issues', *Journal of Sports Sciences*, 19: 777–809.

Bourbousson, J., Poizat, G., Saury, J., and Sève, C. (2010) 'Team coordination in basketball: Description of the cognitive connections between teammates', *Journal of Applied Sport Psychology*, 22: 150–66.

Bourbousson, J., Sève, C., and McGarry, T. (2010a) 'Space-time coordination patterns in basketball: Part 1. Intra- and inter-couplings among player dyads', *Journal of Sports Sciences*, 28: 339–47.

Bourbousson, J., Sève, C., and McGarry, T. (2010b) 'Space-time coordination patterns in basketball: Part 2. The interaction between the two teams', *Journal of Sports Sciences*, 28: 349–58.

Bourbousson, J., Poizat, G., Saury, J., and Sève, C. (2011) 'Description of the dynamic shared knowledge: An exploratory study during competitive sports interaction', *Ergonomics*, 54: 120–38.

Clot, Y. and Kostulski, K. (2011) 'Intervening for transforming: The horizon of action in the Clinic of Activity', *Theory and Psychology*, 21: 681–96.

Clot, Y., Fernandez, G., and Carles, L. (2002) 'Crossed self-confrontation in the Clinic of Activity', in S. Bagnara, S. Pozzi, A. Rizzo, and P. Wright (eds), *Proceedings of the 11th European Conference on Cognitive Ergonomics* (pp. 8–13). Roma, Italy: Istituto di Science e Technologie Della Cognizione.

Côté, J., Salmela, J.H., Trudel, P., Baria, A., and Russel, S. (1995) 'The coaching model: A grounded assessment of expert gymnastic coaches' knowledge', *Journal of Sport and Exercise Psychology*, 17: 1–17.

Dale, G.A. (1996) 'Existential phenomenology: Emphasising the experience of the athlete in sport psychology research', *The Sport Psychologist*, 10: 307–21.

Gal-Petitfaux, N., Adé, D., Poizat, G., and Seifert, L. (in press) 'L'intégration de données biomécaniques et d'expérience pour comprendre l'activité et concevoir un dispositif technologique: étude d'une situation d'évaluation avec des nageurs de haut-niveau', *Le Travail Humain*.

Gilbert W.D. and Trudel P. (2001) 'Learning to coach through experiences: Reflection in model youth sport coaches', *Journal of Teaching in Physical Education*, 21: 16–34.

Gouju, J.L., Vermersch, P., and Bouthier, D. (2007) 'A psycho-phenomenological approach to sport psychology: The presence of the opponents in hurdle races', *Journal of Applied Sport Psychology*, 19: 173–86.

Hauw, D. and Durand, M. (2004) 'Elite athletes' differentiated action in trampolining: A qualitative and situated analysis of different levels of performance using retrospective interviews', *Perceptual and Motor Skills*, 98: 1139–52.

Hauw, D. and Durand, M. (2007) 'Situated analysis of elite trampolinists' problems in competition using retrospective interviews', *Journal of Sport Sciences*, 25: 173–83.

Hauw, D. and Durand, M. (2008) 'Temporal dynamics of acrobatic activity: An approach of elite athletes specious present', *Journal of Sports Science and Medicine*, 7: 8–14.

Hauw, D., Berthelot, C., and Durand, M. (2003) 'Enhancing performance in elite athlete through situated-cognition analysis: Trampolinists' course of action during competition', *International Journal of Sport Psychology*, 34: 299–321.

Hauw, D., Renault, G., and Durand, M. (2008) 'How do aerial freestyler skiers land on their feet? A situated analysis of athletes' activity related to new forms of acrobatic performance', *Journal of Science and Medicine in Sport*, 11: 481–6.

Hughes, M. (2004) 'Performance analysis – a 2004 perspective', *International Journal of Performance Analysis in Sport*, 4(1): 103–9.

Hughes, M. and Bartlett, R.M. (2002a) 'Editorial', *Journal of Sport Sciences*, 20: 735–7.

Hughes, M. and Bartlett, R.M. (2002b) 'The use of performance indicators in performance analysis', *Journal of Sports Sciences*, 20: 739–54.

Hughes, M. and Franks, I.M. (2004) *Notational Analysis of Sport: Systems for Better Coaching and Performance in Sport*, London: Routledge.

Johnson, R.B. and Onwuegbuzie, A.J. (2004) 'Mixed methods research: A research paradigm whose time has come', *Educational Researcher,* 33: 14–26.

Knudson, D.V. and Morrison, C.S. (2002) *Qualitative Analysis of Human Movement*, Champaign, IL: Human Kinetics.

Lafont, D. (2007) 'Towards a new hitting model in tennis', *International Journal of Performance Analysis in Sport*, 7: 106–16.

Lees, A. (2002) 'Technique analysis in sports: A critical review', *Journal of Sports Sciences*, 20: 813–28.

Lees, A., Graham-Smith, P., and Fowler, N. (1994) 'A biomechanical analysis of the last stride, touchdown, and takeoff characteristics of the men's long jump', *Journal of Applied Biomechanics*, 10: 61–78.

McGarry, T. (2004) 'Searching for patterns in sports contests', in S. Butenko, J. Gil-Lafuente, and P.M. Parlados (eds), *Economics, Management and Optimization in Sports* (pp. 203–23). Berlin: Springer-Verlag.

McGarry, T. (2009) 'Applied and theoretical perspectives of performance analysis in sport: Scientific issues and challenges', *International Journal of Performance Analysis of Sport*, 9: 128–40.

McGarry, T. and Franks, I.M. (2003) 'The science of match analysis', in T. Reilly and A.M. Williams (eds), *Science and Soccer 2* (pp. 265–75). London: Routledge.

McGarry, T., Khan, M.A., and Franks, I.M. (1999) 'On the presence and absence of behavioural traits in sport: An example from championship squash match-play', *Journal of Sports Sciences*, 17: 297–311.

McGarry, T., Anderson, D.I., Wallace, S.A., Hughes, M.D., and Franks, I.M. (2002) 'Sport competition as a dynamical self-organizing system', *Journal of Sports Sciences*, 20: 771–81.

O'Donoghue, P. (2004) 'Match analysis in racket sports', in A. Lees, J.-F. Kahn, and I.W. Maynard (eds), *Science and Racket Sports 3* (pp. 155–62). London: Routledge.

O'Donoghue, P. (2010) *Research Methods for Sports Performance Analysis*, Abingdon, UK: Routledge.

O'Donoghue, P. and Ingram, B. (2001) 'A notational analysis of elite tennis strategy', *Journal of Sports Sciences*, 19: 107–15.

Passos, P., Araujo, D., Davids, K.W., Milho, J., and Gouveia, L. (2009) 'Power law distributions in pattern dynamics of attacker-defender dyads in the team sport of rugby union: Phenomena in a region of self-organized criticality?', *Emergence: Complexity and Organization*, 11: 37–45.

Poizat, G., Adé, D., Seifert, L., Toussaint, H., and Gal-Petitfaux, N. (2010) 'Evaluation of the Measuring Active Drag system usability: An important step for its integration into training sessions', *International Journal of Performance Analysis in Sport*, 10: 170–86.

Sève, C. (2006) 'Les dispositifs d'aide à la performance sportive basés sur l'utilisation de la vidéo', in L. Robène and Y. Léziart (eds), *L'Homme en Mouvement: Histoire en Anthropologie des Techniques Sportives – Tome 2* (pp. 227–56), Paris: Chiron.

Sève, C. and Poizat, G. (2005) 'Table tennis scoring systems and expert players' exploration activity', *International Journal of Sport Psychology*, 36: 320–36.

Sève, C., Saury, J., Theureau, J., and Durand, M. (2002) 'Activity organisation and knowledge construction during competitive interaction in table tennis', *Cognitive Systems Research*, 3: 501–22.

Sève, C., Saury, J., Ria, L., and Durand, M. (2003) 'Structure of expert players' activity during competitive interaction in table tennis', *Research Quarterly for Exercise and Sport*, 74: 71–83.

Sève, C., Saury, J., Leblanc, S., and Durand, M. (2005) 'Course-of-action theory in table tennis: A qualitative analysis of the knowledge used by three elite players during matches', *European Review of Applied Psychology*, 55: 145–55.

Sève, C., Poizat, G., Saury, J., and Durand, M. (2006) 'A grounded theory of elite male table tennis players' activity during matches', *The Sport Psychologist*, 20: 58–73.

Sève, C., Nordez, A., Poizat, G., and Saury, J. (in press) 'Performance analysis in sport: Contributions from a joint analysis of athletes' courses of experience and of mechanical indicators', *Scandinavian Journal of Medicine and Science in Sports*, doi: 10.1111/j.1600-0838.2011.01421.x.

Stelter, R., Sparkes, A., and Hunger, I. (2003, February) 'Qualitative research in sport sciences – an introduction [electronic version]', *Forum Qualitative Soziaforschung [Forum: Qualitative Social Research]*, 4, Art. 2, http://nbn-resolving.de/urn:nbn:de:0114-fqs030124.

Tashakkori, A. and Teddlie, C. (1998) *Mixed Methodology: Combining Qualitative and Quantitative Approaches*, Thousand, CA: Sage.

Tashakkori, A. and Teddlie, C. (2003) *Handbook of Mixed Methods in Social and Behavioural Research*, Thousand Oaks, CA: Sage.

Theureau, J. (2003) 'Course of action analysis and course of action centered design', in E. Hollnagel (ed.), *Handbook of Cognitive Task Design* (pp. 55–81). Mahwah, NJ: Lawrence Erlbaum Associates.

Zhang, H. and Hohmann, A. (2004) 'Table tennis after the introduction of the 40 mm ball and the 11 point format', in A. Lees, J.-F. Kahn, and I.W. Maynard (eds), *Science and Racket Sports 3* (pp. 227–32). London: Routledge.

Applied sports performance analysis

26

SOCCER

Albin Tenga

NORWEGIAN SCHOOL OF SPORT SCIENCES, NORWAY

Summary

Soccer is one of the most analysed sports and has a relatively long history of performance analysis (Reep and Benjamin, 1968). The ultimate objective of performance analysis in soccer is to enhance player and team performance within the specific context of competition or training. Therefore, the quality of performance analysis may be considered fundamental to the coaching process in soccer.

Research on performance analysis in soccer serves two functions: the descriptive function, in which information about past performance is produced for coaching feedback; and the prescriptive function, where information about future performance is generated for outcome projection and performance optimization. Undoubtedly, the accumulated information from soccer performance analysis has contributed to a substantial increase in our specific knowledge on technical, tactical, physical and psychological aspects of the game over the years. This has led researchers to offer advice to soccer practitioners about different topics of interest, such as detailed understanding of important skills, the positional demands technically, how to play effectively, correct behavioural and mental states in stressful situations and even how these diverse skills can be acquired.

However, applied research in soccer needs to pay further attention to critical issues related to conceptual and methodological shortcomings in order to meet its intents and purposes effectively. In addition to the consideration of opposition relationship, other areas recommended for future research include development of theoretical framework, research on critical behaviours, consideration of situational and playing contexts and inclusion of spatial and temporal dynamics.

Introduction

Soccer is one of the most extensively analysed sports and the use of the 'Reep system' (Reep and Benjamin, 1968) of analysis has had a big influence on the development of its performance analysis (McGarry and Franks, 2003).

Most of the research done on performance analysis in soccer is of an applied nature, based on observational research. Its ultimate objective is to enhance player and team performance by providing knowledge which has meaning within the specific context of competition or training. Performance analysis provides the coach and player with information about past performances (descriptive function) and may be useful also in generating data for predictive model development (prescriptive function). The information about skill performance, presented in the form of feedback, is among the critical factors affecting the learning and hence the proficiency of a motor skill (Franks, 2004; McGarry and Franks, 2003).

The second function of facilitating model development moves the role of match performance analysis from descriptive analysis to a prescriptive function. This is because not only can likely outcome be projected through competing playing profiles, but the profiles can also be optimized to promote successful performance. However, the descriptive function of performance analysis in soccer presupposes that the analysed events are not all completely random. Soccer-playing events are assumed to exhibit some inherent organization and explanation (Franks, 1988). Here, the term organization implies stable (or invariant) soccer performance, while explanation implies reliable transfer to future applications based on inductive reasoning. The challenge for performance analysis in soccer becomes, therefore, to identify the stable (or invariant) soccer performance in order to satisfy the necessary condition for its prescriptive function.

Most of the studies on performance analysis in soccer are typically described on the basis of probability (McGarry and Franks, 2003), with the exception of a few studies on perturbations (Hughes and Reed, 2005; Hughes *et al.*, 1998; Hughes *et al.*, 2001) and opposition relationship (Tenga *et al.*, 2010a, 2010b), which incorporated dynamic concepts in their analyses. Some researchers argue that it is difficult if not impossible to have valid data unless sports performance is considered as a complex dynamic process with self-organizing properties (e.g. McGarry *et al.*, 2002; Perl, 2001, 2002). McGarry and Perl (2004) and Hughes (2004) present a good overview of such alternative system descriptions for sports contests. However, so far, these potentially useful analysis approaches are mainly either incomplete or incapable of yielding practical results (Hughes, 2004). Hence, neither the system description based on probability (random processes) nor the one based on dynamical systems so far alone managed to capture all complexities involved in describing a soccer match play. Therefore, further research using various types of system descriptions, separately or together as a hybrid, is warranted.

Research on performance analysis in soccer

The aspects of soccer performance commonly analysed in contemporary research include technical, tactical, physical and psychological aspects. In the past, as for sports performance analysis in general, soccer performance analysis has been limited to notational analysis and biomechanics (O'Donoghue, 2010: 2). The current text will also include research from physiological and psychological investigations, provided that their data were recorded during actual soccer performance in training or competition. Therefore, studies on injury risk and injury mechanism as well as studies on physiological responses and those on the influence of different psychological factors will also be included. In this chapter, applied research on performance analysis in soccer will therefore be organized into five groups according to their contributions.

Analysis of technique

Analysis of technique examines the mechanical aspects of technique and is concerned with the execution of a particular skill in terms of kinetic and kinematic details of the movement involved. This can also be accomplished with the help of qualitative analysis of mechanical properties of a particular soccer skill using video recordings of the player performing the skill. According to O'Donoghue (2010: 2), analysis of technique can include laboratory-based biomechanical analysis if the technique under investigation is an important skill for performance within the context of a particular sport. Examples of such skills in soccer may include shooting at goal, heading, throwing-in and keeper-related techniques. Kicking technique, with its many variants, is the skill which defines soccer and it is undoubtedly the most analysed technique in soccer (Lees, 2003).

Four stages of a mature kicking motion that have been suggested by Lees (2003) include the retraction of the leg during the backswing; the rotation of both thigh and shank forwards; the thigh deceleration and shank acceleration leading to ball impact; and the follow through. In another study, the trend in the data indicating the effect of different angled approaches to kick a stationary ball suggested that the maximum swing velocity of the kicking leg was achieved with an approach angle of 30 degrees and maximum ball velocity with an approach angle of 40 degrees (Isokawa and Lees, 1988). However, this finding is contested by a more recent study using 3D analysis of kinematics, which reported that approach angle had no effect on ball speed (Kellis et al., 2004).

More recently, detailed analyses of kicking technique including 3D aspects of the skill have been reported as a result of the increasing availability of suitable analysis equipment (Lees, 2009). Lees and Nolan (2002) concluded that slower and more precise action leads to greater consistency in accuracy, while the increases in ball speed were associated with increases in range of motion at the pelvis, hip and knee joints. Ball velocities of 32 and $27 \, m.s^{-1}$ with foot velocities of 22 and $20 \, m.s^{-1}$ were reported for the preferred and non-preferred foot, respectively, in skilled amateur players (Nunome et al., 2006). From these results, it was concluded that the better performance of the preferred foot was due to strength rather than coordination. Elsewhere, a full-body model and a 3D optoelectronic motion capture system was used to analyse selected kinematic variables (Shan and Westerhoff, 2005). This study concluded that the arm contralateral to the kicking leg has a role to play in influencing the efficiency of the kick. Kristensen and Bull (2009) found that the approach velocity influences the ball velocity and that optimal subject-specific velocity of approach does exist in soccer kicking. In another study, players displayed similar kinematic strategies in knee flexion but not ankle extension at the ball contact and follow-through phases of the instep penalty kick when targeting four different corners of the goal (Goktepe et al., 2010). These researchers concluded that the area of the goal targeted affects the kinematics of ankle extension but not knee flexion. Katis and Kellis (2011) reported kinematic differences between straight approach soccer kicks and kicks performed following a cutting manoeuvre action. In specific, these researchers found that a double-cutting manoeuvre reduces ball and foot speed.

The use of fast automatic and reliable data collection systems based on optoelectronic motion analysis is still new to the analysis of kicking and other soccer skills (Lees, 2009). Thus, many more studies on analysis of soccer techniques are to be expected in the near future.

Technical effectiveness

Technical effectiveness is concerned with the assessment of the effect of the skills performed by players during match play and it is expressed by using positive-to-negative ratios. Olsen and Larsen (1997) reported the use of frequency profiles of positive and negative applications of different skills for every player's ball involvement as first attacker and first defender. Their instrument (DOMP) included defensive plus (e.g. winning the ball by reading the game; D), offensive plus (e.g. passing an opponent with the ball; O), offensive minus from losing the ball (e.g. losing the ball during dribbling; M) and offensive minus from passing errors (e.g. square or back pass to the opponent; P). The resulting ratios show good correlation with match result

($r = 0.764$) and created scoring opportunity ($r = 0.49$) and the total number of ball involvements for individual players reflected well the demands of different positional roles according to the style of play in attack (direct play) and in defence (zone-oriented) employed by the Norwegian national team. Hughes and Probert (2006) found no significant difference in either number or quality of different techniques employed by outfield players between successful and unsuccessful teams. Unfortunately, this study used a single scale to represent two different concepts (i.e. quality of skill execution and pressure), something which is simply not correct.

As is evident from the limited number and quality of studies available, despite its potential to be used directly by the squads, it seems apparent that considerable research on technical effectiveness will be beneficial for the enhancement of soccer performance.

Tactical analysis and evaluation of decision making

Tactical analysis attempts to identify effective strategy and tactics of play employed by a player, a group of players or a whole team. A strategy refers to a plan agreed in advance in order to make best use of the player's or team's strengths, while limiting the effects of any weaknesses. At the same time, the strategy should seek to exploit any known weaknesses of the opposition, while avoiding situations where the opposition can make use of their strengths. On the other hand, tactics relate to a punctual adaptation to new configurations of play and to the circulation of the ball, and therefore tactics are adaptations to opposition. This means tactics relate to the positions taken in reaction to an adversary in a match situation, as well as the adaptation of the team to the conditions of players' (for details of the different aspects of strategy and tactics, see Gréhaigne et al., 1999).

The strategy that has been agreed prior to the match and tactical decisions made during the match are not directly observable. Instead, the observation of different skills performed by players, the locations on the pitch where they are performed as well as the timing of these actions during a match play can give an indication of the strategy and tactics being applied. The evaluation of decision making through observational means is a natural extension of tactical analysis, often implicitly accomplished within tactical analysis. The decisions made by a player during a match play can only be observed indirectly. This requires an understanding of different options available, their relative chance of success and any risks involved, as well as the situational pressure that a player was under when making a decision. However, despite its potential to influence soccer performance directly, research on decision-making processes during real soccer matches is very scarce. Only a study by Jordet (2005) is available in the literature. Using post-intervention questionnaires and interviews to support the video analyses, Jordet concluded that ecological imagery training can improve visual exploratory ability in elite players, but without clear improvement of players' performance with the ball.

The original work of Reep and Benjamin (1968) is considered to be a landmark in match performance analysis in soccer (McGarry and Franks, 2003). This research was based on the analysis of data collected from 3213 matches played between 1953 and 1968. These data on goal scoring and the length of passing sequences were analysed statistically and appeared to follow a probability structure. Two main findings from this research were: first, approximately 80 per cent of goals resulted from a sequence of three passes or less and, second, a goal is scored in every ten shots. These findings have been reconfirmed by several different studies (e.g. Bate, 1988; Franks, 1988; Hughes, 1990). In short, Reep and his colleague showed that a successful style of play can be built by maximizing the 'chance' elements of the game (Reep and Benjamin, 1968). For example, Bate (1988) concluded that, to increase the number of scoring opportunities, a team should play the ball forward as often as possible, reduce square and back passes to a minimum, increase the number of long passes forward and forward runs with the ball, and play the ball into forward space as often as possible. Indeed, the adoption of these recommendations by some soccer managers in England has been responsible for what has come to be known as the 'direct play' style of attack (Franks and McGarry, 1996). However, McGarry and Franks (2003) maintain that the nature of the good association between successful match performance and the direct style of play is still not well understood.

Research on playing effectiveness concentrates mainly on how goals are scored and comparisons between successful and unsuccessful teams. The question of whether longer or shorter passing sequences are more effective in goal scoring has long been disputed in the soccer community, including among performance analysis researchers (e.g. Bate, 1988; Hughes *et al.*, 1988; Olsen and Larsen, 1997; Reep and Benjamin, 1968). Literature shows mixed findings, with studies supporting either longer passing sequences (e.g. Hughes and Churchill, 2004; Hughes and Snook, 2006; Hughes *et al.*, 1988) or shorter passing sequences (e.g. Bate, 1988; Hughes, 1990; Olsen and Larsen, 1997; Reep and Benjamin, 1968) as a more effective attacking style. Furthermore, the most recent studies demonstrated that more goals were scored from shorter passing sequences, but also that there were more instances of shorter passing sequences than longer ones (Hughes and Franks, 2005; Hughes and Snook, 2006; Tenga *et al.*, 2010a, 2010b). Thus, the difference between these studies appears to be due to the different interpretations of effectiveness and that, if the data are normalized, the longer passing sequences indeed become more effective than shorter ones.

Furthermore, team possessions originating from the final third of the playing field were found to be effective in goal scoring (Bate, 1988; Garganta *et al.*, 1997; Hughes, 1990; Hughes and Snook, 2006; Tenga *et al.*, 2010a, 2010b). Bate (1988), for example, reported 50 to 60 per cent of all possessions leading to shot on goal originated in the attacking third. This finding favoured the approach of direct play as this tactic is expected to decrease the likelihood of a team losing possession in the defending third of the field (Bate, 1988). More recently, compared to the unsuccessful teams, successful teams were reported to score more goals from possessions started in the midfield zone, but not in the attacking third (Tenga and Sigmundstad, 2011). Hook and Hughes (2001) reported similar results, showing that successful teams were more able to start with the ball in their own defensive half and end with a shot at goal compared to unsuccessful teams.

Several studies have reported that possessions with relatively longer duration were related with successful teams (Hook and Hughes, 2001; Hughes and Churchill, 2004; Jones *et al.*, 2004; Tenga and Sigmundstad, 2011). Hughes and Churchill (2004) found that successful teams in Copa America 2001 kept the ball for longer durations and created shots after possessions lasting more than 20 seconds more frequently than unsuccessful teams. Also, significantly longer possessions were performed by successful rather than unsuccessful teams from the 2000 European Championships (Hook and Hughes, 2001). The same was found for teams from the English Premier League (Jones *et al.*, 2004) and from the Norwegian top professional league (Tenga and Sigmundstad, 2011). Hughes *et al.* (1988) also reported that successful teams used more touches per possession than unsuccessful teams in the 1986 World Cup finals. Moreover, style of play seems to influence possession duration as well. Carling *et al.* (2005) reported that the majority of goals (53 per cent) in 1998 and 2002 FIFA World Cup finals were scored after possessions lasting between 6 and 15 seconds, while more than 55 per cent of all goals scored in the English Premier league in the 1997–98 season were from possessions of less than five seconds. The authors suggested that international teams are more likely to score goals after long passing sequences and that English Premiership teams tend to employ a more direct attacking strategy.

More qualitative possession characteristics, indicating high and low degrees of offensive directness (counter-attacks and elaborate attacks, respectively), have been used in more recent studies (Tenga and Sigmundstad, 2011; Tenga *et al.*, 2010a, 2010b). Counter-attacks were found to relate to success in goal-scoring. The authors argued that the inclusion of qualitative evaluation improves the ability to describe team possessions in soccer because it enables the analysis of temporal and spatial dimensions of soccer performance, which usually are difficult to measure directly. However, most of the studies on tactical analysis use unidimensional frequency data based on analyses done in isolation from the match context. Since the opposition is responsible for the 'unexpected' in a match, requiring constant adaptation to constraints due to the confrontation between two teams (Elias and Dunning, 1966; Gréhaigne *et al.*, 1997), tactical analysis must consider the relationship between the two opposing teams to be a more valid analysis.

Only a few studies on tactical analysis in soccer have considered, directly or indirectly, opposition relationship in their analyses (Table 26.1). Harris and Reilly (1988) showed that defence against attacks with a shot on target, compared to the ones without a shot, tended to involve higher attacker-to-defender ratios and greater average distances between the attacker in possession and the nearest defender throughout the attack.

According to Gréhaigne (1991), the overall attacking configuration with adequate space and time against an opponent's defence which is out of balance had a positive effect on goal-scoring in 10 out of 33 goals. Elsewhere, it was reported that the defending performances, directly measured through distances and angles between attackers and defenders and the number of players, were related to delaying and diverting attacks, and covering attacking space (Suzuki and

Table 26.1 Examples of studies on tactical analysis in soccer that directly or indirectly consider opposition interaction in their analyses

Reference	Sample size	Opposition relationship
Taylor *et al.* (2008)	40 matches (20 strong; 20 weak opposition)	Opposition quality[a]; Match status[b]
Lago and Martin (2007)	340 observations from 170 matches between league teams of different quality	Opposition quality; Match status
Seabra and Dantas (2006)	112 shot situations from 7 matches	Opposition interaction[c]
Bloomfield *et al.* (2005)	22 team performances (7 Arsenal; 8 Chelsea; 7 Man. United)	Match status
Jones *et al.* (2004)	3544 team possessions from 24 matches (12 successful; 12 unsuccessful teams)	Opposition quality; Match status
Suzuki and Nishijima (2004)	439 defending performances from one match	Opposition interaction
Olsen and Larsen (1997)	28 counter-attacks (25 scoring chances; 3 goals) from 14 matches	Indirect opposition interaction[d]
Gréhaigne (1991)	36 goals from 14 matches	Opposition interaction
Harris and Reilly (1988)	180 randomly selected shot and non-shot attacks from 24 matches	Opposition interaction

Notes

a Analysis of team's performance according to the quality of opposing team (i.e. strong and weak).

b Analysis of team's performance according to ongoing status of the match (i.e. winning, drawing and losing).

c Simultaneous analysis of offensive and defensive performances (i.e. in relation to each other) within a match-play situation.

d Indirect analysis of offensive performance in relation to defensive performance (i.e. by observing opponent's degree of control over the ball prior to ball winning).

Nishijima, 2004). Seabra and Dantas (2006) reported a higher proportion of successful shooting attempts for ball receptions and shots originating from zones of low defensive confrontation than high defensive confrontation. Moreover, though indirectly, Olsen and Larsen (1997) showed more scoring opportunities and goals in counter-attacks started when the opponent defence was imbalanced rather than balanced. Similarly, Bloomfield *et al.* (2005), Jones *et al.* (2004), Lago and Martin (2007) and Taylor *et al.* (2008) reported the influence of match status and opposition quality on ball possession and frequency of technical behaviours. In summary, these studies (Table 26.1) report promising effects of considering opposition relationship to better understand tactical performance in soccer. However, only Suzuki and Nishijima (2004) have used a multivariate analysis approach. Some studies did not use any statistical method to compare sets of data (Bloomfield *et al.*, 2005; Gréhaigne, 1991; Olsen and Larsen, 1997), while the remaining studies employed univariate data analyses. In addition, most of these studies have small sample sizes, making the study power too low to obtain significant results.

The more recent studies by Tenga *et al.* (2010a, 2010b) presented empirical evidence of opposition relationship between offensive and defensive playing tactics in soccer by using analytical study designs. For example, counter-attacks were associated with a higher odds ratio for producing a score box possession than elaborate attacks when playing against an imbalanced defence, but not against a balanced defence (Tenga *et al.*, 2010a). Similarly, counter-attacks were associated with a higher odds ratio for producing a goal than elaborate attacks when playing against an imbalanced defence (Tenga *et al.*, 2010b). Thus, the fact that these two studies produced very similar results, irrespective of the design (cohort-like vs. case-control-like) and outcome variable (score-box possession vs. goal) used, strengthened the evidence.

Work-rate analysis and evaluation of injury risk and mechanism

Physical aspects of soccer performance analysis include time-motion analysis and supplemented data from heart rate and blood lactate measurements taken during soccer training or competition. Time-motion analysis involves evaluation of player movement throughout the entire game in terms of time spent, distance covered and speed of different movement activities during match play (Bangsbo, 1994a). Data from player movement research provide guidelines for efficient and specific fitness training programmes and tactical elements which can enhance a player's performance and reduce the risk of injury during a match (Bangsbo, 1996).

Time-motion analysis in soccer using hand notation combined with an audio tape recorder was first described by Reilly and Thomas (1976). They were able to specify in detail the work rates of players in different positions, distances covered in a game and the percentage of time in different categories of activity, classified according to intensity, duration (or distance) and frequency. A summary of the research on such work-rate characteristics indicates that outfield players cover 8–13 km during the course of a match, and with as many as 1000 different activities in a game, there is a break in the level or type of activity every six seconds. The overall distance covered by outfield players during a match consists of 24 per cent walking, 36 per cent jogging, 20 per cent cruising sub-maximally (striding), 11 per cent sprinting, 7 per cent moving backwards and 2 per cent moving with possession of the ball (Williams *et al.*, 1999; Reilly, 2003). The vast majority of actions are 'off the ball', such as a jump for the ball or a tackle of an opponent (Reilly, 2003).

The game of soccer has experienced a tremendous increase in tempo of play over the years (Table 26.2). Table 26.2 reveals a parallel increase in the number of short sprints (2–3 s, covering about 10–15 m), which suggests that an increase in the tempo of play over the years is the most likely reason behind the huge distances covered during matches in modern soccer.

Table 26.2 Total distance covered and number of sprints performed per match over the years (Bangsbo, 1994a; Bangsbo *et al.*, 1991; Bradley *et al.*; 2011; Ekblom, 1986; Dufour, 1993; Dupont *et al.*, 2010; Ohashi *et al.*, 1988; Reilly and Thomas, 1976)

Year	Distance in km	Year	Number of sprints
1954	4.5	1947	70
1976	8.7	1970	145
1986	10.1	1985	185
1988	10.3	1989	195
1991	10.8 (9–14)★	1991	196★
2010	11.9†	2010	13†
2011	10.8 ± 1.0‡	2011	120 ± 39‡

Notes

★ Data for the outfield players (HI≥15 km.h^{-1}); † Data for the central midfield players (sprint>24 km.h^{-1}); ‡ Data for the outfield players in 4-3-3 formation (HI≥14.4 km.h^{-1}).

Using more sophisticated methods (e.g. Bloomfield *et al.*, 2004; Robinson and O'Donoghue 2008), recent studies have applied detailed time-motion techniques allowing details of accelerations, decelerations, turns, swerves and jumps to be recorded. For example, studies on path changes during player movements for the understanding of agility requirements of soccer have been conducted (e.g. Bloomfield *et al.*, 2007a, 2007b; Robinson *et al.*, 2011). In an analysis of the physical demands when running with the ball in professional soccer, Carling (2010) found that players ran a mean total distance of 191 ± 38 m with the ball, of which 34.3 per cent was covered at speeds of >19.1 km.hour^{-1}. Further, mean time in possession, duration and touches per possession were 53.4 ± 8.1 s, 1.1 ± 0.1 s and 2.0 ± 0.2, respectively, with significant differences across playing positions for all variables. Dupont *et al.* (2010) reported that physical performance, as characterized by total distance covered, high-intensity distance, sprint distance and number of sprints, was not significantly affected by the number of matches per week (one versus two), whereas the injury rate was significantly higher when players played two matches per week as opposed to one match per week (25.6 versus 4.1 injuries per 1000 hours of exposure). Elsewhere, midfield players were reported to cover a significantly greater total distance than defenders and forward players. Also, more distance was covered in the first half compared to the second in medium intensities (11.1 – 19 km.hour^{-1}), but no difference between the two halves was found in either total distance or distances covered at submaximal and maximal intensities (Di Salvo *et al.*, 2007). High-intensity activity was also related to team success, with teams finishing in the bottom five (919 ± 128 m) and middle ten (917 ± 143 m) league positions completing significantly more total high-intensity running distance per outfield player per match compared with teams in the top five (885 ± 113 m) from three seasons of the English Premier League (Di Salvo *et al.*, 2009).

Buchheit *et al.* (2010) found similar position-dependent results in highly trained young (U13–U18) soccer players, showing midfielders covered the greater total distance and centre-backs covered the lowest. Also, distance for very high-intensity activities (>16.1 km.hour^{-1}) was lower for centre-backs compared with all other positions, while wide midfielders and strikers displayed the highest very high-intensity activities. In elite female soccer, Andersson *et al.* (2010) reported more high-intensity running and sprinting in international compared with domestic games. Further, female midfielders covered longer distances with high-intensity running in international than in domestic games over the entire game and in the most intense five-minute period of the games, whereas no differences were observed between the game types for defenders. Carling and Dupont (2011) found no reduction in skill-related performances during professional soccer match play as a result of a decline in physical performance. The study by Bradley *et al.* (2011) showed that attackers in 4-3-3 formations covered about 30 per cent more high-intensity running than attackers in 4-4-2 and 4-5-1 formations. Moreover, despite the fact that no differences were found in overall ball possession, the number of passes performed was higher for players in 4-4-2 compared with 4-3-3 and 4-5-1 formations. Thus, this study is the first to demonstrate that physical performance across playing positions is also dependent upon the team formation employed.

Heart-rate data observed during match play generally confirm that the circulatory strain during match play is relatively high, with patterns closely related to the distances covered by the players in a match (Ali and Farally, 1991; Bangsbo, 1994b). The heart rate varied with the work rate and differed between playing positions and between first and second halves. Mean values of 155 beat.min^{-1} for a centre-back and a full-back player, 170 beat.min^{-1} for a midfield player, and 168 and 171 beat.min^{-1} for two forward players have been reported for a team at university level (Van Gool *et al.*, 1983). The same study reported 169 beats.min^{-1} in the first half and 165 beat.min^{-1} in the second half. However, these heart-rate values are likely to overestimate the players' work rate since other factors, such as dehydration, hyperthermia and mental stress, also contribute in elevating the heart rate during a soccer match (Bangsbo and Krustrup, 2009). Measurements of blood lactate concentration were also used to indicate the severity of soccer match play. The mean values of 2–10 mM, with individual values of above 12 mM were reported during soccer matches (Bangsbo and Krustrup, 2009). Ekblom (1986) reported progressively higher lactates in matches from the lower to the top divisions of the Swedish league. According to Bangsbo and Krustrup (2009), blood lactate values can be high even though the muscle lactate concentration is relatively low due to the higher lactate clearance rate in the muscle than in blood.

Other research investigating injury risk (e.g. Andersen *et al.*, 2004c; Hawkins and Fuller, 1998; Rahnama *et al.*, 2002) and injury mechanism (e.g. Andersen *et al.*, 2004a, 2004b) has used observational analysis of match events. Hawkins and Fuller (1998) found that the playing position has no influence on the rate of injury. Assessing the exposure of players to playing actions during English Premier League matches, Rahnama *et al.* (2002) found that more than one third of the playing actions were judged to have some level of injury potential (assessed subjectively on the likelihood of the actions to produce an injury). Andersen *et al.* (2004c) provided a more detailed description of high-risk playing actions by using video-based methods that combine soccer-specific and medical information to represent a different approach. No single classic playing situation typical for soccer injuries or incidents could be recognized in this study. However, in most cases, the exposed player seemed to be unaware of the opponent challenging him for ball possession. Further, this study shows that, of the 121 injuries during matches from the top professional league in Norwegian soccer, 43 per cent were identified on video. Among these, serious, moderate and minor injuries were distributed equally. Sixty-nine injuries were not identified on video. Of these, about half were minor and one-fifth serious. Most of the injuries (75–87 per cent) affected the lower extremities. Sprains of the ankle or knee were the most common injury types seen on video, whereas muscle strains to thigh or lower leg accounted for nearly half of the injuries reported but were not identified on video. This implies that there was no stoppage in play, the player did not go down on the pitch but was able to continue and the player was not given treatment until half-time or after the match. These results suggest that a video analysis alone, as previously used in Hawkins and Fuller (1998) and Rahnama *et al.* (2002), without simultaneous access to medical information from team medical staff, may result in a biased description of how injuries occur in soccer. A similar conclusion was produced by Rahnama and Zareei (2010) in another video analysis-based study. However, this study reported higher incidence of injuries in the Asian Cup of 2007 than that recorded for the World Cup competitions in 1998, 2002 and 2006 and that goalkeepers sustained more injuries than players in other positional roles. Rahnama and Zareei suggested that the higher incidences of injury in this study might reflect the relatively lower level of skill evident in Asian soccer players compared to players at international level, as well as differences in physical characteristics.

Andersen *et al.* (2004a, 2004b) attempted to avoid the shortcomings of recall bias in previous research and studied injury mechanism using video recordings of the incidents cross-referenced with reports of acute time-loss injuries from the team medical staff. They reported two mechanisms for ankle injuries thought to be specific to soccer: 1) player-to-player contact, with impact by an opponent on medial aspect of the leg just before or at foot strike, resulting in a laterally directed force, causing the player to land with the ankle in a vulnerable, inverted position; and 2) forced plantar flexion, where the injured player hit the opponent's foot when attempting to shoot or clear the ball (Andersen *et al.*, 2004a). For the mechanisms for head injuries, elbow-, arm- or hand-to-head contact was the most common mechanism observed. In most of these contacts, the upper arm of the player causing the incident was at or above shoulder level, and the arm use was considered to be active (Andersen *et al.*, 2004b).

Behavioural and psychological analysis

The idea that tactics can be inferred from observed patterns of behaviour during competition or training can also be extended to behavioural and psychological aspects of performance (O'Donoghue, 2010: 7). In soccer, observational technique has been used to investigate the effect of importance of the kicks (Jordet *et al.*, 2007; McGarry and Franks, 2000) and public status (Jordet, 2009a, 2009b; Jordet *et al.*, 2009) on the performance of a penalty kick.

In penalty shootouts, the later kicks are argued to be more important than early kicks (McGarry and Franks, 2000). The authors argued further that, if each kick was to be performed independently of the others, all kicks would be of equal importance. However, in reality, each kick is performed in awareness of both the outcome of the previous kicks and the current standings between the teams. Penalty kicks are also perceived to be important due to the fact that their outcome determines whether a team advances or is eliminated from the tournament, or alternatively, they determine a team's final rank – that is either winning a tournament or being placed third (Jordet *et al.*, 2007). Thus, one reason as for why penalty kicks are experienced as stressful is that the importance of their outcome is assumed to be indicative of stress and anxiety.

Investigating how the order of the shooters would affect the outcome, McGarry and Franks (2000) found that the goal probabilities of each kick from the first to the sixth kick follows an inverted-U, with the least successful kicks early and late. However, this study used a small sample size and the data used may be confounded by the bias of selected line-up order, with coaches picking the best player to take the first kick. In contrast, another study using a larger data set found that goal probability in penalty shootouts follows a negatively linear curve, with higher anxiety progressively resulting in a poorer outcome (Jordet *et al.*, 2007). In addition, Jordet *et al.* (2007) demonstrated that importance of the kicks was negatively related to the outcomes of the kicks, whereas skill and fatigue were less, or not, related to outcome.

The phenomenon of choking under pressure was also investigated in relation to poor performance in penalty shootouts. Jordet (2009a) examined links between public status and performance in penalty shootouts and found that players with high current status performed worse and seemed to engage more in self-defeating behaviours than players with future status. Further, there were indications that some performance reduction may be stemmed from misdirected self-regulation of low response time. Similarly, players from countries with higher public status (England and Spain) spent less time preparing their shots and were less successful in penalty shootouts than players from countries with lower public status (Jordet, 2009b). Jordet *et al.* (2009) demonstrated that the phenomenon of choking under pressure may indeed be a type of self-defeating behaviour. The authors argued that players may attempt to escape unpleasant emotional distress induced by extreme levels of performance pressure by getting the situation over with as soon as possible, leaving their performance to suffer as a result. In another study, individually displayed post-shot behaviours involving celebration with both arms after success-ful soccer penalty kicks were found to be associated with winning the shootout (Moll *et al.*, 2010). According to Moll and colleagues, this finding showed that the transference of emotions from individuals onto teammates and opponents is an important process in the context of elite sport performance.

The presented findings indicate a promising potential and therefore further work is needed to explore more behavioural and psychological factors directly associated with performance, especially at high levels of play.

Future work

Research on performance analysis in soccer over the past years has undoubtedly advanced our understanding of game behaviour. However, the validity of data generated from most studies, especially on the prescriptive function of tactical analysis, can be questioned due to the lack of assessment of opposition relationship in their analyses. Other critical issues related to conceptual and methodological shortcomings of the contemporary research that need attention in future research may include development of theoretical framework, research on critical behaviours, consideration of situational and playing contexts, and inclusion of spatial and temporal dynam-ics (McGarry, 2009). The more access to the positional data from automated player tracking systems, covering the entire on-field activity of all players throughout the match, will ensure more efficient and reliable research in the future. This will benefit especially the analysis of time-motion, tactics and decision-making processes during match play. In the past, most time-motion investigations suffered from the limited number of players that could be analysed, as well as the reliability with which they could be analysed. In addition, the availability of move-ment data for all players throughout the entire match will enrich the time-motion analysis by relating players' movement data to the performance during match play, as well as enable a more holistic tactical analysis.

Research on technical effectiveness and decision-making processes, as well as observational research on penalty shootouts, serves a direct purpose in enhancing player and team perform-ance in soccer. However, to date, the applied research in these areas appears most limited. More research on technical effectiveness, decision-making processes and observational research within behavioural and psychological aspects of soccer match performance is therefore espe-cially recommended.

Concluding remarks

The chapter provides evidence that research on performance analysis in soccer has raised our level of knowledge about technique and technical effectiveness, tactics and evaluation of deci-sion making, work-rate and evaluation of injury risk and mechanism, and behavioural and psychological aspects of player and team performance. The substantial knowledge has been produced for coaching feedback (descriptive function) as well as for outcome projection and performance optimization (prescriptive function). This has led researchers to offer advice to soccer practitioners about different topics of interest, such as detailed understanding of important skills, the positional demands technically, how to play effectively, correct behavioural and mental states in stressful situations and even how these diverse skills can be acquired.

However, applied research in soccer needs to pay further attention to critical issues related to conceptual and methodological shortcomings in order to meet its intentions and purposes effectively. Nevertheless, more efficient and reliable research on soccer performance analysis in general, particularly on the analysis of time-motion, tactics and decision-making processes during match play, is expected in the future. This is due to the easier availability of positional data from more accurate player-tracking technology. Further, there is a need for more research on technical effectiveness, decision-making processes and observational research within behavioural and psychological aspects of player and team performance. To date, these areas remain most limited, yet necessary, for the enhancement of soccer performance.

References

Ali, A. and Farally, M. (1991) 'Recording soccer players' heart rate during matches', *Journal of Sports Sciences*, 9: 183–9.

Andersen, T.E., Arnason, A., Engebretsen, L. and Bahr, R. (2004a) 'Mechanisms of head injuries in elite football', *British Journal of Sports Medicine*, 38: 690–6.

Andersen, T.E., Floerenes, T.W., Arnason, A. and Bahr, R. (2004b) 'Video analysis of the mechanisms for ankle injuries in football', *The American Journal of Sports Medicine*, 32: 69–79.

Andersen, T.E., Tenga, A., Engebretsen, L. and Bahr, R. (2004c) 'Video analysis of injuries and incidents in Norwegian professional football', *British Journal of Sports Medicine*, 38: 626–31.

Andersson, H.A., Randers, M.B., Heiner-Møller, A., Krustrup P. and Mohr, M. (2010) 'Elite female soccer players perform more high-intensity running when playing in international games compared with domestic league games', *Journal of Strength and Conditioning Research*, 24: 912–9.

Bangsbo, J. (1994a) *Fitness Training in Football: A Scientific Approach*, Bagsværd, Denmark: HO+Storm.

Bangsbo, J. (1994b) 'The physiology of soccer – with special reference to intense intermittent exercise', *Acta Physiologica Scandinavica*, 151(619): 1–155.

Bangsbo, J. (1996) 'Physiology of training', in T. Reilly (ed.), *Science and Soccer* (pp. 51–64). London: E and FN Spon.

Bangsbo, J. and Krustrup, P. (2009) 'Physical demands and training of top-class soccer players', in T. Reilly and F. Korkusuz (eds), *Science and Football VI* (pp. 318–30). London: Routledge.

Bangsbo, J., Nørregaard, L. and Thorsøe, F. (1991) 'Activity profile of competition soccer', *Canadian Journal of Sports Science*, 16: 110–6.

Bate, R. (1988) 'Football chance: Tactics and strategy', in T. Reilly, A. Lees, K. Davids and W.J. Murphy (eds), *Science and Football* (pp. 293–301). London: E and FN Spon.

Bloomfield, J.R., Polman, R.C.J. and O'Donoghue, P.G. (2004) 'The "Bloomfield Movement Classifications": Motion analysis of individual players in dynamic movement sports', *International Journal of Performance Analysis in Sport*, 4: 20–31.

Bloomfield, J.R., Polman, R.C.J. and O'Donoghue, P.G. (2005) 'Effects of score-line on team strategies in FA Premier League soccer', *Journal of Sports Sciences*, 23: 192–3.

Bloomfield, J.R., Polman, R.C.J. and O'Donoghue, P.G. (2007a) 'Physical demands of different positions in FA Premier League soccer', *Journal of Sports Science and Medicine*, 6: 63–70.

Bloomfield, J., Polman, R., O'Donoghue, P. and McNaughton, L. (2007b) 'Effective speed and agility conditioning methodology for random intermittent dynamic type sports', *Journal of Strength and Conditioning Research*, 21: 1093–100.

Bradley, P.S., Carling, C., Archer, D., Roberts, J., Dodds, A., Di Mascio, M., Paul, D., Diaz, A.G., Peart, D. and Krustrup, P. (2011) 'The effect of playing formation on high-intensity running and technical profiles in English FA Premier League soccer matches', *Journal of Sports Sciences*, 29: 821–30.

Buchheit, M., Mendez-Villanueva, A., Simpson, B.M. and Bourdon, P.C. (2010) 'Match running performance and fitness in youth soccer', *International Journal of Sports Medicine*, 31: 818–25.

Carling, C. (2010) 'Analysis of physical activity profiles when running with the ball in a professional soccer team', *Journal of Sports Sciences*, 28: 319–26.

Carling, C. and Dupont, G. (2011) 'Are declines in physical performance associated with a reduction in skill-related performance during professional soccer match-play?', *Journal of Sports Sciences*, 29: 63–71.

Carling, C., Williams, A.M. and Reilly, T. (2005) *Handbook of Soccer Match Analysis*, London: Routledge.

Di Salvo, V., Baron, R., Tschan, H., Calderon Montero, F.J., Bachl, N. and Pigozzi, F. (2007) 'Performance characteristics according to playing position in elite soccer', *International Journal of Sports Medicine*, 28: 222–7.

Di Salvo, V., Gregson, W., Atkinson, G., Tordoff, P. and Drust, B. (2009) 'Analysis of high intensity activity in premier league soccer', *International Journal of Sports Medicine*, 30: 205–12.

Dufour, W. (1993) 'Computer-assisted scouting in soccer', in T. Reilly, J. Clarys and A. Stibbe (eds), *Science and Football II* (pp. 160–6). London: E and FN Spon.

Dupont, G., Nedelec, M., McCall, A., McCormack, D., Berthoin, S. and Wisløff, U. (2010) 'Effect of 2 soccer matches in a week on physical performance and injury rate', *The American Journal of Sports Medicine*, 38: 1752–8.

Ekblom, B. (1986) 'Applied physiology of soccer', *Sports Medicine*, 3: 50–60.

Elias, N. and Dunning, E. (1966) 'Dynamics of group sports with special references to football', *British Journal of Sociology*, 17: 388–402.

Franks, I.M. (1988) 'Analysis of association football', *Soccer Journal*, September/October: 35–43.

Franks, I.M. (2004) 'The need for feedback', in M. Hughes and I.M. Franks (eds), *Notational Analysis of Sport* (pp. 8–16). London: Routledge.

Franks, I.M. and McGarry, T. (1996) 'The science of match analysis', in T. Reilly (ed.), *Science and Soccer* (pp. 363–75). London: E and FN Spon.

Garganta, J., Maia, J. and Basto, F. (1997) 'Analysis of goal-scoring patterns in European top level soccer teams', in T. Reilly, J. Bangsbo and M. Hughes (eds), *Science and Football III* (pp. 246–50). London: E and FN Spon.

Goktepe, A., Ak, E., Karabork, H., Cicek, S. and Korkusuz, F. (2010) 'Knee flexion and ankle extension strategies at instep penalty kick', in B. Drust, T. Reilly and A.M. Williams (eds), *International Research in Science and Soccer* (pp. 39–45). London: Routledge.

Gréhaigne, J.F. (1991) 'A new method of goal analysis', *Science and Football*, 5: 10–6.

Grehaigne, J.F., Bouthier, D. and David, B. (1997) 'Dynamic-system analysis of opponent relationships in collective actions in soccer', *Journal of Sport Sciences*, 15: 137–49.

Gréhaigne, J.F., Bouthier, D. and Godbout, P. (1999) 'The foundations of tactics and strategy in team sports', *Journal of Teaching in Physical Education*, 18: 159–74.

Harris, S. and Reilly, T. (1988) 'Space, team work and attacking success in soccer', in T. Reilly, A. Lees, K. Davids and W.J. Murphy (eds), *Science and Football* (pp. 322–8). London: E and FN Spon.

Hawkins, R.D. and Fuller, C.W. (1998) 'An examination of the frequency and severity of injuries and incidents at three levels of professional football', *British Journal of Sports Medicine*, 32: 326–32.

Hook, C. and Hughes, M. (2001) 'Patterns of play leading to shots in "Euro 2000"', in M. Hughes and I.M. Franks (eds), *Proceedings of Pass.com* (pp. 295–302). Cardiff: CPA UWIC Press.

Hughes, C. (1990) *The Winning Formula*, London: William Collins Sons and Co. Ltd.

Hughes, M. (2004) 'Notational analysis – a mathematical perspective', *International Journal of Performance Analysis in Sport*, 4: 97–139.

Hughes, M. and Churchill, S. (2004) 'Attacking profiles of successful and unsuccessful teams in Copa America 2001', *Journal of Sports Sciences*, 22: 505.

Hughes, M. and Franks, I.M. (2005) 'Analysis of passing sequences, shots and goals in soccer', *Journal of Sports Sciences*, 23: 509–14.

Hughes, M. and Reed, D. (2005) 'Creating a performance profile using perturbations in soccer', in D. Milanovic and F. Prot (eds), *4th International Scientific Conference on Kinesiology* (pp. 34–53). Zagreb: University of Zagreb.

Hughes, M. and Probert, G. (2006) 'A technical analysis of elite male soccer players by position and success', in H. Dancs, M. Hughes and P.G. O'Donoghue (eds), *Proceedings of World Congress of Performance Analysis of Sport 7* (pp. 89–104). Cardiff: CPA Press, UWIC.

Hughes, M. and Snook, N. (2006) 'Effectiveness of attacking play in the 2004 European Championships', in H. Dancs, M. Hughes and P.G. O'Donoghue (eds), *Proceedings of World Congress of Performance Analysis of Sport 7* (pp. 46–62). Cardiff: CPA Press, UWIC.

Hughes, M., Robertson, K. and Nicholson, A. (1988) 'Comparison of patterns of play of successful and unsuccessful teams in the 1986 World Cup for soccer', in T. Reilly, A. Lees, K. Davids and W.J. Murphy (eds), *Science and Football* (pp. 363–7). London: E and FN Spon.

Hughes, M., Dawkins, N., Reed, D. and Mills, J. (1998) 'The perturbation effect and goal opportunities in soccer', *Journal of Sports Sciences*, 16: 20.

Hughes, M., Langridge, C. and Dawkins, N. (2001) 'Pertubation actions not leading to shots on goal in soccer', in M. Hughes (ed.), *Notational Analysis of Sport IV* (pp. 23–32). Cardiff: UWIC CPA Press.

Isokawa, M. and Lees, A. (1988) 'A biomechanical analysis of the instep kick motion in soccer', in T. Reilly, A. Lees, K. Davids and W.J. Murphy (eds), *Science and Football* (pp. 449–55). London: E and FN Spon.

Jones, P.D., James, N. and Mellalieu, S.D. (2004) 'Possession as a performance indicator in soccer', *International Journal of Performance Analysis in Sport*, 4: 98–102.

Jordet, G. (2005) 'Perceptual training in soccer: An imagery intervention study with elite players', *Journal of Applied Sport Psychology*, 17: 140–56.

Jordet, G. (2009a) 'When superstars flop: Public status and choking under pressure in international soccer penalty shootouts', *Journal of Applied Sport Psychology*, 21: 125–30.

Jordet, G. (2009b) 'Why do English players fail in penalty shootouts? A study of team status, self-regulation, and choking under pressure', *Journal of Sports Sciences*, 27: 97–106.

Jordet, G., Hartman, E., Visscher, C. and Lemmink, K.A.P.M. (2007) 'Kicks from the penalty mark in soccer: The roles of stress, skill, and fatigue for kick outcomes', *Journal of Sports Sciences*, 25: 121–9.

Jordet, G., Hartman, E. and Sigmundstad, E. (2009) 'Temporal links to performing under pressure in international soccer penalty shootouts', *Psychology of Sport Exercise*, 10: 621–7.

Katis, A. and Kellis, E. (2011) 'Is soccer kick performance better after a "faking" (cutting) manoeuvre task?', *Sports Biomechanics*, 10: 35–45.

Kellis, E., Katis, A. and Gissis, I. (2004) 'Knee biomechanics of the support leg in soccer kicks from three angles approach', *Medicine and Science in Sports and Exercise*, 36: 1017–28.

Kristensen, L.B. and Bull, T. (2009) 'Effect of approach velocity in soccer kicking', in T. Reilly and F. Korkusuz (eds), *Science and Football VI* (pp. 47–9). London: Routledge.

Lago, C. and Martin, R. (2007) 'Determinants of possession of the ball in soccer', *Journal of Sports Sciences*, 25: 969–74.

Less, A. (2003) 'Biomechanics applied to soccer skills', in T. Reilly and A.M. Williams (eds), *Science and Soccer* (pp. 109–19). London: Routledge.

Lees, A. (2009) 'The biomechanics of football skills', in T. Reilly and F. Korkusuz (eds), *Science and Football VI* (pp. 11–17). London: Routledge.

Lees, A. and Nolan, L. (2002) 'Three dimensional kinematic analysis of instep kick under speed and accuracy conditions', in W. Spinks, T. Reilly, and A. Murphy (eds), *Science and Football IV* (pp. 16–21). London: Routledge.

McGarry, T. (2009) 'Applied and theoretical perspectives of performance analysis in sport: Scientific issues and challenges', *International Journal of Performance Analysis of Sport*, 9: 128–40.

McGarry, T. and Franks, I.M. (2000) 'On winning the penalty shoot-out in soccer', *Journal of Sports Sciences*, 18: 401–9.

McGarry, T. and Franks, I.M. (2003) 'The science of match analysis', in T. Reilly and A.M. Williams (eds), *Science and Soccer* (pp. 265–75). London: Routledge.

McGarry, T. and Perl, J. (2004) 'Models of sports contests: Markov processes, dynamical systems and neural networks', in M. Hughes and I.M. Franks (eds), *Notational Analysis of Sport* (pp. 227–42). London: Routledge.

McGarry, T., Anderson, D.I., Wallace, S.A., Hughes, M.D. and Franks, I.M. (2002) 'Sport competition as a dynamical self-organizing system', *Journal of Sports Sciences*, 20: 771–81.

Moll, T., Jordet, G. and Pepping, G.-J. (2010) 'Emotional contagion in soccer penalty shootouts: Celebration of individual success is associated with ultimate team success', *Journal of Sports Sciences*, 28: 983–92.

Nunome, H., Ikegami, Y., Kozakai, R., Apriantono, T. and Sano, S. (2006) 'Segmental dynamics of soccer instep kick with the preferred and non-preferred leg', *Journal of Sports Sciences*, 24: 529–41.

O'Donoghue, P. (2010) *Research Methods for Sports Performance Analysis*, London: Routledge.

Ohashi, J., Togari, H., Isokawa, M. and Suzuki, S. (1988) 'Measuring movement speeds and distances covered during soccer match-play', in T. Reilly, A. Lees, K. Davids and W.J. Murphy (eds), *Science and Football* (pp. 329–33). London: E and FN Spon.

Olsen, E. and Larsen, O. (1997) 'Use of match analysis by coaches', in T. Reilly, J. Bangsbo and M. Hughes (eds), *Science and Football* (pp. 209–20). London: E and FN Spon.

Perl, J. (2001) 'Artificial neural networks in sports: New concepts and approaches', *International Journal of Performance Analysis in Sport*, 1(1): 106–21.

Perl, J. (2002) 'Game analysis and control by means of continuously learning networks', *International Journal of Performance Analysis in Sport*, 2: 21–35.

Rahnama, N. and Zareei, M. (2010) 'Video analysis of football injuries at the Asian Cup 2007', in B. Drust, T. Reilly and A.M. Williams (eds), *International Research in Science and Soccer* (pp. 123–30). London: Routledge.

Rahnama, N., Reilly, T. and Lees, A. (2002) 'Injury risk associated with playing actions during competitive soccer', *British Journal of Sports Medicine*, 36: 354–9.

Reep, C. and Benjamin, B. (1968) 'Skill and chance in association football', *Journal of Royal Statistical Society, Series A*, 131: 581–5.

Reilly, T. (2003) 'Motion analysis and physiological demands', in T. Reilly and A.M. Williams (eds), *Science and Soccer* (pp. 59–72). London: Routledge.

Reilly, T. and Thomas, V. (1976) 'A motion analysis of work rate in different positional roles in professional football match play', *Journal of Human Movement Studies*, 2: 87–97.

Robinson, G. and O'Donoghue, P.G. (2008) 'A movement classification for the investigation of agility demands and injury risk in sport', *International Journal of Performance Analysis in Sport*, 8: 127–44.

Robinson, G., O'Donoghue, P.G. and Wooster, B. (2011) 'Path changes in the movement of English Premier League soccer players', *Journal of Sports Medicine and Physical Fitness*, 51: 220–6.

Seabra, F. and Dantas, L. (2006) 'Space definition for match analysis in soccer', *International Journal of Performance Analysis in Sport*, 6: 97–113.

Shan, G. and Westerhoff, P. (2005) 'Full-body characteristics of the maximal instep kick by male soccer players and parameters related to kick quality', *Sports Biomechanics*, 4: 59–72.

Suzuki, K. and Nishijima, T. (2004) 'Validity of a soccer defending skill scale (SDSS) using game performances', *International Journal of Sport and Health Science*, 2: 34–49.

Taylor, J.B., Mellalieu, S.D., James, N. and Shearer, D.A. (2008) 'The influence of match location, quality of opposition, and match status on technical performance in professional association football', *Journal of Sports Sciences*, 26: 885–95.

Tenga, A. and Sigmundstad, E. (2011) 'Characteristics of goal-scoring possessions in open play: Comparing the top, in-between and bottom teams from professional soccer league', *International Journal of Performance Analysis in Sport*, 11: 545–52.

Tenga, A., Holme, I., Ronglan, L.T. and Bahr, R. (2010a) 'Effect of playing tactics on achieving score-box possessions in a random series of team possessions from Norwegian professional soccer matches', *Journal of Sports Sciences*, 28: 245–55.

Tenga, A., Holme, I., Ronglan, L.T. and Bahr, R. (2010b) 'Effect of playing tactics on goal scoring in Norwegian professional soccer', *Journal of Sports Sciences*, 28: 237–44.

Van Gool, D., Van Gerven, D. and Boutmans J. (1983) 'Heart rate telemetry during a soccer game: A new methodology', *Journal of Sports Sciences*, 1: 154.

Williams, A.M., Lee, D. and Reilly, T. (1999) *A Quantitative Analysis of Matches Played in the 1991– 1992 and 1997–1998 Seasons*, London: The Football Association.

27

RUGBY

Sebastian Prim[1] and Michele van Rooyen[2]

[1] SOUTH AFRICAN RUGBY UNION, SOUTH AFRICA
[2] UNIVERSITY OF STELLENBOSCH, SOUTH AFRICA

Summary

Rugby is an extremely physically demanding game. With the implementation of law changes, ball-in-play time and the number of events players are involved in have increased dramatically over the last 20 years. Modern rugby training regimes are often restricted to archaic methodologies, based upon outdated information. The aim of this chapter is to provide greater insight into the demands of modern rugby in order to provide coaches and conditioning coaches with better information from which they can make more informed decisions regarding training regimes. This activity profile and work-rate information has been provided by a number of studies using either time-motion analysis or Global Positioning System (GPS) technology. Pertinent and practical technical and tactical information for coaches will be provided. The literature investigating the basic skills required by rugby players will be reviewed. More advanced technical skills, such as evasion techniques and the tackle situation, will also be investigated. The chapter will be concluded with a review examining the key tactical outcome of rugby – scoring points – in order to provide novel information that might help teams to be more successful.

Introduction

Due to rugby's increasing level of professionalism, rugby performance analysis is in a rapid state of evolution. Coaches, media, administrators and players are demanding greater access to more detailed analysis of team and player performance. The key element to achieve success in rugby is to be able to replicate and often exceed performance in training, to that which occurs in competition. In order to accurately replicate match-day performance in training, you require accurate, longitudinal and reliable information about all aspects of match performance. These aspects include mentality, decision making, technical and tactical expertise and work rate.

Jim Greenwood stated that a 'team's efficiency is a product of its work rate, governed by its physical preparation but conditioned by its freshness and attitude and its technical and tactical expertise' (Greenwood, 2003: 315). Performance analysis has been used extensively in rugby to evaluate the physical demands, and technical and tactical performances, with the goal of determining the winning formula for success. Data from the International Rugby Board (IRB) is used in this chapter as it comes from a respected source and it provides the most up-to-date information. Although it is acknowledged this data is not from peer-reviewed scientific sources, it is used by coaches to modify performance and thus impacts on future research.

Rugby union

The following three sections survey research that has been done in rugby union in the areas of physical demands, technical aspects and tactical aspects of the game.

Physical demands

Work-to-rest ratios

Due to the highly intermittent nature of rugby union, the patterns of work-to-rest ratios are an important determinant of the physical demands of the game. Deutsch *et al.* (1998) investigated *real-time* time-motion analysis with heart rate in elite under-19 rugby players. The authors observed that there were noticeable differences between the work rates of forwards and backs. Work rates were defined as 'those when a player was cruising, sprinting, rucking, mauling or scrummaging, with the remaining activities classified as rest'. Forwards and backs had work-to-rest-ratios of 1:1.4 and 1:2.7, respectively. The forwards performed approximately three times more high-intensity work (11.2 ± 0.9 min; mean ± standard error of the mean) than backs (3.6 ± 0.5 min), despite the backs (5640 m) covering greater total distances than the forwards (4240 m). Regarding the heart-rate data, the percentage time spent in higher intensity activities was greater for props and locks, and back row forwards (58.4 per cent and 56.2 per cent, respectively) than the inside and outside backs (40.5 per cent and 33.9 per cent). The greater percentage of time spent in the higher intensity zone for forwards may also be a result of the forwards being involved in rucking and mauling, as well as frequent bouts of work such as scrumming and lifting.

Deutsch *et al.* (2002) compared work rates between elite club and Super 12 rugby players using a player position classification system and found work-to-rest ratios of approximately 1:7 and 1:21 for Super 12 forwards and backs, respectively, compared to 1:6 and 1:18 for elite club teams. The major differences that were found between elite club and Super 12 players were that Super 12 backs had lower frequencies of work events (46.9 ± 9.0 events compared to 54.8 ± 10.8 events per game) and longer rest periods (99.5 ± 3.5 s compared to 78 ± 3.5 s per game).

Duthie and Pyne (2005) measured the movement patterns of Super 12 rugby players in order to examine differences between first and second halves of the game, as well as between positional groups. No differences were found between work duration and frequency between the first and second halves. There were, however, significant differences between forwards and backs, with forwards performing more work, at a higher frequency, for longer durations. The forwards and backs had work-to-rest ratios of 1:6.3 and 1:17.2, respectively. The majority of the work efforts lasted 0–4 s (approximately 49 per cent) and 4–8 s (approximately 33 per cent), with only 5 per cent of work durations lasting more than 16 s. Rest periods of less than 20 s were most common.

Deutsch and Kearney (2007) examined the frequency, mean and maximum durations of work bouts during the 1996 and 1997 Super 12 seasons (Tables 27.1 and 27.2). It was observed that forwards (121.9 events) participated in significantly more work bouts than backs (46.9 events) and performed greater amounts of work, 10.5 min compared to 3.6 min. The work-to-rest ratio of forwards (1:7.4) was also significantly higher than that of backs (1:21.8).

All the studies discussed thus far have used time-motion analysis in conjunction with video footage to evaluate work rates and activity profiles. The advent of GPS has allowed work-to-rest ratios and activity profiles to be measured more objectively. Cunniffe *et al.* (2009) used GPS and heart-rate monitors to measure the physiological demands of players participating in a match between two elite club teams. They observed a work-to-rest ratio of 1:5.8 for the forward and 1:5.7 for the back.

Activity profiles

A summary of the results from the most recent and relevant studies investigating activity profiles can be found in Tables 27.1 and 27.2. Generally, backs covered more distance than forwards. They covered this additional distance predominantly by walking, cruising/striding, in utility movements and sprinting. Due to the substantial time spent in utility movements, Deutsch and Kearney (2007) recommended that these movements should form an integral part of physical conditioning for back-line players. Further recommendations were that acceleration should be a key area for forwards as their sprint durations generally lasted less than 5 s (Duthie and Pyne, 2005). This would equate to sprint distances of less than 40 m. Backs had sprint durations of approximately 6 s in duration. This has implications for conditioning, with forwards focusing predominantly on sprints of 30 m or less, with backs of 50 to 60 m.

With a number of rule changes instituted by the IRB leading to an increase in ball-in-play time, the number of rucks and mauls has increased dramatically. McLean (1992) reported an average of 73 rucks and mauls in Five Nations rugby. In Six Nations matches in 2011, there were on average 194 rucks and mauls, an increase of 266 per cent (IRB, 2011).

Roberts *et al.* (2008) quantified the total distances run and changes in high-intensity activity during match play. They measured static exertion (rucks, mauls, scrums, lineout lifts and tackles) and discovered that forwards work more frequently and for longer durations than backs. Forwards covered 5581 ± 692 m per match, compared to 6127 ± 724 m for backs, and were more frequently involved in static exertions. Additionally, the investigators discovered that there was greater distance travelled in the first ten minutes of the match compared with the periods of 50–60 minutes and 70–80 minutes. This was due to an increased volume of low-intensity activity rather than a drop in high-intensity work. They hypothesised that fatigue, even though not reflected in high-intensity running, may be observed in the intensity of static exertion activities.

Hartwig *et al.* (2011) compared activity profiles in adolescent matches and training. The key finding was that training sessions did not simulate the high-intensity repeat sprint demands of rugby at the adolescent level. The authors therefore recommended that coaches modify on-field training sessions to incorporate more high-intensity sprint activities.

Venter *et al.* (2011) used GPS units to measure distances covered, activity profiles and impacts from collisions during five semi-professional club matches (Tables 27.1 and 27.2). Back-row forwards had the highest frequency of impacts 683 ± 295, while the outside backs had the fewest (474 ± 82). Inside backs experienced the majority of the severe impacts (>10; 12 ± 3), while front-row forwards had the least (8 ± 5) severe impacts per match.

With the IRB allowing GPS to be used in match play, researchers will strive for a better understanding of the physical demands of rugby. Future studies should incorporate video analysis and performance indicators with GPS data to provide a holistic idea of match play. Training should also be compared to the match data for homology.

Table 27.1 Summary of activity profiles for forwards (units)(% time spent in each activity)

Activity	Duthie and Pyne. (2005) (mean [SD])			Deutsch and Kearney (2007) (mean [SD])			Venter et al. (2011) (mean [SD])		Cunniffe et al. (2009)		Hartwig et al. (2011) (mean [SD])		
	FR	BR	Com	FR	BR	Com	FR	BR	FR	BR	FR	BR	Com
Standing	43 (10)	39 (10)	41 (10)	—	—	47.7 (4.6)	21.7 (2.1)	23.0 (4.9)	—	—	—	—	44.5 (4.3)
Walking	25 (8)	29 (6)	27 (7)	—	—	17.9 (4.7)	42.2 (10.0)	46.9 (6.5)	—	66.5	—	—	35.5 (4.2)
Jogging	20 (3)	19 (5)	20 (4)	23 (3)	19 (2)	21.0 (2.9)	26.1 (3.8)	23.6 (5.9)	—	24.3	—	—	14.5 (2.7)
Cruising/striding	1.5 (0.8)	2.0 (0.5)	1.7 (0.9)	0.7 (0.5)	1.8 (1)	1.2 (1.0)	9.6 (4.6)	6.0 (1.8)	—	3.4	—	—	3.6 (3.5)
Sprinting	0.4 (0.4)	0.7 (0.5)	0.5 (0.4)	0.11 (0.09)	0.31 (0.24)	0.20 (0.2)	0.48 (0.23)	0.47 (0.14)	—	0.8	—	—	0.9 (2.1)
Utility	—	—	—	1.1 (0.9)	1.9 (0.7)	1.4 (0.9)	—	—	—	—	—	—	—
Rucking and mauling	—	—	—	—	—	—	—	—	—	—	—	—	—
Scrummaging	—	—	—	4.00 (1.14)	3.65 (0.92)	3.8 (1.0)	—	—	—	—	—	—	—
Static high intensity	10 (2)	11 (4)	10 (3)	—	—	—	—	—	—	—	—	—	—

Notes

FR = Front row; BR = Back row; Com = Forwards combined

Table 27.2 Summary of activity profiles for backs (% time spent in each activity)

Activity	Duthie and Pyne (2005) (mean [SD])			Deutsch and Kearney (2007) (mean [SD])			Venter et al. (2011) (mean [SD])		Cunniffe et al. (2009)		Hartwig et al. (2011) (mean [SD])		
	IB	OB	Com	IB	OB	Com	IB	OB	IB	OB	IB	OB	OB Com
Standing	43 (11)	38 (13)	41 (12)	—	—	47.7 (4.6)	21.0 (3.5)	20.7 (1.4)	—	77.8	—	—	32.7 (7.3)
Walking	34 (8)	43 (9)	38 (10)	—	—	17.9 (4.7)	53.6 (5.8)	60.3 (3.9)	—	—	—	—	48.8 (7.6)
Jogging	17 (3)	15 (5)	16 (4)	18.8 (2.9)	15.5 (4.4)	17.3 (3.7)	20.0 (3.0)	15.6 (2.3)	—	13	—	—	13.6 (2.5)
Cruising/striding	2.5 (0.7)	1.7 (0.7)	2.1 (0.8)	2.4 (1.4)	2.6 (0.7)	2.5 (1.1)	6.2 (3.7)	2.8 (0.5)	—	3.4	—	—	3.1 (1.8)
Sprinting	1.6 (0.5)	1.4 (0.5)	1.5 (0.5)	0.35 (0.24)	0.87 (0.51)	0.59 (0.44)	0.7 (0.3)	1.11(1.2)	—	1.4	—	—	1.3 (0.8)
Utility	—	—	—	4.8 (2.5)	4.1 (2.8)	3.6 (1.1)	—	—	—	—	—	—	—
Rucking and mauling	—	—	—	—	—	—	—	—	—	—	—	—	—
Scrummaging	—	—	—	—	—	—	—	—	—	—	—	—	—
Static high intensity	1.8 (0.8)	1.0 (0.4)	1.5 (0.8)	—	—	—	—	—	—	—	—	—	—

Notes

IB = Inside backs; OB = Outside backs; Com = Backs combined

Ball in play and events per game

McLean's calculated average game time was 29 min (McLean, 1992). The IRB measured ball-in-play time as 39 minutes 10 seconds during Six Nations matches (IRB, 2011), an increase of almost 75 per cent over the 20-year period. Williams *et al.* (2005) studied the effect of rule changes implemented in 1999. They noticed that ball in play increased, on average, from 30 minutes 7 seconds in 1999 to 33 minutes 16 seconds in 2003. These values are lower than the 43 minutes of ball in play reported from Tri Nations matches in 2010 (IRB, 2010; see Figure 27.1).

There has been a more than 200 per cent increase in the frequency of rucks and mauls recorded during international matches between 1990 and 2011 – a 266 per cent increase in the Five/Six Nations from 1990 to 2011 and a 200 per cent increase in the Tri Nations between 1999 and 2010 (see Figure 27.1). This increase has tremendous implications for the conditioning of players, as these are the most physically demanding aspects of the game. Training should be updated regularly to include adaptations to rule changes and consequent player demands.

Technical analysis

Running, passing and kicking

Rugby requires players to be proficient at a number of skills in order to participate. Open play skills consist of running, evasion, tackling, passing, catching, rucking and mauling and set-piece skills consist of scrummaging, restarts, lineouts and kicking to goal. Pavely *et al.* (2010) examined the effect of hand delivery used during ball delivery for bilateral punt kicking and discovered that *suboptimal* kicking biomechanics resulted in significantly less distance and greater trajectory variation than kicks with the preferred foot. Pavely *et al.* (2009) studied bilateral passing skills in elite rugby players. They found that passes to the non-preferred side resulted in a greater number (57 per cent vs. 15 per cent) of forward passes, less distance (13.5 m vs. 15.4 m), longer reaction times and shorter movement times.

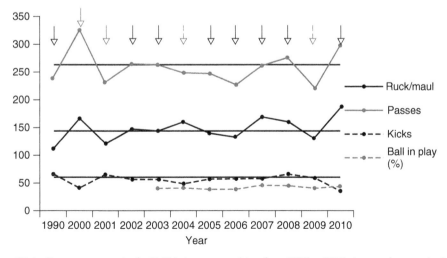

Figure 27.1 Events per game in the Tri Nations competition from 1999 to 2010. Arrows denote winning team (black – New Zealand, grey – Australia and grey dashed – South Africa)

Walsh *et al.* (2007) examined the effect of ball-carrying technique on sprint speed between experienced and inexperienced amateur players outdoors on a rugby field. They found that carrying the ball in both hands produced significantly slower sprint times. However, they indicated that practice will allow players to adjust to running with the ball and reduce the effect of ball carriage on running speed (Walsh *et al.*, 2007).

Evasion

Sayers and Washington-King (2005) observed how different running activities used in 2003 Super Rugby created different phase outcomes. They identified reception speed, intensity of effort, running pattern and evasion techniques as key aspects that determine positive outcomes. The lack of evasive techniques had the greatest chance of resulting in a negative outcome (yet is still widely coached at elite level), whereas the forward step had the greatest chance to produce a positive outcome.

Sayers and Washington-King (2005) noted that backs produced the most positive phase outcomes. They received the ball at greater speeds, ran with greater intensity and at more angles and were more evasive. Forwards had a greater percentage of tackled ball carries and less positive phase outcomes. This was due to the forwards' proximity to the opposition, resulting in less acceleration time or time to use evasive strategies to beat defenders.

Sayers (2007) presented a model for effective ball carries. His study consisted of three parts: biomechanics of evasion; systematic analysis of offensive play; and the validation of the performance indicators obtained by the systematic analysis of offensive play. The biomechanics analysis indicated that smaller steps leading up to and at the point of direction change enhanced the ability of the centre of mass (CoM) velocity to be maintained. Conversely, post-direction change or at the reacceleration phase, larger strides were more advantageous to maintaining CoM velocity.

Second, positive phase outcomes were associated with receiving the ball at cruising and sprinting speeds, then accelerating into the contact zone, while negative phase outcomes were associated with receiving the ball while jogging or walking, and then failing to accelerate into the contact zone (Sayers, 2007).

The third part of the study used the two key performance indicators obtained from the first two parts – 1) Players must accelerate after receiving the ball, striving to maintain CoM in the contact zone, and 2) Players must avoid running directly at defenders and use an evasion technique that maintains CoM in the contact zone – and developed three additional performance indicators for offensive ball carrying success, 3) Players should strive to offload the ball prior to contact, or in contact, 4) Players should avoid going to ground unnecessarily, and 5) Players should strive for deception by disguising their intentions (Sayers, 2007). Sayers' study has tremendous implications for coaches and players at all levels and provides a simple model for effective evasion techniques and successful offensive play.

The tackle contest is a key determinant of success in rugby (McKenzie *et al.*, 1989). Wheeler and Sayers (2009) examined defenders' body positions when attempting to tackle the ball carrier, along with the contact intensity of the ball carrier, the attacking pattern of play and the tackle result of the ball carry. Their results indicated that 71 per cent of breakdown losses occurred when the tackler was in a *good* defensive body position. Using a *good* -quality fend and running with *good* contact intensity resulted in 96 per cent of breakdown wins. The ball carrier's quality of fending combined with contact intensity were key predictors of the defender's body position, with 86 per cent of *poor* defensive positions successfully predicted with these contact skills. The importance of the ball carrier having effective fending skills was demonstrated by the fact that *strong* fending strategies created opportunities for the ball carrier to offload the ball in the tackle, and 40 per cent of tackle breaks were achieved with a *moderate* or *good* fending strategy.

Tactical analysis

The first objective of a rugby match is to score as many points as possible through tries, conversions, penalties and drop goals. The second objective is to restrict the number of points that the opposition score. Data collected by the IRB demonstrates that the majority of points come from tries, then penalties, conversions and drop goals (Table 27.3; IRB, 2007, 2010 and 2011).

In an average of 70 per cent of matches, the number of tries scored determined the winning team (IRB, 2007, 2010 and 2011). It would therefore make sense to examine the factors that lead to tries being scored and the possible differences between winning and losing performances.

Statistical comparisons of IRB data from international matches (Tri Nations and Six Nations) show the importance of maintaining a high degree of possession from your own set pieces and having the ability to disrupt and steal ball from the opposition's set pieces. Teams that are higher in the IRB's ranking system have on average an 80 per cent plus success rate on retaining their own lineout ball and an average rate of over 20 per cent for stealing their opposition's lineout ball. This finding was similar for scrums, with more successful teams retaining possession on their own scrum feed an average of 92 per cent of the time and winning ball on the opposition's scrum on average 14 per cent of the time.

Quantitative studies have been conducted to determine the factors that discriminate winning teams from losing ones. Jones *et al.* (2004) found that only 2 of 22 performance indicators measured were statistically different between winning and losing. These were the percentage of tries scored out of the total tries scored and the percentage of steals from the opposition's lineout ball. Other differences were noted for winning teams but did not reach statistical significance, such as more effective execution of first-phase play, an increased success rate at the breakdown and a greater number of turnovers won during open play. No statistically different performance indicators were found when the point difference between international teams was 15 or less (Vaz *et al.*, 2010). However, there were statistical differences when the teams were separated by a point's difference of between 16 and 34 (Vaz *et al.*, 2011). Lineout performance was a discriminating factor for winning teams, along with the frequency of tackles missed, of possession kicked away and of passes made. Lineout, tackling and kicking effectiveness have repeatedly been shown to be factors that distinguish winning performances from losing ones (Ortega *et al.*, 2009; van den Berg and Malan, 2010). Whilst this is a useful starting point for a tactical analysis of rugby, a try is composed of more variables than set pieces and requires additional information regarding elements that resulted in successful versus unsuccessful behaviours.

Table 27.3 Summary of the breakdown of points scored from IRB statistical reports

	World Cup 2007	Tri Nations 2010	Six Nations 2011
% Points scored from tries	60	53	43
% Points scored from penalties	21	32	41
% Points scored from conversions	17	15	13
% Points scored from drop goals	2	0	3

With teams utilising a more scientific pre-match preparation and there being fewer differences between winning and losing matches, coaches need a different approach to the classical statistical analysis of match play. The average number of tries per match has also decreased over the last ten years (Sasaki *et al.*, 2007) and is illustrated by IRB data (Figure 27.2), despite the actual ball-in-play time increasing (Figure 27.1). This puts extra pressure on players to score tries whenever possible. Therefore, more in-depth information is required for teams to maximise their attacking potential.

van Rooyen *et al.* (2006) and van Rooyen and Noakes (2006a) have found that the amount of time taken to score points is significantly greater than the amount of time for turnovers to occur. The average point-scoring movement was 33 s and turnover movements lasted 18 s (van Rooyen *et al.*, 2006; van Rooyen and Noakes, 2006a). Additional work by van Rooyen and Noakes (2006b) found that the overall length of a movement had an influence on the final placing in the World Cup. In a breakdown of the number of points scored per movement category (Table 27.4), there is a trend of points per movement increasing as the movement extends.

The movements that were 80 s or longer were randomly distributed across the match time (Figure 27.3) and occurred throughout the tournament, especially during the knockout stages.

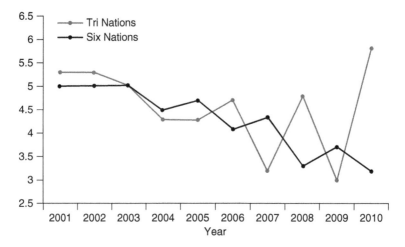

Figure 27.2 The average number of tries that have been scored in the Six Nations and Tri Nations over the last ten years. Data from IRB (2010)

Table 27.4 Summary data showing the number of points scored per movement for each team

Movement length (s)	England	Australia	New Zealand	South Africa
0–20	0.8	0.4	0.5	0.7
20–40	1.2	1.8	1.8	1.3
40–60	2.2	2.5	1.3	1.3
60–80	1.6	3.7	3.1	2.3
80+	3.0	3.3	2.2	0.0
Mean	**1.2**	**1.2**	**1.2**	**0.9**

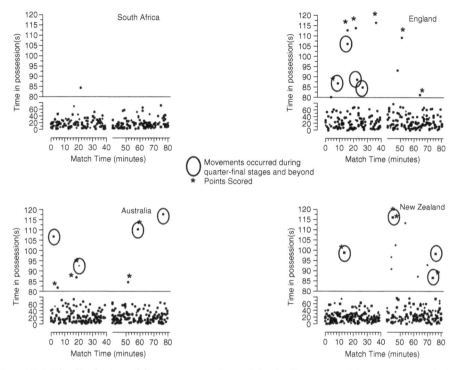

Figure 27.3 The distribution of the movements observed for the four teams with respect to match time. Data above the line indicates that movements are longer than 80 s. Circled data represents movements that occurred during the quarter-final or later in the tournament. ★ illustrates that points were scored during those specific movements

Rugby league

Rugby union and Rugby league both originated from the same sport and share many similarities, especially with regards to the technical skills discussed above, but despite this there is little work published on rugby league. In particular, technical aspects of rugby league have been neglected by the academic community. The next two sections will cover physical demands and tactical aspects.

Physical demands

Work-to-rest ratios

Meir *et al.* (1993, 2001) used video analysis to determine the work-to-rest ratios of players before and after the introduction of the 10 m offside rule in 1993. They found changes in these ratios for both the forwards (pre-rule change 1:6 vs. 1:10 [hooker] and 1:7 [prop] post-rule change) but more significantly to the backs (1:8 pre-rule change vs. 1:12 [halfback] and 1:28 [wingers] post-rule change) (Meir *et al.*, 2001). These changes were suggested to be as a result of increased workloads that demanded longer periods of recovery (Meir *et al.*, 2001).

More recent studies have utilised more sophisticated hardware and software technologies to determine the average work-to-rest ratios of a variety of positional groupings. These data are summarised in Table 27.5.

Table 27.5 Summary of work-to-rest ratios

Author	Technology	Work:rest ratio	
Beck and O'Donoghue (2004)	CAPTAIN system (O'Donoghue, 1998)	Forwards	1:13.3
		Backs	1:15
King *et al.* (2009)	Hand-notation game-analysis system	Hit-up forwards	1:5.1
		Adjustables	1:5.3
		Outside backs	1:4.9
Sirotic *et al.* (2009)	Computer-based tracking (Trak Performance)	Elite players	1:3.2
		Semi-elite	1:4
Sykes *et al.* (2009)	Semi-automated tracking (ProZone)	Attacking	1:7.8
		Defending	1:6.8
McLellan *et al.* (2010)	Global positioning systems (GPS)	Forwards	1:19
		Backs	1:5.6
McLellan *et al.* (2011)	Global positioning systems (GPS)	Forwards	1:7
		Backs	1:6
Sykes *et al.* (2011)	Semi-automated tracking (ProZone)	Props	1:3.8
		Back row	1:3.1
		Pivots	1:3.8
		Outside backs	1:3.1
Gabbett *et al.* (2012)	Global positioning systems (GPS)	Hit-up forwards	1:14.2
		W-R forwards	1:12.3
		Adjustables	1:13.7
		Outside backs	1:10.7

Note
W-R forwards = Wide-running forwards

There are vast disparities in the work-to-rest data presented in Table 27.5. However, there are consistencies noted between studies. Rugby league forwards are on average observed more frequently in contact activities and standing; their overall low intensity work rate is considerably less than the backs but so is the volume of sprinting that they are involved in (Gabbett *et al.*, 2012; King *et al.*, 2009; Waldron *et al.*, 2011). The rate of repeated high-intensity work for the forwards is more intense (one bout every 4.8 minutes) than that of the backs (one bout every 9.1 minutes) (Gabbett *et al.*, 2012). The sprinting volumes recorded for the backs range from 0.36 sprint.min to 0.44 sprint.min⁻¹, which equates to a sprint every two minutes of playing time (Waldron *et al.*, 2011). These match-based findings illustrate that different training activities are required for the forwards and the backs. Forwards should focus on repeated high-intensity efforts that are combined with physical collisions, and the backs need to devote time to repeated high-speed sprinting (Gabbett *et al.*, 2012).

Activity profiles

A summary of the results from studies of rugby league matches that have investigated activity profiles using various different methodologies can be found in Table 27.6. Comparisons across these studies are difficult as each author used their own movement and player grouping definitions.

In rugby league, the forwards, especially the hit-up forwards, are more frequently interchanged than the backs generally because of the greater volume of physical contacts and short-distance repeated sprinting they are involved in during matches (Austin *et al.*, 2011; Gabbett *et al.*, 2012). Studies have presented data indicating that backs covered more distance than forwards during the 80-minute match (Gabbett *et al.*, 2012; King *et al.*, 2009). However, this is due to differences in total match time per player rather than actual positional differences. Once the data is normalised for match time, players cover similar distances of $\pm$ 100 m.min^{-1} (Gabbett *et al.*, 2012).

The importance of high-intensity (HI) work was highlighted by Sirotic *et al.* (2009). They found that this was a distinguishing feature between elite and semi-elite players. Elite players spent almost 3 per cent more game time (specifically during the first half) in HI activities than their semi-elite counterparts, even though the skill demands for all players were similar (Sirotic *et al.*, 2009).

Austin *et al.* (2011) found that hit-up forwards (HU) were most frequently involved in bouts of repeated high-intensity exercise (RHIE) per match (9–17 hit-up backs vs. 2–8 adjustables [ADJ] and 3–7 outside backs [OB]), had the longest average duration (53 $\pm$ 8 vs. 39 $\pm$ 16 and 34 $\pm$ 11 for HU, ADJ and OB, respectively) and had the shortest average recovery (376 $\pm$ 205 s for HU) between bouts when compared to the other two positional groups (442 $\pm$ 304 for ADJ and 820 $\pm$ 567 for OB). These bouts of RHIE were analysed further by dividing the bouts into the percentage of time spent tackling or sprinting. It was found that the HU spent approximately 60 per cent RHIE tackling and 40 per cent sprinting, compared to the ADJ who had a 50:50 division of tackling vs. sprinting. This all provides coaches with an outline of the basic requirements of training drills, which, according to Gabbett *et al.* (2012), are not currently matching the physical demands of match situations.

The physiological data need to be interpreted more frequently in conjunction with the video analysis of matches. This will help to determine how different movement categories are associated with the various skill events that occur during matches. For example, Austin *et al.* (2011) have shown that RHIE bouts are related to try scoring. They found that 70 per cent of total RHIE bouts were within five minutes of a try being scored. This combination of data analysis can help to interpret the findings of Sykes *et al.* (2011), who found that there were differences in locomotive rates of players between the different quarters of a match. The OB were found to have a lower locomotive rate during the final 20 minutes of the match when compared to the first 20 minutes. Additionally, high-intensity and very high-intensity running were significantly lower in the final quarter when compared to the first quarter (Sykes *et al.*, 2011), even though the rate of tackling remained consistent across the match.

Ball in play and events per game

There are limited data presented giving the percentage ball-in play time during rugby league matches. Data from Eaves *et al.* (2008) show that there has been a 5 per cent decrease in ball in play from 60.3 $\pm$ $\pm$ 5.1 per cent in 1988 to 55.6 $\pm$ 6.0 per cent in 2002. However, more recent data from Sykes *et al.* (2011) indicate that there has been a 3 per cent increase in ball-in-play time over this period as they recorded values of 63.3 $\pm$ 6.4 per cent.

Comparisons of skill analysis in rugby league are very difficult as there are limited studies that have quantified these events (Sirotic *et al.*, 2009; Sykes *et al.*, 2011) and the only commonalities between these data are tackle and hit-up frequencies. Both studies found tackle rates of approximately 0.3 tackle.min^{-1} – 0.25 $\pm$ 0.16 for elite and 0.28 $\pm$ 0.16 for semi-elite players (Sirotic *et al.*, 2009) and 0.27 $\pm$ 0.13 for elite players (Sykes *et al.*, 2011). The same finding was true of the hit-up frequency data – 0.12 $\pm$ 0.07 for all players (Sirotic *et al.*, 2009) and 0.17 $\pm$ 0.07 (Sykes *et al.*, 2011).

Table 27.6 Summary of activity profiles for rugby league players (% time spent in each activity)

Activity	Beck and O'Donoghue (2004)		King et al. (2009)			Sykes et al. (2009) (mean [SD])	McLellan et al. (2010) (mean [SD])		McLellan et al. (2011) (mean [SD])		Sirotic et al. (2011) (mean [SD])				
	Fwd	Back	Hit-up	Adj	OB	All	Fwd	Back	Fwd	Back	Bks	Fd	Fbk	Hook	Serv
Standing	33.9	25.4	44.5	22	30	2.3 (1.1)	—	—	—	—	8.5 (2.7)	10.8 (2.5)	8.0 (1.8)	9.7 (1.7)	9.7 (2.4)
Walking	10.9	42.1	29	42	35	53.9 (7.3)	42.3 (10.4)	41.9 (9.4)	42.7 (8.9)	43.0 (10.5)	26.0 (3.4)	21.8 (2.5)	23.6 (2.2)	20.5 (2.7)	22.2 (3.2)
Jogging	40.2	17.3	15.5	19	17	30.5 (5.4)	36.4 (9.6)	27.9 (7.4)	34.7 (9.5)	29.2 (7.7)	11.7 (1.5)	13.0 (1.7)	13.5 (1.2)	15.2 (1.9)	14.5 (2.1)
Low intensity	—	—	—	—	—	—	—	—	—	—	46.3 (3.6)	45.4 (3.8)	45.4 (2.4)	46.0 (3.8)	45.6 (4.6)
Crusing/running	—	—	5	10	12	6.7 (1.4)	8.8 (2.4)	7.1 (2.3)	8.8 (2.6)	7.6 (2.7)	—	—	—	—	—
Striding	—	—	—	—	—	—	7.7 (2.1)	7.7 (2.5)	7.5 (2.4)	7.7 (3.1)	5.2 (1.2)	6.7 (1.4)	6.4 (1.4)	6.7 (2.6)	5.9 (1.3)
Highintensity	—	—	—	—	—	1.8 (0.5)	3.1 (0.7)	5.0 (1.2)	3.1 (0.6)	5.3 (1.0)	1.8 (0.6)	1.9 (0.4)	2.3 (2.3)	1.5 (1.8)	1.6 (1.4)
Sprinting	—	—	1	3	3	0.4 (0.3)	1.7 (0.4)	2.3 (0.9)	1.6 (0.6)	2.6 (0.8)	0.6 (0.3)	0.5 (0.1)	0.8 (0.4)	0.4 (0.3)	0.4 (0.2)
Utility	7.9	3.7	5	4	3	4.2 (4.2)	—	—	—	—	—	—	—	—	—
Backing	5.6	8.9	—	—	—	—	—	—	—	—	—	—	—	—	—
Running	0.5	0.5	—	—	—	—	—	—	—	—	—	—	—	—	—
Shuffling	1.0	2.1	—	—	—	—	—	—	—	—	—	—	—	—	—

Notes

All = All players; Fwd = Forwards (shirt no. 8–13); Hit-up = Hit-up forwards (shirt no. 8, 10–12); Fd = Forwards (shirt no. 8, 10–12); Hook = Hooker (shirt no. 9); Adj = Adjustables (shirt no. 6, 7, 9, 13); Back = Backs (shirt no. 1–5); Bks = Backs (shirt no. 2–5); Fbk = Fullback (shirt no.1); Serv = Service (shirt no. 6, 7, 13).

Tactical analysis

There is little work published on the tactical analysis of rugby league. Eaves and Evers (2007) looked at how disruptions in the flow of the game (and possible point-scoring opportunities) were influenced by the choice of post-ruck plays. There was an increased frequency in play-disrupting incidents when pass plays were used after a ruck rather than play from hit ups or dummy runs. Thus pass plays can be associated with scoring tries and winning behaviour. Further investigation by Eaves and Broad (2007) showed that Australian teams were more adept at confining their opponents to the defensive area of the field than their British counterparts and they played a more expansive game in the middle of the field. It is suggested that, in order to become more successful against Australian teams, the British have to develop ways to restrict the territory their opposition gain and learn to play a more expansive game (Eaves and Broad, 2007). An additional skill that is associated with winning teams is the ability to effectively execute an offload of the ball during a tackle. Higher-ranked teams have been shown to score more tries following an offload than lower ranked teams (Wheeler *et al.*, 2011). The quality of the offload also contributed to tries being scored. Thus players should develop a tactical awareness to identify appropriate situations when offloads can be effectively executed (Wheeler *et al.*, 2011).

Rugby union sevens

Rugby sevens is 'an abbreviated variant of rugby union' (Higham *et al.*, 2012: 1) played by two teams of seven players and predominantly lasts for two seven-minute halves. The game follows the majority of the rugby union's regulations, with additional adaptations to compensate for the fewer players. Thus the game will have many of the physiological and technical characteristics previously described under the 15-man version. At present, there is a dearth of peer-reviewed research on rugby sevens. However, this is expected to change with the increasing popularity and Olympic status this version of the sport now has.

Physical demands

Work-to-rest ratios

One of the earliest studies published on work rates in rugby sevens was by Rienzi *et al.* (1999). They found that, on average, matches were 17.4 minutes long and comprised of 80 per cent activity and 20 per cent rest (players were static). This indicates average work-to-rest ratios of 1:0.26 for the forwards and 1:0.20 for the backs in a 1996 international rugby sevens tournament.

Since Rienzi *et al.* (1999), no further studies were published until Higham *et al.* (2012) and Suraez-Arrones *et al.* (2011a, 2011b). These most recent studies have used GPS to monitor performance. All of these studies grouped static activity and walking in the same category, so work-to-rest ratios from these studies can only be presented as high:low intensity work. Higham *et al.* (2012) and Suraez-Arrones *et al.* (2011a) calculated high–to-low intensity ratios of 1:0.5 for male sevens players and 1:0.4 for females (Suraez-Arrones *et al.*, 2011b). A recalculation of Rienzi *et al.* (1999) data shows that their high:low intensity ratios were 1:0.9 for forwards and 1:0.8 for backs. This could indicate that the game has become faster over the last 15 years and that training drills need to be changed to reflect this.

Activity profiles

A summary of the results from the four studies investigating activity profiles of sevens rugby players can be found in Table 27.7.

The differences between the activity profiles of the forwards and backs were highlighted by Rienzi *et al.* (1999). They found that the forwards spent more time engaged in static or jogging movements than the backs. However, the relevance of this finding to the modern game is unclear (Rienzi *et al.*, 1999).

Higham *et al.* (2012) established that there were several variations between domestic and international competitions. These were especially focused around the high-intensity demands the players had to perform. International matches were played at a higher intensity and placed a greater physical load on the players (Higham *et al.*, 2012). It was suggested from these findings that playing in domestic competitions does not adequately prepare players for the demands of international competition.

Players have been recorded running on average 1580.8 ± 146.3m during a single match (Suarez-Arrones *et al.*, 2011a). The distance covered (137.7 ± 84.9m) at speeds of >20km.hour^{-1} comprised of 7.4 ± 3.9 sprints that were on average 18 ± 7.6m (range 9.1 ± 5.7m to 29.5 ± 11.7m). A tournament requires that teams play five or six matches over a two-to-three-day period. If these data are scaled up to reflect a tournament, it suggests that players have to be conditioned to not only perform repeated bouts of sprinting within a match (7.4 ± 3.9 × 18.0 ± 7.6m) but also across multiple matches (5 or 6 × [7.4 ± 3.9 × 18.0 ± 7.6m]), with only a few hours rest in between. This presents the most successful teams with potential playing demands (per player) of 9.5km to cover with 800m covered at speeds of >20km.hour^{-1} (based on a squad of seven players). In addition to this, players can be faced with between 70 and 90 minutes of total rugby exposure per tournament (Suarez-Arrones *et al.*, 2011b). Training regimes need to be designed to reflect these needs.

Ball in play

Hughes and Jones (2009) calculated ball-in-play time during the 2001 IRB World Sevens Series to be on average 40 per cent. Fuller *et al.* (2010) later reported ball-in-play data to be 50 per cent and van Rooyen *et al.* (2008) found it to average 52 per cent. This would suggest that the ball-in-play time has increased by 10 per cent from 2001 to 2004.

Table 27.7 Summary of activity profiles for sevens players (% time spent in each activity)

Activity	Rienzi et al. (1999)		Higham et al. (2012)		Suraez-Arrones et al. (2011a, 2011b)	
	Forwards	Backs	Domestic	International	Men	Women
Static	20.7	16.7	33.8	34.9	34.8	29.7
Walking	26.0	26.9				
Jogging	20.5	19.6	27.6	25.5	26.2	33.2
Cruising	—	—	21.0	19.6	9.8	11.6
Striding	—	—	—	—	15.5	16.4
High-intensity running	5.9	7.4	8.4	9.3	5	3.7
Sprinting	—	—	9.2	10.6	8.7	5.4
Moving sideways	11.4	14.1	—	—	—	—
Walking backwards	13.3	13.0	—	—	—	—
Jogging backwards	2.1	2.5	—	—	—	—

Tactical analysis

The studies of rugby sevens have concentrated on determining factors that distinguish winning from losing performances. Hughes and Jones (2009) found that the majority of differences between winning and losing related to open-play actions rather than set-piece actions. There were more dummy and miss passes used by winning teams, they had more effective evasive techniques (side steps and swerves) and they completed more clean breaks than their counterparts. On the other side, winning teams were involved in fewer rucks/mauls, made fewer kicks, normal and loop passes and had fewer passes per try than losing teams. In addition, winning teams had a greater percentage of both possession and territory (Hughes and Jones, 2009). A study by van Rooyen *et al.* (2008) also concluded that the possession accumulated during a match distinguishes teams, especially during the knockout stages of a tournament. They concluded that, to reach the finals or semi-finals of a tournament, teams needed to be able to secure and maintain possession for periods of 30 to 60 s and, of these individual possessions, more than 30 per cent must result in points being scored (van Rooyen *et al.*, 2008).

A simple description of events that occur during rugby matches does not provide modern coaches with enough tactical information for them to determine how to win matches. More in-depth profiles are required of the events that lead to successful or unsuccessful behaviours, including where they occur on the field, when they occur during a match and how they occur.

Concluding remarks

This chapter has reviewed the use of performance analysis in monitoring the physical demands and the technical and tactical aspects of rugby. Modern-day rugby is physically demanding, with high work-to-rest ratios, increased ball-in-play time and greater events per match than 20 years ago. Studies by Cunniffe *et al.* (2009), Gabbett *et al.* (2012), McLellan *et al.* (2011), Suarez-Arrones *et al.* (2011a, 2011b) and Venter (2011) have used current GPS technology to evaluate the physical demands of matches. This and the previous literature indicate that forwards are involved in more high-intensity work than backs. However, backs cover more distance during matches, especially at the higher speeds. Basic sport-specific skills, such as running with the ball (Walsh *et al.*, 2007), passing (Pavely *et al.*, 2009) and kicking (Pavely *et al.*, 2010), have also been investigated. It was found that these skills need to be trained using both the dominant and the non-dominant sides of the body. More complex skills, such as tackling, are a key component of the modern game and have a significant influence on a team's ability to score tries and win matches. This is demonstrated by the ability of the ball carrier to receive the ball at speed, use evasive running techniques and dominate the tackle situations to create point-scoring opportunities for the attacking team (Wheeler and Sayers, 2009; Wheeler *et al.*, 2010, 2011). Another area of play that distinguishes successful from unsuccessful play is the ability to maintain possession. Try scoring occurs more frequently when teams are able to maintain possession for longer periods (van Rooyen and Noakes, 2006a, 2006b; van Rooyen *et al.*, 2008). This trend is particularly evident in close or knockout matches. Achieving success in rugby is complex and requires an interdisciplinary approach. However, performance analysis has assisted coaches to physiologically, technically and tactically develop more successful teams.

References

Austin, D.J., Gabbett, T.J. and Jenkins, D.G. (2011) 'Repeated high-intensity exercise in professional rugby league', *Journal of Strength Conditioning Research*, 25: 1898–904.

Beck, C. and O'Donoghue, P.G. (2004) 'Time-motion analysis of intervarsity Rugby League competition', in P.G. O'Donoghue and M.D. Hughes (eds), *Performance Analysis of Sport VI: Proceedings of the World Congress of Performance Analysis of Sport VI* (pp. 150–5). Cardiff, UK: CPA, UWIC Press.

Cunniffe, B., Proctor, W., Baker, J.S. and Davies, B. (2009) 'An evaluation of the physiological demands of elite rugby union using Global Positioning System tracking software', *Journal of Strength and Conditioning Research*, 23: 1195–203.

Deutsch, M. and Kearney, G. (2007) 'Time-motion analysis of professional rugby union players during match-play', *Journal of Sports Sciences*, 25: 461–72.

Deutsch, M., Maw, G., Jenkins, D. and Reaburn, P. (1998) 'Heart rate, blood lactate and kinematic data of elite colts (under-19) rugby union players during competition', *Journal of Sports Sciences*, 16: 561–70.

Deutsch, M., Kearney, G. and Rehrer, N. (2002) 'A comparison of competition work rates in elite club and "Super 12" rugby', in W. Spinks, T. Reilly and A. Murphy (eds), *Science and Football IV* (pp. 160–6). London, UK: Routledge.

Duthie, G. and Pyne, D. (2005) 'Time motion analysis of 2001 and 2002 super 12 rugby', *Journal of Sports Sciences*, 23: 523–30.

Eaves, S. and Broad, G. (2007) 'A comparative analysis of professional rugby league football patterns between Australia and the United Kingdom', *International Journal of Performance Analysis in Sport*, 7(3): 54–66.

Eaves, S. and Evers, A. (2007) 'The relationship between the "play the ball" time, post-ruck action and the occurrence of perturbations in professional rugby league', *International Journal of Performance Analysis in Sport*, 7(3): 18–25.

Eaves, S.J., Lamb, K.L. and Hughes, M.D. (2008) 'The impact of rule and playing season changes on time variables in professional rugby league in the United Kingdom', *International Journal of Performance Analysis of Sport*, 8(2): 44–54.

Fuller, C.W., Taylor, A. and Molloy, M.G. (2010) 'Epidemiological study of injuries in international Rugby Sevens', *Clinical Journal of Sport Medicine I*, 20(3): 179–84.

Gabbett, T.J., Jenkins, D.G. and Abernethy, B. (2012) 'Physical demands of professional rugby league training and competition using microtechnology', *Journal of Science and Medicine in Sport*, 15: 80–6.

Greenwood, J. (2003) *Total Rugby: Fifteen Man Rugby for Coach and Player*, 5th ed., London, UK: A and C Black.

Hartwig, T., Naughton, G. and Searl, J. (2011) 'Motion analyses of adolescent rugby union players: A comparison of training and game demands', *Journal of Strength and Conditioning Research*, 25: 966–72.

Higham, D.G., Pyne, D.B, Anson, J.M. and Eddy, A. (2012) 'Movement patterns in rugby sevens: Effects of tournament level, fatigue and substitute players', *Journal of Science and Medicine in Sport*, 15(3): 277–82.

Hughes, M. and Jones, R. (2009) 'Patterns of play of successful and unsuccessful teams in men's 7-a-side rugby union', in T. Reilly and F. Korkusuz (eds), *Science and Football V: The Proceedings of the Fifth Congress on Science and Football* (pp. 247–52). London: Routledge.

International Rugby Board (2007) 'Statistical review and match analysis: 2007 Rugby World Cup'. Online. Available at www.irb.com/mm/document/newsmedia/0/071026ctirbanalysisrwc2007report%5f3830. pdf.

International Rugby Board (2010) 'Statistical review and match analysis: 2010 Tri Nations'. Online. Available at ww.irb.com/mm/document/newsmedia/mediazone/02/04/06/08/2040608%5fpdf.pdf.

International Rugby Board (2011) 'Statistical review and match analysis: 2011 RBS 6 Nations'. Online. Available at www.irb.com/mm/document/newsmedia/mediazone/02/04/23/63/2042363_pdf.pdf.

Jones, N., Mellalieu, S. and James, N. (2004) 'Team performance indicators as a function of winning and losing rugby union', *International Journal of Performance Analysis in Sport*, 4: 61–71.

King, T., Jenkins, D. and Gabbett, T. (2009) 'A time-motion analysis of professional rugby league match-play', *Journal of Sports Sciences*, 27(3): 213–9.

McKenzie, A., Holmyard, D. and Docherty, D. (1989) 'Quantitative analysis of rugby: Factors associated with success in contact', *Journal of Human Movement Studies*, 17: 101–13.

McLean, D. (1992) 'Analysis of the physical demands of international rugby union', *Journal of Sports Sciences*, 10: 285–96.

McLellan, C., Lovell, D. and Gass, G. (2010) 'Creatine kinase and endocrine. Responses of elite players pre, during, and post rugby league match play', *Journal of Strength and Conditioning Research*, 24(11): 2908–19.

McLellan, C., Lovell, D. and Gass, G. (2011) 'Performance analysis of elite rugby league match play using Global Positioning Systems', *Journal of Strength and Conditioning Research*, 25(6): 1703–10.

Meir, R., Arthur, D. and Forrest, M. (1993) 'A time motion analysis of professional rugby league: A case study', *Strength and Conditioning Coach*, 1: 24–9.

Meir, R., Colla, P. and Milligan, C. (2001) 'Impact of the 10-meter rule change on professional rugby league: Implications for training', *Strength and Conditioning Journal*, 23: 42–6.

O'Donoghue, P.G. (1998) 'The CAPTAIN system', in M. Hughes and F. Tavares (eds), *Performance Analysis of Sport V: Proceedings of the World Congress of Performance Analysis of Sport V* (pp. 213–19). Cardiff, UK: CPA, UWIC Press.

Ortega, E., Villarejo, D. and Palao, J. (2009) 'Differences in game statistics between winning and losing rugby teams in the six nations tournament', *Journal of Sports Science and Medicine*, 8: 523–7.

Pavely, S., Adams, R., Di Francesco, T., Larkham, S. and Maher, G. (2009) 'Execution and outcome differences between passes to the left and right made by first-grade rugby union players', *Physical Therapy in Sport*, 10: 136–41.

Pavely, S., Adams, R., Di Francesco, T., Larkham, S. and Maher, C. (2010) 'Bilateral clearance punt kicking in rugby union: Effects of hand used for ball delivery', *International Journal of Performance Analysis of Sport*, 10: 187–96.

Rienzi, E., Reilly, T. and Malkin, C. (1999) 'Investigation of anthropometric and work-rate profiles of Rugby Sevens players', *Journal of Sports Medicine and Physical Fitness*, 39(2): 160–4.

Roberts, S., Trewartha, G., Higgitt, R., El-Abd, J. and Stokes, K. (2008) 'The physical demands of elite English rugby union', *Journal of Sports Sciences*, 26: 825–33.

Sasaki, K., Furukawa, T., Murakami, J., Shimozono, H., Nagamatsu, M., Miyao, M., Yamamoto, T., Watanabe, I., Yasugahira, H., Saito, T., Ueno, Y., Katsuta, T. and Kono, I. (2007) 'Scoring profiles and defense performance analysis in rugby union', *International Journal of Performance Analysis in Sport*, 7(3): 46–53.

Sayers, M. (2007) 'Development of an offensive evasion model for the training of high performance rugby players', in T. Reilly and F. Korkusuz (eds), *Science and Football VI: Proceedings of the 6th World Congress of Science and Football* (pp. 278–84). Oxon, UK: Routledge.

Sayers, M. and Washington-King, J. (2005) 'Characteristics of effective ball carries in Super 12 rugby', *International Journal of Performance Analysis in Sport*, 5(3): 92–105.

Sirotic, A.C., Coutts, A.J., Knowles, H. and Catterick, C. (2009) 'A comparison of match demands between elite and semi-elite rugby league competition', *Journal of Sports Sciences*, 27(3): 203–211.

Sirotic, A.C., Knowles, H., Catterick, C. and Coutts, A.J. (2011) 'Positional match demands of professional rugby league competition', *Journal of Strength and Conditioning Research*, 25(11): 3076–87.

Suarez-Arrones, L.J., Nuñez, F.J., Portillo, J. and Mendez-Villanueva, A. (2011a) 'Running demands and heart rate responses in Men Rugby Sevens', *Journal of Strength and Conditioning Research*, doi:10.1519/JSC.0b013e318243fff7.

Suarez-Arrones, L.J., Nuñez, F.J., Portillo, J. and Mendez-Villanueva, A. (2011b) 'Match running performance and exercise intensity in elite female Rugby Sevens', *Journal of Strength Conditioning Research*, doi:10.1519/JSC.0b013e318238ea3e.

Sykes, D., Twist, C., Hall, S., Nicholas, C. and Lamb, K. (2009) 'Semi-automated time-motion analysis of senior elite rugby league', *International Journal of Performance Analysis of Sport*, 9: 47–59.

Sykes, D., Twist, C., Nicholas, C. and Lamb, K. (2011) 'Changes in locomotive rates during senior elite rugby league matches', *Journal of Sports Sciences*, 29(12): 1263–71.

van den Berg, P. and Malan, D. (2010) 'Match analysis of the 2006 super 14 rugby union tournament', *African Journal for Physical Health Education, Recreation and Dance*, 16: 580–93.

van Rooyen, M. and Noakes, T. (2006a) 'An analysis of the movements, both duration and field location, of 4 teams in the 2003 Rugby World Cup', *International Journal of Performance Analysis in Sport*, 6(1): 30–9.

van Rooyen, M. and Noakes, T. (2006b) 'Movement time as a predictor of success in the 2003 Rugby World Cup Tournament', *International Journal of Performance Analysis in Sport*, 6(1): 40–56.

van Rooyen, M.K., Lambert, M.I. and Noakes, T.D. (2006) 'Too many errors and too little possession: A retrospective analysis of the South African performance in the 2003 Rugby World Cup', *International Journal of Performance Analysis in Sport*, 6: 57–72.

van Rooyen, M.K., Lombard, C. and Noakes, T.D. (2008) 'Playing demands of Sevens Rugby during the 2005 Rugby World Cup Sevens Tournament', *International Journal of Performance Analysis in Sport*, 8(2): 114–23.

Vaz, L., Sampaio, J. and van Rooyen, M.K. (2010) 'Rugby game-related statistics that discriminate between winning and losing teams in IRB and Super twelve close games', *Journal Sport Science and Medicine*, 9: 51–5.

Vaz, L., Mouchet, A., Carreras, D. and Morente, H. (2011) 'The importance of rugby game-related statistics to discriminate winners and losers at the elite level competitions in close and balanced games', *International Journal of Performance Analysis in Sport*, 11: 130–41.

Venter, R., Opperman, E. and Opperman, S. (2011) 'The use of Global Positioning System (GPS) tracking devices to assess movement demands and impacts in Under-19 Rugby Union match play', *African Journal for Physical, Health Education, Recreation and Dance*, 17: 1–8.

Waldron, M., Twist, C., Highton, J., Worsfold, P. and Daniels, M. (2011) 'Movement and physiological match demands of elite rugby league using portable Global Positioning Systems', *Journal of Sports Sciences*, 29(11): 1223–30.

Walsh, M., Young, B., Hill, B., Kittredge, K. and Horn, T. (2007) 'The effect of ball carrying technique and experience on sprinting in rugby union', *Journal of Sports Sciences*, 25: 185–92.

Wheeler, K. and Sayers, M. (2009) 'Contact skills predicting tackle-breaks in rugby union', *International Journal of Sports Science and Coaching*, 4: 535–44.

Wheeler, K., Askew, C. and Sayers, M. (2010) 'Effective attacking strategies in rugby union', *European Journal of Sport Science*, 10(4): 237–42.

Wheeler, K., Wiseman, R. and Lyons, K. (2011) 'Tactical and technical factors associated with effective ball offloading strategies during the tackle in rugby league', *International Journal of Performance Analysis in Sport*, 11: 392–409.

Williams, J., Hughes, M. and O'Donoghue, P. (2005) 'The effect of rule changes and ball in play time in rugby union', *International Journal of Performance Analysis in Sport*, 5: 1–11.

28

BASKETBALL

Jaime Sampaio[1], *Sérgio Ibáñez*[2] *and Alberto Lorenzo*[3]

[1] UNIVERSITY OF TRÁS-OS-MONTES AND ALTO DOURO, PORTUGAL

[2] UNIVERSITY OF EXTREMADURA, SPAIN

[3] TECHNICAL UNIVERSITY OF MADRID, SPAIN

Summary

Preparing basketball teams to perform at the highest standard of competition is a complex process dependent upon the interactions of technical, tactical, fitness and anthropometric characteristics of available players. In general, basketball performance depends offensively on shooting field goals and defensively on securing defensive rebounds (Ibáñez *et al.*, 2003; Ittenbach *et al.*, 1992; Karipidis *et al.*, 2001). In closely contested games, fouls and free throws have also been reported to be important (Kozar *et al.*, 1994). Other game-related statistics, such as turnovers, steals, assists and blocked shots, are not reported consistently as discriminators between winning and losing teams. It has also been suggested that the best breakdown of offensive and defensive performances can be obtained by analyzing four factors in the following order of importance: (1) effective field-goal percentage, (2) offensive rebounding percentage, (3) turnovers per ball possession and (4) free-throw rate (Kubatko *et al.*, 2007). This chapter will cover the research on performance indicators addressed in basketball research and how the results of static, dynamic and self-organized complexity studies are contributing to model basketball performance.

Overview of performance indicators in basketball

All persons involved in basketball, at some point, have looked into a boxscore, searching for reasons to help explain the game's outcome. In general, these boxscores contain information that describes the frequency of actions performed by players of both teams in a game. This description is actually considered a very complete record of the game and provides an idea of how players and teams performed based on the raw data. Therefore, the popularity of basketball statistics with coaches, players, fans and the media should be no surprise.

This massive usage created a need to ensure data reliability – for example, at the time of comparing performances based on data gathered by different operators. In all professional and amateur leagues, the data gathering process is regulated by the operational definitions and criteria published in the *Basketball Statisticians Manual* (FIBA, 2009). The game actions (variables) presented and defined in this official manual are the following: free throws, field goals, rebounds, assists, steals, turnovers, blocked shots and fouls. This is an excellent contribution to ensure intra- and inter-operator reliability; but by having reliable data, the assumption of validity is not necessarily comprised – that is, although the data may be consistent, it is not obvious that most of these actions are really performance indicators. In addition, there is a major methodological concern related to the contamination of game pace in the frequencies of the gathered variables. For example, the performance of a team A that makes 35 field goals in an 80-possession game must be different to the performance of a team B that makes the same 35 field goals in a 90-possession game. A solution for this problem was found by redefining ball possessions, as described earlier in non-academic websites (i.e. Journal of Basketball Studies) and published later (Kubatko *et al.*, 2007; Oliver, 2004). According to this redefinition, a ball possession starts when one team gains control of the ball and ends when that team gives up control of the ball. The teams can give up possession in several ways, such as making field goals or free throws that lead to the other team taking the ball out of bounds, defensive rebounds and turnovers. Securing an offensive rebound does not start a new possession, although it does start a new play. At the end of the game, ball possessions are guaranteed to be approximately the same for the two teams, providing a normalized basis for evaluating the teams' efficiency. From this point forward, the points scored per 100 ball possessions were used as a performance indicator, enabling a comparison of performances between games that were played at different paces (Oliver, 2004). In addition, Sampaio and Janeira (2003) normalized all the other variables (rebounds, fouls, assists, etc.) according to the standard measure of 100 ball possessions.

With some of these concerns carefully addressed, the search for valid basketball performance indicators has been a hot topic for several international research teams, either in the academic or in the professional fields. The main aim of most authors was to produce reliable and valid performance indicators and consequently provide their use to coaching staffs for improving player and team performances. The nature of the basketball game is complex, dynamic and non-linear (Davids *et al.*, 2003; Glazier, 2010; Lames and MacGarry, 2007); therefore, the performance indicators used in the modeling process should be able to capture most of these properties. In general, this process can be carried under static, dynamic and self-organized complexity perspectives.

Static complexity in basketball

This is the simplest form of complexity, mainly because it assumes that the studied structure does not change with time. The approach analysis of the system is analogous to a photograph (Lucas, 1999). Also, it is a structure-oriented observation model that enables the researcher to register isolated elementary actions of a game, but it does not allow data to be obtained about the process (Pfeiffer and Perl, 2006). Most of the studies carried out in basketball performance analysis have been carried under this approach, with the goal of identifying the variables that most discriminate between winning and losing teams by using the variables' averages during the 40-minute game (Csataljay *et al.*, 2009; Gomez *et al.*, 2006, 2009; Lorenzo *et al.*, 2010; Ortega *et al.*, 2007; Sampaio and Janeira, 2003; Trninic *et al.*, 2002; Ziv *et al.*, 2010). In very general terms, results show that basketball performance depends offensively on shooting field goals and defensively on securing defensive rebounds (Ibáñez *et al.*, 2003; Karipidis *et al.*, 2001; Sampaio and Janeira, 2003; Trninic *et al.*, 2002). In closely contested games, fouls and free throws have been reported to be important for game outcome (Kozar *et al.*, 1994). Other game-related statistics, such as offensive rebounds, turnovers, steals and assists, are not reported consistently as discriminators between winning and losing teams.

Trninic *et al.* (2002) studied 36 games from nine final FIBA European Club Championship tournaments. The differences between winning and losing teams were identified in the defensive rebounds, in the field-goal percentages and in free-throw percentages. According to the authors, the results suggest that winning teams showed better tactical performance in controlling inside positions for defensive rebounds. They were also better at controlling the ball in offense in searching for an optimal chance to shot, which considerably reduces risks and results in fewer turnovers and higher shooting percentages (Trninic *et al.*, 2002). The same results were found in Junior World Championship games that ended with less than a 12-point margin (Ibáñez *et al.*, 2003). However, these authors obtained different results when analyzing two other groups of games (with differences in scoring between 13 and 24 and above 24 points).

The idea behind this approach of analyzing different groups of games is that analyzing performance according to a static complexity perspective means that several other variables need to be controlled, in order to have not one but several descriptive photographs. For example, a physiological analysis of exercise effects needs an accurate definition of the performed workload (e.g. heart-rate responses to 20 minutes performed in a cycle ergometer at 60 RPM). In basketball, there is a need to describe accurately what kinds of games were analyzed. In the previous physiological example, it makes little sense to analyze a sample mixing workloads performed at 60, 70 and 80 RPM. In fact, this control seems to be one of the most important points of using static complexity models in basketball performance analysis. Thus, the analyzed games should be properly described using several (situational) variables, in order to reduce the variability to comprehensible stages and ensure minimal internal validity.

Subsequent research has attempted to improve the validity of most performance indicators by controlling the effects of several other variables, such as game-score differences (Gomez *et al.*, 2008; Lorenzo *et al.*, 2010; Sampaio and Janeira, 2003), type (Sampaio and Janeira, 2003) and location (Gomez *et al.*, 2008; Sampaio and Janeira, 2003). The game-score difference is an important variable to take into account in the first place. In fact, in static modeling designs, the teams' performances should be analyzed when the game outcome is still uncertain. For example, a game that ends with a difference of more than 25 points had probably no uncertainty in the outcome (at least in the final minutes) and probably many minutes were assigned to less important players and their actions will be averaged with all the previous ones from the game. Also, when the game is probably lost, the teams trailing in the score take risky decisions, such as systematically forcing three-point field-goal opportunities and ball steals, and they commit a higher number of fouls to stop game time. On the other hand, the teams that lead are now less pressured and just have to control game time. The sum of these decisions favor the leading team, so it seems likely that score differences will probably increase. All these issues are confirmed by substantial differences in all variables between winning and losing teams identified in unbalanced games (Gomez *et al.*, 2006; Sampaio and Janeira, 2003). In fact, in unbalanced games, most of the variables can differentiate between winning and losing teams, but, at the end, they have no practical utility. Therefore, the usage of classification procedures to differentiate between balanced and unbalanced games seems a very adequate procedure.

Game type is an important factor to take into account in basketball teams' strategic behavior. The regular season is comprised of games played between all teams and it is a contest in accumulating points, enabling teams to reach the playoffs and better classifications (for home-advantage purposes). The playoff games are substantially different. The lowest-level teams are no longer playing and, therefore, each confrontation is always between higher-ranked teams in a series of three, five or seven consecutive games, where the importance of winning is much higher. Therefore, it is no surprise that playoff games may be played slower, with the consequence of having fewer scored points by field goals, due to a less risky strategic behavior. However, committed fouls are higher because it is better to stop the offense immediately through fouling, which leads to more points being scored from free throws and increases the importance of these statistics. In general, playoff home games are won by teams who exhibit fewer committed fouls and secure fewer offensive rebounds, probably as a consequence of having missed fewer field goals or of a faster defensive repositioning, which prevents players being positioned to secure offensive rebounds. When playing away, winning playoff games seems to be related to missing fewer and making more free throws and securing more offensive rebounds. In these cases, securing offensive rebounds may suggest that away teams succeed in reactivating unsuccessful ball possessions and simultaneously stopping the home team from fast breaking and gaining momentum (Sampaio and Janeira, 2003).

Home advantage in basketball has consistently been between 60 percent to 64 percent (Courneya and Carron, 1992; Pollard and Pollard, 2005). There are several problems with identifying the variables that might be responsible for this effect because it is likely that most causes will be interacting in difficult to ways to isolate and quantify. Although some earlier studies have identified that home teams outperformed away teams in functional aggression variables, such as rebounds, blocks and steals (Varca, 1980), it is not obvious that these behaviors occurred only by the effect of playing at home. Nevertheless, available research relates home teams' performances to better field-goal percentages, more defensive rebounding and fewer committed fouls (Sampaio and Janeira, 2003). When interacting with game outcome, the home winning teams secured more defensive rebounds and performed fewer assists. Conversely, the away winning teams secured more defensive rebounds, performed more assists and were more successful in two- and three-point field goals (Gomez *et al.*, 2008).

Contrasting winners' and losers' performances can only provide a measure of team success at a given instant because successful teams can also lose some games and unsuccessful teams can also win some games (Ibáñez *et al.*, 2008; Madrigal and James, 1999). Therefore, other authors have used teams' classification ranks to measure season-long success (Ibáñez *et al.*, 2008; Ittenbach and Esters, 1995; Ittenbach *et al.*, 1992). The first attempts at relating basketball game statistics to success identified the points per game and the points allowed as the most significant predictor variables (Ittenbach and Esters, 1995; Ittenbach *et al.*, 1992). Although, the results were not surprising, it was interesting to see that the variables used (points per game, points allowed, field-goal percentage, number of free throws, three-point field-goal percentage and number of rebounds) explained less than 50 percent of the variance. In these results, the effect of game pace is clear because a team may score 50 points and be a winner or score 80 points and lose the game. Later on, Ibáñez *et al.* (2008) aimed to identify the game-related statistics that discriminate between season-long successful and unsuccessful basketball. The obtained results were much different than those obtained when contrasting winners and losers. The most powerful performance indicators were assists, steals, and blocks, highlighting the importance of overall passing skills, as well as outside and inside defensive performance. Curiously, these results are likely to confirm that offensive variables are more related to short-term success (winning games) and defensive variables to mid- and long-term success (winning championships). The probable reason for these results may be the lower variability in defensive performances (Oliver, 2004) because these are less influenced by all environmental factors (such as game location).

More recently, Ziv *et al.* (2010) analyzed seven consecutive seasons with the aim of examining the relationship between game statistics and team rankings, when controlling for multicollinearity. The results suggested that a number of on-court statistics do not reliably predict team ranking at the end of the season and that condensing the correlated variables can lead to better predictions. The authors used a factor analysis on the 12 on-court variables, which were reduced to three components by a factor analysis. Out of these three components, four new independent variables were created in order to improve the accuracy of teams' performance analysis: score, condensing assists, field-goal and free-throw percentages; defense, condensing defensive rebounding and blocks; gain possession, condensing steals and received fouls; and lose possession, condensing turnovers and committed fouls.

In fact, the search for an accurate group of performance indicators is really a hot topic. It has also been suggested that the best breakdown of offensive and defensive performances can be obtained by analyzing four factors in the following order of importance: (1) effective field-goal percentage, (2) offensive rebounding percentage, (3) turnovers per ball possession, and (4) free-throw rate (Kubatko *et al.*, 2007; Oliver, 2004). Offensively, a team wants to minimize turnovers per possession and maximize all the other factors. These factors are not all equivalent. For example, it was suggested that for NBA games the relative weights of these are approximately 10, 6, 3, and 3, respectively, for each factor (Kubatko *et al.*, 2007).

Sampaio *et al.* (2010b) analyzed these four factors, attempting to explain the United States of America's dominance at the Beijing Olympic Games (2008). The authors stated that USA's fast pace was the main reason for their dominance (81.1 ± 3.0 ball possessions per game versus 70.7 ± 2.1 for the remaining tournament). Therefore, they aimed to identify the game-related statistics that discriminated between fast- and slow-paced games, as well as to identify key performance factors relating to point differentials. The findings indicated that an increase in game pace for the USA team resulted in more recovered balls and a higher number of successful two-point field goals, while not hindering performance substantially in any of the other game-related statistics. In contrast, when the opponent teams increased the pace of the game, only the number of fouls they committed increased. The effects of the four independent variables were inspected for the whole game and for the first- and second-half quarters. For the whole-game model, the outcome was explained by the four factors, but the recovered balls appeared as the second most important factor in explaining the differences in game-quarter scores. For each recovered-ball-per-possession more than the opponent, the USA team increased game quarter outcome by 16.9 ± 5.1 points. These measures of assertive play on both offensive (offensive rebounding) and defensive (recovered balls) play were important factors in the first half but not in the second, indicating that USA's assertive play diminished in the second half. These results may represent a strategic decision to play more conservatively at the end of the game in order to promote the adequate and needed recovery when facing a concentrated schedule such as the Olympics. Nevertheless, the differences obtained between the first- and second-half quarters help to emphasize that performance do changes with time and, therefore, approaching performance analysis by using dynamic complexity may be an interesting complement to understand the game determinants.

Dynamic and self-organized complexity in basketball

Dynamic complexity allows the dimension of time to be addressed in our understanding of the phenomenon. Often, time is modeled as a continuous variable; however, for this particular situation, the attempts to model the basketball game by using time as a discrete variable will also be considered (although they are not dynamic in a straight sense).

It is a fact that time is a fundamental dimension for understanding basketball performance. Nevertheless, the game is better described by the performance indicators that do not change with time (or do so more predictably). From a dynamic perspective, it is possible to find literature describing the importance of initial strong performances by the early success models (Isoahola and Blanchard, 1986). Other perspectives are that starting to lead the game may be understood as a measure of performance accomplishment and hence might have an effect on players' subsequent efforts (Bandura, 1997).

Basketball research on this topic is very scarce. Cooper *et al.* (1992) investigated whether initial and late-game scores are good predictors for the final outcome. It was found that teams who were winning in the first quarter of the game ended up winning 70 percent of the time, whereas the teams who were winning at the end of the third quarter ended up winning 80 percent of the time. More recently, Sampaio *et al.* (2010c) found that the greater the difference in accumulated score at the beginning of each quarter, the more points were recovered by the teams who were losing. In these cases, only when differences in score were above eight points did the lead in the game quarter either have a detrimental effect on the winning team or a motivational effect on the losing team, or both. In fact, the results showed that game quarter outcomes in the whole game, in the second, third and fourth game quarters, were explained by the difference in the accumulated score at the beginning of the quarter. For each point of difference in the accumulated score at the beginning of each quarter, the teams decreased game quarter outcome by 0.27, 0.30, 0.21 and 0.29 points, respectively (Sampaio *et al.*, 2010c). That is, if a team was leading by ten points at half-time, the most likely result at the end of the third quarter was for them to maintain only a seven-point lead.

Other perspectives suggest that the last moments of the games are the most determinant (Bar-Eli and Tenenbaum, 1988a, 1988b; Bar-Eli and Tractinsky, 2000). Obviously, in these last moments of the game, all positive actions, like steals or blocks, and negative actions, like fouls or turnovers, acquire an increased importance. In fact, if a team is winning by one point in the final ball possession and manages to block the opponents' shot, this block may be considered a decisive action. However, it would have much less importance anywhere else in the game. For example, basketball free-throw performance indicators acquire much higher importance in the final moments of these balanced games, where the game is to be decided and the frequency of fouling increases (Kozar *et al.*, 1994). In this study, the authors identified that about 20 percent of all points were scored from free throws. Also, the free throws comprised a significantly higher percentage of total points scored during the last five minutes than during the first 35 minutes of the game, both for winning and for losing teams. The results of Bar-Eli and Tractinsky (2000) were obtained from a sample of 57 ball possessions in the last five minutes of the game indicated that final moments are characterized as comprising twice as many highly critical possessions than low-criticality possessions. Also, the number of highly critical possessions increased strongly toward the end of the game. As should be expected, the results also indicated that highly critical possessions were characterized by a lower quality of decision making compared to low-criticality possessions.

In this topic of criticality, research has also investigated the origin and the validity of common beliefs regarding the 'hot hand' phenomenon. Probably the majority of basketball players and fans tend to believe that a player's probability of hitting a field goal is higher following a hit than following a miss on the previous shot. However, research has systematically failed to provide such evidence (Gilovich *et al.*, 1985). According to Gilovich *et al.* (1985), the belief in the 'hot hand' may be attributed to a general misconception of chance, according to which even short random sequences are thought to be highly representative of their generating process. After several years of research on this topic, a review has been made and, still, the question of whether success breeds success and failure breeds failure remains unsolved (Bar-Eli *et al.*, 2006). In essence, the empirical research supports the non-existence of a relationship between future success and past performance. The authors also point to the need for further developments around the structure of the environment in which a hot hand belief is likely to emerge. As proposed earlier by Burns (2004), an important step forward would be detecting situational factors that enable us to judge the value of the belief either as a fallacy or an adaptive strategy for decision making. In fact, it seems possible that the 'hot hand' may be an adaptive behavior flowing from a fallacious belief, suggesting that there should be a connection in the mind of players between the belief and the behavior, and that this connection should be stronger in expert players. Nevertheless, the structure of the environment needs to be considered in order to improve understanding of this topic – for example, by using self-organizing complexity procedures.

Self-organizing complexity aims to combine the internal constraints of closed systems with the creative evolution of open systems (Lucas, 1999). Therefore, the performance in a basketball game is analyzed as a result of co-evolving interactions between the player, the task and the environment (Newell, 1986). The main idea here is the possibility of designing the environment rather than the system itself and letting the system evolve toward a solution, without trying to impose one. At the end, the aim is to predict the emergent solutions that may occur from different configurations and constraints of the environment. Available literature using the game of basketball is very limited. Although speculating without using game data, Schmidt *et al.* (1999) have described dynamic self-organization and dyadic intra- and interactions, providing several examples from basketball. The authors demonstrated how spontaneous strategic changes could occur – for example, in a backdoor play – and how these could be measured by using variables like the distance of the attacker or ball from the attacking basket and the distance between the defender and the attacker.

Only a couple more studies are available, by Bourbousson *et al.* (2010a) and Bourbousson *et al.* (2010b). In the first study, the authors examined space–time patterns of basketball players during competition by analyzing positional data. Strong, coordinated in-phase relations were identified in the longitudinal (basket-to-basket) direction for all playing dyads, suggesting that these movements were very constrained by the game demands. In the second study, the authors examined space–time coordination dynamics of two basketball teams during competition. They used as variables the geometric team center and a stretch index, obtained from the mean distance of team members from the center. Non-linear relative-phase analysis of the centers demonstrated in-phase stabilities in both the longitudinal and the lateral directions, with more stability in the longitudinal direction. Stretch index results demonstrated in-phase attraction in the longitudinal direction and no attraction in the lateral direction. Overall, the findings demonstrated that space–time movement patterns in basketball seem to present a uniform description, in keeping with universal principles of dynamical self-organizing systems. Also, these results may open up interesting perspectives in providing explanations for several results obtained by performance analysis undergrounded in static complexity models.

Concluding remarks

The framework presented in Figure 28.1 resumes this chapter. Basketball performance indicators should be able to capture global or partial aspects of complex, dynamic and non-linear

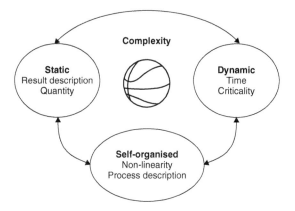

Figure 28.1 Complexity and research in the basketball game

Table 28.1 Overview of recent studies carried out within static, dynamic and self-organized complexity in basketball

Study	Complexity	Criteria	Normalization and variability	Statistics
Bourbousson et al. (2010a)	Self-organized	—	—	Relative phase
Bourbousson et al. (2010b)	Self-organized	—	—	Relative phase
Cooper et al. (1992)	Dynamic	—	—	Probability models
Csataljay et al. (2009)	Static	Winners/losers	Clustered game final differences	Wilcoxon signed ranks
Gomez et al. (2006)	Static	Winners/losers	Clustered score final differences	One-way ANOVA Discriminant analysis
Gomez et al. (2009)	Static	Winners/losers	Player status	One-way ANOVA Discriminant analysis
Gomez al. (2008)	Static	Winners/losers	Team quality Ball possessions	Independent t-test Discriminant analysis
Ibanez et al. (2003)	Static	Winners/losers	Clustered score final differences Ball possessions	Independent t-test Discriminant analysis
Ibanez et al. (2008)	Static	Team rankings	Clustered score final differences Ball possessions	Independent t-test Discriminant analysis
Lorenzo et al. (2010)	Static	Winners/losers	Ball possessions Clustered score final differences	Repeated measures ANOVA Discriminant analysis
Ortega et al. (2007)	Static	Winners/losers	—	Chi-square Independent t-test
Ittenbach and Esters (1995)	Static	Team rankings	—	Multiple regression
Sampaio and Janeira (2003)	Static	Winners/losers	Ball possessions Clustered score final differences Game location Game type	One-way ANOVA Discriminant analysis
Sampaio et al. (2010a)	Static	Within-season variation	Ball possessions Clustered team quality and player duration on court	Factor analysis Mixed linear model
Sampaio et al. (2010b)	Static	USA team vs. others	Ball possessions Game pace	Multiple regression Discriminant analysis
Sampaio et al. (2010c)	Static/dynamic	—	Clustered score final differences Game quarters Game location Team quality	Linear regression
Trninic et al. (2002)	Static	Winners/losers	—	Discriminant analysis
Ziv et al. (2010)	Static	Team rankings	—	Factor analysis Stepwise multiple regressions

properties of performance. Static complexity and structure-oriented observation models enable a higher quantity of isolated elementary actions of a game to be registered. These are suitable for result-description purposes, but limited when there is a need to obtain data about the process. Dynamic complexity modeling has been used to address the time dimension to understand performance either by early success models of criticality or by the final moments of the game (criticality). Finally, self-organizing complexity seems to be emerging, with the need to combine the co-evolving interactions between the player, the task and the environment.

Table 28.1 presents a very brief description of how recent studies are addressing these previously presented issues. In particular, attention should be paid to the criteria used in assessing the performance indicators' validity and also to the control made by addressing normalization and/or variability.

References

Bandura, A. (1997) *Self-Efficacy: The Exercise of Control*, New York: Freeman.

Bar-Eli, M. and Tenenbaum, G. (1988a) 'The interaction of individual psychological crisis and time phases in basketball', *Perceptual and Motor Skills*, 66(2): 523–30.

Bar-Eli, M. and Tenenbaum, G. (1988b) 'Time phases and the individual psychological crisis in sports competition: Theory and research findings', *Journal of Sports Sciences*, 6(2): 141–9.

Bar-Eli, M. and Tractinsky, N. (2000) 'Criticality of game situations and decision making in basketball: An application of performance crisis perspective', *Psychology of Sport and Exercise*, 1(1): 27–39.

Bar-Eli, M., Avugos, S. and Raab, M. (2006) 'Twenty years of "hot hand" research: Review and critique', *Psychology of Sport and Exercise*, 7(6): 525–53.

Bourbousson, J., Sève, C. and McGarry, T. (2010a) 'Space–time coordination dynamics in basketball: Part 1. Intra- and inter-couplings among player dyads', *Journal of Sports Sciences*, 28(3): 339–47.

Bourbousson, J., Sève, C. and McGarry, T. (2010b) 'Space–time coordination dynamics in basketball: Part 2. The interaction between the two teams', *Journal of Sports Sciences*, 28(3): 349–58.

Burns, B.D. (2004) 'Heuristics as beliefs and as behaviors: The adaptiveness of the "hot hand"', *Cognitive Psychology*, 48(3): 295–331.

Cooper, H., DeNeve, K. and Mosteler, F. (1992) 'Predicting professional game outcomes from intermediate game scores', *Chance: New Directions for Statistics and Computing*, 5(3–4): 18–22.

Courneya, K.S. and Carron, A.V. (1992) 'The home advantage in sport competitions – a literature-review', *Journal of Sport & Exercise Psychology*, 14(1): 13–27.

Csataljay, G., O'Donoghue, P., Hughes, M. and Dancs, H. (2009) 'Performance indicators that distinguish winning and losing teams in basketball', *International Journal of Performance Analysis in Sport*, 9(1): 60–6.

Davids, K., Glazier, P., Araújo, D. and Bartlett, R. (2003) 'Movement systems as dynamical systems: The functional role of variability and its implications for sports medicine', *Sports Medicine*, 33(4): 245–60.

FIBA (2009) *Basketball Statisticians Manual*, Geneva: International Basketball Federation.

Gilovich, T., Vallone, R. and Tversky, A. (1985) 'The hot hand in basketball – on the misperception of random sequences', *Cognitive Psychology*, 17(3): 295–314.

Glazier, P.S. (2010) 'Game, set and match? Substantive issues and future directions in performance analysis', *Sports Medicine*, 40(8): 625–34.

Gomez, M.A., Lorenzo, A., Sampaio, J. and Ibáñez, S.J. (2006) 'Differences in game-related statistics between winning and losing teams in women's basketball', *Journal of Human Movement Studies*, 51(5): 357–69.

Gomez, M.A., Lorenzo, A., Sampaio, J., Ibáñez, S.J. and Ortega, E. (2008) 'Game-related statistics that discriminated winning and losing teams from the Spanish men's professional basketball teams', *Collegium Antropologicum*, 32(2): 451–6.

Gomez, M.A., Lorenzo, A., Ortega, E., Sampaio, J. and Ibanez, S.J. (2009) 'Game related statistics discriminating between starters and nonstarters players in Women's National Basketball Association League (WNBA)', *Journal of Sports Science and Medicine*, 8(2): 278–83.

Ibáñez, S.J., Sampaio, J., Saenz-Lopez, P., Gimenez, J. and Janeira, M.A. (2003) 'Game statistics discriminating the final outcome of Junior World Basketball Championship matches (Portugal 1999)', *Journal of Human Movement Studies*, 45(1): 1–19.

Ibáñez, S.J., Sampaio, J., Feu, S., Lorenzo, A., Gomez, M.A. and Ortega, E. (2008) 'Basketball game-related statistics that discriminate between teams' season-long success', *European Journal of Sport Science*, 8(6): 369–72.

Isoahola, S.E. and Blanchard, W.J. (1986) 'Psychological momentum and competitive sport performance – a field-study', *Perceptual and Motor Skills*, 62(3): 763–8.

Ittenbach, R. and Esters, I. (1995) 'Utility of team indices for predicting end of season ranking in two national polls', *Journal of Sport Behavior*, 118(3): 216–24.

Ittenbach, R., Kloos, E. and Etheridge, J. (1992) 'Team performance and national polls – the 1990–91 NCAA Division I basketball season', *Perceptual and Motor Skills*, 74(3): 707–10.

Karipidis, A., Fotinakis, P., Taxildaris, K. and Fatouros, J. (2001) 'Factors characterizing a successful performance in basketball', *Journal of Human Movement Studies*, 41(5): 385–97.

Kozar, B., Vaughn, R.E., Whitfield, K.E., Lord, R.H. and Dye, B. (1994) 'Importance of free-throws at various stages of basketball games', *Perceptual and Motor Skills*, 78(1): 243–8.

Kubatko, J., Oliver, D., Pelton, K. and Rosenbaum, D. (2007) 'A starting point for analyzing basketball statistics', *Journal of Quantitative Analysis in Sports*, 3(3): 1–22.

Lames, M. and MacGarry, T. (2007) 'On the search for reliable performance indicators in game sports', *International Journal of Performance Analysis in Sport*, 7: 62–79.

Lorenzo, A., Gomez, M.A., Ortega, E., Ibanez, S.J. and Sampaio, J. (2010) 'Game related statistics which discriminate between winning and losing under-16 male basketball games', *Journal of Sports Science and Medicine*, 9(4): 664–8.

Lucas, C. (1999) *Quantifying Complexity Theory*. Online. Available at www.calresco.org/lucas/quantify. htm (accessed 1 May 2012).

Madrigal, R. and James, J. (1999) 'Team quality and the home advantage', *Journal of Sport Behavior*, 22(3): 381–98.

Newell, K. (1986) 'Constraints on the development of coordination', in M. Wade and H. Whiting (eds), *Motor Development in Children: Aspects of Coordination and Control* (pp. 341–60). Dordrecht, Germany: Martinus Nijhoff.

Oliver, D. (2004) *Basketball on Paper: Rules and Tools for Performance Analysis*, Dulles: Brassey's Inc.

Ortega, E., Palao, J.M., Gomez, M.A., Lorenzo, A. and Cardenas, D. (2007) 'Analysis of the efficacy of possessions in boys' 16-and-under basketball teams: Differences between winning and losing teams', *Perceptual and Motor Skills*, 104(3): 961–4.

Pfeiffer, M. and Perl, J. (2006) 'Analysis of tactical structures in team handball by means of artificial neural networks', *International Journal of Computer Science in Sport*, 5(1): 4–14.

Pollard, R. and Pollard, G. (2005) 'Long-term trends in home advantage in professional team sports in North America and England (1876–2003)', *Journal of Sports Sciences*, 23(4): 337–50.

Sampaio, J. and Janeira, M. (2003) 'Statistical analyses of basketball team performance: Understanding teams' wins and losses according to a different index of ball possessions', *International Journal of Performance Analysis in Sport*, 3(1): 40–9.

Sampaio, J., Drinkwater, E.J. and Leite, N.M. (2010a) 'Effects of season period, team quality, and playing time on basketball players' game-related statistics', *European Journal of Sport Science*, 10(2): 141–9.

Sampaio, J., Lago, C. and Drinkwater, E.J. (2010b) 'Explanations for the United States of America's dominance in basketball at the Beijing Olympic Games (2008)', *Journal of Sports Sciences*, 28(2): 147–52.

Sampaio, J., Lago, C., Casais, L. and Leite, N. (2010c) 'Effects of starting score-line, game location, and quality of opposition in basketball quarter score', *European Journal of Sport Science*, 10(6): 391–6.

Schmidt, R.C., O'Brien, B. and Sysko, R. (1999) 'Self-organization of between-persons cooperative tasks and possible applications to sport', *International Journal Of Sport Psychology*, 30: 558–79.

Trninic, S., Dizdar, D. and Luksic, E. (2002) 'Differences between winning and defeated top quality basketball teams in final tournaments of European Club Championship', *Colleguim Antropollogicum*, 26(2): 521–31.

Varca, P. (1980) 'An analysis of the home and away game performance of male college basketball teams', *Journal of Sport and Exercise Psychology*, 2(3): 245–57.

Ziv, G., Lidor, R. and Arnon, M. (2010) 'Predicting team rankings in basketball: The questionable use of on-court performance statistics', *International Journal of Performance Analysis in Sport*, 10(2): 103–14.

29

INDOOR VOLLEYBALL AND BEACH VOLLEYBALL

Isabel Mesquita[1], José M. Palao[2], Rui Marcelino[1] and José Afonso[1]

[1]UNIVERSITY OF PORTO, PORTUGAL

[2]UNIVERSITY OF MURCIA, SPAIN

Summary

Research on performance analysis in volleyball arose systematically in the literature in the 1990s. This chapter will present the different conceptual perspectives used to study indoor volleyball and beach volleyball performance using notational analysis, taking into account technical and tactical indicators. In this field, chronological analyses have evolved from studies applying descriptive designs to ones with an emphasis on correlation analysis. Recent research in the field of notational analysis tends to follow Thelen's (2005) recommendations, and instead of establishing simple cause-and-effect relationships, it embraces the possibility of profuse non-linear interactions. This supports the need for an ecological approach, considering the match as a complex dynamical system. Studies on indoor volleyball have been progressing in this direction and assessing sequences of events and their timeline, as well as the context of their use. However, beach volleyball is still in the initial stages that indoor volleyball has already gone through. Likewise, studies are becoming more sophisticated in order to contribute to performance modelling, attending to the dynamics and complexity of the game. Moreover, a synthetic description of the characteristics, advantages, and limitations of some available systems that have been specifically designed for performance analysis in indoor volleyball and beach volleyball will be presented, as well as trends for future research in this field.

Introduction

Analysing a team's performance is imperative for optimizing the preparation process and for assisting in the development of concepts and strategies capable of stimulating improvement in the team's efficacy (Jäger and Schöllhorn, 2007). Indeed, notational analysts and coaches commonly employ performance indicators to assess individual and team performances (Hughes and Bartlett, 2002). Research in performance analysis (PA) focused on volleyball has been providing thorough information on the features, patterns, and specificities of teams' behaviours within competitive contexts, providing valuable data for guiding practice and research alike. In indoor volleyball, this trend emerged earlier than in beach volleyball. However, although research lines and methodologies are similar, the state of knowledge and number of studies are greater in indoor volleyball.

This chapter attempts to synthesize evolutionary trends of research in this field, identifying the most common research questions emerging from PA investigation in indoor volleyball and beach volleyball, and also to characterize the most commonly used methods to analyse the data.

Indoor volleyball performance analysis: methodological tools and technical and tactical indicators

Several online databases were searched, including SportDiscus, PubMed, Web of Science, and Medline. Key search terms used included 'volleyball', 'game analysis', 'match analysis', 'notational analysis', 'performance analysis', 'performance indicators', 'tactical analysis', and 'video analysis'. Manual searches were also conducted using the reference lists from the recovered papers. Methodologically, a content analysis strategy was applied. Consequently, 87 papers were selected that fulfilled three criteria: to have been pioneering in the approached themes; to have presented relevant trends for future research; and to have been consistent in the methods applied. The papers were grouped in function of the methods, purposes, and variables (see Figure 29.1). Subsequent encoding allowed discrimination between three types of analysis: descriptive, correlation, and predictive.

Descriptive and correlation-based research

The first papers in scientific journals presented a methodological design that was fundamentally based on a descriptive analysis of tactical and technical indicators. Although these types of studies were pioneering before 1985 (Cox, 1974; Baacke, 1982; Byra and Scott, 1983; Ejem, 1980; Ejem and Horak, 1980; Vojik, 1980), they are still conducted today because they positively contribute to a sound knowledge regarding the evolutionary trends of the game. These studies represent accumulated data in different game actions in function of their effect (e.g. number of points earned with the serve, percentage of errors in the attack). Currently, these analyses tend to be a starting point in each paper, after which different and more sophisticated analyses are

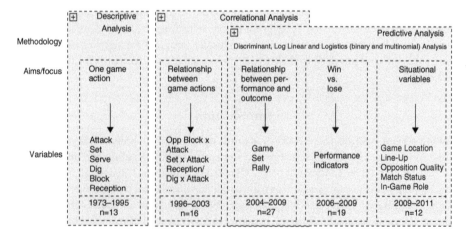

Figure 29.1 Research focused on performance analysis in indoor volleyball in respect of methods, purposes, and variables

conducted. The most widely analysed performance indicators were related to the attack (Castro and Mesquita, 2010; Katsikadelli, 1995), followed by the set (Palao *et al.*, 2004, 2005), serve (Agelonidis, 2004), defence (Mesquita *et al.*, 2007), block (Palao *et al.*, 2004), and reception (Palao *et al.*, 2006). By presenting global measures of performance, these studies proposed to describe and characterize tactical and technical indicators related to performance (Hughes and Franks, 2004).

Jäger and Schöllhorn (2007) authored one of the main papers on the subject, focusing on the players' movements and tactical manoeuvres. They identified specific tactical patterns by different women's national teams, which were probably adapted to the individuality of the team members, and concluded that each team presented their own unique tactical patterns, with implications for the training processes. Approaches using pattern-recognition procedures, allowing analysis of player movements with clustering methods, have only recently had an impact in the specific literature.

Correlational studies followed the descriptive ones in an attempt to identify relationships between different sets of game actions (Katsikadelli, 1996). The major purpose was to understand the extent to which changes in performance in one game indicator would reflect upon performance in the subsequent actions. This line of investigation was predominantly correlative or associative in nature. A considerable body of research applied bivariate statistics (namely the chi-square), with a smaller percentage using sequential lag analysis.

This line of research has shown that volleyball actions exhibit a strong relationship, possibly due to their relative deterministic structure (Afonso and Mesquita, 2011), especially in space and type of action (Afonso *et al.*, 2005a, 2005b; Castro and Mesquita, 2008; Costa *et al.*, 2010). Some of the relationships found were: features of the opponent's block (number of players, cohesiveness, starting positions) and attack efficacy (Mesquita and César, 2007); setting zone and type of set with attack efficacy (Afonso *et al.*, 2010; Laios and Kountouris, 2010); and characteristics of reception and defence with attack efficacy (Costa *et al.*, 2011). Mostly, research has focused on the study of the side-out phase, with few studies focusing on the transition phase. The side-out or complex I (KI) is the attack after serve-reception, consisting of serve-reception, setting, and attack. The transition or complex II (KII) is the counter-attack phase, comprising the block, defence, counter-attack setting, and counter-attack. Overall, these studies have demonstrated the high regularity and stability in defensive and offensive patterns and this should be considered when designing preparation processes for teams. Despite using different samples and variables, attack efficacy has repeatedly been shown to be independent with regard to previous game actions (Castro and Mesquita, 2008; Costa *et al.*, 2010). The ability of the attacker, the tactical and technical quality of the opposing block, and even psychological factors may be stronger predictors of attack efficacy than the type of block of the opposition (Afonso and Mesquita, 2011).

A concurrent line of research was based on correlation analysis, and it searched for significant relationships between the efficacy of certain game actions and the final score, whether in the set (Marcelino and Mesquita, 2008; Marelic *et al.*, 2004; Monteiro *et al.*, 2009) or the match (Marcelino *et al.*, 2008; Palao *et al.*, 2004; Papadimitriou *et al.*, 2004; Zetou and Tsigilis, 2007). Although these studies have provided limited information, since the relationships were bivariate, they have established that performance in attack and reception are highly related to success in volleyball (Marelic *et al.*, 2004; Zetou and Tsigilis, 2007). The diversity of variables used in such studies makes generalization difficult, but the studies have suggested paths for future research.

Some studies have built models presenting performance indicators with discriminatory power concerning the final result (for example, 'Best reception, first set attack'; Zetou and

Tsigilis, 2007). Marcelino *et al.* (2008) have verified that the overall performance of the teams and the performance in each game action differ in function of using absolute data (e.g. number of spike points) or relative variables (e.g. percentage of spike points). Results show that the best teams present better performances in relative variables concerning the attack (coefficient of spike, percentage of spike points, and percentage of spike errors), the serve (percentage of serve points), and the block (percentage of block points). Therefore, it seems that relative variables present greater explanatory power of success than absolute variables.

Predictive analysis of performance

Research studies that have focused on the development of predictive models of performance, using multivariate statistics, are still scarce, especially in volleyball (Marcelino *et al.*, 2011a). The additional value of these methods is related to the predictive potential to regulate training and match performance alike, but excessive speculation should be avoided, as warned by Heazle-wood (2006: 541–2):

> Mathematics and science are based on principles of description and more importantly prediction. The ability to make substantive and accurate predictions of future elite level sports performance indicates that such approaches reflect 'good' science. Often these predictions are purely speculative and are not based on any substantial evidence.

One of the first scientific works, if not the first, that focused on volleyball (Cox, 1973) analysed the relationship between team performance and the skill components of serving, serve reception, setting, spike, spike defence, and free-ball passing, as measured by adapted charting procedures. The spike was the most influential skill in predicting team success, followed by spike defence, serve reception, setting, serving, and free-ball passing. This trend was corroborated by other studies (Marcelino *et al.*, 2008; Marelic *et al.*, 2004; Zetou and Tsigilis, 2007).

Recently, relationships between performance indicators and the final outcome of the match have been established. Applying a logistic regression, Rocha and Barbanti (2006) concluded that it is possible to predict 77.7 per cent of the set outcomes in volleyball using only the number of attack errors and the teams' performance in blocking and serving. In the same vein, João *et al.* (2010) identified gender differences in volleyball game-related statistics using a discriminant analysis. Considerable variability was evident in the game-related statistics profile, as men's volleyball matches were more strongly associated with terminal actions (errors of service), while women's volleyball matches were characterized by continuous actions (in defence and attack). This suggests an influence of the anthropometric and physiological differences between women and men on performance profiles.

Marcelino *et al.* (2009a) analysed 65,000 actions of the 2005 World League using logistic regression and demonstrated that victory within sets is significantly associated with performance in each of the game actions (serving, reception, setting, attack, defence, and blocking). Likewise, they concluded that playing at home increases the likelihood of winning each set, an advantage that is greater for the first, fourth, and fifth sets.

The comparison of performances between winning and losing teams has also been granted attention from research in order to find the most relevant performance indicators associated with success in volleyball (Drikos and Vagenas, 2011; Marelic *et al.*, 2004; Rocha and Barbanti, 2006), mainly applying discriminant functions. Certain performance indicators have emerged as more powerful in explaining performance than others. Overall, attack effectiveness (Drikos and Vagenas, 2011), the spike in the attack phase (Marelic *et al.*, 2004), as well as blocking performance, serve performance and attack errors performance (Rocha and Barbanti, 2006) have been demonstrated as largely influencing the final result.

Multivariate models capable of integrating the effects of different explanatory variables and their interactions on a target variable have recently been used in volleyball match analysis (Afonso *et al.*, 2010) in order to understand how space, time, and task-related variables relate to match performance. The first papers published within this scope were authored by Eom and Schutz (1992a, 1992b). The aim of their first study (Eom and Schutz, 1992a) was to investigate playing characteristics of team performance in international men's volleyball using discriminant analysis. Significant differences between *team standing* and *game outcome* were due to better performances in the game skills used in the counter-attack process. The block and the spike were the most important skills in determining team success. The aim of the second paper (Eom and Schutz, 1992b) was to develop and test a method to analyse and evaluate sequential skill performances in a team sport. Log-linear procedures were used to investigate the nature and degree of the relationship in the first-order (pass-to-set, set-to-spike) and second-order (pass-to-spike) transition plays. Results showed that there was a significant dependency in both the first-order and second-order transition plays, indicating that the outcome of a skill performance is highly influenced by the quality of a preceding skill performance. In addition, the pattern of transition plays was stable and consistent, regardless of the classification status: *game outcome*, *team standing*, or *transition process*. These studies represented a hallmark, a changing point, as they moved forward to more comprehensive and ecological models of performance, surpassing the simple counting of game actions and their efficacy.

More recently, studies using multinomial logistic regression have evidenced regularities in the team behaviours and presented relevant contributions for practice. Castro and Mesquita (2010) analysed factors that could predict the attack tempo in the complex II or transition phase of volleyball. The variables dig type, dig efficacy, and setting zone demonstrated predictive power of the attack tempo. An increasing dig efficacy and stabilization of dig type improved the quality of dig action and the setting action increased the use of quicker attack tempos. Following this trend, two studies have analysed tactical determinants of attack efficacy. Castro *et al.* (2011) and Costa *et al.* (2011) demonstrated that speed (*attack tempo*) and power (*attack type*) have a relevant impact in determining complex II attack success. However, quicker attacks increased the chances of scoring only in transition (Costa *et al.*, 2011). Afonso and Mesquita (2011) wanted to further study this, so they analysed the probabilistic relationships that assisted in predicting outcomes relating to block cohesiveness and attack efficacy in elite-level women's volleyball. Particular emphasis was placed on anticipation movements (Williams, 2009), as they are grounded on a well-timed extraction of relevant information (Bar, 2007). On many occasions, this mental anticipation translates into motor anticipation as the player and/or the team start moving ahead of the predicted stimulus. The authors concluded that the availability of the middle-player to run quick attacks was a key variable in inducing motor anticipation in the blockers. In fact, motor anticipation in blocking a quick attack successfully diminished the likelihood of opposition success in several types of quick attacks or combination plays.

Teams should be thought of as self-organized dynamic systems under pressure from external constraints, a tenet that has been leading research towards a new research pathway (McGarry *et al.*, 2002). Some sports will most likely exhibit a lack of static game patterns (McGarry *et al.*, 2002), but they should present probabilistic patterns from where the game will unfold (Walter *et al.*, 2007). Notational analysis might be successful in highlighting the dynamic stability inherent in each team and/or game. Following these recommendations, recent research in the field of notational analysis is embracing the reality of non-linear interactions, highlighting the dynamic stability inherent to each team and/or game (Hale, 2001).

Based on these assumptions, more recent models of analysis tend to contemplate situational constraints as influencing game performance (Laios and Kountouris, 2010; Marcelino *et al.*, 2011a). Among the analysed variables, venue (Marcelino *et al.*, 2009a, 2009b), line-up (Laios and Kountouris, 2010), the level/quality of the opposition (Marcelino *et al.*, 2010, 2011a) and the match status (Marcelino *et al.*, 2011a) have been emphasized in volleyball. Research based on the quality of the opposition has demonstrated that it is difficult to proceed to a symmetric separation of groups of teams according to their ranking in the competition (Marcelino *et al.*, 2011b; Taylor *et al.*, 2008). Attempting to skirt this problem, it is proposed that the numeric difference between the rankings of the teams may be a more sensitive variable (Lago, 2009; Lago *et al.*, 2010).

Match status represents the match score at the specific moment of the observation. It is hypothesized that game behaviours and their performance vary throughout the game and change according to temporary variations in the result (Mesquita and Marcelino, in press). In most studies, the categories for match status were defined a priori and contained a considerable amount of data. Usually, the adopted intervals were: losing $[-\infty; -1]$, tied $[0]$ and winning $[1; +\infty]$. This system, which is suitable for low-scoring team sports such as soccer and field hockey, appears limited for high-scoring sports such as handball, basketball, and volleyball. In these cases, the stipulated categories should differentiate losing and winning situations where the difference in the score is small or large. In volleyball, to our knowledge, only one paper was published so far that addressed this.

Marcelino *et al.* (2011a) examined the effects of quality of opposition and match status on technical and tactical performance in volleyball, as measured by block, attack, serve, and set actions related to the tasks, space, players, and efficacy of selected game actions (2007 Men's World Cup). In an attempt to obtain a more reliable measure concerning the quality of opposition, teams were classified through cluster analysis as 'high', 'intermediate', or 'low' quality. The difference between points scored and points conceded was used to define match status. By and large, match status affected tactical performance indicators and this was influenced by the quality of the opposition, as had been previously identified (Lago, 2009). In contrast to these findings, technical variables were unaltered by situational variables, as previously reported in volleyball (Eom and Schutz, 1992a). Results further suggested that volleyball teams took more risky decisions in unbalanced situations. They also carried less risk through technical and tactical decisions in balanced and moderate situations whether they had the advantage or not. Therefore, strategic behaviour was affected by the interaction of quality of opposition and match status, providing a better understanding of volleyball game performance and new insights for practice, competition, and research.

Beach volleyball performance analysis: methodological tools and technical and tactical indicators

The online databases used to find the articles about performance analysis in beach volleyball were SportDiscus®, PubMed, Web of Science, Google Scholar, Sponet, and Dialnet. The key terms used in the search were 'beach volleyball', 'game analysis', 'match analysis', 'notational analysis', 'performance analysis', 'performance indicators', technical analysis', 'tactical analysis', and 'video analysis'. Only papers from peer-reviewed journals were considered in the search. An initial revision of the papers was done by analysing the title and abstracts of the papers. A total of 17 papers were selected (2003–2011). The papers were grouped according to methods, purposes, and variables. Subsequent encoding allowed for discrimination between three types of analysis: descriptive, correlation, and predictive.

Descriptive and correlation analysis

The first papers related to performance analysis in beach volleyball were focused on analysis of technique from a biomechanical perspective (manner of execution, reference values, and differences between the techniques used in indoor and beach volleyball – e.g. skills, jumping, landing, etc.). Specifically, in relation to technical and tactical analysis of beach volleyball, most of the studies have used a correlational analysis of the data. The differences found with the first stage of the development of indoor volleyball showed that, despite the later start, the studies done in beach volleyball present more complex analyses. However, it may be that the analysed articles are from peer-reviewed journals that only accept this type of analysis. These aspects can be viewed as positive (state of the research used to study PA in beach volleyball) and at the same time as negative (risk of absence of reference values in beach volleyball; descriptive stage of a problem).

With regard to the studies that do a correlational analysis, three lines of study can be seen after analysing the articles found: a) studies that analyse the relationship between game actions; b) studies that analyse game actions in different contexts; and c) studies that analyse game actions and outcome.

Concerning the relationships between game actions, the studies that were reviewed showed:

- A relationship between the way the serve is executed and its efficacy (Martinez-López and Palao, 2009). The technique used is significantly associated with serve efficacy (points and error), but not with rally outcome (Koch and Tilp, 2009a; Martinez-López and Palao, 2009). The type of serve execution with the greatest efficacy was the serve directed towards the zone of interference between receivers.
- No relationship was found between the set and attack (Koch and Tilp, 2009a).
- A relationship between reception and attack (type and efficacy) for males and female players (Lacerda and Mesquita, 2003). When the reception conditioned the attack, female players tended to execute a hard attack (more effective options), and when the reception was perfect, more variability in the attack type was found (Koch and Tilp, 2009a).
- A relationship between the way the attack was executed and its efficacy, the opposition block, and the chances to win the rally (Martinez-López and Palao, 2010; Mesquita *et al.*, 2003; Mesquita and Teixeira, 2004a, 2004b). The zone of execution (origin and ending) affects the attack effectiveness. For males, the most used and most effective technique is the power spike. There are significant associations between the previous action and the type of attack with its quality (higher reception efficacy, higher attack efficacy), as well as between the block opposition and attack effectiveness (type of attack used). For female players, similar effectiveness using different types of attack was found. Significant associations between ranking and game outcome and type of attack were also found. The spike had its greatest efficacy when it was directed to lateral and deep zones of the court.

With regard to the studies that analyse game actions in different contexts, two groups of studies can be differentiated: a) studies about the rule changes made by the FIVB; and b) studies about the differences between the ways in which the two sexes play. Several studies have been done on how the rule changes made by FIVB in 2000 have affected game performance. The rule changes made by the FIVB involved a reduction of the court surface (9×9 m to 8×8 m), a change in the score point system (side-out system to rally point), and the serve is now allowed to touch the net. The goal of the changes was to make the game more understandable for the public, increase the continuity in the game (duration of the rallies) and standardize the match duration. Besides these generic goals, several studies have been done to analyse the effect of these changes in the rules on the way in which the game is played. Giatsis and Tzetzis (2003) studied the reception and attack in the men's Hellenics Championship. They did not find differences in attack efficacy before and after the rule changes, despite the court reduction. The authors justified these results because they also found an increase in the reception efficacy, which allowed the players to do the attack under better conditions and because teams are using different types of offensive tactics. Ronglan and Grydeland (2006) also studied the effect of the rule changes on the serve, reception, set, attack, block, and defence efficiency by analysing matches of the men's FIVB World Tour. The researchers found a significant reduction in serve points (4 per cent), serve errors (3 per cent), and attack points (6 per cent), and a significant increase in block actions and block points (4 per cent). No significant differences were found in defensive actions (frequency or efficiency). Investigations about rule changes that studied the relationship between game actions using a correlational analysis do not allow us to establish whether the change in the score system and court dimension has increased the continuity of the game – one of the FIVB's intentions.

Yiannis (2008) briefly compared the technique and efficacy of the different skills performed by male and female players in the 2004 Olympic Games. The results of this study revealed differences between the way the game is played by men and women (e.g. use of power jump serve, hard attack, etc.). Koch and Tilp (2009b) also studied these differences in the way that males and females play in matches from the FIVB World Tour competition. Their results also indicated that top male and female players apply different techniques for success. Differences were found in the technique and quality of serve (men use more jump serves and women use more float serves); in the technique of the reception (men use the lateral reception more than women), set (women use the forearm pass more than men), block (men use the active block more and women use the fake block more), and defence (women defend more shots and men defend more spikes); and in technique and quality of attack (men use the cross-court spike more than women and men make more points and errors than women).

In relation to the studies that analysed game actions and outcome (match, set, or team classification) in the Hellenic Championship, Giatsis and Tzetsis (2003) found that the changes in the court size and the scoring system affected the performance of skills that contributed to winning the match. Before the changes, the skill that was most correlated with winning was the quality of the reception and, after the changes, the winners were the ones that had better attack efficiency and fewer errors (especially in the serve and set). Also in the Hellenic Championship, Michalopoulou *et al.* (2005) found that the winning team had a higher efficacy in the serve and the attack than the losing team. No differences were found in the reception, set, block or defence.

Predictive analysis of performance

In the review that was carried out, only two studies were found that used predictive modelling to study performance. This type of analysis allows for establishing models of performance and relationships between several variables or aspects of the game. The first study was done by Grgantov *et al.* (2005). They studied the impact of the different skills on game outcome in relation to winning or losing after and before the rule changes in the men's Croatian Championship. The results showed that the rule changes have modified the structure of performance. Before the changes, the side-out attack was the most influential skill in predicting the team's success; followed in order by serve reception, court defence, block, counter-attack, and serve. After the changes, the side-out attack was still the most influential skill in predicting the team's success; followed in order by block, counter-attack, court defence, and serve. The attack was the action with the highest predictive power for obtaining a victory with the block and counter-attack. The importance of the serve reception was reduced, according to this study. These results are different from some of the previous studies analysed that used a bivariate analysis. Now the skills that contribute more to winning the match are the ones done above the net (side-out attack, counter-attack, and block). The reasoning for the reduction in the importance of serve reception could be the combination of the reduction in the court size and the fact that an error in the serve gives a point to the opponent.

The second study was done by Giatsis and Panagiotis (2008). They studied the importance of the serve, attack, block, and dig skills on game outcome in relation to winning or losing and the type of match (two or three sets) in the FIVB men's World Tour. They used a discriminant analysis to determine which skill(s) contributed significantly to winning two-set and three-set matches. They found that in 2–0 matches, the winners had better performances than the losers in almost all technical skills. Six parameters discriminated between winners and losers in matches with a 2–0 score: error in attacks, other errors, aces, counter-attacks, kills, and blocks. Opponents' attack errors were the most important factor contributing to a team winning. In 2–1 matches, it was not possible to establish a model that would indicate that a technical skill could act as a predictor of the winning team in a match.

The differences found between these studies are probably due to the difference in the levels of the samples studied (national championship vs. World Tour). It is possible that in the national championship the differences between players are larger than at the international level. In fact, if this theory is true, when teams are closer in skill level, it is more difficult to find differences between winning and losing teams. Another possible difference is that the two studies did not analyse the same variables. Grgantov and collaborators studied all the skills (serve, reception, set, attack, block, and dig), while Giatsis and Panagiotis studied four skills (serve, attack, block, and dig). From the review done of the articles available, it appears that the study of performance has started in beach volleyball, but more studies are required to establish patterns, structure, and tendencies.

Trends and future tendencies in volleyball and beach volleyball performance analysis

Chronologic analysis of PA in indoor volleyball has evidenced the evolution of predominantly descriptive studies towards more complex, multivariate analyses attempting to predict performance. Initially, players' and teams' behaviours were analysed as finished, static products, as if they were fingerprints of the sport. This was done regardless of the nature of the opposition and of the moment of the match in which they were expressed. Traditionally, research was conducted through the accumulation of data concerning efficacy of performance.

The search for linear relationships between variables assumed simple and reductionist connections, reducing ecological validity, in face of the complex and changeable nature of team sports. One of the most important limitations was the neglect of the sequential aspect of the game and its situational specificity (Lames and McGarry, 2007).

More recently, there has been a change in emphasis towards more predictive analyses, with the purpose of modelling performance in volleyball. This was based on the recognition that team sports obey the principles of complex systems (Bar-Yam, 2003; García-Manso *et al.*, 2010; Noakes *et al.*, 2004; Volossovitch, 2008) and now represents a strong line of research in PA in volleyball. *Complex systems* are understood as 'complex structures that consist of *several* elements, usually numerous, whose *relationships are nonlinear*' (García-Manso *et al.*, 2010: 14). García-

Manso *et al.* argued that a relationship is not linear when the response is not proportional to the impulse, or the outcome is not equal to the input. The authors added that non-linearity means that there may be more than one answer to the same stimulus and that in many cases the answer is not at all predictable. They concluded that 'in a non-linear world certainties disappear and move onto probable' (García-Manso *et al.*, 2010: 14). Including the assumptions of complex systems' analysis in the study of team sports has found several limitations when actually designing the methodological approaches. More often than not, there is a simplification of the teams' behaviours, resulting in an effort of methodological sophistication more than in producing relevant knowledge (Morin, 2007).

The broad use of computer technologies in sports and the utilization of advanced mathematical models still defy research in PA in volleyball. The challenge is to provide interactive data that keep the original sense of the game. Therefore, proper video sequences must be obtained, and robust and consistent coding processes should be collected over time with consideration of multiple interactions.

The reality of beach volleyball is completely different. Beach volleyball is still taking its first steps regarding the study of performance. This line of research has been carried out for less than ten years. The path taken and reference provided by indoor volleyball acts as a guide in establishing the next steps in the study of PA in beach volleyball. From the review carried out, future trends in the study of beach volleyball involve studying women's beach volleyball, increasing the variables studied, and combining descriptive, correlational, and predictive analyses in order to obtain reference values and game patterns.

Concluding remarks

An overview clearly highlights that the improvement of volleyball performance has been accomplished by knowledge of match regularities, reinforcing the role of notational analysis in the understanding of match constraints and in guiding practice.

This chapter described research trends within the scope of PA in volleyball. A parallel between the evolution of research and the development of more sophisticated methodological designs was evident, both attempting to grasp the complex and dynamic nature of the game.

In indoor volleyball, the path covered by research has attempted to identify and quantify patterns in the teams' tactical and technical performance, considering the interaction between sets of game actions and their relation with the competitive success. More recently, contextual factors have been considered in their contribution for performance outcomes. In beach volleyball, there is still a lot of work to do to establish reference values and game patterns, instruments of analysis, and aspects that affect performance. However, the structural similarities between the two sports allow us to apply similar methods to some of the problems of indoor volleyball and beach volleyball. The highly deterministic nature of *volleyball* action sequences has facilitated the construction of predictive models of performance, and future research should provide a more thorough approach to this purpose.

References

Afonso, J. and Mesquita, I. (2011) 'Determinants of block cohesiveness and attack efficacy in high-level women's volleyball', *European Journal of Sport Science*, 11(1): 69–75.

Afonso, J., Mesquita, I., and Palao, J.M. (2005a) 'Relationship between spike tempo and zone on the number of blockers in a variety of men's national team game phases', *International Journal of Volleyball Research*, 8(1): 19–23.

Afonso, J., Mesquita, I., and Palao, J.M. (2005b) 'Relationship between the use of commit-block and the numbers of blockers and block effectiveness', *International Journal of Performance Analysis in Sport*, 5(2): 36–45.

Afonso, J., Mesquita, I., Marcelino, R., and Silva, J. (2010) 'Analysis of the setter's tactical action in high-level women's volleyball', *International Journal of Fundamental and Applied Kinesiology*, 42(1): 82–9.

Agelonidis, Y. (2004) 'The jump serve in volleyball: From oblivion to dominance', *Journal of Human Movement Studies*, 47: 205–13.

Baacke, H. (1982) 'Statistical match analysis for evaluation of players' and teams' performances', *Volleyball Technical Journal*, 7(2): 45–56.

Bar, M. (2007) 'The proactive brain: Using analogies and associations to generate predictions', *Trends in Cognitive Sciences*, 11(7): 280–9.

Bar-Yam, Y. (2003) 'Complex system insights to building effective teams', *International Journal of Computer Science in Sport*, 2(2): 8–15.

Byra, M. and Scott, A. (1983) 'A method for recording team statistics in volleyball', *Volleyball Technical Journal*, 7: 39–44.

Castro, J. and Mesquita, I. (2008) 'Estudo das implicações do espaço ofensivo nas características do ataque no Voleibol masculino de elite [Implications of offensive spacing in elite male volleyball attack characteristics]', *Revista Portuguesa de Ciências do Desporto*, 8(1): 114–25.

Castro, J. and Mesquita, I. (2010) 'Analysis of the attack tempo determinants in volleyball's complex II: A study on elite male teams', *International Journal of Performance Analysis in Sport*, 10: 197–206.

Castro, J., Souza, A., and Mesquita, I. (2011) 'Attack efficacy in volleyball: Elite male teams', *Perceptual and Motor Skills*, 113(2): 395–408.

Costa, G., Mesquita, I., Greco, P., Ferreira, N., and Moraes, C. (2010) 'Relação entre o tempo, o tipo e o efeito do ataque no voleibol masculino juvenil de alto nível competitivo [Relationship between tempo, type and effect of attack in male young volleyball players from high competitive level]', *Rev Bras Cineantropom Desempenho Hum*, 12(6): 401–34.

Costa, G., Ferreira, N., Junqueira, G., Afonso, J., and Mesquita, I. (2011) 'Determinants of attack tactics in youth male elite volleyball', *International Journal of Performance Analysis in Sport*, 11: 96–104.

Cox, R.H. (1973) 'Relationship between selected volleyball skill components and team performance of men's Northwest Double A volleyball teams', Ph.D., College of Health, Physical Education and Recreation, University of Oregon.

Cox, R.H. (1974) 'Relationship between selected volleyball skill components and team performance of men's northwest "AA" volleyball teams', *Research Quarterly of the American Association for Health, Physical Education and Recreation*, 45(4): 441–6.

Drikos, S. and Vagenas, G. (2011) 'Multivariate assessment of selected performance indicators in relation to the type and result of a typical set in men's elite volleyball', *International Journal of Performance Analysis in Sport*, 11: 85–95.

Ejem, M. (1980) 'Some theoretical aspects of statistical game analysis utilization in player's performance evaluation', *Volleyball Technical Journal*, 5(3): 43–8.

Ejem, M. and Horak, J. (1980) 'Selected findings from statistical analysis of individual play in Czechoslovak championships', *Volleyball Technical Journal*, 5(3): 17–30.

Eom, H. and Schutz, R. (1992a) 'Statistical analyses of volleyball team performance', *Research Quarterly for Exercise & Sport*, 63(1): 11–18.

Eom, H. and Schutz, R. (1992b) 'Transition play in team performance of volleyball: A log-linear analysis', *Research Quarterly for Exercise & Sport*, 63(3): 261–9.

García-Manso, J., Martín-González, J., and Silva-Grigoletto, M. (2010) 'Los sistemas complejos y el mundo del deporte' [Complex systems and the sport world], *Revista Andaluza de Medicina del Deporte*, 3(1): 13–22.

Giatsis, G. and Tzetzis, G. (2003) 'Comparison of performance for winning and losing beach volleyball teams on different court dimensions', *International Journal of Performance Analysis in Sport*, 3(1): 65–74.

Giatsis, G. and Panagiotis, Z. (2008) 'Statistical analysis of men's FIVB beach volleyball team performance', *International Journal of Performance Analysis in Sport*, 8(1): 31–43.

Grgantov, Z., Katic, R., and Marelic, N. (2005) 'Effect of new rules on the correlation between situation parameters and performance in beach volleyball', *Collegium Antropologicum*, 29(2): 717–22.

Hale, T. (2001) 'Do human movement scientists obey the basic tenets of scientific inquiry?', *Quest*, 53(2): 202–15.

Heazlewood, T. (2006) 'Prediction versus reality: The use of mathematical models to predict elite performance in swimming and athletics at the Olympic Games', *Journal of Sports Science and Medicine*, 5(4): 541–7.

Hughes, M. and Bartlett, R. (2002) 'The use of performance indicators in performance analysis', *Journal of Sports Sciences*, 20(10): 739–54.

Hughes, M. and Franks, I. (2004) 'Notational analysis – a review of the literature', in M. Hughes and I. Franks (eds), *Notational Analysis of Sport. Systems for Better Coaching and Performance in Sport*, 2nd ed. (pp. 59–106). London: Routledge.

Jäger, J. and Schöllhorn, W. (2007) 'Situation-orientated recognition of tactical patterns in volleyball', *Journal of Sports Sciences*, 25(12): 1345–53.

João, P., Leite, N., Mesquita, I., and Sampaio, J. (2010) 'Gender differences in discriminative power of volleyball game-related statistics', *Perceptual and Motor Skills*, 111(3): 893–900.

Katsikadelli, A. (1995) 'Tactical analysis of the attack service in high level volleyball', *Journal of Human Movement Studies*, 29(5): 219–28.

Katsikadelli, A. (1996) 'Reception and the attack serve of world's leading volleyball teams', *Journal of Human Movement Studies*, 34: 223–32.

Koch, C. and Tilp, M. (2009a) 'Analysis of beach volleyball action sequences of female top athletes', *Journal of Human Sport and Exercise*, 4(3): 272–83.

Koch, C. and Tilp, M. (2009b) 'Beach volleyball techniques and tactics: A comparison of male and female playing characteristics', *Kinesiology*, 41(1): 52–9.

Lacerda, D. and Mesquita, I. (2003) 'Análise do processo ofensivo no voleibol de praia de elite em função da qualidade da recepção, do passe e do ataque [Analysis of the offensive process on the side-out in elite beach volleyball]', *EF Deportes*, No. 65 (October).

Lago, C. (2009) 'The influence of match location, quality of opposition, and match status on possession strategies in professional association football', *Journal of Sports Sciences*, 27(13): 1463–9.

Lago, C., Casais, L., Dominguez, E., and Sampaio, J. (2010) 'The effects of situational variables on distance covered at various speeds in elite soccer', *European Journal of Sport Science*, 10(2): 103–9.

Laios, A. and Kountouris, P. (2010) 'Association between the line-up of the players and the efficiency of the serving team in volleyball', *International Journal of Performance Analysis in Sport*, 10: 1–8.

Lames, M. and McGarry, T. (2007) 'On the search for reliable performance indicators in game sports', *International Journal of Performance Analysis in Sport*, 7(1): 62–79.

Marcelino, R. and Mesquita, I. (2008) 'Associations between performance indicators and set's result on male volleyball', paper presented at the 5th International Scientific Conference on Kinesiology, Zagreb, Croatia.

Marcelino, R., Mesquita, I., and Afonso, J. (2008) 'The weight of terminal actions in volleyball. Contributions of the spike, serve and block for the teams' rankings in the World League 2005', *International Journal of Performance Analysis in Sport*, 8(2): 1–7.

Marcelino, R., Mesquita, I., Palao, J., and Sampaio, J. (2009a) 'Home advantage in high-level volleyball varies according to set number', *Journal of Sports Science and Medicine*, 8(3): 352–6.

Marcelino, R., Mesquita, I., Sampaio, J., and Anguera, M. (2009b) 'Home advantage in high-level volleyball', *Revista de Psicologia del Deporte*, 18(2): 181–96.

Marcelino, R., Mesquita, I., and Sampaio, J. (2010) 'Efficacy of the volleyball game actions related to the quality of opposition', *The Open Sports Sciences Journal*, 3: 34–5.

Marcelino, R., Mesquita, I., and Sampaio, J. (2011a) 'Effects of quality of opposition and match status in volleyball high-level performances', *Journal of Sports Sciences*, 29(7): 733–41.

Marcelino, R., Mesquita, I., and Sampaio, J. (2011b) 'Investigação centrada na Análise do Jogo: Da modelação estática à modelação dinâmica [Research on the game analysis: From static to dynamic modeling]', *Revista Portuguesa de Ciências do Desporto*, 11(1): 481–9.

Marelic, N., Resetar, T., and Jankovic, V. (2004) 'Discriminant analysis of the sets won and the sets lost by one team in A1 Italian volleyball league – a case study', *Kinesiology*, 36(1): 75–82.

Martinez-López, A.B. and Palao, J.M. (2009) 'Effect of serve execution on serve efficacy in men's and women's beach volleyball', *International Journal of Applied Sports Sciences*, 21(1): 1–16.

Martinez-López, A.B. and Palao, J.M. (2010) 'Incidencia de la forma de ejecución del remate sobre el rendimiento en voley playa [Effect of spike execution on performance in beach volleyball]', *Kronos*, IX(18): 61–70.

McGarry, T., Anderson, D., Wallace, S., Hughes, M., and Franks, I. (2002) 'Sport competition as a dynamical self-organizing system', *Journal of Sports Sciences*, 20(10): 771–81.

Mesquita, I. and Teixeira, J. (2004a) 'Caracterizacao do processo ofensivo no voleibol de praia masculino de elite mundial, de acordo com o tipo de ataque, a eficacia e o momento de jogo [Characteristics of the offensive process in male peak performance beach volleyball with the attack type, efficacy, and game moment]', *Revista Brasileira de Ciencias do Esporte*, 26: 33–49.

Mesquita, I. and Teixeira, J. (2004b) 'The spike, attacks zones and the opposing block in elite male beach volleyball', *International Journal of Volleyball Research*, 7(1): 57–62.

Mesquita, I. and César, B. (2007) 'Characterisation of the opposite player's attack from the opposition block characteristics. An applied study in the Athens Olympic Games in female volleyball teams', *International Journal of Performance Analysis in Sport*, 7(2): 13–27.

Mesquita, I. and Marcelino, R. (in press) 'O efeito da Qualidade de Oposição e do *Match Status* no rendimento das equipas', in A. Volossovitch and A. Ferreira (eds), *Fundamentos e aplicações em análise do jogo.* Lisboa: FMH-Edições.

Mesquita, I., Moreno, M.P., and Teixeira, J.M. (2003) 'Asociación entre la eficacia en el ataque y la adaptación al bloqueo contrario en voley playa de élite mundial [Relationship between attack efficacy and adaptation to opponent block in peak performance beach volleyball]', *Red: Revista de Entrenamiento Deportivo*, 17(4): 15–22.

Mesquita, I., Manso, F., and Palao, J. (2007) 'Defensive participation and efficacy of the libero in volleyball', *Journal of Human Movement Studies*, 52(2): 95–107.

Michalopoulou, M., Papadimitriou, K., Lignos, N., Taxildaris, K., and Antoniou, P. (2005) 'Computer analysis of the technical and tactical effectiveness in Greek Beach Volleyball', *International Journal of Performance Analysis in Sport*, 5(1): 41–50.

Monteiro, R., Mesquita, I., and Marcelino, R. (2009) 'Relationship between the set outcome and the dig and attack efficacy in elite male volleyball game', *International Journal of Performance Analysis in Sport*, 9(3): 294–305.

Morin, E. (2007) 'Restricted complexity, general complexity', in C. Gershenson, D. Aerts, and B. Edmonds (eds), *Science and Us: Philosophy and Complexity* (pp. 1–25). Singapore: World Scientific.

Noakes, T., Gibson, A., and Lambert, E. (2004) 'From catastrophe to complexity: A novel model of integrative central neural regulation of effort and fatigue during exercise in humans', *British Journal of Sports Medicine*, 38(4): 511–14.

Palao, J., Santos, J., and Ureña, A. (2004) 'Effect of the setter's position on the block in volleyball', *International Journal of Volleyball Research*, 6(1): 29–32.

Palao, J., Santos, J., and Ureña, A. (2005) 'The effect of the setter's position on the spike in volleyball', *Journal of Human Movement Studies*, 48: 25–40.

Palao, J., Santos, J., and Ureña, A. (2006) 'Effect of reception and dig efficacy on spike performance and manner of execution in volleyball', *Journal of Human Movement Studies*, 51(4): 221–38.

Papadimitriou, K., Pashali, E., Sermaki, I., Mellas, S., and Papas, M. (2004) 'The effect of the opponent's serve on the offensive actions of Greek setters in volleyball games', *International Journal of Performance Analysis in Sport*, 4: 23–33.

Rocha, C. and Barbanti, V. (2006) 'An analysis of the confrontations in the first sequence of game actions in Brazilian volleyball', *Journal of Human Movement Studies*, 50(4): 259–72.

Ronglan, L.T. and Grydeland, J. (2006) 'The effects of changing the rules and reducing the court dimension on the relative strengths between game actions in top international beach volleyball', *International Journal of Performance Analysis in Sport*, 6(1): 1–12.

Taylor, J., Mellalieu, S., James, N., and Shearer, D. (2008) 'The influence of match location, quality of opposition, and match status on technical performance in professional association football', *Journal of Sports Sciences*, 26(9): 885–95.

Thelen, E. (2005) 'Dynamic systems theory and the complexity of change', *Psychoanalytic Dialogues*, 15(2): 255–83.

Vojik, J. (1980) 'Several remarks to a system of accumulating data in volleyball', *Volleyball Technical Journal*, 5(3): 35–41.

Volossovitch, A. (2008) 'Análise dinâmica do jogo de andebol. Estudo dos factores que influenciam a probabilidade de marcar golo', Ph.D., Universidade Técnica de Lisboa, Lisbon.

Walter, F., Lames, M., and McGarry, T. (2007) 'Analysis of sports performance as a dynamical system by means of relative phase', *International Journal of Computer Science in Sport*, 6(2): 35–41.

Williams, A.M. (2009) 'Perceiving the intentions of others: How do skilled performers make anticipation judgments?', *Mind and Motion: The Bidirectional Link Between Thought and Action*, 174: 73–83.

Yiannis, L. (2008) 'Comparison of the basic characteristics of men's and women's beach volleyball from the Athens 2004 Olympics', *International Journal of Performance Analysis in Sport*, 8(3): 130–7.

Zetou, E. and Tsigilis, N. (2007) 'Does effectiveness of skill in complex I predict win in men's Olympic volleyball games?', *Journal of Quantitative Analysis in Sports*, 3(4): 1–9.

30

HANDBALL

Anna Volossovitch

TECHNICAL UNIVERSITY OF LISBON, PORTUGAL

Summary

This chapter aims to review the literature regarding performance analysis in handball. Different approaches to throwing analysis, goalkeeper assessment, characterization of physical activity profiles of players and time-motion analysis are presented and discussed.

The static and dynamical approaches in handball match analysis are compared. The static approach is structure-oriented and represented by descriptive and comparative studies based on the summarized game statistics data; the dynamical approach is oriented to the match process and uses play-by-play data, which are promising for addressing chronological changes of the performance and complex assessment of factors that influence a handball team's efficiency. The chapter finishes with suggestions for further investigation in handball performance.

Brief description of the game and major issues of performance analysis in handball

Handball is a time-dependent invasion game, played by two teams of seven players each (six outfield players and a goalkeeper). Each team attempts to score by throwing the ball into the opposing team's goal during a 60-minute match (two halves of 30 minutes each). The opposing teams alternate possession of the ball, so each team has about the same number of opportunities to score by the end of the match. The ball possession ends when a team attempts a field shot, when a seven-metre throw is not rebounded by the offence (possession continues after an offensive rebound) or in the case of a turnover. Handball is a high-scoring game, where the majority of ball possessions end with a shot. This very brief description of handball focuses on some important aspects of the game, which provides a rationale for some of the quantitative and qualitative performance analysis techniques applied to handball that are discussed in this chapter.

This is a review of studies selected from ISI Web Knowledge All Databases based on the criteria that the studies involved performance analysis in handball during the last two decades with a tendency to focus on the following issues:

1. Throwing performance analysis;
2. Goalkeeper performance assessment;

3. Physical activity profiles of players and time-motion analysis; and
4. Match analysis and modelling of team's performance.

Hierarchical structure of performance in handball can be represented by four groups of performance factors: 1) basic anthropological characteristics; 2) specific abilities and skills of handball players; 3) situation-related parameters of competition activities or playing efficiency; and 4) outcome of a match (Vuleta *et al.*, 2003). The next three sections of this chapter are related to the first two groups of performance factors and the fourth section concerns the last two groups.

Throwing performance analysis

One of the key subjects in individual handball performance analysis is the study of the throwing patterns used by players. The throwing ability of players is a critical factor for success in handball, which is why there is a lot of interest in research on this issue. Maximal ball velocity and precision of throwing are considered primary characteristics that influence shot effectiveness (Fradet *et al.*, 2004; Gorostiaga *et al.*, 2005; Granados *et al.*, 2007; van den Tillaar and Ettema, 2007).

Several studies have concluded that ball velocity depends on the type of throw technique, sequences and timing of body segment actions, such as trunk flexion and rotation, shoulder flexion, elbow extension and wrist deviation, as well as on muscle strength and power (Rivilla-Garcia *et al.*, 2011; Wagner and Muller, 2008).

The shot in handball has been analysed from a biomechanical perspective, by measuring 3D kinematic parameters (maximal joint velocity, angle range and maximal angular velocity) and quality of movement (throw accuracy), based on the following factors:

1. Type of throw – jump throw, standing throw, with and without run-up, and the pivot throw (Fradet *et al.*, 2004; Gorostiaga *et al.*, 2005; Granados *et al.*, 2007; Ohnjec *et al.*, 2010; Wagner *et al.*, 2011);
2. Parameters of muscular force of throwers (Bayios *et al.*, 2001; Gorostiaga *et al.*, 2005; Granados *et al.*, 2007; van den Tillaar and Ettema, 2004);
3. Target locations in the handball goal (Bourne *et al.*, 2011; Schorer *et al.*, 2007);
4. Level of players (Bourne *et al.*, 2011; Schorer *et al.*, 2007; Wagner *et al.*, 2010); and
5. Influence of opposition – goalkeeper and defensive player (Gutiérrez *et al.*, 2006; Párraga *et al.*, 2002; Rivilla-Garcia *et al.*, 2011).

The above-mentioned studies confirmed significant differences in ball velocity between different throwing techniques. The highest ball velocity was achieved in the standing throw with a three-step run-up, followed by the standing throw without a run-up and then the jump throw (Gorostiaga *et al.*, 2005; Granados *et al.*, 2007; van den Tillaar and Ettema, 2003, 2004; Wagner *et al.*, 2010, 2011).

In order to study the speed–accuracy trade-off in handball throwing, van den Tillaar and Ettema (2003) applied five types of instructions that emphasized velocity or accuracy, or both, of throwing. When the instruction prioritized accuracy, the ball velocity was changed. In general, instructions which focused on speed and/or accuracy of throw did not influence the throwing technique and relative timing of the different body segments involved in the throwing of experienced handball players.

With reference to parameters that influence throwing accuracy, the recent study of Bourne *et al.* (2011) did not find any significant differences in the dynamical structure of handball penalty shots directed at four separate targets located at each corner of the goal. Also, the study did not observe any differences in complete time-series data analysis or in the analysis of different phases of shots (the wrist and finger mechanics were not registered during the experiment). According to the authors, these findings could possibly denote the importance of the last phase of the shot for speed and accuracy, which had been suggested by previous studies (Wagner and Muller, 2008).

The study of throw-movement patterns according to players' expertise has revealed a significant relationship with the skill level of players, both male and female. Schorer *et al.* (2007) reported a high correlation between a shooter's expertise and throw-movement duration ($r=0.76$, $p<0.01$), as well as the ball-flight duration ($r=0.71$, $p<0.01$). In the same study, the authors also registered a high correlation between thrower's expertise and accuracy of shots assessed by hit–miss ratio ($r=0.90$, $p<0.04$). According to Wagner *et al.* (2010), an increase in trunk flexion, trunk rotation, shoulder internal rotation and angular velocity during throw execution resulted in an increase in ball velocity. High-level handball players demonstrated better results for ball velocity than their less-experienced colleagues. The fact that elite players were taller and heavier was given as one of the reasons that influenced handball throwing performance. Similar results were described by Gorostiaga *et al.* (2005) and Granados *et al.* (2007), who found higher ball velocity in standing throws and three-step running throws of male and female elite players compared to amateurs. This result was associated with higher absolute maximal strength and muscle power of elite players.

The comparison of intra-individual movement patterns in penalty throws performed by novice, advanced and elite handball players indicates that novice motor performance is characterized by higher random variability. Advanced players demonstrated the most stable patterns of throwing, while elite players showed more variability in various aspects of movement patterns (Schorer *et al.*, 2007). The authors differentiated between the active functional variability of experts' throwing from the random variability of novices. According to Schorer *et al.* (2007), the variability in expert execution could be explained by players' intention to reduce the visual information and deceive the opposition.

An analysis of segmental organization of the throwing arm, based on linear velocities of the joints, had revealed that the temporal sequence of the segments used in the handball throw was different from the usual sequencing pattern (from proximal to distal) of throwing activities, like baseball pitching and javelin throwing (Fradet *et al.*, 2004; van den Tillaar and Ettema *et al.*, 2009). This fact could also be related to the need to adapt throwing execution to the constraints imposed by the defenders and goalkeeper.

The ability to conceal the movement pattern is crucial for successful throwing performance in the goalkeeper-and-thrower duel. However, the literature review reveals the predominance of opposition-free conditions in studies of handball throwing. Only a few studies analysed the influence of opposition on ball velocity in handball throwing (Gutiérrez *et al.*, 2006; Párraga *et al.*, 2002; Rivilla-Garcia *et al.*, 2011).

Párraga *et al.* (2002) demonstrated that ball velocity was influenced by the goalkeeper position. When the goalkeeper was diagonally opposite to the thrower's attacking arm, the ball velocity was reduced.

Gutiérrez *et al.* (2006) observed no kinematic differences in the technical execution of handball throws with and without opposition, with the exception of time of run-up before throw, which was shorter when a defensive player was involved. A small sample (11 players) of sub-elite athletes and some measurement limitations could possibly explain this result.

The recent findings of Rivilla-Garcia *et al.* (2011) showed a negative effect of opposition on ball velocity in the jump throw of three groups of handball players (elite, amateur and adolescent). It has also been observed that the effect of opposition on throwing velocity does not vary according to the expertise level of players.

The majority of studies in handball throwing appear to focus on identifying the factors that influence ball velocity and shot accuracy in experimental protocols that exclude the goalkeeper and opposition, and subsequently do not consider the influence of misleading skills, perception and anticipation on handball shot effectiveness. Further research should try to analyse the handball throw in more representative designs that allow the players to explore the dynamic and time-constrained context of interaction between throwers and their opponents, as in real play.

Goalkeeper performance evaluation

The great influence of the goalkeeper's effectiveness on the game outcome in handball has been highlighted in several studies (Fuertes *et al.*, 2010; Pori *et al.*, 2009; Volossovitch and Gonçalves, 2003). This fact explains the wide research interest in the goalkeeper's performance, which has been analysed by using virtual reality technology (Bideau *et al.*, 2003, 2004, 2010; Bolte *et al.*, 2010; Vignais *et al.*, 2009, 2010), eye-tracking systems (Schorer, 2005), 3D kinematic analysis (Gutiérrez-Davila *et al.*, 2011; Rogulj and Papić, 2005), force platforms (Gutiérrez-Davila *et al.*, 2011) and observational methodology followed by sequential data analysis (Prudente *et al.*, 2010).

Comparing goalkeeper performance according to different levels of expertise in the penalty throws, Schorer (2005) revealed significant differences in reaction quality, movement time and number of goalkeepers' gaze fixations. In successful trials, elite goalkeepers were faster and needed a lower number of gaze fixations than their less-experienced colleagues. The results of the study suggest that experienced goalkeepers delayed their movement to the ball, but moved significantly faster. This strategy, to start later, helped them to obtain more information about the ball trajectory without revealing their own intentions.

Rogulj and Papić (2005) analysed speed variation in a specific goalkeeper's movement (low side-step) during the low shot from long distances. The authors also found that initial and medium phases of goalkeeper movement were slower, while there was a considerable acceleration in the final phase.

In several recent studies, the goalkeeper's performance has been analysed in virtual environments from a perception–action coupling perspective (Bideau *et al.*, 2004, 2010; Bolte *et al.*, 2010; Vignais *et al.*, 2009, 2010). It was shown that the handball goalkeeper's behaviour was similar in real and virtual situations, making it possible to extrapolate results obtained in computer-generated situations to interception actions in the real game (Bideau *et al.*, 2003, 2004). Focusing on the real-time interactions between goalkeeper and virtual thrower, virtual reality systems provide standardized experimental situations that allow reliable measurement of performance in reproducible throwing actions. Furthermore, virtual environments help to record the effect of small changes in the thrower's movement and their influence on the goalkeeper's behaviour.

Bideau *et al.* (2010) assessed goalkeepers' anticipation skill in a virtual throw situation and registered a faster response time in successful actions. The computer-generated visual environment enabled systematic variations of throwing parameters, allowing the confirmation of how each particular factor influenced the goalkeeper's behaviour. In order to determine which information was used by the goalkeeper to control his interception actions, the authors dissociated the visual information about the thrower's behaviour from the ball trajectory. Results suggested that ball trajectory is more informative for the goalkeepers, contributing to a higher percentage of successful reactions.

The goalkeeper's perception–action activity in coupled and uncoupled conditions has been analysed by Vignais *et al.* (2009), also using the virtual environment. As in previous research (Dicks *et al.*, 2010; Farrow and Abernethy, 2003), it has been shown that the players' performance was more precise in the motor-task conditions than in judgment reports.

Gutiérrez-Davila *et al.* (2011) investigated the effect of uncertainty on anticipatory goal-keeper strategies. The results suggested that, in greater uncertainty conditions, the goalkeepers started their lateral movement later and slower. Authors classify this goalkeeper behaviour as precautionary. The delay in the action allows the players to conceal their intentions and deceive the opponent, as well as gain time for modifying their movement, in order to adjust it better to the thrower's behaviour. The data suggested that goalkeepers identified more precisely the clues related to the side of throw than the throw height.

Research on handball goalkeepers' performance has shown that visual–motor activity during ball interception is based on the perception–action coupling between thrower and goal-keeper. It has also been demonstrated that the goalkeeper's behaviour is influenced by the defenders' actions (Prudente *et al.*, 2010). Thus, further studies should continue to identify pertinent perceptual information that contributes to the precision of goalkeeper's judgments about throwing actions and ball trajectories. In order to improve goalkeepers' performance, it is also necessary to develop and test different training scenarios based on this relevant visual information.

Activity profiles of handball games

Handball is an intermittent, high-intensity contact sport game. Motor activity of players includes running, jumping, throwing, hitting and blocking, and requires high levels of agil-ity, speed, strength, power and aerobic skills. Anthropometric and physical activity profiles of elite male and female handball players are well reported (Čavala *et al.*, 2008; Čavala and Katić, 2010; Chaouachi *et al.*, 2009; Chelly *et al.*, 2011; Gorostiaga *et al.*, 2006; Granados *et al.*, 2007; Ziv and Lidor, 2009). A higher stature and greater lean body mass are generally considered as advantageous for effectiveness of offensive and defensive players' actions (Milanese *et al.*, 2011; Granados *et al.*, 2007; Wagner *et al.*, 2010).

Previous research has confirmed significant differences between elite and amateur handball players, both male and female, in absolute maximal strength and muscle power (Gorostiaga *et al.*, 2005; Granados *et al.*, 2007). Elite handball players have also demonstrated greater relative maximal power, when compared to untrained subjects or endurance trained athletes (Rannou *et al.*, 2001). These findings suggest that strength and power are imperative attributes for the dynamic and contact competitive activity that distinguishes the handball game.

The physiological measures of players suggest that the anaerobic metabolism is the most relevant for the performance in handball (Delamarche *et al.*, 1987; Granados *et al.*, 2007). The aerobic mechanism is also important and, being requested during low-intensity periods of a match, it enables a faster recovery of players from high-intensity effort (Rannou *et al.*, 2001). However, handball players do not show a high level of aerobic capacity or maximum oxygen consumption (Buchheit *et al.*, 2009; Chaouachi *et al.*, 2009; Gorostiaga *et al.*, 2005; Ziv and Lidor, 2009) because, during the match, they perform many more short- and high-intensity actions which do not demand a high aerobic capacity. Rannou *et al.* (2001) reported that $\dot{V}O_{2max}$ of elite male handball players was similar to sprint-trained athletes, higher than the $\dot{V}O_{2max}$ of untrained subjects and lower than the $\dot{V}O_{2max}$ of endurance-trained athletes. Similar results have been reported by Granados *et al.* (2007) for female players, suggesting only some impor-tance of aerobic capacity for handball performance. In the review of physiological attributes of handball players, Ziv and Lidor (2009) concluded that maximum oxygen consumption as well as endurance capacity *per se* do not differentiate players according to their competitive level.

Position-related differences in anthropometric and physical profiles of players have been reported in male and female handball. Wings were shorter and lighter than players from other positions, and goalkeepers had a greater percentage of body fat (Chaouachi *et al.*, 2009; Luig *et al.*, 2008; Milanese *et al.*, 2011; Rogulj *et al.*, 2005; Sibila and Pori, 2009).

Research has reported conflicting results related to differences among playing position in physical performance. While some studies have claimed significant differences between the physical profile of wings and other playing positions (Čavala and Katić, 2010), others have not (Chaouachi *et al.*, 2009). These conflicting results may be due to some particularities of observed samples and differences between female and male handball and should be addressed in future studies.

The literature review has clearly revealed a lack of time-motion analysis data recorded in handball match-play. Delamarche *et al.* (1987) monitored seven under-18 handball players during the first half of a handball game in a study that also evaluated blood lactate concentration and heart rate of players. Data were recorded every five minutes, and after a ten-minute rest period, suggesting frequent changing of heart rate of players during the game and variation of blood lactate concentration from 4 to 9 mmol.L^{-1}.

Recently, the motion profile of elite players who participated in the 2007 Men's World Championship has been provided by Luig *et al.* (2008). Results obtained from the computer-based match analysis system (SAGIT) suggest significant position-related differences in motion profiles. The greatest distance was covered by wing players (3710.6 ± 210.2 m), followed by backcourt players (2839.9 ± 150.6 m), pivot players (2786.6 ± 238.0 m) and goalkeepers (2058.1 ± 290.2 m). The analysis of motion intensity revealed that 34.3 ± 4.9 per cent of the total distance the players covered was by walking, 44.7 ± 5.1 per cent by slow running and 17.9 ± 3.5 per cent by fast running and 3.0 ± 2.2 per cent by sprinting. As expected, wing players covered significantly longer distances by fast running and sprinting.

Chelly *et al.* (2011) confirmed that elite adolescent players covered a smaller distance and performed fewer technical actions in the second half of a match. These authors reported quite different results than Luig *et al.* (2008) with respect to the total distance covered on average per handball match (1777 ± 264.0 m) and intensities of players' displacement. The fact that the study focused on elite adolescent and not adult players could be one of the many reasons (such as influence of match equilibrium or teams' strategy, for example) that justifies the differences between the results reported by Luig *et al.* (2008) and Chelly *et al.* (2011).

In addition to scarce data about the running profile of handball players, none of the available analysis has taken into account the context of competition, quality of opposition and match equilibrium, which influence players' motion activity, as has been shown in soccer (Lago *et al.*, 2010).

Match analysis and modelling of team's performance

The need for objective, accurate and relevant feedback on the individual and team performance has led to the development of technologically advanced match analysis systems that enable the recording of large amounts of quantitative data in sports games in general and in handball in particular. However, it should be recognized that the quantity of statistical and scientific work in handball match analysis lags far behind that done for basketball, baseball, ice hockey and soccer.

The review of research problems, methodologies and main results allows classification of the approaches used in handball match analysis into two core groups:

1. Static approach (also named 'structure-oriented' by Pfeiffer and Perl, 2006); and
2. Dynamical process-oriented approach.

Static, structure-oriented approach to handball match analysis

The static approach in handball match analysis is represented by descriptive and comparative studies that relate the teams' performance profiles to the game or completion outcome. This analysis makes it possible to 'roughly' detect the principal components of success in handball.

In static, structure-oriented analysis, the patterns of play are traditionally represented by frequencies of several performance variables registered during a game. These summarized data in most cases are evaluated without taking into account the context of the match. The research that has been carried out according to the static approach could be categorized as:

1. Descriptive analysis of the frequency of events that characterize the performance of elite handball teams (Czerwinski, 2000; Feldmann, 2001; Mocsai, 2002; Pollany, 2006; Rogulj et al., 2011; Taborsky, 2008); and
2. Comparative analysis of match statistics and play patterns of winning and losing teams (Rogulj et al., 2004; Srhoj et al., 2001; Vuleta et al., 2003).

The majority of descriptive analyses of elite teams' performances are based on primary descriptive statistics. The results of these analyses are available in European Handball Federation Web Periodicals. Although these publications do not properly represent scientific studies, their results could be useful for coaches, providing them with information from the observation of behaviours of national teams.

The comparative analysis typically uses discrete variables containing information about teams' actions associated with their outcome. Using 12 indicators of scoring efficiency, Vuleta et al. (2003) determined that the winning teams of the 2000 Men's European Handball Championship were significantly more efficient than losing teams in practically all types of shots: back-court shots, six-metre shots and seven-metre throws.

Rogulj et al. (2004) analysed differences between tactical offensive patterns of winners and losers in 90 games of the Croatian First League of Handball. Nineteen indicators that characterized duration, continuity, systems, structure and spatial direction of the attack have been used in the study. The results of multivariate analysis of variance (MANOVA) and canonical discriminant analysis have shown that winning offensive patterns of play was distinguished by more frequent use of fast break and fast position attack with up to 25 s duration. According to the authors, it was not possible to identify any type of offensive system, organization or spatial direction of the attack that could significantly differentiate winning from losing teams in positional attack due to a great variability of teams' actions.

In order to identify the set of relevant game indicators that discriminate winning from losing teams in the 2003 Men's World Handball Championship, Volossovitch and Gonçalves (2003) used binomial logistic regression. The final model included four variables that had a significant effect on the game output: goalkeeper efficiency ($p = 0.001$), field shot efficiency ($p = 0.024$), fast break efficiency ($p = 0.045$) and number of assists ($p = 0.073$).

The analysis of key indicators which distinguish winning from losing teams' performance in handball has revealed that the majority of studies reported a quite evident importance of field shot and goalkeeper efficiency.

Although there is enough evidence that home advantage influences the team's performance, there is a lack of studies that address this issue in handball. We could identify only one study that has evaluated and confirmed the home advantage in games of the Spanish Handball League from 2005–2006 to 2009–2010 seasons (Gómez *et al.*, 2011).

Some problems related to the data of static approach studies should be acknowledged. One of these problems deals with the relevance of information gathered from the summarized data accumulated by the end of the match. The examples of balanced games show that, in some cases, it is not possible to establish a direct and linear relationship between the quantity of actions and the match outcome. The isolated registration of actions analysed out of the context of the competition does not provide valid information about the match process and frequently does not enable understanding of the reasons for the final result.

Dynamical, process-oriented approach to handball match analysis

Tactical process analysis

The dynamical, process-oriented approach is based on the recording of substantial tactical actions in a chronological, sequential order and provides a deeper insight into the tactical models used by a team during a match (Pfeiffer and Perl, 2006). The studies carried out according to this approach aim to estimate the probability of occurrence of determinate actions in order to identify the sequential behavioural patterns that lead to success (Pfeiffer and Perl, 2006; Prudente *et al.*, 2008).

Pfeiffer and Perl (2006) used neural networks to analyse tactical organizations in youth female handball and have managed to reduce the huge volume of data related to complex tactical behaviour to a small number of processes with similar tactical structures. Each offensive attempt was represented as the sequence of stages based on handball-specific concepts; offensive formation followed by four tactical actions registered on their chronological order. The Dynamically Controlled Network, used in the study, enabled the identification of typical tactical processes of 12 teams which participated in 15 matches of the Women's Junior World Championship (2001).

Prudente *et al.* (2008) verified the relationship between type, area of ball recovery and path of the first offensive action with the ball, using the sequential analysis technique. The probabilistic analysis of data from 25 games of the eight best-placed teams that participated in the final phases of the 2002 European Championship and the 2003 World Championship allowed the dependence between the area and type of ball recovery as well as the first action with the ball to be determined.

Probabilistic analysis of handball match result evolution

One of the aims of match analysis is to provide an opportunity to predict sport performance in order to be well prepared for the future competitive scenarios. Vuleta *et al.* (2005) analysed the score evolution in 60 matches from the 2003 Men's World Handball Championships to evaluate the predictive value of the goals scored in the different time periods of a match for the final outcome. The results of regression analysis showed that goals scored in the second and the first 15 minutes of a match have the greatest impact on the final score. In this study, the match equilibrium and round of competition were not considered. In addition, it was assumed that all periods of 15 minutes were independent, and the possible influence between subsequent game episodes was not taken into account. In this sense, the study of Vuleta *et al.* (2005) can be classified as being on the static–dynamical approach boundary of match analysis.

The dynamical approach should take into account the time evolution of performance during the match, which implies considering how prior events influence subsequent ones. Thus, in order to evaluate more precisely the probability of winning, first it is necessary to calculate the probability of scoring and verify whether it varies as the match unfolds. This step implies checking if the probability of scoring is constant during the game and understanding what factors influence, and how, the probability of scoring; in other words, it is necessary to verify the hypothesis of independence and identical distribution of goals scored during a match. For solving this problem, the model with time-varying parameters for the probability of scoring based on the past performance of the opposing team and the current match result has been estimated (Dumangane et al., 2009; Volossovitch et al., 2010). A total of 32,273 observations of ball possession from 224 matches from the 2001, 2003 and 2005 Men's World Handball Championships were used for model estimation. The influence of the match equilibrium and the rhythm of alternating ball possession on the dynamic of parameters of the model was evaluated later (Volossovitch et al., 2010). The results of model estimation suggest that the probability of scoring does not depend on the past offensive performance of one's own team, but on the past offensive performance of the opponent (the own-team defensive performance) and on the point difference. It has been noted that the effects of the recent past performance of the opponent and of the point difference on the probability of scoring in handball are time-varying during the game and influenced by the quality and by the pace of the match.

There is no doubt that the teams' behaviour and consequently the score evolution are products of dynamical interactions between the players of both teams. Thus, for a more complete understanding of the factors that influence success in handball, it is necessary to use mathematical models that incorporate information about offensive and defensive actions and their evolution in time. Dynamic modelling has great potential for solving this problem.

Future work

Many pertinent issues in handball performance analysis require further investigation. In order to better understand the factors that influence throwing effectiveness and goalkeeper efficiency in a real-game situation, it is necessary to study the handball throw and goalkeeper activity in more representative designs and in-situ experimental tasks that reproduce the functional coupling thrower–defender and thrower–goalkeeper.

A more substantial research effort is needed for time-motion analysis of handball players in different game contexts. In match analysis, it is crucial to focus more on the defensive activity. The identification of critical game periods that have a significant influence on the final outcome is also a relevant issue for research in handball.

More studies assessing the influence of contextual variables (quality of opposition, home advantage and score-line) on the handball teams' performance should be carried out. More data are required to characterize position-related playing performance profiles. A further challenge for future research is to create techniques for individual player evaluation and their contribution to the team's success. As a general suggestion, future research should be more focused on the female game.

Concluding remarks

Research work in handball performance analysis has been reviewed in this chapter. Studies regarding throwing performance are focused on identifying the factors that influence ball velocity and shot accuracy. The research results suggested that, along with the throwing technique and players' muscular force, external stimuli (such as opposition) have also influenced the throwing kinematics and thus should be included in future experimental designs.

The goalkeeper's performance has been analysed by using virtual reality technology, eye-tracking systems, 3D kinematic analysis and force platforms. It has been shown that players perform better in motor-task conditions than in judgment reports, that the reaction quality, movement time and number of goalkeepers' gaze fixations are related to the goalkeeper expertise and that virtual reality offers promising tools for studying goalkeeper's activity.

Elite and amateur players showed different physical activity profiles, but their movement activity during competition should continue to be studied. Studies in handball match analysis have been carried out using static, structure-oriented and dynamical, process-oriented approaches. A criticism of the first group of studies is that they do not consider the interaction between different performance variables and the context of competition. On the other hand, the models are oriented to the match process and, based on the play-by-play data, are promising for addressing chronological changes of the performance and complex assessment of factors that influence a team's efficiency.

References

Bayios, I., Anastasopoulou, E., Sioudris, D. and Boudolos, K. (2001) 'Relationship between isokinetic strength of the internal and external shoulder rotators and ball velocity in team handball', *Journal of Sports Medicine and Physical Fitness*, 41: 229–35.

Bideau, B., Kulpa, R., Menardais, S., Fradet, L., Multon, F., Delamarche, P. and Arnaldi, B. (2003) 'Real handball goalkeeper vs. virtual handball thrower', *Presence: Teleoperators and Virtual Environments*, 12(4): 411–21.

Bideau, B., Multon, F., Kulpa, R., Fradet, L., Arnaldi, B. and Delamarche, P. (2004) 'Using virtual reality to analyze links between handball thrower kinematics and goalkeeper's reactions', *Neuroscience Letters*, 372(1–2): 119–22.

Bideau, B., Kulpa, R., Vignais, N., Brault, S., Multon, F. and Craig, C. (2010) 'Using virtual reality to analyze sports performance', *IEEE Computer Graphics and Applications*, 30(2): 14–21.

Bolte, B., Zeidler, F., Bruder, G., Steinicke, F., Hinrichs, K., Fischer, L. and Schorer, J. (2010) 'A virtual reality handball goalkeeper analysis system', in T. Kuhlen, S. Coquillart and V. Interrante (eds), *Joint Virtual Reality Conference of EuroVR-EGVE – VEC*, (pp. 1–2). Stuttgart: Eurographics Association.

Bourne, M., Bennett, S., Hayes, S. and Williams, A. (2011) 'The dynamical structure of handball penalty shots as a function of target location', *Human Movement Science*, 30(1): 40–55.

Buchheit, M., Laursen, P.B., Kuhnle, J., Ruch, D., Renaud, C. and Ahmaidi, S. (2009) 'Game-based training in young elite handball players', *International Journal of Sports Medicine*, 30: 251–8.

Čavala, M. and Katić, R. (2010) 'Morphological, motor and situation-motor characteristics of elite female handball players according to playing performance and position', *Collegium Antropologicum*, 34(4): 1355–61.

Čavala, M., Rogulj, N., Srhoj, V., Srhoj, L. and Katić, R. (2008) 'Biomotor structures in elite female handball players according to performance', *Collegium Antropologicum*, 32(1): 231–9.

Chaouachi, A., Brughelli, M., Levin, G., Boudhina, N., Cronin, J. and Chamari, K. (2009) 'Anthropometric, physiological and performance characteristics of elite team-handball players', *Journal of Sports Sciences*, 27(2): 151–7.

Chelly, M., Hermassi, S., Aouadi, R., Khalifa, R., van den Tillaar, R., Chamari, K. and Shephard, R. (2011) 'Match analysis of elite adolescent team handball players', *Journal of Strength and Conditioning Research*, 25(9): 2410–7.

Czerwinski, J. (2000) 'Statistical analysis and remarks on the game character based on the European Championship in Croatia', *EHF Periodical*. Online. Available at http://home.eurohandball.com/ehf_files/Publikation/Czerwinski-StatisticalAnalysisandRemarksontheGameCharacterBasedontheEChinCRO.pdf (accessed 14 July 2011).

Delamarche, P., Gratas, A., Beillot, J., Dassonville, J., Rochcongar, P. and Lessard, Y. (1987) 'Extent of lactic anaerobic metabolism in handballers', *International Journal of Sports Medicine*, 8(1): 55–9.

Dicks, M., Button, C. and Davids, K. (2010) 'Availability of advance visual information constrains association-football goalkeeping performance during penalty kicks' *Perception*, 39: 1111–24.

Dumangane, M., Rosati, N. and Volossovitch, A. (2009) 'Departure from independence and stationarity in a handball match', *Journal of Applied Statistics*, 36(7): 723–741.

Farrow, D. and Abernethy, B. (2003) 'Do expertise and the degree of perception-action coupling affect natural anticipatory performance?', *Perception*, 32: 1127–39.

Feldmann, K. (2001) 'An analysis of the Men's World Championship in France', *EHF Periodical*. Online. Available at http://home.eurohandball.com/ehf_files/Publikation/feldmann-ananalysisofthemen-sworld.pdf (accessed 20 July 2011).

Fradet, L., Botcazou, M., Durocher, C., Cretual, A., Multon, F., Prioux, J. and Delamarche, P. (2004) 'Do handball throws always exhibit a proximal-to-distal segmental sequence?', *Journal of Sports Sciences*, 22: 439–47.

Fuertes, X., Lago, C. and Casáis, L. (2010) 'La influencia de la eficacia del portero en el rendimiento de los equipos de balonmano', *Apunts, Educación Física y Deportes*, (99): 72–81.

Gómez, M., Polard, R. and Luis-Pascual, J. (2011) 'Comparison of the home advantage in nine different professional team sports in Spain', *Perceptual and Motor Skills*, 113(1): 150–6.

Gorostiaga, E.M., Granados, C., Ibáñez, J. and Izquierdo, M. (2005). 'Differences in physical fitness and throwing velocity among elite and amateur male handball players', *International Journal of Sports Medicine*, 37: 225–32.

Gorostiaga, E.M., Granados, C., Ibáñez, J., González-Badillo, J. and Izquierdo, M. (2006) 'Effects of an entire season on physical fitness changes in elite male handball players', *Medicine and Science in Sports and Exercise*, 38(2): 357–66.

Granados, C., Izquierdo, M., Ibáñez, J., Bonnabau, H. and Gorostiaga, E.M. (2007) 'Differences in physical fitness and throwing velocity among elite and amateur female handball players', *International Journal of Sports Medicine*, 28(10): 860–7.

Gutiérrez, M., Garcia, P.L., Párraga, J. and Rojas, F.J. (2006) 'Effect of opposition on the handball jump shot', *Journal of Human Movement Studies*, 51: 257–75.

Gutiérrez-Davila, M., Rojas, F.J., Ortega, M., Campos, J. and Párraga, J. (2011) 'Anticipatory strategies of team-handball goalkeepers', *Journal of Sports Sciences*, 29(12): 1321–8.

Lago, C., Casais, L., Dominguez, E. and Sampaio, J. (2010) 'The effects of situational variables on distance covered at various speed in elite soccer', *European Journal of Sport Sciences*, 10: 103–9.

Luig, P., Manchado-Lopez, C., Perse, M., Kristan, M., Schander, I., Zimmermann, M., Henke, T. and Platen, P. (2008) 'Motion characteristics according to playing position in international men's team handball', in J. Cabri, F. Alves, D. Araújo, J. Barreiros, J. Diniz and A. Veloso (eds), *Book of Abstracts – 13th Annual Congress of the European College of Sports Science 9–12 July 2008, Estoril* (pp. 241–2). Cruz Quebrada: Edições FMH.

Milanese, C., Piscitelli, F., Lampis, C. and Zancanaro, C. (2011) 'Anthropometry and body composition of female handball players according to competitive level or the playing position', *Journal of Sports Sciences*, 29(12): 1301–9.

Mocsai, L. (2002) 'Analysing and evaluating the 5th men's European Championship', *EHF Periodical*. Online. Available at http://home.eurohandball.com/ehf_files/Publikation/Analysis.pdf (accessed 20 July 2011).

Ohnjec, K., Antekolović, L. and Gruić, I. (2010) 'Comparison of kinematic parameters of jump shot performance by female handball players of different ages', *Acta Kinesiologica*, 4(2): 33–40.

Párraga, J., Gutiérrez-Davila, M., Rojas, F.J. and Ona, A. (2002) 'The effects of visual stimuli on response reaction time and kinematic factors in the handball shot', *Journal of Human Movement Studies*, 42(6): 421–39.

Pfeiffer, M. and Perl, J. (2006) 'Analysis of tactical structures in team handball by means of artificial neural networks', *International Journal of Computer Science in Sport*, 5(1): 4–14.

Pollany, W. (2006) '7th European Championship for men, Switzerland 2006. Qualitative trend analysis', *EHF Periodical*. Online. Available at http://home.eurohandball.com/ehf_files/Publikation/WP_Pollany_Euro06_Trend_Analysis.pdf (accessed 15 September 2011).

Pori, P., Mohorič, U., Tomazini, D. and Šibila, M. (2009) 'Differences in goalkeepers' performance indicators at three consecutive Men's European Championships held in 2002, 2004 and 2006', in A. Hökelmann, K. Witte and P. O'Donoghue (eds), *Current Trends in Performance Analysis: World Congress of Performance Analysis of Sport VIII* (pp. 56–9). Aachen: Shaker Verlag.

Prudente, J., Garganta, J. and Anguera, T. (2008) 'Analysis of tactical performance in top level handball setting the relation between type, area of ball recover and path of first attacking action', in J. Cabri, F.

Alves, D. Araújo, J. Barreiros, J. Diniz and A. Veloso (eds), *Book of Abstracts – 13th Annual Congress of the European College of Sports Science 9–12 July 2008, Estoril* (p. 564). Cruz Quebrada: Edições FMH.

Prudente, J., Garganta, J. and Anguera, M. (2010) 'Methodological approach to evaluate interactive behaviors in team games: An example in handball', in A. Spink, F. Grieco, O. Krips, L. Loijens, L. Noldus and P. Zimmerman (eds), *Proceedings of Measuring Behavior 2010* (pp. 16–18). Wageningen, Netherlands: Noldus Information Technology.

Rannou, F., Prioux, J., Zouhal, H., Gratas-Delamarche, A. and Delamarche, P. (2001) 'Physiological profile of handball players', *Journal of Sports Medicine and Physical Fitness*, 41(3): 349–53.

Rivilla-Garcia, J., Grande, I., Sampedro, J. and van den Tillaar, R. (2011) 'Influence of opposition on ball velocity in the handball jump throw', *Journal of Sports Science and Medicine*, 10: 534–9.

Rogulj, N. and Papić, V. (2005) 'Low side-step kinematic characteristics of handball goalkeeper', in K.P. Adlassnig and M. Bracale (eds), *Biomedical Engineering – 2005* (p. 458). Innsbruck: IASTED.

Rogulj, N., Srhoj, V. and Srhoj, L. (2004) 'The contribution of collective attack tactics in differentiating handball score efficiency', *Collegium Antropologicum*, 28(2): 739–46.

Rogulj, N., Srhoj, V., Nazor, M., Srhoj, L. and Čavala, M. (2005) 'Some anthropologic characteristics of elite female handball players at different playing positions', *Collegium Antropologicum*, 29: 705–9.

Rogulj, N., Vuleta, D., Milanović, D., Čavala, M. and Foretić, N. (2011) 'The efficiency of elements of collective attack tactics in handball', *Kinesiologia Slovenica*, 17(1): 5–14.

Schorer, J. (2005) 'Being right-on-time shows the sensory-motor expertise of national team handball goalkeepers', *Journal of Sport and Exercise Psychology*, 27: 135.

Schorer, J., Baker, J., Fath, F. and Jaitner, T. (2007) 'Identification of inter-individual and intra-individual movement patterns in handball players of varying expertise levels', *Journal of Motor Behavior*, 39(5): 409–21.

Sibila, M. and Pori, P. (2009) 'Position-related differences in selected morphological body characteristics of top-level handball players', *Collegium Antropologicum*, 33: 1079–86.

Srhoj, V., Rogulj, N., Padovan, M. and Katić, R. (2001) 'Influence of the attack end conduction on match result in handball', *Collegium Antropologicum*, 25(2): 611–7.

Taborsky, F. (2008) 'Cumulative indicators of team playing performance in handball (Olympic Games Tournaments 2008)', *EHF Web Periodical*. Online. Available at www.eurohandball.com/publications (accessed 14 September 2011).

van den Tillaar, R. and Ettema, G. (2003) 'Instructions emphasizing velocity, accuracy, or both in performance and kinematics of overarm throwing by experienced team handball players', *Perceptual and Motor Skills*, 97: 731–42.

van den Tillaar, R. and Ettema, R. (2004) 'A force-velocity relationship and coordination patterns in overarm throwing', *Journal of Sports Science and Medicine*, 3(4): 211–19.

van den Tillaar, R. and Ettema, G. (2007) 'A three-dimensional analysis of overarm throwing in experienced handball players', *Journal of Applied Biomechanics*, 23(1): 12–19.

van den Tillaar, R. and Ettema, G. (2009) 'Is there a proximal-to-distal sequence in overarm throwing in team handball?', *Journal of Sports Sciences*, 27(9): 949–55.

Vignais, N., Bideau, B., Craig, C., Brault, S., Multon, F. and Kulpa, R. (2009) 'Virtual environments for sport analysis: Perception-action coupling in handball goalkeeping', *The International Journal of Virtual Reality*, 8(4): 43–8.

Vignais, N., Kulpa, R., Craig, C. and Bideau, B. (2010) 'Virtual thrower versus real goalkeeper: The influence of different visual conditions on performance', *Presence: Teleoperators and Virtual Environments*, 19(4): 281–90.

Volossovitch, A. and Gonçalves, I. (2003) 'The significance of game indicators for winning and losing team in handball', in E. Müller, H. Schwameder, G. Zallinger and V. Fastenbauer (eds), *Proceedings of the 8th Annual Congress of European College of Sport Science* (p. 335). Salzburg: ECSS.

Volossovitch, A., Dumangane, M. and Rosati, N. (2010) 'The influence of the pace of match on the dynamic of handball game', *International Journal of Sport Psychology*, 41(4): 117.

Vuleta, D., Milanovic, D. and Sertic, H. (2003) 'Relations among variables of shooting for a goal and outcomes of the 2000 Men's European Handball Championship matches', *Kinesiology*, 35(2): 168–83.

Vuleta, D., Milanović, D., Gruić, I. and Ohnjec, K. (2005) 'Influence of the goals scored on final outcomes of matches of the 2003 World Handball Championships for Men in Portugal', in D. Milanović and F. Prot, (eds), *Proceedings Book of the 4th International Scientific Conference on Kinesiology 'Science and Profession – Challenge for the Future'* (pp. 470–3). Zagreb: Faculty of Kinesiology, University of Zagreb.

Wagner, H. and Muller, E. (2008) 'The effects of differential and variable training on the quality parameters of a handball throw', *Sports Biomechanics*, 7(1): 54–71.

Wagner, H., Buchecker, M., von Duvillard, S. and Muller, E. (2010) 'Kinematic description of elite vs. low level players in team-handball jump throw', *Journal of Sports Science and Medicine*, 9(1): 15–23.

Wagner, H., Pfusterschmied, J., von Duvillard, S. and Muller, E. (2011) 'Performance and kinematics of various throwing techniques in team-handball', *Journal of Sports Science and Medicine*, 10(1): 73–80.

Ziv, G. and Lidor, R. (2009) 'Physical characteristics, physiological attributes, and on-court performances of male handball players – a review', *European Journal of Sport Sciences*, 9: 375–86.

31

CRICKET

Carl Petersen[1] *and Brian Dawson*[2]

[1]UNIVERSITY OF CANTERBURY, NEW ZEALAND

[2]UNIVERSITY OF WESTERN AUSTRALIA, AUSTRALIA

Summary

Until recently, cricket had not been the focus of much applied scientific research. The advent of a new form of the game (Twenty20) and rule changes (e.g. powerplays for both batting and bowling sides in one-day games) have brought an increased demand for knowledge about the game activities and physiological strain experienced by players in all forms of the game. By understanding better the game demands placed upon batsmen, bowlers (fast and spin) and fielders (wicketkeepers and infielders/outfielders) in Test/first-class, one-day and Twenty20 matches, the training and preparation of players to compete in the various forms of the game, and their ability to recover appropriately between matches, should be improved. In the shorter forms of the game, some statistical research from recent World Cups has also examined team performance and provided some potential strategic and tactical information which may relate to success within Twenty20 and one-day cricket matches. Notwithstanding the physiological demands of the different game formats, cricketers must often compete in hot and humid climates, usually without sufficient time for natural heat acclimatisation. Not only can these conditions affect the physical performance of players, but the concentration and anticipation necessary for the skills of batting, bowling and fielding can also be negatively affected. These skills have also been recently investigated, employing new technology such as instrumented bats, visual occlusion goggles and video projection.

This chapter will review the recent research on all forms of the game of cricket, which, in particular, has provided detailed information on the match workloads of fast bowlers and batsmen. This research has primarily used data from video and GPS analysis, and in some cases has been extended to training practices, allowing a comparison of these physiological demands against game data. Applied recommendations regarding training and preparation for games in hot/humid conditions will be made. Comments on the use of Hawk-Eye ball-tracking technology, the video logging and tagging of every ball in professional cricket, and how performance analysts are presenting and utilising this information to gain a competitive advantage over their opposition will also be made. Possible team tactics for the shorter versions of the game will also be mentioned.

Introduction

Unlike most sports, cricket has three game formats played at the elite level, the duration of these ranging from 3–30 hours. Subtle rule differences exist between game formats, in fielding restrictions (powerplays), scoring of extras (no balls), and the number of overs and short-pitched deliveries a bowler can bowl. First class is the name given to multi-day cricket played between domestic sides over four days with teams having two innings each; when two international teams are involved, the game is played over five days and is called a Test match. One-day cricket (~7 hours) involves each team having one innings, which is limited in the number of overs, usually 50. The shortest and most recent form of cricket, Twenty20 (~3 hours) limits each side to only 20 overs.

Prior to 2001, the sport of cricket had limited scientific performance analysis. Several studies investigated the high prevalence of injuries to fast bowlers, with particular emphasis on fast-bowling technique and the mechanism(s) of lower-back injuries (Burnett et al., 1995; Elliott and Foster, 1984; Foster et al., 1989; Portus et al., 2000). Simulations of single 6, 8 or 12-over bowling spells were used to investigate the physiological demands of fast bowling (Burnett et al., 1995; Portus et al., 2000; Stretch and Lambert, 1999), with only one study investigating the physiological responses of fast bowlers during actual competition (Gore et al., 1993). Batting research focused on visual performance and reaction times (Campbell et al., 1987; Land and McLeod, 2000; McLeod, 1987), anticipatory or advanced cue recognition (Abernethy and Russell, 1984; Deary and Mitchell, 1989; Penrose and Roach, 1995), hitting technique (Gibson and Adams, 1989) and moods and anxiety (Thelwell and Maynard, 1998; Totterdell, 1999). Despite wicketkeeping being the most specialised fielding position in the game, only one study was published prior to 2001, investigating anticipatory cue utilisation (Houlston and Lowes, 1990). Other fielding research looked at technique of the sliding stop (Von Hagan et al., 2000) and overhead throwing (Cook and Strike, 2000), while movement initiation times of slips catchers were also investigated with different coloured balls and light levels (Scott et al., 2000).

Cricket specific fitness results have been reported for junior (14–19 years) English (Venning et al., 1999) and elite South African (Noakes and Durandt, 2000), English (Johnstone and Ford, 2010) and Australian (male and female) cricketers (Bourdon et al., 2000). Anthropometric characteristics of elite cricketers have also been reported and linked to skilled performance, such as bowling speed (Portus et al., 2000). Historically, the estimated hourly energy expenditure (650 kJ.hour^{-1}) of cricketers was published over 50 years ago (Fletcher, 1955), but this is unlikely to be accurate for the modern game.

Recent research: physiological demands on players

The physiological demands on cricketers vary considerably between positions, performance level and game format (Petersen et al., 2011b). The first time-motion studies of cricket used video-based methods to investigate a single position – for example, batsmen or the cover point fielding position (Duffield and Drinkwater, 2008; Rudkin and O'Donoghue, 2008). The long duration (~6 hours per day) and wide playing field of cricket meant that video-based methods could analyse only one player at a time and were extremely time-consuming. The advent of Global Positioning System (GPS) player-tracking technology has made time-motion data collection both practical and time-efficient, with multiple players analysed simultaneously within the same match. An increased knowledge of cricketers' positional movement patterns combined with their physiological demands provides the data required for conditioning coaches to design position-specific conditioning drills. A recent longitudinal 14-week study of training practices included an analysis of 28 common training drills and compared these to published game demands (Petersen *et al.*, 2011a). The authors reported that conditioning drills exceeded game demands, but skill and game simulation drills failed to replicate these for all positions. Careful planning of training drills will ensure a closer match of game and training demands.

The volume of cricket played at the elite level is a major factor influencing player fatigue levels and the subsequent need for recovery practices. Comprehensive studies have documented bowling (Dennis *et al.*, 2003) and throwing (Saw *et al.*, 2009) workloads of cricketers in both matches and training, and how these workloads may relate to injury risks. In contrast, very few intervention studies directed at enhancing either cricket bowling or throwing velocity have been conducted (Petersen *et al.*, 2004; Freeston and Rooney, 2008). Studies focused towards injury prevention and/or performance enhancement provide coaches with practical guidelines to follow. However, the application of these guidelines often requires coaches to break with or modify their traditional approach, which some will be unwilling to do.

Table 31.1 provides a summary of published time-motion measures and demonstrates that fast bowlers cover the greatest total distance at sprinting intensities, whereas wicketkeepers seldom perform at these speeds. The physiological requirements of cricket have also been investigated using a range of measures during actual match play (Brearley, 2003; Brearley and Montgomery, 2002; Gore *et al.*, 1993; Soo and Naughton, 2007) or during simulated components of match play (Burnett *et al.*, 1995; Christie *et al.*, 2008; Duffield *et al.*, 2009; Stretch and Lambert, 1999). Table 31.2 provides a summary of published physiological demands by position and illustrates that there are still limited data on positional sweat rates, core temperature and blood lactate responses.

Hot/humid climates and game play

Cricket is a global summer game and players frequently travel across the world from one tour to the next and often experience large differences in climatic conditions. Cricketers are often required to play in hot/humid climates for extended durations (six hours per day) with little time for prior heat acclimation. Their physical and skilled performance (i.e. bowling velocity, line and length) may be compromised in the heat (Brearley, 2003; Devlin *et al.*, 2001). Several studies have measured the physiological responses of cricketers performing in the heat (Brearley, 2003; Brearley and Montgomery, 2002; Gore *et al.*, 1993; Soo and Naughton, 2007), by recording indices of sweat rate, dehydration and core body temperature. Specific heat acclimatisation for pace bowlers gained via playing a one-day tournament conferred progressive cardiovascular adaptations, but was also shown to have negative consequences (decline in bowling velocity and increase in ratings of muscle soreness) due to inadequate recovery between games (Brearley, 2003).

In addressing preparations for playing in the heat, two recent studies investigated the effectiveness of a short duration (four-day) intensive cycling acclimation protocol on the key physiological indicators of heat acclimation in cricketers (Petersen *et al.*, 2010b, 2010c). With moderate to large decreases in sweat electrolyte concentrations (Na^+, K^+, Cl^-), and exercising heart rate, but only trivial changes in core and skin temperatures recorded, the authors concluded that only partial heat acclimation had been achieved. Traditional methods of heat acclimation commonly employ protocols of 10–14 days of repeated heat exposure to achieve 95 per cent of the maximal acclimation response. However, this length of protocol is not feasible for most cricketers given the short time-frame between tours and their need for skilled training.

A comparison of the usual approach (heat acclimatisation) versus an alternative (pre-tour heat acclimation) was recently investigated in touring elite cricketers (Petersen *et al.*, 2010c).

Table 31.1 Hourly values (mean ± sd) of published time-motion variables for different cricket positions

Source and observations (#)	Level	Format	Total distance (m)	Sprint distance (m)	Sprints (#)	High-intensity efforts (#)	% distance from walking and jogging
Batsmen							
Petersen et al. (2009a) n = 6	State	Twenty 20	4866 ± 900	322 ± 166	24 ± 10	77 ± 34	83
Petersen et al. (2010a) n = 26	Academy	Twenty 20	2429 ± 516	175 ± 97	15 ± 9	45 ± 16	81
Petersen et al. (2010a) n = 36	Academy	One-day	2476 ± 618	149 ± 94	13 ± 9	39 ± 16	84
Duffield and Drinkwater (2008) n = 5	International	One-day					94★
Petersen et al. (2010a) n = 9	Academy	Multi-day	2064 ± 550	86 ± 28	8 ± 3	28 ± 6	87
Duffield and Drinkwater (2008) n = 13	International	Test					96★
Fast bowlers							
Petersen et al. (2009a) n = 4	State	Twenty 20	6367 ± 1120	542 ± 126	32 ± 6	122 ± 33	76
Petersen et al.(2010a) n = 18	Academy	Twenty 20	4172 ± 671	406 ± 230	23 ± 10	61 ± 25	80
Petersen et al. (2010a) n = 24	Academy	One-day	3833 ± 594	316 ± 121	18 ± 5	54 ± 14	82
Petersen et al. (2009b) n = 12	International	One-day	4544 ± 729	326 ± 70	19 ± 3	55 ± 9	84
Petersen et al. (2010a) n = 10	Academy	Multi-day	3773 ± 669	230 ± 149	17 ± 11	56 ± 29	83
Fielders							
Petersen et al. (2009a) n = 14	State	Twenty 20	6106 ± 981	416 ± 265	23 ± 13	97 ± 43	79
Petersen et al.(2010a) n = 26	Academy	Twenty 20	3447 ± 717	129 ± 91	8 ± 5	42 ± 20	86
Petersen et al. (2010a) n = 52	Academy	One-day	3081 ± 550	81 ± 51	5 ± 3	27 ± 11	89
Petersen et al. (2010a) n = 20	Academy	Multi-day	2477 ± 506	52 ± 33	3 ± 2	19 ± 8	91
Rudkin and O'Donoghue (2008) n = 27	First-class	Multi-day	2580				92★
Spin bowlers							
Petersen et al. (2009a) n = 3	State	Twenty 20	6430 ± 1176	115 ± 108	7 ± 6	42 ± 26	93
Petersen et al. (2010a) n = 10	Academy	Twenty 20	3293 ± 447	81 ± 55	5 ± 4	25 ± 12	91
Petersen et al. (2010a) n = 8	Academy	One-day	3130 ± 293	58 ± 37	4 ± 1	29 ± 10	91
Wicketkeepers							
Petersen et al. (2009a) n = 3	State	Twenty 20	4825 ± 570	46 ± 33	4 ± 2	37 ± 9	93
Petersen et al. (2010a) n = 3	Academy	Twenty 20	2483 ± 482	59 ± 23	5 ± 2	30 ± 18	86
Petersen et al. (2010a) n = 4	Academy	Multi-day	2766 ± 347	23 ± 30	2 ± 4	12 ± 6	96

Notes

★ % time spent walking and jogging, not distance.

Sprinting is defined as locomotion movement above 5 m s^{-1}, and a high-intensity effort is defined as movement greater than 3.5 m s^{-1} for more than one second.

Table 31.2 Physiological demands of batting, fast bowling, fielding, spin bowling and wicket keeping

Source and observations (#)	Level	Format	Mean HR (bpm)	Peak HR (bpm)	Sweat rate (L.h⁻¹)	Peak core temp. (°C)	Peak lactate (mmol.L⁻¹)
Batsmen							
Christie *et al.* (2008)¤ (n = 10)	Club	One-day	145 ± 11	155 ± 19	—	—	—
Petersen *et al.* (2010a) (n = 16)	Academy	Twenty 20	149 ± 17	181 ± 14	—	—	—
Petersen *et al.* (2010a) (n = 5)	Academy	One-day	144 ± 13	180 ± 13	—	—	2.4 ± 0.4
Gore *et al.* (1993) (n = 6) – Warm¤	Club	Multi-day	129 ± 2	—	0.60 ± 0.05	38.6 ± 0.03	—
Gore *et al.* (1993) (n = 6) – Cool¤	Club	Multi-day	110 ± 2	—	0.47 ± 0.04	38.3 ± 0.03	—
Brearley and Montgomery (2002) (n = 5)	Academy	One-day	167 ± 4	174	1.00 ± 0.10	38.5 ± 0.2	3.1 ± 0.8
Fast bowlers							
Duffield *et al.* (2009)¤ (n = 6)	State	First-class	162 ± 12★	—	—	38.8 ± 0.8	5.0 ± 1.5
Petersen *et al.* (2010a) (n = 10)	Academy	Twenty 20	133 ± 12	181 ± 10	—	—	—
Gore *et al.* (1993) (n = 3) – Hot	Club	Multi-day	—	—	1.67 ± 0.08	38.0 ± 0.03	—
Gore *et al.* (1993) (n = 5) – Warm¤	Club	Multi-day	116 ± 2	—	0.69 ± 0.05	38.3 ± 0.03	—
Gore *et al.* (1993) (n = 7) – Cool¤	Club	Multi-day	131 ± 2	—	0.71 ± 0.04	38.3 ± 0.03	—
Brearley and Montgomery (2002) (n = 7)	Academy	One-day	—	174	0.81 ± 0.20	38.7	3.3 ± 0.8
Brearley (2003) (n = 4)	Academy	One-day	—	—	0.72	39.2 ± 0.3	3.5 ± 0.6
Burnett *et al.* (1995) (n = 9)¤	Academy	One-day	171 ± 4★	176 ± 12	—	—	5.1 ± 2.5
Stretch and Lambert (1999)¤	Junior		158 ± 10	—	—	—	—
Stretch and Lambert (1999)¤	Senior		158 ± 8	—	—	—	—
Devlin *et al.* (2001)¤	Club		154 ± 14	—	—	—	—
Fielders							
Petersen *et al.* (2010a) (n = 7)	Academy	Twenty 20	115 ± 20	159 ± 14	—	—	—
Petersen *et al.* (2010a) (n = 5)	Academy	One-day	109 ± 8	166 ± 5	—	—	—
Spin bowlers							
Petersen *et al.* (2010a) (n = 3)	Academy	Twenty 20	135 ± 6	176 ± 10	—	—	—
Wicketkeepers							
Petersen *et al.* (2010a) (n = 3)	Academy	Twenty 20	135 ± 19	165 ± 13	—	—	—
Brearley and Montgomery (2002) (n = 1)	Academy	One-day	—	—	—	37.6	—

Notes
★ Post-over heart rate, ¤ Simulation study. Cool, warm and hot conditions had wet bulb globe temperature indices (°C) of 22.1, 24.5 and 27.1, respectively.

This work identifies the expected physiological changes within a four-day time-frame and provides data for the modification of future physical preparation strategies. The authors concluded that typical physiological adaptations can be fast-tracked with exercise–heat acclimation prior to a sub-continent (India) tour; however, only partial thermoregulatory adaptations should be expected after only four sessions.

For cricketers touring hot/humid countries, performing a heat acclimation programme will improve physical preparation and can also improve match performance. Other strategies being employed in elite cricket requiring specific research on their effectiveness include the application of cold towels, ingesting crushed ice drinks and other cooling methods both before and during breaks in play.

Skill and technical analysis

Cricket's fundamental skills of batting, bowling and fielding have recently been investigated using new technology. Often high and lesser skilled performers are compared to gain an insight into the potential distinguishing characteristics of the higher skilled players. Utilising high-speed digital video combined with realistic projected footage, higher skilled batsmen were found to position their head further forward of their centre base point, thereby resulting in their centre of mass also being further forward during the predicted bat–ball contact (Taliep *et al.*, 2007). In addition, research utilising temporally occluded video has indicated that higher skilled batsmen process relevant sources of information earlier, especially from the bowling arm and hand (Muller *et al.*, 2006). This advanced cue utilisation also relates to the previous experience of batsmen, as reported when facing different types of spin deliveries (Renshaw and Fairweather, 2000). Between the ages of 13 and 15 years, high performers in occlusion video-projected batting tasks were found to have accumulated a greater number of hours in structured cricket activity than lower performers in this age bracket (Ford *et al.*, 2010). However, for those aged less than 13 years, the volume of accumulated cricket training hours did not differentiate between the high- and low-skilled performers (Ford *et al.*, 2010).

Technology has also been used to determine how bowlers might gain a performance advantage. By using an instrumented bat, researchers have suggested that bowlers can gain an advantage by forcing batsmen to play strokes slightly wider on the pitch. By achieving this, for several shots, including the off- and cover drive (on the off-side), the on-drive and leg glance (on-side), the bat impact point is usually further from the midline, which may increase the batsman's risk of dismissal (Stretch *et al.*, 2004).

Further work has investigated the forces and timing of the fast-bowling delivery action, which may prove useful for sports medicine personnel and strength and conditioning coaches. When fast-bowling ground reaction forces during the delivery stride were quantified simultaneously using two force platforms, researchers found a greater impact on the front foot, with peak impact occurring 24 ms after contact, than on the back foot, where peak impact occurred 16 ms after foot contact (Hurrion *et al.*, 2000). The maximal vertical ground reaction forces recorded were 2.4 times bodyweight for the back foot and 5.8 times bodyweight for the front foot (Hurrion *et al.*, 2000). Interestingly, the front foot contact phase of the delivery stride also coincided with the greatest proportion of lower trunk extension, contralateral side flexion and ipsilateral rotation (Ranson *et al.*, 2008). The relationship between technique and bowling speed variation has also been investigated with a within-subject design; 88 per cent of the within-bowler variation in ball release speed can be attributed to the factors of run-up velocity, angular velocity of the bowling arm, vertical velocity of the non-bowling arm and stride length (Salter *et al.*, 2007).

Video projection has also been used to supplement fielding training. The projection of realistic video footage successfully improved skilled cricketers' anticipatory decision-making skills. Furthermore, the fielding improvements were greater following six weeks of the combined video and on-field training than achieved with traditional on-field training only (Hopwood *et al.*, 2011).

Tactical considerations

Cricket players have many statistics recorded on their batting, fielding and bowling performances (strike rates, averages, boundaries, catches, dot balls, etc.), and teams also have similar statistics measuring their performance, such as real-time progress towards a run target (the required run rate), which is often displayed graphically on television. Investigators have also used computer modelling to determine optimal scoring rates when batting second (chasing a total; Clarke, 1988) and the most strategic way to rotate batsmen with different strike rates at the end of an innings to maximise a team's score (Clarke and Norman, 1999). It would be interesting to see if these models have ever been practically applied in a real match situation.

Analysing statistics can reveal information about particular team tactics and strategies, especially in the shorter versions of the game. Petersen *et al.* (2008a) reviewed the 2007 Cricket World Cup results to reveal the relative importance of team performance indicators between winning and losing teams. Identifying performance indicators that are most highly correlated with a successful match outcome provides a scientific basis for developing and implementing individual and team strategies. The findings from this tournament included that winning teams take more wickets and maintain a higher run rate, while losing teams score a higher proportion of their runs from singles. A similar analysis was performed for the 2008 Indian Premier League (IPL; Petersen *et al.*, 2008b). The results suggested that more success may be achieved using wicket-taking bowling and field placements in the first and last six overs, while run-restrictive field placings should be utilised in the middle eight overs. An analysis of the 2009 Twenty20 World Cup revealed similar findings; teams should try to maximise the wickets taken in the powerplays and restrict the runs scored in the middle eight overs (Douglas and Tam, 2010).

Based on these findings, coaches could select players that are most capable of executing certain parts of these successful game strategies and should concentrate on improving wicket-taking and run-saving strategies (field placements, bowling deliveries associated with the highest wicket-taking success rates and amount of bowling variation a bowler should employ), as these factors have the largest influence on overall match success.

Ball-tracking technology and software

Over the past decade, television has encouraged the growth of video-based performance analysis in cricket. Television has trialled a number of innovations that have gradually become accepted into the game through the Decision Review System (DRS). Innovations include: Hot Spot, an infra-red imaging system used to determine if a ball contacted the bat or batsman's clothing; Snickometer, a system that graphically analyses sound and video recordings to determine whether a fine noise occurs as the ball passes the bat; and various ball-tracking technologies (Hawk-Eye [Hawk-Eye Innovations, Basingstoke, UK] and Virtual Eye [Animation Research Ltd., Dunedin, New Zealand]) that use calibrated multiple cameras to triangulate the ball trajectory and allow predictions as to whether a ball would have hit the wicket if it had not first hit the batsman. Indeed, most professional and international cricket sides now recognise the value of video recordings by employing a professional match analyst.

While most performance analysts do not have access to the sophisticated television software, detailed match analysis is still possible via video cameras and laptop-based software. A camera is used to log each ball that is bowled, which is then coded by various software applications to enable quick database retrieval. During a game, players and coaches can often then review a decision or a passage of play immediately after it has happened. More detailed notational analysis is undertaken by an analyst in preparation for a game, where they may examine match-to-match performance of opposition players and teams. These data are often communicated in a statistics pack and/or video-based presentation which identifies opposition players' strengths and weaknesses and potential strategies to be implemented against them.

Several different computer programs (including Feedback Cricket [Feedback Sport, Christch-urch, New Zealand], CrickStat [CSIR, Pretoria, South Africa] and Gamebreaker [Sportstec, Warriewood, New South Wales, Australia]) are used throughout the world to analyse matches. In Australia, most state teams use the Cricket Analyst programme (Fairplay Sports); however, one team uses a rival product, namely Gamebreaker (Sportstec, Warriewood, New South Wales, Australia). An agreement exists whereby the home team provides the match analysis service and opposition teams can request particular game footage to prepare for their upcoming game. In England, the English and Wales Cricket Board (ECB) has supplied each first-class county with the CrickStat program, thereby ensuring the standardisation of information uploaded to a central repository. This coded match footage is available to all counties, as well as the national selectors, for more detailed analysis.

The data coded to each ball include general match data (including who was bowling, the batsmen facing and the resultant runs or dismissal method), plus specific positional and shot data for each ball. In English county cricket, each ball is assigned one of 24 different shot types, with positional data then subjectively given (with a mouse click) on where the ball pitched on the wicket and where on the field the ball was hit. At international level, more precise ball-track-ing information is usually imported by replacing the subjective coding of the ball pitch position with automated ball-tracking technology (Virtual Eye or Hawk-Eye).

Using ball-tracking technology, bowling skill has been analysed by recording pitching lengths, bowling lines (width) and velocity (Justham et al., 2008). Fast bowlers exhibited only subtle differences in style between the different formats of cricket (Twenty20, one-day and five-day Test matches). The variability of the bowling deliveries during a six-over spell was also investigated previously using the Hawk-Eye system (Justham et al., 2006), but these two studies did not include any physiological measurements.

Recently, some international level teams have collected video footage of opposition bowlers to use with bowling machines, such as the Probatter (Probatter Sports, Milford, CT). Modi-fied from their original baseball use, the Probatter bowling machine is a video-based bowling simulator that allows a batsman to experience facing a particular opposition bowler and become familiar with the bowler's action and variations before they face them in a match.

Concluding remarks

After little research attention in the twentieth century, the sport of cricket has recently enjoyed much scientific investigation. These studies have focused on quantifying the movement demands of players during the various forms of the game, finding that fast bowlers experience the great-est physiological strain. They commonly perform more sprints and high–intensity efforts, plus cover more total distance when playing than batsmen, spin bowlers, wicketkeepers or fielders. Matching these game demands with training drill intensities is now possible and can be moni-tored by coaches using GPS units, allowing a full squad of players to be tracked simultaneously and in real time. As cricket is a summer sport, acquiring some degree of heat acclimation prior to touring is often necessary, as games are normally scheduled before full acclimatisation can be naturally achieved. Recent research (Petersen *et al.*, 2010b, 2010c) has demonstrated that partial acclimation can be achieved with four sessions of non-specific (cycling) exercise in warm conditions. In addition, the use of cooling methods such as cold towels and crushed ice (slushy) drinks should be further investigated with regard to reducing heat strain and potentially enhancing performance. Notational analysis has also suggested successful team strategies, especially in Twenty20 cricket, where containing runs in the middle eight overs and taking wickets in the first and last six overs has been identified with winning performances. Both team selection and tactics might be influenced by these and similar findings from future notational analysis studies. Lastly, the recent advent of various software systems for ball-tracking purposes offers much scope for use in scouting opponents and providing sophisticated performance feedback to both batsmen and bowlers.

References

Abernethy, B. and Russell, D. (1984) 'Advanced cue utilisation by skilled cricket batsmen', *Australian Journal of Science and Medicine in Sport*, 16: 2–10.

Bourdon, P., Savage, B. and Done, R. (2000) 'Protocols for the physiological assessment of cricket players', in C. Gore (ed.), *Physiological Tests for Elite Athletes* (pp. 238–43). Champaign, IL: Human Kinetics.

Brearley, M. (2003) 'Responses to pace bowling in warm conditions cricket', *Australia Final Coaches Report*, 23–30 August.

Brearley, M. and Montgomery, P. (2002) 'Responses to cricket in hot conditions', *Australian Cricket Board Coaches Report*, 25–29 August.

Burnett, A., Elliott, B. and Marshall, R. (1995) 'The effect of a 12-over spell on fast bowling technique in cricket', *Journal of Sport Sciences*, 13: 329–41.

Campbell, F., Rothwell, S. and Perry, M. (1987) 'Bad light stops play', *Ophthalmic Physiological Optics*, 7: 165–7.

Christie, C., Todd, A. and King, G. (2008) 'Selected physiological responses during batting in a simulated cricket work bout: A pilot study', *Journal of Science and Medicine in Sport*, 11: 581–4.

Clarke, S. (1988) 'Dynamic programming in one-day cricket optimal scoring rates', *The Journal of Operational Research Society*, 39: 331–7.

Clarke, S. and Norman, J. (1999) 'To run or not? Some dynamic programming models in cricket', *The Journal of the Operational Research Society*, 50: 536–45.

Cook, D. and Strike, S. (2000) 'Throwing in cricket', *Journal of Sports Sciences*, 18: 965–73.

Deary, I. and Mitchell, H. (1989) 'Inspection and high speed ball games', *Perception*, 18: 789–92.

Dennis, R., Farhart, P., Goumas, C. and Orchard, J. (2003) 'Bowling workload and the risk of injury in elite cricket fast bowlers', *Journal of Science and Medicine in Sport*, 6: 359–67.

Devlin, L., Fraser, S., Barras, N. and Hawley, J. (2001) 'Moderate levels of hypohydration impairs bowling accuracy but not bowling velocity in skilled cricket players', *Journal of Science and Medicine in Sport*, 4: 179–87.

Douglas, J. and Tam, N. (2010) 'Analysis of team performances at the ICC World Twenty20 Cup 2009', *International Journal of Performance Analysis in Sport*, 10: 47–53.

Duffield, R. and Drinkwater, E. (2008), 'Time-motion analysis of Test and One-Day international cricket centuries', *Journal of Sports Sciences*, 26: 457–64.

Duffield, R., Carney, M. and Karpinnen, S. (2009) 'Physiological responses and bowling performance during repeated spells of medium-fast bowling', *Journal of Sports Sciences*, 27: 27–35.

Elliott, B. and Foster, D. (1984) 'A biomechanical analysis of the front-on and side-on fast bowling techniques', *Journal of Human Movement Studies*, 10: 83–94.

Fletcher, J. (1955) 'Calories and cricket', *Lancet*, 268: 1165–6.

Ford, P., Low, J., McRobert, A. and Williams, A. (2010) 'Developmental activities that contribute to high or low performance by elite cricket batters when recognizing type of delivery from bowlers' advanced postural cues', *Journal of Sport and Exercise Psychology*, 32: 638–54.

Foster, D., John, D., Elliott, B., Ackland, T. and Fitch, K. (1989) 'Back injuries to cricket fast bowlers in cricket: A prospective study', *British Journal of Sports Medicine*, 23: 150–4.

Freeston, J. and Rooney, K. (2008) 'Progressive velocity throwing training increases velocity without detriment to accuracy in sub-elite cricket players: A randomized controlled trial', *European Journal of Sport Science*, 8: 373–8.

Gibson, A. and Adams, R. (1989) 'Batting stroke timing with a bowler and a bowling machine: A case study', *Australian Journal of Science and Medicine in Sport*, 21: 3–6.

Gore, C., Bourdon, P., Woolford, S. and Pederson, D. (1993) 'Involuntary dehydration during cricket', *International Journal of Sports Medicine*, 14: 387–95.

Hopwood, M., Mann, D., Farrow, D. and Nielsen. T. (2011) 'Does visual-perceptual training augment the fielding performance of skilled cricketers?', *International Journal of Sports Science and Coaching*, 6: 523–35.

Houlston, D. and Lowes, R. (1990) 'A preliminary investigation into the anticipatory cue-utilization process for expert and non-expert wicketkeepers in cricket', *Journal of Sport Sciences*, 8: 69–70.

Hurrion, P., Dyson, R. and Hale, T. (2000) 'Simultaneous measurement of back and front foot ground reaction forces during the same delivery stride of the fast-medium bowler', *Journal of Sports Sciences*, 18: 993–7.

Johnstone, J. and Ford, P. (2010) 'Physiologic profile of professional cricketers', *Journal of Strength and Conditioning Research*, 24: 2900–7.

Justham, L., West, A., Harland, A. and Cork, A. (2006) 'Quantification of the cricket bowling delivery; a study of elite players to gauge variability and controllability', in E. Moritz and S. Haake (eds), *The Engineering of Sport 6, volume 1: Developments for Sports* (pp. 205–10). New York: Springer Science.

Justham, L., West, A. and Cork, A. (2008) 'An analysis of the differences in bowling technique for elite players during international matches', in F. Fuss, A. Subic and S. Ujihashi (eds), *The Impact of Technology on Sport II* (pp. 331–6). London: Taylor and Francis Group.

Land, M. and McLeod, P. (2000) 'From eye movements to actions: How batsmen hit the ball', *Nature Neuroscience*, 12: 1340–5.

McLeod, P. (1987) 'Visual reaction time and high speed ball games', *Perception*, 16: 49–59.

Muller, S., Abernethy, B. and Farrow, D. (2006) 'How do world-class cricket batsmen anticipate a bowler's intention?', *The Quarterly Journal of Experimental Psychology*, 59: 2162–86.

Noakes, T. and Durandt, J. (2000) 'Physiological requirements of cricket', *Journal of Sport Sciences*, 18: 919–29.

Penrose, J. and Roach, N. (1995) 'Decision making and advance cue recognition by cricket batsmen', *Journal of Human Movement Studies*, 29: 199–218.

Petersen, C., Wilson, B. and Hopkins, W. (2004) 'Effects of modified-implement training on fast bowling in cricket', *Journal of Sports Sciences*, 22: 1035–9.

Petersen, C., Pyne, D.B., Portus, M.R., Cordy, J. and Dawson, B. (2008a) 'Analysis of performance at the 2007 Cricket World Cup', *International Journal of Performance Analysis in Sport*, 8(1): 1–8.

Petersen, C., Pyne, D.B., Portus, M.R. and Dawson, B. (2008b) 'Analysis of Twenty/20 cricket performance during the 2008 Indian Premier League', *International Journal of Performance Analysis in Sport*, 8(3): 63–9.

Petersen, C., Pyne, D., Portus, M. and Dawson, B. (2009a) 'Quantifying positional movement patterns in Twenty/20 cricket', *International Journal of Performance Analysis in Sport*, 9: 165–70.

Petersen, C., Pyne, D., Portus, M., Karppinen, S. and Dawson, B. (2009b) 'Variability in movement patterns during One Day Internationals by a cricket fast bowler', *International Journal of Sports Physiology and Performance*, 4: 278–81.

Petersen, C., Pyne, D.B., Dawson, B., Portus, M.R. and Kellett, A. (2010a) 'Movement patterns in cricket vary by both position and game format', *Journal of Sports Sciences*, 28, 1: 45–52.

Petersen, C., Pyne, D.B., Dawson, B., Portus, M.R., Kellett, A. and Cramer, M. (2010b) 'Partial heat acclimation in cricketers using a 4-day high intensity cycling protocol', *International Journal of Sports Physiology and Performance*, 5: 535–45.

Petersen, C., Pyne, D., Dawson, B. and Portus, M.R. (2010c) 'Heat acclimation and acclimatisation of elite cricketers', presentation at New Zealand Sports Medicine and Science Conference, Wellington, New Zealand, November.

Petersen, C., Pyne, D.B., Dawson, B., Kellett, A. and Portus, M.R. (2011a) 'Comparison of training and game demands of national level cricketers', *Journal of Strength and Conditioning Research*, 25(5): 1306–11.

Petersen, C., Pyne, D.B., Dawson, B. and Portus, M.R. (2011b) 'Comparison of player movement patterns between 1-day and Test cricket', *Journal of Strength and Conditioning Research*, 25(5): 1368–73.

Portus, M., Sinclair, P., Burke, S., Moore, D. and Farhart, P. (2000) 'Cricket fast bowling performance and technique and the influence of selected physical factors during an 8-over spell', *Journal of Sports Sciences*, 18: 999–1011.

Ranson, C., Burnett, A., King, M., Patel, N. and O'Sullivan, P. (2008) 'The relationship between bowling action classification and three-dimensional lower trunk motion in fast bowlers in cricket', *Journal of Sports Sciences*, 26: 267–76.

Renshaw, I. and Fairweather, M. (2000) 'Cricket bowling deliveries and the discrimination ability of professional and amateur batters', *Journal of Sports Sciences*, 18: 951–7.

Rudkin, S. and O'Donoghue, P. (2008) 'Time-motion analysis of first-class cricket fielding', *Journal of Science and Medicine in Sport*, 11: 604–7.

Salter, C., Sinclair, P. and Portus, M. (2007) 'The associations between fast bowling technique and ball release speed: A pilot study of the within-bowler and between-bowler approaches', *Journal of Sports Sciences*, 25: 1279–85.

Saw, R., Dennis, R., Bentley, D. and Farhart, P. (2009) 'Throwing workload and injury risk in elite cricketers', *Journal of Science and Medicine in Sport*, 12: 63–4.

Scott, K., Kingsbury, D., Bennett, S., Davids, K. and Langley, M. (2000) 'Effects of cricket ball colour and illuminance levels on catching behaviour in professional cricketers', *Ergonomics*, 43: 1681–8.

Soo, K. and Naughton, G. (2007) 'The hydration profile of female cricket players during competition', *International Journal of Sport Nutrition and Exercise Metabolism*, 17: 14–26.

Stretch, R. and Lambert, M. (1999) 'Heart rate response of young cricket fast bowlers while bowling a six-over spell', *South African Journal of Sports Medicine*, 6: 15–19.

Stretch, R., Nurick, G., Balden, V. and Mckellar, D. (2004) 'The position of impact of the ball striking a cricket bat: Assisting coaches with performance analysis of cricket technique and skill levels', *International Journal of Performance Analysis in Sport*, 4: 74–81.

Taliep, M., Galal, U. and Vaughan, C. (2007) 'The position of the head and centre of mass during the front foot off-drive in skilled and lesser skilled cricket batsmen', *Sports Biomechanics*, 6: 345–60.

Thelwell, R. and Maynard, I. (1998) 'Anxiety-performance relationships in cricketers: Testing the zone of optimal functioning hypothesis', *Perceptual and Motor Skills*, 87: 675–89.

Totterdell, P. (1999) 'Mood scores: Mood and performance in professional cricketers', *British Journal of Psychology*, 90: 317–32.

Venning, E., Brewer, J. and Stockill, N. (1999) 'Pre-season characteristics in junior county cricketers', *Journal of Sports Sciences*, 17: 992–3.

Von Hagen, K., Roach, R. and Summers, B. (2000) 'The sliding stop: A technique of fielding in cricket with a potential for serious knee injury', *British Journal of Sports Medicine*, 34: 379–81.

32

RACKET SPORTS

Peter O'Donoghue[1], Olivier Girard[2] and Machar Reid[3,4]

[1]CARDIFF METROPOLITAN UNIVERSITY, UK

[2]ASPETAR – QATAR ORTHOPAEDIC AND SPORTS MEDICINE HOSPITAL, DOHA, QATAR

[3]TENNIS AUSTRALIA

[4]UNIVERSITY OF WESTERN AUSTRALIA, AUSTRALIA

Summary

Performance analysis research has been carried out on the four main racket sports: tennis, squash, badminton and table tennis. This chapter surveys the research that has been completed since the last main reviews of science and racket sports by Hughes (1998), Lees (2003) and O'Donoghue (2004). Analysis of shot technique has been carried out using kinetic and kinematic analyses, with methods following advances in technology. Technical effectiveness is a broader analysis of tennis performance, assessing winner-to-error ratios and percentages of different point types that are won. Point sequences have been used to investigate momentum, stationarity and independence of points. Tactical analysis has been applied in racket sports using modern eye-tracking systems, as well as more broadly by examining point profiles. The physical demands of racket sports can be estimated using observational techniques, rally and rest timings, heart–rate responses, blood lactate concentration and perceived exertion.

Introduction

There are four main racket sports (tennis, badminton, squash and table tennis), with some other racket sports being played to a lesser extent. Racket sports can be played with a net dividing the players or, in the case of squash, with the players moving in a common court area. The common aspects of racket sports are that shots are played by competitors in alternation, forming rallies. There are singles and doubles games in all four main racket sports. The purpose of this chapter is to review performance analysis research in racket sports. There have been previous reviews of notational analysis and performance analysis in racket sports (Hughes, 1998; O'Donoghue, 2004) and a review of science and racket sports that includes performance analysis research (Lees, 2003). The current chapter covers recent contributions that have been made since these reviews were completed.

The review is structured into four parts to deal with four of the purposes of performance analysis that are relevant to the study of racket sports. Technique analysis is concerned with mechanical aspects of technique and how skills are performed. Technical effectiveness, on the other hand, is concerned with outcomes of skills performed, irrespective of how correctly a skill has been performed. Tactical analysis is concerned with strategies and tactical decisions that are manifested in observable patterns of play. Finally, physical aspects of performance can be investigated through analysis of rally lengths and estimates of game intensity. Direction for future research efforts in performance analysis of racket sports is given at the end of the chapter.

Technique analysis

Performance analysis typically involves analysis of data gathered during actual sport competitions. However, there are occasions where detailed analysis of technique requires data collection during controlled laboratory experiments. Such research still falls under the umbrella of performance analysis of sport where the techniques being investigated are key aspects of the sport that cannot be studied to the required level of detail during actual competition (O'Donoghue, 2010: 2). This section covers the main research developments in technique in racket sports. The studies reviewed have to manage the balance between the need for experimental control and the need for ecological validity in order to investigate relevant aspects of racket sport skills. There are numerous biomechanical principles, yet those proposed to be most relevant to understanding stroke technique are the stretch–shorten cycle, the use of coordinated segment rotations (kinematic chain principle) and the distance over which racket speed can be developed (Elliott, 2006). Two- and three-dimensional videography, force plate/plantar loading analysis and electromyography have been employed to critique the biomechanics of different strokes.

Kinematic analyses of racket sport skills have generally shown that segment endpoint velocities increase in proximal to distal fashion. This has been demonstrated to characterise the tennis serve and groundstrokes (Reid and Elliott, 2002; Reid *et al.*, 2008), the squash forehand (Elliott *et al.*, 1996) and the table tennis forehand (Iino *et al.*, 2008; Iino and Kojima, 2009), and it is only long axis (or more specifically internal rotation) of the upper arm that has been reported to occur out of sequence (Takahashi *et al.*, 1996). It is intuitive that there are some similarities in the kinematic sequencing that epitomises the stroke production of the different racket sport skills. However, the disparate dimensions of the court as well as differences in equipment (inertia of racket and ball/shuttlecock) presumably contribute to subtle variation in each of the shot's swing shapes and associated joint coordination. For example, where Iino *et al.* (2008) and Iino and Kojima (2009) have focused on the role of wrist flexion in the table tennis backhand and forehand, tennis studies have generally attended to whole-body kinematics to inform a coach's view of how end-point velocity is developed from the 'ground up'. Kinematic analysis has provided evidence that, while tennis players reproduce broad techniques when returning serve, they also adapt technique to deal with specific serve return situations (Gillet *et al.*, 2010). Landlinger *et al.* (2010) used kinematic analysis to show that level of player was a further source of variability in forehand technique in tennis.

Evaluations of the kinetics of stroke or movement production in racket sports have employed force transducers, force platforms and three-dimensional modelling techniques. Researchers have often focused on kinetics, which explain the forces that produce movement, to better understand the relationship between stroke production and injury. The type of serves or hitting stance of groundstrokes are known to produce higher trunk and upper-limb loading conditions (Bahamonde and Knudson, 2003; Reid *et al.*, 2008). The generation of ground reaction force, which helps to account for players' lower limb drive to the ball and plays an important role in the production of all strokes and movements, has been shown to increase with expertise in specific racket sport skills (Girard *et al.*, 2005). In badminton, Kuntze *et al.* (2010) investigated the kinematics and ground reaction forces of three common types of lunges: the kick lunge, the step-in lunge and the hop lunge. The results suggested that the step-in lunge may be beneficial for reducing the muscular demands of lunge recovery, while the hop lunge allows higher positive power output. Where ground reaction forces provide insights into a player's lower-limb drive, the use of pressure insoles provides researchers and coaches with more specific data to describe the interaction between the shoe and the surface on which racket sport players compete. By using pressure insoles divided into nine areas, Girard et al. (2007a) reported that hard versus clay courts induced higher loading in the hallux and lesser toe areas but lower relative load on the medial and lateral mid-foot in competitive players during tennis-specific movements. In-shoe loading patterns in each foot (back and front) were also shown to differ between two types of tennis serve (first and second serve) and two service stance styles (foot-up and foot-back techniques) (Girard et al., 2010a). Interestingly, the type of court surface was observed to have a significant effect on plantar pressures characterising the first serve in tennis. Compared to hard courts, a reduced asymmetry in peak and mean pressures between the two feet was found on clay, suggesting a greater need for stability on this surface (Girard et al., 2010b). The differences in loading patterns are important for understanding potential injury mechanisms and designing appropriate preventive strategies.

Information concerning the timing and magnitude of muscular activity during the different phases of a particular movement can be gained from electromyography (EMG) recordings. Recent efforts have been made to include EMG data during tennis strokes, such as the serve (Girard et al., 2005), the forehand (Rogowski et al., 2011) and the volley (Chow et al., 2007), while the research attention afforded to the other racket sports has been less extensive. Indeed, the work of Sakurai and Ohtsuki (2000) represents one of very few studies to have examined the EMG characteristics of a badminton stroke, the smash. In comparing the smash of skilled and unskilled players, they revealed similar proximal upper-limb EMG patterns but with significantly more variability in the distal upper-limb EMG characteristics of the unskilled players. Although trunk (Chow et al., 2003) and lower-limb (Girard et al., 2005) muscular activity levels have been investigated, most of the EMG analyses of tennis strokes have focused on the muscles of the hitting arm and shoulder region (Rogowski et al., 2011; Seeley et al., 2008; Wei et al., 2006). Pre- and post-impact activation of five upper extremity muscles in the tennis volley were compared across conditions of ball speed and ball type in a group of 24 recreational tennis players (Chow et al., 2007). In this study, oversize tennis balls did not significantly increase upper extremity muscle activation compared to regular size balls during a tennis volley. Of further interest was the highest post-impact activation observed in the *extensor carpi radialis*, which is indicative of vigorous wrist stabilisation that may irritate players with lateral epicondylalgia. To this end, EMG can also inform sports medicine professionals and coaches about the injury potential of different players or techniques.

Technical effectiveness

Technical effectiveness provides an abstract portrayal of the performance of skills within sport using positive-to-negative ratios, percentage of successful executions and, specifically in racket sports, winner-to-error ratios. This type of analysis does not go into mechanical detail of the skills that are applied, but technical effectiveness can be used in a complementary fashion with technique analysis, as described by Bartlett's (2001) unified approach. The simplest type of technical effectiveness examines point outcomes. For example, Gale (1971) proposed the model shown in equation (32.1) for the probability of winning a point. In this equation, $p1$ and $p2$ are the probabilities of the first and second serves being played in, respectively, while $q1$ and $q2$ are the conditional probabilities of the point being won by the server given that the first or second serve is in, respectively.

$$P = p1.q1 + (1 - p1).p2.q2 \qquad (32.1)$$

O'Donoghue (2009a) applied this equation to published statistics for 427 completed women's singles matches in the 2007 and 2008 Australian and US Open tournaments. This analysis showed that 242 of the 854 serving performances would have won more points if the second serve was played like the first serve, 265 would have been more effective if the first serve was played like the second serve and two performances would have been more effective if the first serve was played like the second serve and vice versa. This left a minority of 345 of 854 serving performances where the observed strategy was the most effective for winning points on serve.

Models for the probability of winning service games in tennis have been used to investigate different scoring systems (Croucher, 1982, 1998). These models are based on the assumptions of stationarity and independence of points. Stationarity means that the probability of winning a point is the same irrespective of the score within the game. Independence means that the probability of winning a point is the same no matter what happened in the preceding points. Recently, Knight and O'Donoghue (in press) challenged the assumption of stationarity, finding that players were significantly more likely to win break points than non-break points when receiving serve. However, O'Donoghue and Brown (2009) were unable to challenge the assumption of independence of points when they analysed 26 serving performances from 13 men's singles matches of over 200 points played at Grand Slam tournaments. This research suggests that momentum in tennis is a misperception of players, coaches, spectators and commentators. There has been some speculation about momentum in squash (Davies *et al.*, 2008; Hughes *et al.*, 2006); however, these studies failed to use inferential statistical procedures to demonstrate that there were more longer sequences of winning (or losing) points than would be expected by chance.

In tennis, the effectiveness of net play and baseline play has been analysed using the percentage of points won in Grand Slam singles tennis (O'Donoghue and Ingram, 2001). Stroke effectiveness has been analysed in table tennis (Djokic, 2002), squash (Brown and Hughes, 1995) and badminton (Cabello-Manrique and González-Badillo, 2003; Oswald, 2009) by counting winners, faults and unforced errors. This is very challenging and requires knowledgeable observers to classify errors during data collection. The percentage of unforced errors is a valid performance indicator in all racket sports when the data are reliable. However, at the elite level, some errors may appear to be unforced but observers need to take into consideration the quality of the shot that a player is trying to return. It was for this reason that O'Donoghue and Ingram (2001) decided to classify point outcomes as winners or errors without distinguishing between forced and unforced errors.

Tactical analysis

Technique analysis can be thought of as investigating whether a skill is being performed correctly. Tactical analysis, on the other hand, is concerned with whether the correct skill is being performed. Irrespective of the quality of execution of a skill, tactical analysis is concerned with the decision to select the skill rather than the other options that may have been available in the given situation. Performance analysis typically uses observational techniques, which cannot directly observe the strategy decided prior to a match or moment-to-moment tactical decisions that are made within a match. However, patterns of play in sports allow inferences to be made about the strategies and tactics adopted by players. The types of events performed, the location of events and timings of events all give indications of strategic and tactical decisions that are made by players.

In racket sports, tactics can be inferred from player positioning (Underwood and McHeath, 1977), point profiles (O'Donoghue and Liddle, 1998), rally duration (O'Donoghue and Ingram, 2001; Ming et al., 2008), shot types (Oswald, 2009) and shot placement (Hughes and Clarke, 1995). Service strategy is an important aspect of table tennis that has been analysed by examining the use of forehand and backhand serves, direction of serve, application of spin and depth of serve (Drianovski and Otcheva, 2002). Service placement has also been used as an indicator of strategy in tennis, with players showing a tendency to serve to the backhand of both right-handed and left-handed opponents (O'Donoghue, 2009b). Unierzyski and Wieczorek (2004) found that serve placement may also be influenced by court surface, with fast tennis courts favouring serves to the 'T', while slower courts favour more serves played to wide areas to open up the court.

The profile of shots played is also an indicator of strategy. This was one of the indicators of strategy that showed similarities in 21 and 15-point (11-point for women) badminton matches (Ming et al., 2008). Another indicator of strategy is the proportion of points of two or more shots where players attack the net (O'Donoghue and Ingram, 2001). The exclusion of aces, double faults, serve winners and return winners means that only those points where players had an option to approach the net were considered.

Player movement is dictated by tactical concerns, with squash players seeking to position themselves around the 'T' in between shots to give the optimal chance of reaching whatever shot the opponent plays. Vučković et al. (2009) used the SAGIT/Squash player-tracking system to compare the movement patterns of squash players in a world team championship with players in Slovenian national championships and a local recreational tournament. The system uses image-processing techniques to analyse play filmed by a camera located on the ceiling of the squash court. The clearest finding of this study was that players at higher levels of the game spent more time in the 'T' area when the opponents were playing shots than players at lower levels. Furthermore, winning players in Slovenian national championships and the local recreational tournament spent more time at the 'T' than losing players at these tournaments. A later paper by Vučković et al. (2010) revealed limited reliability of the SAGIT/Squash system; however, much of the measurement error reported may be systematic error that can be corrected during analysis, rather than random error.

Although much tactical analysis research in racket sports has been done using data from actual competition, there is still scope for controlled experimental investigation in the study of decision making and tactics in racket sports. An example in table tennis used kinematic analysis as well as line of gaze to investigate visual and motor behaviour during forehand strokes (Rodrigues et al., 2002). Mobile eye-tracker technology was used with an image mixer to present the eye image, the player's view and an observer's view of forehands played. A serving player fed balls consistently, with pre-, early and late cues indicating the target location that forehands were to be played to. 'Quiet eye' was defined as the duration of final fixation on a crucial location before the initiation of action. This study showed that lower-skilled players had a later 'quiet eye' onset during missed shots than successful shots, while higher-skilled players had similar 'quiet eye' onset between missed shots and successful shots.

Tactical analysis can be limited when using event frequencies and summary data for whole performances. Temporal analysis is concerned with sequences of events and probabilities of options being chosen in different situations. One example of such research in table tennis is the Markov chain model of table tennis strokes developed by Pfeiffer et al. (2010). This model showed states within rallies and the events which resulted in state transitions. The model covered game actions, stroke position, the direction shots were played and detail of the technique used. The temporal information was displayed in the form of transition matrices and state charts.

Physical aspects of play

The physical demands of racket sports can be investigated using observational methods to evaluate movement characteristics as well as estimates of game intensity, including heart-rate response (HR), measures of oxygen consumption ($\dot{V}O_2$), blood lactate concentration ([La]) and rating of perceived exertion (Fernandez Fernandez *et al.*, 2006; Gomes *et al.*, 2011). The average physiological responses to tennis match play have been reported to be rather modest, with mean exercise intensities of 60–70 per cent $\dot{V}O_{2max}$ and 60–80 per cent HR_{max}. In general, [La] values do not exceed 4 mmol.l⁻¹. In squash, the mean intensity is higher: 70–85 per cent $\dot{V}O_{2max}$ and 80–90 per cent HR_{max} with [La] up to 8–9 mmol.l⁻¹ (Girard *et al.*, 2007b). Game intensity in badminton (75–85 per cent $\dot{V}O_{2max}$; 75–90 per cent HR_{max}; 3 <[La] < 6 mmol.l⁻¹) is generally lower than in squash but higher than in tennis (Faude *et al.*, 2007). To date, the limited data available during table tennis match play in internationally competing juniors have demonstrated low cardiorespiratory and metabolic demands ($\dot{V}O_2$ = 26 ml.kg⁻¹.min⁻¹; HR = 126 beat.min⁻¹; [La] = 1.1 mmol.l⁻¹) (Sperlich *et al.*, 2011). Thus the physical and physiological demands in racket sports can vary to a large extent and can be influenced by a multitude of factors, such as the style of the player, the gender, the level and style of the opponent, the surface, the equipment (i.e. missile and racket characteristics) and the environmental factors (i.e. temperature and humidity) (Fernandez Fernandez *et al.*, 2006). In tennis, being female, slower surfaces, type 3 balls, longer match duration and baseline play increase the aerobic demands, whereas being male, fast surfaces, type 1 balls, shorter match duration, serve and volley play increase the anaerobic demands.

The duration of competition in racket sports varies from 30 to 60 minutes in squash and badminton to more than five hours in tennis, but average durations of 30–90 minutes are common in all racket sports. A broad analysis of the demands of racket sports can be done using rally times and inter-rally breaks; this has been done in tennis (O'Donoghue and Ingram, 2001), badminton (Cabello-Manrique and González-Badillo, 2003) and squash (Girard *et al.*, 2007b). In most high-level matches, the rallies last on average between 2 and 20 s and the work-to-rest ratio between 1:1.1 and 1:1.5. Nevertheless, match activity varies widely across racket sports. In Grand Slam tennis, the mean duration of rally and resting periods are approximately 4–8 s and 20 s, respectively (O'Donoghue and Ingram, 2001). Rally times have been found to be longer (9 s) in regional and national level tennis tournaments but resting periods are still about 20 s (Torres-Luque *et al.*, 2011). The average effective playing time ranges usually between 10 per cent and 30 per cent of the game duration, whereas, in squash, the point duration is longer (10–20 s) and the resting period is shorter (7–8 s), so the effective playing time is 50–70 per cent (Girard *et al.*, 2007b; Montpetit, 1990). The mean rally length fails to portray the demands of a game as there can be a full range of rally lengths. For example, in international badminton singles, the mean rally duration has been measured at 6.4 s (Cabello-Manrique and González-Badillo, 2003). However, only 61.7 per cent of rallies were between 3 s and 9 s in duration. Similarly, the mean rest duration in international badminton was measured at 12.9 s but only 48.6 per cent of rests were between 9 s and 15 s (Cabello-Manrique and González-Badillo, 2003).

A tennis player typically runs an average of 3 m per shot and a total of 8–12 m in the course of a point, completing 300–500 high-intensity efforts during a best-of-three set match (Fernandez Fernandez *et al.*, 2009). The number of directional changes in an average point is four. About 80 per cent of all strokes are played within 2.5 m of the player's ready position, while about 10 per cent of strokes are made with 2.5–4.5 m of movement. Liddle *et al.* (1996) used notational analysis to estimate that male badminton players cover 18.6 m during a singles rally and 9.5 m during a men's doubles rally. Distances covered in squash can now be measured using automatic player-tracking systems such as SAGIT/Squash (Vučković *et al.*, 2010). The reliability of this system has been reported without breaking the error down into systematic bias and random error components. It is therefore difficult to assess whether SAGIT/Squash is sufficiently reliable for different types of study, but further analysis of reliability data should be able to analyse those types of study where the system can be applied.

The activity within rallies is difficult to characterise using the locomotive movement classes typically used in time-motion studies of field games. Therefore, researchers have developed more specific movement classifications to describe the activity within rallies in racket sports. Richers (1995) introduced the concept of continuous footstep movements to study movement within tennis rallies. She found that there were between five and six footsteps taken within average footstep movements during rallies on clay, grass and cement surfaces. However, the 2.5 continuous footstep movements made per rally on grass was lower than the 3.6 movements on clay and the 3.9 movements on cement. Robinson and O'Donoghue (2008) compared path changes, accelerations and decelerations made by Roger Federer and Rafael Nadal on grass and clay courts. This showed that there were more path changes of 45 to 135 degrees to the left on grass than on clay. Clay-court play was characterised by more braking movements and accelerations from a stationary state than grass-court play. This was because a player making a shot on clay was able to move back to the centre of the baseline and pause before having to decide where to move to play the next shot. On a grass court, the players often had to move directly from one side of the baseline to the other without pausing in the middle. Experimental research has shown that performing path changes during movements elevates the oxygen cost of movements (Botton *et al.*, 2011). Performing 50 path changes per minute involved a greater oxygen cost than 33 path changes per minute, which in turn involved a greater oxygen cost than 22 path changes per minute at a range of running speeds. Further, the concept of 'velocity coupling' behaviour, which is a perceptual motor behaviour that occurs during coincident timing tasks such as racket sports, has been found to increase oxygen uptake, blood lactate concentration, heart rate, rating of perceived exertion and perceived task difficulty in tennis (Cooke and Davey, 2007).

Fatigue impairs racket sports performance and is manifested by mistimed shots, altered on-court movements and wrong cognitive (i.e. tactical) choices. For example, Mitchell *et al.* (1992) have reported that fatigue after a three-hour tennis match play is manifested by a decreased velocity of the serve and longer time to complete tennis pattern shuttle-runs. Girard *et al.* (2006) reported progressive reductions in maximal voluntary strength (10–13 per cent decrease in quadriceps) and leg stiffness highly correlated with increases in perceived exertion and muscle soreness throughout a three-hour tennis match, whereas explosive strength was maintained and decreased only after exercise. Furthermore, a 16 per cent decrease in knee extensor isometric maximum voluntary contraction torque was observed after a one-hour squash match play (Girard *et al.*, 2010c). The aetiology of muscle fatigue in racket sports is a complex phenomenon (i.e. distinction between temporary fatigue and fatigue occurring in the final stage of a competition) that involves impairment in both neural (suboptimal muscle activation) and contractile (accumulation of metabolites) processes (Girard and Millet, 2008; Girard *et al.*, 2010c). Hot environments and dehydration worsen fatigue, whereas carbohydrate supplementation before or during competitions may delay the development of fatigue (Hornery *et al.*, 2007).

Future research directions

Further research in racket sport performance needs to take advantage of technological advances. For example, the Hawk-Eye system (Hawk-Eye Innovations, Basingstoke, UK) is accurate ball-tracking technology that is applied during real matches rather than being restricted to controlled experiments.

Because the segmental coordination of movement execution may be rearranged with fatigue (Forestier and Nougier, 1998), future experiments should consider changes in kinematics, kinetics or EMG signals of body segments involved in the kinetic chain to explain the decrease in stroke effectiveness during prolonged match play. However, there is more to performance analysis of sport than notational analysis and biomechanics. An expanded array of methods can be used in performance analysis of sport (O'Donoghue, 2010: 2). There have already been examples of other ways of analysing actual sports performance in racket sports. Buscombe *et al.* (2006) analysed body language, demonstrating that opponent body language could affect the perceptions of a player. Other research using new types of data from actual sports performance includes the research of Poziat *et al.* (2009), who have analysed verbalisations made during table tennis matches. There is other research into racket sports which is covered elsewhere in this handbook. For example, squash has been used as an exemplar of sport as a dynamic self-organising system (McGarry *et al.*, 2002). Feedback systems for table tennis have been developed using ball impact detection technology (Baca and Kornfeind, 2009) and interactive video analysis of shot types (Leser and Baca, 2009). Further development and evaluation of such systems in all racket sports is another important area for future research.

Finally, the increasing interest in performance analysis in tennis must be expanded to the other racket sports. Future experiments must be done in a context appropriate to game play (specificity of the experimental situation) with, in parallel, a high level of standardisation and reliability of the measures.

Concluding remarks

A considerable volume of research has been done in racket sports performance, with some of the earliest notational analysis research being applied in squash (Hughes, 1998). However, as sports science has emerged, more ambitious studies have used a greater variety of methods in the investigation of different aspects of racket sports. These include kinematic analysis, ground reaction force measures, plantar pressure data, physiological measures and player tracking data.

References

Baca, A. and Kornfeind, P. (2009) 'Feedback systems in table tennis', in A. Lees, D. Cabello and G. Torres (eds), *Science and Racket Sports IV* (pp. 208–13). London: Routledge.

Bahamonde R. and Knudson D. (2003) 'Kinetics of the upper extremity in the open and square stance tennis forehand', *Journal of Science and Medicine in Sport*, 6(1): 88–101.

Bartlett, R. (2001) 'Performance analysis: Can bringing together biomechanics and notational analysis benefit coaches?', *International Journal of Performance Analysis of Sport*, 1: 122–6.

Botton, F., Hautier, C. and Eclache, J.P. (2011) 'Energy expenditure during tennis play: A preliminary video analysis and metabolic model approach', *Journal of Strength and Conditioning Research*, 25(11): 3022–8.

Brown, D. and Hughes, M. (1995) 'The effectiveness of quantitative and qualitative feedback on performance in squash', in T. Reilly, M. Hughes and A. Lees (eds), *Science and Racket Sports* (pp. 232–7). London: E and FN Spon.

Buscombe, R., Greenlees, I., Holder, T., Thelwell, R. and Rimmer, R. (2006) 'Expectancy effects in tennis: The impact of opponents' pre-match non-verbal behaviour on male tennis players', *Journal of Sports Sciences*, 24: 1265–72.

Cabello-Manrique, D. and González–Badillo, J.J. (2003) 'Analysis of the characteristics of competitive badminton', *British Journal of Sports Medicine*, 37: 62–6.

Chow, J.W., Carlton, L.G., Lim, Y.T., Chae, W.S., Shim, J.H., Kuenster, A.F. and Kokubun, K. (2003)

'Comparing the pre- and post-impact ball and racquet kinematics of elite tennis players' first and second serves: A preliminary study', *Journal of Sports Sciences*, 21: 529–37.

Chow, J.W., Knudson, D.V., Tillman, M.D. and Andrew, D. (2007) 'Pre- and post-impact muscle activation in the tennis volley: Effects of ball speed, ball size and side of the body', *British Journal of Sports Medicine*, 41: 754–9.

Cooke, K. and Davey, P.R. (2007) 'The energy cost during velocity coupling during tennis groundstrokes', *Journal of Sports Sciences*, 25: 815–21.

Croucher, J.S. (1982) 'The effect of the tennis tie-breaker', *Research Quarterly for Exercise and Sport*, 53: 336–9.

Croucher, J.S. (1998) 'Developing strategies in tennis', in J. Bennett (ed.), *Statistics in Sport* (pp. 157–71). London: Arnold.

Davies, G., Fuller, A., Hughes, M.T., Murray, S., Hughes, M.D. and James, N. (2008) 'Momentum of perturbations in elite squash', presentation at the World Congress of Performance Analysis of Sport VIII, Magdeburg, September.

Djokic, Z. (2002) 'Structure of competitors' activities of top table tennis players', in N. Yuza, S. Hiruta, Y. Iimoto, Y. Shibata, Y. Tsuji, J.R. Harrison, A. Sharara, J.F. Khan, K. Kimura and S. Araki (eds), *Table Tennis Sciences 4 and 5* (pp. 74–90). Lausanne: ITTF.

Drianovski, Y. and Otcheva, G. (2002) 'Survey of the game styles of some of the best Asian players at the 12th World University Table Tennis Championships (Sofia, 1998)', in N. Yuza, S. Hiruta, Y. Iimoto, Y. Shibata, Y. Tsuji, J.R. Harrison, A. Sharara, J.F. Khan, K. Kimura and S. Araki (eds), *Table Tennis Sciences 4 and 5* (pp. 3–9). Lausanne: ITTF.

Elliott, B. (2006) 'Biomechanics and tennis', *British Journal of Sports Medicine*, 40(5): 392–6.

Elliott, B., Marshall, R. and Noffal, G. (1996) 'The role of upper limb segment rotations in the development of racket-head speed in the squash forehand', *Journal of Sports Sciences*, 14: 159–65.

Faude, O., Meyer, T., Rosenberger, F., Fries, M., Huber, G. and Kindermann, W. (2007) 'Physiological characteristics of badminton match play', *European Journal of Applied Physiology*, 100(4): 479–85.

Fernandez Fernandez, J., Mendez-Villanueva, A. and Pluim, B. (2006) 'Intensity of tennis match play', *British Journal of Sports Medicine*, 40(5): 387–91.

Fernandez Fernandez, J., Sanz-Rivas, D. and Mendez-Villanueva, A. (2009) 'A review of the activity profile and physiological demands of tennis match play', *Strength and Conditioning Journal*, 31(4): 15–26.

Forestier, N. and Nougier, V. (1998) 'The effects of muscular fatigue on the coordination of a multijoint movement in human', *Neuroscience Letters*, 252: 187–90.

Gale, D. (1971) 'Optimal strategy for serving in tennis', *Mathematics Magazine*, 5: 197–9.

Gillet, E., Leroy, D., Thouvarecq, R., Megrot, F. and Stein, J.F. (2010) 'Movement-production strategy in tennis: A case study', *Journal of Strength and Conditioning Research*, 24(7): 1942–7.

Girard. O. and Millet, G.P. (2008) 'Neuromuscular fatigue in racquet sports', *Neurologic Clinics*, 26(1): 181–94.

Girard, O., Micallef, J.-P. and Millet, G.P. (2005) 'Lower-limb activity during the power serve in tennis: Effects of performance level', *Medicine and Science in Sports and Exercise*, 37(6): 1021–9.

Girard, O., Lattier, G., Micallef, J.-P. and Millet, G.P. (2006) 'Changes in exercise characteristics, maximal voluntary contraction and explosive strength during prolonged tennis playing', *British Journal of Sports Medicine*, 40(6): 521–6.

Girard, O., Eicher, F., Fourchet, F., Micallef, J.-P. and Millet, G.P. (2007a) 'Effects of the playing surface on plantar pressures and potential injuries in tennis', *British Journal of Sports Medicine*, 41: 733–8.

Girard, O., Chevalier, R., Habrard, M., Sciberras, P., Hot, P. and Millet, G.P. (2007b) 'Game analysis and energy requirements of elite squash', *Journal of Strength and Conditioning Research*, 21(3): 909–14.

Girard, O., Eicher, F., Micallef, J.-P. and Millet, G. (2010a) 'Plantar pressures in the tennis serve', *Journal of Sports Sciences*, 28: 873–80.

Girard O., Micallef, J.-P. and Millet, G.P. (2010b) 'Effects of the playing surface on plantar pressures during the first serve in tennis', *International Journal of Sports Physiology and Performance*, 5: 384–93.

Girard, O., Micallef, J.-P., Noual, J. and Millet, G.P. (2010c) 'Alteration of neuromuscular function in squash', *Journal of Science and Medicine in Sport*, 13(1): 172–7.

Gomes, R.V., Coutts, A.J., Viveiros, L. and Aoki, M.S. (2011) 'Physiological demands of match-play in elite tennis: A case study', *European Journal of Sport Science*, 11(2): 105–9.

Hornery, D., Farrow, D., Mujika, I. and Young, W. (2007) 'Fatigue in tennis. Mechanisms of fatigue and effect on performance', *Sports Medicine*, 37(3): 199–212.

Hughes, M. (1998) 'The application of notational analysis to racket sports', in A. Lees, I. Maynard, M. Hughes and T. Reilly (eds), *Science and Racket Sports II* (pp. 211–20). London: E and FN Spon.

Hughes, M. and Clarke, S. (1995) 'Surface effect on elite tennis strategy', in T. Reilly, M. Hughes and A. Lees (eds), *Science and Racket Sports* (pp. 272–7). London: E and FN Spon.

Hughes, M., Fenwick, B. and Murray, S. (2006) 'Expanding normative profiles of elite squash players using momentum of winners and errors', *International Journal of Performance Analysis Sport*, 6(1): 145–54.

Iino, Y. and Kojima, T. (2009) 'Kinematics of table tennis topspin forehands: Effects of performance level and ball spin', *Journal of Sports Sciences*, 27: 1311–21.

Iino, Y., Mori, T. and Kojima, T. (2008) 'Contributions of upper limb rotations to racket velocity in table tennis backhands against topspin and backspin', *Journal of Sports Sciences*, 26: 287–93.

Knight, G. and O'Donoghue, P.G. (in press) 'The probability of winning break points in Grand Slam men's singles tennis', *European Journal of Sports Sciences*.

Kuntze, G., Mansfield, N. and Sellers, W. (2010) 'A biomechanical analysis of common lunge tasks in badminton', *Journal of Sports Sciences*, 28: 183–91.

Landlinger, J., Lindinger, S., Stoggl, T., Wagner, H. and Muller, E. (2010) 'Key factors and timing patterns in the tennis forehand of different skill levels', *Journal of Sports Science and Medicine*, 9(4): 643–51.

Lees, A. (2003) 'Science and the major racket sports: A review', *Journal of Sports Sciences*, 21: 707–32.

Leser, R. and Baca, A. (2009) 'Practice oriented match analysis in table tennis: A coaching aid', in A. Lees, D. Cabello and G. Torres (eds), *Science and Racket Sports IV* (pp. 214–19). London: Routledge.

Liddle, S.D, Murphy, M.H. and Bleakley, E.W. (1996) 'A comparison of the physiological demands of singles and doubles badminton: A heart rate and time/motion analysis', *Journal of Human Movement Studies*, 30: 159–76.

McGarry, T., Anderson, D.I., Wallace, S.A., Hughes, M.D. and Franks, I.M. (2002) 'Sport competition as a dynamic self-organising system', *Journal of Sports Sciences*, 20: 771–81.

Ming, C.L., Keong, C.C. and Ghosh, A.K. (2008) 'Time-motion and notational analysis of 21 point and 15 point badminton match play', *International Journal of Sports Science and Engineering*, 2: 216–22.

Mitchell, J.B., Cole, K.J., Grandjean, P.W. and Sobczak, R.J. (1992) 'The effect of a carbohydrate beverage on tennis performance and fluid balance during prolonged tennis play', *Journal of Applied Sport Science Research*, 6(2): 174–80.

Montpetit R.R. (1990) 'Applied physiology of squash', *Sports Medicine*, 10(1): 31–41.

O'Donoghue, P.G. (2004) 'Match analysis in racket sports', in A. Lees, J.F. Khan and I.W. Maynard (eds), *Science and Racket Sports III* (pp. 155–62). London: Routledge.

O'Donoghue, P.G. (2009a) 'More than half of women's singles performances would have won more points on serve if the first serve was used for both first and second serve or the second serve was used for both first and second serve', poster presentation at the 3rd International Workshop of the International Society of Performance Analysis of Sport, Lincoln, UK, April.

O'Donoghue, P.G. (2009b) 'Opposition effects in men's singles tennis at the French Open', poster presentation at the 3rd International Workshop of the International Society of Performance Analysis of Sport, Lincoln, UK, April.

O'Donoghue, P.G. (2010) *Research Methods in Performance Analysis of Sport*, London: Routledge.

O'Donoghue, P.G. and Liddle, S.D. (1998) 'A match analysis of elite tennis strategy for ladies' singles on clay and grass surfaces', in A. Lees, I. Maynard, M. Hughes and T. Reilly (eds), *Science and Racket Sports II* (pp. 247–53), London: E and FN Spon.

O'Donoghue, P.G. and Ingram, B. (2001) 'A notational analysis of elite tennis strategy', *Journal of Sports Sciences*, 19: 107–15.

O'Donoghue, P.G. and Brown, E.J. (2009) 'Sequences of service points and the misperception of momentum in elite tennis', *International Journal of Performance Analysis in Sport*, 9(1): 113–27.

Oswald, E. (2009) 'Playing patterns of world elite male and Austrian top male single's badminton players', in A. Lees, D. Cabello and G. Torres (eds), *Science and Racket Sports IV* (pp. 197–203). London: Routledge.

Pfeiffer, M., Zhang, H. and Hohmann, A. (2010) 'A Markov chain model of elite table tennis competition', *International Journal of Sports Science and Coaching*, 5(2): 205–22.

Poziat, G., Bourbousson, J., Saury, J. and Sevè, C. (2009) 'Analysis of contextual information sharing during table tennis matches: An empirical study of coordination in sports', *International Journal of Sport and Exercise Psychology*, 7: 465–87.

Reid, M. and Elliott, B. (2002) 'The one- and two-handed backhands in tennis', *Sports Biomechanics*, 1: 47–68.

Reid, M., Elliott, B. and Alderson, J. (2008) 'Lower-limb coordination and shoulder joint mechanics in the tennis serve', *Medicine and Science in Sports and Exercise*, 40: 308–15.

Richers, T.A. (1995) 'Time-motion analysis of the energy systems in elite and competitive singles tennis', *Journal of Human Movement Studies*, 28: 73–86.

Robinson, G. and O'Donoghue, P.G. (2008) 'Movement in world class tennis on clay and grass courts: A case study', poster presented at the World Congress of Performance Analysis of Sport VIII, Magdeburg, Germany, September.

Rodrigues, S.T., Vickers, J.N. and Williams, A.M. (2002) 'Head, eye and arm coordination in table tennis', *Journal of Sports Sciences*, 20: 187–200.

Rogowski, I., Rouffet, D., Lambalot, F., Brosseau, O. and Hautier, C. (2011) 'Trunk and upper limb muscle activation during flat and topspin forehand drives in young tennis players', *Journal of Applied Biomechanics*, 27(1): 15–21.

Sakurai, S. and Ohtsuki, T. (2000) 'Muscle activity and accuracy of performance of the smash stroke in badminton with reference to skill and practice', *Journal of Sports Sciences*, 18: 901–14.

Seeley, M.K., Uhl, T.L., McCrory, J., McGinn, P., Kibler, W.B. and Shapiro, R. (2008) 'A comparison of muscle activations during traditional and abbreviated tennis serves', *Sports Biomechanics*, 7(2): 248–59.

Sperlich, B., Koehler, K., Holmberg, H.C., Zinner, C. and Mester, J. (2011) 'Table tennis: Cardiorespiratory and metabolic analysis of match and exercise in elite junior national players', *International Journal of Sports Physiology and Performance*, 6(2): 234–42.

Takahashi, K., Elliott, B. and Noffal, G. (1996) 'The role of upper limb segment rotations in the development of spin in the tennis forehand', *Australian Journal of Science and Medicine in Sport*, 28(4): 106–13.

Torres-Luque, G., Cabello-Manrique, D., Hernandez-Garcia, R. and Garatachea, N. (2011) 'An analysis of competition in young tennis players', *European Journal of Sport Science*, 11(1): 39–43.

Underwood, G. and McHeath, J. (1977) 'Video analysis in tennis coaching', *British Journal of Physical Education*, 8: 136–8.

Unierzyski, P. and Wieczorek, A. (2004) 'Comparison of tactical solutions and game patterns in the finals of two grand slam tournaments in tennis', in A. Lees, J.F. Kahn and I.W. Maynard (eds), *Science and Racket Sports III* (pp. 169–74). London: Routledge.

Vučković, G., Perš, J., James, N. and Hughes, M. (2009) 'Tactical use of the T area in squash by players of differing standard', *Journal of Sports Sciences*, 27: 863–71.

Vučković, G., Perš, J., James, N. and Hughes, M. (2010) 'Measurement error associated with the SAGIT/ Squash computer tracking software', *European Journal of Sports Sciences*, 10: 129–40.

Wei, S.H., Chiang J.Y., Shiang, T.Y. and Chang, H.Y. (2006) 'Comparison of shock transmission and forearm electromyography between experienced and recreational tennis players during backhand strokes', *Clinical Journal of Sport Medicine*, 16: 129–35.

33

COMBAT SPORTS

Kerstin Witte

OTTO-VON-GUERICKE-UNIVERSITY MAGDEBURG, GERMANY

Summary

The beginning of this chapter gives an overview of the structures and disciplines of combat sports, as well as samples of combat-specific performance requirements. In contrast to many other sports, only a few authors have focused on performance analysis in combat sports. Known methods and results of several topics of performance analysis (analysis of techniques, modelling and investigation of stress, energy cost, match analysis, and anticipation) will be presented for karate, judo, taekwondo, boxing, and others. The potential to apply these topics to the other combat sports, as well as required modifications, will also be discussed.

Introduction – structure, disciplines of combat sports and performance requirements

Combat sports, specifically martial arts, are characterized by a great manifoldness and have a long history. Their geographical roots can be found in the Asiatic countries: Japan (aikido, judo, ju-jitsu, kendo, iaido, karate, and sumo), China (hung kuen, praying mantis, tai chi chuan, shaolin, jeet kune do, and wing tsun), Korea (taekwondo, hap-ki-do, and taek-kyon), Thailand (muay thai), and others. Many of their sports and arts are practised in Europe and are modified in relation to European tradition and sports rules. One has to distinguish two types: duel (two combatants fight against each other using certain rules of engagement, e.g. kumite in karate) and kata (term referring to a pattern of defence and attack). Further classifications in reference to techniques are: striking (boxing, kick-boxing, full-contact karate, taekwondo), grappling (judo, Brazilian jiu-jitsu, many forms of wrestling), hybrid (shoot boxing, mixed martial arts), and weapons (fencing, kendo, wushu). The focus of this chapter will be on the modern competitive combat sports.

Success in combat sports is influenced by the following factors: coordination, especially exactness and speed of techniques, condition, tactics, and mental load capacity. Many authors focus on condition; McGuigan *et al.* (2006) found that wrestling is a unique combative sport that places high metabolic demands on the body. For instance, isometric strength is a determinant for successful and less successful athletes. An example of a particular requirement for training methods is the execution of techniques with and without contact. Neto *et al.* (2007) and Neto *et al.* (2009) detected differences in the muscle activity by means of surface EMG, which is also a special method in performance analysis. A higher muscle activity could be found in strikes with contact, which is justified by a greater psychological motivation and the need for stabilization of the joints during the impact. Another result showed lower electromyography median frequencies for strikes with impact compared to ones without impact. For strikes without impact, this can be an indication of a better synchronization of the motor units.

But systematic studies have not been undertaken for all factors influencing performance in combat sport. In this chapter, a survey of special research studies for single combat sports and some of the author's own results are presented. In the conclusion, possible knowledge transfer to other combat sports is discussed.

General and specific methods of performance analysis in combat sports

Although it is well-known that mental strength is an important factor influencing the decision on the winner (e.g. a study on kick-boxing by Devonport, 2006, and a study on wushu by Kuan and Roy, 2007), psychological test procedures have generally not been applied. In contrast, measurements of muscle strength are widespread. On the basis of their research, Roschel *et al.* (2009) concluded that international-level karate players' kumite match performance is influenced by upper- and lower-limb power. The hand-grip strength of judo athletes can be determined by a static and dynamic judogi strength test (Franchini *et al.*, 2011). In particular, dynamic grip strength endurance seems to be a discriminating variable between judo athletes.

Franchini *et al.* (2009) and Boguszewska *et al.* (2010) recommended the inclusion of the following items for an optimal training control: biomechanical measurements, physical fitness tests, and special fitness tests for each discipline. The results of an examination with judo athletes showed a significant correlation between the index of special judo fitness test and the absolute and relative power output and velocity in the maximal cyclometer test. The load index is defined by the quotient of the sum of the final heart rate and the heart rate after one minute of the test, divided by the number of throws (ippon seoi nage). Similar sport-specific tests were proposed by Sterkowicz and Franchini (2009) for karate and by Sterkowicz-Przybycien (2009) for ju-jitsu.

Analysis of technique

Movement coordination is an important factor for effective execution of attacks and defence. Several methods have been established to analyse these techniques. Imamura *et al.* (2006) accomplished a three-dimensional kinematical analysis and determined the impulses and momentum of three judo throws: harai-goshi, seoi-nage, and osoto-gari. Based on this, it is possible to gather information about the effectiveness of the behaviour between uke (the person who 'receives' a technique) and tori (meaning 'to take', 'to pick up', or 'to choose') in relation to the phases (kuzushi, tsukuri, kake). However, these imprecise results were produced by the use of only two cameras, with a sample rate of 60 Hz, as well as manually determined position of the joints. Of special interest are the differences between body mass velocities in the temporal course of both judokas in comparison with training and competition (Imamura *et al.*, 2007). The use of motion-capture systems with automatic recognition of markers (e.g. the Vicon system, Vicon, Centennial, Colorado) allows the analysis of fast and complex movements. In order to examine the effectiveness of two executions, Camomilla *et al.* (2009) analysed the jump of the karate kata 'unsu' additionally with surface EMG.

Kinematical investigations are supplemented by measurements of force and acceleration. Examples are analyses of kicks in taekwondo and yongmudo (O'Sullivan *et al.*, 2009) and estimation of effectiveness of several attacks from kung fu using load cell, accelerometers, and high-speed video (Bolander *et al.*, 2009). In this way, Bolander *et al.* (2009) discovered relationships between acceleration and force under different striking conditions (strike distance, type of strike, and height of target).

The most often used in-flight kick is the roundhouse kick. Wasik (2010) characterized the kinetics of a roundhouse kick in taekwondo by means of three-dimensional motion capture. The first stage contains the rotation of the torso, which accelerates the leg. In the second stage, the knee joint is straightened until it reaches the target. Wasik (2010) detected that the dynamics of the kick depends on the velocity of the foot and the rotation moment of the arms, whereas the speed and acceleration of the jump influence the duration of the kick. Emmermacher *et al.* (2007) analysed the foot trajectories of different variations of the roundhouse kick 'mawashi-geri' in karate. From the statistical results, it was concluded that the foot trajectory is shorter when the technique is executed by the front leg than by the rear leg. A higher velocity of the ankle is found for the variant with the kicked rear leg. The purpose of the study by Witte *et al.* (2007) was to identify similarities and differences of various roundhouse kicking techniques in karate in terms of kinematic characteristics. On the basis of the ankle velocity–time-courses of the supporting leg and the kicking leg, an objective phase structuring was given (see Figure 33.1). The subject executed variations of the mawashi-geri and the ura-mawashi-geri. General and individual distinctions were found in relation to the temporal structures of the movements. A characteristic of mawashi-geri (front leg) is the appearance of two maximum values of the ankle (kicking leg) velocity, whereas the relation between them is dependent on the subject. The shortest movement times were found for the mawashi-geri with front leg for all three analysed subjects.

Because kicks and other techniques in combat sports are very complex, many biomechanical parameters are necessary to estimate the similarities between these movements. To consider the whole movement, a possibility is to use nonlinear procedures. Unfortunately, there is no relation to the single biomechanical parameters given. Hence, Witte *et al.* (2010) presented a procedure of visualized movement patterns, which allows a subjective impression of the total movement coordination (see Figure 33.2), and in addition further analyses, by means of statisti-

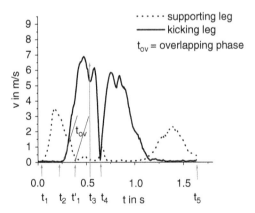

Figure 33.1   Velocity–time-courses of the ankles of mawashi-geri with the front leg. The time points $(t_1–t_5)$ represent essential movement points: $t_1–t'_1$: preparatory or introductory phase by supporting leg, $t_2–t_3$: start-up phase of the thigh of the kicking leg, $t_3–t_4$: snapping phase of the lower leg, $t_4–t_5$: returning to a balanced stance (source: Witte *et al.*, 2007)

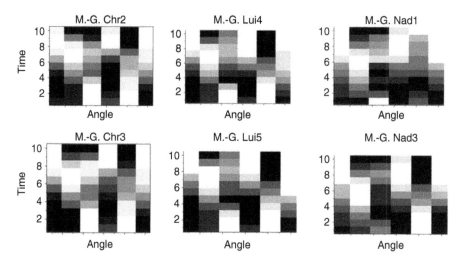

Figure 33.2 Visualized contour plots of movement pattern of mae-geri for three athletes: Chr, Lui, and Nad, two trials per athlete. White: angle-maximum, black: angle-minimum. From left to right, the angles are: hip, knee, ankle, spine, dorsiflexion of pelvis, internal rotation of pelvis

cal tools, confirmed similarities and variability between the movements. Based on this, advice for training optimization can be given.

Modelling and investigations of stress

Baker and Davies (2006) established that the maximum performance on a bicycle ergometer for international karate practitioners depends more on fat-free mass than on body mass index. A simple variant to observe overstress in joints uses a high-speed video. Witte and Emmermacher (2009) discovered an overstretching of the elbow joint and wrist of elite karatekas.

A method to estimate the joint stress is biomechanical modelling. Simulations can be used, based on the biomechanical model, in order to find the optimal movement exercise. Witte and Jackstien (2008) modelled the karate kick mae-geri and stepping movements. The full-body human model was created using the ADAMS software package (Multibody Dynamics Simulation) with its LifeMOD plug-in using the Plug-in-gait marker set. To determine the input data and control parameters, extensive investigations were necessary (cf. Witte and Jackstien, 2008). For mae-geri, it is necessary to distinguish between the supporting leg and the kicking leg. While the supporting leg is loaded by the body weight, the kicking leg is loaded by the acceleration and deceleration during movement and the demanded inertia force. Figure 33.3 shows the calculated forces of the knee for both legs. It can be seen that, for the knee of the supporting leg, the greatest values occur at the beginning of the movement; that means in the phase of raising the leg. However, for the kicking leg, we find the greatest stress in the stretching phase, when the foot reaches the target.

Table 33.1 shows the simulated forces and torques (maximum values) of the ankles for uniform and non-uniform step-movements which are common in karate-kumite competition for one karate fighter. As expected, the highest joint loads occur for the non-uniform steps in relation to the transverse component.

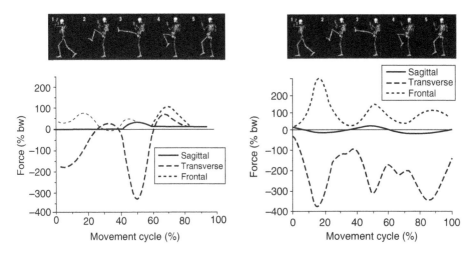

Figure 33.3   Knee forces for the mae-geri. Left diagram: supporting leg, right diagram: kicking leg

Table 33.1 Simulated joint forces and torques of both ankles and for both executions in uniform and non-uniform step movements

Ankle	Force (% BW)		Torque (% BWm)	
	Uniform	*Non-uniform*	*Uniform*	*Non-uniform*
Sagittal				
Left	24	42	52	42
Right	17	36	40	49
Transverse				
Left	317	327	5.1	7.2
Right	256	328	2.4	6.0
Frontal				
Left	23	50	10	14
Right	64	76	8	7.5

Energy cost

It can be assumed that there is a relationship between energy cost and the execution of combat sport techniques, for example, in judo. Franchini *et al.* (2005) established that blood lactate after general (arm Wingate test) and specific (Special Judo Fitness Test) tests correlated with blood lactate after combat, indicating the similarity of metabolic demands in these events. Lech *et al.* (2010) proposed that the level of anaerobic capacity plays a specific role in the course of the fight between judo athletes. Individual functional abilities of judo competitors should be taken into consideration during technical and tactical training. In general, elite judo athletes presented higher upper body anaerobic power and capacity than non-elite athletes. Although aerobic power and capacity are crucial for judo performance, the available data do not reveal differences between judo athletes of different competitive levels (Emerson *et al.*, 2011). Typical maximal oxygen uptake values for male athletes are around 50–55 ml.kg^{-1}.min^{-1}, and 40–45 ml. kg^{-1}.min^{-1} for female judo athletes (Emerson *et al.*, 2011). Santos *et al.* (2010) designed a specific, simple and non-invasive field test to determine the individual aerobic–anaerobic transition zone in judokas. In this test, which is as close as possible to a real judo combat, the judoka has to perform a determined judo technique in a certain time while a portable gas analyser records spirometric data. Santos *et al.* (2011) checked the validity of the test in relation to a laboratory test. However, Almansba *et al.* (2010) warned against overstating the importance of $\dot{V}O_{2max}$ because this parameter can vary in between individual training periods and hence cannot be considered a physiological indicator determining the competition level of each judoka.

Blood lactate measurements and spirometrical research have also been carried out in taekwondo (Matsushigue *et al.*, 2009) and wrestling (Karninčić *et al.*, 2009). Beekley *et al.* (2006) compared the maximum oxygen uptake of several sports with sumo wrestling. They found that sumo wrestlers have a lower $\dot{V}O_{2max}$ than athletes from other sports. One reason may be the large fat mass of these athletes.

Nunan (2006) developed an aerobic fitness assessment test for competitive karate practitioners, wearing a portable spirometrical device. A protocol simulating common attack strikes used in competitive karate sparring was developed from video analysis. In addition, a specific sequence of strikes and timings for the test was created out by means of a pilot study. Anecdotal reports revealed that the new test accurately simulates the actions which are used in competitive karate (Nunan, 2006). Witte and Emmermacher (2011) determined spirometrical data during karate-kumite competition under training conditions. The results of the three calculated energy balance components revealed that 60 to 80 per cent of aerobic capacity was used. This agrees with the results of Beneke *et al.* (2004) and Doria *et al.* (2009) and should be taken into account during the training process. Based on video and synchronous recording of applied techniques, the coach can conclude energetic reserves of the workout of the athlete.

Match analysis

Today, video-based equipment is often used for analysing sport activities. During a judo competition, special forms give information about the executed attacks or actions and their efficiency (Adam *et al.*, 2011). Silva *et al.* (2011) analysed the time structure of muay thai and kick-boxing, focusing on three levels of effort: observation, preparation, and interaction. Ashker (2011) researched technical and tactical aspects that differentiate between winning and losing performances in boxing. He found that winners were more highly developed than losers in performing offensive skills directed to the head or body, total, lead and rear hand punches, boxing combinations, defensive skills, and technical performance effectiveness.

Marcon *et al.* (2010) performed a video analysis by means of the self-developed judo analysis software Saats™ (Structural Analysis of Action and Time in Sports), which computes the precise duration of activities, allowing analysis of the following actions: break, grip, technique, fall, and groundwork. It was concluded that the use of this computer software for notational analysis in judo greatly assists in detailing the actions performed by athletes.

In summary, it can be concluded that no systematic match analysis software exists. One example of a video-based software package for karate-kumite has been described by Emmermacher *et al.* (2010). After loading a video sequence into the program, the user can select the frame and the point of time of the actual event (attack or others) by a key press. A statistical analysis and the creation of a database of the athlete are parts of the match analysis. In the first feasibility study, 16 fights from the under 63 kg weight division for youth (male), 15 fights from the under 52 kg (male), and 11 fights from the open class (male) were analysed to find out which techniques are the most often used in each respective weight class. The results showed that hand techniques, especially gyaku-zuki, are most often used for attacks (up to 60 per cent).

Boguszewski (2011) defined and determined the effectiveness of defensive actions applied in judo. All actions, including attacks, counter-attacks and defence without counter-attack, were recorded and their effectiveness, preparatory actions, breaks, and the referees' decisions were evaluated. Boguszewski (2011) defined 12 different types of defence without counter-attack. For each technique, he determined the frequency of application and the effectiveness.

In the research study by Del Vecchio *et al.* (2011), performance analysis quantified the effort–pause ratio (EP) and classified effort segments of stand-up or groundwork to identify the number of actions performed per round in mixed martial art (MMA) matches. In consideration of the duration of the match, they found only one significant difference between rounds: time spent in groundwork at a low intensity was longer in the second round compared to the third round. Another result was the decrease of EP ratio (between high-intensity effort to low-intensity effort plus pauses) from 1:2 to 1:4 in accordance with other combat sports (judo, wrestling, karate, and taekwondo).

Anticipation and perception

Hristovski *et al.* (2006) used a nonlinear dynamical approach for decisions to punch a target. This theory shows that the behaviour of the fighter is influenced by many factors, including environmental, task, and individual constraints. This study focused on the importance of the distance between the boxer and the bag. A study by Wasik (2009) found that an attack (punch in taekwondo) with a duration of 0.1 s could not be prevented because of the reaction time of 0.2 s. So the anticipation of the attack is very important for the competitor. To determine the ability of anticipation and to improve the skill of observing movements, video-based test equipment was developed by Witte and Emmermacher (2010). This protocol contains a practical test and two PC tests in real time and slow motion. The protocol includes the following steps: video selection, creation of a subject database, single tests with analysis, a video database of athletes, several tests and analysis routines, and reports for the coach (see Figure 33.4). The results of

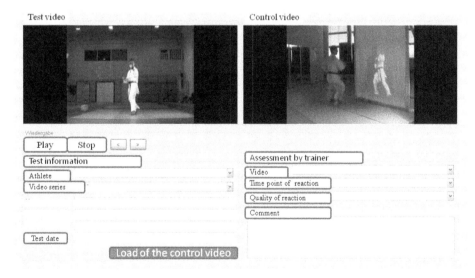

Figure 33.4 Screenshot of the trainer mode to evaluate the practice test (source: Witte and Emmermacher, 2010)

a pilot study showed that the gyaku-zuki and its variants, as well as combinations with other techniques, were the least anticipated techniques (Witte and Emmermacher, 2010).

To enhance a near-to-reality reaction of the athlete using a three-dimensional attacker, virtual reality technology has been developed using a measuring station. This is advantageous over a two-dimensional presentation of an attacker on a video screen or monitor (Witte *et al.*, 2011). In this study, a virtual environment for karate was developed by means of a CAVE (Cave Automatic Virtual Environment). The results of a comparison between reality, video projection, and virtual reality based on participants' reaction times to karate attacks showed shorter reaction times in the virtual environment than with the video projection. It was concluded that the virtual environment is more similar to reality than video projection and hence induces more realistic reactions in the athletes.

Concluding remarks

There is great diversity in performance analysis in combat sports. The reason for this is that each martial art has its own techniques and rules, meaning generalization is complicated. Nevertheless, the following conclusions can be drawn:

- Modern motion-capture systems allow three-dimensional analyses of techniques and should be used for their optimization.
- High-speed video allows the detection of faults in technique.
- It is worth considering whether nonlinear methods are suitable for analysing techniques of combat sport.
- Biomechanical analysis of joint loads can be carried out and the effectiveness of techniques can be estimated.
- Methods for determining energy balance are necessary for optimal training. The tests should be done while performing under near-to-competition conditions.
- Special software is necessary to simplify the work of the coach for match analysis and to populate a statistical database for each athlete.
- To improve anticipation, special measurement stations are necessary which allow the study of cues from attacks which are used for anticipation.

References

Adam, M., Smaruj, M., and Tyszkowski, S. (2011) 'The diagnosis of the technical-tactical preparation of judo competitors during the World Championships (2009 and 2010) in the light of the new judo sport rules', *Archives of Budo/Science of Martial Arts*, 7(1): 5–9.

Almansba, R., Sterkowicz, S., Sterkowicz-Przybycien, K., and Belkacem, R. (2010) 'Maximal oxygen uptake changes during judoist's periodization training', *Archives of Budo/Science of Martial Arts*, 6(3): 117–22.

Ashker, S.E. (2011) 'Technical and tactical aspects that differentiate winning and losing performances in boxing', *International Journal of Performance Analysis in Sport*, 11(2): 356–64.

Baker, J.St. and Davies, B. (2006) 'Variation in resistive force selection during brief high intensity cycle ergometry: Implications for power assessment and production in elite practitioners', *Journal of Sports Science and Medicine*, Combat Sports Special Issue 1: 42–6.

Beekley, M.D., Abe, T., Kondo, M., Midorikawa, T., and Yamauchi, T. (2006) 'Comparison of normalized maximum aerobic capacity and boy composition of sumo wrestlers', *Journal of Sports Science and Medicine*, Combat Sports Special Issue 1: 13–20.

Beneke, R., Beyer, T., Jachner, C., Erasmus, J., and Hütler, M. (2004) 'Energetics of karate kumite', *European Journal of Applied Physiology*, 1(92): 518–23.

Boguszewska, K., Boguszewski, D., and Busko, K. (2010) 'Special judo fitness test and biomechanics measurements as a way to control of physical fitness in young judoists', *Archives of Budo/Science of Martial Arts*, 6(4): 205–9.

Boguszewski, D. (2011) 'Defensive actions of world's top judoists', *Journal of Human Kinetics*, 27(1): 111–22.

Bolander, R., Neto, O.P., and Bir, C.A. (2009) 'The effects of height and distance on the force production and acceleration in martial arts strikes', *Journal of Sports Science and Medicine*, Combat Sports Special Issue 3: 47–52.

Camomilla, V., Sbriccoli, P., Mario, A.D., Arpante, A., and Felici, F. (2009) 'Comparison of two variants of a Kata technique (Unsu): The neuromechanical point of view', *Journal of Sports Science and Medicine*, Combat Sports Special Issue 3: 29–35.

Del Vecchio, F.B., Hirata, S.M., and Franchini. E. (2011) 'A review of time-motion analysis and combat development in mixed martial arts matches at regional level tournaments', *Perceptual and Motor Skills*, 112(2): 639–48.

Devonport, T.J. (2006) 'Perceptions of the contribution of psychology to success in elite kickboxing', *Journal of Sports Science and Medicine*, Combat Sports Special Issue 1: 99–107.

Doria, C., Veicsteinas, A., Limonta, E., Maggioni, M.A., Aschieri, P., Eusebi, F., Fano, G., and Pietrangelo, T. (2009) 'Energetics of karate (kata and kumite techniques) in top-level athletes', *European Journal of Applied Physiology*, 107: 603–10.

Emerson, F., Del Vecchio, F.B., Matsushigue, K.A., and Artioli, G.G. (2011) 'Physiological profiles of elite judo athletes', *Sports Medicine*, 41(2): 147–66.

Emmermacher, P., Witte, K., Bystrzycki, S., and Potenberg, J. (2007) 'Different variations of karate technique Mawashi-Geri', in H.-J. Menzel, and M.H. Chagas (eds), *Proceedings of the XXVth International Symposium on Biomechanics in Sports* (pp. 289–92), Ouro Preto, Brazil.

Emmermacher, P., Witte, K., Tietze, R., and Hiller, R. (2010) 'Video supported fight analysis in karate – K-WETT-A', presentation at the Asian Conference on Computer Science in Sports (ACCSS), Tokyo, September.

Franchini, E., Takito, M.Y., and de Moraes Bertuzzi, R.C. (2005) 'Morphological, physiological and technical variables in high level college judoists', *Archives of Budo*, 1: 1–7.

Franchini, E., Del Vecchio, F.B., and Sterkowicz, S. (2009) 'A special judo fitness test classificatory table', *Archives of Budo*, 5: 127–9.

Franchini, E., Miarka, B., Matheus, L., and del Vecchio, F.B. (2011) 'Endurance in judogi grip strength test: Comparison between elite and non-elite judo players', *Archives of Budo/Science of Martial Arts*, 7(1): 1–4.

Hristovski, R., Davids, K., Araújo, D., and Button, C. (2006) 'How boxers decide to punch a target: Emergent behaviour in nonlinear dynamical movement systems', *Journal of Sports Science and Medicine*, Combat Sports Special Issue 1: 60–73.

Imamura, R.T., Hreljac, A., Escamilla, R.F., and Edwards, W.B. (2006) 'A three-dimensional analysis of the center of mass for three different judo throwing techniques', *Journal of Sports Science and Medicine*, Combat Sports Special Issue 1: 122–31.

Imamura, R.T., Iteya, M., Hreljac, A., and Escamilla, R.F. (2007) 'A kinematic comparison of the judo throw Harai-goshi during competitive and non-competitive conditions', *Journal of Sports Science and Medicine*, 6: 15–22.

Karninčić, H., Tocilj, Z., Uljević, O., and Erceg, M. (2009) 'Lactate profile during Greco-Roman wrestling match', *Journal of Sports Science and Medicine*, 8(3): 17–19.

Kuan, G. and Roy, J. (2007) 'Goal profiles, mental toughness and its influence on performance outcomes among Wushu athletes', *Journal of Sports Science and Medicine*, 6(2): 28–33.

Lech, G., Palka, T., Sterkowicz, S. Tyka, A., and Krawczyk, R. (2010) 'Effect of physical capacity on the course of fight and level of sports performance in cadet judokas', *Archives of Budo/Science of Martial Arts*, 6(3): 123–8.

Marcon, G., Franchini, E., Jardim, J.R., and Neto, T.L.B. (2010) 'Structural analysis of action and time in sports: Judo', *Journal of Quantitative Analysis in Sports*, 6(4): article 10.

Matsushigue, K.A., Hartmann, K., and Emerson, F. (2009) 'Taekwondo: Physiological responses and match analysis', *Journal of Strength and Conditioning Research*, 23(4): 1112–17.

McGuigan, M.R., Winchester, J.B., and Erickson, T. (2006) 'The importance of isometric maximum strength in college wrestlers', *Journal of Sports Science and Medicine*, Combat Sports Special Issue 1: 108–13.

Neto, O.P., Magini, M., and Pacheco, M.T.T. (2007) 'Electromyographic study of a sequence of

Yau-Man Kung Fu palm strikes with and without impact', *Journal of Sports Science and Medicine*, 6(2): 23–7.

Neto, O.P., Carolina, A., and Marzullo, M. (2009) 'Wavelet transform analysis of electromyography Kung Fu strikes data', *Journal of Sports Science and Medicine*, 8(3): 25–8.

Nunan, D. (2006) 'Development of a sports specific aerobic capacity test for karate – a pilot study', *Journal of Sports Science and Medicine*, 5 (CSSI): 47–53.

O'Sullivan, D., Chung, Ch., Lee, K., Kim, E., Kang, S. Kim, T., and Shin, I. (2009) 'Measurement and comparison of Taekwondo and Yongmudo turning kick impact force fort two target heights', *Journal of Sports Science and Medicine*, 8(3): 13–16.

Roschel, H., Batista, M., Monteiro, R., Bertuzzi, R.C., Barroso, R., Loturco, I., Ugrinowitsch, C., Tricoli, V., and Franchini, E. (2009) 'Association between neuromuscular test and Kumite performance on the Brazilian Karate National Team', *Journal of Sports Science and Medicine*, 8(3): 20–4.

Santos, L., Gonzalez, V., Iscar, M., Brime, J.I., Fernandez-Rio, J., Egocheaga, J., Rodriguez, B., and Montoliu, M.A. (2010) 'A new individual and specific test to determine the aerobic-anaerobic transition zone (Santos Test) in competitive judokas', *Journal of Strength and Conditioning Research*, 24(9): 2419–28.

Santos, L., Gonzalez, V., Iscar, M., Brime, J.I., Fernandez-Rio, J., Rodriguez, B., and Montoliu, M.A. (2011) 'Retesting the validity of a specific field test for judo training', *Journal of Human Kinetics*, 29: 141–50.

Silva, J.J.R., del Vecchio, F.B., Merseburger Picanco, L., Takito, M.Y., and Franchini, E. (2011) 'Time-motion analysis in Muay-Thai and Kick-Boxing amateur matches', *Journal of Human Sport and Exercise*, 6(3): 490–6.

Sterkowicz, S. and Franchini, E. (2009) 'Testing motor fitness in karate', *Archives of Budo*, 5: 29–34.

Sterkowicz-Przybycien, K. (2009) 'Special fitness testing in sport ju-jitsu', *Archives of Budo*, 5: 131–7.

Wasik, J. (2009) 'Chosen aspects of physics in martial arts', *Archives of Budo/Science of Martial Arts*, 5: 11–14.

Wasik, J. (2010) 'The structure of the roundhouse kick on the example of a European Champion of tae-kwon-do', *Archives of Budo/Science of Martial Arts*, 6(3): 211–16.

Witte, K. and Jackstien, M. (2008) 'Application of the BRG (Biomechanical Research Group). LifeMOD for simulations of step-movements and kicks and estimation of joint stress', presentation at the ISBS Conference, Seoul, Korea, July.

Witte, K. and Emmermacher, P. (2009) 'Biomechanical analysis in karate', in A. Hökelmann, K. Witte, and P. O'Donoghue, (eds), *Current Trends in Performance Analysis: World Congress of Performance Analysis of Sport VIII* (pp. 200–13). Aachen: Shaker-Verlag.

Witte, K. and Emmermacher, P. (2010) 'Software package for assessment of visual perception and anticipation ability in combat sport', *International Journal of Computer Science in Sport*, 10(1): 51–62.

Witte, K. and Emmermacher, P. (2011) 'Spirometrie im Karate-Kumite unter Berücksichtigung der Kampfaktivitäten', Symposium Kampfkunst and Kampfsport, Bayreuth, April.

Witte, K., Emmermacher, P., Bystrzycki, S., and Potenberg, J. (2007) 'Movement structures of round kicks in karate', in H,-J. Menzel and M.H. Chagas (eds), *Proceedings of the XXVth International Symposium on Biomechanics in Sports* (pp. 302–5). Ouro Preto, Brazil.

Witte, K., Emmermacher, P., and Langenbeck, N. (2010) 'Method to visualize and analyze similarities of movements – using the example of karate kicks', in R. Jensen, W. Ebben, E. Petushek, Ch. Richter, and K. Roemer (eds), *Proceedings of the 28th Conference of the International society of Biomechanics in Sports* (pp. 186–90). Marquette, Michigan, USA.

Witte, K., Bandow, N., Emmermacher, P., and Masik, St. (2011) 'Using VR technology for studying anticipation in combat sport', in Y. Jiang and H. Zhang (eds), *Proceedings of the 8th International Symposium on Computer Science in Sport* (pp. 45–8). Liverpool: World Academic Union (World Academic Press).

34

TARGET SPORTS

Mario Heller and Arnold Baca

UNIVERSITY OF VIENNA, AUSTRIA

Summary

In the first part of this chapter, performance indicators in target sports are defined and justified. A focus is put on Olympic sports (archery, rifle – specifically, biathlon – shooting, and pistol shooting). In particular, aspects of movement kinematics in terms of postural balance and aiming stability are discussed. After that, an overview of psychophysiological research in the area of precision shooting is given and other aspects which influence the shooting performance are reviewed. Methods for acquisition and analysis of respective parameters and/or time courses of parameter values are presented.

Introduction

Target sports in terms of (Olympic) precise shooting disciplines can be classified into four summer categories (rifle, pistol, shotgun, and archery) and biathlon shooting in winter. Despite various types of guns (firearms, airguns, bows), positions (prone, standing, kneeling), distances (10, 25, 50, and 70 m), physical conditions (cardiorespiratory load, strength and endurance of the upper body), and weather (temperature, wind speed, wind direction), all have in common that the environmental goal is to hit the center of the target. In some cases, the shooting score describes how well this goal is achieved. Obviously, the assessment of shooting results is a relatively unambiguous and useful index of successful and less successful task performance (Mononen *et al.*, 2007), but to gain deeper understanding of the underlying mechanisms causing successful performance, some specific factors of influence become apparent: postural and aiming stability, psychophysiological aspects, and other effects affecting shooting outcome. Within the following sections, a survey of important performance indicators in target sports will be given, without, however, claiming to be exhaustive.

Postural and aiming stability

There are a number of studies in the field of postural and aiming stability in precision shooting disciplines that identified (widely) necessary but not sufficient prerequisites for good shots. Mononen *et al.* (2007) give a good summary of the state of the art regarding postural and aiming stability: highly skilled rifle shooters produced smaller body sway amplitudes both during bipedal standing (Aalto *et al.*, 1990; Niinimaa and McAvoy, 1983) and during shooting (Era *et al.*, 1996; Konttinen *et al.*, 1999) compared to inexperienced shooters. Among inexperienced rifle shooters, postural balance was significantly worse for the less successful shots (Era *et al.*, 1996), whereas no such differentiation was found among top-level shooters (Ball *et al.*, 2003a; Era *et al.*, 1996). Another prerequisite for successful performance seems to be minimal movement of the gun barrel during the aiming phase (Ball *et al.*, 2003b; Konttinen *et al.*, 1998; Mason *et al.*, 1990; Mononen *et al.*, 2003; Zatsiorsky and Aktov, 1990). With regard to skill level, elite shooters were able to keep their rifle more stable during the aiming period compared to novices (Konttinen *et al.*, 2000; Mononen *et al.*, 2003). The degree of gun barrel stability discriminated among high-scoring and low-scoring shots both among novice and among elite rifle shooters (Konttinen *et al.*, 1998; Mason *et al.*, 1990; Mononen *et al.*, 2003).

Significantly larger slow-drift movements were observed compared to tremor for neck, shoulder, elbow, wrist, and gun among air pistol athletes (Pellegrini and Schena, 2005; Tang *et al.*, 2008). This was particularly the case for lateral movements.

Herpin *et al.* (2010) performed one of the very few experimental studies to analyze balance control and the related neurosensory organization. They found out that shooters yielded a better balance control during tests with eyes open and eyes closed than fencers and controls, but fencers showed a better balance control in tests with eyes closed with sway-referenced support surface than shooters and controls.

In recurve archery, where the archer has to cope with the breakdown of the static balance of forces between the external tension and his muscular forces at the moment of shooting, body stability (Hinze *et al.*, 2004; Mason and Pelgrim, 1986) and a stable aiming process seem to play an important role. Gruber *et al.* (2002) analyzed the German junior and national team. The members of the national team showed significantly smaller holding areas and a significantly higher shooting score. Individual analysis revealed no dependence of the result on the stability of targeting in the junior national team but seven archers out of nine showed that dependence in the national team. Moreover, the draw-length should be nearly constant during aiming (Edelmann-Nusser *et al.*, 2006). At the end of the aiming phase, the archer has to pull the arrow back smoothly and steadily (also called 'regularly'; see Edelmann-Nusser *et al.*, 2006; Leroyer *et al.*, 1993).

Insights on performance may also be gained by analyzing surface electromyographic activation patterns. Soylu *et al.* (2006) showed that FITA scores in recurve archery were significantly correlated to the variance ratios of musculus flexor digitorum superficialis and extensor digitorum, investigating similarity of the EMG signals. EMG linear envelopes were more repeatable among archers compared to non-archers. A longitudinal analysis of the German national and junior teams revealed two very stable amplitude activation patterns of musculus trapezius pars transversa (Heller *et al.*, 2004). For ten out of twelve archers, a decreasing rectified smoothed EMG and mean power of the musculus trapezius pars transversa could be found immediately before the contact-loss of the arrow with the bowstring; for two archers, the activity increased. However, the median frequency of EMG signals indicated both longitudinal stability and instability among all athletes.

Psychophysiological aspects

Psychophysiology, defined as 'the scientific study of cognitive, emotional and behavioral phenomena as related to and revealed through physiological principles and events' (Cacioppo and Tassinary, 1990: ix), can provide an objective and relatively non-invasive method of examining the complex processes involved in sports performance (Collins, 1995: 154). Electroencephalography, electromyography, and measures of heart rate, skin conductance and temperature, gaze behavior, respiration, and blood pressure are usually used to reflect changes in the central and autonomic nervous system (cf. Collins, 1995: 155).

Based on the fundamental work by Hatfield *et al.* (1984), there are a number of reports in which the EEG patterns of expert performers have been described when challenged with visuospatial and motor coordination demands during aiming periods in rifle shooting (Deeny *et al.*, 2003; Doppelmayr *et al.*, 2008; Hatfield *et al.*, 1987; Haufler *et al.*, 2000; Holmes *et al.*, 2006; Janelle *et al.*, 2000; Konttinen *et al.*, 2000), pistol shooting (Loze *et al.*, 2001), and archery (Landers *et al.*, 1994; Salazar *et al.*, 1990). A number of these studies revealed that skilled performers exhibit less activation of the left hemisphere (as indexed by an increase in alpha power), relative to that observed in the right, during the preparatory period for self-paced motor tasks. Some authors also report on observed poorer performance when accompanied by the highest observed levels of alpha and low-beta spectral power in the left hemisphere prior to arrow release in archery (Salazar *et al.*, 1990) or in marksmen before shots rejected when compared to shots executed (Hillman *et al.*, 2000).

A slow reduction in heart-rate levels prior to the shot has been shown for elite pistol shooters (Tremayne and Barry, 2001), elite rifle shooters (Hatfield *et al.*, 1987; Konttinen and Lyytinen, 1992), and elite archers (Keast and Elliot, 1990). These findings were not apparent in novice pistol shooters (Tremayne and Barry, 2001). Pre-shot electrodermal levels for the experts were also lower for the best compared to the worst shots, and the duration of the pre-shot cardiac deceleration was longer and more systematic for best than for worst shots (Tremayne and Barry, 2001). With regard to timing of the triggering action of shooting, there are contradictory findings: elite pistol and rifle shooters triggered consistently late in the cardiac cycles, whereas the novice shooters triggered randomly (Helin *et al.*, 1987). Among the novice shooters, better shooting scores were achieved when they triggered during the late phase. However, the timing of the trigger pull in relation to the cardiac cycle is questioned to be a determinant of superior shooting performance in competitive junior elite rifle shooters (Mets *et al.*, 2007) and novice rifle shooters (Konttinen *et al.*, 2003). Konttinen and Lyytinen (1992) describe the typical respiration pattern in rifle shooting consisting of breath holding with slow expiration preceding the trigger pull.

In a more recent study assessing changes in heart-rate variability, Carrillo *et al.* (2011) found that experienced adolescent archers tend to show higher values for low-frequency activity, square root of the mean of squared differences between successive R-R intervals, and percentage of successive normal-to-normal intervals greater than 50 milliseconds than novice archers during a competition.

Since the 1990s, eye movement analysis has been applied in order to study human movement behavior during different interceptive tasks. Already defined in 1996 (Vickers), a visual phenomenon called 'quiet eye' period denotes the final fixation on a specific location or object in the visuomotor workspace within 3 degrees of the visual angle for a minimum of 100 ms. It has been reported that the onset of the quiet eye period occurs earlier and its duration is longer in the elite compared to the sub-elite athletes in small-bore rifle shooters (Janelle *et al.*, 2000), biathlon rifle shooters (Vickers and Williams, 2007), as well as shotgun shooters (skeet, trap, and double trap disciplines; see Causer *et al.*, 2010). Moreover, in all three shotgun disciplines, quiet eye duration was longer and onset earlier during successful compared to unsuccessful trials for elite and sub-elite shooters (Causer *et al.*, 2010).

Other effects influencing the performance

Besides movement kinematics and psychophysiological aspects, there are also other effects influencing the performance in target shooting. Hoffman *et al.* (1992) investigated shooting performance among elite American biathletes immediately after exercise of various intensities. They found that exercise intensity had minimal effect on shooting accuracy and precision for prone shooting, but did affect these measures for shooting in the standing position. The latter is in line with the result of Grebot and Groslambert (2003) and Vickers and Williams (2007). In addition, stability of hold was affected more by exercise intensity for shooting in the standing position compared to prone shooting (Hoffman *et al.*, 1992).

Grebot and Burtheret (2007) examined the influence of negative temperatures on the trigger mechanism and on the ballistic responses of the bullet in biathlon shooting. The results showed that from +20°C until –8°C, the triggering force was equal to 5 N, whereas at –20°C, a triggering force of 8 N was required. The authors suppose the increase of the triggering force that was found under –8°C to be caused by the difference between the coefficients of expansion of the different materials constituting the trigger mechanism. Concerning the ballistic measurements, group diameter at room temperature was significantly lower ($p<0.05$) than –3°C, –10°C, and –20°C. Furthermore, shooting score was significantly better at –20°C ($p<0.05$) compared to –3°C, –10°C, and –20°C conditions.

Yuan and Lee (1997) examined the effects of rifle weight and handling length on aiming stability in a simulated aiming exercise and the relationship between aiming stability and shooting accuracy in a live-fire test. It was shown that different rifle designs led to an alteration of rifle-holding postures and muscle activation levels in order to maintain the system in balance, thereby affecting aiming stability. Furthermore, in the live-fire study, smaller aiming fluctuations, smaller shot group dispersions, and a higher shot group accuracy could be observed for the rifle with smaller length and lesser weight.

Methods for acquisition and analysis

Methods

To overcome the problem of measuring aiming stability with experimental settings which are entirely unrelated to the real-life shooting situation, Alain and Avon (1976) first developed a measurement technique to take a still photograph of an infrared diode attached to the end of a rifle barrel. The stability score was defined as the total area covered by the diode's image on the film during aiming. To provide exact information on the spatial orientations of the aiming axis, Hadani and Bergman (1980) improved the technique, taking successive movie photographs of part of the target as reflected by a mirror mounted on the aiming device. Since the beginning of the 1980s, companies like Noptel, SCATT, RIKA, and SAM Trainer have been developing optoelectronic training devices, allowing training, diagnostics, and research in rifle and pistol shooting disciplines. Moreover, a Noptel-ST-2000 system was adapted for archery (Edelmann-Nusser *et al.*, 2002). All systems have in common that a laser device is attached to the rifle – either in combination with a laser-sensitive grid in order to obtain visual information on the deviation from the center of a target in real time or by using image-processing algorithms to reconstruct the movement of a laser point on a secondary target (Chandrapal *et al.*, 2009). Even though these systems are widely used for assessing the aiming process in shooting disciplines, the specificity of shooting training results with an optoelectronic target has been questioned (Zanevskyy *et al.*, 2009).

Nitzsche and Koch (2000) used a different approach; they fixed a small infrared light-reflecting device directly onto the barrel for measuring the movement of the muzzle. A drawback of all these methods for analyzing the aiming process lies in the necessity of attaching devices to the rifle and the expense of calibrating the system.

Alternatively, optoelectronic motion-capturing systems can be used to track and record the rifle and the athlete's 3D movements in real time by attaching active (Silva *et al.*, 2009) or passive markers (Heller *et al.*, 2006a) to both rifle and athlete (see Figure 34.1).

However, such systems are expensive and difficult to use outdoors. To overcome these problems, Baca and Kornfeind (2006) developed a video-based system which allows the reconstruction of the horizontal and vertical motion of the muzzle using image-processing algorithms (see Figure 34.2). The usefulness of the system was investigated by Heller *et al.* (2006b). The results suggested considerable correspondence of the on-target trajectory and the 2D movement of the muzzle, in particular in the vertical direction. However, translation movements of the shoulder during aiming, which are rather difficult to diagnose, may cause differences in the horizontal plane.

A modified version of the video-based system is able to track the sight of the bow from behind the archer (Edelmann-Nusser *et al.*, 2008). This enables the analysis of the aiming process during competition – for example, the German Archery National Championships in 2007

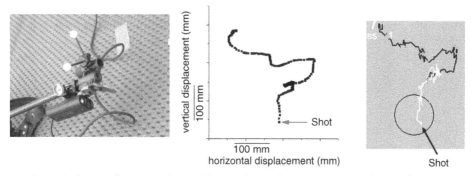

Figure 34.1   Left: Noptel system and two of four passive markers mounted onto the air rifle. Middle and right: Comparison of the calculated aiming point trajectory during the last three seconds before the shot and the Noptel trajectory

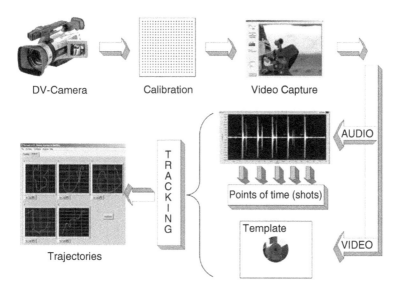

Figure 34.2   Biathlon feedback system MOTRACK

(Ganter *et al.*, 2009) and the World Outdoor Archery Championships in Leipzig, Germany in 2007 (Edelmann-Nusser *et al.*, 2008). Figure 34.3 shows the use of the system and the bow sight which is used for image analysis.

In order to measure additional performance indicators in archery (e.g. the reaction time of an archer to clicker's fall [see also Figure 34.3], arrow velocity, and external factors that may affect arrow velocity), Ertan *et al.* (2005) developed an archery chronometer. They concluded that the chronometer could be used for technical evaluation and enhancing one's shooting technique in archery. A real-time motion analysis system that is able to analyze hand stability of users was developed by Loke *et al.* (2009). The system uses smart ultrasound sensors and is reasonably satisfactory and acceptable in terms of cost, hardware set-up, functionality, and durability.

A robust compact mobile EEG system has been developed by Alpha-Active Ltd specifically for sports applications. Their HeadCoach™ product provides stable EEG output, especially in the alpha-wave region, even when the athlete is moving. Figure 34.4 shows alpha brainwave trends (6.5 Hz–16 Hz/0.5 Hz–32 Hz) for the left and right side of the front of the head of an experienced archer. Recently developed mobile eye-tracker systems (e.g. ASL Mobile Eye-XG) are acquiring eye movements and point of gaze information during the activity, allowing the analysis of unconstrained eye, head, and hand movements under variable conditions.

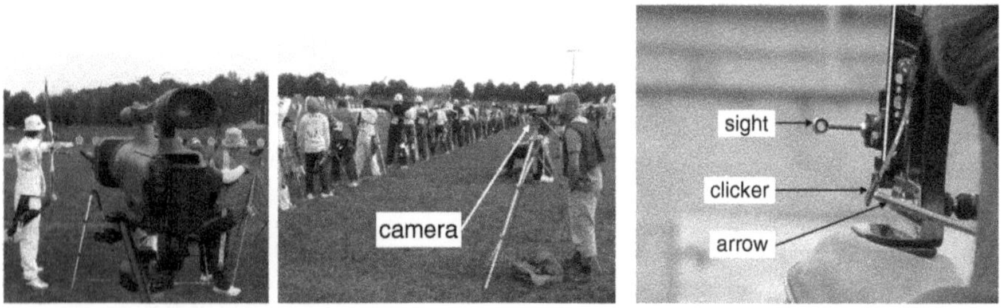

Figure 34.3 Left and middle: Use of the video-based system during the World Outdoor Archery Championship in 2007. Right: Camera view from left behind the archer. The bow sight is used for automatic tracking of the movement of the bow

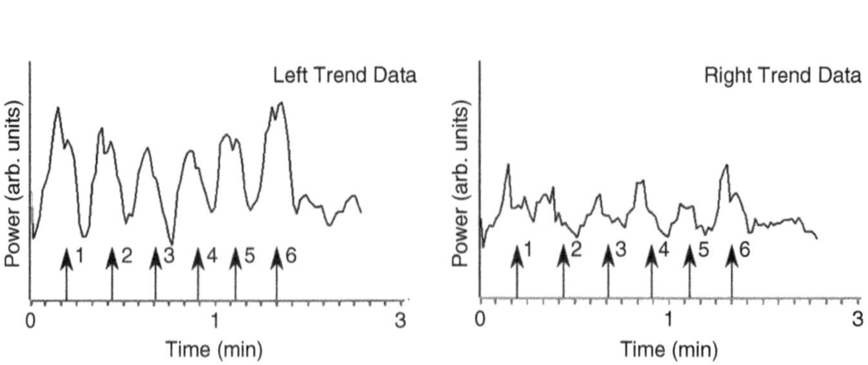

Figure 34.4 Alpha brainwave trends (6.5 Hz–16 Hz/0.5 Hz–32 Hz) for left and right side of the front of head of an experienced archer (Alpha-Active Ltd, used with permission)

Analysis

Almost all of these technologies provide time series of positional data and/or instantaneous velocities. Parameters in data analysis are values normally calculated from time series, including sample means and dispersion values of discrete times, displacements, rotations, and their derivatives. However, there are some other approaches published in the field of shooting performance: three of them are shortly figured out.

Goodman *et al.* (2009) examined regular and random components in aiming point trajectory and discriminated two phases. The first phase was regular approximation to the target accompanied by substantial fluctuations obeying the Weber–Fechner law. In the second phase, beginning at 0.6–0.8 s before the trigger pull, shooters applied a different control strategy: they waited until the following random fluctuation brought the aiming point closer to the target and then initiated triggering. This strategy is tenable when sensitivity of perception is greater than the precision of the motor action, and could be considered a case of stochastic resonance. The strategies that both novices and experts used distinguished only in the parameter values of linear regression models and distances (see Goodman *et al.*, 2009).

Hwang *et al.* (2008) adopted the linear time invariant auto-regressive moving average exogeneous (ARMAX) process to model the aiming trajectory of skilled archers at a distance of 70 m. Both of the vertical and the horizontal deviations were studied instead of the radius or score only. The proposed order-three auto-regressive part was used to represent the stable exponential decay and the oscillation of the aiming trajectory. The magnitude of associated poles of the auto-regressive part whether slightly greater than one was used to determine the fairness of the proposed model. Subsequently, the moving average part was related to the muscle strength and stability of archers. The exogenous part was initially designed to model the adjustment of the deviation between the aiming point and the center of target (Hwang *et al.*, 2008).

Baca and Kornfeind (2012) analyzed the stability of the aiming process of elite biathlon athletes using a special variant of an artificial network of type SOM (self-organizing map; DyCoN, Perl 2004a, 2004b; Figure 34.5). The horizontal and vertical motion of the muzzle was divided into ten time intervals of equal duration. Eight kinematic parameters were calculated describing the motion in these intervals and the artificial network was trained. Similar neurons were combined into clusters. For each shot, the ten data sets describing the aiming process were then mapped to the corresponding neurons. The sequence of the related clusters in the respective succession was used as a representation of the complex aiming motion. In a second processing step, types of shots were identified, applying a second net. A more stable pattern could be inferred for the members of the national squad compared to the biathletes classified in the next best performance level. Only small differences between the two tested shooting conditions (one target five times or all five targets) could be observed.

Perspectives

Virtually every aspect in athletes' performance and preparation could be dissected analyzed and improved. However, it seems that the balance has been tilted towards technological developments that are pushed on athletes and support staff and then have been frequently changed, creating confusion and discomfort.

(Baca et al.*, 2009)*

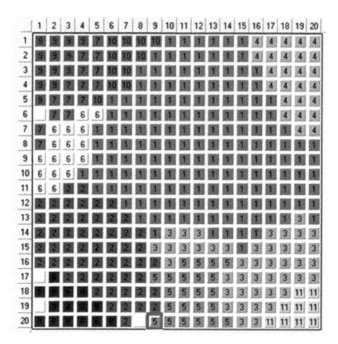

Figure 34.5 Artificial neural network for analyzing the aiming process in biathlon shooting

When performance needs to be analyzed at a more specific level, the results of research studies assessing athletes' performance have to be brought into praxis. This applies for most sports and is particularly true for shooting disciplines.

However, the level of complexity rises if systems are to provide useful information derived from the collected data rather than passing just the sensor data. Such systems perform deeper computational and logical analysis by detecting patterns and complex relationships and by extracting summary-type information that addresses directly users' needs (Baca *et al.*, 2009). They directly supply a higher level of organized information, leaving only the decision making to the end users.

In performance analysis of target shooting, one first attempt was presented by Silva *et al.* (2009). Their prototype system for air rifle/pistol shooting provides recommendations to the coach based on some input data from the shooter and fuzzy rules.

There will be continuing progress towards intelligent systems due to the availability of algorithms for fast and/or accurate data processing (Baca *et al.*, 2009). This will also enable automatic feedback provision.

Concluding remarks

This chapter has described performance indicators in different target sport disciplines with a focus on Olympic sports. After a short introduction, movement kinematics in terms of posture balance and aiming stability has been reviewed for air rifle, pistol, shotgun, and archery shooting. Besides several psychophysiological aspects of shooting, there are also other external and internal effects influencing the performance. The main methods for acquisition have been presented and some remarkable ideas of analysis have been introduced. A development towards intelligent systems is expected in future.

References

Aalto, H., Pyykkö, I., Ilmarinen, R., Kähkönen, E., and Starck, J. (1990) 'Postural stability in shooters', *Journal for Oto-Rhino-Laryngology and its Related Specialties*, 52(4): 232–8.

Alain, C. and Avon, G. (1976) 'A measurement technique for stability as applied in rifle shooting', *Behavior Research Methods and Instrumentation*, 8(1): 5–7.

Baca, A. and Kornfeind, P. (2006) 'Rapid feedback systems for elite sports training', *IEEE Pervasive Computing*, 5(4): 70–6.

Baca, A. and Kornfeind, P. (2012) 'Stability analysis of motion patterns in biathlon shooting', *Human Movement Science*, 31(2): 295–302.

Baca, A., Dabnichki, P., Heller, M., and Kornfeind, P. (2009) 'Ubiquitous computing in sports: A review and analysis', *Journal of Sports Sciences*, 27(12): 1335–46.

Ball, K., Best, R., and Wrigley, T. (2003a) 'Body sway, aim point fluctuation and performance in rifle shooters: Inter- and intra-individual analysis', *Journal of Sports Sciences*, 21: 559–66.

Ball, K., Best, R., and Wrigley, T. (2003b) 'Inter- and intra-individual analysis in elite sport: Pistol shooting', *Journal of Applied Biomechanics*, 19(1): 28–38.

Cacioppo, J.Y. and Tassinary, L.G. (1990) *Principles of Psychophysiology: Physical, Social and Inferential Elements*, Cambridge: Cambridge University Press.

Carrillo, A.E., Christodoulou, V.X., Koutedakis, Y., and Flouris, A.D. (2011) 'Autonomic nervous system modulation during an archery competition in novice and experienced adolescent archers', *Journal of Sports Sciences*, 29(9): 913–17.

Causer, J., Bennett, S.J., Holmes, P.S., Janelle, C.M., and Williams, A.M. (2010) 'Quiet eye duration and gun motion in elite shotgun shooting', *Medicine and Science in Sports and Exercise*, 42(8): 1599–608.

Chandrapal, M., Senanayake, A., and Suwarganda, E. (2009) 'Laser aiming monitoring system for archery', *Proceedings of the IEEE/ASME International Conference on Advanced Intelligent Mechatronics*, 2009: 1154–9.

Collins, D. (1995) 'Psychophysiology and sport performance', in S.J.H. Biddle (ed.), *European Perspectives on Exercise and Sport Psychology* (pp. 154–78). Champaign, IL: Human Kinetics.

Deeny, S.P., Hillman, C.H., Janelle, C.M., and Hatfield, B.D. (2003) 'Cortico-cortical communication and superior performance in skilled marksmen: An EEG coherence analysis', *Journal of Sport and Exercise Psychology*, 25(2): 188–204.

Doppelmayr, M., Finkenzeller, T., and Sauseng, P. (2008) 'Frontal midline theta in the pre-shot phase of rifle shooting: Differences between experts and novices', *Neuropsychologia*, 46(5): 1463–7.

Edelmann-Nusser, J., Gruber, M., and Gollhofer, A. (2002) 'Measurement of on-target-trajectories in Olympic archery', in S.J. Haake (ed.), *The Engineering of Sport I* (pp. 487–93). Oxford: Blackwell Science.

Edelmann-Nusser, J., Heller, M., Hofmann, M., and Ganter, N. (2006) 'On-target trajectories and the final pull in archery', *European Journal of Sport Science*, 6(4): 213–22.

Edelmann-Nusser, J., Heller, M., Ganter, N., Link, D., and Staudinger, J. (2008) 'Erfassung der Visierbewegung bei der Weltmeisterschaft im Bogenschießen 2007 [Aiming trajectories of the sight in the Archery World Championships 2007]', in J. Edelmann-Nusser, E.F. Moritz, V. Senner, and K. Witte (eds), *Sporttechnologie zwischen Theorie und Praxis V* (pp. 67–78). Aachen: Shaker Verlag.

Era, P., Konttinen, N., Mehto, P., Saarela, P., and Lyytinen, H. (1996) 'Postural stability and skilled performance – a study on top-level and naive rifle shooters', *Journal of Biomechanics*, 29(3): 301–6.

Ertan, H., Kentel, B.B., Tümer, S.T., and Korkusuz, F. (2005) 'Reliability and validity testing of an archery chronometer', *Journal of Sports Science and Medicine*, 4(2): 95–104.

Ganter, N., Link, D., Heller, M., and Edelmann-Nusser, J. (2009) 'Aiming trajectories of the sight in the German Archery National Championships', in A. Hökelmann, K. Witte, and P. O'Donoghue (eds), *Current Trends in Performance Analysis: World Congress of Performance Analysis VIII* (pp. 189–194). Aachen: Shaker Verlag.

Goodman, S., Haufler, A., Shim, J.K., and Hatfield, B. (2009) 'Regular and random components in aiming-point trajectory during rifle aiming and shooting', *Journal of Motor Behavior*, 41(4): 367–84.

Grebot, C. and Groslambert, A. (2003) 'Effects of exercise on perceptual estimation and short-term recall of shooting performance in biathlon', *Perceptual and Motor Skills*, 97: 1107–14.

Grebot, C. and Burtheret, A. (2007) 'Effects of temperature changes on the mechanical and ballistic responses in biathlon shooting', *Journal of Applied Mechanics*, 74(5): 1037–41.

Gruber, M., Edelmann-Nusser, J., Seelig, H., and Gollhofer, A. (2002) 'An analysis of the holding area in

Olympic archery', in K.E. Gianikellis (ed.), *Proceedings of the XX International Symposium on Biomechanics in Sports* (pp. 218–21). Cáceras, Spain: ISBS.

Hadani, I. and Bergman, Y. (1980) 'An improved measurement technique for human operator stability in aiming tasks', *Behavior Research Methods and Instrumentation*, 12(5): 571–3.

Hatfield, B.D., Landers, D.M., and Ray, W.J. (1984) 'Cognitive processes during self-paced motor performance: An electroencephalographic profile of skilled marksmen', *Journal of Sport Psychology*, 6(1): 42–59.

Hatfield, B.D., Landers, D.M., and Ray, W.J. (1987) 'Cardiovascular–CNS interactions during a self-paced, intentional attentive state: Elite marksmanship performance', *Psychophysiology*, 24(5): 542–9.

Haufler, A.J., Spalding, T.W., Santa Maria, D.L., and Hatfield, B.D. (2000) 'Neuro-cognitive activity during a self-paced visuospatial task: Comparative EEG profiles in marksmen and novice shooters', *Biological Psychology*, 53(2–3): 131–60.

Helin, P., Sihvonen, T., and Hänninen, O. (1987) 'Timing of the triggering action of shooting in relation to the cardiac cycle', *British Journal of Sports Medicine*, 21(1): 33–6.

Heller, M., Witte, K., Edelmann-Nusser, A., and Zech, A. (2004) 'Longitudinal analysis of surface electromyogram in archery using time-variant spectral analysis', in E. Van Praagh, J. Coudert, N. Fellmann, and P. Duché (eds), *Proceedings of the 9th Annual Congress of the European College of Sport Science* (p. 76). Clermont-Ferrand: University Press.

Heller, M., Baca, A., and Kornfeind, P. (2006a) 'Feedbacksystem im Biathlon – Untersuchungen zum Bewegungsverhalten beim Zielvorgang im Schießen mittels 3D-Bewegungsanalyse [Feedback system in biathlon – 3D motion analysis of the aiming process in shooting]', in K. Witte, J. Edelmann-Nusser, A. Sabo, and E.F. Moritz (eds), *Sporttechnologie zwischen Theorie und Praxis IV* (pp. 259–66). Aachen: Shaker Verlag.

Heller, M., Baca, A., Kornfeind, P., and Baron, R. (2006b) 'Analysis of methods for assessing the aiming process in biathlon shooting', *Proceedings of the XXIV International Symposium on Biomechanics in Sports*, volume 2 (pp. 817–20). Salzburg, Austria: Salzburg University Press.

Herpin, G., Gauchard, G.C., Lion, A., Collet, P., Keller, D., and Perrin, P.P. (2010) 'Sensorimotor specificities in balance control of expert fencers and pistol shooters', *Journal of Electromyography and Kinesiology*, 20(1): 162–9.

Hillman, C.H., Apparies, R.J., Janelle, C.M., and Hatfield, B.D. (2000) 'An electrocortical comparison of executed and rejected shots in skilled marksmen', *Biological Psychology*, 52(1): 71–83.

Hinze, E., Edelmann-Nusser, J., Witte, K., and Heller, M. (2004) 'Körperschwerpunktsschwankungen beim Zielvorgang im Bogenschießen [Oscillations of the body centre of mass during aiming in archery]', in H. Gros, J. Edelmann-Nusser, K. Witte, E.F. Moritz, and K. Roemer, K. (eds), *Sporttechnologie zwischen Theorie und Praxis III* (pp. 165–8). Aachen: Shaker Verlag.

Hoffman, M.D., Gilson, P.M., Westenburg, T.M., and Spencer, W.A. (1992) 'Biathlon shooting performance after exercise of different intensities', *International Journal of Sports Medicine*, 13(3): 270–3.

Holmes, P., Collins, D., and Calmels, C. (2006) 'Electroencephalographic functional equivalence during observation of action', *Journal of Sports Sciences*, 24(6): 605–16.

Hwang, C.K., Lin, J.H., Wu, C.F., and Lin, K.B. (2008) 'Aiming trajectory analysis based on Armax model', *Proceedings of the Seventh International Conference on Machine Learning and Cybernetics*, 2008: 3817–22.

Janelle, C.M., Hillman, C.H., Apparies, R., Murray, N.P., Meili, L., Fallon, E.A., and Hatfield, B.D. (2000) 'Expertise differences in cortical activation and gaze behavior during rifle shooting', *Journal of Sport and Exercise Psychology*, 22(2): 167–82.

Keast, D. and Elliott, B. (1990) 'Fine body movements and the cardiac cycle in archery', *Journal of Sports Sciences*, 8(3): 203–13.

Konttinen, N. and Lyytinen, H. (1992) 'Physiology of preparation: Brain slow waves, heart rate, and respiration preceding triggering in rifle shooting', *International Journal of Sport Psychology*, 23(2): 110–27.

Konttinen, N., Lyytinen, H., and Viitasalo, J. (1998) 'Rifle-balancing in precision shooting: Behavioral aspects and psychophysiological implications', *Scandinavian Journal of Medicine and Science in Sports*, 8: 78–83.

Konttinen, N., Lyytinen, H., and Era, P. (1999) 'Brain slow potentials and postural sway behavior during sharpshooting performance', *Journal of Motor Behavior*, 31(1): 11–20.

Konttinen, N., Landers, D.M., and Lyytinen, H. (2000) 'Aiming routines and their electrocortical concomitants among competitive rifle shooters', *Scandinavian Journal of Medicine and Science in Sports*, 10: 169–77.

Konttinen, N., Mets, T., Lyytinen, H., and Paananen, M. (2003) 'Timing of triggering in relation to the cardiac cycle in novice rifle shooters', *Research Quarterly for Exercise and Sport*, 74(4): 395–400.

Landers, D.M., Han, M., Salazar, W., Petruzzello, S.J., Kubitz, K.A., and Gannon, T.L. (1994) 'Effects of learning on electroencephalographic and electrocardiographic patterns in novice archers', *International Journal of Sport Psychology*, 25(3), 313–30.

Leroyer, P., van Hoecke, J., and Helal, J.N. (1993) 'Biomechanical study of the final push-pull in archery', *Journal of Sports Sciences*, 11(1): 63–9.

Loke, Y.L., Gopalai, A.A., Khoo, B.H., and Senanayake, S.M.N.A (2009) 'Smart system for archery using ultrasound sensors', *IEEE/ASME International Conference on Advanced Intelligent Mechatronics*, 2009: 1160–4.

Loze, G.M., Collins, D., and Holmes, P.S. (2001) 'Pre-shot EEG alpha-power reactivity expert air-pistol shooting: A comparison of best and worst shots', *Journal of Sport Sciences*, 19(9): 727–33.

Mason, B.R. and Pelgrim, P.P. (1986) 'Body stability and performance in archery', *Excel*, 3(2): 17–20.

Mason, B.R., Cowan, L.F., and Gonczol, T. (1990) 'Biomechanical factors affecting accuracy in pistol shooting', *Excel*, 6(4): 2–6.

Mets, T., Konttinen, N., and Lyytinen, H. (2007) 'Shot placement within cardiac cycle in junior elite rifle shooters', *Psychology of Sport and Exercise*, 8(2): 69–177.

Mononen, K., Viitasalo, J., Konttinen, N., and Era, P. (2003) 'The effects of augmented kinematic feedback on motor skill learning in rifle shooting', *Journal of Sports Sciences*, 21(10): 867–76.

Mononen, K., Konttinen, N., Viitasalo, J., and Era, P. (2007) 'Relationships between postural balance, rifle stability and shooting accuracy among novice rifle shooters', *Scandinavian Journal of Medicine and Science in Sports*, 17: 180–5.

Niinimaa, V. and McAvoy, T. (1983) 'Influence of exercise on body sway in the standing rifle shooting position', *Canadian Journal of Applied Sport Sciences*, 8(1): 30–3.

Nitzsche, K. and Koch, M. (2000) 'Entwicklung eines Messplatzes zur Objektivierung der Biathlon-schießleistung [Development of a measuring station for objectively assessing shooting performance in biathlon]', *Leipziger Sportwissenschaftliche Beiträge*, 41(1): 58–89.

Pellegrini, B. and Schena, F. (2005) 'Characterization of arm-gun movement during air pistol aiming phase', *Journal of Sports Medicine and Physical Fitness*, 45(4): 467–75.

Perl, J. (2004a) 'Artificial neural networks in motor control research', *Clinical Biomechanics*, 19(9): 873–5.

Perl, J. (2004b) 'A neural network approach to movement pattern analysis', *Human Movement Science*, 23(5): 605–20.

Salazar, W., Landers, D.M., Petruzzello, S.J., and Han, M. (1990) 'Hemispheric asymmetry, cardiac response, and performance in elite archers', *Research Quarterly for Exercise and Sport*, 61(4): 351–9.

Silva, H.L.K., Uthuranga, S.D., Shiyamala, B., Kumarasiri, W.C.M., Walisundara, H.B., and Karunarathne, G.T.I (2009) 'A trainer system for air rifle/pistol shooting', Proceedings of the Second International Conference on Machine Vision, ICMV 2009: 236–41.

Soylu, A.R., Ertan, H., and Korkusuz, F. (2006) 'Archery performance level and repeatability of event-related EMG', *Human Movement Science*, 25(6): 767–74.

Tang, W.T., Zhang, W.Y., Huang, C.C., Young, M.S., and Hwang, I.S. (2008) 'Postural tremor and control of the upper limb in air pistol shooters', *Journal of Sports Sciences*, 26(14): 1579–87.

Tremayne, P. and Barry, R.J. (2001) 'Elite pistol shooters: Physiological patterning of best vs. worst shots', *International Journal of Psychophysiology*, 41(1): 19–29.

Vickers, J.N. (1996) 'Visual control when aiming at a far target', *Journal of Experimental Psychology: Human Perception and Performance*, 22(2): 342–54.

Vickers, J.N. and Williams, A.M. (2007) 'Performing under pressure: The effects of physiological arousal, cognitive anxiety, and gaze control in biathlon', *Journal of Motor Behavior*, 39(5): 381–94.

Yuan, C.H. and Lee, Y.H. (1997) 'Effects of rifle weight and handling length on shooting performance', *Applied Ergonomics*, 28(2): 121–7.

Zanevskyy, I., Korostylova, Y., and Mykhaylov, V. (2009) 'Specificity of shooting training with the opto-electronic target', *Acta of Bioengineering and Biomechanics*, 11(4): 63–70.

Zatsiorsky, V.M. and Aktov, A.V. (1990) 'Biomechanics of highly precise movements: The aiming process in air rifle shooting', *Journal of Biomechanics*, 23(1): 35–41.

35

SWIMMING, RUNNING, CYCLING AND TRIATHLON

Daniel A. Marinho[1,2], Tiago M. Barbosa[2,3], Henrique P. Neiva[1,2], Mário J. Costa[2], Nuno D. Garrido[2,4] and António J. Silva[2,4]

[1]UNIVERSITY OF BEIRA INTERIOR, PORTUGAL

[2]RESEARCH CENTRE IN SPORTS, HEALTH AND HUMAN DEVELOPMENT, PORTUGAL

[3]NANYANG TECHNOLOGICAL UNIVERSITY, SINGAPORE

[4]UNIVERSITY OF TRÁS-OS-MONTES AND ALTO DOURO, VILA REAL, PORTUGAL

Summary

This chapter covers performance in cyclic sports activities, specifically swimming, running, cycling and triathlon, and the relevant performance indicators in each sport. Different approaches to monitoring performance in each sport are covered, as well as how coaches and athletes can use scientific evidence within coaching practice. Hence, the challenges of different strokes in swimming, the transitions in triathlon and different types of tactics at different distances in running and in cycling will be addressed during this chapter.

Introduction

Enhancing performance is the main goal for athletes, coaches, performance directors and researchers. Indeed, sports performance research has helped them to understand factors that determine athlete performance and to address several concerns regarding how one can control and evaluate these factors. The success of a training program is largely dependent upon satisfying the performance aims associated with it. Therefore, the evaluation and control of the training process can be used to: (i) try to predict future performance; (ii) identify athletes' weaknesses; (iii) measure improvements; (iv) place the athlete in an appropriate training group and with appropriate training tasks; and (v) motivate the athlete (Marinho *et al.*, 2009a).

This chapter presents a background to sports performance and to different approaches to monitoring performance, considering the role of performance indicators in individual, closed and cyclic sports. The authors will focus on underlying similar characteristics between swimming, running, cycling and triathlon, but will also identify differences between each sport that can influence performance. Practical implications for sports performance that can help athletes and coaches enhance performance will also be covered. In fact, how coaches and athletes can use scientific evidence in their daily activity, using coach-friendly language, will be reinforced within this book chapter.

In sports such as swimming, running, cycling and triathlon, the performance is mainly dependent on the interaction between several factors. Biomechanical and energetic factors are regularly considered to be the most important for performance (Barbosa *et al.*, 2010a; Leirdal and Ettema, 2011). Biomechanics comprises kinematics, kinetics, neuromuscular analysis, biological maturation and anthropometric characteristics. Energetic variables comprise variables related to aerobic and anaerobic performance, cardio-respiratory profile, energy cost and efficiency (Barbosa *et al.*, 2011; Costa *et al.*, 2011). However, biomechanical and physiological factors are influenced by domains such as genetics, motor control and anthropometrics (Figure 35.1).

A large part of the research dedicated to competitive sports aims to identify variables that determine performance. This can be considered as an exploratory research trend. The aim of exploratory research is to identify which of several biomechanical and physiological variables are associated with or related to performance. This type of research has been developed based on: (i) applying exploratory regression models; (ii) comparing cohort groups; and (iii) implementing neural network procedures (Barbosa *et al.*, 2010b).

One possibility is to develop statistical models to identify the best predictors of athlete performance (González-Badillo and Marques, 2010; Young *et al.*, 2002). Another option is to compare cohort groups using mean values or analyzing the variation of some selected biomechanical and physiological variables between athletes of different competitive levels. For example, one can compare expert versus non-expert athletes (Baker *et al.*, 2005; Seifert *et al.*, 2007), national-level versus international/elite-level athletes (Hanon *et al.*, 2011; Jesus *et al.*, 2011) or the performances of World Championship and Olympic Games finalists versus non-finalists (Bourgois *et al.*, 2000; Cappaert *et al.*, 1996). Artificial neural networks are a recent approach to solving complex problems, and attempts have been made to predict sports performance using them (Hahn, 2006; Perl, 2004). Neural networks have also been used in talent identification processes, helping to make judgments about future performance levels based on the present individual skills and abilities. This is in contrast to contemporary cybernetic approaches to sports sciences where athletes are viewed as closed circuits and, thereby, an incoming training stimulus drives an equivalent outcome response represented as improved performance (Shestakov, 2005; Silva *et al.*, 2007).

More recently, confirmatory data analysis has become a topic of interest for sports scientists. Such research designs aim to understand the relationships between the variables identified in previous studies and to model the links between them and performance (Barbosa *et al.*, 2010a). This approach consists of a mathematical model for testing and estimating causal

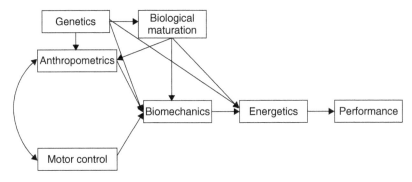

Figure 35.1 Relationships between swimming, running, cycling and triathlon performance and determinant domains

relationships using both statistical data and qualitative causal assumptions, previously hypothesized by researchers, that need to be confirmed or otherwise.

This procedure not only identifies variables, but also indicates the types of interactions between them (Barbosa et al., 2010b). Structural equation modeling analyses the hypothetical relationships between several biomechanical and energetic variables and sports performance and evaluates the resulting model's goodness-of-fit. Although this approach is used on a regular basis in sports psychology (Haney and Long, 1995; Spreitzer and Snyder, 1976), it is not so popular regarding energetics and biomechanical influence on sports performance; this is the case in swimming, running, cycling and triathlon. However, some attempts have been made to apply this procedure in these sports (Barbosa et al., 2010a; Morais et al., in press).

Swimming

Energetics of swimming

Aerobic and anaerobic profile

Swimming performance has been related to maximal total energy release and energy cost (Barbosa et al., 2006; Zamparo, 2006). Indeed, Wakayoshi et al. (1995) reported that energy expenditure correlated negatively with swimming performance. Moreover, considering energetic variables, swimming performance is dependent on aerobic and anaerobic parameters (Laffite et al., 2004). Several authors have reported that maximal oxygen uptake ($\dot{V}O_{2max}$) and lactate threshold were considered good swimming performance predictors (Rodriguez and Mader, 2003; van Handel et al., 1988). Additionally, some authors have reported the analysis of the accumulated oxygen deficit or peak post-exercise blood lactate and the subsequent anaerobic contribution to total energy expenditure for swimming performances (Figueiredo et al., 2011; Reis et al., 2010; Troup, 1992). Hence, physiological profile is one of the most relevant factors to enhance swimming performance.

In swimming, the contribution of the aerobic and anaerobic energy sources to total energy expenditure was shown to be independent of swimming technique, gender and skill (Zamparo et al., 2010). This contribution depends mostly on the duration of the race event (Capelli et al., 1998). At 45.7, 91.4 and 182.9 m (i.e. 50, 100 and 200 yards), Capelli et al. (1998) found that the aerobic component had a contribution to total energy expenditure of 15.3, 33.3 and 61.5 percent, respectively, for the front crawl stroke, 17.4, 36.4 and 59.2 percent, respectively, for the backstroke, 27.1, 46.5 and 67.9 percent, respectively, for the breaststroke and 16.9, 33.3 and 61.1 percent, respectively, for the butterfly. Capelli et al. (1998) also reported that the anaerobic alactic system contributed 20–25 percent (50 yards), 18–20 percent (100 yards) and 10–13 percent (200 yards) of the total energy for swimming different distances. These authors highlighted the important role of the anaerobic component to short-distance events (50 m and 100 m) and the major role of the aerobic component to events lasting at least two minutes (200 m). More recently, Figueiredo et al. (2011) reported a mean contribution of 65.9 ± 1.57 percent of aerobic sources during a 200 m front crawl test, which is similar to the 65 percent found by Ogita (2006) for a 2–3 min bout. Moreover, for the 400 m event, Rodriguez and Mader (2003), Laffite et al. (2004) and Reis et al. (2010) reported an aerobic contribution of 83.2, 81.1 and 95 percent, respectively. Some differences in the percentage contributions reported in the above-mentioned studies have to be attributed to the athlete samples used and their performance levels, but also to the methods used to estimate each of the energy components, particularly the alactic anaerobic one (Figueiredo et al., 2011). Although, as has been indicated by Gastin

(2001), the methods by which energy release is determined have a significant influence on the relative contribution of the energy systems during periods of maximal exercise, these data seem to be relevant for swimming coaches when preparing training protocols. The relative contribution of each energy system to overall energy of different events can be used to focus special care on different training sessions (Marinho *et al.*, 2006).

Biomechanics of swimming

Kinematics

Swimming velocity can be described by its independent variables: stroke length and stroke rate. Increases or decreases in swimming velocity are determined by combined increases or decreases in stroke rate and stroke length, respectively (Craig *et al.*, 1985; Kjendlie *et al.*, 2006; Toussaint *et al.*, 2006). Stroke length is defined as being the distance that the body travels during a full stroke cycle, and stroke rate is defined as being the number of full strokes performed within a given period of time. The relationship between stroke length, stroke rate and swimming velocity for different events (race distance and stroke technique) has been one of the major points of interest in biomechanical research of competitive swimming since the pioneering study of East (1970). Throughout an event, the decrease in swimming velocity is related to a decrease in stroke length in all swimming strokes (Craig *et al.*, 1985; Hay and Guimarães, 1983). Moreover, swimmers try to increase velocity, maintaining stroke length as high and constant as possible and increasing the stroke rate (Craig *et al.*, 1985). Stroke length seems to represent an important parameter to verify differences between elite and non-elite swimmers. Indeed, for a given event, high-level swimmers have higher values for stroke length than lower-level swimmers (Leblanc *et al.*, 2007; Seifert *et al.*, 2008). Comparing several race distances, in longer events, all stroke parameters have a tendency to decrease (Craig and Pendergast, 1979; Seifert *et al.*, 2008). Comparing swimming strokes by distance, there is a trend for stroke rate and velocity to decrease and a slight maintenance of stroke length with increasing distances (Jesus *et al.*, 2011; Chollet *et al.*, 1996).

One other variable often used to assess stroke cycle kinematics is the stroke index, considered as an estimator for overall swimming efficiency (Costill *et al.*, 1985). This parameter assumes that, at a given velocity, the swimmer with greater stroke length has the most efficient swimming technique. Regarding swimming techniques, the front crawl is the one with the highest stroke index, followed by backstroke, butterfly and breaststroke (Sánchez and Arellano, 2002). Regarding swimming distance, Sánchez and Arellano (2002) reported a trend for stroke index decrease from the 50 m to the 200 m events, except in the breaststroke. Nevertheless, Jesus *et al.* (2011) did not find the same decrease in stroke index from shorter to longer distances in World Championship finalists. There was only a significant effect of distance on stroke index for the female swimmers. Regarding swimming level, higher-level swimmers have higher efficiency, which is reflected by a higher stroke index (Jesus *et al.*, 2011; Sánchez and Arellano, 2002).

When comparing World Championship medalists and remaining finalists, there were no significant differences in stroke kinematics between medalists and non-medalists (Jesus *et al.*, 2011). Jesus *et al.* (2011) suggested that differences between them might be explained by other variables, such as limb kinematics and anthropometrics. However, some papers report that the prediction of children's swimming performance can be based on kinematic variables. Saavedra *et al.* (2003) and Vitor and Böhme (2010) reported that the stroke index for boys and the mean velocity of a 50 m maximal bout for girls were included in final prediction models. Moreover, in both genders, from 9 to 22 years old, increases in the swim velocity for the 50 m freestyle event occur due to increases in stroke length and stroke index (Morales *et al.*, 2010).

Stroke length, stroke rate and stroke index depend on limb kinematics. For all swimming techniques, the last phases of the underwater stroke cycle have been presented as having a determinant role for propulsion (Schleihauf, 1979). Higher swimming velocities are achieved by increasing the partial duration and the propulsive force during the final actions of underwater curvilinear trajectories (Barbosa *et al.*, 2011), especially during the insweep and upsweep phases of the front crawl and butterfly, the insweep phase of the breaststroke and the downsweep phase of the backstroke. Even if most of the propulsion (85 to 90 percent) is generated by upper-limb actions in front crawl (Deschodt, 1999; Hollander *et al.*, 1988), lower-limb propulsion should not be disregarded. Therefore, Arellano *et al.* (2006) suggested that the reduction of the kick amplitude and the increase in kick frequency combined with the increase of knee angle during the downbeat to increase the swimmer's velocity. This remark can also be applied in the other swimming techniques, with the exception of breaststroke, since lower-limb actions in this technique are very different. During the breaststroke, analysis has been done on the total time gap between upper- and lower-limb propulsive actions (Seifert and Chollet, 2008) and on the differences between undulation and flat variation of this technique (Persyn *et al.*, 1991). However, Lyttle and Keys (2006) modeled swimmers performing two kinds of underwater dolphin kick and demonstrated an advantage of using a high-amplitude and low-frequency dolphin kick over a small, fast kick based on the velocity range with which underwater dolphin kicks are used. In addition, changes were also made to the input kinematics (ankle plantar flexion angle) to demonstrate that when gliding at 2.18 m.s^{-1}, a 10° increase in ankle plantar flexion could create greater propulsive force during the kick cycle. These results demonstrated that increasing angle flexibility could increase stroke efficiency during lower-limb actions.

Swimming velocity and the swimming energy cost are also dependent on the intra-cyclic variation in horizontal velocity. Higher velocities lead to lower intra-cyclic variation in horizontal velocity. In addition, increasing intra-cyclic variation in horizontal velocity leads to an increase in the energy cost of swimming, even when controlling for the effect of the velocity (Barbosa *et al.*, 2006). Lower intra-cyclic variation in horizontal velocity leads to higher swim efficiency in all swimming techniques. However, in breaststroke and butterfly, higher intra-cyclic variation can be observed. For instance, during the breaststroke, more pronounced body waving imposes a decrease in intra-cyclic variation in horizontal velocity (Sanders *et al.*, 1998; Silva *et al.*, 2002). During the butterfly stroke, a low velocity during hand entry, a high hand velocity during the upsweep and a high velocity of the second downbeat will decrease the intra-cyclic variation and thus lower the energy cost and enhance swimming performance (Barbosa *et al.*, 2008).

Kinetics

Kinetic analysis in swimming has addressed the understanding of two main topics of interest: (i) the propulsive force generated by the propelling segments; and (ii) the drag forces resisting forward motion, since the interaction between both forces will influence the swimmer's velocity.

Regarding propulsive force, most research has been developed on upper-limb propulsion and less attention has been given to the lower limbs. This is probably because of difficulties involving direct measurement of propulsive forces acting on a free swimming subject (Marinho *et al.*, 2009b) and because of the minor relative importance of the lower limbs to overall swimming propulsion (Deschodt, 1999). Thus, one of the most discussed issues in swimming hydrodynamics research is the relative contribution of drag and lift forces to overall upper-limb propulsion. Sato and Hino (2002) used a numerical approach, finding values for drag coefficient to be higher than those for lift coefficient at all angles of attack. From the results of these simulations, the authors concluded that the resultant force was maximal with an angle of attack of the hand of 105° and the direction of the resultant force in that situation was −13°. Based on this analysis, Sato and Hino (2002) suggested that swimmers should stroke backward and with a little-finger-ward, outsweep motion, to produce the maximum thrust during the stroke. Schleihauf (1979) also reported that lift coefficient values increased up to an attack angle around 40° and then decreased. Drag coefficient values increased when the attack angle was increased and they were less sensitive to sweepback angle changes. In a more detail analysis, Bixler and Riewald (2002) found that hand drag had a minimum value near angles of attack of 0° and 180° and a maximum value was obtained near 90°, when the hand was nearly perpendicular to the flow. Hand lift was almost negligible at 95° and peaked near 60° and 150°. Recently, Marinho *et al.* (2011a) confirmed the supremacy of the drag component of the propulsive force, although an important contribution of lift force to the overall propulsive force production by the hand/forearm, in swimming phases when the angle of attack was close to 45°.

Understanding the basis of the propulsive force production can play an important role in swimmers' technical training and performance. The fingers' relative position during the underwater path of the stroke cycle is one of these cases. A large inter-subject range for fingers' relative position can be observed during training and competition, with respect to finger-spreading and thumb position (Marinho *et al.*, 2010a, 2009c). Marinho *et al.* (2010a) found that for angles of attack higher than 30°, the model with little distance between fingers presented higher values for drag coefficient compared to the models with fingers closed and with a large finger spread. For attack angles of 0°, 15° and 30°, the values of drag coefficient were very similar in the three models of the swimmer's hand. In addition, the lift coefficient seemed to be independent of finger spread, showing few differences between the three models. However, Marinho *et al.* (2010a) were able to note slightly lower values for lift coefficient for the position with larger distance between fingers. These results suggested that swimmers create more propulsive force with the fingers slightly spread. Moreover, Marinho *et al.* (2010b) showed that the position with the thumb adducted yielded slightly higher values for drag coefficient compared to thumb-abducted positions. Furthermore, the position with the thumb fully abducted allowed an increase of the lift coefficient of the hand at angles of attack of 0° and 45°. Although there are some differences in the results of different studies (Schleihauf, 1979; Takagi *et al.*, 2001; Marinho *et al.*, 2010b), the main results seem to indicate that, when the thumb leads the motion (sweep back angle of 0°), especially during insweep phases, a hand position with the thumb abducted would be preferable to an adducted thumb position.

Regarding drag, this force can be defined as an external force that acts on the swimmer's body parallel to, but in the opposite direction to, their movement direction. It depends on the swimmer's anthropometric characteristics, equipment characteristics, physical characteristics of the water and the swimming technique (Marinho *et al.*, 2011b). Kjendlie and Stallman (2008) found that active drag in adults was significantly higher than in children. This difference between adults and children was mostly due to different size and velocity during swimming. In addition, Marinho *et al.* (2010b) also studied active drag comparing boys and girls, reporting that there were no differences between them. This was due to the similar values of body mass and height in boys and girls found in this particular study.

Total drag consists of the frictional, pressure and wave drag components. Frictional drag is dependent on water viscosity and generates shear stress in the boundary layer. The intensity of this component is mainly due to the wet surface area of the body, the characteristics of this surface and the flow conditions inside the boundary layer. Pressure or form drag is the result of a pressure differential between the front and the rear of the swimmer, depending on velocity, the density of water and the swimmer's cross-sectional area. Near the water surface, due to the interface between two fluids of different densities, the swimmer is constrained by the formation of surface waves, leading to wave drag (Toussaint and Truijens, 2005).

The contribution of friction, pressure and wave drag components to total drag during swimming is an interesting research issue in sports biomechanics. It is mostly accepted that frictional drag is the smallest component of total drag, especially at higher swimming velocities, although this drag component should not be disregarded in elite-level swimmers. Bixler *et al.* (2007), using a numerical approach, found that friction drag represented about 25 percent of total drag when the swimmer is gliding underwater. Zaidi *et al.* (2008) also reported an important contribution of friction drag (~20 percent) to the total drag when the swimmer is passively gliding underwater. Hence, matters related to sports equipment, shaving and the decrease of immersed body surface should be considered in detail, since this drag component seems to influence performance, especially during the underwater gliding after starts and turns (Barbosa *et al.*, 2011). On the other hand, pressure and wave drag represent the major part of total hydrodynamic drag, thus swimmers must emphasize the most hydrodynamic postures during swimming (Maglischo, 2003; Marinho *et al.*, 2009d). Although wave drag represents a large part of total drag during swimming (Kjendlie and Stallman, 2008), this drag component diminishes significantly when gliding underwater. Lyttle *et al.* (1999) concluded that there is no significant wave drag when a standard adult swimmer is at least 0.6 m under the water's surface. Moreover, Vennell *et al.* (2006) found that a swimmer must be deeper than 1.8 and 2.8 chest depths below the surface for velocities of $0.9\,\mathrm{m.s^{-1}}$ and $2.0\,\mathrm{m.s^{-1}}$, respectively, to avoid significant wave effects.

Neuromuscular response during swimming

Compared to kinematic and kinetic research studies, neuromuscular assessments have not been used as much in competitive swimming research (Barbosa *et al.*, 2010c). The main aim of this approach is to understand the dynamics of neuromuscular activity between strokes during limb and trunk actions. Ikai *et al.* (1964), in their pioneering study of neuromuscular activity in swimming, showed that the bicep braquialis, the triceps braquialis, the deltoid and grand dorsal were highly activated during strokes, with the elbow extensors presenting a higher activation than the elbow flexors during front crawl, butterfly and breaststroke. Following this study, Lewillie (1973) compared different strokes at different velocities and observed the highest neuromuscular activation for the butterfly when swimming at maximum velocity. Moreover, increasing velocity led to an increase in anterior rectum and triceps surae activation in all strokes. Nuber *et al.* (1986) observed high activation of the latissimus dorsi and pectoralis major during underwater phases of the stroke cycle, whereas supraspinatus, infraspinatus, middle deltoid and serratus anterior showed high activation during the recovery phases of the front crawl, breaststroke and butterfly. Additionally, Pink *et al.* (1991) reported similar activation for the pectoralis major and latissimus dorsi to propel the body and for the infraspinatus to externally rotate the arm at the middle of the arm's recovery during the front crawl. Pink *et al.* (1991) also observed high activation for the three heads of the deltoid and the supraspinatus during the arm's entry and exit. These authors presented an important concern regarding injury problems, especially related to high levels of activation of the serratus anterior and the subscapularis. Therefore, coaches and swimmers should be aware of this to help prevent injuries. Barthels and Adrian (1971) suggested that the trunk movement during the butterfly stroke is associated with lower-limb actions, reflected by the greater activity of the rectus abdominus and the spine erector. In breaststroke, Ruwe *et al.* (1994) demonstrated consistent activation for the serratus anterior and teres minor muscles throughout the stroke cycle.

More recently, neuromuscular response has been used to study muscle fatigue and its relationship to limb kinematics, using spectral analysis procedures, which can give important data to coaches and swimmers (Dimitrov *et al.*, 2006; Figueiredo *et al.*, 2010). For instance, Aujouannet *et al.* (2006) reported that, in a fatigued state, the spatial hand path remained unchanged, with a greater duration of the catch, the insweep and the outsweep phases during the front crawl. Moreover, fatigue analysis showed an increase in latissimos dorsi and triceps braquialis during all-out 100 m front crawl swimming (Stirn *et al.*, 2010). When increasing distance to 200 m, the inability to maintain swimming velocity in the last laps was related to the increase of fatigue indices for the flexor carpi radialis, biceps brachii, triceps brachii, pectoralis major, upper trapezius, rectus femoris and biceps femoris (Figueiredo *et al.*, 2010).

Running

Ageing and gender as factors of running performance

In adults, the time to complete a race gradually increases with age. Marathon running among men and women is generally fastest, as indicated by world records, when individuals are 25–35 years old (Trappe, 2007). Nevertheless, a gradual performance decline should be expected in further years (Leyk *et al.*, 2007; Trappe, 2007). This pattern can be associated with age-related declines in maximal and submaximal cardiorespiratory variables (Quinn *et al.*, 2011). A decline in cardiovascular capacity of 0.5 percent per decade occurs in highly trained distance runners, while a 1.0 percent and 1.5 percent decline per decade occurs in moderately trained and untrained individuals, respectively (Trappe, 2007). Decline in sprint performances are expected with age as well. Sprint performance decline is only in the range of 2.6–4.4 percent per decade in 50–69 year-olds (Leyk *et al.*, 2007). However, this decline becomes more apparent around 65–70 years (Korhonen *et al.*, 2003). The deterioration of overall performance with age is primarily related to reduction in running velocity (5 to 7 percent per decade), stride length and an increase in contact time (Korhonen *et al.*, 2003). Reductions in muscular strength and power may be the cause of this performance decline throughout sprint runners' careers (Quinn *et al.*, 2011). Despite the trend of performance declining with age in both endurance and sprint events, continued running late into life attenuates a decline in physiological function with age and is beneficial for overall health (Trappe, 2007).

Gender-specific differences are also apparent. Female times are about 10 percent (marathon) and 13 percent (half-marathon) above the corresponding times of their age-matched peers (Leyk *et al.*, 2007). Traditionally, $\dot{V}O_{2max}$ has been the most important factor related to endurance running (Morgan and Daniels, 1994; Sjodin and Svedenhag, 1985). Earlier observations reported $\dot{V}O_{2max}$ values of 70–85 (ml.kg^{-1}.min^{-1}) and 60–75 (ml.kg^{-1}.min^{-1}) for international male and female runners, respectively (Davies and Thompson, 1979; Smith *et al.*, 2000). Due to this data, distance performance differences are expected to remain fairly constant in the future (Sparling *et al.*, 1998). In contrast to endurance running, the gap between men and women in sprint running has increased since 1952 (Seiler *et al.*, 2007). Performance differences increased from 10.3 percent in the period 1976–1988 to 11.5 percent for the period 2000–2005 (Seiler *et al.*, 2007). This observed change cannot be explained by declining women's participation in sport, poorer training practice or reduced access to technological developments, but it does coincide with dramatic improvements in the scope and sensitivity of drug testing (Seiler *et al.*, 2007). Added to that, underlying differences in muscle mass may also reflect the true sprint performance differences between males and females (Perez-Gomez *et al.*, 2008).

Tactical factors and running performance

Due to their elite nature, top athletes are known to participate in a substantial number of competitions within the year. In most cases, they compete at the same distance several times within and between major competitions. So, small enhancements in performance from race to race are of trivial importance to be well placed or even win a medal in the most important events. Hopkins and Hewson (2001) determined a smallest worthwhile change of ~1 percent for half and full marathons and ~0.5 percent for shorter endurance events in faster adult male distance runners within one competitive season. Authors also stated that female runners, older runners and faster runners are less variable in their performance than male runners, younger runners and slower runners, when comparing within these three groups. Nevertheless, there are some tactical aspects of racing that runners can improve on from one event to another in order to achieve greater enhancements in performance.

The definition of the optimal pacing strategy during the race is one of the most important topics for long-distance runners. Since pacing strategy is regulated by a complex system that balances the demand for optimal performance, it is important to preserve homeostasis during exercise. Pacing strategies should only be used in exercises lasting longer than 80–100 s (van Ingen Schenau et al., 1994). Based on earlier observations, it seems that the optimal pacing strategy differs between events. Greater running speeds in the 800 m event are achieved in the first lap, and the ability to increase running speed on the second lap is limited (Tucker et al., 2006). On the other hand, in the 5,000 m and 10,000 m events, the first and final kilometers are significantly faster than the middle-kilometer sections (Tucker et al., 2006). The pace during the initial stage of a 5,000 m race can be 3 to 6 percent greater than the average race pace, without negatively impacting performance (Gosztyla et al., 2006). Added to this, conserving energy in the middle part of the race allows higher velocities to be reached in the final stages. This trend to demonstrate an 'end spurt' in the final stage of the race is common in world record breakers. Noakes et al. (2009) observed that, in their quickest mile races, world record athletes run the final lap faster than the second and third laps to overcome their opponents. World-class runners adopt a more aggressive pacing strategy requiring greater efforts than the less experienced runners, probably due to a greater mental commitment and/or a better capacity to run under fatigue (Hanon and Gajer, 2009). So, the acquisition of self-selected pace according to a runner's ability is a major strategy for long-distance running. Faster marathoners tend to run at a more consistent pace compared with slower runners (March et al., 2011). They also have greater aptitude for 'recalling pace' throughout the race. 'Recalling pace' helps runners accurately approach their self-set target pace in a race (Takai, 1998). Competitive runners who used cognitive strategies to monitor their running pace and fatigue reproduced more accurate self-set target times during a 20 km intercollegiate race (Takai, 1998). Age and sex can also be considered determinant factors for pacing in a long-distance race. A recent investigation by March et al. (2011) determined that older athletes and female marathon runners are better pacers than younger and male marathon runners, respectively. Based on this evidence, it seems that the pacing strategy is not purely the result of developing fatigue throughout the race. Instead, it is an aspect that runners should regulate in anticipation, based on individual ability, in order to optimize performance.

Endurance races have a large number of participants. Competitors in such events tend to form groups throughout the race. While most of those groups are characterized by having runners from similar competitive levels, the positioning in a group is a factor determining performance. Approximately 95 percent of elite runners participating in the Fukuoka and Tokyo Marathons maintained a minimum distance of 0.5–1.5 m from other competitors and avoided occupying an angle of ±15 degrees either ahead or behind other runners (Yamaji and Shephard, 1987). It is possible that runners with strategic positioning will benefit from a drafting effect and save more energy during the race. This is even more common if athletes are attempting to win a medal in more than one event during a major championship. In this case, athletes need to run each event several times during the competition, which requires a sufficient recovery between races. Strategically, runners need to find other ways of preserving energy from one event to another. Brown (2005) observed that the female middle-distance runners who competed in both the 800 m and 1,500 m at the 2004 Olympic Games ran at the back of the leading group during the early stages, with the purpose of saving energy for further races. This tactical approach of track positioning will also determine the total distance covered in the race. Despite the race distance being initially determined, runners can run wide on bends to overcome their opponents. This suggests that different runners can cover different distances within the same race. Indeed, the fact of going wide to overtake other runners will require an increase in running velocity and will require a higher amount of energy. Jones and Whipp (2002) observed that the winners of the 800 m and 5,000 m finals during the 2000 Olympic Games were the runners who were able to ration their metabolic resources to better effect by running closer to the actual race distance. So, runners should be conscious of minimizing the distance covered in races and have a good positioning in the group if they wish to optimize their performance.

The tactical factors affecting endurance performance differ from those affecting sprint races. For sprinters, the reaction time to the starter's gun should be especially important, as this is a greater factor in determining the outcome of the race than it would be in longer distance races. Collet (1999) observed that most world-class sprinters try to anticipate the start signal. The procedures presently used to start the Olympic sprint events may also influence reaction time.

Sprint performance also relies strongly on a fast acceleration at the start and on the capacity to maintain a high velocity in the remainder of the race. In this case, the best pacing strategy is an all-out effort, even if this strategy causes a strong reduction in velocity at the end (van Ingen Schenau *et al.*, 1994). The acquisition of maximal speed is mainly limited by the ability to accelerate the legs in forward and backward directions, determining the stride frequency and stride length during the race. Salo *et al.* (2011) reported a large variation in performance patterns among the elite sprinters in terms of stride frequency or stride length reliance. Running velocity seems to be highly dependent on the running technique according to the runners' individual characteristics. In this sense, coaches should take this reliance into account in their training.

Environmental factors and running performance

External factors such as environmental conditions can also influence race finish time. In running events, air temperature, humidity, air pollution (particularly in the marathon) and wind direction should be considered in detail. There is evidence that air temperature has a strong correlation ($r = 0.66$–0.73) with finishing time of races (Vihma, 2010). Marathon performance times are progressively slow in races where temperatures rise above 5–10°C (Ely *et al.*, 2007; Montain *et al.*, 2007). Indeed, elite male and female performances seem to be affected by race temperature similarly (Montain *et al.*, 2007). The results of three Japanese Championship Marathons showed that the difference between the first and one-hundredth-placed finishers was the same in cool (5–10°C) as in warm (15.1–21°C) conditions (Ely *et al.*, 2008). By contrast, increases in air temperature induce a greater penalty in the performance of slower runners (Ely *et al.*, 2007; Vihma, 2010). This negative effect of warmer weather on the finishing times of slower runners remains even throughout races, while in faster runners, the effect of higher race temperatures is a deceleration in the latter stages (Ely *et al.*, 2008). In some cases, withdrawal from the race is an option more likely to be taken by non-elite runners in hot conditions. Vihma (2010) reported that the percentage of non-finishers in the annual Stockholm Marathon from 1980 to 2008 was significantly affected (r = 0.72) by the air temperature and specific humidity. Air pollution is also an important external aspect to be considered during long-distance races since performance depends on an optimal lung function. The air pollution present during marathons rarely exceeds health-based national standards and levels known to affect lung function in laboratory situations (Marr and Ely, 2010). However, air pollution levels above the minimum known to affect lung function during exercise may decline performance by 1.4 percent in the marathon, especially for women (Marr and Ely, 2010).

The effect of wind on sprint times is also of considerable interest to runners and coaches. This environmental factor is a particular problem in outdoor sprint running events, which start and finish at different points on a 400 m track. In some circumstances, wind conditions can delay runners reaching their maximum velocity. The disadvantage of headwind seems to be greater than the benefit of tailwind of the same magnitude (Linthorne, 1994). Several authors used mathematical models to gain new insights into the effect of wind assistance on sprinting performance. The most favorable wind conditions are shown to be a wind speed of no more than 2m.s^{-1}, assisting the athlete in the back straight and around the second bend (Quinn, 2010). In the case of headwind, runners should adopt new tactical approaches or modify certain performance patterns to minimize these conditions. Changes in body lean angle in windy situations have little effect on improving performance (Ward-Smith, 1999a). In addition, the outside lane (lane 8) is shown to be considerably faster than the favored center lanes (Quinn, 2010). The use of improved clothing or covering the hair may also lower wind resistance and, as a consequence, aerodynamic drag (Kyle and Caiozzo, 1986).

In summary, studies in real competition conditions are a more accurate way of analyzing performance behavior than laboratory or field tests. Based on scientific evidence from such studies, coaches and runners can manipulate their training and race strategies accordingly.

Cycling

Energetics of cycling

Cycling performance would appear to be largely dictated by the ability of the cyclist to produce high power outputs at minimal metabolic cost. Physiological factors are known to influence mechanical power production and consequently the cycling performance.

Anaerobic

Anaerobic power in cycling is relevant for sprint cycling. A very high power output during 30 s of cycle sprinting uses essential sources of phosphocreatine degradation and glycogenolysis, ending in lactate production. Phosphocreatine degradation reaches a maximal rate within 10 s and ceases to contribute to energy production (Gaitanos *et al.*, 1993).

High lactate production may be due to contributions of anaerobic glycogen and glucose metabolism (Ward-Smith, 1999b) or due to aerobic overproduction of pyruvate and subsequent conversion to lactate (Conley *et al.*, 2001). The higher the exercise intensity, the higher the rate of energy uptake and release of lactate. For example, it is interesting to note that at three and five minutes after completion of the one-hour world record, lactate levels were 5.2 and 5.1 mmol.L^{-1} (Padilla *et al.*, 2000). Nevertheless, it is well documented that lactate reaction is important for maintaining the cytosolic redox and letting glycolysis continue during intensive exercise. Thus, for a given $\dot{V}O_2$ during cycling, high lactate production is beneficial and its production is even more beneficial if accompanied by a high capacity for lactate and proton transport from the cell. These factors are known to increase with endurance and sprint training (Juel, 1998).

Analyzing the biomechanics of cycling, a higher pedal rate requires greater $\dot{V}O_2$ for a given output because of an increase in internal work for repetitive limb movements (Brisswalter *et al.*, 2000). The contraction time is reduced and blood flow to the type I fiber muscles is enhanced. At the same time, muscle fatigue is reduced in muscle type II fibers. However, when pedal cadence is increased without reduction in force to the pedal, type II muscle fibers become progressively recruited. Increasing type II muscle fiber recruitment will contribute to acidosis because they have less mitochondrial mass to facilitate ATP regeneration and the uptake of protons (Roberts *et al.*, 2004).

Aerobic

Cyclists in long-distance events are well known to have high aerobic power and capacity, in order to accomplish their competition events. There is substantial scientific evidence demonstrating that successful cyclists possess high values of $\dot{V}O_{2max}$ and their lactate threshold (that corresponds to the exercise intensity, eliciting a lactate concentration of $4\,mmol.L^{-1}$) is equivalent to a high percentage of $\dot{V}O_{2max}$ of the cyclist (Fernandez-Garcia *et al.*, 2000). For male cyclists, the mean $\dot{V}O_{2max}$ during Le Tour de France and La Vuelta a España was found to be 73.5 mL. $kg^{-1}.min^{-1}$ and the lactate threshold was observed to be 90 percent of $\dot{V}O_{2max}$ (Fernandez-Garcia *et al.*, 2000). This last parameter has been reported as the highest possible steady state of work intensity that can be maintained for a long period of time. As one could note, the best cyclists could perform high-intensity exercise without increasing blood lactate concentration. Padilla *et al.* (2000) studied road-racing cyclists and found that they have obtained high values of $\dot{V}O_{2max}$ ($78.8\pm3.7\,mL.kg^{-1}.min^{-1}$), high values of maximal heart rate ($192\pm6.0\,beat.min^{-1}$) and high values of peak power ($431.8\pm42.8\,W$).

Pfeiffer *et al.* (1993) have demonstrated that $\dot{V}O_{2max}$ is a strong predictor (r = –0.91) of cycling performance in a 14-day stage race among trained female cyclists. Accordingly, it appears that a reduced $\dot{V}O_{2max}$ may be indicative of fatigue or overtraining, helping coaches to adjust and to re-plan the training process. However, it seems that lactate parameters provide a better predictor of endurance performance than oxygen consumption. $\dot{V}O_{2max}$ is limited by the oxygen supply to the muscle mitochondria (Saltin and Strange, 1992; Wagner, 1995). On the other hand, lactate levels are related to the capacity to transport lactate and hydrogen ions or proton (H^+) out of the muscle fibers, and the capacity of skeletal muscle to utilize lactate. Central factors are expected to limit $\dot{V}O_{2max}$, while the lactate response to exercise is primarily related to peripheral factors in trained athletes. Muscle performance is dependent on the percentage of slow-twitch fibers, the activities of key oxidative enzymes and respiratory capacity (Sjodin and Jacobs, 1981).

Additionally, the power related to the weight of the cyclist is considered determinant to competitive cyclists. A power/weight ratio of more than $5.5\,W.kg^{-1}$ is considered a necessary prerequisite for top-level performance (Palmer *et al.*, 1994). Lucía *et al.* (2001a, 2001b) assessed this variable during the most important cycling road races, and data suggest that high power output to body mass ratio ($\geq6\,W.kg^{-1}$) at maximal or close to maximal intensity is a prerequisite in professional cyclists.

Regarding the efficiency of cycling, recent studies indicated that mechanical efficiency seemed to increase with rising exercise intensity in professional cyclists (Lucía *et al.*, 2002). It seems that these cyclists acquire a high cycling efficiency, allowing them to sustain high work-loads for extended periods of time. This is only possible because they reveal substantial resistance to fatigue of recruited motor units at high submaximal intensities (Lucía *et al.*, 2001a, 2001b). Total volume and workloads, alongside the years dedicated to cycling, could have some impact in this efficiency. Professional riders generally cycle 35,000 km per year and compete for 90 days (Lucía *et al.*, 2002). These facts certainly help to develop different physiological and mechanical adaptations, which improve efficiency. During heavy exercise, the efficiency appears to be positively related to the percentage of type I fibers in the vastus lateralis muscle (Horowtiz *et al.*, 1994). A higher proportion of type I fibers in the muscle is associated with a lower submaximal oxygen cost, and thus a greater gross efficiency (Coyle *et al.*, 1992). This efficiency is a reflection of the increase in aerobic metabolism and related increases in muscle power output.

When cycling, breathing pattern can also influence energy expenditure. The oxygen cost of breathing can be very meaningful in highly fit individuals and has been estimated to be about 15 percent of $\dot{V}O_{2max}$ (Harms, 2000). The work of breathing during heavy exercise compromises leg blood flow to working limb muscle. Consequently, a more efficient breathing pattern may avoid reduction in blood flow to the working muscles.

Heart-rate response seems to be related to course profile. In individual time trial stages of a tour, cyclists have been found to reach a mean value of approximately 171 beat.min⁻¹, while in flat stages they reached an average of 125 beat.min⁻¹. During a mountain stage, mean heart rate values are approximately 132 beat.min⁻¹ (Fernandez-Garcia *et al.*, 2000).

Another important concern is related to dehydration and hyperthermia during endurance cycling performance. Coyle (1999) stated that dehydration during exercise promotes hyperthermia by reducing skin blood flow, sweating rate and thus heat dissipation. The combination of dehydration and hyperthermia during exercise causes large reductions in cardiac output and blood flow to the exercising musculature, and thus has a large potential to prejudice endurance performance (Coyle *et al.*, 1992). Therefore, coaches and cyclists should be aware of nutrition during training and competition to prevent hypoglycemia and attenuate dehydration and hyperthermia, especially in long cycling events.

Biomechanics of cycling

One of the greatest points of interest to researchers is the biomechanics of cycling. Pedaling technique, aerodynamics of the system, bicycle equipment and cyclist and anthropometric characteristics are some of the most important determinants of cycling performance.

Pedaling technique

Pedal rate can influence both the ability to produce power as well as the rate of energy consumption. Abbiss *et al.* (2009) suggested that cadence selection could have a significant influence on cycling performance. Although there is no agreed criterion to support the optimal cadence, the existing literature suggests that it can influence neuromuscular fatigue in active muscle groups (Takaishi *et al.*, 1994). There is a trend for racing cyclists to ride at more than 90 RPM, whereas novice cyclists tend to use lower pedal rates (Garnevale and Gaesser, 1991). Additionally, when the cyclist is using the various gear ratios, cadence varies between 70 and 100 RPM. Optimal and self-selected cadences have been found to be influenced by cycle intensity (Marsh and Martin, 1997), course geography (road slope) (Lucía *et al.*, 2001a) and cycling experience (Marsh and Martin, 1997). Maximal aerobic output allows the cyclist to use higher cadence (Nesi *et al.*, 2005). At the same time, higher cadence causes a higher mechanical power output.

When compared to road cycling, uphill cycling typically corresponds to a higher cadence (Millet *et al.*, 2002) and this higher cadence is also used during drafting (Hausswirth *et al.*, 1999). A single pedal rate is not expected to be beneficial for all cyclists. In its place, the optimal cadence during cycling depends on central (i.e. $\dot{V}O_{2max}$) and peripheral physiological characteristics (i.e. muscle fiber contraction). Much more research is still required in this area since there is considerable discrepancy in the existing literature.

Cadence is shown to affect force effectiveness (Candotti *et al.*, 2007; Loras *et al.*, 2009) and gross efficiency (i.e. Foss and Hallen, 2004, 2005). These are two parameters usually used to indicate the quality of pedaling technique (i.e. Candotti *et al.*, 2007; Korff *et al.*, 2007; Zameziati *et al.*, 2006). Force effectiveness is the ratio between the forces directed 90° on the crank arm and the total force on the pedal. In a mechanically effective pedaling technique, a large component of the generated force is directed perpendicularly on the crank arm. Forces directed otherwise do not contribute to mechanical work rate and the associated energy cost is wasted. However, mechanical constraints within the rider–bicycle system can cause the generation of considerable radial forces (Kautz and Hull, 1993).

Gross efficiency is viewed as an indicator of the total metabolic rate, and it is believed that high gross efficiency is related to good technique in general (Candotti *et al.*, 2007; Zameziati *et al.*, 2006). Some studies have demonstrated a moderate-to-strong relationship between force effectiveness and gross efficiency (Candotti *et al.*, 2007; Zameziati *et al.*, 2006). Leirdal and Ettema (2011) verified that cadence has a negative and similar effect on both force effectiveness and gross efficiency. When the cyclists used higher cadence, force effectiveness was lower and consequently gross efficiency decreased. Higher pedaling rates increase the non-muscular component of the pedal forces and this increasing inertial force affects force effectiveness in a negative way (Kautz and Hull, 1993). Leirdal and Ettema (2011) found no effects regarding body orientation or seat position on gross efficiency, force effectiveness or on the relationship between them.

Aerodynamics

Aerodynamic drag force is composed of two forms of drag: pressure and skin-friction drag (Millet and Candau, 2002). Air resistance while cycling is the primary energy cost factor at high speeds. It is the most determinant performance variable at 50 km.hour^{-1} (Gross *et al.*, 1983; Kyle, 1991) and it represents more than 90 percent of the total resistance of cycling at 30 km.hour^{-1} (Kyle, 1991). Therefore, the configuration of the bicycle and its components, as well as body position of the cyclist, are of great importance, and ways to reduce this drag force have been deeply studied. For a constant power output, decreasing aerodynamic drag would result in an increase in velocity of the cyclist–bicycle system. Considering that the mechanical power output can be assumed to be the sum of the energy used to overcome the total resistive forces (De Groot *et al.*, 1995; di Prampero, 2000), the optimization of aerodynamic drag could be fundamental in enhancing the cyclist's performance. Some of the most important parameters influencing aerodynamic drag are: (i) the combined projected frontal area of cyclist and bicycle; (ii) the drag coefficient; (iii) air density; and (iv) the velocity relative to the air (di Prampero *et al.*, 1979).

The effective frontal area is the dominant component of aerodynamic drag and its estimation allows assessment of the cyclist's profile and the optimal riding position for the drag decrease to be determined (Debraux *et al.*, 2011). Frontal surface area represents the portion of the body which can be seen by an observer placed exactly in front of the body. This pressure drag resultant represents the differential air pressures that exist between the front and rear of a moving body. This is mainly dependent on the general size and shape of the body. Skin-friction drag is the resistance generated by the friction of fluid molecules directly on the surface of the body in motion (Millet and Candau, 2002). Grappe (2009) showed that the relationship between effective frontal area and the air velocity was hyperbolic. Regarding skin drag, a special wax cover allows an increase in the velocity of the cyclist–bicycle system at the same mechanical output for the range of cycling velocities between $8.7\,\text{m.s}^{-1}$ and $11\,\text{m.s}^{-1}$ (Grappe, 2009). The importance of the cyclist cover was confirmed by Oggiano *et al.* (2009), who observed the aerodynamic drag to be dependent on the velocity and the roughness of the textile. However, for greater velocities, these differences were not observed. These findings demonstrated the complexity of the relationship between drag coefficient, air velocity and surface roughness.

It was verified that the drag coefficient decreases when body mass increases (Heil, 2001). It was supposed that a higher body mass corresponds to higher body surface area and consequently should correspond to a higher drag coefficient. However, in road racing, when related to body weight, the frontal drag of the smaller cyclists was greater than larger cyclists (Swain, 1994). Moreover, the ratio of body surface to frontal area is larger in smaller cyclists and creates a greater relative air resistance (Cappeli *et al.*, 1993; Swain, 1994). The variation in the drag coefficient is more complex than evaluating the projected frontal area. Its relation with velocity remains difficult to understand and more research is needed to study its characteristics (Debraux *et al.*, 2011).

Added to the air resistance, one cannot neglect the resistance caused by the rolling wheels. Rolling resistance is caused by the compression of the wheel and/or the ground (di Prampero *et al.*, 1979). At low velocity, this affects power output more than air drag (Faria and Cavanagh, 1978). A small-wheeled bicycle demonstrated more resistance to motion than a large-wheeled one, and thus resistance seemed to be inversely proportional to the radius of the wheel (Faria and Cavanagh, 1978). Tire pressure and the specific characteristics of the tire can also have an effect on rolling resistance. Higher pressure and sew-up tires increase cycling efficiency (Faria and Cavanagh, 1978).

It is important to recognize that the drafting effect is a component that tends to reduce the air forces opposing the cyclists and the energy utilization by approximately 40 percent (Lucía *et al.*, 2001b). Hausswirth *et al.* (1999) verified that at a velocity of $39.3\,\text{km.hour}^{-1}$ drafting resulted in a 14 percent reduction for oxygen consumption, a 7.5 percent reduction for heart rate and a 30 percent reduction for expiratory volume. However, these parameters do not change when the cyclists constantly alternate the lead. Drafting reduces the air resistance in the middle of the pack by as much as 40 percent (McCole *et al.*, 1990), and consequently reduces the energy cost. These details could be important to the race, considering that cyclists can use this information to optimize their performance. The tactics used in interaction with the other cyclists, knowing the importance of energy saving, can lead the cyclist to achieve better results. When racing, the cyclist is integrated in a group of elements competing against each other. At the same time, this group is a dynamical and self-organizing system within which the system's elements also have periods of cooperative interaction (McGarry *et al.*, 2002). Waldron *et al.* (2011) introduced the effect of 'swarming' in cycling, demonstrating the presence of attract-and-repel elements during different points of the race. Simultaneously, they verified that breakaways caused longer attract-and-repel phases, perturbing the system complex. A perturbation is considered an event that causes a disruption in the reciprocal rhythm and stability of a system. This incident can result in a turn of events affecting the performance of cyclists.

Equipment: bicycle and cycle vest

The equipment configuration, bicycle and even the cyclist's clothing influence the cyclist's performance (Gonzales and Hull, 1989; Too, 1991). The seat tube angle is an important variable of equipment configuration that has an effect on performance. Increasing this angle (above 78.5° for the smaller cyclists and above 73.2° for the tallest cyclists) leads to changes in the hip angle and, consequently, changes in the length of the muscles crossing the hip joint. An increased seat height allows a forward and more crouched position, resulting in a decreased air resistance. Subsequently, cycling velocity will increase (Heil *et al.*, 1995). The use of aerodynamic frame and wheels also affects the cyclist's performances. Jeukendrup and Martin (2001) showed improvements of more than two seconds in a 40 km time trial. This improvement in time trials demonstrates the importance of the utilization of correct and appropriate equipment. Moreover, it is also necessary to consider the weight of the equipment and the cyclist's vest in order to get better performances.

Anthropometrics

Time-trial cyclists are usually taller and heavier than uphill cyclists (Padilla *et al.*, 1999). When climbing, the cyclist moves slowly and the force of gravity is the main resistance to overcome. Therefore, an increased body mass has a negative effect on the cyclist's velocity (Swain, 1994). In shorter cycling events, taller cyclists seem to be more successful, while shorter cyclists are more successful at longer distances (Craig and Norton, 2001). The cyclist's anthropometric characteristics are essential and can have an important impact on other biomechanical aspects, as seen before (e.g. aerodynamics), and also on bioenergetics. For instance, Coyle (2005), when analyzing Lance Armstrong, reported that, during the months leading up to each of his seven Tour de France victories, he reduced body mass and body fat by 4–7 kg. Therefore, over a seven-year period, an improvement in muscular efficiency and reduced body fat contributed to a remarkable 18 percent improvement in his steady-state power per kilogram of body mass when cycling at a given O_2. (Editor's note: the US Anti-doping agency stripped Armstrong of the seven Tour de France titles in August 2012.)

Triathlon

Anthropometrics, energetics and biomechanics

An excess of body fat in swimming decreases the body's need to expend more energy to increase the buoyancy and thermal resistance to cold water, due to the subcutaneous layer of adipose tissue. However, during running, energy expenditure is related to body mass by the need to raise and lower the body's center of mass and to accelerate and decelerate the legs, moving the total body weight. In cycling, the athlete has to move their body mass and the mass of the bicycle to produce movement (Bentley *et al.*, 2002; Gnehm *et al.*, 1997). It is possible that smaller triathletes may perform better, taking advantage of the drafting effects in swimming and cycling. However, there is not sufficient scientific evidence for this. The triathlon is a long-duration sport (about two hours) and it is associated with typical aerobic physiological characteristics. Maximal heart rate in triathletes has been observed to be 6 to 10 beat.min^{-1} lower in cycling compared to runners (Roecker *et al.*, 2003). However, there is also evidence that heart rate may not differ between cyclists and runners (Bassett and Howley, 2000). Aerobic capacity has been identified as the main component to maintain high exercise intensity, especially during the running section of the triathlon (Dengel *et al.*, 1989). Athlete performance in the Olympic triathlon is highly correlated with anaerobic threshold (De Vito *et al.*, 1995; Holly *et al.*, 1986). It is suggested that $\dot{V}O_{2max}$ sets the upper limit of the aerobic capacity and the performance depends on the ability of the triathlete to exercise at a higher fractional utilization of the $\dot{V}O_{2max}$ (Coyle,

1995). In contrast to other endurance sports, such as cycling and running, only a few studies reported $\dot{V}O_2$ kinetics parameters in triathletes, and more research is needed on this matter. It is important to notice that a great part of the existing research in triathlon separates the sports when testing, and it is important to be cautious about the possible effects of swimming prior to cycling and of cycling prior to running.

Regarding movement kinetics, the existing literature on triathletes is very scarce. According to Toussaint (1990), the swimmers have a greater distance per stroke and a lower stroke frequency than the triathletes (1.23 m vs. 0.92 m), providing a higher swimming velocity (1.17 m. s^{-1} vs. 0.95 m.s^{-1}). Triathletes require more power to produce movement (~45 W) than swimmers (~32 W). Regarding running, kinematics and muscle recruitment were altered in 46 percent of moderately trained triathletes after a 45-minute cycle (Bonacci et al., 2010). There were registered changes in the angle of the ankle and these were associated with the changing running economy after cycling. On the other hand, in cycling, it has been shown that freely chosen cadence in triathletes is about 90 RPM in submaximal exercise (Lepers et al., 2001), which is close to the cadence used in elite cycling (Lucía et al., 2001b).

Swimming, cycling and running

A successful triathlete takes between one hour 45 minutes and two hours to complete the total Olympic distance. The swimming split is suggested to be 15 percent of their total competition time, with 55 percent spent on the bicycle and 29 percent running (Landers et al., 2008). The two initial sections, swimming and cycling, are important for getting into a good position for the running section. The running section is the section most correlated with the overall performance in the Olympic-distance triathlon (Fröhlich et al., 2008).

Swimming is performed in open water and the conditions (temperature, water salinity, turbulence) are highly variable. When the water is below 20°C, triathletes are allowed to use a wetsuit of a maximum of 5 mm thickness. These wetsuits are believed to increase athletes' performances by reducing drag (Chatard et al., 1995), increasing buoyancy and hydrostatic lift (Chatard and Millet, 1996). Regarding swimming technique, elite swimmers are more efficient than elite triathletes (Toussaint, 1990). Though having a similar stroke rate, the swimmers presented higher stroke length, resulting from greater propelling efficiency (Toussaint, 1990). Therefore, stroke length could be a good parameter to assess the technical improvement of a triathlete during the season. Another important variable which has gathered scientific attention is drafting. This occurrence is related to the effects of the displacement of the athlete when he is immediately behind another. The depression made in the water by a leading swimmer seems to decrease the passive drag of the following swimmers by 10 to 26 percent (Chollet et al., 2000; Millet et al., 2000a). Silva et al. (2008) used computational fluid dynamics to verify lower values of drag coefficient in the back swimmer until ~8 m of distance between the swimmers. Thus, drafting could be beneficial to the energy cost of the swimmer when exposed to suction effect (Bassett et al., 1991; Chatard and Wilson, 2003; Hausswirth et al., 2001). Blood lactate concentration is reduced (from a mean value of 5.0±0.5 to 3.4±0.6 mmol.L^{-1}), as well as rating of perceived exertion (from a mean value of 14.9±0.5 to 11.7±0.4) in the back swimmer (Bassett et al., 1991). Improved swimming economy is also reflected in oxygen consumption (from a mean value of 3.12±0.66 to 2.85±0.63 L.min^{-1}).

In cycling, drafting effect is also experienced by the triathletes. Energy expenditure is correlated with the drag that the cyclist has to overcome during displacement. On the other hand, this depends on the effects of the gravity and the air resistance (di Prampero et al., 1979). Air resistance, and consequently energy expenditure, is reduced by drafting behind another cyclist or a group of cyclists. It was evidenced that drafting behind only a leader or a group of cyclists lowered VO_2, heart rate and blood lactate concentration (Hausswirth *et al.*, 1999). It can also be speculated that weaker athletes can utilize this drafting effect to achieve better performances. Another important parameter usually assessed in cycling is the pedaling cadence. Despite the scarce literature in this matter, it has been observed that pedaling cadence used by triathletes is above 80 RPM (Hausswirth *et al.*, 1999), close to optimal cadence suggested (90 RPM).

After cycling, the athletes have to complete the running distance. This involves some challenges, since the triathletes have to run after having already performed two different sports and have to manage the resulting energy expenditure. Triathletes typically experience a decrease in running economy when running after cycling compared to isolated running (Hausswirth *et al.*, 1997). However, this is related to competitive level. Better triathletes exhibit less impairment in running economy than their lesser performing counterparts (Millet *et al.*, 2000b).

Subsequent effects of each discipline

Millet and Vleck (2000) suggested that the ability to optimally link each discipline (or triathlon segment) is important to the success of the triathlete. Therefore, it is fundamental to know and understand the transitions between sections and the effects of each discipline on the subsequent one.

The transitions between swimming and cycling and between cycling and running correspond to less than 1.3 percent of the overall race time (Millet and Vleck, 2000). Regarding their effect on overall performance, the first transition seems to be negligible. Nevertheless, triathletes can best improve the swimming–to-bicycle change by practicing and developing the techniques involved in equipment changeover (Borchers and Buckenmeyer, 1987). Although the importance of the second transition is unclear, it is known that biomechanical, physiological and sensorial adaptations are required for the cycle–to-run transition (Millet and Vleck, 2000). Leaving their bicycle, taking off their helmet and putting on their running shoes takes about eight seconds and the higher the athlete is placed after that, the greater the importance for finishing position (Millet and Vleck, 2000).

Cycling could be influenced by the previous swimming performance. Energy saving by drafting while swimming can be used as an advantage in later phases of the competition. This could result in improvements in pedaling technique and efficiency during cycling (Delextrat *et al.*, 2003). When comparing cycling performance after drafting swimming, Delextrat *et al.* (2005) observed a lower pedal cadence in association with a higher apparent gross efficiency and greater torque production. Swimming intensity affects the physiology and biomechanics of subsequent cycling and total triathlon performance. Although it is possible that long-course triathlon could not experience these effects, as the race duration decreases, swimming intensity above a given threshold can negatively affect subsequent cycling and running (Peeling and Landers, 2009). Reducing swimming intensity to values of 80–95 percent of the maximum leads the athletes to better overall performance results (Peeling *et al.*, 2005). However, they should be cautious, since the swimming section has great importance in the final triathlon result (Landers *et al.*, 2008).

As shown, previous swimming can affect cycling performance, but it also appears that running could be more affected by previous cycling. Cycling exercise is predominantly concentric, in contrast to running, which involves largely eccentric muscle contractions (or stretching contraction cycles – CAE movements). It seems that, in the first moments after transition, the biomechanics of running during a triathlon is quite different from the biomechanics of running performed in isolation. Nevertheless, the current literature has found no differences in running biomechanics after cycling (Hue *et al.*, 1998). Regarding the energy cost of running at the end of a triathlon event, energy cost is significantly higher when compared to isolated running (Hausswirth *et al.*, 1997; Hue *et al.*, 1998). Negative changes in running performance can occur when preceded by high-intensity cycling. However, these effects are dependent on the level of the athlete, being greater for recreational triathletes than for professional ones (Millet *et al.*, 2000b; Millet and Bentley, 2004). Professional triathletes are well trained and are able to maintain higher relative intensity during the cycling stage, causing minor changes in subsequent exercise. Specific training of cycle–run repetitions, at high intensity, can improve the efficiency of running after cycling (Hue *et al.*, 2002). The drafting within the cycling section is an opportunity for the triathlete to reduce intensity and save energy. This metabolic saving has been shown to influence subsequent running performance (Hausswirth *et al.*, 1999, 2001.) Under these conditions, Hausswirth *et al.* (1999) found an improvement of 4 percent in running performance. At the same time, running time at 85 percent of maximal velocity was significantly increased by adopting a slow cadence (74 RPM) for the final minutes of a 30-minute cycling bout, when compared to a freely chosen cadence or even high cadence (Vercruyssen *et al.*, 2005). These findings suggest that triathletes should use lower pedal cadence at the end of the cycling stage, in order to get more benefits during running performance.

Concluding remarks

During this chapter, the authors have attempted to present different approaches to monitoring performance, considering the role of performance indicators in individual, closed and cyclic sports. Similar characteristics exist between swimming, running, cycling and triathlon but there are also differences between each sport. Performance in these sports is related to biomechanical and physiological aspects. Coaches and athletes should consider kinematics, kinetics, neuromuscular analysis, anthropometrics, aerobic and anaerobic performance, energy cost and efficiency to enhance sports performance. An important focus was carried out to present practical implications for sports performance using scientific evidence to monitor and evaluate the training process.

Moreover, the authors attempted to make some contribution to the dissemination of the main results, stimulating young researchers in the fulfillment of the existing gap between sports science and mainstream sciences and also to bridge the gap between theory and practice.

Acknowledgments

The authors thank Helena Maria Gil for her important help in editing this chapter.

References

Abbiss, C.R., Quod, M.J., Levin, G., Martin, D.T. and Laursen, P.B. (2009) 'Accuracy of the velotron ergometer and SRM power meter', *International Journal of Sports Medicine*, 30: 107–12.
Arellano, R., Nicoli-Terrés, J.M. and Redondo, J.M. (2006) 'Fundamental hydrodynamics of swimming propulsion', *Portuguese Journal of Sport Science*, 6(2): 15–20.
Aujouannet, Y.A., Bonifazi, M., Hintzy, F., Vuillerme, N. and Rouard, A.H. (2006) 'Effects of a high-intensity swim test on kinematic parameters in high-level athletes', *Applied Physiology Nutrition and Metabolism*, 3: 150–8.
Baker, J., Deakin, J. and Côté, J. (2005) 'On the utility of deliberate practice: Predicting performance in ultra-endurance triathletes from training indices', *International Journal of Sport Psychology*, 36: 225–40.
Barbosa, T.M. (in press) *Swimming, Encyclopedia of Exercise Medicine in Health and Disease* (ed.), Berlin: Springer.
Barbosa, T.M., Fernandes, R.J., Keskinen, K.L., Colaço, C., Cardoso, C., Silva, J. and Vilas-Boas, J.P.

(2006) 'Evaluation of the energy expenditure in competitive swimming strokes', *International Journal of Sports Medicine*, 27: 894–9.

Barbosa, T.M., Fernandes, R.J., Morouço, P. and Vilas-Boas, J.P. (2008) 'Predicting the intra-cyclic variation of the velocity of the centre of mass from segmental velocities in butterfly stroke: A pilot study', *Journal of Sports Science and Medicine*, 7: 201–9.

Barbosa, T.M., Costa, M.J., Coelho, J., Moreira, M. and Silva, A.J. (2010a) 'Modeling the links between young swimmers' performance: Energetic and biomechanics profile', *Pediatric Exercise Science*, 22: 379–91.

Barbosa, T.M., Bragada, J.A., Reis, V.M., Marinho, D.A., Carvalho, C. and Silva, J.A. (2010b) 'Energetics and biomechanics as determining factors of swimming performance: Updating the state of the art', *Journal of Science and Medicine in Sports*, 13: 262–9.

Barbosa, T.M., Pinto, E., Cruz, A.M., Marinho, D.A., Silva, A.J., Reis, V.M. and Queirós, T.M. (2010c) 'Evolution on swimming science research: Content analysis of the "Biomechanics and Medicine in Swimming" Proceeding Books from 1971 to 2006', in P.L. Kjendlie, R.K. Stallman and J. Cabri (eds), *Book of Proceedings of the XIth International Symposium on Biomechanics and Medicine in Swimming* (pp. 312–13). Oslo, Norway: Norwegian School of Sport Science.

Barbosa, T.M., Marinho, D.A., Costa, M.J. and Silva, A.J. (2011) 'Biomechanics of competitive swimming strokes', in V. Klika (ed.), *Biomechanics in Applications* (pp. 367–88). Rijeka: InTech.

Barthels, K.M. and Adrian, M.J. (1971) 'Variability in the dolphin kick under four conditions', in L. Lewillie, and J.P. Clarys (eds), *First International Symposium on "Biomechanics in Swimming, Waterpolo and Diving* (pp. 105–18). Brussels: Université Libre de Bruxelles, Laboratoire de L'effort.

Bassett, D.R. and Howley, E.T. (2000) 'Limiting factors for maximum oxygen uptake and determinants of endurance performance', *Medicine and Science in Sports and Exercise*, 32(1): 70–84.

Bassett, D.R., Flohr, J., Duey, W.J., Howley, E.T. and Pein, R.L. (1991) 'Metabolic responses to drafting during front crawl swimming', *Medicine and Science in Sports and Exercise*, 23(6): 744–7.

Bentley, D.J., Millet, G.P., Vleck, V.E. and McNaughton, L.R. (2002) 'Specific aspects of contemporary triathlon: Implications for physiological analysis and performance', *Sports Medicine*, 32(6): 345–59.

Bixler, B.S. and Riewald, S. (2002) 'Analysis of swimmer's hand and arm in steady flow conditions using computational fluid dynamics', *Journal of Biomechanics*, 35: 713–17.

Bixler, B., Pease, D. and Fairhurst, F. (2007) 'The accuracy of computational fluid dynamics analysis of the passive drag of a male swimmer', *Sports Biomechanics*, 6: 81–98.

Bonacci, J., Green, D., Saunders, P.U., Blanch, P., Franettovich, M., Chapman, A.R. and Vicenzino, B. (2010) 'Change in running kinematics after cycling are related to alterations in running economy in triathletes', *Journal of Science and Medicine in Sport*, 13(4): 460–4.

Borchers, G.E. and Buckenmeyer, P.J. (1987) 'Triathlon: The swim to bicycle transition', *Medicine and Science in Sports and Exercise*, 19: 49.

Bourgois, J., Claessens, A.L., Vrijens, J., Philippaerts, R., Van Renterghem, B., Thomis, M., Janssens, M., Loos, R. and Lefevre, J. (2000) 'Anthropometric characteristics of elite male junior rowers', *British Journal of Sports Medicine*, 34(3): 213–16.

Brisswalter, J., Hausswirth, C., Smith, D., Vercruyssen, F. and Vallier, J.M. (2000) 'Energetically optimal cadence vs. freely-chosen cadence during cycling: Effect of exercise duration', *International Journal of Sports Medicine*, 20: 1–5.

Brown, E. (2005) 'Running strategy of female middle distance runners attempting the 800m and 1500m double at a major championship: A performance analysis and qualitative investigation', *International Journal of Performance Analysis in Sport*, 5(3): 73–88.

Candotti, C.T., Ribeiro, J., Soares, D.P., de Oliveira, A.R., Loss, J.F. and Guimarães, A.C.S. (2007) 'Effective force and economy of triathletes and cyclists', *Sports Biomechanics*, 6(1): 31–43.

Capelli, C., Rosa, G., Butti, F., Ferretti, G., Veicsteinas, A. and Di Prampero, P.E. (1993) 'Energy cost and efficiency of riding aerodynamic bicycles', *European Journal of Applied Physiology and Occupational Physiology*, 67(2): 144–9.

Capelli, C., Pendergast, D.R. and Termin, B. (1998) 'Energetics of swimming at maximal speeds in humans', *European Journal of Applied Physiology and Occupational Physiology*, 78(5): 385–93.

Cappaert, J., Pease, D. and Troup, J. (1996) 'Biomechanical highlights of world champion and Olympic swimmers', in J. Troup, A. Hollander, D. Strasse, S. Trappe, J. Cappaert and T. Trappe (eds), *Biomechanics and Medicine in Swimming VII* (pp. 76–80). London: E and FN Spon.

Chatard, J.C. and Millet, G. (1996) 'Effects of wetsuit use in swimming event: Practical recommendations', *Sports Medicine*, 22(2): 70–5.

Chatard, J.C. and Wilson, B. (2003) 'Drafting distance in swimming', *Medicine and Science in Sports and Exercise*, 35(7): 1176–81.

Chatard, J.C., Senegas, X., Selles M., Dreanot, P. and Geyssant, A. (1995) 'Wet suit effect: A comparison between competitive swimmers and triathletes', *Medicine and Science in Sports and Exercise*, 27(4), 580–6.

Chollet, D., Pelayo, P., Tourney, C. and Sidney, M. (1996) 'Comparative analysis of 100 m and 200 m events in the four strokes in top level swimmers', *Journal of Human Movement Studies*, 31: 25–37.

Chollet, D., Hue, O., Auclair, F., Millet, G. and Chatard, J.C. (2000) 'The effects of drafting on stroking variations during swimming in elite male triathletes', *European Journal of Applied Physiology*, 82(5-6): 413–17.

Collet C. (1999) 'Strategic aspects of reaction time in world-class sprinters', *Perceptual and Motor Skills*, 88(1): 65–75.

Conley, K.E., Kemper, W.F. and Crowther, G.J. (2001) 'Limits to sustainable muscle performance: Interaction between glycolysis and oxidative phosphorylation', *Journal of Experimental Biology*, 204: 3189–94.

Costa, M.J., Marinho, D.A., Bragada, J.A., Silva, A.J. and Barbosa, T.M. (2011) 'Stability of elite freestyle performance from childhood to adulthood', *Journal of Sports Science*, 29(11): 1183–9.

Costill, D.L, Kovaleski, J., Porter, D., Fielding, R. and King, D. (1985) 'Energy expenditure during front crawl swimming: Predicting success in middle-distance events', *International Journal of Sports Medicine*, 6: 266–70.

Coyle, E.F. (1995) 'Integration of the physiological factors determining endurance performance ability', *Exercise and Sport Sciences Reviews*, 23: 25–63.

Coyle, E.F. (1999) 'Physiological determinants of endurance exercise performance', *Journal of Science and Medicine in Sport*, 2(3): 181–9.

Coyle, E.F. (2005) 'Improved muscular efficiency displayed as Tour de France champion matures', *Journal of Applied Physiology*, 98(6): 2191–6.

Coyle, E.F., Sidossis, L.S., Horowitz, J.F. and Beltz, J.D. (1992) 'Cycling efficiency is related to the percentage of type I muscle fibers', *Medicine and Science in Sports and Exercise*, 24(7): 782–8.

Craig, A. and Pendergast, D. (1979) 'Relationships of stroke rate, distance per stroke and velocity in competitive swimming', *Medicine and Science in Sports and Exercise*, 11: 278–83.

Craig, N.P., and Norton, K.I. (2001) 'Characteristics of track cycling', *Sports Medicine*, 31(7): 457–68.

Craig, A., Skehan, P., Pawelczyk, J. and Boomer, W. (1985) 'Velocity, stroke rate and distance per stroke during elite swimming competition', *Medicine and Science in Sports and Exercise*, 17: 625–34.

Davies, C.T. and Thompson, M.W. (1979) 'Aerobic performance of female marathon and male ultramarathon athletes', *European Journal of Applied Physiology and Occupational Physiology*, 41: 233–45.

Debraux, P., Grappe, F., Monolova, A.V. and Bertucci, W. (2011) 'Aerodynamic drag in cycling: Methods of assessment', *Sports Biomechanics*, 10(3): 197–218.

De Groot, G., Sargeant, A. and Geysel, J. (1995) 'Air friction and rolling resistance during cycling', *Medicine and Science in Sports and Exercise*, 27: 1090–5.

Delextrat, A., Tricot, V., Bernard, T., Vercruyssen, F., Hausswirth, C. and Brisswalter, J. (2003) 'Drafting during swimming improves efficiency during subsequent cycling', *Medicine and Science in Sports and Exercise*, 35(9): 1612–19.

Delextrat, A., Tricot, V., Bernard, T., Vercruyssen, F., Hausswirth, C. and Brisswalter, J. (2005) 'Modification of cycling biomechanics during a swim-to-cycle trial', *Journal of Applied Biomechanics*, 21(3): 297–308.

Dengel, D.R., Flynn, M.G., Costill, D.L. and Kirwan, J.P. (1989) 'Determinants of success during triathlon competition', *Research Quarterly for Exercise and Sport*, 60(3): 234–8.

Deschodt, V. (1999) 'Relative contribution of arms and legs in humans to propulsion in 25 m sprint front crawl swimming', *European Journal of Applied Physiology*, 80: 192–9.

De Vito, G., Bernardi, M., Sproviero, E. and Figura, F. (1995) 'Decrease of endurance performance during Olympic Triathlon' *International Journal of Sports Medicine*, 16(1): 24–8.

Dimitrov, G.V., Arabadzhiev, T.I., Mileva, K.N., Bowtell, J.L., Crichton, N. and Dimitrova, N.A. (2006) 'Muscle fatigue during dynamic contractions assessed by new spectral indices', *Medicine Science and Sports Exercise*, 38: 1971–9.

di Prampero, P.E. (2000) 'Cycling on earth, in space and on the moon', *European Journal of Applied Physiology*, 82: 345–60.

di Prampero, P.E., Cortili, G., Mognoni, P. and Saibene, F. (1979) 'Equation of motion of a cyclist', *Journal of Applied Physiology*, 47: 201–6.

East, D. (1970) 'Swimming: An analysis of stroke frequency, stroke length and performance', *New Zealand Journal of Health, Physical Education and Recreation*, 3: 16–27.

Ely, M.R., Cheuvront, S.N., Roberts, W.O. and Montain, S.J. (2007) 'Impact of weather on marathon-running performance', *Medicine and Science in Sports and Exercise*, 39(3): 487–93.

Ely, M.R., Martin, D.E., Cheuvront, S.N. and Montain, S.J. (2008) 'Effect of ambient temperature on marathon pacing is dependent on runner ability', *Medicine and Science in Sports and Exercise*, 40(9): 1675–80.

Faria, I.E. and Cavanagh, P.R. (1978) *The Physiology and Biomechanics of the Determinants of Cycling*, New York: John Wiley and Sons.

Fernandez-Garcia, B., Pérez-Landaluce, J., Rodríguez-Alonso, M. and Terrados, N. (2000) 'Intensity of exercise during road race pro-cycling competition', *Medicine and Science in Sports and Exercise*, 32: 1002–6.

Figueiredo, P., Sousa, A., Goncalves, P., Pereira, S.M., Soares, S., Vilas-Boas, J.P. and Fernandes, R.J. (2010) 'Biophysical analysis of the 200m front crawl swimming: A case study', in P.L. Kjendlie, R.K. Stallman and J. Cabri (eds), *Biomechanics and Medicine in Swimming XI* (pp. 79–81). Oslo: Norwegian School of Sport Sciences.

Figueiredo, P., Zamparo, P., Sousa, A., Vilas-Boas, J.P. and Fernandes, R.J. (2011) 'An energy balance of the 200m front crawl race', *European Journal of Applied Physiology*, 111(5): 767–7.

Foss, O. and Hallen, J. (2004) 'The most economical cadence increases with increasing workload', *European Journal of Applied Physiology*, 92: 443–51.

Foss, O. and Hallen, J. (2005) 'Cadence and performance in elite cyclists', *European Journal of Applied Physiology*, 93: 453–62.

Fröhlich, M., Klein, M., Pieter, A., Emrich, E. and Gießing, J. (2008) 'Consequences of the three disciplines on the overall result in Olympic-distance triathlon', *International Journal of Sports Science and Engineering*, 2(4): 204–10.

Gaitanos, G.C., Williams, C., Boobis, L.H. and Brooks, S. (1993) 'Human muscle metabolism during intermittent maximal exercise', *Journal of Applied Physiology*, 75(2): 712–19.

Garnevale, T.G. and Gaesser, G.A. (1991) 'It seems that this cyclists fibrlimiting oxygen, stry, erformace. rmance for.es to contribute to enervegradation and glycogenolys. Effects of pedaling speed on the power–duration relationship for high-intensity exercise', *Medicine and Science in Sports and Exercise*, 23(2): 242–6.

Gastin, P.B. (2001) 'Energy system interaction and relative contribution during maximal exercise', *Sports Medicine*, 31(10): 725–41.

Gnehm, P., Reichenbach, S., Altpeter, E., Widmer, H. and Hoppeler, H. (1997) 'Influence of different racing positions on metabolic cost in elite cyclists', *Medicine and Science in Sports and Exercise*, 29(6): 818–23.

Gonzales, H. and Hull, M.L. (1989) 'Multivariable optimization of cycling biomechanics', *Journal of Biomechanics*, 22(11–12): 1151–61.

González-Badillo, J.J. and Marques, M.C. (2010) 'Relationship between kinematic factors and counter-movement jump height in trained track and field athletes', *Journal of Strength and Conditioning Research*, 24(12): 3443–7.

Gosztyla, A.E., Edwards, D.G., Quinn, T.J. and Kenefick, R.W. (2006) 'The impact of different pacing strategies on five-kilometer running time trial performance', *Journal of Strength and Conditioning Research*, 20(4): 882–6.

Grappe, F. (2009) 'Résistance totale qui s'oppose au de´placement en cyclisme', in F. Grappe (ed.), *Cyclisme et Optimisation de la Performance, Collection Science et Pratique du Sport* (p. 604). Paris: De Boeck Université.

Gross, A.C., Kyle, C.R. and Malewicki, D.J. (1983) 'The aerodynamics of human-powered land vehicles', *Scientific American*, 249: 142–5.

Hahn, M.E. (2006) 'Feasibility of estimating isokinetic knee torque using a neural network model', *Journal of Biomechanics*, 40(5): 1107–14.

Haney, C.J. and Long, B.C. (1995) 'Coping effectiveness: A path analysis of self-efficacy, control, coping, and performance in sport competitions', *Journal of Applied Social Psychology*, 25: 1726–46.

Hanon, C. and Gajer, B. (2009) 'Velocity and stride parameters of world-class 400-meter athletes compared with less experienced runners', *Journal of Strength and Conditioning Research*, 23(2): 524–31.

Hanon, C., Rabate, M. and Thomas, C. (2011) 'Effect of expertise on postmaximal long sprint blood metabolite responses', *Journal of Strength and Conditioning Research*, 25(9): 2503–9.

Harms, G.A. (2000) 'Effect of skeletal muscle demand on cardiovascular function', *Medicine and Science in Sports and Exercise*, 32: 94–9.

Hausswirth, C., Bigard, A.X. and Guezennec, C.Y. (1997) 'Relationships between running mechanics and energy cost of running at the end of a triathlon and a marathon', *International Journal of Sports Medicine*, 18(5): 330–9.

Hausswirth, C., Lehénaff, D., Dréano, P. and Savonen, K. (1999) 'Effects of cycling alone or in a sheltered position on subsequent running performance during a triathlon', *Medicine and Science in Sports and Exercise*, 31: 599–604.

Hausswirth, C., Vallier, J.M., Lehenaff, D., Brisswalter, J., Smith, D., Millet, G. and Dreano, P. (2001) 'Effect of two drafting modalities in cycling on running performance', *Medicine and Science in Sports and Exercise*, 33(3): 485–92.

Hay, J. and Guimarães, A. (1983) 'A quantitative look at swimming biomechanics', *Swimming Technology*, 20: 11–17.

Heil, D.P. (2001) 'Body mass scaling of projected frontal area in competitive cyclists', *European Journal of Applied Physiology*, 85: 358–66.

Heil, D.P., Wilcox, A.R. and Quinn, C.M. (1995) 'Cardiorespiratory responses to seat-tube angle variation during steady-state cycling', *Medicine and Science in Sports and Exercise*, 27(5): 730–5.

Hollander, A.P., de Groot, G., van Ingen Schenau, G., Kahman, R. and Toussaint, H. (1988) 'Contribution of the legs to propulsion in front crawl swimming', in B. Ungerechts, K. Wilke and K. Reischle (eds), *Swimming Science V* (pp. 39–43). Champaign, IL: Human Kinetics Books.

Holly, R.G., Barnard, R.J., Rosenthal, M., Applegate, E. and Pritikin, N. (1986) 'Triathlete characterization and response to prolonged strenuous competition', *Medicine and Science in Sports Exercise*, 18(1): 123–7.

Hopkins, W.G. and Hewson, D.J. (2001) 'Variability of competitive performance of distance runners', *Medicine and Science in Sports and Exercise*, 33(9): 1588–92.

Horowitz, J.F., Sidossis, L.S. and Coyle, E.F. (1994) 'High efficiency of type I muscle fibers improves performance', *International Journal of Sports Medicine*, 15(3): 152–7.

Hue, O., Le Gallais, D., Chollet, D., Boussana, A. and Préfaut, C. (1998) 'The influence of prior cycling on biomechanical and cardiorespiratory response profiles during running in triathletes', *European Journal of Applied Physiology and Occupational Physiology*, 77(1–2): 98–105.

Hue, O., Valluet, A., Blonc, S. and Hertogh, C. (2002) 'Effects of multicycle-run training on triathlete performance', *Research Quarterly for Exercise and Sport*, 73(3): 289–95.

Ikai, M., Ishii, K. and Miyashita, M. (1964) 'An electromyographic study of swimming', *Journal of Physical Education*, 7: 47–54.

Jesus, S., Costa, M.J., Marinho, D.A., Garrido, N.D., Silva, A.J. and Barbosa, T.M. (2011) '13th FINA World Championship finals: Stroke kinematics and race times according to performance, gender and event', *Portuguese Journal of Sport Sciences*, 11(Suppl. 2): 275–8.

Jeukendrup, A.E. and Martin, J. (2001) 'Improving cycling performance: How should we spend our time and money', *Sports Medicine*, 31(7): 559–69.

Jones, A.M. and Whipp, B.J. (2002) 'Bioenergetic constraints on tactical decision making in middle distance running', *British Journal of Sports Medicine*, 36(2): 102–4.

Juel, C. (1998) 'Muscle pH regulation: Role of training', *Acta Physiologica Scandinavica*, 162: 359–66.

Kautz, S.A. and Hull, M.L. (1993) 'A theoretical basis for interpreting the force applied to the pedal in cycling', *Journal of Biomechanics*, 26(2): 155–65.

Kjendlie, P.L. and Stallman, R. (2008) 'Drag characteristics of competitive swimming children and adults', *Journal of Applied Biomechanics*, 24: 35–42.

Kjendlie, P.L., Haljand, R., Fjortoft, O. and Stallman, R.K. (2006) 'Stroke frequency strategies of international and national swimmers in 100m races', *Portuguese Journal of Sport Science*, 6(Suppl. 2): 52–4.

Korff, T., Romer, L.M., Mayhew, I. and Martin, J.C. (2007) 'Effect of pedaling technique on mechanical effectiveness and efficiency in cyclists', *Medicine and Science in Sports and Exercise*, 39(6): 991–5.

Korhonen, M.T., Mero, A. and Suominen, H. (2003) 'Age-related differences in 100-m sprint performance in male and female master runners', *Medicine and Science in Sports and Exercise*, 35(8): 1419–28.

Kyle, C.R. (1991) 'The effect of crosswinds upon time trials', *Cycling Science*, 3(3–4): 51–6.

Kyle, C.R. and Caiozzo, V.J. (1986) 'The effect of athletic clothing aerodynamics upon running speed', *Medicine and Science in Sports and Exercise*, 18(5): 509–15.

Laffite, L.P., Vilas-Boas, J.P., Demarle, A., Silva, J., Fernandes, R. and Billat, V.L. (2004) 'Changes in physiological and stroke parameters during a maximal 400-m free swimming test in elite swimmers', *Canadian Journal of Applied Physiology*, 29: 17–31.

Landers, G.J., Blanksby, B.A., Ackland, T.R. and Monson, R. (2008) 'Swim positioning and its influence on triathlon outcome', *International Journal of Exercise Science*, 1(3): 96–105.

Leblanc, H., Seifert, L., Tourny-Chollet, C. and Chollet, D. (2007) 'Intra-cyclic distance per stroke phase, velocity fluctuation and acceleration time ratio of a breaststroker's hip: A comparison between elite and non-elite swimmers at different race paces', *International Journal of Sports Medicine*, 28: 140–7.

Leirdal, S. and Ettema, G. (2011) 'The relationship between cadence, pedaling technique and gross efficiency in cycling', *European Journal of Applied Physiology*, 111(12): 2885–93.

Lepers, R., Millet, G.Y., Maffiuletti, N.A., Hausswirth, C. and Brisswalter, J. (2001) 'Effect of pedalling rates on physiological response during endurance cycling', *European Journal of Applied Physiology*, 85(3–4): 392–5.

Lewillie, L. (1973) 'Muscular activity in swimming', in S. Cerquiglini, A. Venerando and J. Warten-weiler (eds), *Biomechanics III* (pp. 440–5). Basel: Karger Verlag.

Leyk, D., Erley, O., Ridder, D., Leurs, M., Rüther, T., Wunderlich, M., Sievert, A., Baum, K. and Essfeld, D. (2007) 'Age-related changes in marathon and half-marathon performances', *International Journal of Sports Medicine* , 28(6): 513–17.

Linthorne, N.P. (1994) 'Wind assistance in the 100-m sprint' *Track Technique*, 127: 4049–51.

Loras, H., Leirdal, S. and Ettema, G. (2009) 'The muscle force component in pedaling retains constant direction across pedaling rates', *Journal of Applied Biomechanics*, 25: 1–9.

Lucía, A., Hoyos, J. and Chicharro, J.L. (2001a) 'Physiology of professional road cycling', *Sports Medicine*, 31(5): 325–37.

Lucía, A., Hoyos, J. and Chicharro, J.L. (2001b) 'Preferred pedalling cadence in professional cycling', *Medicine and Science in Sports and Exercise*, 33(8): 1361–6.

Lucía, A., Hoyos, J., Pérez, M., Santalla, A. and Chicharro, J.L. (2002) 'Inverse relationship between $\dot{V}O_{2max}$ and economy/efficiency in world-class cyclists', *Medicine and Science in Sports and Exercise*, 34(12): 2079–84.

Lyttle, A.D. and Keys, M. (2006) 'The application of computational fluid dynamics for technique prescription in underwater kicking', *Portuguese Journal of Sport Science*, 6(2): 233–5.

Lyttle, A.D., Blanksby, B.A., Elliott, B.C. and Lloyd, D.G. (1999) 'Optimal depth for streamlined gliding', in K.L. Keskinen, P.V. Komi and P.A. Hollander (eds), *Biomechanics and Medicine in Swimming VIII* (pp. 165–70). Jyvaskyla: Gummerus Printing.

Maglischo, E. (2003) *Swimming Fastest*, Champaign, IL: Human Kinetics.

March, D.S., Vanderburgh, P.M., Titlebaum, P.J. and Hoops, M.L. (2011) 'Age, sex, and finish time as determinants of pacing in the marathon', *Journal of Strength and Conditioning Research*, 25(2): 386–91.

Marinho, D.A., Vilas-Boas, J.P., Keskinen, K., Rodríguez, F., Soares, S., Carmo, C. and Fernandes, R. (2006) 'Behaviour of the kinematic parameters during a time to exhaustion test at $\dot{V}O_{2max}$ in elite swimmers', *Journal of Human Movement Studies*, 51: 1–10.

Marinho, D.A., Garrido, N., Barbosa, T.M., Canelas, R., Silva, A.J., Costa, A.M. and Marques, M.C. (2009a) 'Monitoring swimming sprint performance during a training cycle', *Journal of Physical Education and Sport*, 25(4): 1–6.

Marinho, D.A., Barbosa, T.M., Kjendlie, P.L., Vilas-Boas, J.P., Alves, F.B., Rouboa, A.I. and Silva, A.J. (2009b) 'Swimming simulation: A new tool for swimming research and practical applications', in M. Peters, (ed.), *Lecture Notes in Computational Science and Engineering – CFD for Sport Simulation* (pp. 33–62). Berlin: Springer.

Marinho, D.A., Reis, V.M., Alves, F.B., Vilas-Boas, J.P., Machado, L., Silva, A.J. and Rouboa, A.I. (2009c) 'The hydrodynamic drag during the gliding in swimming', *Journal of Applied Biomechanics*, 25(3): 253–7.

Marinho, D.A., Rouboa, A.I., Alves, F.B., Vilas-Boas, J.P., Machado, L., Reis, V.M. and Silva, A.J. (2009d) 'Hydrodynamic analysis of different thumb positions in swimming', *Journal of Sports Science and Medicine*, 8(1): 58–66.

Marinho, D.A., Barbosa, T.M., Reis, V.M., Kjendlie, P.L., Alves, F.B., Vilas-Boas, J.P. and Silva, A.J. (2010a) 'Swimming propulsion forces are enhanced by a small finger spread', *Journal of Applied Biomechanics*, 26: 87–92.

Marinho, D.A., Barbosa, T.M., Costa, M.J., Figueiredo, C., Reis, V.M., Silva, A.J. and Marques, M.C. (2010b) 'Can 8-weeks of training affect active drag in age-group swimmers?', *Journal of Sport Science and Medicine*, 9: 71–8.

Marinho, D.A., Silva, A.J., Reis, V.M., Barbosa, T.M., Vilas-Boas, J.P., Alves, F.B. and Rouboa, A.I. (2011a) 'Three-dimensional CFD analysis of the hand and forearm in swimming', *Journal of Applied Biomechanics*, 27(1): 74–80.

Marinho, D.A., Barbosa, T.M., Rouboa, A.I. and Silva, A.J. (2011b) 'The hydrodynamic study of the swimming gliding: A two-dimensional computational fluid dynamics (CFD) analysis', *Journal of Human Kinetics*, 29: 80–9.

Marr, L.C. and Ely, M.R. (2010) 'Effect of air pollution on marathon running performance', *Medicine and Science in Sports and Exercise*, 42(3): 585–91.

Marsh, A.P. and Martin, P.E. (1997) 'Effect of cycling experience, aerobic power, and power output on preferred and most economical cycling cadences', *Medicine and Science in Sports and Exercise*, 29(9): 1225–32.

McCole, S.D., Claney, K. and Conte, J.C. (1990) 'Energy expenditure during bicycling', *Journal of Applied Physiology*, 68: 748–52.

McGarry, T., Anderson, D.I., Wallace, S.A., Hughes, M.D. and Franks, I.M. (2002) 'Sport competition as a dynamical self-organizing system', *Journal of Sports Sciences*, 20(10): 771–81.

Millet, G.P. and Vleck, V.E. (2000) 'Physiological and biomechanical adaptations to the cycle to run transition in Olympic triathlon: Review and practical recommendations for training', *British Journal of Sports Medicine*, 34(5): 384–90.

Millet, G.P. and Candau, R. (2002) 'Mechanical factors of the energy cost in three human locomotions', *Science and Sports*, 17: 166–76.

Millet, G.P. and Bentley, D.J. (2004) 'The physiological responses to running after cycling in elite junior and senior triathletes', *International Journal of Sports Medicine*, 25(3): 191–7.

Millet, G.P., Chollet, D. and Chatard, J.C. (2000a) 'Effects of drafting behind a two- or a six-beat kick swimmer in elite female triathletes', *European Journal of Applied Physiology*, 82(5–6): 465–71.

Millet, G.P., Millet, G.Y., Hofmann, M.D. and Candau, R.B. (2000b) 'Alterations in running economy and mechanics after maximal cycling in triathletes: Influence of performance level', *International Journal of Sports Medicine*, 21(2): 127–32.

Millet, G.P., Tronche, C., Fuster, N. and Candau, R. (2002) 'Level ground and uphill cycling efficiency in seated and standing positions', *Medicine and Science in Sports and Exercise*, 34(10): 1645–52.

Montain, S.J., Ely, M.R. and Cheuvront, S.N. (2007) 'Marathon performance in thermally stressing conditions', *Sports Medicine*, 37(4–5): 320–3.

Morais, J.E., Costa, M.J., Jesus, S., Mejias, J.E., Moreira, M., Garrido, N., Silva, A.J., Marinho, D.A. and Barbosa, T.M. (in press) 'Is underwater gliding test a valid procedure to estimate the swimmer's drag?', *Journal of Sports Science and Medicine*.

Morales, E., Arellano, R., Famia, P. and Mercades, J. (2010) 'Regression analysis model applied to age-group swimmers: Study of stroke rate, stroke length and stroke index', in P.L. Kjendlie, R.K. Stallman and J. Cabri (eds), *Biomechanics and Medicine in Swimming XI* (pp. 129–32). Oslo: Norwegian School of Sport Sciences.

Morgan, D.W. and Daniels, J.T. (1994) 'Relationship between O_2 max and the aerobic demand of running in elite distance runners', *International Journal of Sports Medicine*, 15(7): 426–9.

Nesi, X., Bosquet, L. and Pelayo, P. (2005) 'Preferred pedal rate: An index of cycling performance', *International Journal of Sports Medicine*, 26: 372–5.

Noakes, T.D., Lambert, M.I. and Hauman, R. (2009) 'Which lap is the slowest? An analysis of 32 world mile record performances', *British Journal of Sports Medicine*, 43(10): 760–76.

Nuber, G.W., Jobe, F.W., Perry, J., Moynes, D.R. and Antonelli, D. (1986) 'Fine wire electromyography analysis of muscles of the shoulder during swimming', *American Journal of Sports Medicine*, 14: 7–11.

Oggiano, L., Troynikov, O., Konopov, I., Subic, A. and Alam, F. (2009) 'Aerodynamic behaviour of single sport jersey fabrics with different roughness and cover factors', *Sports Engineering*, 12: 1–12.

Ogita, F. (2006) 'Energetics in competitive swimming and its application for training', *Portuguese Journal of Sport Science*, 6(2): 117–21.

Padilla, S., Mujika, I., Cuesta, G. and Goiriena, J.J. (1999) 'Level ground and uphill cycling ability in professional road cycling', *Medicine and Science in Sports and Exercise*, 31(6): 878–85.

Padilla, S., Mujika, I., Angulo, F. and Goiriena, J.J. (2000) 'Scientific approach to the 1-h cycling world record: A case study', *Journal of Applied Physiology*, 89(4): 1522–7.

Palmer, G.S., Hawley, J.A., Dennis, S.C. and Noakes, T.D. (1994) 'Heart rate response during a 4-d cycle stage race', *Medicine and Science in Sports and Exercise*, 26: 1278–83.

Peeling, P. and Landers, G. (2009) 'Swimming intensity during triathlon: A review of current research and strategies to enhance race performance', *Journal of Sports Sciences*, 27(10): 1079–85.

Peeling, P., Bishop, D., Landers, G. and Boone, T. (2005) 'Effect of swimming intensity on subsequent cycling and overall triathlon performance', *British Journal of Sports Medicine*, 39(12): 960–4.

Perez-Gomez, J., Rodriguez, G.V., Ara, I., Olmedillas, H., Chavarren, J., González-Henriquez, J.J., Dorado, C. and Calbet, J.A. (2008) 'Role of muscle mass on sprint performance: Gender differences?', *European Journal of Applied Physiology*, 102(6): 685–94.

Perl, J. (2004) 'A neural network approach to movement pattern analysis' *Human Movement Science*, 23(5): 605–20.

Persyn, U., Colman, V. and Van Tilborgh, L. (1991) 'Movement analysis of the flat and the undulating breaststroke pattern', in D. Maclaren, T. Reilly and A. Lees (eds), *Swimming Science VI* (pp. 75–80). London: E and FN Spon.

Pfeiffer, R.P., Harden, B.P., Landis, D., Barber, D. and Harper, K. (1993) 'Correlating indices of aerobic capacity with performance in elite women road cyclists', *Journal of Strength and Conditioning Research*, 7: 201–5.

Pink, M., Perry, J., Browne, A., Scovazzo, M.L. and Kerrigan, J. (1991) 'The normal shoulder during freestyle swimming. An electromyographic and cinematographic analysis of twelve muscles', *American Journal of Sports Medicine*, 19: 569–76.

Quinn, M.D. (2010) 'External effects in the 400-m hurdles race', *Journal of Applied Biomechanics*, 26(2): 171–9.

Quinn, T.J., Manley, M.J., Aziz, J., Padham, J.L. and MacKenzie, A.M. (2011) 'Aging and factors related to running economy', *Journal of Strength and Conditioning Research*, 25(11): 2971–9.

Reis, V.M., Marinho, D.A., Policarpo, F.B., Carneiro, A.L., Baldari, C. and Silva, A.J. (2010) 'Examining the accumulated oxygen deficit method in front crawl swimming', *International Journal of Sports Medicine*, 31(6): 421–7.

Robergs, R.A., Ghiasvand, F. and Parker, D. (2004) 'Biochemistry of exercise induced metabolic acidosis', *American Journal of Physiology – Regulatory, Integrative and Comparative Physiology*, 287: 502–16.

Rodriguez, F.A. and Mader, A. (2003) 'Energy metabolism during 400 and 100m crawl swimming: Computer simulation based on free swimming measurement', in J.C. Chatard (ed.), *Biomechanics and Medicine in Swimming IX* (pp. 373–8). Saint-Etienne: University of Saint-Etienne.

Roecker, K., Striegel, H. and Dickhuth, H.H. (2003) 'Heart-rate recommendations: Transfer between running and cycling exercise?', *International Journal of Sports Medicine*, 24(3): 173–8.

Ruwe, P.A., Pink, M., Jobe, F.W., Perry, J. and Scovazzo, M.L. (1994) 'The normal and the painful shoulders during the breaststroke. Electromyographic and cinematographic analysis of twelve muscles', *American Journal of Sports Medicine*, 22: 789–96.

Saavedra, J., Escalante, Y. and Rodriguez, F. (2003) 'Multidimensional evaluation of peripubertal swimmers: Multiple regression analysis applied to talent selection', in J.C. Chatard (ed.), *Biomechanics and Medicine in Swimming IX* (pp. 551–6), Saint-Etienne: University of Saint-Etienne.

Salo, A.I., Bezodis, I.N., Batterham, A.M. and Kerwin, D.G. (2011) 'Elite sprinting: Are athletes individually step-frequency or step-length reliant?', *Medicine and Science in Sports and Exercise*, 43(6): 1055–62.

Saltin, B. and Strange, S. (1992) 'Maximal oxygen uptake: "Old" and "new" arguments for a cardiovascular limitation', *Medicine and Science in Sports and Exercise*, 24(1): 30–7.

Sánchez, J. and Arellano, R. (2002) 'Stroke index values according to level, gender, swimming style and event race distance', in Gianikellis, K. (ed.), *Proceedings of the XXth International Symposium on Biomechanics in Sports* (pp. 56–9). Cáceres: Universidad de Extremadura.

Sanders, R., Cappaert, J. and Pease, D. (1998) 'Wave characteristics of Olympic breaststroke swimmers', *Journal of Applied Biomechanics*, 14: 40–51.

Sato, Y. and Hino, T. (2002) 'Estimation of thrust of swimmer's hand using CFD', in *Proceedings of 8th Symposium on Nonlinear and Free-Surface Flows* (pp. 71–5), Hiroshima.

Schleihauf, R.E. (1979) 'A hydrodynamic analysis of swimming propulsion', in J. Terauds and E.W. Bedingfield (eds), *Swimming III* (pp. 70–109). Baltimore: University Park Press.

Seifert, L. and Chollet, D. (2008) 'Inter-limb coordination and constraints in swimming: A review', in N.P. Beaulieu (ed.), *Physical Activity and Children* (pp. 65–93). New York: Nova Science Publishers.

Seifert, L., Chollet, D. and Chatard, J.C. (2007) 'Kinematic change during a 100m front crawl: Effects of performance level and gender', *Medicine Science Sports Exercise*, 39: 1784–93.

Seifert, L., Boulesteix, L., Chollet, D. and Vilas-Boas, J.P. (2008) 'Differences in spatial-temporal parameters and arm-leg coordination in butterfly stroke as a function of race pace, skill and gender', *Human Movement Science*, 27: 96–111.

Seiler, S., de Koning, J.J. and Foster, C. (2007) 'The fall and rise of the gender difference in elite anaerobic performance 1952–2006', *Medicine and Science in Sports and Exercise*, 39(3): 534–40.

Shestakov, M.P. (2005) 'Modeling of technical training of discus throwers in the period of significant changes of their mass-inertia characteristics', *Journal of Physiological Anthropology and Applied Human Science*, 24(4): 367–70.

Silva, A.J., Colman, V., Soons, B., Alves, F. and Persyn, U. (2002) 'Movement variables important for effectiveness and performance in breaststroke', in K. Gianikellis (ed.), *Proceedings of the XXth International Symposium on Biomechanics in Sports* (pp. 39–42). Cáceres: Universidad de Extremadura.

Silva, A.J., Costa, A.M., Oliveira, P.M., Reis, V.M., Saavedra, J., Perl, J., Rouboa, A.I. and Marinho, D.A. (2007) 'The use of neural network technology to model swimming performance', *Journal of Sports Science and Medicine*, 6: 117–25.

Silva, A.J., Rouboa, A., Moreira, A., Reis, V.M., Alves, F., Vilas-Boas, J.P. and Marinho, D.A. (2008) 'Analysis of drafting effects in swimming using computational fluid dynamics', *Journal of Sports Science and Medicine*, 7(1): 60–6.

Sjodin, B. and Jacobs, I. (1981) 'Onset of blood lactate accumulation and marathon running performance', *International Journal of Sports Medicine*, 2: 23–6.

Sjodin, B. and Svedenhag, J. (1985) 'Applied physiology of marathon running', *Sports Medicine*, 2: 83–99.

Smith, D., Telford, R., Peltola, E. and Tumilty, D. (2000) 'Protocols for the physiological assessment of high-performance runners', in C.J. Gore (ed.), *Physiological Tests for Elite Athletes* (pp. 334–44). Australian Sports Commission, Champaign IL: Human Kinetics.

Sparling, P.B., O'Donnell, E.M. and Snow, T.K. (1998) 'The gender difference in distance running performance has plateaued: An analysis of world rankings from 1980 to 1996', *Medicine and Science in Sports and Exercise*, 30(12): 1725–9.

Spreitzer, E. and Snyder, E. (1976) 'Socialization into sport: An exploratory path analysis', *Research Quarterly*, 47(2): 238–45.

Stirn, I., Jarm, T., Kapus, V. and Strojnik, V. (2010) 'Fatigue analysis of 100 meters all-out front crawl using surface EMG', in P.L. Kjendlie, R.K. Stallman and J. Cabri (eds), *Biomechanics and Medicine in Swimming XII* (pp. 168–70). Oslo: Norwegian School of Sport Sciences.

Swain, D.P. (1994) 'The influence of body mass in endurance cycling', *Medicine and Science in Sports and Exercise*, 26: 58–63.

Takagi, H., Shimizu, Y., Kurashima, A. and Sanders, R. (2001) 'Effect of thumb abduction and adduction on hydrodynamic characteristics of a model of the human hand', in J. Blackwell and R. Sanders (eds), *Proceedings of Swim Sessions of the XIX International Symposium on Biomechanics in Sports* (pp. 122–6). San Francisco: University of San Francisco.

Takai, K. (1998) 'Cognitive strategies and recall of pace by long-distance runners', *Perceptual and Motor Skills*, 86(3): 763–70.

Takaishi, T., Yasuda, Y. and Moritani, T. (1994) 'Neuromuscular fatigue during prolonged pedalling exercise at different pedalling rates', *European Journal of Applied Physiology and Occupational Physiology*, 69(2): 154–8.

Too, D. (1991) 'The effect of hip position/configuration on anaerobic power and capacity in cycling', *International Journal of Sports Biomechanics*, 7: 359–70.

Toussaint, H. (1990) 'Differences in propelling efficiency between competitive and triathlon swimmers', *Medicine and Science in Sports and Exercise*, 22: 409–15.

Toussaint, H. and Truijens, M. (2005) 'Biomechanical aspects of peak performance in human swimming', *Animal Biology*, 55(1): 17–40.

Toussaint, H., Carol, A., Kranenborg, H. and Truijens, M. (2006) 'Effect of fatigue on stroking characteristics in an arms-only 100-m front-crawl race', *Medicine Science Sports Exercise*, 38: 1635–42.

Trappe, S. (2007) 'Marathon runners: How do they age?', *Sports Medicine*, 37(4–5): 302–5.

Troup, J. (1992) 'Aerobic characteristics of the four competitive strokes', in J. Troup (ed.), *International Center for Aquatic Research Annual. Studies by the International Center for Aquatic Research (1990–1991)*, (pp. 9–16). Colorado Spring: US Swimming Press.

Tucker, R., Lambert, M.I. and Noakes, T.D. (2006) 'An analysis of pacing strategies during men's world-record performances in track athletics', *International Journal of Sports Physiology and Performance*, 1(3): 233–45.

Van Handel, P., Katz, A., Morrow, J., Troup, J., Daniels, J. and Bradley, P. (1988) 'Aerobic economy and competitive performance of US elite swimmers', in B. Ungerechts, K. Wilke and K. Reischle (eds), *Swimming Science V* (pp. 219–27). Champaign, IL: Human Kinetics Books.

van Ingen Schenau, G.J., de Koning, J.J. and de Groot, G. (1994) 'Optimisation of sprinting performance in running, cycling and speed skating', *Sports Medicine*, 17(4): 259–75.

Vennell, R., Pease, D.L. and Wilson, B.D. (2006) 'Wave drag on human swimmers', *Journal of Biomechanics*, 31: 664–71.

Vercruyssen, F., Suriano, R., Bishop, D., Hausswirth, C. and Brisswalter, J. (2005) 'Cadence selection affects metabolic responses during cycling and subsequent running time to fatigue', *British Journal of Sports Medicine*, 39(5): 267–72.

Vihma, T. (2010) 'Effects of weather on the performance of marathon runners', *International Journal of Biometeorology*, 54(3): 297–306.

Vitor, F.M. and Böhme, M.T. (2010) 'Performance of young male swimmers in the 100-meters front crawl', *Pediatric Exercise Science*, 22: 278–87.

Wagner, P.D. (1995) 'Muscle O2 transport and O2 dependent control of metabolism', *Medicine and Science in Sports and Exercise*, 27(1): 47–53.

Wakayoshi, K., D'Acquisto, J., Cappaert, J.M. and Troup, J.P. (1995) 'Relationship between oxygen uptake, stroke rate and swimming velocity in competitive swimming', *International Journal of Sports Medicine*, 16: 19–23.

Waldron, M., Worsfold, P., White, C. and Murray, S. (2011) 'Swarming behaviour in elite race bunch cycling: A case study', *International Journal of Performance Analysis in Sport*, 11(1): 14–25.

Ward-Smith, A.J. (1999a) 'New insights into the effect of wind assistance on sprinting performance', *Journal of Sports Science*, 17(4): 325–34.

Ward-Smith, A.J. (1999b) 'Aerobic and anaerobic energy conversion during high-intensity exercise', *Medicine and Science in Sports and Exercise*, 31: 1855–60.

Yamaji, K. and Shephard, R.J. (1987) 'Grouping of runners during marathon competition', *British Journal of Sports Medicine*, 21(4): 166–7.

Young, W.B., James, R. and Montgomery, I. (2002) 'Is muscle power related to running speed with changes of direction?', *Journal of Sports Medicine and Physical Fitness*, 42(3): 282–8.

Zaidi, H., Taiar, R., Fohanno, S. and Polidori, G. (2008) 'Analysis of the effect of swimmer's head position on swimming performance using computational fluid dynamics', *Journal of Biomechanics*, 41: 1350–8.

Zameziati, K., Mornieux, D.R. and Belli, A. (2006) 'Relationship between the increase of effectiveness indexes and the increase of muscular efficiency with cycling power', *European Journal of Applied Physiology*, 96: 274–81.

Zamparo, P. (2006) 'Effects of age and gender on the propelling efficiency of the arm stroke', *European Journal of Applied Physiology*, 97: 52–8.

Zamparo, P., Capelli, C. and Pendergast, D. (2010) 'Energetics of swimming: A historical perspective', *European Journal of Applied Physiology*, 111(3): 367–78.

36

FIELD ATHLETICS

José Campos

UNIVERSITY OF VALENCIA, SPAIN

Summary

Field athletics is a group of disciplines which involves jumping and throwing events. This chapter presents the performance indicators of field athletics and their usefulness for coaching and performance optimization. The biomechanical approach appears as a useful strategy for the evaluation of technical patterns in field athletics and their relevance as controllable, trainable and transferable aspects of training.

A methodological strategy for performance analysis in field athletics is presented, underlining the coordination of force application as an important contributor to jumping and throwing ability. In the last part of the chapter, we present the results obtained in the biomechanical analysis of the javelin throw and the long jump, after having considered some of the aspects of the methodology mentioned above.

Introduction

The group of disciplines known as field athletics involves jumping and throwing events, with the main objective of projecting the athlete's body or an implement, respectively. Jumping includes the long and triple jump, the high jump and pole vaulting, and throwing includes shot put, discus, javelin and hammer. These specialities are characterized by the use of acyclic actions, together with a high level of explosive force and a high projection component aimed at projecting the jumper's body (jumping events) or an implement (throwing events) as far as possible.

In jumps, the goal is to project the jumper's mass as far or as high as possible from a fixed projection point. The result of the jump is related to the jumper's physical ability and capacity to adequately transform and handle, at take-off, the forces generated in the approach run.

In throwing events, the goal is to throw an implement as far as possible. Technical actions are considered to be kinetic chains based on the sequential acceleration of segments in a proximal-to-distal sequence, contributing to the object's momentum (Putnam, 1993). Based on their characteristics, in some throws, the effect of air resistance on the implement in the flight phase is minimal (shot put and hammer), while in others it is decisive to reaching the longest possible distance (javelin and discus).

Performance in these specialities can be explained by a number of parameters which together make up a specific performance profile. The variables included within sports performance profiles are typically performance indicators such as selection, combination or action variables that aim to define some or all aspects of performance (Hughes and Bartlett, 2002).

In sports coaching, the general trend is to consider performance and technical achievement synonymous, which implies that good performance requires good technique. However, reality proves that technique alone cannot account for performance. In practice, there are other factors, apart from technique, which add to performance, such as the athlete's physiological, anthropometric and neuromuscular features (Lees, 2002). As a consequence, the interpretation of the links between technical level and performance must be cautious, especially when the reference is that of an athlete's individual model (Bartlett, 1999).

The aim of this chapter is to underline the most relevant aspects to bear in mind for performance analysis in field athletics disciplines. As practical examples of this process, long jump and javelin throw are presented as cases, describing the performance indicators used in both specialities.

Performance analysis of field athletics: a biomechanical approach

The technical level of the athletes is considered to be a clear determinant of performance. The evaluation of the elements which define a technical pattern of athletes is a fundamental step in sport training. The biomechanical approach appears as a useful strategy for the evaluation of technical patterns in field athletics and their relevance as controllable, trainable and transferable aspects of training. Basically, biomechanics is the *science concerned with the internal and external forces that act on a human body and the effects produced by these forces* (Hay, 1993).

The importance of biomechanics for coaching and the improvement of performance depend on the sport involved and the level of the athlete:

- **The mechanical characteristics of the sport**. The greater the technical complexity of the actions involved in the sport, the larger the implication of biomechanics. Field athletics groups together a number of disciplines whose technical actions have a high level of complexity.
- **The level of the athlete**. The higher the athlete's level, the more important his/her technical level. In these cases, performance improvement depends on small details that are difficult to control just through observations by the coach. Biomechanics is therefore essential for an adequate control of the coaching process.

The biomechanical understanding and evaluation of technique involve the consideration of kinematical, kinetic and temporal variables (performance indicators). These include body segment speed or angles, linear and rotational position, displacement and different kinetic variables, such as momentum, force and torque.

The performance profile of a speciality is expressed by hierarchical models based on a cause–effect structure in which parameters are arranged at different levels according to their degree of correlation and influence. All these parameters can be considered as performance indicators, provided that they do meaningfully contribute to the performance. These deterministic models are, in many cases, the best approach to identifying critical features of a movement if we can formulate a clear performance criterion. As examples of such models, Figure 36.1 shows the hierarchical model suggested by Morriss and Bartlett (1996) for the javelin throw.

On the other hand, a biomechanical analysis also implies evaluating the forces generated. Technical actions in field athletics require athletes to use muscular tension of an explosive nature, typical of fast movements and conditioned by a number of factors, such as the following:

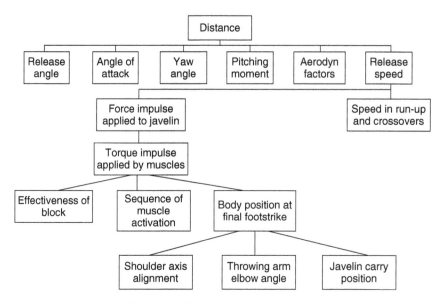

Figure 36.1 Hierarchical model of the javelin throw

- Resistance to be overcome.
- Weight of the throwing artefact. With light weights (javelin throw), maximum tension is reached earlier and decreases as the movement speed grows.
- Force application time. Both in jumping and in throwing events, the application of forces occurs over a very short time. For example, a long jumper who reaches a horizontal velocity in the run-up between 10 and 10.2 m.s^{-1} uses a touchdown time at take-off between 112 and 136 ms to apply the force (Koyama *et al.*, 2008). This ratio requires a specific physical capacity and ability in the jumper, to be able to transform the horizontal velocity of the run-up into vertical impulse.

In jumping events, the muscular intervention process is more dependent on the participation of the segments involved in the lower kinetic chain:

1. In the take-off phase, the lower kinetic chain (open) makes the most of the action–reaction principle to obtain the take-off force, under Newton's third law.
2. The small muscle groups take part in the first contact of the foot with the ground, followed by the large and slow ones during the braking of the take-off, and then by the small and fast muscle groups again, thus completing the take-off.

The muscular intervention process in throws is more complex, as a higher number of body segments are involved from both the upper and the lower kinetic chains:

1. At the start of the release phase, the lower kinetic chain (closed) stays in position to take advantage of the action–reaction principle and so obtain the impulse force during the double support phase.
2. Then, the upper kinetic chain (open) works in a sequential way until the most distal segment (the hand) reaches the maximum velocity needed to throw the implement. Thus, it is the large and slow muscle groups of the lower chain that come into action first, followed

by the upper chain and finally by the small and fast muscular groups of the arm's most distal segments (i.e. the forearm and the hand) to throw the artefact.

Performance analysis strategy in field athletics

Performance analysis is part of the general planning process in coaching and follows a strategic and systematic plan implemented at two levels: (1) evaluation of the athlete's physical and technical condition; and (2) assessment of performance while competing (jump distance/height and throw distance). The information derived from these two levels of analysis allows us to monitor the athlete's evolution in the season and to identify the effects of coaching on the improvement of his/her performance.

A. As far as *physical condition* is concerned, different parameters are evaluated, basically in relation to strength and muscular power:

- general strength for the analysis of the force component of power;
- special strength for the analysis of the capacity to convert general strength into specific strength;
- specific strength for the analysis of the capacity to develop the velocity component of power and to provide power improvement in a way which is specific to the required technique of an athlete.

B. Regarding *technique*, the goal focuses on *evaluation and diagnosis to know what's right and wrong in a movement* (Bartlett, 2007): (1) *evaluation of performance*; and (2) *diagnosis of movement errors*. Different performance indicators are used depending on the goal set:

1. **Determination of the individual technical pattern**. The goal is to describe the athlete's individual model from performance indicators that can be compared with those of the reference theoretical model. Athletes tend to copy the currently most successful performer. Further evidence to this effect has come from research using artificial neural networks – Kohonen self-organizing maps – for javelin and discus throwing by Schöllhorn and Bauer (1998).
2. **Inter-subject analysis**. The goal is to analyse performance indicators of individual models to be able to compare differences between athletes with a different sports level (novice, club, elite).
3. **Intra-subject analysis**. The goal is to determine the internal consistency of the athlete's individual model, underlining the factors with the greatest influence on his/her performance. For novice, club and elite javelin throwers, Bartlett *et al.* (1996) reported that intra-individual differences were greater for the novice and the elite throwers than for the club throwers. Neither of these findings, which were again reinforced by the results of Schöllhorn and Bauer (1998), supports the notion of intra-individual movement consistency. Even elite athletes appear unable to produce invariant movement patterns after many years of practice (Bartlett, 2008).

C. On the other hand, the analysis of the *evolution of performance in competition* consists of describing the reproducibility of competitive performance of athletes and deriving the smallest worthwhile enhancements of performance. An estimate of the smallest change comes from an analysis of reliability (reproducibility or variability) of competitive performance (Hopkins, 2005). We must focus on within-athlete variability from competition to competition to obtain the athlete's typical percentage variation in performance from competition to competition as a coefficient of variation.

Performance indicators in jumping and throwing

Performance indicators in jumping: the long jump

The first performance indicator in jumping is *jump distance or height*, for a horizontal jump (long and triple jump) or a vertical one (high jump and pole vault), respectively. Jump distance/height is conditioned by the values obtained in these performance indicators:

- run-up speed
- force and wind direction
- take-off velocity
- take-off angle
- take-off height
- the gain of vertical velocity
- the loss of horizontal velocity.

Each jumping discipline requires differentiated values in accordance with its specificity. For instance, the projection angle of the jumper's centre of mass (CM) in the triple jump ranges from 14° to 18°; between 18° and 22° in the long jump; and between 60° and 65° in the high jump. As a general criterion, the greater the horizontal velocity, the smaller the angle of projection, and vice versa. The larger the angle of projection, the greater the need for adequately holding the horizontal forces generated in the run-up.

Jumping disciplines must also take into account the *foot/ground contact time during the take-off*. The time of contact between the foot and the ground at take-off (take-off time) depends on the technique used and on the jumper's physical ability. Take-off time correlates negatively with the velocity of the approach run and with the jump distance (Hay, 1986). Therefore, the faster the run-up, the shorter the take-off time and the longer the jump.

Performance in the long jump depends on the actions taken at two decisive phases – that is, the run-up and the take-off. Numerous papers have reported that jump distance depends, to a great extent, on the velocity of the approach run as well as on factors like the projection height, angle and velocity of the jumper's centre of mass at take-off (Alexander, 1990; Bridgett and Linthorne, 2006; Graham-Smith and Lees, 2005; Hay and Nohara, 1990; Hay and Reid, 1988; Lees *et al.*, 1994; Seyfarth *et al.*, 2000). Regarding the approach run, athletes attempt to strike the take-off board accurately with minimum loss of speed and in an optimum body position for take-off (Hay, 1988). Thus, if the jumper is fast, this condition should be made the most of by increasing the length of the run-up. In the long jump, the run-up distance varies from 45 to 60 m. The athlete's speed is reduced in the last 5 m and especially in the last two steps of the run prior to the take-off.

The length of the last three strides is also altered in order to favour the transition from running to taking off. In general terms, the structure is such that the second-to-last stride is longer than the other two, the last one being the shortest. It was stated by Hay and Nohara (1990) that elite long jumpers lowered their CM during the flight phase of the second-to-last stride and stayed low until they raised it for the instant of take-off during the support phase of the jump itself.

Regarding the take-off phase, in the long jump, the efficiency of the jump demands a technical strategy based on making the most of the spring behaviour of the take-off leg (Seyfarth *et al.*, 1999). Several studies have stated that performance in the long jump is directly related to different mechanical and muscular mechanisms that occur from the touch-down to the take-off phase. It is well-known that the greatest gain in vertical velocity occurs during the compression phase, which is associated with a loss of horizontal velocity (Lees *et al.*, 1993).

Table 36.1 shows different performance indicators in the long jump from elite jumpers in a situation of real competition, where the total gain in vertical velocity was $3.41\pm0.36\,\text{m.s}^{-1}$, most of it occurring by the end of the compression phase (from touch-down to maximum knee flexion). During the take-off, the athlete's horizontal velocity is reduced by $1.33\,\text{m.s}^{-1}$ – that is 12 per cent of the velocity of the approach run (Campos *et al.*, 2008).

In long jump, the data analysis focused on three discrete temporal instants associated with the take-off phase (Figure 36.2):

- instant of the touch-down, when the take-off foot touches the ground (board) (*TD*)
- instant of the maximum knee flexion (*MKF*)
- instant of the take-off, in which the foot loses contact with the ground (*TO*).

Thus, the following take-off phases can be differentiated in the jump:

- **compression phase**: from touch-down to maximum knee flexion (*TD–MKF*)
- **extension phase**: from maximum knee flexion to take-off (*MKF–TO*).

Table 36.1 Basic data for official and effective distance, approach speed (V_run), take-off velocity of centre of mass at take-off instant (Vcm_to), angle of projection at take-off instant (Ato) and loss in horizontal velocity (Vy) and gain in vertical velocity (Vz) from the instant of touch-down to take-off (n=22) (Campos *et al.*, 2008)

Variables	Mean±SD
Official distance (m)	7.85±0.14
Effective distance (m)	7.97±0.14
V_run (m.s^{-1})	10.48±0.24
Vcm_to (m.s^{-1})	9.54±0.32
Ato (°)	20.8±2.08
Vz gain TD–TO (m.s^{-1})	3.41±0.36
Vy loss TD–TO (m.s^{-1})	1.33±0.28

Figure 36.2 Representative instants of touch-down, maximum knee flexion and take-off for the long jump (adapted from Campos *et al.*, 2008)

The landing of the foot of the driving leg on the board generates an energy exchange that is fundamental for the jump performance, especially in the braking impulse (compression phase), when the knee extensor muscles work eccentrically. This phase has been described as a pivot mechanism, characterized by an increase in the vertical velocity of the jumper's CM at the expense of a reduction of their horizontal velocity; more than 60 per cent of the athlete's vertical velocity at the take-off is achieved in this phase (Lees *et al.*, 1994). Basically, the jumper's goal is to generate vertical velocity of CM at take-off without losing too much horizontal velocity of CM.

In the compression phase (TD–MKF), the highest increase in the vertical velocity of the athlete's CM is achieved, with a subsequent marked decrease in horizontal velocity. Figure 36.3 shows the values of the spatial velocity components of the CM during the take-off phases for a world-class jumper.

Figure 36.3 shows the changes in magnitude of the medio-lateral, horizontal and vertical velocities of the CM for the jumper with the best effective distance result. The lowest values are those of the medio-lateral velocity. The horizontal velocity lowers from the instant of the touch-down and until the end of the compression phase, but its lowest value is reached after the instant of the maximum knee flexion of the take-off leg ($8.42\pm0.30\,\mathrm{m.s^{-1}}$). Then, it recovers slightly throughout the extension phase until the instant of the take-off, when a mean value of $8.96\,\mathrm{m.s^{-1}}$ is reached. In turn, the vertical velocity of the CM shows the opposite behaviour, progressively growing from $-0.07\,\mathrm{m.s^{-1}}$ at touch-down to $3.17\,\mathrm{m.s^{-1}}$ at take-off.

Performance indicators in throwing: the javelin throw

In throwing disciplines, the preferred performance criterion is *throwing distance*. However, the throwing distance is the consequence of interactions between a number of parameters:

- release velocity (Vo)
- release angle (αo)
- height of release (ho)
- rotation of implement
- air resistance and aerodynamic characteristics of the implement

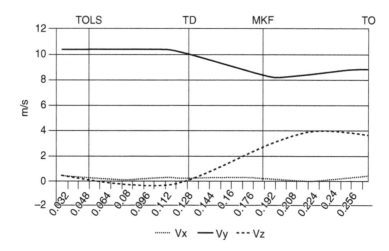

Figure 36.3 Medio-lateral, horizontal and vertical velocities of CM in the last stride and take-off phase

- force and wind direction
- air density
- gravitational coefficient.

If gravity is considered a general constant (9.81 m·s⁻²), in throws in which air resistance has no influence – as is the case with specialties whose artefacts have no aerodynamic features (shot put and hammer) – attention must be paid to release velocity, release angle and release height. In these cases, the distance travelled by the artefact (R) can be estimated by means of equation (36.1):

$$R = \frac{Vo^2 \times \cos\alpha_o}{g} \tag{36.1}$$

The angle of projection of the athlete's CM is conditioned by the horizontal and vertical components of the CM at the take-off instant. It is calculated by the equation (36.2), where Vz = vertical velocity and Vy = horizontal velocity:

$$Projection\ angle\ (\alpha o) = \arctan\frac{Vz}{Vy} \tag{36.2}$$

The performance of a javelin throw is determined by the velocity, direction and height of the javelin at the release, as well as factors affecting the aerodynamics of javelin flight (Bartlett *et al.*, 1996; Hay, 1993). The pattern of motion used in the javelin throw is similar to that used in other movements when striking or throwing an object. These movements are characterized by the fact that the body segments act sequentially to attain the maximum speed in the most distal segment of the system in the instant when the object is struck or thrown (Atwater, 1979; Menzel, 1987). Many studies have described the javelin throwing technique, including those by Bartlett *et al.* (1996), Best *et al.* (1993), Campos *et al.* (2004), Hay (1993) and Whiting *et al.* (1991).

The biomechanical analysis in javelin throwing for each athlete focused on the period illustrated for the preparatory and final throwing phases. The most important factors for javelin release occur during these decisive periods, which offer the best conditions for comparing the athletes' techniques.

It is precisely at this final throwing stage that the acceleration of the javelin starts. The upper extremity joint centre linear velocities are the result of the proximal segment and joint angular motions (Gordon and Dapena, 2006). Hence, performance depends on:

1. the optimum position of the kinetic chain at the start of the final throwing phase;
2. the sequence of kinetic power transmission during the final throwing phase.

A factor that influences the quality of energy transfer to the javelin is the coordinated motion of the upper limb, starting from the acceleration–deceleration of the sequences in the upper kinetic chain. Typically, several body segments, in a proximal-to-distal sequence, contribute to the object's momentum (Putnam, 1993). These sequential motions from the proximal to the distal segments are one of the fundamental keys to performance in overarm throwing. Hip, shoulder, elbow, hand and javelin velocities are taken into account to analyse these power transmission sequences in the final phase.

Figure 36.4 shows hip, shoulder, elbow and javelin velocities in the Finnish thrower Parvi-anen's winning 89.52 m throw in the final of the World Championship in Athletics held in Seville in 1999. The analysis of how the maximum peak velocities for each marker are reached at the instant of release (T3) provides a more detailed description of the timing used by the throwers to structure their individual motion models for the upper limb.

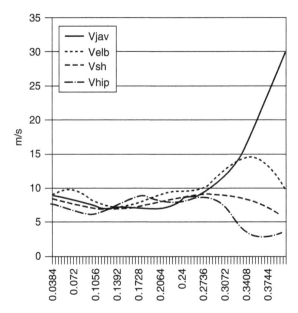

Figure 36.4　Trajectory of hip, shoulder, elbow and javelin markers along the final throwing phase in a world-class athlete

The trajectories of the markers presented in Figure 36.4 show that the general throwing model stated by Menzel (1987) is repeated. As a point of reference, an adequate throw is one in which the order of the joint points described reach their maximum velocity peak as follows: first/hip; second/shoulder; third/elbow; fourth/javelin. Two joint points reaching their maximum velocity peak at the same instant is considered to be a sequence error that hinders power transmission towards the most distal segments.

A more recent study has shown that, despite the fact that elite javelin throwers developed maximum joint centre linear velocities of their throwing arm in a proximal-to-distal sequence, throwers did not start their throwing arm segment and joint angular velocities in a proximal-to-distal sequence (Liu *et al.*, 2010). This is an interesting issue that needs further research but one that should be noted for the technical training of javelin throwers.

However, in javelin throwing, there are other factors that affect performance, such as aerodynamic factors. Due to its special design, the javelin has aerodynamic features that affect the flight phase and subsequently the throwing distance. Table 36.2 shows the values of a number of performance indicators of the finalists of the 1999 World Championships held in Seville.

Table 36.2 Kinematic release parameters in elite throwers (Adapted from Campos *et al.*, 2004)

Athlete	Distance (m)	Release velocity (m.s⁻¹)	Height of release (m)	Attitude angle (°)	Release angle (°)	Attack angle (°)
Parvianen	89.52	29.71	2.14	35.7	36.6	−0.9
Gatsioudis	89.18	29.6	1.90	37.5	31.6	5.9
Zelezny	87.67	29.21	1.80	36.9	31.1	5.8
Hecht	85.24	28.54	2.09	41.7	40.1	1.6
Henry	85.43	28.12	1.99	25.3	32.1	−6.8
González	84.32	29.37	1.83	36.5	27.7	8.8
Backley	83.84	28.5	2.08	40.8	35.3	5.5

Each thrower uses differentiated values. The German thrower Hecht used the largest release angle (40.1°) and the Cuban González the smallest (27.7°). González had the largest resulting attack angle (8.8°) and Parvianen (−0.9°) and Hecht (1.6°) the smallest. Overall, Table 36.2 shows that the athlete who came closest to the reference values was the World Champion, the Finn Parvianen, who was capable of throwing at a release velocity of over 29.5 m.s^{-1}, with a release angle of 36.6°, resulting in a negative attack angle of almost zero.

Concluding remarks

Performance analysis is part of the general planning process in coaching and follows a strategic and systematic plan for the evaluation of the athlete's physical, technical condition and performance while competing (jump distance/height and throw distance).

Technical level of the athletes is considered to be a clear determinant of performance in field athletics. However, reality proves that technique alone cannot account for performance. This chapter has summarized some relevant aspects of performance analysis in field athletics and has pointed out the potential benefits of the biomechanical approach in analysing different performance indicators in jumping and throwing events.

From the technical point of view, it has been demonstrated that intra-individual differences are greater for the novice and the elite athletes than for the club athletes (Bartlett *et al.*, 1996), supporting the notion of intra-individual movement consistency (Schöllhorn and Bauer, 1998). Even elite athletes appear unable to produce invariant movement patterns after many years of practice (Bartlett, 2008).

The performance analysis for long jump and javelin throwing shows that an adequate energy transformation requires an adaptive technical model that can solve the problems that athletes face at the time of jumping and throwing based on their strength and ability. Therefore, training should be addressed from an open, individualized perspective to help athletes build an efficient individual technical pattern.

References

Alexander, R.M. (1990) 'Optimum take-off techniques for high and long jumpers', *Philosophical Transactions of the Royal Society of London*, 329: 3–10.

Atwater, E.A. (1979) 'Biomechanics of overarm throwing movements and of throwing injuries', *Exercise and Sport Science Review*, 7: 43–85.

Bartlett, R. (1999) *Sports Biomechanics: Reducing Injury and Improving Performance*, London: E and FN Spon.

Bartlett, R. (2007) *Introduction of Sports Biomechanics, Analyzing Human Movement Patterns* (2nd ed.), London: Routledge.

Bartlett, R. (2008) 'Movement variability and its implications to sports scientists and practitioners: An overview', *International Journal of Sports Science & Coaching*, 3(1): 113–24.

Bartlett, R., Müller, E., Lindinger, S., Brunner, F. and Morris, C. (1996) 'Three-dimensional evaluation of the kinematic release parameters for javelin throwers of different skill levels', *Journal of Applied Biomechanics*, 12(1): 58–71.

Best, R.J., Bartlett, R. and Morris, C.J. (1993) 'A three-dimensional analysis of javelin throwing technique', *Journal of Sports Sciences*, 11(4): 315–28.

Bridgett, L.A. and Linthorne, L.P. (2006) 'Changes in long jump take-off technique with increasing run-up speed', *Journal of Sports Sciences*, 24(8): 889–97.

Campos, J., Brizuela, G. and Ramón, V. (2004) 'Three-dimensional kinematic analysis of elite javelin throwers at the 1999 IAAF World Championships in Athletics', *New Studies in Athletics*, 21: 47–57.

Campos, J., Gámez, J. and Encarnación, A. (2008) 'Kinematical analysis of the men's long jump at the 2008's IAAF World Indoor Championships in Athletics', in A. Hökelmann, K. Witte and

P. O'Donoghue (eds), *Current Trends in Performance Analysis: World Congress of Performance Analysis of Sport VIII* (pp. 185–9). Aachen: Shaker-Verlag.

Gordon, B.J. and Dapena, J. (2006) 'Contributions of joint rotations to racquet speed in the tennis serve', *Journal of Sports Sciences*, 24: 31–49.

Graham-Smith, P. and Lees, A. (2005) 'A three-dimensional kinematical analysis of the long jump take-off', *Journal of Sports Sciences*, 23(9): 891–903.

Hay, J.G. (1986) 'The biomechanics of the long jump', *Exercise and Sport Sciences Reviews*, 14: 401–43.

Hay, J.G. (1988) 'Approach strategies in the long jump', *International Journal of Sport Biomechanics*, 4: 114–29.

Hay, J.G. (1993) *The Biomechanics of Sports Techniques*, Englewood Cliffs, NJ: Prentice-Hall.

Hay, J.G. and Reid, J.G. (1988) *Anatomy Mechanics and Human Motion*, Englewood Cliffs, NJ: Prentice-Hall.

Hay, J.G. and Nohara, H. (1990) 'Techniques used by elite long jumpers in preparation for takeoff', *Journal of Biomechanics*, 23(3): 229–39.

Hopkins, W. (2005) 'Competitive performance of elite track-and-field athletes: Variability and smallest worthwhile enhancements', *Sportscience*, 9: 17–20. Online. Available at http://sportsci.org/jour/05/wghtrack.htm.

Hughes, M. and Bartlett, R. (2002) 'The use of performance indicators in performance analysis', *Journal of Sports Science*, 20: 739–54.

Koyama, H., Muraki, Y., Takamoto, M. and Michiyoshi, A. (2008) 'Kinematics of takeoff motion of the world elite long jumpers', in Y. Kwon, J. Shim, J. Kum and I. Shin (eds), *Coaching and Sports Performance, XXVI International Conference on Biomechanics in Sport* (p. 695). Seoul, Korea: ISBS.

Lees, A. (2002) 'Technique analysis in sports: A critical review', *Journal of Sports Sciences*, 20: 813–28.

Lees, A., Fowler, N. and Derby, D. (1993) 'A biomechanical analysis of the last stride, touch-down and take-off characteristics of the women's long jump', *Journal of Sports Sciences*, 11: 303–14.

Lees, A., Graham-Smith, P. and Fowler, N. (1994) 'A biomechanical analysis of the last stride, touchdown, and takeoff characteristics of the men's long jump', *Journal of Applied Biomechanics*, 10: 61–78.

Liu, H., Leigh, S. and Yu, B. (2010) 'Sequences of upper and lower extremity motions in javelin throwing', *Journal of Sports Sciences*, 28(13): 1459–67.

Menzel, H.J. (1987) 'Transmission of partial momenta in javelin throw', in B. Johnsson (ed.), *Biomechanics X-8* (pp. 643–7). Champaign, IL: Human Kinetics.

Morriss, C. and Bartlett, R. (1996) 'Biomechanical factors critical for performance in the men's javelin throw', *Sports Medicine (Auckland, NZ)*, 21(6): 438–46.

Putnam, C.A. (1993) 'Sequential motions of body segments in striking and throwing skills: Descriptions and explanations', *Journal of Sports Biomechanics*, 26: 125–35.

Schöllhorn, W.I. and Bauer, H.U. (1998) 'Identifying individual movement styles in high performance sports by means of self-organizing Kohonen maps', in H.J. Riehle and M.M. Vieten (eds), *Proceedings of the XVI Congress of the International Symposium on Biomechanics in Sport* (pp. 574–7). Konstanz: Konstanz University Press.

Seyfarth, A., Friedricks, A., Wank, V. and Blickhan, R. (1999) 'Dynamics of the long jump', *Journal of Biomechanics*, 32: 1259–67.

Seyfarth, A., Blickhan, R. and Van Leeuwen, J.L. (2000) 'Optimum take-off techniques and muscle design for long jump', *Journal of Experimental Biology*, 203: 741–50.

Whiting, W.C., Gregor, R.J. and Halushka, M. (1991) 'Body segment and release parameter contributions to new rules javelin throwing', *International Journal of Sport Biomechanics*, 7(2): 111–24.

37

RHYTHMIC GYMNASTICS

Anita Hökelmann, Gaia Liviotti and Tina Breitkreutz

OTTO-VON-GUERICKE UNIVERSITY MAGDEBURG, GERMANY

Summary

Rhythmic gymnastics is characterised by numerous qualitative and quantitative factors, but only the quantitative factors can be objectified in order to identify performance indicators. Due to high creativity of gymnasts and modifications of the Code of Points, the respective influence of particular performance indicators has changed in the past years. Choreography analyses aim to identify tendencies of the development of the performance structure. This is important for the creation of competitive routines and for the coaching process.

Generalities about rhythmic gymnastics

Rhythmic gymnastics belongs to the group of acyclic technical-compositional sports, with the main purpose 'to perform the movement of the own body with involvement of apparatus and perhaps partners according to the norms' (Kirchner and Stöber, 1994). It is mainly performed by women and is, according to the former IOC President Juan Antonio Samaranch, the 'most charming and feminine sport of the world' (Welkow-Jusek and Labner, 2011).

The evaluation rules are specified in the Code de Pointage (Federation International de Gymnastique, 2009), which represents the official guidelines for this sport discipline. Competitions are characterised by 'numerous, difficult movement structures [Balances, Flexibilities and Waves, Jumps and Leaps, Pivots, Pre-Acrobatics] and choreography compositions including the apparatus Rope, Hoop, Ball, Clubs, and Ribbon' (Schwabowski *et al.*, 1992: 9). It links high athletic performance with body control, concentration, sense for space and time, aesthetics, grace, creativity and artistic skills on a very high level. Therefore, it combines culture of movements, art and sport, which makes it a very complex athletic performance.

In rhythmic gymnastics, individual and group competitions are performed. Both are Olympic disciplines (individual since 1984; group since 1996). Choreographies have to be presented within a certain time span (individual: 1 min 15 s to 1 min 30 s; group: 2 min 15 s to 2 min 30 s) and need to be demonstrated on a specific floor area (13 m × 13 m).

Due to the complexity and versatility of the performance in rhythmic gymnastics, the choreographies are evaluated by three different juries; Difficulty (D), Artistry (A) and Execution (E). The Difficulty judge evaluates the quantity and quality of body and apparatus difficulties performed, while the Execution judge assesses the expression and the stability of the chore-ographies. This includes the expressiveness of the gymnast, the harmony between music and movements, and the accuracy of the performance. The artistic aspect of this sport is evaluated by the Artistry judge. It is described as the artistic value of the choreography, which means that the harmony between music, rhythm, space utilisation, colour effects (leotards, apparatus colour, etc.), the choice of apparatus and body techniques, and for the groups, synchrony and collaboration between the gymnasts, is evaluated. All of these elements need to express/tell the same story. The performance in rhythmic gymnastics is characterised by a high concentration of qualitative and quantitative factors. Qualitative factors include the artistic image/value of the exercise, musical accompaniment and the choice of body and apparatus elements, whereas quantitative factors are: the number of body and apparatus techniques (including originalities), stability of the exercise, use of space, formations and synchrony (group composition). Accord-ing to Graf (2004), quantitative factors can be objectified by certain parameters (performance indicators; see the next section), while qualitative factors of an exercise are highly influenced by subjective impressions and, therefore, 'it is really difficult to rate a performance fairly' (Hökelmann and Blaser, 2009). These difficulties do not only influence the work of the judges, but they also influence the work of coaches, experts, sport scientists and performance analysts in terms of evaluating and analysing performances in rhythmic gymnastics. Those analyses may help to rank performances, to create data bases and performance profiles for individual gym-nasts and groups, and thus to support the coaching process. Additionally, they may identify the most important performance indicators and tendencies in the development of rhythmic gymnastics.

While most choreography analysis methods are hand notation-based and concerned with individual exercises (Krug and Wagner, 1983; Rauchfuß, 1985; Heinß, 1993; Graf, 2004), Hökelmann *et al.* developed a computer-based notation system with the main purpose of ana-lysing group choreographies in rhythmic gymnastics in 2005 (Hökelmann *et al.*, 2006). Addi-tionally, Breitkreutz (2011) tried to make this computer-based method more effective by utilis-ing different software (Utilius VS, CCC-Software, Germany).

Performance indicators in rhythmic gymnastics

As performance indicators are the basis of a successful notational analysis, the first step in choreography analyses should be their determination. They may be defined in the exist-ing literature or during exchanges of expert knowledge (interviews of coaches etc.). These performance indicators are still evaluated and discussed in the literature today. According to Stark (1980), components, technique, composition design, expression and stability indicate the performance in technical-compositional sports. Schwabowski *et al.* (1992) adapted those indicators to rhythmic gymnastics and tried to describe the performance-influencing factors in more detail. Later, Liviotti and Hökelmann (2010) modified this model to group composi-tions, including the evaluation criteria (Figure 37.1). As already stated, there are a variety of qualitative and quantitative factors. Additionally, the composition of rhythmic gymnastics is characterised by the dualism of content and form. Therefore, the content is represented by music, composition design and choice/combination of body and apparatus elements. On the contrary expression, stability, dynamics and – only for group compositions – synchrony determine the form (Liviotti and Hökelmann, 2010). Based on this, it makes it even more dif-ficult to determine the specific performance indicators of this very complex sport. In general, only quantitative performance indicators can be analysed using notational analysis methods as currently no valid methods for the analysis of qualitative indicators exist. Hence, the number

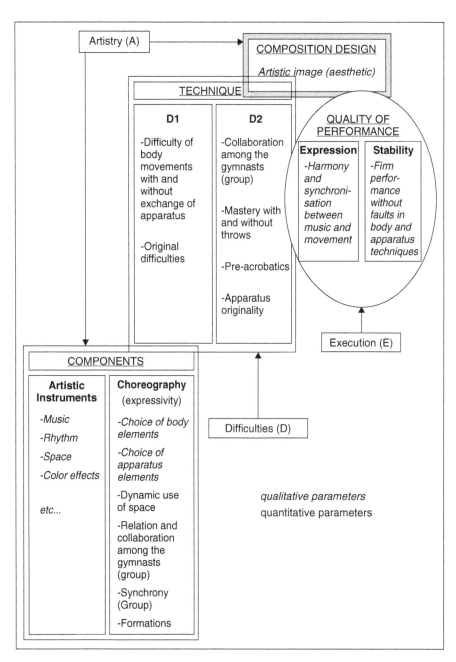

Figure 37.1 Performance indicators in group competitions in rhythmic gymnastics

of body and apparatus techniques, risks, originalities and the space utilisation may be defined as specific quantitative performance indicators for individual competitions. For group choreographies, the number of formations and collaborations, and synchrony can be added to the list of performance indicators.

Methods of data collection

In this section, a short introduction to the working method will be given, followed by an example representation of some possible results of a choreography analysis. As already stated, there are several hand notation systems which can be applied to technical-compositional sports such as rhythmic gymnastics. Unfortunately, most of these methods are very difficult to use and thus ineffective. In recent years, computer-based notational analysis tools for choreography analyses have been developed, which facilitate a more effective analysis process and reliable results.

Additionally, the software supports the creation of databases. These can be useful in terms of determining tendencies in performance development of the discipline, as well as of particular athletes/teams. One of these tools is SimiScout (SIMI Reality Motion Systems GmbH, Unterschleißheim, Germany). SimiScout enables group choreography analyses in rhythmic gymnastics. This video-based notation software utilises a self-defined attribute list (the list of performance indicators shown in Figure 37.2) to describe the observed sporting actions. The list may contain as many attributes as needed for the description. These attributes may be logically distributed across several levels, which are connected to each other in a horizontal hierarchy. Furthermore, the software allows the representation of the positions and the use of the floor area (Figure 37.2) based on a previous calibration of the video. Therefore, it is necessary to record all four corners of the competition area. Thus, the camera position must

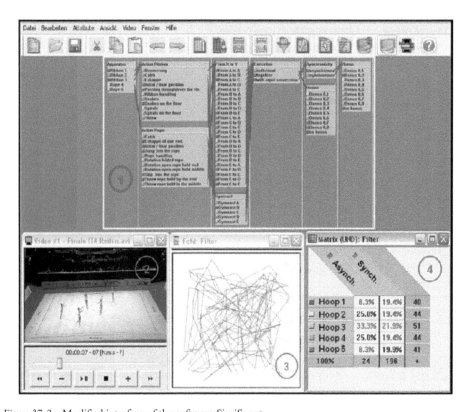

Figure 37.2   Modified interface of the software SimiScout

be fixed. However, zoomed footages may also be utilised. In this case, no calibration is possible. The first step of the analysis process is to document the running paths of the gymnasts and apparatus. This can be done by hand- or computer–based notation and is especially useful in the choreography analysis of group competitions. The second step is to choose/create an appropriate attribute list for the planned analysis. After the footage is uploaded to SimiScout, the analyst may click on the gymnasts in the displayed video when an interesting event is observed. After the video stops, the event can be described using the attribute list. After one event is coded, footage can be played again until a new event is observed by the analyst. Thus, the group and apparatus distances and the other relevant performance indicators can be coded and analysed.

In terms of a first overview of the collected data, the system offers a simple matrix which summarises selected data as absolute or percentage values (Figure 37.2).

In the following example, the attribute list is set up with regards to the Code de Pointage. In order to achieve a simplified data analysis, the attributes are clustered as followed: jumps, other movements (including body techniques which are performed in contact with the floor area – balances, pivots, flexibilities/waves), apparatus techniques where the body controls the apparatus permanently, apparatus techniques where the apparatus abandons the body, apparatus catches, apparatus exchanges, the distances covered by groups and apparatus, respectively and synchrony of performing body and apparatus techniques (Table 37.1).

The aim of the following example is to compare the medallists of the group exercise with five hoops (Russia [RUS], Italy [ITA] and Belarus [BLR]) at the European Championship 2010 in Bremen (Germany).

Representation and interpretation of the results

The national team which presented the highest number of the performance indicator 'other movements' was Italy (9.20 ± 0.45), the one performing the fewest was Russia (7.00 ± 0.00). The Kruskal-Wallis H Test explains significant differences among groups in relation to this variable ($p<0.05$). By analysing the situation in more detail by means of a series of Mann-Whitney U Tests ($p=0.05$), those differences become evident by all possible comparisons ($p<0.05$; Table 37.1, Figure 37.3). On the contrary, differences related to the variable 'jumps' are significant neither in the comparison among groups nor in that between groups (Table 37.1, Figure 37.3). By comparing the techniques with the apparatus, there are significant differences especially when the hoop is permanently controlled by the body (H Test, $p<0.05$). In detail, those differences appear in the comparison between the Russian (14.60 ± 2.51) and the Italian groups (18.60 ± 2.07; U Test, $p<0.05$; Table 37.1).

The same quantity of apparatus techniques where the hoop abandons the body and catching actions can be considered as a test for the objectivity and the correctness of the performed analysis (Table 37.1). In fact, the apparatus must be caught as many times as it is thrown.

A further difference concerns the apparatus exchanges. While the Russian gymnasts showed up to 17.40 ± 2.51 exchanges, the athletes from Belarus performed on average 13.00 ± 2.24 (Mann-Whitney U-Test, $p<0.05$; Table 37.1).

The performed Kruskal-Wallis H Test explains differences regarding the covered distances by both gymnasts and apparatus ($p<0.05$). In particular, those differences occur between the Italian gymnasts, who covered on average 136.79 ± 8.81 m, and the Russian gymnasts, who on the contrary covered only 107.77 ± 13.33 m on average ($p<0.05$; Table 37.1). Additionally, significant differences between the Belarusian (95.72 ± 6.78 m) and the Italian team (136.79 ± 8.81 m) could be detected for the covered distances of the gymnasts (Table 37.1). With regards to the

Table 37.1 Descriptive statistics (mean, standard deviation [SD]) and inferential statistics (Kruskal–Wallis Test [H Test], Mann–Whitney Test [U Test])

Movement	RUS		ITA		BLR		H-Test (p=0.05)	U-Test (p=0.05)
	Mean	SD	Mean	SD	Mean	SD		
Other movements	7.0	0.00	9.2	0.5	8.2	0.8	0.004	RUS vs. ITA (0.004) RUS vs. BLR (0.018) ITA vs. BLR (0.045)
Jumps	11.0	0.7	11.0	0.0	10.2	1.1	—	—
App. controlled by body★	14.6	2.5	18.6	2.1	16.6	1.1	0.034	RUS vs. ITA (0.025) RUS vs. BLR (0.025)
App. abandons body★★	21.4	2.2	20.6	1.7	18.4	1.5	—	—
App. catches	21.4	0.9	20.6	1.7	18.4	2.5	—	—
App. exchanges	17.4	2.5	16.4	0.9	13.0	2.2	0.019	RUS vs. BLR (0.021) ITA vs. BLR (0.020)
Group distance (m)	107.8	13.3	136.8	8.8	95.7	6.8	0.007	RUS vs. ITA (0.016) ITA vs. BLR (0.009)
App. distance (m)	177.0	9.7	194.6	9.5	146.4	15.9	0.004	RUS vs. ITA (0.047) RUS vs. BLR (0.009) ITA vs. BLR (0.009)
Group synchrony (%)	95.9	1.7	92.3	2.2	97.7	3.2	0.027	RUS vs. ITA (0.021) ITA vs. BLR (0.034)
App. synchrony (%)	91.9	2.6	95.0	2.4	91.8	1.6	—	—

Notes

★ Passing into the Hoop, Large Roll over the Body, Unstable Balance of the Apparatus, Rotation around the Fingers, Passing over the Apparatus

★★ Throwing, Roll on the Floor, Rotation on the Floor, Passing over the Apparatus, Handing Apparatus to other Gymnast

distances covered by the apparatus, significant differences between all groups could be found. The apparatus of the Italian team covered 194.57 ± 9.51 m. Compared to the teams of Russia and Belarus, a significant difference could be found (RUS: 177.02 ± 9.71; BLR: 146.47 ± 15.88). Furthermore, the distances covered by the apparatus of the Russian and the Belarusian team differed significantly (Table 37.1).

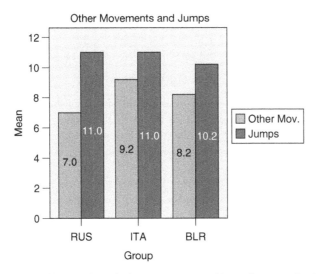

Figure 37.3 Comparison of the number of other movements and jumps between the three medallists

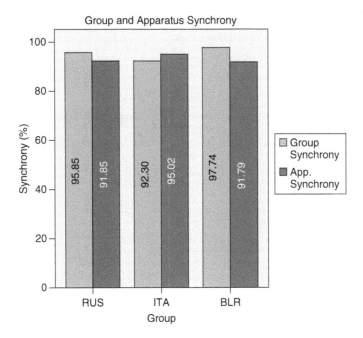

Figure 37.4 Comparison of the group and apparatus synchrony between the three medallists

The comparison of the three medallists of the European Championship with regards to execution synchrony of both body and apparatus techniques showed significant differences only in relation to the synchrony of performing body elements ($p<0.05$). Those differences are better explained by comparing Italy (92.30 ± 2.26 per cent) with Russia (95.85 ± 1.72 per cent), as well as with Belarus (97.74 ± 3.27 per cent; Table 37.1, Figure 37.4).

As the above-presented and discussed data show, there are significant differences among the analysed teams in relation to six out of ten considered variables (Table 37.1). Referring to this, it is clear that the gold-medal winner is the team which neither performed the highest number of body and apparatus techniques, nor covered the longest distance, nor showed the highest execution synchrony.

Concluding remarks

The analysis points out that the most successful choreography does not include the highest number of quantitative parameters. Thus, it is possible to conclude that, in rhythmic gymnastics, the performance is influenced by the quantity as well as by the quality. Despite several attempts to objectify the evaluation of performances in this sport discipline, it is not yet possible to estimate it in all its aspects. That is due to the fact that too much is left to the individual/subjective opinion of the observer (who can be a judge, the audience, a coach or an analyst). As a consequence, the aim for future studies should be to try to objectify the qualitative indicators. In doing so, it would then be possible to find out which parameter(s) influences the final score the most.

However, the quantitative information gained by choreography analyses may support the coaching process through: investigations of individual gymnasts or groups (strengths and weaknesses) and estimation of their degree of performance development, determination of the international performance level, and creation of extensive databases. Additionally, the coach and the choreographer may extrapolate tactical information to create a promising composition. Moreover, the International Committee can utilise the results of the analyses to deduce the possible adaptations of the Code de Pointage and, thus, create a more attractive and audience-friendly sport discipline.

References

Breitkreutz, T. (2011) *Development of a Choreography Analysis Template for Rhythmic Gymnastics*, unpublished Master Thesis, Otto-von-Guericke University Magdeburg.

Federation International de Gymnastique (2009) *Code of Points – Rhythmic Gymnastics, 2009–2012*, Lausanne: FIG.

Graf, S. (2004) *Wettkampfanalysen in der Rhythmischen Sportgymnastik. Anteil der leistungskennzeichnenden Merkmale Choreographie und Ausdruck an der Wettkampfleistung* (Schriften zur Sportwissenschaft, Bd. 56), Hamburg: Verlag Dr. Kovač.

Heinß, M. (1993) 'Schallpegeldiagramme – ein Hilfsmittel für die Leistungsdiagnostik in der Rhythmischen Sportgymnastik', *Leistungssport*, 23(5): 26–9.

Hökelmann, A. and Blaser, P. (2009) 'Bewegungssynchronität als Zielstellung der Individualgenese leistungsrelevanter Techniken im Spitzensport der Rhythmischen Sportgymnastik. Antrag auf Fortsetzung der finanziellen Förderung des prozessbegleitenden Projektes in der "Rhythmischen Sportgymnastik" (Gruppenklassement) für den Zeitraum von 2010 bis 2012', Otto-von-Guericke University Magdeburg.

Hökelmann, A., Blaser, P., Scholz, S., Plock, S. and Veit, S. (2006) 'Quantitative und qualitative Weltstandsanalyse im Gruppenklassement der Rhythmischen Sportgymnastik', in J. Edelmann-Nusser and K. Witte (eds), *Sport und Informatik IX* (pp. 159–64). Aachen: Shaker Verlag.

Kirchner, G. and Stöber, K. (1994) 'Ordnung in der Vielfalt – taxonomische Ansätze und Anforderungsprofile', in P. Hirtz, G. Kirchner and R. Pöhlmann (eds), *Sportmotorik. Grundlagen, Anwendung und Grenzgebiete* (pp. 335–55). Kassel: Universität-Gesamthochschule.

Krug, J. and Wafner, K. (1983) 'Die Struktur der Wettkampfleistung im Gerätturnen', *Theorie und Praxis Leistungssport*, 21(7): 3–21.

Liviotti, G. and Hökelmann A. (2010, December) 'Performance analysis of group competition in modern rhythmic gymnastics – European Championship 2010', oral presentation at the 6th ICCE Continental Coach Conference in Arnhem, Netherlands.

Rauchfuß, M. (1985) 'Entwicklung orgineller Elemente und Verbindungen in der Rhythmischen Sportgymnastik', Dissertation A, Forschungsinstitut für Körperkultur und Sport, Leipzig.

Schwabowski, R., Brzank, R. and Nicklas, I. (1992) *Rhythmische Sportgymnastik. Leistung – Technik – Methodik*, Aachen: Meyer und Meyer Verlag.

Stark, G. (1980) 'Stellung der technischen Sportarten innerhalb der Olympischen Sportarten und Disziplinen', *Theorie und Praxis Leistungssport*, 18(1): 3–25.

Welkow-Jusek, G. and Labner, R. (2011, 3rd January) 'Rhythmische Gymnastik in Österreich. Plattform für Expertinnen und Insider', available at www.oeft.at/rg/basis-info.htm (accessed 2 March 2011).

SUMMARY

Tim McGarry, Jaime Sampaio and Peter O'Donoghue

This Handbook on Sports Performance Analysis is one of a few Routledge International Handbooks that have allowed invited leading international academics to produce state-of-the-art reviews and reports on various aspects in the sport and exercise sciences. The handbooks are an excellent repository of secondary material directing scholars to primary research material as appropriate. Sports performance analysis has received and continues to receive increasing attention and recognition within the sports and coaching sciences, as well as in sports practice, as evidenced in increasing publication in scientific journals, and presentations and attendances at international congresses, conferences and symposia. Thus, publication of this first Handbook on Sports Performance Analysis is both relevant and timely.

In editing this handbook, we (the editors) aimed to provide scholars with contemporary, comprehensive and leading-edge material regarding theoretical, methodological and applied advances in sports performance research and practice. To this end, we are indebted to the invited contributions from all authors who volunteered their time and efforts in producing the articles that comprise this handbook. As with all things, this project was undertaken within various constraints on both editors and authors, not the least of which being space (length) and time (deadlines). As such, early selection decisions were required regarding chapter topics and authors, keeping in mind the wisdom in the aphorism that one cannot please all people all the time. The consequence is absent coverage on some aspects of sports performance, most notably perhaps in the fifth section of the handbook, which concerns research in different sports types.

Knowledge presented by authors of this handbook is relevant to the sports and coaching sciences. In respect of the sports sciences, the theoretical aspects are important for advancing basic understanding of sports performance. They are also important for sports practitioners too. The performance analyst abreast of developing relevant sports performance theory will presumably be more effective when plying his (or her) trade than without such knowledge. Indeed, sports practitioners can play an integral part in assisting theory development by engaging in on-going dialogue with sports scientists to the benefit of all parties. With respect to the coaching process, the nature of feedback, communication in coaching contexts, factors associated with strategies and tactics, decision making and skill development are covered in various places in this handbook. Finally, both scientific and coaching processes use new technologies for data capture and subsequent analysis and these undertakings will doubtless continue with further technological developments of both hardware and software, including wireless communication and portable information devices, including video and other medium. These developments will open new possibilities for sports performance analysis in future.

INDEX